Eastern
Mennonite
University

Eastern Mennonite University

A Century of Countercultural Education

Donald B. Kraybill

The Pennsylvania State University Press
University Park, Pennsylvania

Unless otherwise noted, all images are
courtesy of Eastern Mennonite University.

This publication has been made possible by generous
support from Eastern Mennonite University.

All Scripture quotations are taken from
the King James Version of the Bible.

Library of Congress Cataloging-in-Publication Data

Names: Kraybill, Donald B., author.
Title: Eastern Mennonite University : a century of
    countercultural education / Donald B. Kraybill.
Description: University Park, Pennsylvania : The
    Pennsylvania State University Press, [2017] |
    Includes bibliographical references and index.
Summary: "Traces the socio-cultural transformation
    of Eastern Mennonite University from a
    fledgling religious separatist school in 1917
    to a flourishing, world-engaged university
    populated by many faith traditions, cultures,
    and nationalities"—Provided by publisher.
Identifiers: LCCN 2017032944 |
    ISBN 9780271079134 (cloth : alk. paper)
Subjects: LCSH: Eastern Mennonite University—
    History. | Eastern Mennonite College
    (Harrisonburg, Va.)—History. | Mennonites—
    Education—Pennsylvania—History.
Classification: LCC LD1741.E464 K73
    2017 | DDC 378.755/921—dc23
LC record available at https://lccn
    .loc.gov/2017032944

Typeset by
SCRIBE INC.

Printed and bound by
SHERIDAN BOOKS

Composed in
ADOBE CASLON PRO

Bound in
ARRESTOX

The Pennsylvania State University Press is a member
of the Association of American University Presses.

It is the policy of The Pennsylvania State University
Press to use acid-free paper. Publications on
uncoated stock satisfy the minimum requirements
of American National Standard for Information
Sciences—Permanence of Paper for Printed
Library Material, ANSI Z39.-1992.

Contents

Preface

President Loren Swartzendruber was "over the moon" when he learned that Leymah Gbowee, a 2007 alumna of Eastern Mennonite University (EMU), was to receive the Nobel Peace Prize in November 2011.[1] The news was especially sweet to Swartzendruber's ears because EMU was rather small as universities go. After its modest founding in 1917, it had remained obscure for decades as school officials tried to shelter plain-dressing, fresh-from-the-farm students from worldly evils. It was not until the mid-twentieth century that the school became an accredited four-year college.

The EMU community was pleased that Gbowee, a Liberian peace activist and graduate of EMU's Center for Justice and Peacebuilding, had credited the center for rekindling her passion for peacebuilding. In 2002, she had played a leading role in forming Women of Liberia Mass Action for Peace, a movement of women who locked arms, protested, and prayed to halt a bloody fourteen-year civil war. The group's witness forced President Charles Taylor to resign, opening the door for Ellen Johnson Sirleaf to become Liberia's president and Africa's first female head of state.[2]

Using confrontational tactics to pursue peace would have been unthinkable for students in EMU's early decades, when the words *justice* and *protest* were missing from their lexicon. Mennonites in those days much preferred to be the "quiet in the land," as some outsiders called them. This centennial history chronicles this transformation in Mennonite understandings of peacemaking, along with a host of other transitions in academic freedom, educational philosophy, race relations, gender roles, and the performing arts. In EMU's first four decades, the faculty and students were white, rural Germanic Mennonites. By the end of the school's first century, a third of the traditional undergraduates were people of color, and two-thirds—as well as most graduate students—were not Mennonites.

The Spirit of Progress

Historian Jackson Lears, in *The Rebirth of a Nation: The Making of Modern America*, calls the decades between 1880 and 1920 a formative period for American culture.

A sense of optimism permeated national life as people laid aside memories of the dreadful Civil War and turned to building a modern America. In the last quarter of the nineteenth century, visionary educators, many of whom were religiously motivated, established hundreds of public and private academies (high schools) to meet the needs of an expanding industrial society. Many of these ventures evolved into two- and four-year colleges, but others failed. The majority of those that did survive lost their religious moorings.

Most turn-of-the-century Mennonites in the eastern states were plain-dressing agrarian pacifists who spoke German and English. They were religious separatists with a deep distrust of education beyond the elementary grades. The spirit of progress—propelled by growing numbers of immigrants, incipient urbanization, the westward spread of the nation, emerging industrialization, new forms of communication, and mass-produced garments and household products—troubled the tradition-minded Mennonites.

They would surely have agreed with one scholar's pronouncement that "the forces of modernization [had] descended like a gigantic steel hammer upon all the old communal institutions—clan, village, tribe, region—distorting or greatly weakening them, if not destroying them altogether."[3] These disruptions energized some Mennonites to participate more fully in mainstream American society. Yet even they squabbled for decades over the merits of higher education. Mennonites everywhere faced a quandary: advanced education was coming, and unless they wanted to shun progress completely, they needed to engage it. Some of their most ambitious youth, already invigorated by an education in secular schools, were leaving the Mennonite fold. This sobering fact put Mennonites in a predicament.

At the beginning of the twentieth century, the two largest Mennonite denominations in the United States were the Mennonite Church and the General Conference Mennonite Church. The latter was formed in 1860 by several different Mennonite groups. Their members had both Swiss-German and Dutch-Russian origins. The membership of this denomination, which totaled about 11,600 in 1906, lived mostly in the midwestern and prairie states. As early as 1868, members of the General Conference Mennonite Church established the Wadsworth Institute in Ohio. Kansas Mennonites opened a small preparatory school at Halstead in 1882. Both institutions were short-lived, but Mennonites soon founded permanent schools in those states: Bethel College (Kansas) opened in 1893 and Central Mennonite College (Ohio) opened six years later (and became Bluffton College in 1913).[4] These initiatives by members of the General Conference Mennonite Church were a step ahead of those in the East.

The other denomination, the Mennonite Church, consisted of thirteen regional conferences whose members had Swiss–South German origins. By 1910, about 75 percent of its twenty thousand members lived in Pennsylvania, Maryland, and Virginia.[5] In 1898, the Mennonite Church organized a representative body—the General Conference—that held an annual meeting and operated various church agencies. Because their names were similar, the General Conference established by the Mennonite Church was easily confused with the General Conference Mennonite Church. In 2002, the two binational denominations merged to become two new church bodies, Mennonite Church USA and Mennonite Church Canada. (In this book, unless otherwise noted, references to Mennonites, the Mennonite world, or the church before 2002 refer to the Mennonite Church. After 2002, they refer to Mennonite Church USA.)

In 1894, a Mennonite Church businessman established the Elkhart Institute of Science, Industry, and the Arts in northern Indiana. The institute was renamed Goshen College when it moved to the town of Goshen in 1903. Members of the Mennonite Church also founded Hesston College in Kansas in 1909. EMU, which opened in 1917 as Eastern Mennonite School, was the third educational institution in the Mennonite Church. Because Eastern Mennonite's founders considered Bluffton and Bethel more "worldly" given their alignment with the General Conference Mennonite Church, neither was a direct threat to EMU. Goshen College, with its place in the same Mennonite Church orbit, was another story.

A Faltering Start

Facing attrition and fearing higher education, eastern leaders in the Mennonite Church searched for some middle ground. Distressed by the liberalism they saw in the western schools, a small band of Mennonite Church leaders in the East decided to establish a church-controlled school to safeguard their youth from the wiles of the world. Education, in their judgment, was a dangerous albeit necessary venture to preserve the church. Even so, they believed that with proper supervision, "the experiment," as some of them called it, could succeed and serve the church.

The first two attempts to establish a school in Virginia failed. Six weeks after a groundbreaking ceremony in 1913 for a school near Norfolk, leaders abruptly proposed buying a colonial mansion built by George Washington near Alexandria, 190 miles north. Unresolved conflicts and tepid support from patrons soon crushed that proposal. All prospects for a school seemed to vanish until Mennonite bishop L. J. Heatwole and a handful of followers in Harrisonburg, Virginia, established Eastern Mennonite School (EMS) there in 1917. The fledgling school—which began with five teachers and nineteen students enrolled in Bible courses and the first level of high school—eventually grew into a flourishing university with nearly 1,900 students.

The words *Eastern Mennonite School* carried clout in the Mennonite world. An educational institution in the *East*, operated by *eastern* men, promised to be a safe haven for young Mennonites—one that would not spoil their minds with dangerous ideas or lead them astray. That this school, unlike Goshen and Hesston, had *Mennonite* in its name signaled its religious affiliation with a church that promoted simplicity, plainness of dress, nonviolence, and cultural separation from the larger society. And it was a *school*, an academy that would provide Bible training and high school courses to prepare young people for church-related activities.

The school intended, said Bishop Heatwole, "to uphold the principles of plainness and simplicity of doctrine of the Mennonite church [and] to advocate and defend the faith . . . from the first verse of Genesis to the last verse in Revelation." Moreover, he pledged, "The school is to be subject to and will serve the church. . . . All its teachers shall be examples of and advocates of the plain garb of the church."[6] In its early years, EMS had a host of restrictions on fashionable dress, intercollegiate sports, drama, musical instruments, and "modernist" textbooks on religion and evolution. These defensive tactics, leaders hoped, would safeguard their youth from the perils of modernity and prepare them to serve the church.

In the course of its century-long journey, the school evolved through five phases—from a Bible school, to a high school, to a junior college, to a four-year liberal arts college, and eventually to a university that included Eastern Mennonite Seminary, the Center for Justice and Peacebuilding, graduate programs, and a satellite site in Lancaster, Pennsylvania. Though it still held claim to its Christian identity in 2017, EMU had grown into a vibrant learning community serving Mennonites and people from many other faith traditions, cultures, and nationalities.

Conceptual Lenses

Institutional histories like this one are social constructions—stories crafted by the researchers who write them. As educational histories go, this is not a conventional one. As a cultural sociologist, I explore how the social construction of meaning, identity, and ritual guides human behavior. I am particularly interested in how the moral order—the distinctions between good and evil, right and wrong, sin and virtue—offers us meaning and motivates us to act. In this story, I pay special attention to how those lines shifted in the moral sand over the course of a century.

Cultural analysis also attends to the meaning of words and how the ideas they signify change over time. For example, the early founders frequently used the terms *indoctrination* and *safeguard*. By the mid-twentieth century, those words had vanished. New ideas, embedded in words like *discipleship, Anabaptism, citizenship,* and *student rights*, came into parlance at EMU in the last half of the twentieth century. Symbolic bridging, another variation of cultural change, occurs as the meaning of a word like *nonresistance* gradually morphs into *peacebuilding*, as it did at EMU.

Change is a constant theme in any centennial history. But what aspects of change merit attention? In telling this story, I pursue two sets of questions. First, how did EMU mediate the forces of modernity that contested traditional Mennonite values and identity? How did its leaders sort out what they would embrace, reject, or modify? And how did those *negotiations* transform a separatist ethnic community in 1917 into a world-engaged people by the early twenty-first century? Second, what is Mennonite about Eastern Mennonite? What did it mean to be a Mennonite at the school's founding, and how was that identity being expressed in new ways by 2017?

This tale recounts how culturally conservative Mennonites bargained with modern life through an institution of higher education that was irresistibly drawn into modernity while also trying to shield its students from it. Higher education is often seen as an engine of social change, but this story shows how Eastern Mennonite tried to arrest change for a half century and then later began to promote it. The school was, dialectically, both a product of a changing Mennonite identity and a producer of it. Moreover, religion was central to mediating change, and in that process, religion itself was transformed rather than declining or merely persisting over the course of a century.

Organizations live in social environments and engage with them in a variety of ways. In the course of its history, EMU's patron Mennonite community experienced a metamorphosis from rural farm folk to a more educated, occupationally mixed, and culturally diverse people. The theological developments, changing currents in American society, national trends in higher education, accrediting agencies, alumni interests, and the growing influence of donors shaped EMU from the outside. All these factors complicated, enriched, and tempered the thinking and decision making of faculty and administrators.

Every college coming of age in the twentieth century, religious or not, has had to "contend with modernity"—to borrow from the title of a book on Catholic higher education.[7] Eastern Mennonite University, however, offers a unique laboratory in which to investigate how a separatist community mediated the modernizing forces of specialization, individuation, pluralism, and ubiquitous technology, all of which threatened long-standing Mennonite beliefs. How did EMU officials view the larger culture and respond to the growing impact of technology, the rise of individualism, and the ever-expanding choices in the cultural smorgasbord of American life?

Mennonite educators also had to contend with potent currents that contested the core of Mennonite faith. These included Fundamentalism, modernism, evolution, higher criticism of the Bible, scientific challenges to religion, interfaith claims, and moral relativism. In the crucible of EMU's story, educators negotiated with these threats, which imperiled entrenched Mennonite values of humility, obedience, community, loyalty to the church, and cultural separatism. How would Christian beliefs and Mennonite convictions fare in a setting that privileged academic freedom, liberal learning, and spirited inquiry in the search for truth? Would the college's motto, Thy Word Is Truth, be able to endure for a century?

Of the thousands of documents stashed in the recesses of the EMU archives, I paid particular attention to those that provided clues to the evolving nature of Mennonite identity. Social identities are fluid, ever-changing human constructions of meaning. Mennonite identity is no exception; it was sculpted and resculpted in the transformation of this separatist school into a globally engaged one by 2017. That redo also brought a more individualistic ethos to campus.

Community has always been a core value in Mennonite life, as it is in most agrarian societies. When the school began, Mennonites privileged the church community above individual interests. Faculty and students were expected to deny self-interest, obey the church, and serve as its loyal servants. As the years unfolded, the campus culture increasingly spotlighted individual rights, achievements, and liberties. Even so, in an age where individualism looms large, some communal obligations still linger at EMU. All of these currents, and the tensions among them, are the stuff of this account.

Organization and Sources

I have organized the narrative into five sections that reflect the natural contours of the story. Part 1 serves as a prelude. It unpacks the ferment in the Mennonite world during an age of American progress (1880–1920) in which Mennonites founded new institutions, including mission agencies, publishing companies, schools, and service organizations. It also introduces the four men who would eventually collaborate in founding EMU.

Part 2 chronicles the *school* phase (1917–1947), following the two aborted starts that almost squashed all prospects for a Mennonite school in the East. During the three decades of this phase, Eastern Mennonite School operated a Bible institute, a high school, a correspondence program, a Special Bible Term, and, eventually, a junior college.

The third part explores the *college* phase, which spans the four decades from 1948 to 1986. These years brought enormous changes in the academic program and the professionalization of the faculty. They also saw new freedoms in student life related to dress and intercollegiate sports, and greater independence from the church. During these years, the high school became autonomous and a seminary was established on the campus.

Part 4 focuses on the institution's expansion as a *university*. In addition to changes in the academic curriculum, student life, and the seminary, EMU developed new graduate programs. The Center for Justice and Peacebuilding took flight and soon garnered worldwide recognition, and a branch of the university opened in Lancaster County, Pennsylvania.

The fifth part is a postlude that summarizes the transfiguration of Mennonite identity over the century, explores the results of EMU's "experiment" in Christian higher education, and interprets some of the significant changes that transformed the institution in its first century. Throughout the narrative, I focus on the evolving story of the undergraduate program rather than on other sectors of the university.

I was fortunate to have access to bountiful sources. Hubert Pellman's well-crafted history of the first fifty years, *Eastern Mennonite College, 1917–1967*, provides greater detail of that era than does this book. The massive cache of documents in the university archives could easily have supported a five-volume centennial history. In-depth interviews with some forty people knowledgeable about EMU's past also offered valuable insights.

A word on terminology is also in order. The institution has had four different names at various times: Eastern Mennonite School (EMS), Eastern Mennonite College (EMC), Eastern Mennonite College and Seminary (EMC&S), and Eastern Mennonite University (EMU). EMS, the acronym for Eastern Mennonite School, also applies to Eastern Mennonite Seminary, which was established in EMU's later history. Eastern Mennonite High School (EMHS) became a separate institution in 1982 and later became Eastern Mennonite School (EMS) with grades K–12. Finally, I use the term *EMU* two ways in the text: to describe the university era (1994–2017) and to refer to the institution's entire history.

Transformed and Rooted

In the universe of some 4,700 degree-granting postsecondary institutions in the United States in 2017, EMU stood out with its countercultural accent. EMU's countercultural posture varied in different phases of its history, from its early sectarianism to its active cultural engagement in the later twentieth century. This unconventional institutional history explores how EMU's distinctive cultural features were transformed in the course of its first century.

Among Mennonite colleges, for example, EMU was the only one established in the South. That location meant the school was immersed in a deeply racist environment, which severely tested Mennonite beliefs. And yet, just a few years into the twenty-first century, Leymah Gbowee became EMU's star alumna—a black international non-Mennonite. In its first thirty years, EMU would have refused to admit her. Had she gained entrance, she might have been expelled for being an outspoken woman and a peace activist.

Recent graduation ceremonies provide many snapshots of the transformation and continuity that have marked EMU since 1917. They celebrate features that were forbidden in the first forty commencements. Onstage participants in recent years include women in prominent leadership and ministerial roles. The music of pianos, organs, and other instruments resound in the air. The service includes participation by nonwhite, nonstraight, and non-Mennonite students and families. Graduates and faculty wear once-banned academic regalia. The speeches and sermons affirm higher education and "modern" ideas that were once suspect. Individual achievements in the arts, academics, and intercollegiate sports are praised—in some cases, by wearing honors sashes.

At the same time, the deep roots established during the early years are also evident. In step with the first commencement in 1919, prayers, hymns, and other expressions of Christian faith remain prominent. Honorary doctorates are not awarded. The American flag is not visible, nor is there a single strain of the national anthem. Welcome to the history of a countercultural university.

PART I

Mennonites in a Turbulent Nation, 1880–1920

CHAPTER 1

The Cyclone
of Modernity

A humble common man is worth more . . .
than a high-minded intellectual giant.
—Two Mennonite leaders, 1908

A Temple of Reason (Paris, 1899)

Amos Daniel "A. D." Wenger arrived in Paris on February 10 with a well-churned stomach from his choppy ride across the Channel.[1] The thirty-one-year-old farmer-preacher had just spent ten days in England on the first leg of a fourteen-month around-the-world trip. He would be the second American Mennonite to circumnavigate the globe.[2]

The agitation in his body matched the upheaval in his mind and spirit as he visited England and France. At Oxford University, strange feelings overcame him as he walked the stately halls where John Wycliffe, translator of the Bible into English, and John and Charles Wesley, founders of the Methodist Church, had trod. The British Museum in London impressed him with its "wonderful collections of antiquities of every age and country," but the "cold and formal style" of the Anglican Church did not warm his heart.

He decried London's 7,500 saloons and brothels, which "deal[t] out woe and misery," and its slums, where "women lie, swear, fight and get drunk as well as the men." This "maelstrom of iniquity," he wrote, birthed the Salvation Army. Such "open blackness of sin" and the "haughtiness" of the higher classes made it "a very wicked city"—so wicked that only a "small number" of Londoners would likely "get to heaven."

In Paris, Wenger marveled at some 1,700 splendid boulevards, long blocks of cream-colored stone buildings, windows filled with artistic arrangements of beautiful goods, spacious parks, magnificent palaces, costly monuments, and the world's then largest Ferris wheel, prepared for the 1900 Paris Exposition Universelle. Yet despite its grandeur, the city, in Wenger's eyes, was "full of pomp, display, pride, and skepticism."

Furthermore, its moral climate repulsed him. "[It's] like a sepulcher, outwardly polished and beautiful white," he wrote, "but within, it's full of dead men's bones and the vilest corruption. . . . Hundreds of life-size nude human figures abound in public places." Besides, he noted, the government permitted prostitution, and only 1 percent of the people attended church. Theaters were more plentiful than churches. The shameful, "wicked women of Paris [led] the world in fashionable dress" and wore "the most ornamental and gaudy apparel." For Wenger, such fashion was "contrary to the word of God!"

Why, Wenger wondered, did Paris "sink so shamefully low?" He blamed the Enlightenment and the worship of reason. "The minds of the French people" were shaped by "Voltaire and other infidel writers" who ignored God and the Bible and "enthroned carnal reason as their guide." He wrote, "This sin-reveling city—a mass of corruption gilded with fine art—is but the natural outcome of the teachings of infidelity." For more evidence, he pointed to the Cathedral of Notre Dame, which, during the French Revolution in 1793, had been "converted into a Temple of Reason [with] the busts of great infidels and a statue representing Reason seated on the throne." Four days in Paris was long enough for a Mennonite preacher, he wrote, "especially for one who does not enjoy it."

Paris was far from Wenger's farm in southeastern Pennsylvania, a few miles west of Lancaster City. He began his journey alone after kidney failure snatched away the life of Mary Hostetter, his bride of but a year. Overwhelmed with grief, Wenger sailed to relieve his "intense loneliness." As he traveled, he mailed vivid descriptions of his observations to John F. Funk, editor of *Herald of Truth* in Elkhart, Indiana. Founded in 1864, *Herald of Truth* was the first nationally circulated Mennonite paper to cover Mennonite communities from eastern Pennsylvania to Oregon. Wenger's travelogues attracted a large audience of readers who eagerly awaited each dispatch of his moral commentary on the exotic cultures he saw.

Wenger traveled to India, Ceylon, China, and Japan, where he often observed what he considered heathen idolatry. He was especially eager to visit the Netherlands, Germany, and Switzerland, where his Mennonite ancestors had "fled from a martyr's death." He stopped in Friesland, home of Menno Simons, a Catholic priest who converted to the fledgling Anabaptist faith in 1536. Menno's prolific writings and prominent leadership had made him the namesake of Mennonites. There, in the very womb of the Mennonite faith, Wenger was shocked to hear a Mennonite minister-professor call the Dutch Mennonites "Unitarians" and the American Mennonites "heretics." Worse yet, the professor deemed certain Bible verses spurious because they first appeared as scribal edits in the fifth century. In still another jolt, Wenger heard that a Mennonite scholar in northern Germany had allegedly found eighty thousand mistakes in the Bible.

Wenger did find a few pockets of warm spirituality in European Mennonite communities, but for the most part, he concluded that they were "not faithful and zealous in the cause of Christ" and did not keep "the self-denying principles of God's word." Never before had he seen "such a cold, spiritless faith" among Mennonites. Most of them, he noted, "have been led astray by higher criticism, questioning the origin and authenticity of Scripture . . . even rejecting the divinity of Christ." In Wenger's view, it would be better for those who "don't accept and obey the humble teachings of Jesus" to simply abandon the Mennonite ship. For him, *obedience* to the humble teachings of Jesus and "the *self-denying* principles of God's Word" were the core of the Mennonite faith.[3] The spiritual decadence he found among highly educated Mennonite leaders in Europe appalled him. He had expected to find heathens worshiping idols but not "Mennonite infidels" demeaning the Bible.

That such slippage from Mennonite orthodoxy could happen so quickly in the birthplace of his church—the region where several thousand Mennonite forebears were tortured in the vilest ways, beheaded by the executioner's sword, and torched at the stake—deeply troubled Wenger. The specter of this spiritual decline shaped his view of the church, his fear of higher education, and his commitment to keeping Mennonites separate from American popular culture. The insights from his trip galvanized many convictions that guided his later life as president of Eastern Mennonite School.

Wenger's intellectual curiosity and awareness of the Enlightenment were remarkable for a lightly educated rural Mennonite in 1899. A farmer at heart, he meticulously recorded his observations about vegetation, crops, weather, and natural beauty throughout the trip. In his chronicles, he deplores the immorality of city life, mourns the ubiquity of heathen religions, and prays that God will send American missionaries to save the lost souls in pagan lands. His observations candidly express his love for the Mennonite Church, his commitment to the peaceful teachings of Jesus, and his anticipation of eternal salvation for all those who confess Jesus as their Savior.[4]

Wenger also loved America. Arriving in San Francisco on February 16, 1900, after a tumultuous sea voyage, he was thrilled to see broad, clean streets, fine carriages and horses, electric cable cars, and magnificent buildings "much grander" than anything he had seen abroad. "The conveniences of our own country are superior to those of any other," he opined. "The United States is not the only country, as someone has said, but it is the best one." With these words of admiration for the Progressive Era under way in his homeland, he boarded a train for Lancaster County, visiting Mennonite communities in Iowa, Illinois, and Indiana before arriving home on March 10. The price tag of his fourteen-month trek of nearly forty thousand miles was about $1,000 ($29,000 in 2017 dollars).

"The Burning" (Rockingham County, Virginia, 1867)

It's hard to imagine a deeper cultural chasm than the one separating Paris and Greenmount, Virginia, where A. D. Wenger was born on a farm in the beautiful Shenandoah Valley, bracketed by the Blue Ridge Mountains on the east and the Alleghenies on the west. The majestic Massanutten Peak protrudes into the valley from Front Royal south to Harrisonburg. Wenger described the hamlet of Green-mount, about six miles north of Harrisonburg, as "a tiny village . . . the scene of many [of my] dreams and fond memories with its log house school, shoemaker shop, blacksmith shop, store with post office, and a few dwellings."[5]

Wenger was born in November 1867, three years after Major General Philip Sheridan, a Union commander, had decimated much of the northern Shenandoah Valley in raids locals still call "the Burning." For more than three months in the autumn of 1864, Sheridan's forces scorched the breadbasket of the Confederacy. They burned 1,200 barns and 71 flour mills; confiscated or destroyed some 4,000 bushels of wheat and 10,000 beef cattle, sheep, and swine; and even torched civilian homes. More than four hundred wagonloads of refugees fled north into West Virginia and Maryland. Others, especially sixteen- and seventeen-year-old pacifists who were mostly Mennonites and Dunkers (members of the Church of the Brethren, religious cousins of the Mennonites), escaped the valley to avoid conscription. Two Mennonite historians writing in 2007 noted that never before—or since—had Mennonites in the United States experienced such rampant destruction of their property.[6] Memories of this horrific burning of the valley, which had severely tested their pacifism, lingered long in Mennonite memories.

A. D. Wenger was the eighth of Jacob and Hannah Brenneman Wenger's eleven children. He grew up hearing frightful accounts of the Burning, though his own family's property was spared. As a child, Wenger attended several five-month terms of common (elementary) school. At age nineteen, he enrolled in the normal school (for training elementary schoolteachers) established in 1880 by the Dunkers at Bridgewater, about eight miles south of Harrisonburg.[7] After attending four weeks, he received a teaching certificate. Wenger was "too bashful," however, to look for a teaching job, so he worked on the family farm. Despite the shyness, he said, "I received a conviction one Sunday morning at church [at twelve years of age] that I should someday preach the gospel [and] that conviction never left me."

At age twenty-two, the tug of adventure pulled him westward to visit relatives and explore pioneering Mennonite settlements. It was not unusual for young men at that time to move west for adventure as well as for higher wages and cheaper land. In February 1890, Wenger traveled to Elida, Ohio, to live with his married sister and her husband and work on their farm for six months. During his sojourn there, he immersed himself in biblical studies and religious books, including *Martyrs Mirror*, a hefty 1,200-page book with graphic accounts of the torture of Mennonite martyrs in the sixteenth century. While living with his sister, he was baptized and officially joined the Mennonite Church.

Two weeks after his baptism, he set off alone in a small cart pulled by a wild Texas pony and headed for Iowa to live with his oldest brother, Sol. He traveled by pony cart because of his "fondness for adventure" and in order to see the country better. Along the way, he stopped at Elkhart, Indiana, the midwestern intellectual center for Mennonite Church leaders and religious innovators. Arriving in Iowa, he discovered that one of the few Mennonite congregations in the entire state was near Sol's home. After working for a year on his brother's farm and teaching in a nearby school, he boarded a train to Newton, Kansas, home to a General Conference Mennonite Church community.

Mennonites there welcomed Wenger warmly and engaged him in spirited conversations about religion. In Newton, he met twenty-year-old George R. Brunk, a precocious young leader whose parents had escaped Virginia in the aftermath of the Civil War. Wenger soon headed off to Missouri to visit L. J. Heatwole, a thirty-nine-year-old minister from Rockingham County, Virginia, who had moved near Garden City, Missouri. A recently ordained bishop, Heatwole served the Bethel Mennonite congregation. Wenger then traveled to Versailles, Missouri, to visit relatives. There he met twenty-six-year-old Daniel Kauffman, whose family had moved from Pennsylvania when he was a boy. Kauffman had abandoned a political career as county commissioner after joining the Mennonite Church in 1890 under the persuasive preaching of prominent Mennonite revivalist John S. "J. S." Coffman. Fifteen years later, the quartet of Brunk, Heatwole, Kauffman, and Wenger would collaborate in founding Eastern Mennonite School.

Two pivotal events shaped Wenger's life during the time he lived in Missouri: a summer in Chicago and his ordination as a Mennonite minister. In the summer of 1894, after teaching for a year at the Sugarcreek School near Garden City, he traveled to Chicago, where he attended lectures at Moody Bible Institute each morning. He heard preaching by leading non-Mennonite revivalists, including evangelist Dwight L. Moody as well as C. I. Scofield, who would later become famous as editor of the popular *Scofield Reference Bible*. At Moody, Wenger learned "many valuable lessons" that were a "source of great satisfaction and blessing" for the rest of his life. In the afternoons and evenings, he worked at the recently founded Mennonite mission in the city's slums—the first urban Mennonite mission venture in North America. Wenger's summer in Chicago thus exposed him to prominent Christian leaders outside the Mennonite orbit and immersed him in urban ministry.

Returning to Missouri in the fall of 1894, Wenger once again taught at the Sugarcreek School and participated in the Bethel Mennonite congregation, where L. J. Heatwole had served as bishop. Prompted by health issues and devastating tornados—one of which almost spun the bishop heavenward as he cowered in a coal bin after his house disintegrated—the Heatwole family had fled home to Virginia in April 1893.[8] After Bishop Heatwole's departure, the Bethel congregation eventually ordained Wenger a minister by a unanimous vote of its forty-seven members. Two weeks later, on his twenty-seventh birthday, the handsome young bachelor preached his first sermon, and he soon earned a reputation as an able and articulate speaker. Meanwhile, Daniel Kauffman had moved to the area as the freshly appointed principal of the Garden City Public School. Already ordained a bishop, Kauffman led Bethel Mennonite Church after Wenger left for Iowa to attend Penn College in September 1895.

Wenger was likely the first ordained minister in the Mennonite Church to attend college. The "fashionable Quaker school" gave the Mennonite farm boy a "cordial welcome," in Wenger's words. He received first prize in the school's annual extemporaneous speaking contest, and on Sundays he preached in nearby Mennonite congregations. At a preaching engagement in Palmyra, Missouri, Anna Mellinger Buckwalter—whose family, along with several others from Lancaster County, Pennsylvania, had recently settled in the area—shared an urgent plea. She wished someone would address the spiritual condition of young adults in Lancaster's Mennonite community, who typically waited to join the church until well after they married.[9] "A sudden conviction gripped me," said Wenger, "that I should go to eastern Pennsylvania to help save souls. I thought perhaps I could attend school at Franklin and Marshall College as I preached and labored for the church."

The chance to preach in the largest Mennonite community in America was quite attractive. So after buying a small black bow tie acceptable in Lancaster, he headed east on a rapid trip that included preaching appointments in Mennonite congregations in Ohio, Ontario, and rural New York, arriving in Lancaster on July 10, 1896.

Within a few days, he had nineteen preaching invitations in the Lancaster area. Such demand for his time dashed his plans to attend Franklin and Marshall College. By the end of July, he was home in Virginia, where he preached in all the Mennonite congregations. Several weeks later, he went to the Franconia Mennonite community, twenty miles northwest of Philadelphia, and preached thirty-five times in the month of October. Wenger's spectacular star as a preacher was rising high and fast.

Despite his popularity, Wenger faced criticism from leaders in Pennsylvania and Virginia who stridently opposed revival meetings because, in Wenger's words, "*personal* work was so new."[10] By "personal work" Wenger meant revival services that included an invitation by the evangelist for individuals to stand or to go to the front of the sanctuary to declare their personal faith in Christ as their Savior. Revival services—borrowed from evangelical Protestantism—were a radical innovation in Mennonite churches of the late nineteenth century.

Wenger's mentor, Virginia-bred J. S. Coffman, was the first prominent Mennonite revivalist preacher. Coffman was ordained in Virginia in 1875 and preached there until 1879 when he moved to Elkhart, Indiana, to become the assistant editor of *Herald of Truth* and later the first president of the Elkhart Institute, the forerunner of Goshen College.[11] When Coffman died in 1899, Wenger was suddenly the leading turn-of-the-century Mennonite revivalist. Wenger's meticulous diaries record his preaching engagements and the number of individuals who converted to the Christian faith and joined the Mennonite Church. From his first sermon in November 1894 until February 1907—when he stopped keeping a record for fear it would make him proud of his achievements—he delivered 1,859 sermons, often three on Sundays. Indeed, he averaged one sermon per day in his first year in Lancaster County.[12]

Wenger's sudden conviction to go east to save souls is more fully explained by his romantic relationship with Mary Hostetter, who lived near Millersville, a town a few miles west of Lancaster City. They met when she was visiting Indiana and soon began corresponding.[13] Within a year of his arrival in Lancaster, they were married. After the ceremony in Millersville on July 1, 1897, they took a wedding trip to the Pacific coast by train, visiting relatives and friends along the way. Wenger preached in a few Mennonite Church congregations in Oregon, the only ones west of Kansas at that time. After returning by way of Virginia, they settled in Millersville. Then, a year and two weeks into their marriage, Mary died. The shock of her sudden death prompted A. D. Wenger to embark on his trip around the world.

No Way to Escape (Dale Enterprise, Virginia, 1887)

For several weeks in June 1887, Lewis James "L. J." Heatwole wrestled with angels and demons. Members of the Weavers congregation near Harrisonburg had nominated the thirty-five-year-old into a pool of candidates for ministry known as "the lot." Inspired by biblical precedent, ordination by lot was the typical way of selecting leaders in nineteenth-century Mennonite congregations.[14] A week or so after being nominated, in what might look like a random lottery to outsiders, nominees drew lots—in this case, hymnbooks—and a few moments later, one of them would discover that God had chosen him to serve as a minister. Heatwole had not volunteered for this job. He had not chosen this path. Moreover, he harbored doubts about the divine efficacy of the lot.[15] Worse yet, there was no escape. He had participated in this ritual before—once for preacher and then for deacon—and on both occasions, the lot "fell" on another candidate, to Heatwole's great relief.[16]

A week before the ordination, Heatwole pleaded with the elders to excuse him from the lot. Besides operating a small farm, he had educational duties and scientific interests. He taught in an elementary school, managed a weather station for the US Signal Service, and enjoyed astronomy. The leaders denied his request. Such earthly excuses could not derail the divine calling already under way. Heatwole knew he would have to relinquish some of the things he loved if the lot fell on him this time. He jotted in his diary, "There's nothing left for me to do but to surrender myself."[17] If chosen, he and his wife, Molly, would bear heavy responsibilities for many years and receive no financial remuneration or theological training.

Molly's brother, revivalist J. S. Coffman, who lived in Elkhart, Indiana, urged Heatwole to stop relying on his own judgment and to "be entirely submissive to the hand of God."[18] Devout Mennonites believed that during this ritual, God would reach down from heaven to select a new servant of the flock. The newly ordained man and his spouse would submit to God's will. Members of the congregation would also yield to divine providence and accept the authority of the new

The meetinghouse of Weavers Mennonite Church near Harrisonburg, Virginia (ca. 1880s), where L. J. Heatwole was ordained minister in 1887. A 1915 meeting at this site led to the decision to locate Eastern Mennonite School in Harrisonburg. Photo: Collection of David and Elizabeth Heatwole.

God-certified minister who would be their shepherd for the rest of his life. Anyone dismayed by the outcome could only grumble silently or argue with God.

That Sunday morning, Heatwole and the twelve other candidates cautiously eyed the thirteen hymnbooks standing upright on the preachers' table at the front of the meetinghouse. The books had been secretly shuffled before the service, and two contained a slip of paper because two ministers would be ordained that morning. Assuming the ordination was typical of other Mennonite churches, each slip bore two messages. On one side was a quote from Proverbs 16:33: "The lot is cast into the lap; but the whole disposing thereof is of the Lord." The other side simply said, "The Lord has chosen you."

Heatwole's father-in-law, Bishop Samuel Coffman (father of Molly and J. S.), conducted the ordination. The silence, the suspense, and the mystery of the solemn moment were palpable. All eyes were on the thirteen hymnbooks. After each candidate had selected one, Bishop Coffman carefully checked each book. He found one of the fateful slips inside Heatwole's book and immediately ordained him. "I was greatly shocked to find myself one of the chosen," Heatwole confided to his diary. "I came home from church in dejected spirits generally. Molly bears up bravely under the circumstances which of itself put me in better cheer."[19]

Heatwole was not enthusiastic about preaching. At first, his fifteen-minute sermons were abruptly short compared to the usual hour-long exhortations. One time he "wilted right at the onset" and sat down after a few minutes.[20] As he honed his homiletic skills, his sermons expanded with thoughtful content and precise words. Somewhat shy, he spoke quietly, with careful enunciation, but he lacked the charm and persuasive passion of his brother-in-law J. S. Coffman.

The sacred ritual of ordination, well ensconced in Mennonite tradition, exposes salient themes of nineteenth-century Mennonite identity and spirituality—*submission, simplicity, humility*, and *community*—that articulated one's spiritual relationship to God and the church, underscoring the dialectic between community and individual. Communal authority and obligations superseded individual preferences. Pride, frequently condemned by preachers as an abomination in the eyes of God, was code for individualism—the flaunting of individual achievements and self-importance that threatened communal harmony. Humility, the supreme virtue, was shown by yielding to God, deferring to others, renouncing self-interest, and minimizing individual opinions and accomplishments.[21]

A Quiet and Peculiar Identity

Nineteenth-century Mennonites in the East, sometimes called the *Stillen im Lande* (quiet in the land), were known as pious, peaceful, plain-dressing, hardworking,

Pennsylvania Dutch–speaking farmers and small business owners.[22] Their faith focused on following the teachings of Jesus, especially his Sermon on the Mount (recorded in Matthew 5–7). Their religious expressions were communal, quiet, sober—not individualistic or emotional—and perhaps even repressed at times. Their modest and meek spirituality was embodied in daily habits rather than in volumes of systematic theology. Two forms of separation guided Mennonite interactions with the larger society: *nonresistance* and *nonconformity*.

Nonresistance entailed separation from the state. Though some voted, Mennonites usually did not engage in political activities or hold public office—except for minor positions in local townships. Their two-kingdom theology, which L. J. Heatwole called "the Kingdom of Peace and the Kingdom of Force," drew a sharp line between church and state.[23] In their view, the ethics of the kingdom of God, articulated by Jesus, rested on a foundation of love and nonviolence, which Mennonites called *nonresistance*. They tried to practice Jesus's admonitions in Matthew 5:38–48 to love enemies and not resist evildoers, even in self-defense. In short, they did not fight back or exact revenge but left vengeance in God's hands.

In sharp contrast, the state, emblematic of this world's kingdom, employed force and violence, or at least the threat of them, to maintain order. Mennonites paid their taxes and respectfully prayed for elected officials. Citing Romans 13:1–7, they believed that government was established by God to punish evildoers and reward those who did good. But Mennonites' primary citizenship was in heaven. As pilgrims and strangers on earth, Mennonites held a halfhearted sense of citizenship in this world. Espousing their two-kingdom theology, they were loath to tell the government what to do or to protest its policies, because it functioned in a separate ethical sphere with different obligations than the kingdom of God. This view posed thorny questions about Christian citizenship in the political realm—questions that Mennonites would wrestle with throughout the twentieth century.[24]

Mennonites also advocated *nonconformity*, refusing to conform to certain cultural practices and values of the larger society, or "worldliness" as they called it. This cultural divide between their church and certain aspects of mainstream culture was underscored by Scriptures that urged Christians not to conform to the world (Rom. 12:1–2) and not to love the world and its things that breed lust, desire, and pride (1 John 2:15–17). Despite their separatist views, Mennonites had many non-Mennonite friends and participated in some civic events. But they typically refrained from holding membership in lodges, labor unions, and granges and from attending or participating in fairs, sporting events, and theatrical performances.[25]

Despite their cultural separation, Mennonites held private property and participated in the American economy. Hundreds of Mennonite entrepreneurs operated small businesses, buying and selling products in the larger marketplace. Even so, most families were engaged in farming. Their communal instincts usually prompted them to generously assist church members in times of tragedy and financial need. The cultural fences around Mennonite life were porous, flexible, and ever-changing. For L. J. Heatwole, the accent on simplicity, separation, and traditionalism gave Mennonites a "peculiar identity" that had prevented the church from "being swept into the open maelstrom of the world" as had happened to many Protestant churches in the last half of the nineteenth century.[26]

Mennonite congregations had no paid church officials and no budgets, only periodic offerings to assist the needy. Each congregation had several ordained ministers—two or three preachers and a deacon who assisted in special rituals such as communion and baptism and attended to the material needs of members experiencing misfortune. A bishop typically supervised several congregations. Congregational authority was vested in "the bench" of ministers who sat at the front of the meetinghouse facing the members during services.

Church organizations—Sunday schools, mission programs, educational ventures, youth projects, church publications, and social service agencies for the needy—were virtually nonexistent on the Mennonite landscape before 1875. The only semblance of organization beyond the congregation was the regional conferences of ministers that gathered once or twice a year.

After L. J. Heatwole was ordained minister, he participated in Virginia Mennonite Conference (established in 1835), a semiannual meeting of the thirty-six ordained officials in the Commonwealth of Virginia. Virginia Conference, with some eight hundred members, had three districts—clusters of congregations—and each one had a supervising bishop.[27] Heatwole's father-in-law, Samuel Coffman, was the bishop of the Middle District, which had four congregations near Harrisonburg.[28]

The word *conference* carried three meanings: the authority of the church, the twice-yearly gatherings of ordained leaders, and the network of congregations under its umbrella. As the highest authoritative body, the conference exercised power over bishops, congregations, and members through its decisions (recorded in minutes). The conference certified ministers for ordination and supervised the bishops, who interpreted—and sought to enforce—its regulations among the members in their district. Among other decisions Virginia Conference made from 1885 to 1890 were those forbidding members from attending worldly conventions and birthday parties, playing croquet, and exhibiting goods at local fairs. The conference also advised members against growing mustaches, wearing gold watch chains, swearing oaths, selling strong cider or wine to minors, and joining secret organizations like the Masons and the Farmers Alliance.[29]

Because no national organization existed, ecclesiastical authority rested in the regional conferences. States like Virginia and Iowa had only one conference, while Pennsylvania, the most populous Mennonite state, had four. The conferences were loosely coupled through kinship ties, letter writing, and occasional visits. The large and prosperous settlements in eastern Pennsylvania, such as Lancaster and Franconia Conferences, were quite different from the fledgling frontier congregations in the Midwest that were sprouting from migrations.

A New Century of Progress (Chicago, 1893)

Mennonites opened their first North American mission in Chicago in 1893, the same year that the city's gigantic World's Columbian Exposition proclaimed the beginning of "a century of progress." The Indiana-Michigan Conference discouraged its members from attending the great fair. Even so, two of its leaders, *Herald of Truth* editor John F. Funk and revivalist J. S. Coffman, found reasons to attend nearby religious events shortly after the fair opened.[30] Apart from piquing Mennonite curiosity, the exposition reflected the sense of optimism permeating national life during this time as people laid aside memories of the dreadful Civil War and turned to building a modern America. The Progressive Era, spanning roughly four decades (1880–1920), emanated a national spirit of hope, optimism, and progress.[31]

The optimism was driven by scientific discoveries, social reforms, and enormous strides in manufacturing that gave consumers a host of new products, from mousetraps and stop signs to vacuum cleaners and steam-driven tractors. New inventions—the airplane, Edison's light bulb, phonographs, motion picture cameras, sound recorders, and electrical distribution systems—sped up industrialization and mass communication. The Mennonite Book and Tract Society circulated a two-page ad recruiting agents to peddle a "cyclopedia" describing hundreds of recent inventions for the "Horseless Age," including "Liquid Air," "Wireless Telegraphy," "Submarines," and "X-Rays."[32] The inventive spirit pulsing across the land made it an exciting time.

Progressivism involved much more than technology. Its broad canopy stretched over advances in social, economic, political, and educational realms designed to regulate child labor, prohibit the sale of alcohol, reduce prostitution, remedy health hazards, eliminate corruption in government, establish federal regulations over banks and industries, and grant women the right to vote and participate in politics.

Three massive forces during this era—industrialization, immigration, and urbanization—combined to transform American society from a rural small-farm economy in 1880 to an urban industrial one by 1920. During these years, the percentage of farmers fell from 43 to 25 percent. Meanwhile, the percentage of urbanites nearly doubled, as more than half of all Americans lived in cities by 1920.[33]

The growing use of machine and electrical power for manufacturing increased the output of mass-produced goods like sewing machines, bicycles, and fashionable clothing.[34] This was also the era of industrial barons such as J. P. Morgan, Andrew Carnegie, Andrew W. Mellon, and John D. Rockefeller.

The urbanization was driven by both immigrants and native-born children from rural areas who abandoned their plows to search for new jobs and opportunities in cities. At the same time, a sizable number of farmers in the East were moving west in search of cheaper land. Both of these turn-of-the-century population shifts uprooted old social patterns across the country.

In the four decades from 1880 to 1920, nearly twenty-four million immigrants arrived in the United States, many settling in northeastern cities and Chicago. The sudden influx of famished outsiders from different countries created ghettos with poorly paid jobs, inadequate education, crowded tenement houses, and overflowing sewers. These dismal factors prepared a seedbed for crime, prostitution, and proliferating vices. Yet despite the obstacles, many immigrants were scrappy enough to succeed. By 1920, one-third of the nation's 105 million people were recent immigrants or first-generation Americans.[35]

The Progressive Era showed its gloomy underbelly in the urban squalor, a squalor that stirred social work heroine Jane Addams to establish Hull House in 1889 in Chicago, where she persuaded middle-class women and men to live in a slum to serve and Americanize impoverished immigrants of Italian, Irish, German, Greek, Russian, and Polish origins.[36] Women such as Addams, energized by religious convictions, actively led many of the urban reform efforts. Her Hull House experiment was replicated in thirty similar initiatives in Chicago and many other cities.

Addams was one of thousands of religious reformers laboring under the broad umbrella of the Social Gospel Movement. Its leaders sought to apply Christian ethics and the primitive tools of social science to address economic inequality, crime, slums, alcoholism, child labor, and poor education. William Stead's 1894 book, *If Christ Came to Chicago!*, urged disciples of Christ to follow his example and serve the city's destitute. Baptist pastor Walter Rauschenbusch argued in *Christianity and the Social Crisis* (1907) that Jesus compels his followers to engage in social reform.

These Social Gospel advocates blended personal salvation with social action, mixing pleas for both individual conversion and systemic change. Alongside their evangelical concern for souls, they sometimes lobbed harsh critiques at social inequality and capitalism. Ever optimistic, the Social Gospel activists envisioned that earnest Christian efforts would improve society, inching it toward an embodiment of the kingdom of God on earth. They expected that Christ would return only after systemic evil was rid by human efforts.[37]

The intellectual developments of the late nineteenth century, which cracked many taken-for-granted assumptions, were soon trickling into public discourse. Charles Darwin's *The Origin of Species* (1859) offered groundbreaking evidence of natural selection and evolving life-forms that sparked fiery discussions in the scientific and theological worlds of Europe and the United States. The emerging ideas shook not only the foundations of science but also deeply rooted religious views of creation. Many German theologians were using higher criticism, a scholarly, analytical approach to Bible study. This method, with its probing questions about the author, cultural context, scribal additions, and original meaning of a particular text, shattered well-entrenched assumptions about the Bible and divine revelation.[38]

These developments created a cauldron of heady and exciting ideas for some scholars but frightened others who embraced age-old orthodox beliefs. The progress spawned by the swelling number of immigrants, urbanization, industrialization, factory-produced products, and especially the ideas spewing from universities and colleges worried traditional Mennonites.

The burgeoning hopes of the Progressive Era were soon dashed on the rocks of brutality when World War I (1914–1918) claimed a toll of sixteen million dead and twenty million wounded, earning it the dismal distinction of being one of the deadliest conflicts in human history. Those hopes would be quickly battered again in the wake of the war when the flu pandemic of 1918 snatched away fifty million lives around the globe.

The Great Mennonite Transformation (Elida, Ohio, 1897)

One of the fruits of progress in Detroit was Henry Ford's assembly line, which by 1913 was rolling out a new Model T every forty seconds of the working day. Known as Fordism, this feat employed specialization, standardization, speed, and central control to revolutionize mass production around the world.[39]

The seeds of Fordism were planted in the Mennonite Church in November 1897 when seventy Mennonite bishops and ministers traveled by train and horse-drawn carriage to Elida, Ohio, for a two-day gathering at the Pike Meetinghouse. The newly married A. D. Wenger, now living in Lancaster, enjoyed mingling with his old friends, Preacher George R. Brunk from Kansas, Bishop L. J. Heatwole from the Shenandoah Valley, and Bishop Daniel Kauffman of Versailles, Missouri.[40]

The participants had gathered to divine the answer to this question: Should the Mennonite Church organize a national church body? Advocates argued that it would unify the sixteen regional conferences and "centralize our powers to build up the church . . . to direct mission, Orphan Homes, Publishing [organizations] etc., etc."[41] Cautionary voices implored their fellow ministers not to rashly form the proposed General Conference.

Daniel Kauffman pleaded for a united effort: "See the tremendous power which other organizations are bringing to bear upon us to draw us away from the plain, peaceable, and self-denying principles of the Bible. . . . Instead of boldly standing up as one solid body, we're going along in a haphazard way, some trying to do one thing and some another, often sparring [with] each other over some trivial matter. . . . Why can't we get together, understand each other better, and do something?"[42]

Representation at the gathering was lopsided. Fifty of the seventy participants came from Ohio and Indiana. Two people spoke for Virginia and only five voices represented Pennsylvania, the mother lode of Mennonites with four regional conferences and 50 percent of the national Mennonite population. Support for a national church body came largely from the Midwest, where newly sprouted congregations were smaller, scattered, and "surrounded by worldly influence and worldly examples of other Christian groups."[43]

L. J. Heatwole explained that the five eastern conferences (including Franconia, Lancaster, and Virginia) were *already* "united by the peculiar ties of kinship, as well as by a bond of fellowship" warmed by frequent visits. Thus none of these conferences needed "the unifying effect" of a Mennonite general conference.[44]

Yet by the end of the second day, "a large majority" agreed to call the first meeting of the General Conference a year later in Wakarusa, Indiana. Although Heatwole, Brunk, and Wenger attended that meeting in 1898, the Franconia, Lancaster, and Virginia Conferences sent no official delegates. The body elected Daniel Kauffman as moderator. Among other matters, the group discussed how to arrest the growing worldliness of members and how to bring the new mission and service organizations under General Conference control.[45]

Establishing the General Conference was a pivotal point in the *Great Transformation* of Mennonite life, which stretched from 1880 to 1920.[46] These were tumultuous years as Mennonites had to reckon with the tentacles of modernization reaching into their rural communities. Daniel Kauffman described modernization as a "relentless war . . . being waged against us" that sucks "many of our young people . . . away in the whirlpool of worldliness."[47]

This turbulence energized many Mennonites to explore new ways of thinking and living in the twentieth century. In rural hamlets from Virginia to Ohio and from Pennsylvania to Iowa, they grappled with the new gadgets spilling from factories, the westward migration of their own people, increasing contact with Protestant churches, growing urbanization, mass markets, transcontinental rail travel, and new educational opportunities. All of these factors enlarged the Mennonite worldview and stoked the Great Transformation of Mennonite life, which some scholars have called an "awakening" or a "quickening" from the slower pace of the staid

mid-nineteenth-century Mennonite communities. These vibrant changes transfig-
ured some separatist Mennonites from being the "quiet in the land" to building
institutions in mainstream life.

Mennonite leaders did not intend to convert the Mennonite Church into a
factory. Still, they did apply some of the principles of Fordism to the General
Conference apparatus, making it a national Protestant-like denomination with
bureaucratic features. Daniel Kauffman, speaking about church institutions, used
the explicit terms of Fordism to argue that Mennonite leaders of colleges and other
organizations should all have the "same type" of template in mind when they "think
of a model Christian . . . and [should] all work together in the *manufacture* of that
kind of *product*."[48] Such central national control, which aimed for uniformity and
standardization of church life, was unprecedented in the Mennonite Church.

The sharp sense of Mennonite identity in older, well-established communities
in the East became blurred as Mennonites shifted from German to English, started
Sunday schools, accepted revival meetings, built dozens of church-wide organizations, and energetically pursued church activities outside the confines of local
congregations. All of these changes signaled assimilation into American society.
Some Mennonites were trading in their old Mennonite passports for new ones
stamped "American Protestant." They were speaking "American" and acting more
Protestant in some ways.[49]

Networks of visionary Mennonite lay members established a host of new institutions during the Progressive Era, often without the endorsement of any regional
conference. These new ventures included mission outposts, orphanages, retirement homes, and publishing operations, as well as Sunday school promotional
meetings and Bible conferences. The mission initiatives included two foreign sites
(India, 1898, and Argentina, 1917) and two "home" missions (Chicago, 1893, and
Philadelphia, 1899).[50] Much of the Mennonite energy poured out of the Midwest,
especially around Elkhart, Indiana, some ninety miles east of Chicago, and the
nearby congregations founded by settlers from the East.

Mennonite activists repeated a four-letter mantra. "Work, work, work on every
hand for every consecrated worker," proclaimed one church leader.[51] *The Christian
Worker's Manual* was published in 1915.[52] The work ethic of nineteenth-century rural
life was now diverted toward building church institutions. "There is a mighty work
before us, and the sooner we get ourselves into shape to do it the easier it is done.
The day is past when we can sit down with folded arms and rely upon the spirit of
inbred Mennonitism to fill our churches," one leader said.[53] And the editor of a
Mennonite periodical lamented that church life had become "all work—one continued earnest, active, hurrying, rushing, hustling, pushing whirl of active work."[54]

EMS professor Ernest G. Gehman portrays blindfolded Mennonite parents sending their offspring to secular colleges. *Source: Sword and Trumpet* 2, no. 2 (Apr. 1930): 19.

Mennonite advocates of progress engaged in personal work, mission work, the Lord's work, and church work. Up-and-coming leaders solicited not just workers but aggressive workers who promoted bold initiatives. Most of this activism, driven by lay members, reached beyond local congregations and for the first time linked Mennonites across different regional conferences and states.

Fashioning a New Mennonite Identity

Beneath the outward signs of the Great Transformation lurked deeper shifts in Mennonite reality. People began appealing to *rational* sources of authority more than *traditional* ones to justify their beliefs and actions.[55] The growing influence of science encouraged scrutiny, questions, doubt, logic, and evidence-based research, which punctured many taken-for-granted assumptions. New sources of authority included the self, science, church organizations, and other religious groups.

Bishop Daniel Kauffman, moderator of the new General Conference, was a prolific author and diplomatic leader. His *Manual of Bible Doctrines*, published in 1898, showcased the principles of Fordism. It was the first logical, organized, and systematic book of Mennonite beliefs, which reflected a rational mind-set quite different from the oral stories and memories that had bestowed authority on the regional conferences for many years.

At about the same time, Mennonites were refashioning their view of God. They began seeing God as a planner and started referring to "God's plan of salvation"—a God-devised plan to save people from their sins. The notion that God was a planner dovetailed nicely with America's new obsession with planning. Mennonites did not invent this phrase. The revivalist J. S. Coffman likely borrowed it from C. I. Scofield, who thought that God had divided history into different dispensations (periods) of time.[56] Even so, the expression "God's plan of salvation" remained ensconced in popular Mennonite views of divine design for decades—giving individuals a choice to accept or reject God's plan.

When thirteen-year-old Suie Garber attended the first revival meetings condoned by Lancaster Conference in 1906, she did a courageous thing: she stood up and walked to the front of the meetinghouse and accepted Christ as her *personal* Savior. Her act overflowed with emotion. During the three-week series of meetings, 124 other people, aged ten through sixty, did the same thing. Garber's choice was quite unlike that of those in her parents' generation, who had dutifully joined the church as twenty- to thirty-year-olds in a rite of passage with few traces of emotion. For the older generation, conversion was a quiet, gradual, communal commitment.

The revival-style conversions were quick, public, and individualistic. They also entailed a new kind of religious experience: a personal relationship with a close-at-hand God. For A. D. Wenger and others, revival preaching and evangelism was "personal work."[57] Unlike the quiet conversions of days past, the emotion-laden ones like Garber's had a personal narrative that went something like this: "I accepted Christ as my personal Savior in February 1906 when I heard the powerful preaching of bishop Noah Mack. It was really something, it seemed so wonderful."[58]

These heartfelt salvation narratives were sincere. Still, the religious code words—"I accepted Christ as my personal Savior"—showed how a new generation of Mennonites had borrowed a script from the broader evangelical world. These conversion narratives accented *choice* and the *individual*: personal salvation, personal Bible study, and personal witness all centered on an individual's feelings, agency, and choice. This transformation of the self unleashed a new energy and activism that was reshaping Mennonite life at the outset of the twentieth century.

Church leaders faced a dilemma, however. As young people felt freed from the constraints of older traditions, would they stay within Mennonite pastures? A new focus on *obedience* and *self-denial* emerged to address that question.[59] Mennonites had always stressed the importance of obeying the teachings of Jesus, one's parents, and the church. Likewise, self-denial was embedded in Mennonite teaching, especially in Jesus's admonition that his disciples must be willing to deny self-interest (Luke 9:23). Now, however, obedience and self-denial were increasingly underscored and codified in Mennonite writing. They had received little attention in Daniel Kauffman's 1898 *Manual of Bible Doctrines*, but his 1914 revision, *Bible Doctrine*, highlighted them. In another book, Kauffman devoted an entire chapter to criticizing self-aggrandizement, followed by a chapter on the virtues of self-denial.[60] With the rise of individualism, the *self* was emerging as a new entity in Mennonite discourse, and an unbridled self could disturb uniformity, humility, and harmony. Invoking obedience and self-denial were guilt-inducing ways of controlling individual impulses.

Coinciding with a greater focus on the individual was self-adornment. Dress became a contentious issue among Mennonites during the Progressive Era. Until then, Mennonite identity had been sculpted by speaking German and wearing simple, plain clothing upon joining the church. (In some regions Mennonite men and women wore trendy clothing prior to baptism and church membership.)[61] Traditional dress practices began to crumble in the course of the Great Transformation, leaving Mennonite identity somewhat vague.

Several developments made fashionable clothing more accessible and more tempting: sized patterns for commercial production, enhancements to the sewing machine, large clothing factories, the rise of mail-order catalogs and women's magazines, and the advent of rural mail delivery in 1902. Most importantly, mass-produced fashions were becoming available in stores in rural areas. All these developments promised access to mass-produced, stylish, ready-to-wear clothing for everyone, everywhere.[62] Greater access to such clothing gave Mennonites greater choice and a new tool of self-expression.

As dress became a flash point among Mennonites, the key question was this: Should the church establish church-wide regulations for garb? Church officials had always encouraged members to wear plain clothing, but they had never prescribed a specific style or uniform. Should the uniformity of Fordism apply to dress? If the church could revitalize nonconformity and codify it using specific dress regulations, perhaps Mennonites could create a new symbol of identity that would also protest popular clothing. A uniform pattern of dress would constrain self-aggrandizement.[63]

In the first two decades of the twentieth century, many Mennonite Church leaders actively promoted a regulation garb consisting of a plain suit (a jacket with a straight-cut standing collar and no lapels) for men and a cape dress (a dress with additional fabric covering the front and back of the bodice) and a head covering for women.[64] Members who wore the regulation garb relinquished their right to self-expression and also signaled their loyalty to the Mennonite team. Moreover, distinctive dress helped strengthen the cultural separation that had eroded with the decline of the German language.

The Great Transformation altered Mennonite consciousness, religious beliefs, and practices. Individuals exercised greater choice. Ironically, as individual moral authority was rising, so was the clout of the newly created organizations, which reached far beyond local congregations for the first time in American Mennonite history. The power of the new education, service, publication, and mission organizations would swell over the course of the twentieth century and refashion Mennonite identity. The growing individualism, reliance on rational authorities, and institution building coalesced in a ripe moment for starting Mennonite schools.

An Educational Quandary

Between 1890 and World War I, members of three Mennonite groups established seven high schools and colleges.[65] Yet Mennonite educational initiatives lagged well behind those of other churches. As religious separatists, many Mennonites held an abiding distrust of education beyond the one-room common schools. Their opposition to higher education reached back to their origins in sixteenth-century Europe, even though some of the earliest Anabaptist leaders were university educated. Well-educated Protestant and Catholic clergy who scorned Anabaptists as "heretics" and interrogated them in religious trials often used clever theological terms to justify torturing them for following the simple teachings of Jesus. Eventually, the rural lineage and fringe social status of Swiss-German Mennonites (both in Europe and the United States) favored practical training over book learning. Besides, American colleges now brought new reasons to fear education.

Many Mennonites were "opposed to higher education," explained two influential Mennonite Church leaders in 1908, because "some of our young people, having acquired a liberal education, . . . [became] puffed up with pride and valueless to the church. . . . Others . . . became avowed skeptics. Recognizing that a humble common man is worth more . . . than a high-minded intellectual giant, many of our most thoughtful people have taken a decided stand against higher education."[66]

Some of the most ambitious youth, invigorated by a progressive education in non-Mennonite colleges, were leaving the Mennonite fold. L. J. Heatwole painfully declared that "no other denomination in America has suffered as fearful reverses" in losing their youth. And because of "this tremendous drain," the Mennonite Church could only count "her adherents by thousands . . . where there might have been millions!"[67]

These sobering facts are not well documented. Still, such widely shared perceptions placed Mennonites in a predicament: advanced education was coming, and unless they wanted to completely shun progress, they had to engage it. And engage it they did. Yet even progress-minded Mennonites squabbled for several decades about the merits of any education beyond the elementary grades.

A Protestant Christian ethos had permeated Harvard, Yale, Princeton, Columbia, and the other colleges founded by churches before the Civil War. These schools had a clergyman at the head, mandatory chapel attendance, courses in Christianity, and occasional religious revivals.[68] All of that changed during an educational revolution in the last quarter of the nineteenth century. The older colleges reinvented themselves as European-style universities, and a host of new ones, including Johns Hopkins, the University of Chicago, Cornell, and Stanford, sprang into prominence. Now funded by wealthy philanthropists and the government instead of by churches, the religious flavor of universities both new and old declined rapidly.

As the nation's population almost doubled between 1870 and 1900, the number of college students spiked as well, rising from 52,000 to 238,000. Faculty numbers also increased. At Harvard, for example, they surged from 60 to 600.[69] Small college start-ups were also plentiful in the nineteenth century. In Pennsylvania, eighty institutions were founded by 1900 (fourteen were state colleges).[70] The majority of private schools were established by churches or visionary educators with religious motivations. In Virginia, sixteen colleges had been founded by churches or religious leaders by 1900.[71] Some religiously motivated educators wanted to retain a particular religious identity and shield their youth from cultural assimilation. Others sought to equip their youth with Bible training for missionary work, and still others aimed to offer a religion-based education to the larger public.

Hundreds of new institutions began as academies (high schools) or normal schools (which trained teachers for elementary schools). Although many of these new ventures eventually became colleges, a considerable number had failed by the early twentieth century, and most of those that did survive gradually lost their religious moorings.

The Dunkers, for example, established some two dozen academies and normal schools between 1860 and 1900. Two-thirds had failed by 1908. Among the survivors, only six still had ties with the church in 1940.[72] One was Bridgewater College in Virginia, established in 1880 as a normal school.[73] Both A. D. Wenger and L. J. Heatwole had attended Bridgewater, located eight miles south of Harrisonburg. Pennsylvania had two surviving colleges founded by the Brethren: Juniata College (1876) and Elizabethtown College (1899) in western Lancaster County.[74] The Brethren in Christ, another religious cousin of the Mennonites, started Messiah College as a Bible school in 1909 near Harrisburg, Pennsylvania.[75]

The Birth of Mennonite Colleges

Members of the General Conference Mennonite Church opened Bethel College (Kansas) in 1893 and Central Mennonite College in Ohio in 1899 (the latter would become Bluffton College by 1913).[76] Dr. Henry A. Mumaw—Mennonite Church member, homeopathic physician, and entrepreneur of Swiss-German roots—founded the Elkhart Institute of Science, Industry, and the Arts in northern Indiana in 1894. The Elkhart Institute offered academic and commercial courses for working adults. Although many of the people who bought stock in the institute's corporation were Mennonites, it was not controlled by the church. When the institute moved fifteen miles southeast to the town of Goshen in 1903, it was renamed Goshen College. In 1905, it came under the jurisdiction of the Mennonite Board of Education, an agency of the Mennonite Church.[77]

Mennonite revivalist J. S. Coffman, the titular president of the institute, titled his inaugural address "The Spirit of Progress." While heralding the new school, Coffman, like many Mennonites, was also anxious about its future. "What will be the result of this transition?" he asked, and then he confessed, "We fear and tremble as we think of what might be. Let us never say, there is no danger!" Yet he asserted that Christian higher education "will form a pavilion round about us in which we can dwell in safety from the encroachments of popular opinion and worldly aspirations that will come dashing against us with the fury of a sweeping cyclone."[78]

Deep within their souls, some Mennonites worried that the furious cyclone of modernity might upend their best intentions and dash their placid communities on the rocks. Indeed, that fear was not an idle one. Within twenty-five years of its founding, turbulence over religious modernism would dash Goshen College on the rocks—prompting church leaders to shutter it for an academic year (1923–1924) until they could regain control.

In 1909, members of the Mennonite Church built a college in Hesston, Kansas. Both Goshen College and Hesston College were established in the Midwest despite the fact that 75 percent of the Mennonite population lived in the eastern heartlands of Pennsylvania, Maryland, and Virginia.[79] Not surprisingly, the most ardent critics of Goshen and Hesston hailed from the old Mennonite strongholds in the East. Distressed by what they considered dangerous modernism in the western schools, a handful of church leaders in the East advocated for a *conservative* eastern school.

When he arrived back in Lancaster County in 1900 from his global trek, A. D. Wenger pondered the prospect of an eastern school but decided the time was "not ripe yet." He later shared the idea of an eastern school with a Mennonite friend at an unlikely spot: Harvard University. N. E. Byers, president of Goshen College, was on

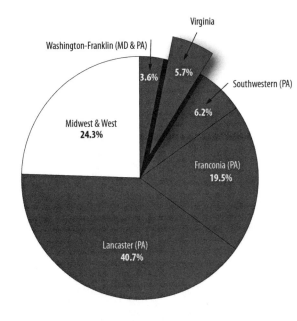

Washington-Franklin (MD & PA)

Virginia

3.6%

5.7%

Southwestern (PA)

6.2%

Midwest & West
24.3%

Franconia (PA)
19.5%

Lancaster (PA)
40.7%

Membership of Mennonite
Church conferences in 1910.
Source: Family Almanac 1910, 56.
Chart: Linda L. Eberly.

a study leave at Harvard in spring 1903. He told Wenger that his school had needed to "make our own faculty" because there were so few Mennonite teachers. Moreover, he advised Wenger to send promising students to universities immediately to get as much "experience and prestige as possible" so that later they could help build a college. Further, Byers suggested collecting funds right away and holding them in reserve until Lancaster Mennonites were ready for a school.

Byers argued against having two competing schools: "The Eastern school can be controlled by Eastern men and the Western school by Western men but we must have one general board to harmonize [their work]." He hoped that "ten years from now [1913] an Eastern institution" could offer four-year college courses and Goshen College could become "a good small college giving only the two first years of regular college courses in addition to a preparatory [high school]."[80]

Caught between their fear of attrition and their suspicion of higher education, eastern Mennonites would resolve their quandary by negotiating a middle ground. By 1912, visionary leaders began planning for a school of advanced learning that would safeguard their youth from the maelstrom of worldliness. Education, in their judgment, was a dangerous yet necessary venture to preserve the church. They hoped and prayed that a church school, with proper supervision, could successfully retain their youth and also serve the church.

PART II

Eastern Mennonite *School* and the Founding Era, 1917–1947

CHAPTER 2

Vision Blurred, Hope Deferred

*[We need] men . . . willing to throw their lives
into the enterprise, and stay with it.*
—EMS trustees, July 17, 1913

"I Feel a Desire"

When his global tour ended in March 1900, A. D. Wenger returned to the home that his late wife, Mary Hostetter, had built in the village of Millersville, a few miles west of Lancaster. Mary's mother and father had died before she was twenty, leaving her a farm and the resources to build a house before she married A. D. at age twenty-nine.

The day after his return, he visited with Bishop Daniel Lehman and Magdalena Lehman, members of Millersville Mennonite Church. The stories of his travels intrigued the Lehmans' eldest child, twenty-one-year-old Anna May "Annie" Lehman. A teacher at Central Manor Common School, she invited A. D. to bring some of his artifacts to her school and speak about his tour.[1]

Wenger's invigorating world trip had not quenched his loneliness or his longing for a soul mate. A few days after visiting Annie's school, he reached out to her: "I have felt a kind of special interest in you. . . . I feel a desire to know more about you. Think and pray over this, but please answer soon. . . . Your reply will reveal to me more fully the will of God." She responded in two days: "I have no objection to you calling some time to see me. Anytime you desire." Five weeks later, while A. D. was conducting revival meetings among the Mennonites of Virginia, the couple confirmed their engagement by letter. A. D. and Annie were married on September 27, 1900, in Millersville.

Two months after their wedding, polio struck Wenger, and he spent the next year recovering while completing his manuscript for *Six Months in Bible Lands and Around the World in Fourteen Months.* Wenger's bout with polio permanently weakened the muscles in both arms and one leg. Annie faithfully helped him in and out of the bathtub for the rest of his life. He walked with a limp and could only eat comfortably if he rested both arms on the table. He was able to drive a horse and carriage but not a car when they came into use.

From their home in the village, A. D. and Annie tried to operate the farm west of Millersville that he had inherited when Mary died, but they faced some problems. Because of his polio, A. D. had trouble tilling the hilly and stony ground. He hired day laborers, but they insisted on using some of the land to raise tobacco—an important cash crop in Lancaster's Mennonite community. Wenger abhorred growing tobacco, yet the couple wanted to raise their children on a farm. Despite A. D.'s prominence as a church-wide evangelist, he had received a cool reception from some of Lancaster's most tradition-minded ministers, who considered him an outsider and disliked his revivalist preaching and openness to education. Thus A. D. and Annie decided to leave Lancaster County. On September 22, 1908, five days shy of their eighth wedding anniversary, the two took a train to Baltimore, where they boarded an overnight boat on the Chesapeake Bay for Norfolk, Virginia, to look for a new home.

At the beginning of the twentieth century, some Mennonites were exploring locations in southeastern states where they could acquire cheap land to establish Mennonite colonies and expand their mission outreach. Mennonites from various states had already begun planting a colony in 1897 near Denbigh, Virginia, a small town close to the city of Newport News. Located near the Warwick River, Denbigh was the seat of Warwick County. The recent arrivals called their new congregation Warwick River Mennonite Church.[2]

A sister settlement was established about the same time at Fentress, about sixteen miles south of the city of Norfolk.[3] The two settlements were separated by Hampton Roads, one of the world's largest natural harbors, which emptied into the Chesapeake Bay and the Atlantic Ocean.[4] The forty-mile, day-long trip from Denbigh to Fentress required a ferry ride across the harbor. The Tidewater area attracted Mennonite settlers with its inexpensive and level land, ample rainfall, easy access to urban markets, and balmy winters ideal for growing apples, grapes, strawberries, and other fruits and vegetables.

A. D. and Annie bought farmland near the village of Fentress. In November 1908, they took their four children by horse and carriage from Lancaster to Baltimore, where they boarded a ferry to Norfolk to join five Mennonite families already living in Fentress, including A. D.'s brother and sister-in-law and their ten children. A. D. served as preacher in the fledgling congregation at Fentress, which by 1909

A. D. Wenger (1867–1935)
and Anna May Lehman
(1878–1955) were married
on September 27, 1900, in
Millersville, Pennsylvania.

claimed thirty-three members. He continued to serve on church-wide committees but curtailed his evangelistic travels in order to cultivate grapes and other fruits and vegetables and to raise his growing family, which eventually numbered eight children. Their youngest son, Chester, later said, "My parents moved to Fentress to raise grapes because they didn't want to raise tobacco in Lancaster."[5]

Crazy about Each Other

From his perch on the preachers' bench facing the congregation of the Lindale church near Harrisonburg, Virginia, Bishop George R. Brunk could easily scan the audience. The twenty-eight-year-old bachelor's gaze froze when he saw a charming young woman stand and walk out to get some water for her mother. It was June 1900, and Brunk had arrived from Kansas to visit and preach for several months.[6] He also attended the semiannual meetings of Virginia Conference, where he mingled with old friends A. D. Wenger of Lancaster and Bishop Daniel Kauffman from Missouri.

Ordained as a preacher in Kansas when he was twenty-one and as a bishop five years later, Brunk was already well known as a riveting revival preacher and up-and-coming leader. Bestowed with persuasive powers and a height of six feet four inches, he had a commanding presence. Brunk had a special knack with words and could articulate big ideas with clarity and simplicity. His keen memory and sharp wit made him an engaging and charming speaker. One historian described him as "a man of strong emotions driven by an equally strong will." Brunk was endowed with "a powerful charisma. His voice, well-modulated and resonant, could project intimacy or intimidation, lyrical sweetness or thunderous severity with equal effect. Whether in sympathy or contempt, his eyes engaged and held you."[7]

This was his first trip to Virginia, and he was eager to meet his Brunk kin. He also looked forward to learning more about how his parents had fled the Shenandoah Valley at great peril during the Civil War and especially how his father, Henry, a conscientious objector, had been captured and imprisoned by the Confederate Army. Henry later opted for noncombatant service but felt so guilty that he deserted the army and remained a fugitive for two and a half years until he left Virginia one night and traveled to Maryland. His wife, Susan (Heatwole), also slipped away and eventually joined him in Hagerstown, Maryland. They resettled in Illinois, where George was born in 1871.[8]

About two years later, the Brunk family moved to Marion Center, Kansas, about forty miles northeast of Hesston. Soon after arriving, Henry died of typhoid fever, as did three of his offspring, leaving Susan and their four remaining children, including two-year-old George, to fend for themselves on the lonely Kansas prairie. A short time later, young George fell ill—so ill that his mother said, "Just lay him away and let him die in peace."[9] But somehow he survived both his illness and the hardscrabble frontier life—an anvil of adversity that would forge his fearless and scrappy spirit. After telling his mother that he would never become a Mennonite, he was converted as a seventeen-year-old, under the influence of J. S. Coffman's preaching.[10]

Brunk had arrived in Virginia in April 1900 not only to explore his roots but also to kindle some revival fires in the conference where, twelve years earlier, J. S. Coffman's evangelistic preaching had stirred up quite a ruckus. The conference had never endorsed revival meetings, but Brunk's powerful preaching crumbled its resistance.[11] Upward of seven hundred people flocked to some of his Sunday services. He boldly broke the unwritten rule that prohibited more than three services in a row by preaching for a week at some places. Brunk noted that many people "favored three or four weeks of meetings just like we do in the West."[12]

By the end of June, he had delivered sixty sermons, yielding some fifty converts in the midst of an icy stalemate between Virginia's progressives and traditionalists. Two years later, the traditionalists withdrew to form an Old Order Mennonite congregation. Brunk recalled that because of his preaching, "the dust of opposition blew inside and outside the church—I was threatened by mobbing from outside and denounced openly in conference by grey beards who afterwards loved and supported me."[13]

George R. Brunk learned that the young woman he saw at Lindale was twenty-five-year-old Katie Wenger, a younger sister of A. D. Wenger. The day after he first spied her in church, he asked an elderly Brunk relative to escort him to her home in Greenmount for introductions. She lived alone with her mother, Hannah. George stayed for several hours, and during that time, the foursome enjoyed a meal and he offered Katie a rose. Six weeks later, in mid-July, they were married in Katie's home by Bishop L. J. Heatwole. The couple took a wedding trip to Washington, DC—catching their first glimpse of a horseless carriage—and then traveled on to Pennsylvania, where George preached in several congregations before returning by boat to visit the newly formed communities in the Tidewater area.

Four days after their wedding, George gushed to family in the West, "We are as happy as it's lawful to be." They carried their exuberance to Pennsylvania, where, according to George, it set off a "big flare up." Two Lancaster bishops were offended by the couple's public affection and George's playing of a mouth organ in an open carriage on their way to a church service. George conceded later that they "were too crazy about each other" to notice the watchful eyes of others.[14] Back in Virginia, the tongues of some folks were clucking about how he had snatched Katie away from Hannah so quickly, forcing her to sell the farm, and then whisked Katie off to the harsh plains of Kansas.

Katie and George arrived in Kansas in the fall of 1900. They first settled in McPherson County and eventually relocated to Comanche County, where they built a house in 1907. However, by 1910, they decided to move back to Virginia, intending to settle in Fentress near Katie's two brothers, Timothy and A. D. Wenger. Although the Brunks had shipped their household goods directly to Fentress, they decided to stop first in Denbigh to visit Katie's sister Anna and several friends. Arriving in Denbigh, they were startled to hear that folks in Fentress stridently opposed their coming and that thirty-year-old Bishop Joseph Wert—who had jurisdiction over congregations in the area—declared that he would leave Fentress if the Brunks came. George and Katie abruptly altered their plans and settled permanently in Denbigh instead.[15]

Why did their plan to live in Fentress provoke anxiety? At thirty-eight, George R. Brunk was already an ecclesiastical giant. He had a national reputation as a decisive leader—having aided frontier settlements and mediated church disputes in Colorado, Idaho, Indiana, Kansas, Missouri, and Pennsylvania, along with maintaining a heavy schedule of preaching, writing, and serving on church-wide committees. Mennonites in the Tidewater area remembered that during his October

1906 visit—even with no jurisdiction in Virginia—he had vigorously urged Virginia Conference to strengthen its separatist stance and, a few days later, fired off an essay to *Herald of Truth* blasting thirty-six inconsistencies in Mennonite life.[16]

Never lacking in self-confidence, Brunk cut a wide swath across the Mennonite world. His influence reached well beyond any single community, conference, or state. The locals worried that if he moved into the area, they would never be the same. And they never were. In May 1910, three months after the Brunks arrived, Virginia Mennonite Conference met in Denbigh and appointed George bishop of the Warwick River congregation, which his family attended. About two years later, the conference also assigned the Fentress congregation to Brunk after Bishop Wert scuttled his own career through sexual improprieties.[17]

If Virginia Conference hoped that its quick embrace of Brunk would boost Virginia's clout in the Mennonite world and inscribe the then obscure communities in Denbigh and Fentress into the annals of Mennonite history, then it succeeded. George R. Brunk did all of that and more from his pulpit in Denbigh for twenty-eight years.

The Brunks probably had multiple reasons for moving to the Tidewater region.[18] George's own roots were in Virginia, and three of Katie's siblings and their families lived in the area. Besides, the small Virginia Conference was more open to change than the older Mennonite settlements in Pennsylvania. The infant congregations in Denbigh and Fentress offered more elbow room for an enterprising bishop than the well-established churches two hundred miles west in the Shenandoah Valley.[19]

But another factor loomed large in George's mind. "One main reason for our coming east," he said, "was to press my campaign against the corrupting influences of Goshen College . . . and counteract the rising tide of Goshenism."[20] When Brunk learned that a Goshen faculty member had quipped that George R. was "pouting in Western Kansas" where he could not "run a church," he retorted, "I have landed in old Virginia ready for war against every high thing that exalts itself against the knowledge of God!!!"[21]

The Mennonite Students' Safeguard and Industrial School

Truth be told, Eastern Mennonite School may never have sprouted, at least not as early as 1917, without the enterprising efforts of George R. Brunk. In December 1912, about two years after he settled in Denbigh, members of his Warwick River congregation started a movement to establish a Mennonite school to counter the "questionable character of [local] public schools." The minutes of the first meeting note that "conviction and enthusiasm have sprung up [about] launching an institution" that would solve "the school problem not only for our immediate community but many others as well."[22]

Mid-Atlantic sites related to the founding of Eastern Mennonite School, ca. 1915. Map: Jonathan P. Gehman.

Ten years after Goshen College president N. E. Byers described his dream of an eastern school, the Warwick River enthusiasts set it in motion. Beginning in December 1912, they held thirteen meetings in rapid succession over five months. By February 1913, they had approved a constitution (drafted by L. J. Heatwole) and organized a "General Board" with five committees, appointing twenty-five men to serve on it.[23] The board was a skeletal network of appointees, some of whom had never agreed to serve and rarely attended meetings.

Four members of the General Board lived outside Virginia, while three lived in state but far from the Tidewater region. The founders hoped that by appointing board members from Ohio and Pennsylvania, they would serve Mennonite students not only in the Denbigh area but also in regions beyond. The board included Bishop John Mosemann of Lancaster and two national heavyweights at the newly minted Mennonite Publishing House in Scottdale, Pennsylvania—Aaron Loucks, financier and CEO, and Daniel Kauffman, now working there as editor of *Gospel Herald*. L. J. Heatwole, living two hundred miles west in Harrisonburg, was the most active non-Denbigh participant. A. D. Wenger, a member of the four-person managing committee, was still farming in Fentress, but he rarely attended meetings despite his strong convictions regarding Mennonite schools.

The school advocates planned to distribute one thousand copies of the constitution, seek the endorsement of Virginia Conference and the newly established (1905) church-wide Mennonite Board of Education, and solicit funds and students from eastern conferences. All five appointees to the faculty committee except Preacher

Daniel Shenk lived outside the Tidewater area. Although these factors underscored the larger-than-Denbigh vision, the energy, funds, and leadership were driven by the Warwick River congregation and Bishop Brunk's passion. Brunk's handwritten minutes of the meetings, his commitment to secure teachers, and his role as temporary chair of the General Board confirm his prominent leadership during the first fourteen months of the venture.

The advocates wanted to establish a school that would receive the "hearty approval of our congregations in the East." They hoped to organize an independent school that later "would operate under the sanction of the Va. conference." They intended to protect the school with "safeguards thrown around this institution [to] ensure its continued orthodoxy." The proposed Mennonite Students' Safeguard and Industrial School aimed to provide a "practical education" with "industrial features" as well as a "spiritual incentive for developing more fully and completely the mind of the student along religious as well as moral and intellectual lines." Finally, the leaders hoped to "foster a mission department [for] the training of the mind as well as the heart and hand of orphaned children." Other prominent features of the school included vocal music and Bible study, as well as elementary, high school, and vocational courses. The earliest draft of the constitution had few restrictions: all teachers were required to be members of the Mennonite Church in good standing, and only those textbooks and "forms of theology" that were "strictly in accord with the faith and doctrine of the [Dordrecht] Mennonite Confession of Faith" would be acceptable.[24]

By the fifth meeting—even before the constitution was approved—the Warwick River congregation voted unanimously to build the school, renamed the Warwick Mennonite Institute, on forty-two acres of Preacher Daniel Shenk's land adjacent to the church.[25] By early June, school proponents had finished plans to construct a temporary building in order to enroll students in the fall. They also continued to solicit funds from church leaders in Virginia and beyond. At the proposed site, Brunk reportedly told bystanders, "Whoever writes the history of the school can say that George R. Brunk hauled the first load of sand for it."[26]

Shortly after their thirteenth meeting, when the school enthusiasts had already acquired land and money and expected to open the school three months later, the project collapsed. A commodious mansion near Washington had suddenly upstaged all the efforts at Denbigh. In Brunk's words, "I arranged a plan to try Alexandria." Sometime around June 7, 1913, Brunk had traveled to Alexandria to certify a new congregation. He installed David Garber (an ordained friend from Kansas) as minister and bishop of a handful of Mennonites who had recently settled near Mount Vernon.[27] During his visit, Brunk discovered that one member, Chris G.

Garber, had purchased Hayfield, an eight-hundred-acre estate formerly owned by George Washington. A spacious colonial mansion equipped with modern fixtures for lighting and heating sat on two acres of beautiful grounds with "buildings nicely arranged by Gen. Washington himself with trees and old-time shrubbery etc."[28]

Brunk thought the site, about twelve miles from Washington and two miles from Mount Vernon, was ideal for a school. Knowing that Chris Garber was under financial stress, Brunk thought the school plan would help Garber, and on a whim, the enterprising bishop proposed an offer as they stood on the porch of the mansion. Brunk explained, "He was in [a] tight pinch when I first went there—I told him he could not make it, he must sell. He said his wife would not do it—said he had just turned a buyer away. . . . At that point, I thot [sic] of the school, and suggested that he donate the house and grounds to the school. And if the school is here once, I feel sure you can sell off your land. He said then that if we would find persons to take the land he would give the donation."[29] The handshake agreement stipulated that Garber would donate the colonial building and two acres to the school board if the school or private individuals would purchase three hundred acres for sixty dollars apiece so that he could satisfy his debt.[30]

Surprisingly, the Warwick advocates, who had worked feverishly over the last five months, accepted Bishop Brunk's proposal when they met on June 17. When he explained that Alexandria was a central location "for the whole East" and the "large commodious, well-furnished building was ready to occupy, [it] appealed [to them] pretty strongly," a testament to the bishop's persuasive powers. Daniel Shenk, who had donated ten acres of his land for the Warwick Mennonite Institute, reported, "The sentiment here was unanimous," with the caveat that donors could request that their past contributions remain in Denbigh for "a small local school here . . . in which nothing above the eighth grade will be taught."

Within days, all eyes turned 170 miles north to the Hayfield estate.[31] Even Washingtonians saw the news, which appeared in a story published in the *Washington Times* on July 14 and a day later in the *Washington Herald*: "Christian Garber, owner of the Hayfield farm, has offered to donate the use of the old mansion at that place, together with [two] acres of land to the Mennonite sect to be used for the establishment of a Mennonite college."[32] The signed-with-a-handshake deal, however, would soon become ensnarled in a bitter two-year dispute that would leave the new school homeless. The plan began to unravel back in Denbigh by late July, when Daniel Shenk learned that Adam Baer, an entrepreneur from Maugansville, Maryland, had diverted his promised $1,000 gift for the Warwick school to Alexandria, "seriously crippling" any school at Denbigh. A year later, Shenk used the word "tragedy" to describe how the school had "slipped away" from the Denbigh area.[33]

Hayfield Mansion in Alexandria, Virginia, location of the first Special Bible Term in January 1915.

The Alexandria Mennonite Institute

On July 17, 1913, a three-person exploratory committee consisting of Daniel Kauffman (chair), L. J. Heatwole, and Adam Baer met at the Hayfield mansion and inspected the property.[34] They found the brick walls of "the Colonial Mansion built 150 years ago . . . by George Washington . . . still firm and compact . . . [without] a single crack or crevice." Moreover, they saw twelve-foot-wide porches skirting three sides of the three-story, nineteen-room building. Enamored, they spoke with Chris Garber and reaffirmed the verbal deal: he would donate the mansion and two acres if the school found buyers for three hundred acres at sixty dollars each, which would raise $18,000 to "lift" his mortgage.[35] In their minds, there were merely two liabilities: poor lighting because of small windows and the two-and-a-half mile distance to the train station. Apart from those drawbacks, it was "about as favorable a location" as they could imagine.[36]

The committee recommended the Hayfield site to the General Board with three qualifications: (1) if a favorable sentiment emerges in the churches, (2) if the small Hayfield congregation grows, and (3) if "men can be found . . . to manage the school, who are capable, consecrated, loyal to God and the church and willing to throw their lives into the enterprise, and stay with it."[37] The investigators hoped to create a new Mennonite colony in Alexandria. To offset Garber's debt, they expected that settlers would buy some of his land and that speculators would buy some as well, in hopes of reselling it to Mennonites moving into the area later.

The Hayfield project was on the agenda when Virginia Conference met in October 1913. David Garber, recently installed as bishop at Alexandria, was welcomed as a new member of the conference. One participant recalled, however, that "no one had a greater influence on the Virginia conference" that day than George R. Brunk.[38] After lengthy discussion, the conference unanimously agreed that "brethren who feel interested" could contribute "their means, patronage and influence" to the proposed school at Alexandria. While granting their permission for individuals to contribute, the conference promised no funding, organizational oversight, or responsibility for the project.[39]

Eleven months and fifteen meetings after the school advocates first met, the General Board held its final meeting in Denbigh on November 12, 1913. They endorsed the recommendations of the exploratory committee (Heatwole, Kauffman, and Baer) and asked these men to promote Alexandria, convene a "mass meeting" to reorganize the board, update the constitution, and "launch the school." The General Board urged the committee to act with "all possible haste" so that friends of the school would "not become sick from hope deferred."[40]

While the surface seemed tranquil, the waters below were turbulent. Since the beginning of the school movement, Brunk had repeatedly invited Samuel Grant "S. G." Shetler, a prominent evangelist, Bible teacher, and organizer of Bible schools, to manage the new school. Shetler declined, severely disappointing Brunk, who said he was "sure that if we could get Shetler the rest would [fall in place]."[41] Furthermore, no settlers or investors had stepped forward to buy land at Hayfield. And most worrisome of all, Chris Garber had become cantankerous, contesting the board's interpretations of "the deal" and blaming the board members for delays and what he considered broken promises—all reasons to become sick from hope deferred.

One spark of hope was John J. "J. J." Wenger, cousin of A. D. Wenger and Katie Wenger Brunk. George R. Brunk had earlier tried to lure J. J., who was a deacon at the Lindale congregation near Harrisonburg and a person with some financial acumen, to Denbigh to be the business manager of the proposed Warwick Mennonite Institute.[42] More recently, Bishop David Garber had invited him to move to Alexandria and serve as deacon of the new congregation.[43] J. J. Wenger visited Alexandria in the fall of 1913 and eventually moved there in early 1914. During his fall visit, he learned of Chris Garber's financial straits and obtained a personal bank loan, giving the money to Garber so he could make payments on his mortgage and avoid bankruptcy, which would have ruined all prospects for the school.[44]

Knowing that his hopes for Alexandria were endangered, Bishop Brunk wrote a blunt letter to Chris Garber two days before Thanksgiving 1913, refuting many of

Garber's charges—particularly the one that Brunk himself had promised to purchase the three hundred acres. Brunk wrote that he could hardly keep his own financial "head above water" given his large family and all his church work. He also explained that the board had not been "idle," as Garber had charged; severe criticism from an unnamed bishop had prohibited the board from purchasing land until Virginia Conference sanctioned the project in October, and the failure to recruit S. G. Shetler was also a setback.

Brunk then clarified several matters. "The board won't blame you if you sell the land to others," he told Garber, also assuring him that the board was not scouting for other sites and was "working as quickly [as possible]." Brunk had hoped that J. J. Wenger's personal loan would help Garber keep his offer open so the group could "get men and money and students." But, he continued, "if you can't wait, withdraw your offer . . . [it] never has been sure that there will be a school *at all*." At the same time, Brunk remained convinced that "if the school stands there," it will bring buyers for the land. In closing, Brunk said, "It's not wise to rush," and stated his hopes that "no one will be *injured*."[45]

The trio promoting the project (Heatwole, Kauffman, and Baer) publicized a mass meeting of eastern church leaders for February 17–18, 1914, at Maugansville, near Hagerstown, Maryland. The turnout was pathetic. According to one count, only thirteen people showed up including the janitor of the meetinghouse—redefining the word *mass*.[46] The attendees reported their home communities' views of the Alexandria project. One observer noted, "There was as much sentiment *against*, as for it."[47] Even the official report noted "grave and doubtful" concerns that the church could ever control a school. Still, the group agreed that a school might benefit the church "if the right kind of teachers . . . and a safe management" could be secured.[48]

Participants reviewed a revised constitution for the school, now renamed the Alexandria Mennonite Institute. They also reorganized the General Board, replacing many Warwick appointees with new ones from a wider area. Bishop L. J. Heatwole was elected chair, replacing George R. Brunk, who had served as acting chair from the outset. Now vice chair, Brunk continued on the faculty committee and, most importantly, chaired the trustee committee, which was responsible for facilities and sites, including the delicate negotiations with Chris Garber. J. J. Wenger, now living in Alexandria, was placed on three committees and appointed business manager. His wife, Isa, was designated matron of the school, which the board hoped to open by fall 1914. A. D. Wenger served on the constitution committee as well as on the trustee committee.

Despite the apathy at the Maugansville meeting, the school proponents plodded on. On February 20, 1914, the new trustee committee took a written proposal to

Garber, asking for a decision within six days.[49] He promptly rejected it as "undesirable for him in every way."[50] Garber requested arbitration and helped select an impartial committee, which, by late spring, cleared the trustee committee of any wrongdoing, including Garber's "unreasonable and unjust charges."[51] Discussions with Garber continued, but he turned recalcitrant, bitter, and volatile.

By early June 1914, Chairman Heatwole had become impatient with the "standstill" and saw no reason to wait and prolong the messy process.[52] He was particularly annoyed that Brunk had conjectured that Hayfield could "be bought cheap before long." David Garber, bishop at Alexandria, was ready to drop the "badly mixed up affair," especially since Mennonites in Maryland and Pennsylvania had no interest in it at all.[53]

Meanwhile, J. J. Wenger had been "praying and laboring much . . . to restore peace and good feeling," and on July 28, he reported some success: Chris Garber had signed a written confession apologizing for his "rashness" and asking for forgiveness.[54] The trustee committee responded with a generous letter of forgiveness, asked his forbearance for any offense, and prayed that "every particle of bitterness" might vanish.[55]

Also in late July, J. J. Wenger announced that he had purchased "a couple hundred acres" at Hayfield "solely on my own will, without any authority." He did it "to save brother G. from foreclosure and also trusting we might yet restore good feeling . . . and hopes for the school."[56] Wenger planned to resell the land with the mansion and barn to individuals and/or the school board. Although this good omen came too late to open the school that fall, it did place the mansion in friendly hands.

Earlier, in June, L. J. Heatwole had despaired of a fall opening, so he proposed holding a four-week Bible school at Hayfield in January 1915. It was a smart move, given the stalemate, the worrisome gossip, and the likelihood that the venture would implode. A short-term Bible school, the easiest kind of school to organize, would surely signal a step forward, test the market for students, and most likely receive a favorable response in the churches. The General Board approved the Bible school on October 9, 1914, when it met at the yearly gathering of Virginia Conference.[57]

The Hayfield Bible School

Nineteen-year-old J. Irvin Lehman met Daniel Kauffman for the first time when Kauffman spoke at a two-week Bible conference in mid-November 1914 at the Marion Mennonite Church near Chambersburg, Pennsylvania. The congregation was in the conservative-minded Washington-Franklin Conference, which straddled Washington County, Maryland, and Franklin County, Pennsylvania. Kauffman told Lehman about the four-week Bible school that would begin in six weeks at Hayfield.

Eager to attend but uncertain how to pay his expenses, Lehman, at Kauffman's suggestion, decided to sell copies of Kauffman's *Bible Doctrines* and A. D. Wenger's *Around the World*. Sometimes traveling by sleigh, Lehman peddled the books and earned twenty-five dollars, which covered his rail fare between Chambersburg and Washington, DC, room and board, textbooks, and other miscellaneous expenses at Hayfield.[58]

Primary instructors for the Special Bible Term that opened on January 12, 1915, were George R. Brunk, Daniel Kauffman, L. J. Heatwole, and E. J. Berkey. All were Virginians except for Kauffman, who lived in Scottdale, Pennsylvania. (In addition to teaching, he rose at 5:00 a.m. each morning to keep abreast of his editorial work for *Gospel Herald*.) According to a promotional flyer, subjects included Bible doctrine, Sunday school (methods of organization), and vocal music. One course called "The Worker's Equipment" reflected the activism in vogue; it covered "qualifications for *workers*. . . . The *worker* at *work* in church . . . personal *work* among the saved and unsaved . . . and the *workers'* library."[59]

Heatwole directed the school.[60] Tuition was free, but students paid three dollars per week for room and board. Heat, electricity, books, stationery, and laundry were extra. Transient boarders paid fifteen cents per meal. Forty-nine pupils—twenty women and twenty-nine men—had registered. Thirty-eight came from Virginia, while the rest hailed from Pennsylvania (six), Maryland (two), Indiana (two), and Ohio (one). J. J. "Uncle Johnny" Wenger was the handyman, business manager, and driver. He met students and visitors at the railway station and conveyed them to the mansion in a horse-drawn carriage. His wife, Isa ("Aunt Isie"), served as matron and cook. "Each day brought 2 to 3 visitors and 'inspectors' from various churches," and all of them "went away well pleased with what they saw and learned," recalled J. J. Wenger.

Student Clarence Shank seemed to adjust quickly. On the third day, he noted in his diary, "School is on the Hayfield farm 6 miles from Alexandria. We are getting along in school right well." Most student reports were glowing. J. Irvin Lehman was impressed by L. J. Heatwole's lectures and "very much impressed" with Daniel Kauffman's presentation on building character. The "stirring sermons" of George R. Brunk had a "profound effect" on him. Students also heard talks on marriage, obedience, and rural missions, among other topics. They savored the chance to interact with influential church leaders for several weeks.

Out-of-class activities included a lot of singing and exploring of the surroundings. One evening, students sang at Chris Garber's home. On another day, J. Irvin Lehman and three friends hiked to Mount Vernon, climbed over the locked back gate, toured the grounds, entered the mansion, and walked down to the Potomac without being noticed. They returned to Hayfield after dark without having paid admission for their after-hours, self-guided tour. School staff soon persuaded the four that integrity was more important than frugality, so the young men sent the one-dollar fee to the shrine keeper, a friend of George R. Brunk. On another occasion, Brunk accompanied some students on a visit to the US Congress. Hearing a debate on prohibition, the bishop became energized, saying, "I wish I had a chance to talk."[61] Had he pursued a career in politics, his oratorical skills, keen mind, persuasive logic, and penchant for debate would have fit the job well.

Many of the students had never been away from home before. They were generally well behaved, apart from one couple, who were enthralled with their newfound affection for each other. However, the pair found their romance thwarted by the woman's parents. Eventually, both sets of parents asked Principal Heatwole to facilitate an agreement between the students to curtail their relationship. It worked so well that the couple never married.

From all reports, students were invigorated by their four-week immersion into Mennonite ecclesiastical culture and thrilled to study in a colonial mansion built by America's first president near the nation's capital. It was heady stuff for a country boy like J. Irvin Lehman, who a few days before his arrival had been hauling hog manure on his family's farm in the hinterlands of Franklin County, Pennsylvania.

Not everyone in the wider church, however, was pleased about the Special Bible Term. When George R. Brunk suddenly departed at the end of the first week because of the birth of a daughter, school leaders appealed to Lancaster Conference to send Bishop John Mosemann, Bishop Noah Mack, or Preacher I. B. Good to pinch hit for Brunk. Reflecting some negative sentiment toward the school, "Mosemann said he *could* not. Another said he *dare* not, and the third one simply *would* not."[62]

The Demise of Hayfield

On the last day of classes, J. Irvin Lehman was unable to get a train to Chambersburg. To his surprise, he was invited to observe the General Board meeting that evening in the mansion on whether to hold another Special Bible Term. Because the broader church showed sparse interest in education, the sentiment was negative until W. W. Hege, a pastor from Lehman's Washington-Franklin Conference, "gave a strong plea" of support, turning the tide for another Bible term.[63]

Even so, the Hayfield project soon became a fiasco. Sentiment for the project soured. Even Aaron Loucks, an influential member of the General Board, said, "I never was convinced that the site was ideal."[64] A multitude of events in the following months unraveled any prospects for a permanent school at Hayfield, and by the end of 1915, all hope had vanished.

By mid-March, George R. Brunk, disheartened by the tart relations with Chris Garber, the lack of investors in the land, and anemic church support, distanced himself, saying, "It all depends now on the eastern people; if they want a school they must dig up some money. . . . I for one am not going to kick the doors down and force a school upon them." He even threatened to return to Kansas: "Unless the Lord opens a way this year for a man [principal] . . . I will take it for granted that the door is shut and subside. I am a western plant anyhow and feel inclined to move in reach of Hesston if this school dies."[65]

The trustee committee owed J. J. Wenger about $700 for the equipment he had purchased for the Special Bible Term. To repay him, Brunk proposed that each of the five members lend Wenger $150. When the four other members refused, Brunk complained of being "tired of holding office with no power attached to it, but the power to carry blame." Tensions also heated up when J. J. Wenger offered, at cost, to sell the board the two hundred acres and the mansion that he had purchased, plus his expenses for the Bible term. Brunk was "UNALTERABLY" opposed to the trustees taking on any debt, saying that he only feared two things: "debt and the devil."[66] J. J. Wenger and his cousin A. D. Wenger disagreed with Brunk, thinking that if the board borrowed funds to purchase Hayfield or another site, they would be more likely to garner contributions.

As a result of these differences, Brunk resigned as chair of the trustee committee. Frustrated by the sluggish support of the church, he lamented, "I think we should have the school, and that the East could easily support and operate it, BUT I DO NOT THINK THAT THEY ARE GOING TO DO IT."[67] He continued to serve as a member of the faculty committee and as vice chair of the General Board. Although he disagreed with Brunk on procedure, A. D. Wenger, as late as July 1915, fully concurred that "the brethren in Virginia alone could pay for it, while Maryland and Pennsylvania could do much more [financially]."[68] The issue was not money. It was uncertainty about location and vision and dwindling confidence in the leadership.

Doubtful that the trustee committee would ever purchase the property, J. J. Wenger made a final but futile attempt in May 1915 to salvage his considerable investment in the Hayfield mansion and the two hundred acres he had bought from Garber. He distributed an attractive flyer with a photo of Hayfield, touting the site as ideal for a school. He offered to sell the land (not the mansion) to investors—promising that it "[would] grow in value." As an added perk, investors were promised free tuition for one or more scholars, commensurate with the amount of land they purchased.[69] Shortly after Wenger had purchased the land the previous year, Bishop Daniel Kauffman had written a well-crafted vision and plan of implementation and financing for the Hayfield school.[70] Nonetheless,

Kauffman's earlier initiative and now Wenger's appeal were too late to avert a disaster.

Particles of Bitterness Everywhere

About two months after the promotion, J. J. Wenger was shocked to discover that the property he had purchased from Chris Garber under a written agreement did not have a clean title.[71] Because of this encumbrance, Garber refused to allow him to sell the property. Their relationship rapidly deteriorated. Transactions were complicated by a trust that held a lien on the property and by real estate agents, lawyers, and Wenger's mortgage holder, who demanded an $800 interest payment by October 10, 1915. Meanwhile, a defiant Garber filed a suit against Mennonite churches in three states and refused to repay the personal loan of $1,300 that Wenger had given him two years earlier.[72] Trying to recover the money, Wenger filed a suit against Garber—not a wise move for a Mennonite deacon in a church that was skittish about lawsuits because they were considered incompatible with principles of nonresistance.

On the strong advice of Bishop David Garber, Wenger nullified the suit the day before his scheduled court appearance and wrote a letter of apology to Chris Garber. Still, Garber accused Wenger of removing a water ram from the property, which Wenger vehemently denied. To inflame matters more, Wenger's cow gored one of Garber's cows, igniting a dispute about the dead cow's value. The row spread particles of bitterness everywhere.[73] Finally, in January 1916, Wenger sold his property on public auction, ending all prospects for a school at Hayfield.

In the spring of 1916, all the Mennonite families in the Alexandria area moved away. A few months later the project literally went up in smoke. Ignited by chimney sparks on its shingled roof, the colonial mansion burned down, removing any remnant of the Mennonite experiment at Hayfield. A century later, some rough bumps in the grass at the edge of a small park in the suburban Hayfield development across from Hayfield High School were all that remained. By then, "Uncle Johnny" Wenger's prediction that the land value would rise had come true: an acre offered for sixty dollars in 1914 now fetched more than a million dollars.

There was plenty of blame to share in the aftermath of Alexandria. Most of those close to the situation pinned the bulk of it on Chris Garber, who had persistently faulted school officials for his troubles, despite their repeated reminders that he was free to sell to other buyers at any time.[74] One outside observer said that Garber's "ungovernable temper has had much to do with the failure. . . . His ugly treatment of church representatives, his inhumane conduct [produced] an ugly troublesome case." At times, he flared up into a rage; he even chased school representatives off his property on one occasion.[75] Even the mild-mannered, slow-to-judge preacher A. D. Wenger described Garber as "a Satan possessed fellow man."[76]

Yet the General Board had plenty of blame to shoulder as well. The founding fathers of the school were mostly farmer-preachers with no experience operating a school or organizing a business. They were propelled by deep desires for an eastern school, but zeal was not enough. The visionaries were caught in a conundrum: they could not begin the school without funding, yet no one wanted to buy land in Alexandria or contribute to the school until they could see exactly what kind of a school it would be and what kind of "products" it would yield.[77] Besides, the never-ending negotiations with Garber sent snippets of gossip across Mennonite enclaves, chilling any enthusiasm for a school. Even with attempts to spin the news in church papers, backyard chatter about Hayfield had turned glum—especially when alternative sites were discussed.

The Hayfield debacle was a bitter disappointment for George R. Brunk. Both school sites he had proposed had fizzled. Neither one was central for eastern Mennonites or situated near a sizable and stable Mennonite community. Both attempts carried Brunk's imprimatur. His gifts were oration, vision, and argumentation, not mediation, compromise, and negotiation. He retreated to Denbigh, exhausted and emotionally wounded, only to face two more difficulties. His reputation was at stake in Indiana, where he was "on trial" at Goshen College for incendiary comments he had made over the years about the school.[78] Added to that concern were serious illnesses that Brunk described as a "nervous breakdown and heart disease," which kept him bedridden during World War I. His condition was so dire that he and his family feared he would die.[79]

Brunk had often said that if the trustees got "the man" and "the place," the dollars and support would come. Unfortunately, the board failed to get either. A deeper flaw, however, was ambiguous authority. Who exactly was in charge? Who had the clout and fiduciary responsibility to make decisions? The self-appointed board was not incorporated. Even within the board and its numerous committees, the authority structure was nebulous without an executive committee empowered to act. The provisional constitution, self-approved in February 1913 and frequently revised, was not adopted until 1923.

Moreover, Virginia Conference had never approved the project, made it a priority, or promised to fund it. When Bishop Brunk made his strong pitch to the conference in October 1913, it did not endorse the venture but merely gave consent for individuals to participate. The Warwick River congregation, which had endorsed the school plan in February 1913, was the only official church body to do so for many years. This crisis of authority dogged the project and partially explains the two failures. While there was much talk about the importance of church support, it was never clear whose support constituted the sponsorship of the church. Which congregations? Which conferences? This ambiguity arose partly because the proposed school was the first cross-conference project of its kind in the East. All of these factors fueled the collapse at Hayfield and underscored the fact that pacifist ideals do not guarantee a conflict-free community.

The founders emphasized that the church needed a school to save its youth, who otherwise would be lost to the world. But what kind of school would save them? And what exactly was the founders' vision for the school? A Bible school? A high school? A vocational school? A liberal arts college? The blurred and ever-changing vision made attracting dollars difficult. Without a clear goal, a principal, and a location, why would anyone want to invest? None of the visionary leaders had thick enough wallets to fund the school, except perhaps Aaron Loucks in Scottdale. Had a Virginia financier been willing to purchase the Hayfield property, the sad saga might have ended quite differently. But this was a Mennonite communal project that did not fit the industrial baron model (where a single entrepreneur would bankroll a new institution), which by 1900 was the new trend in American higher education.

On top of these complications, most Mennonites in the East still saw high school as mere garnish for a farming people. Besides, since 1905, they had been hearing gossip about "bad things" happening at Goshen College, tainting their interest in colleges in general. The thunderclouds of war in Europe, which had been rumbling since July 1914, added more uncertainty to the prospects for an eastern school.

The idea of a sectarian Mennonite school sitting near Alexandria had many ironic wrinkles. Why did rural-loving Mennonites who wanted to be separate from the world—pacifists who denounced participation in military service—relish starting a school near Washington, DC, in a home built by a politician and military general? Bishop Daniel Kauffman, chairman of the committee that proposed the site, later saw the discrepancy. He came to dislike Hayfield because it was too close to the estate of a political hero. "This is no place for a Mennonite school. There's too much militarism here," he reportedly said.[80]

Were the founders also blind to the irony of sectarians—who emphasized separation from the world and were trying valiantly to save their youth from drifting into its clutches—holding the very first Bible school for their offspring sixteen miles from the epicenter of the worldly kingdom? How could Mennonites, folks who explicitly shied away from cities with their worldly fashions and who preached a plain-and-simple lifestyle, study their sacred scriptures and teach their doctrine of nonconformity in a well-adorned colonial mansion without any sense of incongruity? Further, did any Mennonite leaders see the duplicity of planting a school that aimed to "cultivate the instincts of the rural way of life" in the backyard of urban Washington? For a people who preferred living on the fringes of society, the fascination with the colonial mansion and its high status accoutrements unveiled, perhaps, their unspoken desire to travel on the main concourse of American life.

"Where Is the Man?"

The search for a principal, which had stretched over three years, can be summarized in one word: failure. Despite all the energy and publicity for an eastern school, no one with unquestionable conservative credentials would take the job. This fact, plus the two aborted starts and the ongoing search for a site, cast a foreboding shadow over the enterprise.

After the Maugansville meeting in February 1914, the faculty committee rebooted its search for a principal. About a month later, Bishops Heatwole and Brunk traveled to Lancaster County to meet with I. B. Good, a well-regarded schoolteacher, businessman, and minister in Lancaster Conference. For unknown reasons, Good refused the position. Even Daniel Kauffman, a member of the faculty (search) committee with superb administrative credentials and a gigantic churchly stature, declined in order to retain his editorship of *Gospel Herald*. A. D. Wenger also refused. He had promised Annie that he would focus on family and farming until their children left home.[81] Ever confident that S. G. Shetler could lead the school to success, the committee continued to pester him, but to no avail. Brunk, frustrated by the search, asked J. J. Wenger emphatically, "*Where Is the Man?* I think the first thing is to find a man to head the school."[82]

The committee contacted one applicant for teaching who clearly qualified for the principalship. Bishop Daniel Kauffman called this person "one bright ray of promise for the success of the school." Committee members gave the candidate rave reviews: "I am very, very favorably impressed." "I was favorably impressed." "I have no doubts about qualifications. . . . I heartily favor employing." After citing the applicant's "qualifications and fitness . . . recommendations and personal example," Chairman Heatwole enthused, "We would not need to look further [for a principal]," but then noted wistfully, "The one thing lacking is that she is a woman instead of a man."[83] The committee was so enamored of Marion Charlton from Maugansville, Maryland, that it considered appointing her acting principal until Shetler might arrive, at which point she would become vice principal.[84] A few months later, with no offer from the school, Charlton slipped away to teach at Hesston College.

Despite the desperation of their search, it was unthinkable that a woman could head a school and direct the work of ordained men on the faculty in a church where women were denied ordination and in a nation where women would need to wait six more years to gain the right to vote.

Paralleling the search for a principal, the trustee committee in the spring of 1915 began an earnest hunt for alternatives to Hayfield. Six sites were considered, and three of them were dropped with little consideration. The first was Amelia County, Virginia, about thirty-five miles southwest of Richmond.[85] The Hagerstown, Maryland, area offered an ideal central location for eastern Mennonites, but no specific property was investigated.[86] A property at Martinsburg, West Virginia, was also rejected.[87]

Two more mansions near Alexandria emerged as prospects. One property near Hayfield included 270 acres with an eighteen-room house. Priced at $200,000, it reportedly could be bought for $25,000—a tempting bargain for frugal Mennonites.[88] The second property near Alexandria, promoted as "A Magnificent Country Estate, near Washington, D.C.," included a colonial mansion with fourteen rooms, a panoramic view of the surrounding countryside, sixty-seven acres for cultivation, and three hundred fruit trees of various kinds.[89]

The trustee committee gave the most attention to the Waterlick Hotel on the Sulfur Springs property near Strasburg, Virginia. Listed for $10,000, the sixty-room hotel with a thirty-by-sixty-foot swimming pool sat on seventy-five acres of land near the railroad. The owner offered it to the "Mennonites, the church of his grandfather, at their own terms." A committee visited the site in August 1914 and prepared a two-page description, but for unknown reasons, they decided not to pursue it.[90]

Lancaster County, the heartland of eastern Mennonites, was missing from the list and only mentioned in passing as still not ready for a school. Oddly, even Harrisonburg, in the midst of Virginia's old Mennonite settlement, never appeared once in the stream of correspondence during the three-year search for a site. All of that, however, was about to change—and change fast.

As chair of the General Board, L. J. Heatwole had much to fret about in the fall of 1915. After conducting a robust Bible school at Hayfield nine months earlier, things had stalled. Hayfield was doomed, a new location was still elusive, the search for a principal had faltered, the board seemed lethargic, and all prospects for a school were dim. These were all valid reasons to abandon hope. But Heatwole didn't. He plodded on. Tiring of long-distance collaboration and the never-ending zigzags, he took the lead to find a place, any place, where they could replicate the Hayfield model for a Special Bible Term in January 1916, which was fast approaching.

As late as November 19, Heatwole wrote to the General Board asking for permission to speak with one of his friends, Abraham Paul "A. P." Funkhouser, about renting yet another mansion, nicknamed the White House, for a Special Bible Term beginning mid-January 1916.[91] The White House was located in a grove of trees that was part of Assembly Park, a twenty-three-acre plot about a mile north of Harrisonburg. Funkhouser, a United Brethren minister, had developed Assembly

Park on a farm he had purchased in 1892. The site was frequently used for camp meetings, festivals, and horse racing.

The plans went public when Heatwole convened and chaired a meeting on Saturday afternoon, December 4, at Weavers Mennonite Church, west of Harrisonburg, where he had been ordained and now provided bishop oversight. He noted that since Alexandria was not available for another Special Bible Term, the leaders needed to look for a site "at once" so that the school could open a few weeks later. He would need help quickly to raise funds and arrange logistics *if* the White House could be rented from Funkhouser. The gathering appointed an acting committee of seven local men chaired by Christian H. "C. H." Brunk—a farmer, music composer, and deputy in the Rockingham County Clerk's Office—to take on those tasks. The group met with Funkhouser on December 20 and signed an agreement to rent the White House for $150 for a short-term institute in January 1916 and again a year later if desired.[92]

Just three weeks before the Special Bible Term was to open, Heatwole wrote to A. D. Wenger, pleading with him to come as a teacher. George R. Brunk, hibernating in Denbigh, had given a "flat refusal to come," and Daniel Kauffman could not come because his wife was ill. Wenger agreed to be one of the teachers, the rest of whom were local people. Heatwole served as the director. He rushed to print an eight-page promotional program identical to the year-old Hayfield flyer except for the location, dates, and instructors.[93]

Meanwhile, J. J. and Isa Wenger were recalled from Alexandria to serve as business manager and matron at Harrisonburg. In late December, they sent all the school equipment they had purchased for Hayfield, their personal belongings, and one thousand quarts of fruit and other food on two freight cars. Even so, their "curtain top auto" was loaded full. It was a bittersweet journey. They had lost $2,800 and expended bushels of emotional anxiety during the ongoing squabbles with Chris Garber, yet they sensed a glimmer of hope for a school in Harrisonburg, just ten miles south of their old home in Lindale. Upon arrival, they scoured the "big, dirty" White House and arranged all the desks and furniture for the new Special Bible Term.[94]

Gospel Herald announced on December 30 that a "special committee appointed by the Shenandoah Valley brotherhood" was handling the logistics for a Bible school.[95] For the first time, the valley people had taken charge of the fate of N. E. Byer's dream for an "Eastern Mennonite School." The Denbigh players were on the sidelines, as were many of the General Board members who had lost hope. Heatwole, the esteemed senior bishop of the three church districts in the valley, was in charge. Now in familiar territory, he selected his players carefully, aware that this was the third and perhaps the last chance to resuscitate the eastern school project. Ironically, after three

The White House in Assembly Park, north of Harrisonburg, site of the January 1916 Special Bible Term. This former resort hotel provided space for classes, offices, and dormitory rooms until January 1920.

years of logging hundreds of miles on the train to Denbigh, Alexandria, and other potential sites, he finally had found one just six miles from his home.

Perhaps it was that joy that led Heatwole to describe in almost ecstatic words the first day of the Special Bible Term on January 19, 1916.[96] He began by noting the first hymn: "Begin the day with God, / Kneel down to him in prayer, / Lift up thine heart to his abode, / And seek his love to share."[97] Some thirty-five students and a small handful of teachers sang those words as they opened the first page of the history of Eastern Mennonite University at Harrisonburg. To Heatwole's ears, "the volume of voices that broke forth [that morning] rang through the building and echoed through the surrounding woods." At noon the group gathered around a "bounteous" table of food. And after a "fervent invocation," they sang a well-known doxology: "Praise God from whom all blessings flow, / Praise him all creatures here below, / Praise him above, ye heavenly host, / Praise Father Son and Holy Ghost."[98]

Heatwole recalled that the singing that day "seem[ed] so perfect in all parts" that it surprised "everybody [because of] the lofty and inspiring heights to which the voices of the sopranos rose, the rich and soothing tones that came from the altos, and the deep and resounding voices of the basses that seemed to come up from the lower chambers of the earth." Indeed, he raved, "the singing seemed so rapturous and so inspiring as to give the old building and especially the assembly room, a veneration and a sanctity that must continue."[99] Good food, good singing, and invigorating worship opened the doors of EMU's history and helped hold them open for more than a century.

CHAPTER 3

The Experiment at Assembly Park

The school . . . will be an experiment . . .
with our eastern churches.
—C. H. Brunk, trustee chair

A Surprising Announcement

In July 1917, the widely read *Gospel Herald* announced that the long-awaited Eastern Mennonite School (EMS) would open in October without a "permanent head."[1] After a five-year search, the trustees still had not found their man, but engineer or not, this train was leaving the station. That April, desperate to secure a principal because "little could be done toward opening the school" without one, the board of trustees made a final effort to hire S. G. Shetler.[2] Without his consent, they declared him principal of EMS. The bold move was futile because Shetler wanted to continue speaking at Bible schools and Young People's Institutes across the Mennonite world.[3] Undeterred, the trustees proceeded with plans to open the school in the fall.

The year 1917 was a dismal time to open a school. With the Bolshevik Revolution jarring Russia and World War I raging in Europe, anxiety hung heavy in the air. The United States had entered the war in April. Mennonite conscientious objectors, conscripted as part of a 2.8-million-man draft, were jolted by the harsh treatment they received in military camps for refusing to enter even noncombatant service or wear army uniforms. The angry public backlash against the "slackers," "traitors," and "yellowbellies" who refused to fly the flag and fight for their country sharpened Mennonites' sense of otherness in American society. Already seen as peculiar, they now faced new questions about their allegiance and patriotism. Were these Swiss-Germans truly Americans? Nonresistance in the clutch of war recalibrated Mennonite identity in American life as it had during the American Revolution and the Civil War.[4]

Besides dealing with the war, the Mennonite Church had canceled its plans to hold its annual General Conference in Harrisonburg in August 1917 because of a polio epidemic in the region.[5] Undaunted, Bishop Heatwole and his colleagues pressed on. They had been quite busy since holding the six-week Special Bible Term in early 1916.[6] The forty students enrolled initially had swelled to sixty by the last week, with another hundred visitors attending evening lectures. A. P. Funkhouser, the United Brethren minister who had rented his "White House" to the trustees for that Special Bible Term in Harrisonburg, had opened the building each day and attended some lectures. On February 1, 1916, he gave the White House keys to J. J. Wenger, the school's business manager, before taking a train to New York for his winter residency.

Funkhouser—perhaps impressed with the vitality of the Mennonites, their singing, or their food—wrote to L. J. Heatwole from New York on February 12 and offered to sell them Assembly Park.[7] The offer sparked nine months of bargaining. After considering four other sites near Harrisonburg, as well as the Brandon Institute in Augusta County, and trading several offers and counteroffers with Funkhouser, both parties finally agreed to a price of $14,500 for Assembly Park.[8]

Striking the deal was not easy. Annoyed that Funkhouser was haggling over details and worried that the agreement would collapse—adding a third failure to the school's search for a permanent home—C. H. Brunk, chair of the trustees, sent Funkhouser a blunt letter on October 20 explaining that this was the Mennonites' final offer. "It is up to you to say whether you will accept it on the terms and conditions set forth," Brunk wrote. He explained that the Mennonites were rapidly losing interest in the park and "looking around now for another location." Brunk concluded, "If we fail to hear from you soon . . . the deal is off, and we will act accordingly [and will] remove our effects from the park at the end of the next Bible term [January 1917]."[9] Taken aback by Brunk's stern words, Funkhouser accepted the conditions the next day. And with that, the deal for a permanent home for EMS was sealed on October 24, 1916.[10]

An astonishing thing happened in April 1917, about six months after the deal was struck. After years of intense discussions and dozens of declarations about the importance of having a church-operated and church-controlled school in the East, six men from the Harrisonburg area formed a self-perpetuating legal entity that was *independent* of any church connections, requiring only that the trustees be members of the Mennonite Church. These local trustees, whom the General Board of EMS confirmed, executed a charter in order to purchase land and operate a school. Thus, from 1917 to 1923, the six-member independent board that founded EMS operated without an approved constitution under the shell of the General Board, which held a perfunctory annual meeting until it was dismantled in 1923.[11]

Creating a legal charter forced the question of naming the "eastern school." Names on early drafts of the constitution had included "Mennonite Students' Safeguard and Industrial School," "Warwick Mennonite Institute," "Warwick Mennonite Academy," and "Alexandria Mennonite Institute." A big issue was at stake: should the word *Mennonite* be in the name as an explicit statement of denominational identity? C. H. Brunk, chair of the local board, in a letter to the General Board, argued *against* inserting *Mennonite* into the name: "It is not customary to give a school a denominational name . . . some people are more or less prejudiced against denominational institutions." Moreover, he said, a school "can be just as truly denominational without the name." Brunk was not just speaking for himself: "Last evening after the services at Weavers [congregation] about ten of us . . . met for consultation and *unanimously* . . . suggest the name Eastern Institute and Bible School."[12]

The records do not say how the final name was determined. What is clear, however, is that the charter signed in April 1917 said "Eastern Mennonite School." Yet the matter was not entirely settled. Ten years later, the faculty proposed two new names to the trustees—Sharon College and Olivet College—names that would have erased the Mennonite brand. The board deferred action, leaving Mennonite identity inscribed in the name.[13] Even in the twenty-first century, Eastern Mennonite University remains the only Mennonite-related college or university of eight in the United States that carries the denominational name.

A Reluctant President

An announcement in *Gospel Herald* on September 27, 1917, informed the Mennonite world that Eastern Mennonite School "will be ready, the Lord willing . . . for opening exercises on October 9, 1917." It also noted that "Bro. J. B. Smith" had recently agreed to "be in charge of the Bible department."[14]

Worried that they would not have a helmsman for the first year, in August, the trustees had appointed A. G. Heishman manager of the new school. Heishman, who had taught in West Virginia as a seventeen-year-old, was heavily involved with starting EMS at Harrisonburg. A Mennonite minister, he later served as business manager and taught Bible, agriculture, commercial subjects, and eventually correspondence courses. He served as a trustee from 1914 until 1948 and chaired the board for a number of years. Historian Hubert Pellman describes Heishman as a reserved and dignified person with a friendly and fatherly demeanor.[15]

A few days before *Gospel Herald* announced his appointment, Smith had asked Daniel Kauffman how to promote a Bible school that he hoped to open by October 1 in Ohio.[16] Nonetheless, Smith quickly dropped those plans and moved his family to Harrisonburg, arriving on October 9, the day before registration. In late

October, the board elected Smith president of the new school and renamed Heishman vice president. (Smith's formal title was "principal," but most institutional references called him "president.")[17]

Jacob Brubaker "J. B." Smith was born in 1870 in St. Jacobs, Ontario. In 1917, the forty-seven-year-old was one of the few Mennonites who held advanced degrees. He had attended Elkhart Institute and had received a BA from Ohio Northern University, a BD from Temple University, and a doctor of divinity degree from Oskaloosa College in Iowa in 1914. Ordained in 1897, Smith was a preacher in the Bethel Mennonite Church in West Liberty, Ohio, where he earned his living as a potato farmer. In 1910, he moved to Kansas and taught at Hesston College for seven years. Smith returned to Ohio in 1917, hoping to begin a Bible school and take up farming again.

An expert in New Testament Greek, Smith eventually published a concordance. He was fascinated by numerology, word studies, and systematic theology, but his overriding passion was teaching biblical studies. Moreover, he was an ardent opponent of liberal theology and higher criticism. His essays on education were well crafted, intellectually sophisticated, and persuasive.[18] At times, Smith's intense focus on a conversation or an abstract idea left him oblivious to the details at hand, as happened in one oft-repeated tale. While speaking with a neighbor on his farm in Ohio, Smith remarked that he suddenly felt nauseous, to which the neighbor replied, "You'd probably feel better if you took your hands off that electric fence."[19]

When J. B. Smith and his family arrived by train on Tuesday afternoon, October 9, 1917, they settled temporarily in the White House, whose rooms served as student residences, classrooms, and administrative offices. Some months later, the Smiths moved to the Stringtown area (later called Mennonitetown and, eventually, Park View). Their house was near the tollgate at the intersection of Mt. Clinton Pike and State Route 764, where travelers grudgingly paid eight or ten cents, depending on how far they were going.[20]

The morning after his arrival, Smith registered six charter students, two of whom were his daughters, Beulah and Ruth. The other four were Christian Brunk and Harry A. Brunk from Harrisonburg and two out-of-state women: Mary Brubaker from Ohio and Mary Nafzinger from Michigan. A few more students enrolled in the next few days, and on Monday, October 15, the school officially opened.[21] A total of nineteen students attended at least one term in the 1917–1918 school year.

Infant Academics

During the school's first two years, the academic program was basic and informal. The early academic tone reflected the fact that the staff, except for President Smith, had little if any college experience. Their grasp of education mirrored their experience in

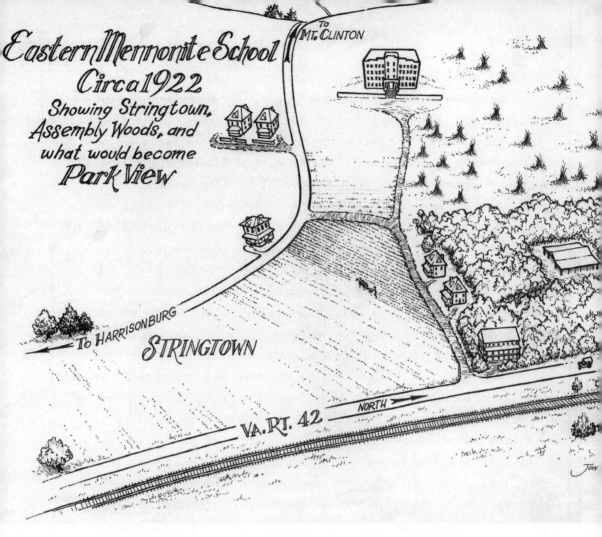

Eastern Mennonite School Circa 1922. Showing Stringtown, Assembly Woods, and what would become Park View

TO MT. CLINTON

To HARRISONBURG   STRINGTOWN

VA. RT. 42   NORTH

Sketch of campus, ca. 1922. Lower right: wooded area of Assembly Park, showing the White House, the Tabernacle, and faculty homes. Upper center: newly constructed administration building. Map: Jonathan P. Gehman.

public normal schools, which were designed to certify teachers for the elementary grades. The EMS staff and the board devoted more energy to establishing the Bible school curriculum than to the academy. In many ways, the first decade of the school reflected the Bible school and Bible institute movement that swept North America and the Mennonite world from 1890 to 1930.[22] The first college-level course was not offered until the fifth academic year. The early catalogs declared that "the church needs many workers and a few scholars." The school aimed to give students "a good knowledge of God's Word . . . [so they would] be staunch defenders of the faith as well as consecrated workers in the Lord's great harvest field."[23]

Though the early catalogs outlined an ambitious curriculum, some of the announced courses were never offered. School officials nevertheless initiated seven educational options within the first two years. The *academy* track promised a four-year sequence of study equivalent to a standard high school. Required courses included English, ancient history, science, Latin, mathematics, and one Bible course per semester. The *Bible* track, with three projected levels (elementary, intermediate, and advanced), had the most extensive menu of courses. The *vocal music* stream aimed to train students to read music and serve as choristers in their home congregations. The *preparatory* department served students who had not completed the seventh or eighth grades in the common schools. In this track, the faculty gave special attention to proficiency in English, grammar, arithmetic, spelling, and penmanship, and all the students were required to take a course in "simple Bible study."

In the first year, President Smith initiated *correspondence* courses in biblical studies, which flourished for many years. In the second academic year, the institution began a *primary* school for children in the elementary grades. Officials hoped it would not only serve their own families and the families of their non-Mennonite neighbors but also become a model for religious primary education elsewhere. The *Special Bible Term*, a midwinter program that school leaders had already had experience operating in 1916 and 1917, continued until 1960.

Few explicit references to Mennonite identity appeared in the curriculum or in the course titles or descriptions. Yet the curriculum was saturated with Mennonite perspectives. The trustees wanted to establish a Bible school and to highlight the Bible in the wider curriculum. The Bible doctrine courses emphasized a distinctive Mennonite interpretation of doctrine. Other religion courses, all taught by Mennonites, were also tinted by their worldview. The vocal music courses aimed to enhance the quality of singing in Mennonite congregations. Besides these academic aspects, Mennonite identity permeated all the other social and religious dimensions of the campus.

J. B. Smith and four colleagues—A. G. Heishman, J. Early Suter, Noah D. Showalter, and Elizabeth Heatwole—constituted the first faculty. President Smith taught advanced courses in Bible and New Testament Greek. His encyclopedic knowledge and enthusiasm for learning inspired and motivated many students to pursue biblical studies after they attended EMS.

Suter, a farmer and minister who had studied for one year at Goshen College, taught English at EMS until March 1918. He and Heishman had pressed the trustees to offer high school subjects beyond Bible studies alone, which the board would have preferred. Finally, the trustees consented to allow the two men to teach high school subjects, with one stipulation: they would only receive remuneration if any funds were left over after the Bible teachers had been paid. For six months of work, Suter received sixty-seven dollars and the satisfaction of seeding high school courses in the new school.[24] Showalter taught music in the spring of 1918 and later solicited funds for a new building. Elizabeth Heatwole, daughter of L. J. Heatwole, served on the faculty until March 1918. She taught preparatory subjects and served as preceptress of the girls living in the White House. She received room and board but no salary for her work.

The resignation of three faculty members—Suter, Showalter, and Heatwole—in early March of the first academic year left Smith with only Heishman on the faculty. The two of them simply taught more classes until Marion Charlton, whom the board had considered appointing acting principal back in 1914, arrived in late March from Hesston. Her training at Shippensburg State College and Columbia Business College at Hagerstown, as well as her teaching experience at Hesston College, enabled her to set high scholastic standards in the English, geography, science, history, and clerical courses. Also, as preceptress she helped rural students acquire the social manners and etiquette fitting for broader public life. Charlton taught until the summer of 1919, when she resigned to care for her ailing mother in Maryland.[25]

The school was closed from October 8 to November 6, 1918, because the Spanish flu pandemic had reached the campus. New teachers that fall included Elizabeth Horsch, John Longacre "J. L." Stauffer, and Herbert N. "H. N." Troyer—an older EMS student who would graduate in spring 1919. Maurice T. "M. T." Brackbill from Michigan joined the faculty in March 1919. Brackbill's diaries record an abrupt and overwhelming immersion into life in Harrisonburg. The day after his arrival, he was already teaching courses in botany, Julius Caesar, and algebra, as well as handling many other tasks. Several days later, Brackbill proposed a demerit system and a tennis court, both of which the faculty endorsed. And by the end of the month, Brackbill reported, "I visited a Jewish synagogue in Harrisonburg [and] for the first time in my life a *Negro* cut my hair."[26]

Total registration in the first two years was 240 students. Seventy were regular students in three departments: academy (37), Bible (20), and preparatory (13). The remaining 170 students were enrolled in Special Bible Terms (80), correspondence courses (59), and the primary school (31). The students came from twelve different states and provinces. The first commencement, on June 2, 1919, celebrated the graduation of three men and four women, one of whom was President Smith's daughter Beulah. Four graduated from the academy and three from the Bible department.[27]

A Shocking Proposal

Maintaining the stately White House, whose grandeur was quickly fading, became a hefty burden for the trustees. In early 1919, fifteen months after Smith had taken the helm, the trustees began planning for a new academic building. About the same time, and at Smith's urging, they decided to purchase the one-hundred-acre Whitman farm directly west of Assembly Park.[28] These were bold moves—even risky ones—at a time when the school, in the midst of its second year, faced a burgeoning

First graduating class, 1919. Back, left to right: Charles Wolford, Lessie Wenger Hershberger, Herbert N. Troyer, Nellie Burkholder Weber, Clayton F. Derstine. Front, left to right: Mary Nafzinger, President J. B. Smith, Beulah Smith.

debt. Enrollment had shrunk because of the war and the flu pandemic, making it "necessary to encumber the property or solicit funds to pay it."[29] The trustees dispatched their venerable fund-raiser, Peter S. "Uncle Pete" Hartman, and J. M. Shenk to increase their solicitation efforts.

Meanwhile, President Smith, without trustee endorsement, proposed raising $250,000 ($3 million in 2017 dollars) for an endowment fund.[30] This was a very progressive idea. Mennonite Church schools did not have endowments at the time because they were considered irreconcilable with the teaching of Jesus in the Sermon on the Mount to "take no thought for the morrow" and were thought to weaken a school's reliance on church contributions. Smith promptly embarked on a tour of Mennonite communities in the East to raise the money. Faculty meetings were canceled for eight weeks in the winter of 1919 and most of the month of April so "Brother Smith could be in the field" raising money.[31]

Smith reached out to A. D. Wenger for help. Wenger responded sarcastically, "I had heard about a 'cocoon' bursting at Assembly Park, but I did not think the butterfly would be so thickly covered with gold dust. Can it fly?" Aghast at the proposition to raise $250,000, Wenger chided Smith, "Will you need so much money? You have it nicely figured out but figures lie so terribly sometimes. I believe it will be very hard to get anything like $250,000. You should assure us what the money will be used for . . . [and] that you are not soon leaving to start a school in Ohio. What if we receive the funds and build a large building, but then Lancaster County builds a school and its students no longer come to Virginia?"[32]

President Smith's gold-dusted butterfly never flew. Skepticism about higher education among eastern Mennonites was so strong that numerous leaders declined to preach the baccalaureate sermon at the first commencement, forcing Smith to do it himself.[33] Such distrust turned off the funding spigots and thrust EMS into a financial dilemma: How could the school move forward given its dubious donors, the rising operational debt, the costs of constructing a new building, and the new mortgage on the Whitman farm? To relieve these financial pressures, Smith concocted yet another plan.

By late April, the trustees had hired a contractor and an architect to develop two site plans for the new building—one on the hillside farm west of Assembly Park and the other within Assembly Park. The next day, President Smith proposed moving Eastern Mennonite School to Martinsburg, Pennsylvania, about 165 miles north of Harrisonburg.[34] He had visited the site of a suitable property that was available at a much lower price than the cost of constructing a new academic building.[35] The trustees were stunned. The proposal especially annoyed the board chair, C. H. Brunk. A few days later, he wrote, "[It's] late in the day now to talk about moving the school: We [Harrisonburg leaders] took up and fostered the school idea when no one else seemed to want it." Speaking directly about Smith, Brunk said, "His whole mind and energy is directed in [moving the school] out of state, which would at this stage create quite a disruption to say the least. We must naturally wonder, *What Next*."[36] These words conveyed the trustees' dismay and loss of confidence in Smith's leadership. After all the efforts to find a suitable site and all the time and energy given to establish the school in Harrisonburg, after all the money spent on purchasing Assembly Park, after all the donations already received for a school *at* Harrisonburg, and after all the well-known zigzags over the past seven years, an out-of-state move would shatter any remaining confidence church officials, local supporters, and donors had in the new venture and would surely toss it into the dumpster of Mennonite history.

Meanwhile, Daniel Kauffman fired off a letter to Smith from Scottdale and, in the most gentle and diplomatic way possible, implied that moving the school was a very foolish idea. After overcoming their shock, the trustees met on May 14, 1919. They noted the proposal's "disturbing effect upon the school and the congregations" and recalled that the school's permanent location had earlier been stipulated by the church, the board, and the charter according to the laws of Virginia. The trustees then declared that they would take the "earliest possible" steps to construct buildings "somewhere *on the grounds* originally designated for the school."[37] With this action, they unequivocally fixed the permanent site for Eastern Mennonite School.

Any confidence that the trustees might have had in Smith's administrative, political, and planning skills quickly evaporated. Sadly, they realized that they still had not found a man with the steady managerial skills required to lead the school.

From a Colonial Mansion to a Cracker Box

The school community debated the merits of the hillside versus Assembly Park for the new three-story building. President Smith supported the "hillsiders," and the trustees chose that location with its magnificent view of Massanutten Mountain to the east. They stipulated that the building be ready for the 1920 January term, just seven months away, and turned to John "Curly John" Kurtz, the boys' dormitory manager, to supervise the construction.

Born Amish in Mifflin County, Pennsylvania, Kurtz had gone west and joined the Mennonites. His wife died in Iowa just eight months after they married, and to deal with his grief he enrolled in the Special Bible Term in January 1917. He liked the Harrisonburg area and soon found himself on the EMS staff. An experienced carpenter, Kurtz was also inventive and entrepreneurial. He needed all those skills and more to manage the tight construction schedule of the new building, which would house administrative offices, classrooms, dormitories, a chapel, and a library. He completed the building on time, but the stress wrought havoc on his body, leaving him near death with flu and severe pneumonia.[38]

The architectural style of the building was severely plain: a three-story concrete block structure standing tall on the bare hillside. Touted as fireproof and plastered with cream-colored stucco, the austere building was quickly dubbed the "Cracker Box." Having tried the colonial mansion in Alexandria and the White House at Assembly Park, the Mennonites finally built a structure befitting their nonconformity to the world. If nothing else, the stark aesthetics of the building underscored the values of simplicity, plainness, and the unadorned life acclaimed in the EMS catalog.

The school faced a financial hurdle in erecting the Cracker Box. According to business manager H. N. Troyer, "It was a large undertaking . . . with limited resources at hand." Sentiment "against church school education" made it difficult to raise funds. "When the building was about three-fourths up," funds were exhausted. The school quickly raised $30,000 when "a number of brethren guaranteed a loan at the bank of $1,000 each, so the work could go on."[39]

The administration building, nicknamed the Cracker Box, was constructed in the summer and fall of 1919 and occupied in January 1920.

Students were responsible for moving their belongings up the hill from the White House to the Cracker Box on January 9, 1920. Mary C. Shenk recalled, "We girls spent a good deal of time and 'elbow grease' cleaning the windows, not only in our own rooms-to-be but all over the building." Like a long line of ants, students straggled up the hill "loaded with suitcases, boxes, dresses and suits on hangers, and possessions of all sorts. Not even the plank steps were in place in the front, so we picked our muddy way around to the back of the building." There they walked across a wooden plank spanning the yawning chasm between the pasture and the back door.[40] M. T. Brackbill's diary notes summed up the day: "Supper in new building. Joy is supreme. Everybody is exceedingly happy." But two weeks later, the joy had fled: "No water often. Building often cold. Workmen in building still making dirt and noise. Business manager curt and inconsiderate. Prices high and salary low."[41] Things gradually improved and the Cracker Box, later known as the administration or "Ad" Building, became the campus centerpiece for sixty some years.

Elizabeth Lehman, sister of Annie (Mrs. A. D.) Wenger, had come to EMS from her home in Millersville, Pennsylvania, in the fall of 1919. Her fiancé had recently died of the flu while at Camp Meade as a conscientious objector. Elizabeth, who taught high school English in the new Ad Building, had taken special interest in Curly John when he was sick. Her love, and an all-night prayer vigil, were said to have helped jumpstart his recovery. Still, his doctor urged him to go to Colorado to recuperate. Elizabeth wanted to join him, so they married and spent their eight-month honeymoon at high altitudes near Pikes Peak. Kurtz later built three-story brick wings on both ends of the Ad Building, one in 1926 and the other in 1941. He also constructed a large chapel (later named Lehman Auditorium) in 1942 and Northlawn, a large women's dormitory, in 1948.[42]

Another campus romance involved Harold S. Bender, a young man from Indiana. In early September 1919, Bender spent a week visiting Elizabeth Horsch, a young faculty member from Scottdale, Pennsylvania. On one of those days, Bender pulled up to the White House in a red roadster with its top down. With her headscarf whipping in the breeze, Elizabeth stepped out of the building and joined Bender for an all-day outing in the mountains.[43] The couple eventually married, and a dozen years later, Harold would return to EMS under less pleasant conditions.

Real Revival, No Foam or Lather

Chester K. "C. K." Lehman, a brother-in-law of A. D. Wenger, served as the school's academic dean from 1923 to 1956. Lehman, the intellectual architect of the academic program, explained, "Eastern Mennonite School has as its first aim the personal salvation of each student; and secondly to give youth the broadest and most comprehensive views of the world." For Lehman, a divine transformation—a conversion—was necessary before students could acquire a true education in other realms. The school's "first and foremost objective" was for each student to have a spiritual regeneration. Using revivalist language typical of the time, the early catalogs intoned that the "transforming power" of personal salvation was essential for a "complete education."[44]

Campus religious life was intense. It included private devotions each morning before breakfast, a daily chapel service, prayer circles, and church services on Sunday, the Lord's Day. In addition, weeklong revival meetings were held each semester. A visiting evangelist would preach in the morning chapels and hold evening services to encourage confessions of sin and recommitments to Christ. Shortly before his death in 1951, J. B. Smith told a relative that the revival conducted by John Mast in the spring of 1919 was a "high spot in his life." Smith's daughter Ruth, a student at the time, recalled that the revival was not "foam or lather." It was a moment that led her from "a doubting, wavering church member . . . to solid ground . . . where I lost all my doubts and fears . . . ever since."[45]

One student remembered the many rows of students standing during the Mast revival "for confession and repentance late in the night until the last ones [had] poured out confessions of their sins, pride, bitterness, hatred, self-righteousness and faithlessness." More than 130 confessions were made publicly in chapel, and others were made in private prayer. "God graciously . . . made EMS a heaven on earth and gave joy," said one student.[46] Another recalled that "throughout the world, some 30 million people had died of the flu; several were sick on the campus; all around the school the disease was raging. Prayer was made to God. The revival continued [as] souls were refreshed, others were restored, many were being saved." Some classes were canceled "because of the intense thirst for spiritual truth." One teacher mused, "How can we teach algebra when God is speaking to hearts?"[47]

On one of the nights, President Smith, overwhelmed with joy, left the chapel hurriedly. The next morning, he explained to a student, "I had to leave the building, I wanted to shout. Passing through the woods, I could hardly restrain myself. . . . [Finally,] when I opened the door at home . . . I shouted."[48]

Falling on a Double-Edged Sword

If the Mast revival was a high point of J. B. Smith's life, an episode in December 1921 was a low one. According to a school legend, Bishop George R. Brunk forced President Smith out of office because he had purchased a used piano for his home. (Brunk opposed the use of musical instruments in church and discouraged ministers from having pianos in their homes.) The story contained a small strand of truth. But Smith's relationship with the trustees was already frayed. Rumors about Smith moving on had begun circulating in 1920.[49] Smith had said earlier that he only intended to stay at EMS for two years because of his two-year leave of absence from the hoped-for Bible school in Ohio.[50]

Moreover, after the Cracker Box was built on the hill, some trustees, faculty, and supporters remained unhappy. According to Smith, "[I] had begun thinking of leaving [because] I was *blamed*" for placing the new building on the hill and causing dissent among those who wanted it in Assembly Park. Smith's fund-raising skills were also receiving mixed reviews, with one bishop claiming that Smith "did more harm than good" on his trip to raise money in Lancaster County. Daniel Kauffman had also scolded him about making "hasty criticisms of Goshen [College]."[51]

Besides J. B.'s own troubles, his wife, Lena, reported a run-in with A. G. Heishman—alleging that he had attended fairs, circuses, and a boxing match, had fallen out with his neighbors, and had a deplorable home life, all of which "injured his influence both as a minister and his association with the school."[52] Heishman apologized for attending a fair and a circus and said he had removed himself immediately from a boxing match on the street when he realized what it was. After a lengthy investigation, a five-member, bishop-appointed committee concluded that most of the charges by Sister Smith via "Bro. Smith against Bro. Heishman were based on rumors, and hearsay, and unproven." The committee urged Smith to "use greater caution in receiving, believing, or discussing similar reports."[53]

Smith's sometimes impulsive comments and behavior, especially his proposal to move EMS out of state, had eroded his political capital with the trustees, despite his superb skills as a scholar and Bible teacher. Any residual confidence likely vanished on December 6, 1921, about four years after Smith had taken office, when Bishop George R. Brunk, vice chair of the General Board and chair of its Religious Welfare Committee, wrote an intimidating letter to Smith about his piano. Brunk was especially perturbed that Smith "gave out the impression that [Brunk] was not opposed to it." In an exchange the two men had had about musical instruments, Brunk had agreed that since Virginia Conference did not prohibit pianos, Smith, as a minister, had "the same right as other preachers and bishops to have one," but that did not mean, he wrote, "I gave my approval to any."[54]

Brunk alleged that people were disappointed that Smith was not a better example of conservatism. "Therefore," he continued, "a great protest has risen which you will be wise to heed—otherwise the school and [the] cause in general will greatly suffer. . . . I would advise you to bend to the conservative sentiment on this matter . . . rather than listen to the voice of luxury and see your usefulness crumble." In response, Smith recalled a conversation in which Brunk could not produce any biblical proof from the Old Testament or the New Testament against having musical instruments in homes: "Here the discussion stopped and Brother Brunk remarked, 'Either you or I have to get out (some such words).'"[55]

Smith wrote a letter of rebuttal listing four ordained officials, including Bishop L. J. Heatwole, who had pianos in their homes. Brunk replied on December 15 saying, "It was disloyal for you to defend the instruments" publicly at EMS. He thought Smith had used him to justify Smith's acceptance of musical instruments. Brunk contended that the four ministers had pianos for unjustifiable reasons and noted, "Jacob Smith [had one] to please and (I am sure in my mind) it will injure his daughters."[56]

Brunk had written a persuasive essay against musical instruments some years earlier, and now at the end of World War I, he was campaigning for church members to sell any organs and pianos in their homes and send the funds overseas to alleviate the hunger of starving children. Brunk insinuated that, by purchasing the used piano, Smith had fallen on a double-edged sword and was both "corrupting the church and permitting children to starve."[57] Meanwhile, as their fathers were contesting musical instruments, Smith's daughter Ruth and Brunk's son Truman, both EMS students, were courting. They were distraught that their fathers' dispute might injure their prospects for marriage—but it didn't.

When A. D. Wenger, pruning his grapes in Fentress, heard about the dustup between Brunk and Smith over the piano, he "felt certain the piano was the climax of dissatisfaction with [Smith] and something would be done."[58] Bishop Brunk wrote to Wenger on January 4, 1922, explaining, "Brother Smith wants to *make peace* with me. [He thinks] there is a movement to oust him" by Troyer, Heishman, and

C. K. Lehman. Indeed, Brunk himself was part of the conspiracy to oust Smith, for the bishop had his eye on his brother-in-law, A. D. Wenger: "I have in mind for *you* to accept the Presidentship and for Chester [C. K. Lehman] to make up what you lack along the line of schoolwork. You would be *sound* and *economical* and Chester could keep up the school standards. What Say You, Answer at Once."[59]

Meanwhile, Wenger himself, in a long chat with J. B. Smith, had learned "that [Smith] would give up his piano and work under another President" if he could stay at EMS. But when Wenger consulted with some faculty and other leaders to see if Smith could be retained as a teacher, he "met so much unfavorable sentiment" that he gave up any hope for Smith staying and even doubted that Smith's daughters would be acceptable as teachers.[60]

Despite his desire to stay on as a teacher, Smith submitted his letter of resignation to the trustees on January 26, 1922. He stopped attending the monthly trustee meetings and began contacting midwestern church leaders about his prospects for teaching at Goshen College, serving as head of its Bible department, or even becoming its president. D. H. Bender, president of Hesston, declared that sending Smith, the arch critic of Goshen, to Goshen would be "unthinkable . . . an injustice to him [Smith], to the school, and to the cause." But he averred that Goshen did need "a conservative teacher like Smith in its Bible department."[61]

By the last year of the Smith administration (1921–1922), 55 percent of EMS students came from states beyond Virginia. One-third came from Pennsylvania, and the remainder named seven other states and Canada as home. All together, they represented ten regional conferences in the Mennonite Church.[62] Smith's ability to attract students from beyond Virginia, his intellectual stature, and his biblical scholarship were important contributions. His most enduring legacy, however, was hiring several key faculty—Dorothy Kemrer, M. T. Brackbill, C. K. Lehman, Daniel "D. W." Lehman, and J. L. Stauffer. All of them would play significant roles in molding the school's mission over the next thirty years.

Before leaving Harrisonburg, Smith sent a six-page confidential letter to the Virginia Department of Education criticizing H. N. Troyer (faculty member and business manager) and EMS in general. In July 1922, J. L. Stauffer and C. K. Lehman learned about the letter during a visit to Richmond to discuss EMS's accreditation. The official who informed them of the letter was so distressed by Smith's handling of the initial accreditation that he planned to visit EMS in the fall to verify its policies.[63]

By late spring 1922, J. B. Smith had returned to Ohio to cultivate his potato patch and otherwise remain busy as a scholar, Bible teacher, and voice of conservatism. "I have no doubt made some blunders," he said in reflection, "but religiously and educationally, I feel the work has been signally blessed."[64] The mismatch between Smith's gifts and the board's expectations paved the path to his exit. Although students applauded his skills as a Bible teacher, he lacked the temperament and administrative skills to manage an institution. And the trustees, for their part, were unrealistic to expect one man to teach, administer, plan, and raise funds, as well as have the political savvy to run the school.

An Irresistible Force

From his farm in Fentress, A. D. Wenger was inclined to accept Bishop Brunk's invitation to consider the presidency of EMS. "The moment I heard about brother Smith's piano, a conviction came on me that I was never able to fully [shake off]," he wrote. Several other factors also nudged Wenger toward the job. President D. H. Bender of Hesston College had already, in early February 1922, turned down an offer to replace Smith. Wenger's children were mostly grown or in school. And during a recent visit to the EMS campus, board members, teachers, students, and a visiting minister from Lancaster County had urged him to take the position, making "the burden grow heavier." Finally, the sight of 150 students leaving a Friday evening chapel service clinched Wenger's calling: "[I saw] a vision of the future of the school and I've mightily felt the presence of God ever since. There seems to be an irresistible force that I am powerless against."[65] With little ado, the trustees unanimously appointed A. D. Wenger president on February 25, 1922, effective at the end of the spring semester.[66]

Finally, after ten years of searching, the trustees had found their man. Wenger was almost without blemish. He was not a scholar with a doctoral degree, but he was a self-educated theologian, a world traveler, a savvy administrator, a business-man, a well-known but nonflamboyant evangelist who had preached throughout the church. Wenger was steadfast and earnest. He had credibility. And he had trust. He knew all the intramural politics of the previous ten years and had developed a deft sense of diplomacy. If anyone could steer a steady course forward, it was Wenger. Moreover, he enjoyed the blessing of his influential brother-in-law, Bishop George R. Brunk, now recovered from his illness. Wenger had promised Annie that he would stay on the farm and help raise their children until they were in school. Having kept his promise, he was now ready to lead the school.

An administrative team of three men—Wenger, Dean C. K. Lehman, and teacher J. L. Stauffer—led EMS for the next thirteen years. President Wenger made steady but significant strides in strengthening the school. His financial skills and constituent support in the first year of his presidency enabled EMS to reduce its debt from $43,000 to $3,000 and balance the operating budget. He wisely gave his brother-in-law C. K. Lehman freedom to shape the academic vision and program. Apart from finances, Wenger's signature contribution was fortifying church relations. He pressed for a revised charter (1923) that placed EMS solidly under the authority of Virginia Conference for the first time. A new board of sixteen trustees—all appointed by the conference—was organized. That board drafted and approved the first official constitution in 1924.[67]

Wenger's clear and compelling vision for EMS was printed in a widely distributed booklet titled *Who Should Educate Our Children?* "The question is no longer, shall we educate or not," said Wenger. With states now requiring high school attendance, the question had become, Who should do it? President Wenger rested his case with this plea:

> Shall we sit still until our church houses stand empty because worldly schools through their pride, pleasure, immorality and evolution have robbed us of our children? If we do not provide for *our own*, others *will*, and they will take them from us. Thus, we have been giving our sons and daughters to other denominations and to the world for over two hundred years. If we ever intend to stop, let us do it now. *It can be done.* If we in this generation cannot solve the school problem as it confronts the Church, how can it be done in the next? We can now *if we will*. Let us solve the problem before *it dissolves us*.[68]

Wenger's vision resonated with church leaders. His articulate and earnest plea bolstered church cooperation, financial support, and student applicants. For many years, Wenger's booklet offered the best sustained argument for a Mennonite-operated school in the East.

In the academic area, Dean Lehman envisioned a college that was "Christian to the core; Mennonite through and through."[69] Yet he desired more than a narrow parochial school. His intellectual dream for a junior college in the mid-1920s had a liberal arts perspective. He wanted students to read and digest the great classics of literature "that have occupied men's minds from times venerable with age." He also hoped that students would gain a grasp of history with its "mighty train of events," observe the "ills of humanity" and their proposed cures, and appreciate philosophy with its "unifying attempts to solve the deep mysteries of life, of the universe, and of God," as well as mathematics and the sciences. Nonetheless, Lehman's vision had limits. He wanted evolution, the "Arch Enemy of Christianity," completely expurgated from the curriculum—reflecting the national mood invigorated by the famous "Scopes Monkey Trial" of 1925.[70]

A spirit of enthusiasm pulsed among the three dozen entry-level college students of 1923–1924. They were enchanted by a lively address M. T. Brackbill gave on learning. "This quest for truth gives us a broader vision," he told them. "It widens our horizon. Distance is annihilated, and time, that heartless, unrelenting wretch, is rebuked. You need not propeller and rudder to touch at Madrid or circle the Mediterranean. Study the past, and you can call it from the grave of centuries and make it live again. Stage the drama anywhere you please. Choose the players at will from the long line of rulers, jurists, statesmen, discoverers, philosophers, poets . . . watch them in battle, on thrones, in legislative assemblies . . . or in the slave market." And then he invited students to "study philosophy and you can curl up your legs on the floor of a philosopher's school in Crotona, six centuries before Christ, and listen from behind the curtain to the white-robed, Golden-crowned Pythagoras."[71] Intellectually curious students, living away from their rural homes for the first time, found such a potpourri of ideas intoxicating, opening up vistas they had never imagined.

The Virginia Board of Education accredited EMS as a junior college in 1930.[72] This important step enabled graduates to transfer to four-year colleges. Two years later, the state certified EMS graduates to teach in public schools. In the first ten years of the Wenger administration (1922–1932), full-time enrollment grew from 119 to 158 while the number of part-time students (Special Bible Term, correspondence, and Summer Term) hovered around 125. In the spring of 1932, 77 percent (121) of the full-time students were in high school and the remaining 23 percent (37) were college-level. After the May 1932 commencement, the alumni association had a total of 331 members. About one-third of them were working as "Home Keepers" (housewives), 15 percent were teaching, 14 percent were farming, 13 percent were in advanced studies, and the remainder were in church work, nursing, and other occupations.[73] Nearly eighty Mennonites, most of whom had graduated from EMS's normal course (the two-year teacher training program), taught in thirty-eight small elementary schools in Rockingham County in the first half of the twentieth century.[74]

Just Common, Humble Folk

Many students participated in literary societies, which served as training camps for public life through debate, oratory, and music, as well as mathematical contests, spelling matches, discussions, and readings of classical literature and students' writing. EMS had three literary societies in the 1920s. College-level students joined the Smithsonians (sons of J. B. Smith). High school students selected either the Philomatheans or the Armerians. As EMS historian Hubert Pellman notes, the term *literary* encompassed a wide range of topics, from current events to science and religion.[75] Students enthusiastically participated in literary activities, which were usually held on Friday evenings.

Many spontaneous music groups—duets, quartets, trios, octets, and choruses—formed by students and faculty added spice to social and religious life. Most students had learned to sing a cappella in their home congregations. At EMS, they sang enthusiastically in music classes and in daily chapel and other church services. Singing was a Mennonite art form that strengthened social solidarity. Alumni from the 1920s recalled "a grand romance" with delightful musical memories. Especially cherished were the songs written by "loyal students" to express their devotion to EMS and receive "relief from their surging poetic natures."[76] Four-part a cappella singing was a ritual enactment that symbolized how the blend of individual voices could create a sublime reality eclipsing individual identity.

A strong mission emphasis across the curriculum and stirring revival meetings propelled students into off-campus mission activities. The student-driven, faculty-guided Young People's Christian Association (YPCA) emerged in 1922. It aimed "to promote growth in Christian character, fellowship, *aggressive* Christian work . . . to train [students] for Christian service . . . and the extension of His Church."[77] Reflecting the modern specialization of spirituality, the young Mennonites organized into nine committees. Over the next three decades, the YPCA would become a powerhouse where EMS students could test their interest in mission work in the Shenandoah Valley and beyond. Citing YPCA projects, teacher Gertrude Nissley enthused that EMS was training students who would have a great impact on the world.[78]

In the first decade, the students were rather ordinary. "We're just common folks here, and it would be a great pity if we would try to be anything else," opined an editorial in the *Journal*, a faculty-student publication for alumni and constituents.[79] Emma Z. Horst remembered that students in the dorms "lived much like a family."[80] And it was not unusual for students to live in the homes of faculty members. Laura Slabaugh resided with J. L. Stauffer's family in their little cabin in Assembly Park. This was the abode that one prospective teacher disparagingly called "a hut"

In the early years, students were transported to off-campus outings and socials in trucks.

and where Mrs. Stauffer's feet were frostbitten one winter.[81] Yet Slabaugh recalled how the Stauffers "graciously took me in and shared their humble abode with me for two years. . . . It was an old log cabin, in its fullest meaning . . . but it was *so much more*, it was a place of love, happiness, peace, contentment and ungrudging hospitality."[82]

The familial theme was both literal and spiritual. Although many employees had no relatives at EMS, some did. Three siblings of President Wenger's wife, Annie Lehman—C. K., D. W., and Elizabeth (married to "Curly John" Kurtz)—worked at EMS. They lived in three adjacent houses on what would become College Avenue. George R. Brunk's wife, Katie Wenger, was a sister of President Wenger. The Wenger-Brunk-Lehman cluster exerted a strong influence on the development of the school.

On the spiritual side, the familial theme of brothers and sisters in Christ was ritualized by prefacing faculty and staff members' last names with "Brother" or "Sister" (e.g., "Sister Horsch" and "Brother Kurtz"). Faculty members and other employees greeted each other with these spiritual salutations. Students addressed staff and faculty, but not other students, in the same way. No other titles were used. These ritualized greetings were continual reminders of the ties that linked everyone in a religious fraternity that was more than just a school.[83]

A little village called Mennonitetown sprouted up around the administration building. It was a *Gemeinschaft* knitted together by daily conversations, a place where backyard chatter kept everyone apprised of all the neighborly goings-on. It even had its own post office: Mennonite Station, Harrisonburg, Virginia. Mennonite ethnicity ran deep in this little hamlet.

EMS esteemed the traditional Mennonite virtues of humility and self-denial. Student programs had titles such as "Pride and Humility," "The Curse of a Haughty Spirit," and "A Humble Heart."[84] "Uncle Pete" Hartman always reminded students to "go home more humble" than they were before attending a meeting, class, or chapel.[85] Young faculty member Elizabeth Gish, writing in the *Journal*, distinguished between two phases of Christian humility: "The Willingness to Serve" and "Submissiveness to Authorities."[86]

EMS leaders stressed the importance of self-denial and the rejection of self-will. They believed that "a rigid and judicious discipline" would promote self-denial. Students were reminded that Jesus had "hurled scathing anathemas . . . upon the self-willed and disobedient." They learned that "self-abnegation and submission to rightful authority can bring about true liberty and happiness." The 1935–1936 catalog explained that "the school encourages self-denial, thrift, submission to and respect for authority."[87] For D. W. Lehman, the aims of public schools were "erroneous because they emphasize self and omit others."[88] The social ethos, with religious blessing, reminded students that communal values should always trump individual freedom.

Humility was ritualized in kneeling for public prayer in chapel and other religious services and also when washing another's feet in the footwashing rite at communion (John 13:1–17). To avoid self-exultation, individual photographs of seniors were forbidden in commencement issues of the *Journal* until 1929. Likewise, until 1935, the faculty appeared only as a group in *Journal* photos.[89] Taboos on playing musical instruments for performance and singing solos provided other ways to restrain self-expression. The ultimate ritual of humility was public confession in chapel. Confessions of sin during revival meetings were voluntary. Administrators, however, sometimes required deviant students to confess their transgressions in front of the entire student-faculty body in chapel. This public shaming was an effective mode of social control.[90]

The Founding Farmers

The founders of EMS were white, rural, and male. Although dozens of men and women energetically operated the school in its formative decade (1915–1925), seven men were especially influential in shaping its mission and policies. This circle included early visionaries L. J. Heatwole, A. D. Wenger, George R. Brunk, and Daniel Kauffman. After EMS opened in Harrisonburg, J. B. Smith and early faculty members C. K. Lehman and J. L. Stauffer actively steered its course.

This cluster of seven, which included the first three presidents, crafted the ideological vision, drafted the policies, and sculpted the school's character for three decades. Men and only men served as trustees and held administrative posts (registrars, academic deans, and presidents) for sixty years. Sadie Hartzler—who was appointed a faculty member in 1926 and part-time librarian in 1928 and then served as full-time librarian from 1945 to 1961—was the lone exception to the male dominance of administrative roles in the school's early decades.

All the founders were or would become ordained ministers (Wenger, Lehman, and Smith) or bishops (Brunk, Kauffman, Heatwole, and Stauffer). They all were leaders in Virginia Conference, except for Daniel Kauffman, who served on the trustee faculty committee until 1944. This tight link between the school and the conference made it difficult to distinguish between the founders' views and those of Virginia Conference. Furthermore, since 1923, the conference controlled the school by appointing the trustees and approving its constitution.

The founders were not professional educators. Their worldviews and convictions were formed more by their churchly roles than by their education. Apart from Daniel Kauffman, J. B. Smith, and C. K. Lehman, who had academic credentials, the others were largely self-educated, ordained churchmen with little or no college experience as students or teachers. Yet they were intelligent, creative, and industrious men who held staunch commitments to conservative Mennonite beliefs.

The founders considered themselves "aggresso-conservatives." This phrase, coined by Daniel Kauffman in 1915, meant conservative in belief but aggressive in method. Such people held conservative views of church practice while aggressively initiating new programs.[91] Although midwestern Mennonites considered the founders conservatives, many traditional conservatives in the East viewed them as progressives because they promoted church-operated schools. The founders were committed to a Bible-based, Mennonite-directed education, which they hoped would silence more traditional Mennonites who claimed that any education beyond the primary grades was a danger that would only cultivate pride, individualism, and heresy. Yet for the founders, an embrace of Mennonite education did not mean an embrace of cultural assimilation and urbanization.

"Go to the farm." That's what President Wenger told the graduating class in the spring of 1935. He implored them to plow because "our ancestors were nearly all farmers." Many who moved to town, Wenger lamented, left the Mennonite faith. After listing the virtues of rural life, he urged students to live "away from the din, dust, and filth of the city."[92] He shared this strong rural bias with the other founders. Wenger raised grapes and produce, J. B. Smith grew potatoes, George R. Brunk operated an orchard, and L. J. Heatwole tended a small farm. The dean of the faculty, C. K. Lehman, raised broilers (chickens for roasting). Rural images peppered the religious vocabulary of the founders, whose use of biblical words—vineyard, field, sowing, seed, ripe, reaping, sheaves, harvest—complemented their rural worldview.

An antiurban ethos permeated EMS's culture until the mid-twentieth century. Among other purposes, the school's charter aimed to guide youth into "the rural walks of life" rather than into "the commercial channels of the cities."[93] In 1920–1921, the school added courses for prospective farmers because "the country which God made is more beautiful than the city which man made [and] life is larger and freer and happier on the farm than in the town." That same year EMS restructured its calendar so students living on farms could leave school in late March to begin spring plowing. This enabled farmers to complete the four-year high school curriculum in five years.[94]

J. L. Stauffer viewed urban life more positively than his colleagues because he had worked in an inner-city mission for several years. Even so, his interests were more aligned with saving souls in the slums than appreciating urban life itself. Mission outreach by EMS students largely targeted rural areas of the Blue Ridge Mountains, from Mutton Hollow, Virginia, to Wildcat, Kentucky.[95]

Despite all the rhetoric about the virtues of rural life, EMS's modest agricultural curriculum sputtered along in the high school until it ran out of gas in the 1950s. The hope of sending many students to the farm largely faded. Instead, EMS provided an on-ramp for many fresh-from-the-farm students to pursue professional careers.

A Fortress Called Safeguard

The Battle Script

It's worth pausing from our story to ponder the fears and hopes of the founders. There was much to fret about during EMS's formative decade (1915–1925). The school was born in a climate of fear—fear of the fast-changing worldly culture, fear of theological liberalism, fear of evolution, fear of urban life, fear of higher education, fear of Goshen College, and fear of secular, state-directed education. Moreover, the founders worried that without a church-run school, young people would leave the Mennonite fold in droves and the church would shrink, if not vanish. In their minds, the very survival of their beloved church was at stake. They also fretted that if they started a school, it might eventually turn away from or, worse yet, work against the church. Yet if the East offered no alternative to Goshen, eastern youth attending Goshen might lose their faith even more quickly than if they had gone to a public college.

Five of the ideological architects of EMS—Brunk, Heatwole, Smith, Stauffer, and Wenger—envisioned their educational efforts as spiritual warfare.[96] This Mennonite version of the epic clash between the forces of good and evil provided potent images that motivated the founders, helped them interpret events, and infused their work with eternal meaning. The image of a battle—a root metaphor—is rife throughout the founders' correspondence. This metaphor explains much of EMS's behavior as an organization. The battle motif inspired a narrative that helped the founders interpret their social world and gave them a repertoire of responses to fast-changing events that impinged on the school.

The founders viewed themselves as fighting for "the Truth" in a great conflict between God and Satan. As warriors for the truth, they resolved never to give up the fight, believing that in the end, God would vanquish evil. Their confidence rested in these words of Scripture: "Put on the whole armour of God, that ye may be able to stand against the wiles of the devil. For we wrestle not against flesh and blood, but against principalities, against powers, against the rulers of the darkness of this world, against spiritual wickedness in high places" (Eph. 6:11–12). For a nonresistant people, the battle motif, albeit biblical, was awash with irony.

Defending the Fortress

The battle metaphor had practical implications. To the founders, the forces of evil were actively at work in the larger society and even within the Mennonite Church.

The Mennonite fight against infidels and modernists outside Mennonite walls, and against "world-lovers" and liberals inside them, as portrayed by Ernest G. Gehman and George R. Brunk. *Source: Sword and Trumpet 2*, no. 4 (Oct. 1930): 7.

The worldly society was *perceived* as hostile. Thus the founders did what most groups—teams, corporations, countries—do in the face of a threat: they took defensive measures to protect themselves. They tried to shield Mennonite youth from the menace of popular culture so that they would "be saved . . . and safeguarded from the pernicious influence" of secular education.[97] Feeling besieged by external forces, the founders built a fortress to shelter students from the wiles of the world and indoctrinate them in Mennonite belief and practice.

At their second meeting, the day after Christmas in 1912, the Warwick school advocates wanted "safeguards . . . thrown around" their proposed school to "insure its continued orthodoxy." The word *safeguard* abounds in the plans leading to the startup at Harrisonburg. Moreover, the first line of the aims and objectives section in the 1917–1918 catalog says, "The Eastern Mennonite School is intended as a *safeguard* for . . . the young people of the Mennonite Church." *Safeguard* also appears in the 1917 charter. The first official constitution in 1924 contains a section titled "By-Laws and Safe-guard Features." The constitution's section on amendments declares that its "safe-guard features for the Mennonite Church and School shall be *unchangeable*" in any future revisions. That safeguard of safeguarding held for nearly forty years until a constitutional revision erased it in 1963.[98] EMS's safeguarding principles, and the policies flowing from them, rested on this fundamental assumption: the dominant culture is hostile, and it will swallow us up if we do not protect our youth from it.

EMS leaders viewed the rapid rise of public high schools in the 1920s as one example of a hostile threat. President Wenger avowed that students in public schools "breathe the atmosphere of heresy, unbelief, immorality, dishonesty, the dance, the movie, fashionable dress, secret societies, cigarette-smoking, card-playing, national patriotism and carnal warfare." Then he added, "Many of the teachers are of the silly, bobbed-hair, dancing, card-playing kind."[99] D. W. Lehman, in a two-part essay, "The 'Scum' of High School Experiences," described fifty-two examples of lewd behavior that he had gathered from public schools in eight states.[100] Worried about falling into the cauldron of popular culture, EMS leaders sprinkled their correspondence and documents with the words *defense*, *defensive*, and *defenders* until the 1940s.

Passwords, Loyalty, and Boundaries

In the midst of battle, loyalty matters. References to loyalty appeared repeatedly in school correspondence and publications.[101] The founders sought loyal troops—teachers and staff who were loyal to the church, loyal to the nonresistant gospel, and loyal to the mission of EMS. Likewise, they hoped to produce loyal students, who would become loyal church members and loyal workers in the Lord's vineyard. Loyalty, a softer word than obedience, nonetheless signaled self-denial—yielding individual interests to community norms.

Plain dress was the litmus test of loyalty. Plain dress for students and teachers signaled not only separation *from* the world but also loyalty *to* the church and the school. Besides, teachers were expected to wholeheartedly promote the regulation garb of the church.

Operating and defending a fortress in a hostile world required regulations, boundaries, and symbols. In the founding era, EMS had a host of restrictions on fashionable dress, sports, drama, and art, as well as on "modernist" books on religion, evolution, and science. This fortress mentality involved a careful selection of faculty, staff, curricular offerings, textbooks, and periodicals in the library. *The Mennonite*, a periodical of the "worldly" General Conference Mennonite Church, was not placed in the library but restricted to the president's office.[102] In 1931, faculty were asked to note errors about evolution "on the margins of all magazines" in the library "to safeguard the readers."[103]

Protective guidelines restricted interaction with other colleges and visiting speakers. One teacher eschewed mixing with the world because it is "so rotten." Bishop Brunk intoned that "the pass-word of the world is mix, mix, mix, but that of the gospel is be ye separate."[104] This caution about mixing too freely with outsiders was also ritualized by the selective use of handshakes and the kiss of peace.[105] On one occasion, President Wenger answered a knock on the door of his home. A young man from Lancaster County, not dressed in plain attire, had come to check in with the president, as required, before visiting with his girlfriend, who was attending one of the school's Special Bible Terms. Wenger began to extend his hand to the visitor but then pulled back and asked, "A Brother?" When the visitor nodded yes, Wenger extended his hand again and also gave him the kiss of peace.[106]

One boundary around the EMS fortress was a bit porous. The first mission statement in 1917 welcomed non-Mennonite students who were in "sympathy with the principles" of the Mennonite Church. This welcome was repeated in the catalogs throughout the twentieth century. Yet the welcome had limits. President Wenger, for example, was uncertain if he should ask a United Brethren minister, who wore a ring and held a lodge membership, to pray in chapel. Because Mennonite women rarely cut their hair (1 Cor. 11:5–6), Wenger was unsure if he should permit a Baptist girl with cut hair to lead devotions in a dormitory prayer circle. From the beginning, mandatory courses pertaining to Mennonite beliefs and dress standards were waived for non-Mennonites. Still, these students were not exactly first-class citizens; they were excluded from holding office in the YPCA and in the Alumni Association.[107] In the first twenty years of the school's history, 1,076 students were enrolled in regular classes, but only 15 (fewer than one a year on average) were not Mennonites.[108] Most of them came from the Harrisonburg area.

The Educational Core: Indoctrination

If a fortress is a fitting metaphor for EMS as an institution, *indoctrination-separation* aptly describes its educational philosophy. Until 1939, the school's catalog asserted that the Mennonite Church was duty-bound "to indoctrinate and establish her young people in her Articles of Faith and Doctrinal Standards."[109] The founders unapologetically sought to immerse students in a Mennonite worldview. Only with indoctrination, they believed, could their educational experiment succeed. They were not interested in cultivating independent thinking in the realm of religion for fear that it might threaten the notion of absolute truth. The faculty, for example, prohibited students from arguing about biblical interpretations in literary debates.[110]

Such defensive tactics, leaders hoped, would safeguard their youth from the perils of modernity and prepare them to serve the church.

The founders expected EMS to be subject to the church and to serve it. The men who tried to establish the school at Denbigh and then at Alexandria envisioned a school under tight church control. Such control was ambiguous, however, until the revised charter placed EMS under the thumb of Virginia Conference in 1923. Over the years, however, state standards and professional associations gradually weakened the church's grip on the school. Already in 1923, Dean Lehman conceded that the church was "able to speak *only generally*" regarding the policies and aims of the school.[111] Serving the church was one thing; being controlled by it was quite another.

By the spring of 1932, the experiment begun at Assembly Park was well under way. In its first fifteen years, EMS had enjoyed relative stability, slow growth, and rising support from churches beyond Virginia Conference. Even so, it remained a modest operation with three dozen students in the junior college, and now it faced a painful economic depression. Meanwhile, officials were engaged in an intercollegiate battle to save the church from the threat of modernism as church colleges became the ideological battleground to define Mennonite identity in the twentieth century. And in the West, the star of Goshen College was shining ever brighter and drawing more youth from the East.

CHAPTER 4

Fighting for
the Truth

Modernism is the Devil's handmaiden.
—Bishop John Mosemann

Fighting the Scourge of Liberalism

Throughout its first two decades, Eastern Mennonite School was entangled in a national theological controversy. While World War I was ravaging millions, liberals and conservatives in American Protestant churches were fighting over the credibility of the Bible. Scholars point to the eight-year period of 1917 to 1925—overlapping with the founding of EMS—as the peak of the national battle between liberalism and Fundamentalism.[1] Mennonite leaders, animated by these Protestant controversies, were sparring over similar issues. This ideological battle shook Mennonite identity, tempted many to take sides, and sparked a clash between EMS and Goshen College.

J. B. Smith's arrival in Assembly Park in October 1917 sent a clear message to the Mennonite world: the new school would staunchly defend the fundamentals of the Christian faith against liberalism. Smith did not disappoint. A week after he arrived at EMS, Virginia Conference welcomed him as a minister and appointed him to the Mennonite Board of Education (MBE). Four months later, he implored the MBE to "drive out the enemy," the liberalism that he blamed Goshen College for spreading across the church. It was rather audacious for the head of a new school to issue such a scathing critique of its twenty-three-year-old sibling. Smith's pungent six-page letter reveals the ideology of the founders' worldview—a mind-set of fear that shaped the school's values and policies well into the mid-twentieth century. Authored by Smith and endorsed by the trustees, it reflected the sentiment of EMS's founders and early leaders.[2]

Always lucid and well organized, Smith began the letter by summarizing the "crisis" posed by liberalism. He then enumerated seventeen tenets of conservatism followed by seventeen of liberalism. Conservatives, explained Smith, claim that the Bible is "divinely inspired in *all* its parts . . . [It] is infallible, authentic, and authoritative." Liberals, in Smith's eyes, consider church doctrines just "an accumulation of traditions perpetrated by an ignorant people." Eventually, with time and intelligence, "the narrow and bigoted tenets will be regulated [*sic*] to the dead past," allowing the church, in the liberal view, to rise to new heights of achievement and splendor.[3]

Smith was not alone in his fear of liberalism. Counting up the curses facing the church in 1919, *Gospel Herald* editor Daniel Kauffman ranked "LIBERALISM" as the top foe of Christianity.[4] Bishop L. J. Heatwole, in an essay titled "How Mennonites Are Confronting the Menace of Modernism," explained how church leaders were combating it in church papers, Bible conferences, sermons, and books and by eventually closing Goshen College, where "students were imbibing the corroding and deadly influences of so-called higher criticism."[5] Lancaster bishop John Mosemann—critic of Goshen College and friend of EMS—charged that "*modernism is the Devil's handmaiden*. It is like a venomous reptile, for wherever it strikes its fangs, it leaves its victims inoculated with its deadly poison."[6]

Used interchangeably in Mennonite writing, *liberalism* and *modernism* referred to theological beliefs, not culture or politics. Liberalism, wrote Daniel Kauffman, is "known by many names such as New Theology, New Thought, Higher Criticism, Free Thought, Unitarianism Etc. Etc." All of these discredit "the idea that the Bible is absolutely reliable."[7] Without doubt, the deepest wedge dividing liberals and conservatives in this battle was their view of divine inspiration. Conservatives believed that the Bible was inspired by God and was "the final authority" on creation, miracles, and the resurrection.[8] A. D. Wenger surely had not forgotten the skepticism he heard Mennonite preachers voice earlier in Holland. He told EMS students that they would need their "Bible knowledge and abiding faith in Christ . . . to combat . . . the *vicious* forms of liberalism, evolution, and atheism."[9] Conservatives also charged that liberal religious views spawned terrible cultural consequences—the teaching of evolution in public schools, women voting and entering politics, and the growing immorality in public life.

This was not a little cultural spat. Gigantic issues were in play. If Christians could not trust the Bible, their faith would crumble. How could they confront the evolutionists without absolute confidence in a literal account of creation? Many conservatives saw the slick fingers of Satan shaping the minds of liberals, whose methods, according to Smith's 1918 letter, involved "secrecy, evasion, equivocation, duplicity, intrigue, and spiritual jugglery." For conservatives, this was a spiritual battle between God and the devil. In George R. Brunk's words, "We have two mighty opposing forces at work, one drawing upward on the souls of men to good and God, and the other downward to Satan and death."[10] A. D. Wenger noted that "Satan is working" in public schools "to get a stranglehold on the rising generation to choke out its conscience for pure and noble things."[11] In light of this grave threat, J. B. Smith called the creeping liberalism in the Mennonite Church an "impending calamity" that would take the church "down to defeat and destruction."[12]

Flirting with Fundamentalism

In Smith's long letter to the MBE, he borrowed some words from the playbook of a growing network of strident conservatives in American Protestant churches. By 1920, the most vociferous conservatives were calling their movement Fundamentalism. In some ways, liberalism and Fundamentalism were two sides of the coin of scientific rationalism. As the modernist-fundamentalist strife intensified, many denominations faced divisive civil wars in their schools, publishing houses, mission programs, and annual conferences.[13] The ideas driving this national movement had been galvanizing for more than a decade. About the time that George R. Brunk was convening the Warwick school advocates in 1913, a wealthy California oil magnate, Lyman Stewart, was distributing three million copies of a set of booklets titled *The Fundamentals: A Testimony to the Truth*.[14] The twelve-volume set stoked fiery debates between theological conservatives and liberals in various denominations.

To buttress their defense against liberalism, Virginia leaders borrowed some ideas from the Fundamentalist movement. Soon after Smith took the helm at EMS, *Gospel Herald* promoted *The Fundamentals* as "a worthy and effective way of combating the flood of liberalism" and "a very valuable asset in every home library."[15] Essays in *Gospel Herald* alerted Mennonites to the ongoing controversy over Fundamentalism.[16]

The entire edifice of Fundamentalism rests on *inerrancy*—the claim that the Bible is error-free. Each word of Scripture is factual and true because God, by divine dictation, spoke directly to the authors of the Bible's sixty-six books, fundamentalists believe. This belief became known as *verbal* (God speaking to the writers) *and plenary* (all words and all books) *inspiration*. If the Bible is free of error, then the virgin birth, the miracles, the resurrection, and the one-day creation of humans are all indisputable facts. Yet theological progressives scoffed at the idea that the biblical accounts were literally true in every detail. How do we know? they asked. The answer was: Because the Bible itself says so.[17]

J. B. Smith wrote a long chapter on the Bible in Daniel Kauffman's 1914 edition of *Bible Doctrine*. He used the words *verbal and plenary inspiration* and even declared that "every book of it, every chapter of it, every word of it, every syllable of it, and every letter of it is the direct utterance of the Most High." With this chapter and other writings, Smith, more than any other churchman, inserted fundamentalist jargon into the Mennonite lexicon.[18] The first EMS catalog (1917–1918), already in print when Smith arrived in Harrisonburg, had no doctrinal statement.

Virginia Conference met in early December 1918, about eight months after J. B. Smith had written his letter to MBE and shortly after the end of the Great War. In the opening session, a bishop warned, "The devil hopes to accomplish a great end in overthrowing the church, especially in this day and age, by introducing false doctrine."[19] The Virginians, however, did not wince about sparring with the devil. They swiftly appointed a committee of three (J. B. Smith, A. D. Wenger, and George R. Brunk) to investigate the "menace of liberalism" and draft measures to safeguard the conference from modernism's "destructive blight." Virginia Conference also pleaded with the church-wide General Conference to oppose "the tenets and delusions of the new theology" and to "purge the Church from this calamitous peril."

The three men were all heavyweights at EMS. Smith was the first and Wenger the soon-to-be second president of the school, and Brunk was vice chair of the school's trustees and chair of its powerful Religious Welfare Committee. The special committee developed eighteen Articles of Faith, which Virginia Conference adopted in October 1919.[20] In a note to Smith three weeks before the meeting, Brunk told him, "Get your fundamentals drafted good, clear and strong, so no liberalist can hide under them and we will put them thru [sic] at our district conference." Smith drafted the statement and Brunk muscled it through the conference.[21]

The statement began with some key fundamentalist words: "We believe in the *plenary, verbal* inspiration of the Bible as the word of God; that it is authentic in its matter, authoritative in its counsels, *inerrant* in its original writings, and the only *infallible* rule of faith and practice."[22] The work of the three-member committee was significant and influential. After Virginia Conference adopted the eighteen points, the Mennonite Church General Conference approved them as the "Christian Fundamentals" in 1921.[23]

The Virginia Articles of Faith first appeared in the 1920–1921 EMS catalog and remained there for forty years. Moreover, the EMS faculty pledged their loyalty to these doctrinal principles at the opening of each school year until 1939.[24] Thereafter, they pledged "periodically" until 1946, when pledging vanished. The articles were replaced in the 1961–1962 catalog by a lengthy statement of philosophy that did not include the words *plenary* and *verbal* but did reference the Bible's inerrancy.[25]

Hybrid Fundamentalists

Leaders of Virginia Conference thought that liberal theology would eventually destroy their church. Wanting to mobilize the best defense against liberalism, they found help in the fundamentalist view of the Bible. Traditional Mennonite

Ernest G. Gehman (vaulting over the pole) and several unidentified students relax in front of the Cracker Box, 1921. Gehman, a 1922 graduate of EMS, returned as a professor of German after receiving degrees from Franklin and Marshall College and later from Heidelberg University.

beliefs were anchored in the Bible—especially in the teachings of Jesus. Mennonites had always assumed the divine inspiration of the Bible, and even before the fundamentalist-modernist controversy, they had accepted its accounts of the virgin birth, miracles, and resurrection as fact. Yet these beliefs had never been codified as doctrine.[26]

The 1632 Dordrecht Confession of Faith, written by Dutch Mennonites—and still authoritative for the Mennonite Church in 1917—did not have an article on the Bible. The confession simply took the Bible's divine inspiration for granted. Each of its eighteen articles was heavily documented with Scripture.[27] Yet if pushed by opponents, Mennonites could not point to one crisp article of faith that unequivocally affirmed divine inspiration. In many ways, Daniel Kauffman's *Bible Doctrine* of 1914 served as a proxy credo.

By adopting the 1919 Articles of Faith, Virginia Conference hoped to plug a hole in their doctrinal dike. The precision of the fundamentalist jargon—*inerrancy, verbal and plenary inspiration*—drew a sharp line against the foe of liberalism and helped bolster Mennonite defenses against it. For the Virginia Mennonites, such borrowing was not a rejection of their faith as articulated in the Dordrecht Confession but an enhancement of it.[28]

While EMS stood categorically against liberalism, it was not a fundamentalist institution. Preserving the Mennonite Church and its peculiar doctrines and practices was foremost on the EMS agenda. To accomplish that, the founders had to muster a strong defense against liberalism. Although the Virginia Conference Articles of Faith were printed in the catalog, two key institutional documents—the constitution and the annual catalog itself—were otherwise free of fundamentalist language.

The school catalogs published from 1918 to 1960 declare that EMS is a *denominational* school. Even after dropping the word *denominational* in 1961, the catalogs identify EMU as a Mennonite institution. These documents never call EMS a fundamentalist school, promote the fundamentals of faith, or mention the word *Fundamentalism*. Still, the early catalogs are unapologetic: the church, through EMS, "has the right to indoctrinate" youth in order to "maintain, propagate, and perpetuate" Mennonite faith and doctrine.[29]

EMS's first constitution served twenty-three years (1924–1947) without using the words *Fundamentalism, fundamentalist, fundamentals, inerrancy*, or *verbal and plenary inspiration*. A reference to the Bible simply says, "The school shall give the Bible a place in each course of study; it shall encourage the students to make it their constant companion." Trustees were expected to be "open defenders of the Bible doctrines peculiar to the Mennonite faith."[30]

For their part, teachers were required to be members of the Mennonite Church "in full sympathy with her doctrines and practices, and free from the unscriptural teaching . . . such as evolution, higher criticism and the new theology." In addition, they were forbidden to teach anything "contrary to the doctrines and practices of the Mennonite Church." Moreover, the constitution prohibited literature and textbooks containing "Higher Criticism, Evolution, Fiction or any other popular forms of error."[31]

Virginia Mennonites were hybrid fundamentalists who borrowed from the fundamentalist crusaders to preserve a conservative Mennonite theology and practice. Rather than eroding Mennonite identity, the borrowing strengthened and enhanced it. Co-opting some language from Fundamentalism was a way to reaffirm and perpetuate certain Mennonite distinctives, which gave EMS strong ballast in the tumultuous seas of modernity.

For Virginia Mennonites, the word *fundamentals* signaled apostolic and historic orthodoxy, while *Fundamentalism* was open to critique. One of EMS's founding faculty members, J. L. Stauffer, for example, wrote an article naming ten errors of Fundamentalism.[32] Using the vocabulary of Fundamentalism—*verbal, plenary, inerrant*—was simply naming what they thought they had always believed but had never declared. Beginning in 1919 and continuing well into the 1950s, Virginia Conference held an annual fundamentals conference to discuss basic Christian and Mennonite beliefs. Certain Mennonite convictions aligned with the views of some fundamentalists: opposition to evolution and separation from worldly activities such as divorce, drinking, dancing, and attending movies.[33]

The EMS founders, however, repeatedly separated themselves from Fundamentalism by contending for a "whole Gospel," a "full Gospel," and by practicing "the all things" taught by Jesus. These three phrases were code for nonresistance and nonconformity, including plain attire and other Mennonite distinctives.[34] Sharply separating conservative Mennonites from fundamentalists, A. D. Wenger considered all Mennonite ordinances, nonresistance, and nonconformity to be fundamentals of the faith.[35] George R. Brunk declared that Mennonites, "if true to a full gospel, must be *against* both [fundamentalists and liberals]."[36] He also lamented that fundamentalists "neglect or refuse the two central pillars of Gospel fundamentalism, *Nonresistance* and *Nonconformity to the world*."[37] Brunk criticized what he called "Worldly Fundamentalists" for a host of evils and urged Mennonites not to fellowship with or cooperate with "the so-called Fundamentalists."[38] Moreover, he was annoyed that some of the "tons of Fundamentalist literature" in circulation "was getting into our own church."[39]

The founders of EMS were first and foremost Mennonites. Church elders were, in truth, more worried about the drift away from traditional teachings than they were about being fundamentalists.[40] Even though Virginia Mennonites were united *against* liberalism, they were not united *with* Fundamentalism. That they had grafted some words of Fundamentalism to the trunk of Mennonite religion to protect it from the onslaught of modernism did not make them fundamentalists. And yet the words that they grafted did articulate a more precise understanding of biblical inspiration than their heretofore folksy view of it.

When Is Jesus Coming?

If EMS was not a fundamentalist school, it certainly was a flagship for premillennialism, with its apocalyptic view of the world's end. In 1898, before his first marriage and trip around the world, A. D. Wenger introduced this novel eschatology into the Mennonite Church at a ten-day Bible conference in western Pennsylvania. Wenger's talk about the Rapture—when Christians would fly like angels to meet Jesus in the skies—engrossed the audience. His description of Jesus's imminent return was the most talked about lecture for months. It cracked the secret code of the biblical prophecies hidden from believers for years. It forecast how the world would end and even identified the unfolding world events that signaled Jesus's imminent return.[41]

Although premillennialism was new to Mennonites, its roots reached back to the early church, before AD 300. Irishman John Nelson Darby repopularized the view when he coined the term *rapture* in 1830. Wenger had learned about premillennialism when he attended lectures by C. I. Scofield at Moody Bible Institute in the summer of 1894. Little did he know then that his spellbinding conference talk years later would stir heated controversy in Mennonite communities and fuel contentious wrangling on the EMS campus for years.

This end-of-world theory, which resurged in the late nineteenth century in England and America, focused on the millennium—the biblical idea of a thousand years of peace and prosperity on the earth.[42] The big question was, would Jesus return to earth before or after the millennium? There were three answers: before, after, and neither. The premillennialists predicted a second coming *before* the thousand years of peace; the postmillennialists expected Jesus *after* the millennium. And the amillennialists agreed that Jesus would return to earth for the final judgment but expected that the millennium would be a spiritual reign, not a literal kingdom on earth.[43]

The three different views hinged on distinctions between literal and figurative interpretations of certain Scriptures. The amillennial view, traditionally held by Mennonites, interpreted words of prophetic Scripture allegorically. For premillennialists, the same passages were literal forecasts of the future.[44] For example, the words "one day is with the Lord as a thousand years" (2 Pet. 3:8) was a figure of speech for amillennialists, while for premillennialists it referred to a literal earthly millennium.

The premillennialists expected three things to happen before Jesus inaugurated the thousand years of peace. First, the Rapture would whisk Christians (dead and alive) away into heaven, leaving unbelievers behind. Second, those left behind would face a seven-year tribulation of terror ruled by the Antichrist. Finally, after a series of wars, the tribulation would culminate in the gigantic battle of Armageddon between the knights of evil and good in a Palestinian valley. Jesus and his saintly comrades would return to Earth, win the battle, and inaugurate a millennium of peace on earth.[45]

Advocates of this view proclaimed, "Jesus is coming" and soon. Their slogan echoed the title of an 1878 book by William E. Blackstone—"the most popular book associated with [premillennialism] through World War I."[46] With funding from fundamentalist oil baron Lyman Stewart, the book was later expanded and republished. It eventually sold more than a million copies in multiple editions in forty-eight languages.[47] Its message was clear: you had better be ready. The Rapture could happen at any moment, and you might be left behind. Fascination and fear about the Rapture continued into the twenty-first century in American culture, evinced by the bestselling *Left Behind* series of sixteen novels and the 2014 film *Left Behind*.[48]

Premillennial views percolated quickly in Mennonite circles after 1910. The Mennonite Publishing House began selling the *Scofield Reference Bible* soon after it was printed.[49] When thirty-seven-year-old preacher J. L. Stauffer joined the faculty of EMS in 1918, he came with impressive premillennial credentials. Five years earlier, he had published a popular twenty-page booklet, *The Coming of the Lord and Practical Christian Living*, which sold ten thousand copies in six months. After topping fifteen thousand, it appeared in a third edition.[50] J. B. Smith had been a strong proponent of premillennialism when he taught at Hesston College (1909–1917).

Now with a larger megaphone at EMS, his voice grew even louder. One Mennonite historian credits the trio of Stauffer, Smith, and A. D. Wenger with popularizing premillennialism in the Mennonite world.[51] Aiding them were the strong voices of Bishop George R. Brunk and Lancaster leaders John Mosemann and Noah Mack. The affiliation of these men with EMS branded it a "pre-mill" school, exposing thousands of students to that view for several decades.

C. K. Lehman, the academic dean, was the lone faculty proponent for historic amillennialism. Despite being lopsided, debates about the "millennial question" were quite animated. Why? The three views offered different forecasts for how and when the world would end, different views of how Christians should engage the world in the meantime, and different ways of interpreting current events. It made a drastic difference whether Jesus's return was just around the corner or a thousand years away.

Postmillennialists had little to fret about because they expected Jesus's return *after* the millennium. Motivated by their Christian convictions, they engaged in reforms to abolish poverty, alcoholism, prostitution, and other societal ills. Doing so, they thought, would eventually usher in God's kingdom on earth. Mennonites, at least those at EMS, gave little credence to this view because they thought such Social Gospel activists were liberals who downplayed personal conversion.

Premillennialists were pessimistic about any human attempts to fix social woes.[52] The ills of poverty, injustice, and warmongering were, for them, sure signs that the Rapture was near, and in their minds, any attempts to ameliorate them would only stall God's plan for Jesus's return. The Bible, for premillennialists, predicted that conditions on earth would wax worse and worse with wars and rumors of wars before Jesus returned. So why engage in social action if Jesus was arriving soon? The most urgent and imperative action was mission work—saving the souls of the lost while they still had a chance of salvation before the Rapture. In 1929, George R. Brunk said, for example, "The crying need of the world today is not the settlement of the *race question* . . . but of bringing lost souls into saving contact with the Gospel."[53]

Amillennialists, sometimes accused of being closet liberals, expected Jesus to literally return to earth, but they believed that no one could predict the time of his arrival. Meanwhile, they sought to obey his commands by preaching the gospel and reaching out to those in need. All the while, they remained watchful and ready for Jesus's return.

Dividing Holy History

To muddle matters more, most premillennialists held a dispensational view of the Bible. Conservative scholars were troubled by thorny contradictions in different sections of Scripture. Influenced by scientific rationalism, they carefully observed facts

This faculty quartet sang on campus and at local churches for many years. Left to right: D. W. Lehman (professor of education, bishop, and brother of C. K.), H. D. Weaver (business manager), C. K. Lehman (academic dean), Ernest G. Gehman (professor of German). Gehman drew sketches for the audience while the quartet sang.

and classified them as natural scientists would—into a taxonomy that might resolve the inconsistencies.[54] Following this procedure, dispensational scholars divided biblical history into seven time periods (dispensations) based on how people had responded to God's overtures. *The Scofield Reference Bible*, published in 1909, included extensive footnotes and occasional comments in the text itself that shaded the biblical story with a subtle dispensational lens. One of Oxford University Press's best-selling books, the Scofield Bible spread dispensationalism around the world.[55] By the early 1920s, most fundamentalists had embraced dispensational premillennialism.

Dispensationalism posed two serious problems for Mennonites.[56] The Scofield Bible postponed the application of Jesus's teachings in the Sermon on the Mount until the earthly millennium. This effectively obliterated the ethical imperatives of the Gospels—nonresistance, love of enemy, nonviolence, and forgiveness. Moreover, Scofield's view of the church as invisible and mysterious scuttled the Mennonite notion that the church was a literal community of believers, accountable to one another for their conduct. Scofield's ideas undercut these twin pillars of Mennonite doctrine.

Bishop Brunk was especially perturbed that J. B. Smith promoted the Scofield Bible on campus. He ventured that "Smith was raised on the Scofield Bible like a baby on a bottle." A convinced premillennialist, Brunk led the charge for a modified dispensationalism. He noted some twenty Scofield errors that "rob the church of the four Gospels and Acts."[57] Brunk accepted the dispensations of the Hebrew Testament but dismissed Scofield's postponement of the ethical teachings of Jesus. Many premillennialists at EMS adopted this modified brand of dispensationalism.

Dispensationalism's toolbox of charts, graphs, numbers, and codes gave it a pseudoscientific appeal. The literal, inspired words of the Bible provided proof for the prophetic interpretations. Not only was the Bible error-free; like science, it could also predict. The power of biblical prophecy to foretell the future was not only alluring, it also dovetailed nicely with the modern penchant to explain and predict. Using scientific-like calculations, premillennialism provided a framework that explained how diverse elements of the biblical story fit harmoniously into God's grand scheme. C. I. Scofield, in the introduction to his reference Bible, noted that the old biblical study guides were "unscientific," but "the remarkable results of the modern study of the prophets . . . [give] a clear and coherent harmony." His analytical summaries, like those of a good scientist, supposedly rejected "merely personal views and interpretations."[58]

Clashing over the Peaceful Millennium

At times, the debates between the "pre-mills" and the "a-mills" at EMS became quite prickly because big theological issues were at stake. The premillennialists accused the amillennialists of not believing in the Bible because they rejected a literal interpretation of its prophecies about the future. On the other side, the amillennialists blamed the premillennialists for rejecting Jesus's Sermon on the Mount—the cornerstone of Anabaptist ethics since the sixteenth century. The animosity ran so deep on campus that Virginia Conference called a cease-fire in 1935 to stop the "dissension" and "harsh contentions" that were estranging people. The conference refused to take sides. Rather, it appealed for "forbearance" and urged respect for those with differing opinions. While agreeing on a literal return of Christ, the conference called both postmillennialism and Scofield's postponement idea erroneous.[59]

EMS's premillennial identity complicated public relations. The Mennonite "East" was not unified on the millennial question. When J. L. Stauffer drew up a list of the "Believers" and "Opposers" of a literal millennium among Mennonite leaders, his tally tilted against premillennialism.[60] That sentiment was so strong in Franconia Conference that premillennialists—including Stauffer, one of its own sons—were barred from preaching there. Likewise, the Washington-Franklin Conference rejected premillennialism in 1916 after Stauffer and Brunk had stirred up a storm when they preached there a year earlier.[61] With some exceptions, including EMS supporters John Mosemann and Noah Mack, most Lancaster Conference leaders stood against the literal reign of Christ on earth.[62] The eastern conferences contained a sizable pocket of potential students and financial gifts, which required EMS leaders to temper their premillennial enthusiasm when preaching in some churches.

Many ironies thread through the EMS saga with premillennialism. While the word peppered the private correspondence of the founders, it never appears in official publications—the *Constitution*, *Catalog*, *Bulletin*, and *Journal*. The phrase "unfulfilled prophecies" was code for premillennialism in course descriptions. Nonetheless, everyone on and off campus knew exactly where EMS stood. Oddly enough, EMS leaders—especially J. B. Smith, A. D. Wenger, and J. L. Stauffer, who were striving hard to establish a conservative school—were at the same time advocating a novel doctrine that alienated them from some traditional Mennonites.

Interestingly, amillennialism appealed to both traditional Mennonites and more progressive ones. Eastern traditionalists affirmed it because it was the church's long-established belief. More progressive and scholarly types, such as C. K. Lehman, rejected premillennialism's method of biblical interpretation. J. L. Stauffer noted that "all the Goshen College professors" were against premillennialism and then lamented that "nearly everything Goshen condemns, the Bible upholds."[63] EMS leaders found themselves strangely at odds with both traditionalists and progressives on the millennial question.

Some scholars suggest that premillennialism provides an antidote for anxiety about rapid social change and uncertainty.[64] There was plenty of angst from 1915 to 1935 with World War I, the influenza epidemic, the liberal-fundamentalist controversies, revolutionary developments in technology, rapid changes in public morality, and the Great Depression. Premillennialism offered some relief from engaging the woes of the world, a guidebook for interpreting God's purposes behind current events, and a sense of clarity—even a sense of awe that true believers had deciphered the secret code to the world's end. Premillennialism helped make sense of perplexing anxieties and confirmed that God had things under control.

By 1941, the EMS faculty had a ratio of sixteen premillennialists to one amillennialist (C. K. Lehman); among the Bible teachers, the ratio was five to one, according to Stauffer's calculation.[65] In terms of faculty views, curriculum, controversy, engagement with social issues, and public identity, the premillennial imprint on campus far exceeded that of Fundamentalism. The ethos of premillennialism cast a pessimistic pall over EMS. It sharpened the school's sense of separation from the world. It generated little energy for social action, political protest, or other engagements in the public square. J. L. Stauffer contended, for example, that Mennonites should have "absolutely nothing to do with the political system of the world."[66] The belief that Jesus was coming soon did, however, spur students and faculty into a host of mission outreach programs to preach the gospel before the Rapture.[67]

Purging Liberalism at Goshen

Goshen College loomed large in the formation of EMS, not as a virtuous model, but as an example of Mennonite education gone awry. From the Harrisonburg perspective, Goshen demonstrated how *not* to do Mennonite education. EMS was fighting a battle against liberalism, and its founders believed that, instead of combating it, Goshen was spreading it in the church. EMS and Goshen were engaged in an ideological battle over conflicting views of Mennonite orthodoxy, Mennonite identity, and Mennonite higher education. Not surprisingly, EMS-Goshen relations were contentious, to put it mildly, until midcentury.

When J. B. Smith fired off his six-page salvo to the Mennonite Board of Education in February 1918, he made a strategic move. For at least ten years, he had scolded Goshen College from afar. Now, as a Virginia Conference appointee on the MBE and as head of the five-month-old EMS, he had institutional clout. And just five weeks earlier, J. E. Hartzler, the second president of Goshen College (1913–1918), had resigned amid a financial crisis and a cloud of criticism from church leaders in the Indiana-Michigan Conference. Smith seized this moment to eradicate liberalism at Goshen.

N. E. Byers had left Goshen for Bluffton College in 1913, having served fifteen years as president of Elkhart Institute and then Goshen College. (Elkhart Institute was renamed Goshen College after it moved to the town of Goshen in 1903.) During Byers's tenure, he and Goshen's academic dean, C. Henry Smith, had considerable freedom to shape the school's direction—at least until 1905, when the church-wide MBE was founded to give oversight to the college. Growing criticism from church leaders in the Indiana-Michigan Conference surrounding Goshen eventually nudged Byers, Smith, and other faculty in the Goshen College brain trust to leave for Bluffton College, which was associated with the General Conference Mennonite Church. There, J. B. Smith noted sarcastically, "they [had] the liberty to ventilate unhindered their liberalistic views" about progressive Mennonite education.[68]

In many ways, the MBE was feeble during its first two decades (1905–1925). The large board met once a year and mostly deferred to Goshen's academic leaders. It had little muscle because the role expectations of the board and the academic staff were vague, the power balance between the school's educated elite and the board's farmer-ministers was skewed, and Mennonites were neophytes at running any kind of organization. The MBE did not have a constitution until 1919, and even then, it was difficult to align it with long-standing campus practices.[69] Hesston College was more attuned to MBE policy because it had been founded under the auspices of the MBE in 1908.

EMS consistently refused to come under the MBE until the organization could control its own institutions—Goshen and Hesston.[70] Some bystanders called EMS "an illegitimate child" for being conceived outside of the MBE.[71] The gap between MBE's rhetoric about promoting church standards and Goshen's actual practice agitated the EMS founders. George R. Brunk mocked the MBE members by calling them "laxitarians" for their loose supervision of Goshen. For more than twenty years, EMS leaders complained bitterly about the lax supervision. As late as 1935, J. L. Stauffer was beating the same old drum after attending an MBE meeting at which it passed a policy at odds with its own constitution and the dress standards of the General Conference. Disgusted, he wrote that Mennonite schools "are headed straight for the rocks of worldliness and sorrowful defeat, with the Lord writing 'Ichabod' over the whole outfit" (an allusion to 1 Samuel 4).[72]

With the exception of J. L. Stauffer, all the founders had traveled in the Midwest and were familiar with the Elkhart Institute and its move to Goshen in 1903. J. B. Smith was a student at the institute when it opened in 1894. Apart from L. J. Heatwole, most of the founders had served on the MBE at different times from 1905 into the mid-1930s as appointees of Virginia Conference or of the MBE itself.[73] As board members, they had easy access to administrative reports, student life policies, and other matters at Goshen, and they sometimes used that information to wage war on Goshen from the East. For conservatives, vigorously criticizing liberalism was more important than forbearance in those years. The attacks by EMS on the MBE and Goshen College were unrelenting for some twenty-five years.[74]

A Jubilee for Hell?

Poison. Cancer. Curse. Those were some of the labels hurled at Goshen from the East. The founders of EMS were not timid. In 1906, Goshen College president N. E. Byers alleged that in a public meeting George R. Brunk had called Goshen "a curse to the Mennonite Church." Unable to recall those exact words, Brunk agreed that they certainly reflected his sentiments.[75] Despite Brunk's persistent criticism of Goshen, he claimed that he "was a real friend of the school, and only an enemy of its LIBERALISM." When officials refused to reform the college, Brunk promised a vigorous public campaign "against their LIBERAL POLICIES, that they would be compelled to hear."[76]

A sentence from Goshen president J. E. Hartzler's inaugural address in 1913 had grated on Bishop Brunk: "Let the college man be a man of the world, but let his world be a world of all time, of all lands, and of all sorts and conditions of man."[77] While serving on the MBE, Brunk charged Goshen College with disloyalty to church standards in four areas: dress, amusements, mixing with the world, and liberal doctrine. He in turn was accused by Goshen officials of making slanderous and false statements about the college. In 1915, the MBE appointed a committee to investigate the charges that Brunk, John Mosemann, and Mennonite historian John Horsch had unfairly denounced Goshen College.[78]

While the investigation was under way, Hartzler visited Brunk's congregation in Denbigh, Virginia. Brunk met him at the train station. Ordained Mennonite men typically greeted each other with a ritual kiss of peace on the lips to signify their spiritual fellowship in the church. Hartzler offered to greet Brunk, but the bishop turned his cheek and refused the kiss. He did, however, shake Hartzler's hand. Brunk had "pretty good" evidence that Hartzler was behind the accusations against him. Although Hartzler said the investigation was not a "personal matter," Brunk considered the charges "personal and ruinous." He told Hartzler, "I do not like to see a man take another by the beard, smilingly, and stab him to death under the fifth rib" (an allusion to 2 Samuel 3:27).[79]

The investigators concluded that Brunk at times was "too severe" and made mistakes based on hearsay, but they found no evidence that he had lied. Still, the ordeal haunted him. On the one hand, he felt good that "the Goshen men had to eat their cruel words." On the other, he worried that "long after I'm dead" in the "dark corners of the church," people will ask, "[Was Brunk] the bishop that Goshen had tried for lying? . . . Was he found guilty, or not?" Brunk's consolation was the coming Judgment Day, when "there will be a trial . . . that will make things right and slippery eels will all be caught."[80]

Before he was president of EMS, Smith had an altercation with President Hartzler over a religious periodical—a squabble serious enough to merit a public letter of mutual apology, which the two men signed in September 1916.[81] With Hartzler's resignation two years later, Smith urged the Mennonite Church to "purge the canker that, octopus-like, has fastened itself upon Goshen's vitals. . . . The supreme hour has come. Delay is dangerous. The pruning knife of God's Word must be applied. The canker must be extricated from its lurking place."[82] In his six-point appeal to the MBE, Smith declared that the Mennonite Church would have been better off if Goshen College had never opened.[83]

By endorsing Smith's epistle in early 1918, the EMS trustees hoped to launch "a supreme effort to purge Goshen College from the insidious and seductive canker of liberalism." The letter asked the MBE to "apply the remedy. Purge Goshen College of the last vestige of higher criticism, evolution, and kindred tenets of the new theology, whether found in textbooks, in magazines, or in living tissue. . . . Shall we despise our priceless heritage and cause *Heaven to mourn and Hell to have a jubilee?*"[84]

As a member of the MBE's textbook committee in 1919, J. B. Smith scoured the Goshen College library for "unsound books." He found one hundred theological works that he considered to be heretical and listed them by title. In addition, the college had on its shelves "scores of books" on sociology, science, and philosophy that were "directly antagonistic to the teachings of the Bible as interpreted by the Mennonite church."[85] Although Smith took some satisfaction in being known as a "heresy hunter," his aggressive attacks did not please everyone in the East.[86] In fact, some thought that his "tearing up Goshen" in public talks had given "Goshen a lot of free advertising."[87]

Smith's narrative about Goshen shaped EMS's corporate culture into the mid-1950s. The theme was always the same: "Goshen is liberal. It's dangerous for young Mennonites to go there. If they do, they'll likely get liberal or even leave the church." Regardless of its accuracy, this yarn shaped EMS's identity as a safe, conservative alternative to liberal Goshen. All of this played well with eastern conservatives and helped EMS to thrive.

In March 1920, the EMS community was settling into the new "Cracker Box" and J. L. Stauffer was in his second year of teaching when he received a letter that startled him. The writer was Harold S. Bender, a new, twenty-three-year-old instructor at Hesston College. The young professor, a 1918 graduate of Goshen College, carefully dismantled the arguments of Stauffer's recent essay in *Gospel Herald* in which he had criticized a conference of young Mennonites in France engaged in reconstruction after World War I. That such a young upstart would take on an ordained minister with a well-established reputation as a conservative leader was unsettling. The intellectual depth and incisiveness of Bender's arguments required a reply.[88]

Stauffer was appalled at Bender's view of separation from the world. "I believe in being unspotted from *sin* but I do *not* believe in making Mennonites separate from the rest of the people in the world," wrote Bender. Moreover, he asserted that one reason "dress restrictions are pushed so hard is because our ministry realizes they do not have the ability, the leadership, the spiritual power, the mental keenness and superiority to accomplish the educational program." Therefore, he continued, they "fall back upon [these restrictions]. . . . I believe our strict regulations have done more harm than good." Even more, Bender blamed "the poverty of the average Mennonite in culture, things of music, literature, art, and beauty" on excessive separation from the world.[89]

Stauffer severely criticized Bender's views on regulation attire, charging him for being "out of harmony with the church" and personally inconsistent for not wearing a plain coat. He chided Bender for "condemning the church standard" and then setting up his own definition of modest dress. Then Stauffer honed in on liberalism: "Down East here we do not know of a single graduate of Goshen College, including yourself, that has spoken against the liberalistic trend of modern churches, social

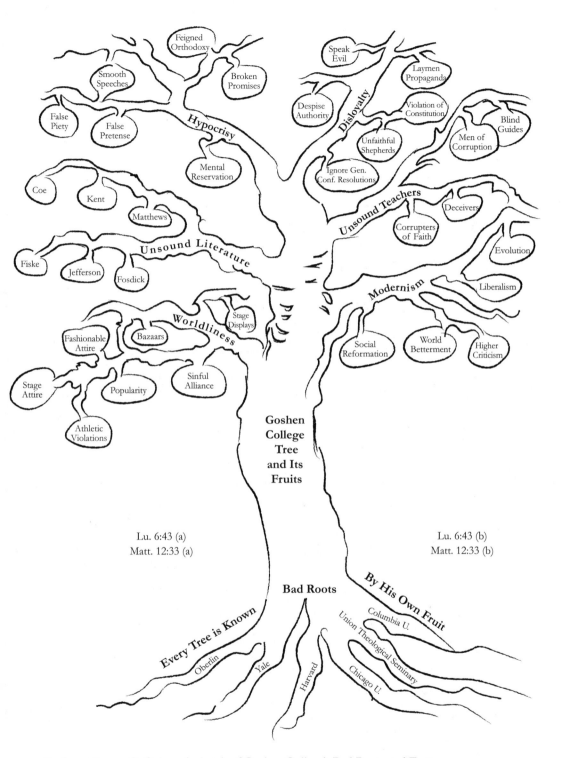

Professor Ernest G. Gehman's sketch of Goshen College's Bad Roots and Fruits, ca. 1930.
Artistic restoration by Linda L. Eberly.

and theological movements. Why do Goshen graduates never denounce higher criticism? [Why do they] constantly kick against the principles and practices of the church? WHY IS THIS?"[90]

As the Bender-Stauffer debate continued, the Virginia brethren *were* speaking against liberalism. In the spring of 1920, 117 leaders in three eastern conferences signed a petition, "Shall the Old Landmarks Stand?" It appealed to the Mennonite Church to "take aggressive action" to safeguard the church and her institutions "from the heresies and delusions of the present-day apostasy." The petition also attacked Goshen College without naming it. To underscore the enemy's rapid gains, the author estimated that liberals in the Mennonite Church had grown from twenty-five in 1910 to possibly one thousand in 1920—a dubious fact, but a good measure of the perceived threat.[91]

In 1921, J. B. Smith advised MBE officials to "close the doors of Goshen College until you *can* begin right."[92] His hopes would soon be realized. After the resignation of President Hartzler in 1918, Goshen was walking on wobbly legs. The next five years saw four presidents and three academic deans pass through the administrative turnstiles until the MBE shuttered "old Goshen" for the 1923–1924 academic year. Goshen's beleaguered alumni association advised students stranded at Goshen to transfer to Bluffton College because it was "best fitted to conserve the fine Christian ideals" of Goshen College—a suggestion that confirmed the suspected alliance between the two colleges to observers in the East.[93]

J. B. Smith considered it a "victory and triumph" if every bit of the "rubbish of liberalism" at Goshen was gone.[94] Adding his jubilation, George R. Brunk proclaimed that Virginia "sank Goshen in the fight against covert disloyalty."[95] Yet eastern critics could claim little credit. Internal problems and pushback from the Indiana-Michigan Conference were the primary forces that shut Goshen down.[96] Virginia critics were heartened by the closure and held high expectations that "new Goshen" would be more theologically conservative and promote plain dress. With these hopes, the frosty EMS-Goshen relations began to thaw—but not for long.

The Battle Intensifies

Several months after Goshen reopened in the fall of 1924, A. D. Wenger received four copies of a one-page memo addressed to the MBE. The memo proposed that representatives of Hesston, Goshen, and EMS form a committee for cooperation among the schools. Each copy was already signed by presidents S. C. Yoder of Goshen and D. H. Bender of Hesston, leaving space for Wenger's signature. He never signed the copies. Even with the détente following Goshen's reopening, collaboration seemed unwise.

Paradoxically, after it reopened, Goshen became even more of a threat to EMS than "old Goshen" ever was. The rebooted school now had the strong, steady leadership of President Yoder and academic dean Noah Oyer. These leaders found diplomatic ways to realign the college with the midwestern conferences, which were more progressive than Virginia Conference. The leaders of "new Goshen" invested in the well-being of the Mennonite Church by hiring faculty with scholarly and churchly credentials.

As both institutions grew in strength, the ideological battle intensified. Correspondence between the schools often included accusations based on hearsay, misrepresentation, and factual errors. Territorial disputes over students and financial supporters exacerbated the tensions. Just one year after Goshen reopened, threats of a schism between the two schools and the eastern and western sections of the church surfaced in interschool correspondence, and they continued into the 1930s.

In August 1925, Dean Oyer was livid. He had worked diligently to restore the church's confidence in the one-year-old "new Goshen." Oyer was a close friend of C. K. Lehman, dean at EMS. As roommates at Princeton Theological Seminary, they had relished late-night discussions of theology. Now they found themselves in the deanships of competing schools. Oyer had just learned that EMS had advised Elizabeth Gish, a gifted young woman teaching temporarily in its high school, to complete her college work at Franklin and Marshall College or Elizabethtown College (both in Lancaster County) instead of at Goshen as she had planned. Although EMS was not yet a two-year college, she hoped to eventually return there to teach.

Writing to Lehman, Oyer said, "I deplore this action on your part. . . . It seems so utterly incredible to me that you should sanction such schools as Franklin and Marshall and even Elizabethtown for your [prospective] teachers and regard us with suspicion. . . . [We] feel the sting in your advice to Elizabeth." Oyer noted that many at Goshen thought "that the East is a bit bigoted and looks with disdain upon us."

In addition, Oyer criticized A. D. Wenger for refusing to work with Goshen and wrote that EMS apparently wants to "break" fellowship and collaboration with Goshen. "That is within your power if you think it best," Oyer wrote to Lehman. "You can drive a wedge between the East and the West which will take generations to heal, or you can be a mighty instrument in keeping things together. Which will you do?"[97]

These were heartbreaking words to hear from an old friend. C. K. Lehman immediately wrote a letter to A. D. Wenger—still tending his grapes in Fentress over the summer break—that was rather critical of him. Lehman confessed that he did not "have peace of mind" ever since he and Wenger had advised Gish against going to Goshen. He worried that his brother-in-law did "not understand the Goshen brethren in some things." Lehman asked Wenger rhetorically if he was unaware that Goshen had a "most difficult and acute problem to solve" in regaining the trust of the church.[98]

EMS faculty, 1923. Back, left to right: Henry Weaver, A. G. Heishman, A. D. Wenger (president), J. L. Stauffer, Henry Keener. Front, left to right: Ira Franck, C. K. Lehman, Elizabeth G. Gish, Dorothy Kemrer, Daniel W. Lehman, Paul Sauder. Gish taught at EMS for three academic years (1922–1925) before becoming the center of a controversy between EMS and Goshen College.

A lack of respect for Goshen, Lehman continued, "will mean a breakup of fellowship with these brethren. Are you ready to part company with them? For myself, Noah Oyer, Sanford Yoder, and Harold Bender are among my most intimate friends. Is this to be broken?" Wenger and Brunk recently had taken a firm noncooperation stance toward Goshen, which Lehman called "unchristian."[99] For Wenger, however, relationships were secondary to faithfulness. "We don't want any break [within the church], but we cannot sacrifice gospel principles," he wrote several weeks later. Wenger hoped that if a schism did occur, it would not divide East and West but would be "along gospel lines."[100]

To mend the rift over Elizabeth Gish, the EMS faculty, at a special meeting on September 2, 1925, reversed course and adopted a statement of neutrality. Before the vote, C. K. Lehman promoted Goshen as a good option for Gish. This annoyed Harvard-trained EMS professor D. Ralph Hostetter. He castigated Lehman personally at the meeting and threatened to resign from the faculty if EMS continued to hire Goshen graduates as it had done since 1918 when it hired Dorothy Kemrer and Elizabeth Horsch.[101] Gish eventually graduated from Goshen and then taught at EMS for a year before commencing a teaching career at Hesston College.

Elizabeth Gish was one of many young people caught in the cross fire as the hunt for students intensified between EMS and Goshen. To minimize the conflict, the MBE had established geographical territories for each school. Yet the boundary lines defining those territories were somewhat blurred for two reasons: the MBE did not have any authority over EMS, and, because Goshen represented the Mennonite Church, the college assumed some license to recruit anywhere. This murky situation tempted both schools to engage in poaching.

As Goshen expanded, its tendrils reached eastward. In 1922, Goshen had no students from eastern Pennsylvania, but within five years, it had three teachers and seven students from Lancaster Conference alone.[102] By the early 1930s, President Wenger opined that "Goshen College [was] getting bold now, so bold" that it had recruited sixteen students from Pennsylvania.[103] He told Bishop Brunk, "[Goshen officials] are determined to Goshenize the church. They are making our territory in the East smaller all the time."[104] Goshen's advance was a primary factor in driving EMS to seek junior college accreditation. Without accreditation, C. K. Lehman predicted that "the westward stream" of students would increase and EMS would decline.[105]

Even with such animosity, EMS leaders perceived themselves closer to Goshen than to Bluffton and Bethel Colleges, which were affiliated with the General Conference Mennonite Church. A. D. Wenger confessed that he was glad to have "Goshen and Hesston, instead of only Bluffton and Newton (Bethel)" on the Mennonite map. He favored Hesston because it was generally "more conservative than Goshen."[106] On one occasion, Wenger told Goshen president S. C. Yoder that Goshen got along so well with Bluffton because they both "practice[d] more of a social Gospel."[107] President Yoder, for his part, was tired of the "campaign of mudslinging, to even up things." Yet slinging some of his own, he told J. L. Stauffer, "Bluffton offers us unfair competition, and fights us hard, but . . . when it comes to competition, the Bluffton crowd are gentlemen in comparison with some of your people."[108]

If Goshen was a bad example of collegiate piety, the Dunker colleges were even worse. The founders frequently pointed to them as foreshadowing what could happen to EMS. In A. D. Wenger's words, "The Dunker church has trodden the path ahead of us . . . their schools are liberal, their members are in the fashions, in the lodges, and their elders are in state legislatures etc."[109] Wenger noted the regret of a Dunker elder who said, "It's too late for us now to clean house." Then he listed "all the evils" which had come into their denomination.[110] Wenger declared, "The Brethren college here at Bridgewater is going by leaps and bounds into worldliness of all kinds." Even so, many of EMS's junior college graduates completed their last two years of college at Bridgewater.[111]

"We Have Enough Wounds Now"

In 1927, Goshen College added a significant asset to its arsenal—a scholarly journal titled the *Mennonite Quarterly Review* (*MQR*). The editor was thirty-year-old

Harold S. Bender, a rising star in Mennonite historical studies. *MQR* was "not a journal of propaganda . . . nor merely one of opinion or comment." Rather, vouched the editor, it was to be "a servant of the truth and to the historic ideals and faith of the Mennonite church." He also hoped it would contribute to historical scholarship both in America and Europe. The distribution of 2,200 gratis copies to university and college libraries and Mennonite ministers both in Europe and America revealed the scope of Bender's ambition.[112] It was a major volley in the battle to define Mennonite identity and orthodoxy. And it certainly would not go unanswered in Virginia.

Exactly two years later, George R. Brunk released the first issue of his own quarterly, the *Sword and Trumpet*. Its subtitle clarified its polemical purpose: *Devoted to the Defense of a Full Gospel, with Special Emphasis upon Neglected Truths, and to an Active Opposition of the Various Forms of Error That Contribute to the Religious Drift of the Times*. That the fifty-eight-year-old editor was poised for battle was clear from the periodical's first paragraph. The *Sword and Trumpet* was stepping into "the arena of religious conflict in the spirit of the Christian soldier, the weapons of whose warfare are not carnal, but mighty through God to the pulling down of strongholds; casting down imaginations in every high thing that exalts itself against the knowledge of God." Without apology for its militant tone, Bishop Brunk said the periodical would combat "the religious drift in general and the evils which promote it." The new publication was sanctioned by and subject to Virginia Conference's direction and control, although that body provided no funding for it.[113]

When Harold S. Bender learned about "brother Brunk's" plans, he worried that such "a radical and a fighter [might] do more harm than good." He hoped that Brunk would not use his quarterly to "fight the church. . . . We have enough wounds now."[114] For his publication, Bender drew on Anabaptist history to legitimate his arguments. Brunk, on the other hand, turned to the Bible and Virginia Conference for credibility. It was a Goliath versus Goliath matchup: a brilliant German-educated scholar soon to receive his doctorate in theology from Heidelberg University versus a brilliant self-taught bishop with only a sagebrush education. Unfortunately for Brunk, the younger scholar had the last word as the battle outran the bishop's life.

For Brunk, ideological warfare was not propaganda, so he used the *Sword and Trumpet* to fight for the truth as vigorously as possible. His lengthy editorial titled "The Drift" in the first issue sharply criticized the Mennonite Church for drifting ever closer to modernism, secularism, and popular American culture. Many EMS leaders wrote for the publication. Writing for Bender's *MQR*, however, was taboo. For example, when Bender invited C. K. Lehman to submit an article, he refused, saying, "It might be used against me [at EMS]."[115] In another instance, the Religious Welfare Committee blocked Professor Harry Brunk from publishing an essay in *MQR*.[116]

Harold S. Bender, dean of Goshen College, founded and edited the *Mennonite Quarterly Review*. *Source:* MC USA Archives.

Bishop George R. Brunk, early proponent of an eastern Mennonite school, founded and edited the *Sword and Trumpet*.

Even more wounds were inflicted between 1930 and 1934 as EMS and its sympathizers continued bombarding the MBE. In early 1931, former president J. B. Smith unleashed a stinging attack: "A Statement of Facts and an Appeal to the Mennonite Board of Education." Trying to publicly shame the MBE, he fired off the broadside to all Mennonite Church ministers. His rant included his well-worn litany against liberalism, charges that the word "safeguard" was deceptively removed from the MBE's constitution, and accusations of "indecent, shocking, and ridiculous" photos of men dressed as women at a Goshen student Halloween masquerade. Smith enclosed photographs of the event, one of which he captioned "Heathenizing Christians at Goshen College." He distributed his jeremiad against Goshen shortly before the MBE meeting scheduled for February 23–24, 1931. On the evening following the meeting, Noah Oyer, Goshen's academic dean, died of typhoid fever. Letters of alarm from ministers, stirred by Smith's broadside and addressed to Oyer, arrived before and after his death.[117]

Harold S. Bender called two-thirds of Smith's accusations false and based on hearsay. He declared the public stunt "unwarranted, untruthful, unchristian," and regrettable: "It is impossible to undo the evil he has done." What good purpose would be served, Bender wondered, by "publishing abroad the moral corruption in J. B. Smith's own family?"[118] Nonetheless, Smith contemplated a second exposé of MBE and Goshen evils, a move supported by J. L. Stauffer and Bishop John Mosemann, but one that never happened.[119]

C. K. Lehman was considered, but not invited, to become dean at Goshen to replace Noah Oyer. Harold S. Bender opined that no one aligned with Smith could "accomplish anything" at Goshen. "We don't need outside interference from the East to solve our problems," said Bender.[120] In the end, Goshen turned to Bender himself to appoint as its dean. Lehman considered Bender one of his intimate friends. They had been teaching colleagues at Hesston for a short time (1918–1919), and they both had attended Princeton Theological Seminary. Serving in identical roles at rival institutions would soon test the tensile strength of their friendship.

After attending his first MBE board meeting in January 1932 as an appointee of Virginia Conference, Lehman was distressed. In response, he wrote a severe assessment of thirteen issues related to the MBE's performance. Among other things, he asked, "Why after a thirty-year experiment with never dying souls" is Goshen College unable to find "loyal Mennonite instructors from her alumni? What an indictment of this institution!"[121]

On December 28, 1932, Lehman sent a second memo to the MBE executive committee. The four-page message targeted the "breach" between the MBE's dress standards and Goshen's noncompliance, which Lehman expected would divide the church.[122] Forty ordained ministers in Virginia Conference (including EMS leaders) signed the memo, which was titled "Concerning an Appeal to the Mennonite Board of Education." The signatories pleaded with the MBE to stop its "serious . . . violations" of its own constitution, which regulated Goshen's policies.[123]

To Lehman's surprise, when the MBE met in January 1933, the executive committee read his memo to the entire board. Harold S. Bender, Goshen's new dean, was astonished by what he heard. Unable to meet at the event, Bender wrote to his old friend a few days later saying he was "shocked" by the memo and "seriously disturbed" about its consequences. Realizing that he would need to deal with a "new Chester Lehman," Bender wrote that he regretted they could not cooperate with "mutual confidence" and that Lehman was "ready to make the break" between the schools.[124]

Soon after the MBE meeting, Bender learned that Ernest G. Gehman, German teacher at EMS and cartoonist for the *Sword and Trumpet*, had written a satirical poem attacking Goshen College, which he read to his students. Bender asked A. D. Wenger for a copy of the poem.[125] In a letter that he never sent, Wenger explained, "Brother Gehman had to slam you [Goshen] for slamming the church to which you are pledged to be a faithful servant. Gehman thought it no sin . . . to speak against evil wherever found, including ourselves as well as you folks." In the same letter, Wenger said he had heard that Goshen gossips were calling EMS "very immoral." Just to clear the record, Wenger noted that no student under EMS supervision had ever "committed fornication" so far as he knew. Wenger sent a revised version of the letter, in which he did not mention slamming or fornication. The letter also claimed that Gehman's poem had been destroyed.[126]

Although a *copy* of Gehman's seven-stanza poem may have been destroyed, the original is in the EMU archives. Here are the first and last stanzas:

> Who Is Responsible?
> Who is responsible? Who must give answer
> For this affliction of spiritual cancer
> Seizing the church through a poisoning potion
> That they've been feeding our children at Goshen?
>   A question we can't shrug away. . . .
>
> Those whom the church has entrusted high duty
> Which they are selling, like Judas, for booty,
> Must reckon, as stewards for faithless devotion,
> To a Judge more austere than the judges at Goshen.
>   And *then* who will shrug it away?[127]

The Virginia brethren mounted yet another attack on Goshen when the MBE met in February 1934. This time, J. L. Stauffer, wearing four hats (EMS faculty member, Virginia Conference appointee to the MBE, moderator of Virginia Conference, and ordained minister), was up to bat. In a two-page letter, Stauffer denounced Goshen for allowing students to present programs in worldly churches and civic organizations. Stauffer's data buttressed his critique. He had scrutinized twelve months of the *Goshen College Record* and attached a list of thirty-one infractions of Goshen students speaking and performing in non-Mennonite churches (Brethren, Methodist, Congregational, Presbyterian, Nazarene, Reformed, United Brethren, Evangelical) and at public high schools, the Chamber of Commerce, the Salvation Army, and ladies missionary organizations.[128]

"A Little Ignorant Institution"

A year after Goshen reopened in 1924, President Wenger had already despaired of it ever becoming a conservative college. His disappointment nudged EMS to turn insular, sectarian, and sour for the next ten years. Territorial disputes over students and dollars increased. Goshen had the advantage of being endorsed by the General Conference. As a four-year college, Goshen attracted Mennonite youth seeking a full degree without needing to transfer. Furthermore, it had a swelling reputation for scholarship led by superstar historian Harold S. Bender. For progressives in the East who were unconcerned about separatist attire, Goshen was an attractive alternative to EMS. President Wenger worried that with Goshen's gains, EMS would shrink and accomplish little for conservatism.[129] In the face of these pressures, EMS struggled with a sense of inferiority.

Somewhat marginalized by their own stance, A. D. Wenger and George R. Brunk endorsed a policy of "let Goshen alone."[130] More than once, C. K. Lehman told Harold S. Bender that Wenger was "definitely committed" to noncooperation and that Brunk would veto any attempts to collaborate.[131] After Bender paid a somewhat awkward visit to EMS in 1932, Wenger hoped that no more Goshen faculty would set foot on campus.[132]

The faculty concurred. Their statement in 1927 advised students not to finish their work at Goshen. Rather, it urged them to attend colleges near their homes so they could relate to conservative congregations. In addition, the faculty agreed to refrain from any contacts with Goshen that would blend the policies of their schools. Trying to leverage their influence to impel Goshen toward conservatism, the EMS faculty would cooperate, the statement said, *if* Goshen required conservative attire, forbade intercollegiate contests, stopped engaging non-Mennonite speakers, and deemphasized sports. More than likely, those caveats were greeted with derision at Goshen.[133]

In 1932, Wenger recalled that, years earlier, the high regard some EMS teachers held for Goshen made it awkward to discuss the school at faculty meetings. "Now it is vastly different," he said, "We can freely discuss any Goshen matters without offending anyone." Clearly, the faculty had turned its back on the West. Even prayer became a ritual way of shunning Goshen. The president said that "for years" faculty who spoke in chapel services would "pray for our sister institutions Goshen and Hesston." Now he realized that such prayers "mislead" students by giving them the impression that "those schools are all right." Thus Wenger advised the faculty to stop praying for Goshen in chapel because it would legitimate the wayward school. But it was OK, he said, to pray for Goshen in private.[134]

Increasingly, President Wenger felt trapped by a generational shift of leadership, new organizational patterns, and a growing vibrancy in Mennonite intellectual life. With only one year of education at a small Quaker college in 1897, he felt outclassed by Goshen's new leaders. Besides, the growing licentiousness in popular culture (movies, short skirts, nightclubs, jazz) and the Mennonite Church's inability to stop the drift into that moral morass weighed heavily upon him. By temperament, Wenger was earnest, sincere, and conscientious. Yet he was fast becoming a man of yesteryear, a man who loved his "dear old church." He even admitted that he was "still earnestly endeavoring to maintain the standards held by practically all of our congregations a generation ago."[135]

Wenger yearned to resolve differences with the old recipe of "brotherly love." He opined to a confidant, "I hate controversy, was sick of it long ago, and avoid it all I possibly can."[136] He found the power politics of organizational life stressful and longed for old-style face-to-face decision making grounded in "cooperation, humility, concessions . . . and respect."[137]

Wenger lamented to Goshen president S. C. Yoder that some people treated him like a "scapegoat . . . perhaps because of my stupidity."[138] He confessed that the Goshen people felt almost like strangers to him: "They may honestly think I'm narrow and ignorant and far in the wrong." In his view, it was "useless for our little board to petition Goshen College. . . . They never yield to us in anything. We are too small and insignificant for such consideration."[139] Besides, in Wenger's eyes, Goshen would not accept criticism from the East. "They flare back every time," he told George R. Brunk. "[They think they] are so far superior in knowledge, wisdom, and ethics. They do not want any help from a *little ignorant institution* like EMS."[140]

One of the president's confidants was Bishop John Mosemann of Lancaster. After several sleepless nights in the fall of 1927, Wenger wrote to Mosemann, "John, I can't help it. I must pour out to somebody, to get relief from [all] that rests heavily upon me. We would better die in the conflict, despised and rejected, with a few faithful ones than to drift with the tide." He fretted about ominous forces undermining the church's "very existence" and pulling it rapidly into the world. He reminded Mosemann that both of them were "intensely interested in keeping the church pure and separate from the world," for their children as well as others.[141] "The awful crop [of liberalism]," Wenger told another friend, "may not be harvested until after we are gone, but I feel so sorry to leave our dear children such a heritage."[142]

On top of these woes, Wenger felt pinched on both sides by his two brothers-in-law. More than Wenger, C. K. Lehman had positive feelings toward Goshen's leaders and was willing to cooperate with them. George R. Brunk stood on the other side. On one occasion, Brunk called Wenger "a scared Kitty" because he was afraid to tackle liberalism publicly. "Better get out of that covert attitude and face the enemy like a man," said Brunk.[143]

Wenger first chided Brunk for not encouraging him "in anything." Then he refuted the "scared Kitty" charges. More than anyone else on campus, Wenger asserted, "I have contended against the evil influences of Goshen College." Indeed, Wenger noted, his criticisms of Goshen were sometimes almost more than "the faculty could stand." After one of his talks to the faculty, he said, some of the "sisters who graduated from Goshen" were so offended that they went to J. L. Stauffer privately "and cried over my remarks about Goshen."[144]

These words of despair came from the man who, thirty-five years earlier, was a prominent Mennonite revivalist, a man whose soul was filled with joy and confidence. In the battle for truth, his perspective was shaded by premillennialism and its view of apostasy in the latter days—which Wenger surely thought had arrived. He worried that the apostasy that had crept into Goshen was now sneaking into pulpits in progressive Mennonite congregations and, God forbid, even some conservative ones. In a letter to Bishop Mosemann, Wenger wrote, "[I hope] something may yet be done to save Lancaster and other conservative Mennonites from the great apostasy that is now in nearly all Christendom. Do you think that the East can yet be saved from a final plunge into the world? I have not given up the fight of faith. [Yet with so] many adversaries against us, how can we draw the lines tighter and save at least a part of the church?"[145]

A Tight and Powerful Web

For some twenty years, EMS expended enormous resources—time, energy, money, manpower, and hundreds of conversations and letters—battling Goshen College and the MBE. The conflict had multiple layers. It was a fight for students and financial support, but it was foremost an ideological battle—perpetuated by the eastern wing of the church—to define Mennonite identity and orthodoxy. Mennonite schools, argued one scholar, were "identity battlegrounds."[146] Goshen was the primary target because of its power to educate the next generation of church leaders and to thwart EMS's ability to recruit students who would become ambassadors of conservatism.

EMS leaders sat on the MBE not as representatives of EMS but as appointees of Virginia Conference. Their prime aim was to retard progressivism and promote conservatism in the Mennonite world. At the MBE table, the Virginia delegates were able to press that agenda as well as the interests of EMS.

To the midwestern eye, it looked like a small bloc of vocal agitators was trying to impose conservative eastern standards, a generation old, on the whole church and particularly on Goshen College. With what authority, midwesterners wondered, were EMS administrators telling Goshen officials how to operate their college? If the East had words like *poison*, *cancer*, and *curse* for Goshen, the Goshen people had names too—*backbiters, extremists, pessimists, ultraconservatives, howlers, knockers, absurdists, mud slingers*—for the pesky eastern hornets that kept stinging them.

The tight nexus between the founders of EMS and Virginia Conference confounded the MBE and Goshen leaders. Because Virginia Conference controlled EMS, it could use its educational institution to fight its battles. Likewise, EMS leaders could claim the blessing of Virginia Conference to accomplish their ends. No other conference or educational institution in the Mennonite Church had the clout to exert itself so powerfully outside its area. By 1925, Virginia had only 4.7 percent of the total Mennonite Church membership and 7.6 percent of the membership of the seven conferences east of Indiana.[147] Had Virginia Conference appointed leaders unaffiliated with EMS, the dynamics would have been different. Without the tight web between EMS and Virginia Conference, the East could not have mounted such a raucous campaign against Goshen.

At times, the Virginia bloc exploited the close school-conference relationship. Some Goshen leaders blamed EMS for soliciting signatures for the 1920 antiliberalism statement, "Shall the Old Landmarks Still Stand?" Smith and Stauffer both retorted that this was a conference initiative, not a school one, and then Smith added, "Of course, the school is heartily in favor of the protest." Their retort wasn't completely true. Virginia Conference never officially endorsed the document. Yet the authors of the statement—Brunk, Smith, Stauffer, and Wenger—were ordained leaders in Virginia Conference with deep loyalty to EMS.[148] In this case, Smith and Stauffer were guilty of the very duplicity of which they accused Goshen. This knotty conflict of interest continued throughout the strife.

Sharp Rebukes

For MBE and Goshen educators, the most vexing aspect of this ideological battle was that the EMS founders refused to compromise—on anything. Again and again, they repeated the no-compromise mantra. J. B. Smith wanted to "follow a rigidly no-compromise policy." J. L. Stauffer put it this way: "I hate the compromise spirit when truth is involved, like I hate snakes." For his part, A. D. Wenger flatly said, "It is wrong to compromise with the world."[149] This rigidity made mediation, negotiation, and collaboration with Goshen futile. The no-compromise posture stood on this bedrock assumption: Truth is a fixed absolute, fully known, and worthy of an aggressive defense. Error is the enemy of Truth. And the Virginians were certain that they knew the truth.[150]

In a letter in 1920, Harold S. Bender told Stauffer that his "closed system of thinking . . . prevent[ed] the possibility of progress and acquiring new truth. A closed system is impervious to new light and learning." To Bender, Stauffer's mind seemed settled: "You tolerate objections only to refute them." For his part, Bender wanted to explore "the truth," not just engage in a defense of each other's "own views."[151]

Without Bender's permission, Stauffer passed a copy of his letter to Bishop Brunk, who could not resist admonishing the twenty-three-year-old Bender: "We have a closed policy," boomed the bishop, "on all that the *Bible teaches*, all that the *church rules* . . . and all that a *Bishop rules* in the interest of spiritual welfare." Outside of those gated areas, Brunk averred, "We always have had an open policy." For example, he wrote, "[We are] open to the Bible doctrine of Christ's reign on earth [premillennialism]. *We are open to more Bible truth, but closed to human error such as evolution, higher criticism, etc.*"[152]

For EMS leaders, heresy always lurked on Goshen's side of the battlefield, never on their own turf. Moreover, in what seemed like righteous arrogance, not only did the founders defend absolute truth; they did so with belligerence. They were unapologetic about their aggressive tactics. And they mustered up ample biblical references to legitimate attacking those who would compromise. "There is a time and place for *gentleness* and for *sharp rebuke*," proclaimed Bishop Brunk, who then cited eight Bible verses that, in his mind, gave leaders license to rebuke error and the people who promote it. Besides, said Brunk, "[the liberals] always talk *charity, charity, charity*," forgetting that the Bible also calls for using "a rod." He told Bender that to protect the flock in his district and across the church, he practiced "open rebuke for the aggressively insubordinate; and excommunication for the persistently rebellious."[153]

In a sizzling letter to Wenger, Smith, and Daniel Kauffman, Brunk attacked Bishop Kauffman for "sticking with the corruptors [who were liberalizing] the Church." Brunk signed off with these words: "FIRST PURE, THEN PEACABLE [*sic*]."[154] Translation: Defending pure doctrine supersedes keeping peaceful relationships. Such rhetoric was a trademark of Brunk's roughshod style. Goshen president S. C. Yoder grew weary of the combative exchanges that didn't seek solutions but just "shifted blame to others." It seemed to him, "that we not only need to stand for the things of God, but we need to do it in a Godly way."[155] Yoder and his dean, Harold S. Bender, were pragmatists, looking for ways to collaborate, even if those ways required compromise. From their perspective, the EMS militants were more interested in polemical diatribes about doctrine than in finding ways to work together.

How did the feisty EMS founders justify the sharp darts they threw at Goshen? They were emboldened by Scripture, Fundamentalism, and premillennialism. As Bishop Brunk noted, certain Scriptures seemed to sanction strong verbal rebuke. Moreover, the language of spiritual warfare lifted from the Bible was filled with fighting images. The founders also had absorbed some of the militancy that was an earmark of Fundamentalism.[156]

The final source of militancy was premillennialism's forecast of apostasy among professed Christians in the last days, when "evil men and seducers shall wax worse and worse, deceiving, and being deceived."[157] Such Scriptures spurred ardent critics of liberalism like J. B. Smith and A. D. Wenger to justify damning and excommunicating liberal, apostate deceivers of orthodoxy within the Mennonite Church.[158]

Especially for Brunk and Smith, Goshen's educational philosophy deceived and seduced students to embrace liberal views. Paradoxically, the founders seemed unaware that their abrasive and militant efforts to protect historic Mennonite doctrine were gross violations of long-standing Mennonite virtues of humility, meekness, forbearance, and nonresistance.

Thy Word Is Truth

In the midst of the strife with Goshen, the May 1928 *Eastern Mennonite School Journal* featured a new front cover: a school seal that bore the motto Thy Word Is Truth. Dean C. K. Lehman explained to readers that the new seal and its message would appear on every official publication of the school to announce "our ideals and aims." The faculty had chosen the motto, and the trustees gladly approved it.

The four words came from Jesus's prayer to his Father in John 17:17. At first glance, the message seemed clear, yet Lehman explained that the meaning of *Word* was flush with ideas—the Bible as a whole, the words of God in the Bible, the words of Jesus, and Jesus himself as God's Word, which was a prominent theme in John's Gospel and in the prayer itself. Furthermore, Jesus told his disciples to continue in his word: "And ye shall know the truth, and the truth shall make you free" (John 8:32). But even these possibilities, said Lehman, do not exhaust the motto, because all nature reveals God and the realm of truth.[159] For many years, an annual chapel service emphasized that "Thy Word Is Truth."

The motto left no doubt about the school's commitment to orthodoxy. Astute observers in Indiana, Virginia, and every Mennonite hamlet in between could not miss the sharp cleavage between Thy Word Is Truth and Goshen's motto, Culture for Service. One was grounded in religion; the other made no explicit reference to it.

Amid the fray of battle, several issues stood prominent. Oblivious to the stark incongruity of peace-preaching Mennonites waging war over the "Truth," both sides ironically agreed on the centrality of nonresistance to Mennonite identity. The letter-writing men, following the Mennonite custom of the time, always addressed their recipient as "dear brother," even if the letter seemed to seethe with anger just beneath the surface. Despite all the talk of war, writers on both fronts continued to mention their "beloved church" as the supreme body worthy of admiration and loyalty. In truth, the animosity was so intense because the two sides held vastly different dreams for their beloved church. In the end, even with all the worries about a "break" between East and West, the sacred body was never broken—a remarkable outcome given the bitter schisms in some denominations induced by the liberal-fundamentalist controversies of the 1920s.

CHAPTER 5

Fortifying the Fortress

The Truth *comes first. Then* students *and* money.
—Bishop George R. Brunk

Swallowing the Dog

The Great Depression hit rock bottom in 1932. George Smoker, an EMS student from western Pennsylvania, saw the despair among the six thousand residents in his hometown of Scottdale. Banks had closed. Twenty-six stores on Main Street sat empty and the merchants were bankrupt. A spirit of desperation pervaded the town. People were stealing without remorse. In some homes, all the salable furnishings had been sold and the water shut off. A service representative arrived at one home to turn off the gas only to find "the mother boiling the last edible thing in the house—the family dog," wrote Smoker. "The future is dark . . . no hope brightens the horizon."[1]

A drought devastated the Shenandoah Valley in the summer of 1930. Trees shed their leaves two months early. Dozens of trees in Assembly Park died, as did ten on J. L. Stauffer's lot. Adding to the troubles, the open-air tabernacle in Assembly Park—the site of commencement since 1919—collapsed under heavy snow in 1932. Struggling to keep EMS afloat during the Depression, one of the trustees at a board meeting said, "Now that we've swallowed the dog, we may as well swallow its tail."[2]

Overall enrollment at EMS dipped to 149 by fall 1929, its lowest in seven years. During the worst years of the Depression, the academic program was trimmed, faculty salaries were voluntarily cut 10 percent, and the teaching staff shrank. In 1932–1933, science teacher M. T. Brackbill agreed to a leave of absence without pay to pursue graduate work. Some faculty were reduced to part-time work. The three single women holding full-time appointments had their work and salaries reduced to the equivalent of two full-time teachers, on the principle that married faculty "should be the last to suffer."[3] In addition, the school urged each faculty member to pay the tuition for one student. Mildred Kauffman from Lancaster County could not have entered in fall 1932 without the tuition and lodging provided by her uncle, teacher D. Ralph Hostetter.[4] The operating ledger showed a loss of about $1,000 for two consecutive years (1929–1931) but then a surplus of some $4,000 two years later, thanks to severe cutbacks. During those bare-bones times, the school continued to carry a $34,000 debt acquired before the Depression.[5]

In the fall of 1933, the junior college applications remained steady at about forty students, but high school applicants had dropped to ten.[6] Students were entering public high schools because EMS's tuition and transportation were too expensive. In response, President Wenger personally canvassed for students in the Harrisonburg area. With his own funds, he purchased an Essex sedan dubbed "the school bus" and hired a driver for it to make transportation more affordable. Local Mennonites canned vegetables and donated them to the dining hall. Chester Wenger, son of the president, remembers his mother diluting cocoa with water because of the financial squeeze.[7]

To provide employment for students in financial straits, President Wenger, teacher Ernest G. Gehman, and local businessman E. C. Shank formed the Sharon Manufacturing Company in 1933 as a private industry in an old campus building. The company made small, two-color, cast-aluminum toys. The entrepreneurs chose toy making because it required minimal skill. They hoped to manufacture ten thousand small cars and trucks a week to provide extra income for as many as fifty students. After producing about two hundred thousand toys, the company closed in 1934 due to the rising cost of aluminum and the restrictive policies of the National Recovery Administration.[8] Despite the company's closure, the special efforts to cut costs and recruit students boosted enrollment to an all-time high of 172 students by 1936–1937.

Lancaster Is Almost Ripe

In the midst of the Depression, President Wenger reported that EMS solicitors in Lancaster County had "found the field more ripe."[9] This was good news for Wenger, who, thirty-two years earlier, had declared Lancaster not yet ripe for a school. Lancaster Mennonites had seriously considered starting their own school in 1908, but the idea never gained traction. Yet Lancaster remained wary of a school in Harrisonburg. Lancaster's senior bishop, Ben Weaver, was still peeved about how L. J. Heatwole had handled a trip to recruit I. B. Good as principal from the Lancaster area in 1914.[10] Nine years later, Heatwole apologized, and by 1927, Weaver was "impressed with EMS" but still thought "it should *be in Lancaster County*."[11] At a meeting of the Lancaster and Virginia bishops in June 1927, the Lancaster leaders refused a generous offer to appoint half of the sixteen EMS trustees. Some leaders adamantly opposed higher education; others thought the church should not operate colleges because students could attend nearby public or private colleges. Still others hoped to build a school in Lancaster County.[12]

Bishop Weaver's death in September 1928, more than any other factor, explained Lancaster Mennonites' new readiness to endorse EMS, according to Oliver Shenk, a proponent of a Lancaster school. He claimed that Weaver and several others planned to start a school there in 1929. Without Weaver's support—and with Shenk's sudden enthusiasm for EMS upon visiting the campus shortly after the bishop's death—the momentum for a school in Lancaster lost steam, at least for a while.[13] Occasional overtures from President Wenger, J. L. Stauffer, and Bishop Brunk, as well as coaxing from Lancaster bishops John Mosemann and Noah Mack, brought the Virginia and Lancaster leaders together again in October 1933. After this cordial meeting, the Lancaster bishops encouraged all of their youth who desired an education beyond the elementary grades to attend EMS.[14] Nine years later, the Lancaster Mennonites opened their own high school and sent many of its college-aspiring graduates to Harrisonburg. Despite their endorsement of EMS, Lancaster leaders still did not accept appointments to the board of trustees until the mid-1960s.

The détente between Lancaster County Mennonites and Eastern Mennonite School was long overdue. It increased the already heavy traffic between "the County" and "the Valley," as the two places were known. Nearly half of the faculty in the mid-1930s had roots in Lancaster, about half of the students in 1933 came from "the County," many Lancaster students attended the Special Bible Term, and some Lancaster leaders supported the annual Ministers Week and other EMS programs.

Sara Weaver, who grew up among the "very starched" Lancaster Mennonites, found the southern-style ethos more relaxed and congenial. After graduating from EMS in 1935, she taught in Fentress, where "it didn't matter if you drove on the lawn. And the people were so nice. They loved me and I loved them. And I had just a delightful time teaching."[15] A midwestern student at EMS carried a stereotype of Lancaster Mennonites as people who "claimed to be very plain, but raised tobacco and drove expensive cars and wore clothes cut from the best of cloth."[16] Grace Showalter, longtime director of EMU's historical library, thought that Virginia Mennonites had "subtle refinements" of etiquette and a quiet and serene spirituality shaped more by "Southern conventionality" than religious conservatism.[17]

In the Twinkling of an Eye

Among his accomplishments as president, A. D. Wenger counted EMS's survival during the Depression and the long-awaited Lancaster endorsement. Current events were worrisome, though, with Adolf Hitler becoming chancellor of Germany in

January 1933 and the new Democratic president, Franklin D. Roosevelt, stimulating the economy with federal mandates. Although the school's fortress mentality seemed to be flourishing, Wenger fretted that the Virginia contributors were too few in number. Writing to Enos Hess, the president of Messiah Bible College in 1933, Wenger expressed doubt that the schools would escape "the severe world depression [following] the cruel war." In the midst of such gloom, he hoped "the Lord will come and take us out in the twinkling of an eye" (an allusion to 1 Corinthians 15:52).[18]

In September 1934, still struggling to shake off the effects of the Depression, President Wenger faced his own set of troubles. Over the next twelve months, he would deal with an attempt to trim his authority, conflicts with two of his brothers-in-law, and mounting pressure to raise money for ambitious projects. While Wenger and Dean C. K. Lehman worked well together on administrative matters, they held disparate views on Christ's millennial reign on earth. In the spring of 1934, Wenger confessed that he had "withstood C. K. a little harder than [he] ever did before." As a result, Lehman approached trustee chair A. G. Heishman, and the two devised a plan to strip many of Wenger's responsibilities in "a quiet and private manner," leaving him a mere "figurehead."[19]

When George R. Brunk heard of the planned coup d'état, he protested to the Religious Welfare Committee (RWC), saying that Wenger had helped the school both "religiously and financially."[20] And the bishop thought "ill of any person" who would try to "crowd out" the president. Yet Brunk averred to Wenger privately, "Maybe the Lord is working and he needs you more at Fentress than at the school next year."[21] Hearing Brunk's protest, Chairman Heishman backed off quickly, claiming he had only hoped to lighten Wenger's load because he was getting "in a rut too deep to get out."[22] The plan to shrink the president's authority failed, but it was nevertheless unsettling to Wenger as well as to his supporters.

Like a father protecting a child, Bishop Brunk did everything he could to safeguard EMS from danger.[23] He was quite distressed in the fall of 1930 when he spoke at EMS and some of the students left his talk early to attend other events. He called it a "mean low trick" that the students were free to leave early. Speaking at an event without required attendance, he felt, made him look like "a *stool pigeon* to draw conservative students." He threatened to resign from the RWC.[24] Later he accused EMS of discriminating against his children who were students there, declaring himself a "discouraged, displeased, and nearly disgusted man."[25] President Wenger quickly refuted the claims of discrimination. Although Bishop Brunk defended Wenger's presidency, on some occasions, he harshly criticized him. In Wenger's words, Brunk was "severe," "harsh," and "too rough." "[He] thrashed me," and "[never] encouraged me in anything." Wenger advised his brother-in-law to follow the Golden Rule more closely.[26]

Even though Brunk pummeled both opponents and friends, his intellectual agility and his grasp of theological movements—and their threat to the school he loved—were incisive. For example, Brunk was a persistent and vociferous critic of Calvinism, a theological tradition named for sixteenth-century church reformer John Calvin, who emphasized the sovereignty of God and downplayed human agency. Calvin's accent on predestination was, for Brunk, a grave theological error that shrank free will too much and promoted "eternal security" based on God's grace alone, apart from ethical practice. The idea of "once saved, always saved" endangered Mennonite imperatives to live a nonresistant and nonconformed life. If Calvinism penetrated Mennonite thinking, Brunk worried that the church's whole-Gospel package of salvation and ethics would unravel.

In Brunk's mind, salvation involved both free will and human choice. He advocated spiritual synergy, a partnership in which humans participated with God in salvation by exercising their free choice to follow Jesus. Synergy, for Brunk, was analogous to rowing a boat. It required two oars—faith and works—to row in a straight line. The belief that predestination guaranteed eternal security eroded individual responsibility for ethical behavior. Prospective faculty were asked to "loyally defend" the school's "standards against all the errors [in Calvinism] contrary to our biblical faith and religious philosophy."[27]

Whenever Brunk spoke at EMS in the 1930s, he plucked the same old chord about the dangers of Calvinism. People soon tired of it. Some faculty who were afraid to speak to Brunk complained to A. D. Wenger. In late 1934, Wenger told Brunk that his audiences would likely dwindle if he kept chipping away at Calvinism. Brunk retorted that EMS must "attack and expose the fallacies of Calvinism unrelentingly or lose." Then he thundered, "The *truth* comes first and *students* and *money emphatically* afterward." The bishop again threatened to resign from the RWC, repeating, "I will not sit as a stool pigeon to draw innocent students" to EMS just to have them "corrupted by Calvinistic" views.[28] Nonetheless, Brunk delivered an eloquent and affectionate commencement address to the 1935 graduates with only a brief mention of Calvinism, "the most dangerous heresy of our time."[29]

If George R. Brunk was tempestuous, C. K. Lehman was predictable, at least when it came to amillennialism. As academic dean, Lehman assigned courses to faculty members and to himself. Some faculty thought he taught certain courses to promote his amillennial views. In spring 1935, A. D. Wenger asked the RWC to investigate the work of the dean—a move similar to the one Lehman had made against Wenger several months earlier. Lehman and Wenger's relationship chilled for three months that spring—neither could sleep well, but both continued to participate in communion services.[30] During this time, Wenger talked with Lehman daily for a week about assigning more classes to premillennialist teachers. Wenger, who first introduced this view to the Mennonites, claimed that Lehman called it a heresy because it was only forty years old and not the orthodox Mennonite stance. In Wenger's view, Lehman was obstinate, strong-minded, overconfident, and unwilling to yield. But Lehman claimed that Wenger had "intruded upon my rights and the duties the board gave me."[31]

What Wenger considered stubbornness was for Lehman a deep religious conviction for traditional Mennonite orthodoxy. Paradoxically, in a supposedly conservative Mennonite school, Lehman stood alone against all his colleagues. Eventually, the two men reconciled. For himself, Wenger was glad that "Chester had been severely checked while some of us older ones are yet on the stage of action."[32] Lehman *was* checked, but not for long.

More than anyone else, C. K. Lehman pushed for EMS to become a four-year college. Without opposition, he put on a full-court press in spring 1935, well aware that it might be a ten-year project.[33] He added physics to the curriculum to complete the premed track and developed a four-year sequence of courses for a Bible degree.[34] In an attempt to upgrade faculty credentials in preparation for the four-year college, Lehman, without success, asked the trustees to provide sabbaticals at half salary so faculty could pursue advanced training.[35]

Prior to that, the faculty had urged President Wenger "to go after funds" to build an addition to the Ad Building and to launch the four-year college.[36] While the faculty and trustees supported these plans, the fund-raising expectations added to the president's bucket of anxieties. Nonetheless he plodded on. In his annual report to the trustees in summer 1935, he noted that the school had suffered no deaths in the past year. He spoke at the General Conference in Ontario in early August and then went to Fentress to harvest grapes before returning to campus on September 11.

About a week later, he became ill yet continued teaching his classes. He came home to rest each day but gradually grew weaker. On Saturday, October 5, after eating breakfast, Wenger pulled up a chair to the wood-burning cook stove in the kitchen and warmed his feet at the open oven. Annie, who was working nearby, heard a noise. Turning, she saw him slumped over. And in an instant, in the twinkling of an eye, he was gone, just as he had hoped. The local community mourned on Monday at an on-campus funeral. Later that evening, Wenger's seventeen-year-old son, Chester, guided the hearse through the night along the 230-mile route to Fentress for a second funeral, followed by the burial near his father's much-loved vineyard. Bishop Brunk's words to Wenger, "Maybe the Lord . . . needs you more at Fentress than at the school," had come true, but not in the way anyone expected.[37]

Two and a half years later, George R. Brunk also left this world quickly, passing away one evening while milking a cow in his barn at Denbigh across the bay from

Fentress.[38] Both men, stricken by heart disease, departed at age sixty-seven. Brunk's daughter Ruth, a recent graduate of EMS, described her grief with these words: "His seat is empty. We miss his counsel and advice, his love and kisses, his singing, smiling, and his prayers. It's painful to go to the table and not hear him pray."[39]

In the short span of five and a half years, three influential founders of the school (Heatwole, Wenger, and Brunk) had died.[40] The curtain on the school's founding era was closing. Yet the battle for truth would continue, as Ernest G. Gehman underscored in his "Dirge" honoring Wenger:

> How are the mighty fallen!
> How as the years go on
> Must warriors leave the battle!
> And now another's gone!
>
> And yet when faith was threatened,
> When error stalked abroad,
> You rose to do it battle,
> Withstood its face, unawed.
>
> How are the mighty fallen!
> Alas, another's gone!
> But, Brethren, in his footsteps
> We'll press the battle on![41]

Squirrels, Prayers, and Bad Books

The risk-averse trustees had no trouble finding Wenger's successor. Two days after Wenger's death, they appointed John Longacre "J. L." Stauffer acting president until November 1936, when he was officially confirmed.[42] The credentials and experience of the forty-six-year-old Stauffer mirrored the school's culture. He was an ardent premillennialist, a critic of Calvinism and eternal security, a minister, the moderator of Virginia Conference since 1932, a recently ordained bishop, a prominent church-wide leader, and a champion of Mennonite conservatism.[43] Moreover, he had served seventeen years as a faculty member and held appointments on the administrative committee and as secretary of the trustees. All of Stauffer's roles in the church solidified the bond between EMS and Virginia Conference.

A son of eastern Pennsylvania's Franconia Conference, Stauffer's formal education included one year of high school, one year of business school, and two correspondence courses from Goshen College. A thoughtful, well-versed biblical scholar, he was largely self-taught in theological knowledge. He worked for the Stetson Hat Company in Philadelphia as a stenographer and salesman from 1906 through 1911 and married Lydia Kolb in 1910. Shortly after their marriage, they moved to Altoona, Pennsylvania, where he directed the Mennonite-operated City Mission until J. B. Smith recruited him to teach at EMS in 1918.[44]

For leisure, Stauffer enjoyed trout fishing. He was also fascinated with squirrels and had trained some to nibble nuts on a window seat inside his home office. Known as an even-tempered, slow-to-anger man, he lost control one day when one of the squirrels scampered up the inside of a trouser leg and bit him. He promptly shot the intruder.[45]

The Stauffers had five children, including J. Mark, who became a longtime music teacher at EMS. On their plot along the dirt road between Assembly Park and the Ad Building, the Stauffers raised chickens, tended a big garden, and hosted student "roomers" for sideline income. During the Special Bible Term each winter, when the campus was flooded with extra students, the Stauffer children slept in their cold attic to provide space for the six-week boarders. A devout family, the Stauffers gathered in the parlor most evenings after supper for a "family altar" of Bible reading, hymn singing, and a kneeling prayer.[46]

Prayer was an important religious ritual in the life of EMS as well. In a rite of humility and submission, students knelt for prayer each morning at the twenty-minute chapel service. Bells, which signaled the change of classes, also rang at 7:20 a.m. for morning watch (a time of personal devotion and prayer) and again at 7:00 p.m., when separate clusters of men and women gathered for thirty-minute prayer circles. Prayers were offered at the beginning of all religious services and before meals. Many faculty members, especially those teaching Bible courses, offered a prayer at the opening of each class. With their piety outstripping that of the faculty, students petitioned to have the "secular courses" open with a prayer as well.[47] An "upper room" provided students a private place to schedule time for meditation and prayer. Early Sunday mornings, a mission prayer meeting was held before the campus church service. On Sunday evenings, another prayer circle included a Bible study followed by a public church service. Student life seemed drenched in prayer and religious events.[48]

During Stauffer's twelve years as president (1936–1948), Bible courses and religious life were preeminent on campus. The president's annual report to the trustees typically noted how many students had "accepted Christ," "were saved," or "had been converted" at the fall and spring revival meetings. Stauffer heartily embraced the indoctrination-separation paradigm, but that grew more difficult as the winds of modernity began to batter the fortress.

The Administration Committee (J. L. Stauffer, C. K. Lehman, and D. Ralph Hostetter) was responsible for "safeguard[ing] students [from] modernistic interpretations of Scripture and other false and erroneous teachings."[49] To prevent such evil from seeping into the curriculum, the committee approved all proposed textbooks. By 1946, the three administrators had grown weary of the "difficult task," because it was "practically impossible to obtain textbooks that [were] 100 percent acceptable." Almost all texts had some objectionable content—erroneous teaching; evolution; modernistic interpretation of the Scripture; wrong views of the church; an emphasis on motion pictures, theater, or the radio; or objectionable pictures of comedians, sculpture, or nude artwork. The censors could not find even one acceptable American literature textbook because of so many "objectionable things" in American life. Despite "exercising the utmost care" in screening textbooks, the committee warned the RWC to expect criticism from parents or students.[50]

"We Probably Would've Had a Riot"

Alongside their academic work, literary societies, and on-campus religious programs, students energetically engaged in off-campus evangelism sponsored by the student-run Young People's Christian Association. YPCA projects provided an apprenticeship for students to practice their convictions and test their long-term interests in mission work. Witness activities drew them out of the white ethnic fortress and into worlds of imprisonment, poverty, rural isolation, mental illness, and racism, which few of them had seen before. The wattage that powered these ventures intensified during President Stauffer's tenure. The fact that YPCA projects were the only permissible mixed-gender activities likely enhanced their popularity.

One student leader boasted that the YPCA "controlled nearly all the school's student activities, both social and religious."[51] Alongside the school's own religious programs, the YPCA conducted Bible studies, Friday morning devotions, and mission meetings on topics as diverse as China, India, Jews, missionary heroes, and personal evangelism. The YPCA's primary aim was to witness to those "in darkness" by leading them to accept Christ as their personal Savior. One enthusiastic student called mission work "a divine boomerang. We go to make others happy and for so doing our Master makes us happy."[52]

YPCA teams held "meetings" consisting of Bible reading, prayer, singing, preaching, and personal testimonies on street corners, in private homes ("cottage meetings"), in prisons, and in almshouses. EMS students gave programs at the Rockingham County prison, a "colored prison camp" near Harrisonburg, and at the Iron Gate Prison Camp about ninety-five miles south of Harrisonburg, where "about fifty Negro men who have fallen prey to the merciless spiritual captivity of Satan . . . work on construction projects."[53]

On campus, students periodically made respectful references to "colored people" in talks and essays. In a 1931 essay titled "The Colored Johnson Family," Ruth Mininger described a Christmastime visit to a local home. A literary program on African American music and culture featured a "stirring debate on the ever-live question: Should the Negro enjoy equal privileges with the white race?" The judges favored the affirmative arguments of Clarence Fretz, a northerner.[54]

Fretz and seven other members of the class of 1937 were instrumental in starting the first Mennonite mission to African Americans south of the Mason-Dixon Line. In 1935, the YPCA proposed a radical idea: open a mission on Gay Street in Harrisonburg to serve African American and white children. Students hoped that a Sunday school and summer Bible school would be more effective than the preach-and-run tactic of street corner meetings, dropping gospel tracts on doorsteps, and holding cottage meetings in the homes of African American people.

Virginia Conference blessed the YPCA's new venture and asked its mission board to supervise it. Even so, the YPCA paid all the rent for the building. A site committee consisting of John R. Mumaw, Ernest G. Gehman, and student Moses Slabaugh found an abandoned restaurant on the corner of Gay Street and Federal Alley. A former beer joint, the place required a lot of soaping, scraping, and scrubbing. The services at the Gay Street Mission that opened in spring 1936 were segregated from the start. Two Sunday schools were held every Sunday—one in the morning for whites and one in the afternoon for African Americans. A children's meeting and preaching service were held on alternate Sunday evenings. Earl Delp, a 1937 graduate, explained that although some Mennonites were against segregation, "You couldn't buck City Hall." Local and state laws forbade integrated meetings. "We probably would've had a riot if we had tried to hold a mixed service." People in Harrisonburg "would have risen up against us."[55] The awkwardness of holding segregated meetings in the same building prompted the mission board to relocate the white services to a vacant church building on Chicago Avenue in fall 1936.

In the summer of 1937, some fifty African American people attended the evening worship service and the four Sunday school classes held in the afternoon. EMS students frequently visited the homes of children who attended the Sunday school classes. One student happily reported that "[one] Colored lady remarked that the Colored children learn more of God's word at our Sunday school then at all the other Colored Sunday schools combined."[56] Although the "Mennonite Mission for the Colored" focused on evangelism, numerous social activities—sewing circles, social gatherings, home economics, woodshop projects—were gradually added.[57]

Summer Bible school at the Gay Street Mennonite Mission for the Colored in Harrisonburg, 1940. The mission was established in 1936 by the YPCA.

The YPCA initiative was the first Mennonite mission venture in Harrisonburg, the first conference-supported African American congregation, and the first Mennonite attempt to establish an African American congregation in the South.[58] And while the segregated services ostensibly supported racist customs, EMS students were quietly violating racial taboos in their routine contacts with African Americans. Historian James O. Lehman called the project "quite a daring move." Some ordained leaders wanted to close the "colored mission" because it was so radical.[59]

It was risky for two reasons: the participating students were breaking racial norms and they were Yankees. Some local Mennonites were annoyed that the out-of-state students energizing the Gay Street initiative seemed to have little respect for long-standing racist customs.[60] All thirteen students and alumni mission enthusiasts (except Ada Bechtel) were non-Virginians. Of the project's three faculty advisors—J. R. Mumaw, Harry Brunk, and Ernest G. Gehman—only Brunk was from Virginia. The other students and faculty advisors hailed from Pennsylvania (eight), Ohio (two), Delaware (one), Maryland (one), Michigan (one), and Ontario (one).[61]

The Pennsylvanians knew that Lancaster Conference had recently commissioned its first missionaries to Africa. The fanfare surrounding that sendoff enticed four hundred Mennonites to reserve a ten-car train from Lancaster to the ports of New York to witness the departure.[62] Some EMS students cringed at the incongruity of sending missionaries thousands of miles to Africa to save dark-skinned people when some Mennonite segregationists refused to drive a few miles into Harrisonburg to aid an African American mission. A chapel speaker sharpened the contradiction with these words: "God is testing our sincerity of working among Negroes in Africa [by how much we work] among Negroes at home." These comments also marked the evolving use of "Negro" instead of "Colored" at EMS.[63]

Charles M. Sheldon's 1896 book, *In His Steps: What Would Jesus Do?*, likely influenced students to get involved in the Gay Street project. The main character in Sheldon's popular fictional work was a pastor who urged parishioners in his white well-to-do congregation to ask, "What would Jesus do?" as they faced daily decisions. Answering that question led the pastor and his parishioners to address racism, poverty, and systemic social inequality. In a down-to-earth style, Sheldon emphasized the socioeconomic implications of Jesus's teachings, thus helping promote the Social Gospel movement.

The front cover of the 1937 commencement issue of the *Journal*, which served as the class yearbook, was themed "In His Steps" and bore an unmistakable resemblance to the cover of the 1899 edition of Sheldon's book. Four members of the editorial staff were involved in the Gay Street mission. The theme appears at the top of each page. The class poem, the class song, and a long essay by Earl Delp were also titled "In His Steps." But although Sheldon's book may have inspired the students, their explanations for initiating the mission focused on saving souls, not changing socioeconomic conditions.

An Incubator for Fordism

Meanwhile, other YPCA activities were flourishing. Gospel tract distribution was a prominent one. The number of tracts distributed ranged upward of 56,000 per year, as shown in table 1. Tracts were dispersed in monthly door-to-door canvassing of Harrisonburg homes as well as through tract dispensers in public places. They were also mailed or rolled and tossed to pedestrians from cars. One tract committee considered "raining tracts" down on Harrisonburg from an airplane, but the plan failed. Another tract committee, interested in Jewish evangelism, sent religious literature to some three hundred Jewish families in Lynchburg, Richmond, Staunton, and Waynesboro.[64]

YPCA gospel teams of four to twelve students traveled to other states during summers and midyear breaks to present programs of preaching, singing, and personal testimony. It was not unusual to have five to ten teams per year, with some of them logging several thousand miles. Some teams used a pop-up trailer purchased by the YPCA. The Ambassador Gospel Team of six men and six women traveled nine thousand miles across Canada and the United States in the summer of 1948.[65]

Off-campus activities inevitably sparked some romance. Chester Wenger and Sara Weaver were on a YPCA team that conducted a street meeting in Grottoes, about fifteen miles south of EMS. On one outing, Chester was preaching on a street corner and Sara was singing in the ladies quartet. Though not dating yet, she had her eye on him as they were singing, and she later confessed that even then she was dreaming of dating him. Back in the EMS cafeteria, her friends whispered

Table 1. YPCA Activities, 1939–1940 and 1947–1948

	Type and Number of Activities per Academic Year	
	1939–1940	*1947–1948*
Bible Programs (On-Campus)	28	27
Devotional Programs (On-Campus)	32	26
Prison Programs	36	31
City Programs	29	636
Rural Programs	56	211
Missions Prayer Meetings	43	43
Almshouse Programs	44	23
Children's Home Programs	—	12
Total Programs and Meetings	268	1,009
Total Student Service Contacts	2,527	4,238
Gospel Outreach Teams	7	12
Gospel Tracts Distributed	42,144	56,127
Off-Campus Conversions	49	38

Sources: Journal, July–Aug. 1940, 22–23; *Bulletin,* June 1948, 1–7.

that Chester's "cat-like eyes" followed her every move.[66] Their marriage, like many others, was a happy byproduct of YPCA activities.

Students invested enormous energy in witness and mission projects. Dressing in plain garb and articulating their faith on street corners, in cottage meetings, and in door-to-door visits reinforced their identity as mission-minded Mennonites. Without exception, YPCA endeavors focused on religious witness and soul saving, not on social work or political activism. Student initiatives assumed that personal conversion was a prerequisite to any social betterment.

Apart from its evangelistic value, the YPCA was an incubator for organizational management. The twenty different YPCA committees during the 1947–1948 school year reflected the specialization of modernity. The YPCA had Fordism written all over it—with central control, standardization, quantification, and an eye on productivity—which was not surprising, since President Stauffer had compared EMS to a corporation that produced products.[67] YPCA president Richard Detweiler's annual report read like the executive summary of a corporate CEO. He had tallied the productivity of each committee's programs, student contacts, and converts. Each student's weekly activities were tracked. All the efforts that school year yielded thirty-eight conversions and 4,238 "service opportunities" (individual

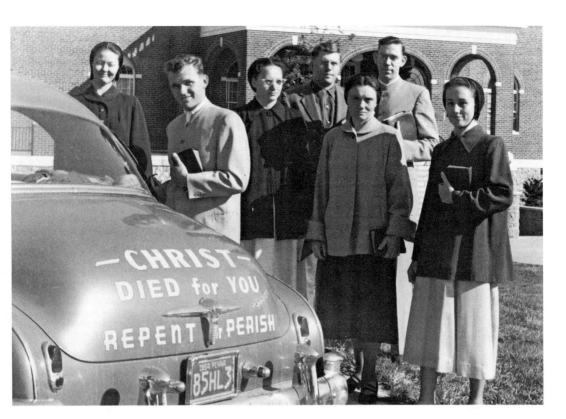

A YPCA gospel team with its mobile religious billboard, ca. 1954.

student contacts). Like a CEO measuring productivity, Detweiler wrote, "This compares favorably with last year's total of 3,361."[68] Among other things, students were learning how to operate complex organizations.

Another Millennial Flare-Up

In the late 1920s and early '30s, A. D. Wenger and C. K. Lehman had locked horns over millennial issues. Again in the late 1930s, while a war was heating up in Europe, the simmering millennial dispute flared up with greater intensity than ever. In an eighteen-paragraph letter to the RWC in June 1941, Dean Lehman laid out nine charges of unfairness caused by the skewed six-to-one Bible faculty ratio, which favored premillennialists. In Lehman's view, the 1935 Virginia Conference statement calling for charity on both sides meant *parity* of millennial perspective in the number of faculty, the curriculum, and public programs. For the premillennialists, however, charity did not mean parity.

Lehman recalled the "awful grillings" he had suffered at the hands of "the brethren Wenger, Stauffer, Brunk, Mack, and others" in 1935. Moreover, amillennial constituents had pressed "hard on him" to rectify the severe imbalance. Lehman lamented that all the "propaganda and misrepresentation" had "marred our fellowship." He told the RWC that he prayed that EMS would become "a true servant of the church and not merely an organ for the dissemination of premillennialism."[69] Despite his position as academic dean and his office's inner door opening into the president's office, Lehman's voice was somewhat muffled. President Stauffer was a diehard proponent of premillennialism and an ex officio member of the RWC. Since the two senior administrators could not resolve their impasse, Lehman turned to the RWC as a court of arbitration.

In a letter to the RWC three times as long as Lehman's, Stauffer refuted his accusations paragraph by paragraph. Almost as annoyed at Lehman as he was at the squirrel that had bitten him, Stauffer deplored the dean for bypassing him and making a direct appeal to the RWC and for calling premillennialism "a system of pessimism in Christian garb" and a "heresy." The president's rebuttal stoked the fire with two incendiary words: modernist and Goshen. "Many amillennialists are modernists," he told the RWC, "but I have never found . . . a premillennialist who was one." Besides, he continued, church leaders do not want the "amillennialism and worldliness of Goshen College" creeping into EMS.[70]

To gather facts, President Stauffer surveyed sixty college students. Half of them had "no idea" of their own minister's millennial stance. Some 58 percent had not changed their millennial view since coming to EMS, and 93 percent saw "no violation" of toleration and charity in campus discourse.[71] Clearly, most students found the debate constructive and were certainly more charitable than their teachers. Time eventually provided a healing balm.[72] Furthermore, a real war was raging in Europe, and EMS faced more urgent matters: dealing with the military draft and developing a strong academic program befitting an accredited college.

War and More

On December 7, 1941, an EMS student slipped out of the dorm, as he often did on Sunday evenings, to enjoy some music on his car radio, since radios were banned on campus. He returned breathless with news: Japan had attacked eight US warships near Hawaii. "That's how we boys learned about Pearl Harbor," recalled Hubert Pellman.[73] The surprise attack thrust the United States into World War II. Preparations for war had already begun after Germany invaded Poland in August 1939. A year later, the United States had begun a national conscription that would eventually induct 10.1 million men into the armed forces. The war disrupted colleges everywhere by shrinking enrollments, raising prices, and imposing rationing.

Mennonites again received jeers of "yellow belly" and other insults because they refused conscription.[74] Harrisonburg officials conducted air raid drills to prepare for possible German air attacks at night. Students Harold D. Lehman and Dwight Hartman were responsible for surveillance (on bicycle) and reporting to civic officials any lights in Park View homes and EMS buildings that remained on during the drills. Wartime rationing severely restricted access to gas and tires. Instead of using buses, students walked to a nearby woods for their all-day school outing in 1943.[75]

After witnessing the horrific treatment of pacifists during World War I, Mennonites, Brethren, and Quakers—known since 1935 as the Historic Peace Churches—had been negotiating quietly with federal officials to ensure alternatives for conscientious objectors (COs) if conscription ever came. Their efforts were fruitful.[76] President Roosevelt issued an executive order in February 1941 allowing religious conscientious objectors to perform alternative service in the national interest through Civilian Public Service (CPS) projects. In these church-run and church-funded service units, COs provided labor without pay for approved public projects with civilian oversight. Some of the units were located at former sites of the Civilian Conservation Corps, a public works program started in 1933.

Draftees could request a deferment from their hometown draft board for jobs of "national importance" in agriculture, medicine, and ministry or to pursue seminary studies. Deferments were based on a draftee's work, not his beliefs. Conscientious objectors without deferments had three options: enter the military as noncombatants, join CPS, or go to prison. Of 690 draftees in Virginia Conference, 76 percent received deferments, 15 percent entered CPS, and 9 percent joined the armed forces.[77]

Seven months before Pearl Harbor, the first CPS site administered by Mennonites opened near Grottoes, south of Harrisonburg. Nearly twelve thousand conscientious objectors served in 151 CPS units during World War II, performing work of national importance in agriculture, forestry, mental health, and social services and serving as human guinea pigs for medical studies. Nearly 40 percent of all CPSers were affiliated with a Mennonite group.[78] General Lewis Hershey, director of Selective Service, called CPS "an experiment" to test America's willingness to preserve minority rights even in the midst of war.[79]

At EMS, some draft-age men were not conscripted; others enrolled in the four-year Bible curriculum; still others left school for CPS or for deferred work at home. Despite all these changes, enrollment more than doubled over the eight years bracketing the war. College attendance spiked nearly fourfold—from 40 to 153 students—and the number of men pursuing a bachelor's degree in biblical studies rose from six to fifty-three.[80]

When the draft began, Selective Service deferred seminarians but not religious studies majors at four-year colleges. EMS officials, trying to qualify students for deferments, faced a quandary: the Mennonite Church had no seminaries because it did not require seminary training for its ministers. Theological students had little chance of ordination because most congregations still used the lot to select ministers. Furthermore, the school was not an accredited four-year college. So for several months EMS could not guarantee four-year Bible students a deferment.[81] Hailing from various states, the drafted students ultimately were accountable to their hometown draft boards, whose sympathy for COs varied greatly.

Some draftees faced hard choices. Most of the congregations with students at EMS excommunicated members who entered the armed forces. Virginia Conference, for example, declared that "our people who have entered the armed forces . . . have forfeited their fellowship in the church by their own choice."[82] Paul Peachey, a twenty-three-year-old Mennonite farm boy from southwestern Pennsylvania, wrestled with a moral dilemma when he arrived at EMS in September 1941. Within two months, the first lottery-based draft chanced upon his name. Conscientiously opposed to killing, he was considering CPS until he learned from Dean Lehman that Selective Service had reclassified Bible students in four-year colleges (without regard to accreditation) as seminarians.

This abrupt shift by Selective Service created a choice for Peachey: enter CPS or pursue biblical studies at EMS. Two months of school had stirred his interest in Christian service but not in preministerial studies. Still undecided two days before his induction date, he called Dean Lehman and halfheartedly said, "I guess I'll stay." Discomfort soon plagued him—knowing that American men were dying on battlefields and fellow Mennonites were performing a civic duty in CPS while he was ostensibly studying to be a minister. Whatever guilt he carried about not entering CPS soon fled after graduation, when he went to Europe for a twenty-seven-month stint distributing food and clothing to war-ravaged people under the auspices of Mennonite Central Committee (MCC), an inter-Mennonite relief and service agency.[83]

Civilian Public Service indirectly changed campus life. By late 1943, forty EMS alumni were serving in CPS in locations from Maine to Oregon and from California to Puerto Rico. Some alumnae worked in CPS units as nurses, dietitians, or matrons. Reports of CPS activities frequently appeared in the *Journal*. One alumnus called the CPSers "priests" who were practicing their "nonresistant Christian way of life."[84] Most students had relatives who were involved in some way with CPS. Several faculty taught courses at CPS sites such as Grottoes and Beltsville, Maryland. Church leaders who had visited CPS projects presented programs on campus. EMS actively recruited former CPS men and offered them admission to the school with a one-year remedial course or a GED for those without high school diplomas. Although the school routinely accepted a few GED applicants, half of the incoming class in 1947 entered on GED tests.[85]

Some CPSers spoke to the student body about their experiences. These interesting stories depicted young Mennonites scattered across the country performing a civic duty of national importance. It was a whole new way of envisioning Mennonite engagement with the world. But not everyone applauded CPS. President Stauffer and some Virginia Conference leaders were not fond of placing conservative Mennonites in CPS units where they rubbed shoulders with worldly Quakers, liberal pacifists, and progressive Mennonites.

In an odd irony, military conscription benefited Mennonites by testing the mettle of their nonresistance in the ferment of war. As it did twenty-five years earlier, the war recalibrated Mennonite identity and hardened the pacifist resolve of many. And as before, World War II propelled Mennonites into service and benevolent activities in the larger society.[86] More than thirty alumni, for example, served in CPS mental health assignments during the war.[87] The prominence of CPS activities reinforced students' Mennonite identity, not only as Christian pacifists, but as a set-apart people in American society. This experience was transformative, not just for CPS participants but for all students on campus.

The CPS experience also formulated a new Mennonite identity—one with a *social conscience* for serving people outside the Mennonite orbit. Mennonites were now engaging the world, not only in missionary work but also in human service, in ways that were completely new to them. CPS opened the shutters of the fortress and offered a new paradigm for social activism—one that was quite different from the YPCA's pattern of mission. Ironically, this transformation was spurred not by Christian conviction but by civic duty required by the country. Similarly, military conscription, more than personal persuasions, prodded EMS leaders to cooperate in new ways with other Mennonite agencies in CPS arrangements and with the Council of Mennonite and Affiliated Colleges, which helped organize the recruitment of international students to EMS.[88]

Bonnets and Buttons

At the same time that new ways of engaging the world were emerging—and perhaps in response to them—expressions of Mennonite identity on campus hardened. Throughout the founding era, EMS's staunch reputation for requiring plain attire branded it as a conservative school. The first three presidents (Smith, Wenger, and Stauffer) were strong proponents of church-regulated dress. Controversy about attire grew in the mid-1940s, peaked in the late 1960s, and then gradually subsided. By 1990, dress regulations had vanished except for those governing attire in the sunbathing areas of campus.

In some sectors of the Mennonite Church and especially at EMS, dressing in plain clothing was a daily social ritual in the first half of the twentieth century. This was particularly true for women, who wore a devotional covering also known as a prayer covering or prayer veiling. Plain-dressing women were also expected to wear a black bonnet over their covering when they left campus. In addition, regulations included dark hose, dark shoes, long dresses, and long hair wrapped in a simple bun under their covering. These daily rehearsals of Mennonite identity underscored loyalty to the church, submission to authority, limits to self-expression with dress, and the line between church and world.

Although church-wide practices of nonconformity relaxed somewhat as World War II receded, they did not change at EMS. There the resolve to protect the ethnic fortress cinched the rules even more. Speaking about plain fashion to the "faculty sisters," President Stauffer reminded them that Mennonites "[were] traveling the narrow road while the world is traveling the broad one." Noting the gradual "break-down of nonconformity," he underscored the ominous biblical warning that those who befriend the world are enemies of God (James 4:4).[89] Any "let down" of dress standards, he warned, would erode constituent confidence in the school.[90]

A few congregations were already allowing hairstyling and wedding rings.[91] Ada M. Zimmerman, dean of college women, saw a "rapid permeation of worldliness" in the church and urged students not to wear fashionable "hairdos."[92] President Stauffer asked, "When does headwear cease to be a bonnet?" He pleaded with the "faculty sisters" to help him stop students from the "wearing of near-hats, near-bonnets, no bonnets or other inconsistent headwear." And he wondered, "How can we eliminate immodest form-advertising dresses?"[93]

To halt such fashion, EMS tightened the screws of separatism during the Stauffer administration. Printed dress standards expanded sevenfold from 1924 to 1946, swelling from 76 to 520 words.[94] The women's dress code had three foci: covering the body, concealing the body's form, and wearing symbols of Mennonite identity in public. The regulations did not mention the prayer covering until 1948 because it was assumed that women would wear one. Although school officials urged young men to wear a plain coat, they never required it, nor did they prohibit neckties. But beginning in 1941, all

The Armerian Literary Society, wearing plain dress, 1942–1943. The YPCA led off-campus mission endeavors, but literary societies energized on-campus student life.

neckties had to be black. Across the years, male students were required to wear black hats off campus. Long socks of plain, dark colors were added to the list in 1943.

Apart from the growing number of rules, other shifts appeared between 1924 and 1946. The familial words "sisters" and "brethren" used for students in the 1924 dress standards had vanished by 1946. To legitimate dress expectations in 1924, leaders turned to the Mennonite General Conference and to each student's regional conference. The 1946 regulations, however, upheld standards with words such as "*our* ideal for young men . . ." and "in young women, *we* look for. . . ."[95] Scripture and the school itself had thus replaced the church as the source of authority, because church-wide practices had become so diverse. Whereas the 1924 guidelines applied to all students, those in 1946 explicitly addressed "church members," thus giving passes to non-Mennonites and unbaptized Mennonites.

President Stauffer in 1947 urged the women's dress committee to find "some remedies" for flesh-colored hose (instead of the required black hose), disgraceful-looking coverings, short dresses, and the remnants of bonnets. He was especially annoyed by one Mennonite student, a chorus member, who wore short dresses, had "a collapsible bonnet [and] a lamentable hairdo," and strutted a restitched dress that revealed a "very objectionable neckline." He forbade her to accompany the chorus unless she made an "internal and external change."[96]

The women's dress committee in 1947–1948 pondered some perplexing questions about bonnet regulations for students: Should every woman be required to own one? May women substitute the bonnet for the covering when doing Christian service with the YPCA? May women borrow someone else's bonnet? Does the bonnet have any spiritual significance? If so, can it substitute for the covering in church?[97] Such questions both agitated and amused some students. One alumna said, "We called the bonnet a 'crash helmet.' It really didn't protect you from the weather, or the wind and rain. It was just an old tradition."[98]

In her letter to students entering EMS in 1948, Dean Zimmerman summarized the school's expectations. Both the covering and the bonnet had to cover the hair in the back. The bonnet could not substitute for a covering during church services. Hose had to be dark and of modest weight with a denier of at least thirty. (The higher the denier, the thicker the fabric.) Dark hose with seams in the back were required to conceal any appearance of attractive legs. Zimmerman's instructions also specified black or brown shoes with heels and closed toes. Full-length sleeves and modest necklines were imperative. Blouses with exceptionally low necklines were prohibited.[99] Marijke Schutte, a Mennonite exchange student from Holland, reflected later to a friend, "They didn't make me wear a covering, but they did make me wear black stockings."[100]

Women play volleyball in the exercise hall, "X-Hall." This cement block structure replaced a wooden-frame building constructed in 1926 that had collapsed in 1930. The X-Hall provided the only indoor space for exercise until the first gymnasium was built in 1958. Women were not permitted to wear special clothing for exercise.

Also in 1948, the men's dress committee prohibited trouser legs rolled above the ankle at any time, overalls [blue jeans], going shirtless in the gym, and white shoes (only black and brown ones were permitted).[101] Overalls were approved later that year because they were washable and economical. Men were allowed to roll up their sleeves a one-quarter length, and the rule for men's hose disappeared. The requirement to wear hats for extended trips was dropped except for YPCA service projects and church meetings.[102] Teacher D. Ralph Hostetter, however, still expected men to wear traditional black hats on field trips for bird-watching and to natural science museums in Washington, DC.[103]

Some men wrestled with whether to wear a plain coat. A former student explained, "If a man wore a necktie, it had to be solidly black. I quickly caught on that an ordinary suit with an ordinary dress shirt was not stylish; my solution was to don a black tie, but not the straight-cut coat." Male students were admonished to be loyal to the church, to the standards of the school, and to the general principle of nonconformity. However, no Bible verses pointed directly to buttoning collars, wearing hats or long-sleeved shirts, or any other aspect of male dress.

When Regulations Backfire

Some of the faculty and staff had the hapless job of enforcing the dress regulations. The dean of men, A. Don Augsburger, bemoaned standing at the chapel door every day just to remind the open-collared men to button up. He told them, "It's just a rule, so let's just do it." The men's dress committee was reluctant to make rules because they "failed to appeal to the minds of our best thinking boys."[104] The rule forbidding white slacks prompted some inventive boys to dye their white slacks pink, a stunt that won the prank-of-the-month award.[105] The committee worried that their efforts were worthless because "many students" conformed outwardly but had no personal convictions. The committee even considered an aggressive button-the-collar promotion that left compliance to *individual conscience*—a provocative proposal that came twenty years before its time.[106]

On matters of dress, the locus of authority was ambiguous. Who held the clout to determine dress standards: EMS, the student's home congregation, Virginia Conference, the Mennonite General Conference, or the student's own conscience?[107] Regardless of where the authority rested, women's dress issues were more highly regulated than men's. Three-fourths of the verbiage on student attire in 1946 targeted women. "The problem," explained alumna Lois B. Bowman, "was that the men made all the rules about dress, and they had no idea of the practical implications for women."[108]

In patriarchal societies, men determine what women may wear. Mennonite men, threatened by the seductive power of women's bodies, created a maze of rules to conceal them. Mennonite writer Sarah Kehrberg notes that "we legislate what threatens us."[109] And legislate they did. At EMS, men held cultural, institutional, and religious power. Besides, they had an arsenal of Bible verses pertaining to women's dress that linked the rules closely with personal faith.

Dean of women Ada M. Zimmerman, in a thoughtful and gracious letter to incoming students, tied wardrobe expectations directly to religious faith and church loyalty. She spoke of expressing spirituality in personal appearance, of practicing *righteousness*, and of upholding the church's true heritage. She reminded women that the devotional covering was an ordinance taught by the Word of God and that hairstyles should reflect the covering's spiritual significance. Finally, she averred that a woman of high Christian integrity should always cover her body so it does not attract attention and should "be aware that her dress does not exhibit a careless *spirituality* in her relationship with the Lord."[110]

The direct line between dress and spirituality encouraged compliance. It also induced the noncompliant to feel guilty. Though men usually crafted and advocated the dress regulations, many women embraced them without protest, sometimes even enthusiastically. For example, in her essay "The Necessity for Regulation of Attire in the Mennonite Church," student Edith Showalter argued that without a standardized dress code, the Mennonite Church "will risk losing her other peculiar doctrines that mark her as a full-gospel church."[111] For other women, the dress code's increasing severity and EMS's enforced compliance, regardless of personal conviction, sowed bitterness toward the school and church leaders.

Refining Rough Mennonites

Some of the button-the-collar type of dress regulations inadvertently polished the rough edges of rural youth and taught them the social graces required for upward social mobility. Because many students "come to us in the *raw*," President Stauffer told the faculty, "it's our responsibility to help them to conduct themselves as Christian ladies and gentlemen."[112] The etiquette and protocol of the dining hall exposed unrefined Mennonites to the distinctions of class—the habits of politeness and poise required for success in middle-class America. In this way, EMS served a bit like a traditional American finishing school that taught young women the charm and etiquette befitting upper-class life. As early as 1918, for example, EMS stipulated that students were "regarded as ladies and gentlemen" until proven otherwise.[113]

Fresh-from-the-country young men required considerable refining. The women's dress committee described them as a "big problem" for not acting like gentlemen in the dining hall, complaining that it is "distasteful for clean, *refined* people to eat at the same table with boys." The faculty women deplored them arriving for meals in "sweatshirts, physical education clothes, unclean work clothes, and uncombed hair . . . directly from athletics or work" without "properly bathing and changing clothes and shoes."[114] Former student C. Norman Kraus recalled hearing "a lot of emphasis on being *properly* dressed. We had to keep our shirt collars buttoned for class because it was proper. We were told not to complain because at Harvard they even had to wear a coat to class."[115]

One midwestern farm boy who knew little about proper table manners described the dining rules this way: "We had starched cloth napkins that we tucked away between meals in little boxes with our names. (Smear grape jam on the napkin, and you had to try to hide it all week!) We were assigned table places . . . to mix us for our own social betterment." Each table had a host whose "job was to demonstrate good manners and guide the conversations." Once a week, "the table group rotated to an adjoining table in one direction, and the hosts and hostesses rotated in the opposite direction."[116]

Students eat their meals family style at assigned seats in the dining hall to learn etiquette and refined manners, 1943–1944.

Student essays rehearsed the importance of manners, personal appearance, and courtesy outside the dining room. Emma Shenk, writing about personal appearance, spotlighted neatness, cleanliness, and scrubbed nails, as did Daniel Hertzler, who added "shiny shoes" in his essay titled "The Well-Groomed Christian Gentleman." Among other things, EMS was transforming young men into gentlemen and young women into ladies.[117] Two student essays enumerated the "marks of a lady" and the "marks of a gentleman." Esther Huber viewed a gentleman as a "polished diamond" with "good etiquette" whose "tastes are refined." Robert Martin portrayed the ideal lady as "reserved, neat, and courteous [with] poise and refinement." He said, "She has what Shakespeare long ago called 'an excellent thing in a woman—a voice that is soft, gentle and low.'"[118] A banner headline in the student handbook declared that literary societies are "Yours to Enjoy for Refinement."[119]

Former student Theron Schlabach recalled "a plethora of students . . . with creased trousers and starched shirts. I had a sense of being among folks who were elite and knew it."[120] Student Daniel Hertzler surmised that "the Christian gentleman who is dressed plainly, but neatly, possesses a dignity that commands attention." Dressing to command attention was far afield from historic Mennonite teaching on humility and simple clothing that aimed to deflect attention, and Hertzler was troubled that "good grooming" could go too far. "The ego in man," he said, "is always glad . . . to focus a spotlight on himself."[121]

If EMS was not running a typical finishing school, it *was* refining young Mennonites to fit the mores of middle-class propriety. Gum chewing was forbidden because it was "not genteel."[122] Some alumni, however, disliked promoting middle-class mores. Clarence Fretz, for example, chided President Stauffer about EMS "conforming to the world's etiquette." Fretz asked, "Do the dining room practices tend to the simple life, or to the life of sophisticated 'refinement' and ostentation?" Furthermore, how could a church school "which stands for the simple gospel, the simple life, and the primacy of evangelism devote itself to the cultivation of taste for refinement, culture, art, classical music, and the world's literature? How long will our young people be satisfied with simple homes, simple recreation, simple church worship, and simple Scripture reading?"[123]

No Touching, Not Even Handholding

The correspondence of EMU leaders is rife with references to "the social problem." Simply stated, the problem was this: How can we keep males and females separate and control their romantic inclinations? Men resided on the third floor and women on the second floor of the Cracker Box, sometimes dubbed "the match box" for its romantic allure. Students were not permitted to enter the floor of the other sex. Beginning in its second year (1918–1919), EMS restricted visiting between men and women to the reception room and then only with advance permission.[124] As late as the 1940s, little had changed. Courtship as well as meeting a prospective date was confined to the reception room because of control, explained Hubert Pellman, a student in the 1940s. "The matron's office adjoined the reception room, and she always kept her door open." The size of a small classroom, "it had some furniture, some chairs," Pellman continued, "but it wasn't a room you wanted to stay in very long. You had to go there to meet your date, but then you'd probably walk around campus."[125]

Relationships "between young men and young women were very tightly controlled," explained Pellman. "No touching, not even handholding—a much violated rule. Chaperones were not only present: they were a system; they came with the Virginia scenery."[126] Forbidden courting activities included conspicuous loitering in the halls, clandestine meetings, visiting a young woman in her home without a parent or guardian present, and smooching on campus. Off-campus dating required advance permission and an approved chaperone. Two or more couples eighteen years of age or older could leave the campus for *a walk* without a chaperone. And double-dating couples twenty years of age or older were free to drive off campus without a chaperone.[127]

Such stringent regulations were not unusual at private religious schools in the early twentieth century. President A. D. Wenger's daughter Anna May found similar ones when she enrolled at Elizabethtown College and lived in the dormitory in summer 1926. Writing to her mother in Fentress, Anna May complained, "This morning they read off a whole list of rules and regulations. The girls must get permission to do about everything except study, eat, and sleep. I wish we had the freedom the boys have here. They seem to trust them more."[128]

EMS promoted a "true character-building education to give students a sense of moral responsibility to foster self-control by reason of principle rather than mere obedience to rules." The school aimed to "foster biblical discipline—*parental*, firm, and positive—self-denial, thrift, submission to, and respect for authority . . . and above all spiritual growth." An EMS diploma ideally signaled "not only intellectual attainments but also good character."[129]

Did the maze of rules foster a moral education? "Yes," said Theron Schlabach, "but not in the way intended. I had high ethical standards when I arrived. What I really learned at EMS about ethics was a sense of humor about treating rules too absolutely." Schlabach had been "campused" for riding a friend's souped-up Cushman Scooter all the way to Roanoke and back on a beautiful day. Yet while he was restricted to campus, he surreptitiously left campus to dig ditches to earn petty cash. "Nobody ever seemed to notice; I did no real mischief . . . nor accumulated a record of incorrigible behavior. Rules, yes, but I learned to pick my way around them carefully." In short, Schlabach learned "that when rules seem too sharp, dull the edges a bit and smear on a little fuzz."[130] By 1950, the complexity of student regulations required a lot of fuzz.

With the Stroke of a Pen

By the mid-twentieth century (1949–1950), 376 women and 303 men were enrolled at the school, which two years earlier had been renamed Eastern Mennonite College (EMC). Regular students numbered 192 in the high school and 252 in the college. Another 235 were enrolled in summer school, the Special Bible Term, and correspondence courses. The students hailed from twenty-two states plus Canada, Germany, Belgium, and Korea. Half were from Pennsylvania and a quarter from Virginia. Faraway states—Alabama, California, Idaho, Kansas, Montana, Oregon—contributed about a dozen students.[131] In the thirty-three years leading up to 1950, total enrollment in the high school, college, Special Bible Term, and correspondence department was 13,000 (which includes double-counted students who attended two or more consecutive years).

The number of regular students had grown over the previous decade. College-level enrollment, which rose from 55 to 252, drove the growth, while high school enrollment declined after peaking at 286 in 1945. The high school faced new competition after Lancaster Mennonite School opened in 1942. On the larger Mennonite educational landscape, Hesston (a junior college) claimed 94 students in 1949–1950, while Bluffton's enrollment of 257 was similar to EMC's 252. The two largest Mennonite four-year colleges were Goshen with 622 students and Bethel (in Kansas) with 415.[132]

Beyond its regular academic offerings, EMC was a hub for a variety of programs for Mennonite young people and church leaders. The six-week Special Bible Term each winter attracted upward of 100 students and as many as 178 in 1949. One romantic couple hoped to spend their honeymoon at the six-week event only to have their ministers forbid it. Eager to help promote their beloved school, Special Bible Term students in 1948 offered to pay for a neon light atop the administration building, only to have it denied.[133]

Many self-employed church leaders attended the annual Ministers Week that overlapped the Special Bible Term. Weekend conferences on topics such as missions, nonconformity, and Christian life often served as bookends to the Bible term. Three-day Young People's Institutes were popular in the summer. Conferences were organized throughout the year on special topics. These public events were important for recruiting regular students and developing a web of ideological and financial supporters. The school served as an intellectual hub for articulating ideas that fueled a conservative movement as participants returned to their homes in various states.

By the 1940s, EMS was aggressively developing a four-year college. For accreditation, the state required schools to have department heads with doctoral or equivalent degrees, a system of faculty rank, an annual compensation of $3,000 for full professors, and five thousand more books than EMS's seven-thousand-volume library contained. Dean Lehman considered the salary requirement completely "out of reach."[134] State accreditation also required a constitutional revision and the renaming of Eastern Mennonite School (EMS) to Eastern Mennonite College (EMC).

As a testament to a remarkable continuity throughout the founding era, the original constitution had never been revised. Even so, as the college now sought to fulfill the state requirements, a reworked constitution was approved by Virginia Conference in 1947.[135] Like its 1924 predecessor, it specified sixteen trustees elected by Virginia Conference. It contained eight "safeguard features" that prohibited hazing, musical instruments, and intercollegiate sports, among other things. It also required textbooks to be as "free as possible" of higher criticism, evolution, Calvinism, and "unwholesome fiction." The revised constitution required conference approval of any EMC plans to join an "educational or accrediting association." Though the president was empowered to function as an "executive officer," the document did not specify who was authorized to appoint him.[136]

In October 1947, the Virginia State Board of Education authorized EMC to grant three degrees—bachelor of arts, bachelor of science, and bachelor of religious education—and gave provisional approval for a seminary-level theology degree with two years of study beyond the four-year degree in biblical studies. Exactly thirty years after its opening in 1917, the stroke of a pen in Richmond turned EMS into EMC.[137]

Earlier that year, an action of Virginia Conference brought celebration and almost dancing to the three music-loving Lehman families living in adjacent homes along South College Avenue. The three ordained men (D. W., C. K., and their brother-in-law,

"Curly John" Kurtz) arrived home on June 6, 1947, with the happy news that the conference had lifted the twenty-year ban on ordained men owning musical instruments. It reiterated, however, its long-standing prohibition of musical instruments in schools and churches for fear they would ruin a cappella singing.

According to family lore, Chester and John bought pianos that very evening. (Professor John R. Mumaw, who lived a block down the street, soon bought an organ.) Later that evening, Daniel W. Lehman, a bishop and a professor of education at EMS, brought his old violin down from the attic and tuned it up to play a jig. Because of their loyalty to the church, these men had deprived themselves and their families of their love of music-making for twenty long years.[138]

Cracks in the Mortar

From a distance, EMC's robust enrollment and recent state accreditation signaled success, yet a closer inspection of the fortress revealed some cracks in the mortar. In 1945, *Eastern Mennonite School Bulletin*, the school's public mouthpiece, ran a three-month series of front-page articles titled "Where Does Eastern Mennonite School Stand?" The essays addressed questions raised by some critics of the school's orthodoxy.[139]

In early 1945, Bishop S. H. Rhodes, who wore three hats—vice chair of the trustees, chair of the RWC, and conference executive committee member—presented twenty-seven complaints to President Stauffer, who was also a bishop and an ex officio member of the RWC. Some of the gripes related to Stauffer's work as a bishop, but fifteen of them focused on the school: the use of a book on sex, clapping after campus programs (which encouraged presenters or performers to be proud), women wearing bandannas instead of coverings, Goshen College speakers at EMS, cooperation with Goshen College, students (women and men) standing behind the pulpit in chapel, and class officers wearing ties, to name a few.[140]

At about the same time, Minister "Curly John" Kurtz wrote a letter to Bishop Rhodes. Kurtz adamantly protested a supplemental text, *Harmony in Marriage*, on library reserve for a Christian family course taught by Professor John R. Mumaw, a minister and the secretary-treasurer of Virginia Conference. Kurtz fussed that the book's description of sex would prompt "lewd, lustful, licentious thinking" in the minds of students whose parents had sent them to EMS to be "guarded and protected" from precisely such abhorrent things.[141]

Within days of Kurtz's letter, John F. Garber, a minister and a son-in-law of the late A. D. Wenger, sent a letter to the RWC. Garber was shocked to find a college library book on pastoral psychology that leveled "a frontal attack on the innocent unsuspecting youth" attending EMS. He also was appalled that John R. Mumaw allegedly condoned telling young children fairytales and myths, which

Garber thought would "pervert their mental appetites."[142] And why, he wondered, was EMS sanctioning women wearing bandannas? The RWC soon banned *Harmony in Marriage* and any other "offensive materials on matters of sex," and it urged the administrative leaders (J. L. Stauffer, J. R. Mumaw, and D. Ralph Hostetter) to stop offering the Christian family course.[143]

These troubles, along with the complexities of operating a surging four-year college and the stressful duties of a bishop—including a bungled ordination he supervised—weighed heavily on the sixty-year-old president.[144] In January 1948, the trustees granted Stauffer a two-year leave of absence for the 1948–1950 school years and appointed forty-four-year-old John R. Mumaw acting president. In December 1949, Stauffer resigned, and a few weeks later, with no fanfare, Mumaw was appointed president, effective July 1, 1950.[145] Having had twenty years to observe him as a faculty member and eighteen months as acting president, the trustees had confidence in Mumaw's educational vision and leadership skills. He was the first alumnus to assume the presidency. In many ways, he was a poster boy for the transformative power of EMS, given his unruly attitude when he first arrived on campus.

A farm boy from Wooster, Ohio, Mumaw had rough edges that required some serious refinement. In the summer of 1920, his mother, Catherine, fretted and prayed about her rebellious son, the youngest of her eleven children. His father had died when he was two, and now the sixteen-year-old was running with a rough crowd in the Smithville public high school. He aspired to be a professional actor—a horrifying thought for a devout Mennonite widow. Over the summer, she gave John two stark choices: drop out of school and run the eighty-acre farm or go to the new Mennonite school in Virginia. One of her older sons advised, "Don't spend any more money on him; he's too far gone!" Over the noon meal on Saturday, August 25, four days before registration at EMS, she asked if he planned to go. "No," he said, "it's too late now." She surprised him by saying she had already mailed his application and arranged for someone to meet him at the Harrisonburg train station at ten o'clock Monday evening. When Mumaw arrived, J. L. Stauffer was on hand to greet him. Smoking a cigarette, Mumaw muttered, "Where is this damn school?" as Stauffer drove the "stinking" boy to campus.[146]

During the fall 1920 revival meetings, Mumaw's name was on the prayer list of "unsaved" students. Eager to rid himself of all the social pressure, he was one of the first to stand and make what he later called "a false confession" of Christian commitment. His remarkable turnabout set off a wave of confessions as more than half the students made new or renewed commitments to Christ. Mumaw, however, soon returned to mischief. Following a tip, President Smith found him and another student "patronizing a back-alley pool room" one afternoon in Harrisonburg. After the students returned to campus, Smith subpoenaed them to a special faculty meeting to explain their transgression. As Mumaw headed down the stairway from the third-floor boy's dorm to the first-floor faculty meeting, he felt like he was descending "into the flames of hell." This frightening image melted his heart, and he confessed his wrongdoings. As punishment, the faculty required a confession the next day in chapel in front of all the students. That night, he "opened his heart to the Lord and with deep penitence, pleaded for mercy and forgiveness," and then made a secret pledge to live for Christ the rest of his life. Mumaw's crisis conversion empowered his lifelong conviction for Christian ministry.[147]

After graduating from the high school in 1922, Mumaw taught elementary school before returning to EMS in 1925 to take college courses and direct the correspondence department. Over the summers, he continued his undergraduate studies at Elizabethtown College, since EMS had no college-level summer courses; also, his girlfriend lived in Lancaster. Within a three-month period in the spring of 1928, Mumaw was ordained a minister in Virginia Conference, received a bachelor of arts degree from Elizabethtown College, and two days later was married to Esther Mosemann, daughter of Lillie and Bishop John Mosemann of Lancaster. The Mumaws raised five daughters on a three-quarter-acre plot with a garden and a cow along South College Avenue in Park View.[148]

After being hired as an EMS faculty member in 1927, Mumaw quickly ascended into administrative roles alongside his teaching of English and Bible courses. He did graduate work in English at the University of Virginia and eventually received a master's in religious education from American Theological Seminary. Mumaw was appointed EMS's first campus pastor in 1941 and gradually shifted his teaching and writing interests to pastoral care and family studies. His gentle manner and gracious ability to transcend conflict engendered trust from his colleagues. A faculty member who knew him well attributed Mumaw's selection as president to his administrative efficiency and dispatch, his relish for work, and his deep dedication to the school and the church. Mumaw's gift of diplomacy and his proficiency as a manager helped him inch the school's culture of indoctrination toward a more liberal arts ethos in a Mennonite world beset by social change. At midcentury, the freshly minted president appeared poised to pivot EMC into a new era.

PART III

Eastern Mennonite *College* and the Big Transformation, 1948–1986

CHAPTER 6

Will the Fortress Stand?

We have a self to discover, to understand, to use.
—Ada M. Zimmerman, dean of women

Can the Fortress Be Reclaimed?

J. R. Mumaw's easy glide to the presidency swerved off course three weeks before
he took office on July 1, 1950. The sudden swerve reflected the spirit of McCarthyism in the national air. US Senator Joe McCarthy's witch hunts—based on false
or incomplete evidence—had accused hundreds of citizens of being communists.
Christian revivalism in the early 1950s, pioneered by evangelist Billy Graham, was
also decidedly anti-Communist. Moreover, the "Red Scare" of this era produced
duck-and-cover exercises in schools to shield students against nuclear bombs.

The suspicious spirit of McCarthyism had already arrived at EMS in 1942. Vir-
ginia Conference organized a one-day hearing on campus to interrogate Orie O.
Miller, general secretary of the Mennonite Central Committee (MCC), the inter-
Mennonite relief agency that administered many of the Mennonite Civilian Public
Service (CPS) camps. Seventeen Virginia Conference members accused MCC and
CPS of collaborating with socialists, communists, liberals, and nonreligious paci-
fists. Their vigorous questioning of Miller produced 117 pages of testimony. Ernest
G. Gehman and "Curly John" Kurtz were two of Miller's leading antagonists.[1]

The suspicion voiced by these arch conservatives resurfaced in 1950 when Virginia Conference met in June. J. L. Stauffer, bishop and outgoing president, made a
surprising motion. He asked the conference to investigate "reported irregularities"
at the recently state-accredited Eastern Mennonite College. Swift approval of the
motion triggered an extensive six-month investigation of Mumaw and the college.[2]
During the investigation, Stauffer continued to serve on the Religious Welfare
Committee (RWC) and on EMC's Administration Committee.

Although students in the late 1940s thought that EMC was tightening regulations, conservative critics thought otherwise. President Mumaw faced twenty

charges spurred by an inquisition that, in his words, cast a "menace of suspicion, misrepresentation, and unkindness" over the school for the next six months—giving him a very awkward presidential welcome.[3] The outcome was fraught with uncertainty. The president might be affirmed—or replaced. The investigators might recommend drastic changes in college personnel and policies. Even worse, they might shutter EMC just as the church had closed Goshen College twenty-six years earlier. The memory of that closure hung heavily over the investigation.

The investigation committee consisted of twenty-six men—sixteen trustees, five members of the RWC, and five members of the conference executive committee. The work of the committee and its four subcommittees involved some thirty days of time, not counting individual meetings, fact-finding, and document preparation, all of which consumed thousands of person-hours. The crisis continued until January 1951, when Virginia Conference called a special two-day session.

Three weeks after Mumaw took office on July 1, 1950, the three-person steering committee directing the investigation listened to thirty-two complainants at a two-day hearing.[4] The presenters included ordained officials, out-of-state leaders, faculty members, and alumni. J. R. Mumaw and C. K. Lehman did not attend the hearing, but J. L. Stauffer did. The presenters offered 130 statements—all but five of which were negative. After the hearing, charges were filed against nine people. John R. Mumaw received twenty and C. K. Lehman ten. Seven other faculty and staff members faced one or more accusations. Additional charges were aimed at the institution as a whole. The four subcommittees developed recommendations that the investigation committee sent to Virginia Conference for action.

What had so quickly gone awry? The conference had recently approved a new college constitution. EMC's rapid growth and new state certification promised a bright future. From all appearances, the sudden inquisition was prompted by Mumaw's appointment as president. Once again, he had become a poster boy for the school—not as a hero of spiritual transformation, but as a closet liberal who some feared would lead the school astray. Yet the discontent driving the investigation was much deeper and more complicated than it appeared. The cord of truth had seven strands.

The Seven Strands

A Generational Shift

A major generational shift in leadership was under way. Most of the founders had passed on: L. J. Heatwole in 1932, A. D. Wenger in 1935, George R. Brunk and John Mosemann in 1938, Daniel Kauffman in 1944, and Noah Mack in 1948. J. B. Smith would die within a year, in 1951. The influence of C. K. Lehman and J. L. Stauffer, who had molded the institution from the start, was waning, although Lehman remained dean until 1956.[5]

A new generation of men contending for leadership included two sons and a son-in-law of Bishop George R. Brunk who were ministers: Truman Brunk (b. 1902), George R. Brunk II (b. 1911), and J. Ward Shank (b. 1904). Later ordained bishop, Truman Brunk was moderator of Virginia Conference during the 1950 investigation. With the stately stature and persuasive voice of his father, George Brunk II was appointed assistant professor of Christian education and practical theology at EMC in 1949. J. Ward Shank, an EMC trustee, was also secretary of Virginia Conference.

Yearning for the Past

George Brunk II, J. Ward Shank, Ernest G. Gehman, and John Kurtz were articulate critics of EMC. They, along with other handwringers, lamented EMC's drift away from the "founding fathers" who, in the words of George Brunk II, had provided "rigid and constant . . . oversight." Ernest G. Gehman wanted to "*return*" to the founders' original "purpose and principles." At the two-day hearing, EMC trustee Henry M. Shenk asked, "How can we *regain* the lost ground?" George Brunk II avowed, "We must take whatever steps are necessary to *recover* it."[6] Pleas to recover, return, and regain underscored the loyalists' nostalgia for "old EMS," as well as their desire to retain the fortress resting on its indoctrination-separation paradigm. This was the last chance for conservatives to turn EMC back to the principles of its mythic past.

Loss of Conference Control

If J. R. Mumaw had been in the room when the trustees elected him president in January 1950, he would have had cause to worry. One trustee reported that "some people" think the conference had "only very remote control over selecting the president" since the revised constitution (1947) gave that authority to the trustee executive committee.[7] That sense of loss helped ignite the investigation. Still, the issue ran deeper. John Kurtz said, "EMC purports to be controlled by the conference, but it's not." For the disenfranchised like Kurtz, the conference had lost the reins of its runaway school. Virginia Conference, declared George Brunk II, "must recover its grasp" of the school and strengthen its "teaching and indoctrination."

Worldly Ties

As the critics lamented the loss of church control, they also groused that EMC was affiliating with national professional organizations and cooperating with colleges like Bridgewater, Goshen, and nearby Madison. Conservatives were especially perturbed that the college was seeking accreditation from the Southern Association of Colleges and Schools (SACS). In their mind, the word *association* violated biblical injunctions against being "unequally yoked" with secular organizations (2 Cor. 6:14). Since EMC already had state certification, the detractors feared that the college would soon be serving a worldly professional association instead of the church. College officials, on the other hand, argued that accreditation was necessary for graduates to enter medical school and other graduate programs.[8] That the flak about professional accreditation came after the conference had approved EMC's plan to apply to SACS suggested that a small minority was pushing the investigation.[9]

Big and Professional

The complainants were unhappy with EMC's rapid growth. They thought the school had become too big too fast and too professional too quickly. It had become, in a word, a bureaucracy with specialized roles, job descriptions, and a hierarchy. Recently, EMC had appointed a paid "field secretary" for development, a director of admissions, and an office of public affairs. The catalog, for the first time in 1949–1950, listed "fancy" titles for faculty that included their ranks, such as assistant professor and associate professor. In the minds of conservatives, the string of degrees and titles behind the names reflected worldly symbols of power and prestige typical of secular colleges. John R. Mumaw, at the request of the faculty, had written a paper distinguishing cultural titles used in educational and secular settings from religious titles used for sacred occasions.[10] The new tone diminished the egalitarian ethos of the 1920s, when "brother" and "sister" were commonly used.

Demise of Nonconformity

Many of the issues raised by the investigation focused on the erosion of nonconformity. Six years earlier, the Mennonite Church had called a special three-day conference to address the breakdown of plain attire across the church.[11] Nearly three hundred ordained leaders, including six bishops and sixteen ministers from Virginia Conference, had attended the meeting. One resolution threatened to exclude members from communion—and expel them—if they persisted in holding life insurance, joining labor unions, donning immodest and worldly attire, wearing jewelry and wedding rings, and attending movies. Thus the allegations of declining safeguards at EMC mirrored, in some ways, a national Mennonite trend.

The investigators heard a litany of concerns about worldliness creeping onto the campus: accepting too many "incorrigible and disobedient" students, permitting women and unordained men to speak from the pulpit, allowing a woman to edit the *Journal*, training young women to be bold, condoning sports and competitive games, relaxing requirements that women wear black hose, permitting outrageous bandannas, permitting the girls' octet to wear worldly clothing, giving chapel talks on modesty instead of on plain attire, hiring new faculty who were disloyal to church standards, permitting worldly magazines in the library, using too many photographs in college publications, allowing too many special music groups, kneeling less for prayer, making fun of plain clothing, inviting outside speakers who questioned conservative values, and creating a climate where fewer men wore plain suits.

A Conspiracy?

The investigation offered intrigue for conspiracy theorists. An odd pattern emerged at the two-day hearing in July 1950. Four of the thirty-two men who spoke uttered half (48 percent) of all the words. Who were these talkative men, and why were they talking so much? In order of verbiage, they were J. Ward Shank, George Brunk II, Henry M. Shenk, and Ernest G. Gehman. All were ministers except Shenk. The quartet shared a conservative mind-set and a close connection to the late Bishop George R. Brunk.

J. Ward Shank, married to Stella Brunk, was one of Brunk's sons-in-law. Shank became an associate editor of the *Sword and Trumpet* in 1943. At the time of the investigation, he was serving as secretary of the conference, which placed him on the investigation committee. George Brunk II was the bishop's son. Henry M. Shenk, who lived in Denbigh, was a son-in-law of the bishop by his marriage to Esther Brunk. Ernest G. Gehman, erstwhile Goshen critic, German teacher, and cartoonist for the *Sword and Trumpet*, had worked closely with Bishop Brunk, whom he highly respected. All four men held official positions with the *Sword and Trumpet*: Brunk and Shank were associate editors, Gehman was the office editor, and Henry M. Shenk was the circulation manager. During the investigation, Shenk wrote a lead article that posed concerns about EMC's ties to the church.[12]

Of the four men, George Brunk II would have been the only one qualified to be president when Mumaw was appointed in January 1950. Brunk held a bachelor's degree in theology from EMS, a bachelor of arts from the College of William and Mary, and a bachelor of divinity from Union Theological Seminary in Richmond. The namesake of the late influential bishop, young George had the persona, conservative convictions, and grasp of his father's vision to make EMC, in his words, "a powerhouse for conservatism." The thirty-nine-year-old Brunk was the only viable Virginian—and the conservatives preferred a president from Virginia.

Defendants Exonerated

Shortly after the hearings in July 1950, the four subcommittees prepared proposals to improve administrative practices and repair the school's relationship with the conference. Simultaneously, the steering committee informed J. R. Mumaw, C. K. Lehman, and the seven other faculty members of the charges against them. Allegations against Mumaw included teaching his Christian family course against the advice of the RWC, actively cooperating with liberal church-wide Mennonite organizations, permitting a student who played competitive sports to lead a youth Bible meeting, being a liberal and supporting liberals (thus tarnishing EMC's conservative reputation), hiring a male faculty member with weak convictions on plain clothing, insinuating that the regulation garb had no scriptural grounds, refusing to stop the decline of dress standards, being self-willed, and displaying a spirit of determination. None of the charges pertained directly to Mumaw's vision for EMC, his management skills, or his presidential qualifications. In a fourteen-page document, Mumaw refuted the charges and declared that he had always supported the decisions of Virginia Conference.[13]

The accusations against C. K. Lehman were about his biblical interpretation of war in the Old Testament and the miracles of Jesus and his use of new translations of the Bible rather than the King James Version. One critic called him a liberal. Other grousers said Lehman's popularity with Goshen-area Mennonites maligned EMC's reputation. And finally, they alleged that he had permitted a "brother to teach Sunday school who wears a tie." Lehman promptly rebutted the ten allegations.[14]

The tepid charges against the other men—Milton G. Brackbill, John Hiestand, B. Charles Hostetter, Paul Martin, Ira Miller, Nevin Miller, and J. Otis Yoder—pertained to their views of Calvinism, remarriage after divorce, and nonconformity. All of the individuals facing charges wrote responses and met with the steering committee in late August. In its interrogation of the nine men, the committee pleaded for a "spirit of charity" and hoped that any "animosity" would not dissuade them from taking communion.[15]

During the fall of 1950, the steering committee developed its report for the special session of Virginia Conference in January.[16] Those deliberations produced four significant outcomes. With the exception of Paul Martin and Milton Brackbill, all defendants were exonerated of the charges against them for lack of sufficient evidence. Martin, a recently hired faculty member, was asked to meet with the RWC to confirm his appointment. Brackbill, an instructor in the Special Bible Term, was dismissed for questioning certain church teachings.[17] J. Irvin Lehman, editor in chief of the *Sword and Trumpet* and a Special Bible Term teacher, was cleared of charges but voluntarily resigned because he had relayed some of Brackbill's views to the investigators and felt responsible for "the dismissal of a beloved colleague."[18]

Eleven recommendations involved operational tweaks that Mumaw considered doable, such as replacing the pulpit with a podium for student speakers in chapel and having the president be an ex officio consultant to—rather than a member of—the RWC. Eight additional recommendations were woven into a constitutional revision in 1952. One required conference approval of future presidential appointments.[19] After endorsing the final report in January 1951, the conference gave EMC, Mumaw, and the faculty "a vote of confidence and moral support." These outcomes vexed the conservatives who had hoped to remove Mumaw from office and rein in what they considered to be an unbridled school.

A Wedge of Estrangement

The records do not reveal why former president J. L. Stauffer called for an investigation. Perhaps he hoped it would rid the air of false rumors so that Mumaw's new administration could more easily lift off the runway. Mumaw was, after all, the cigarette-smoking rebel Stauffer had met at the train station in 1920 and mentored into a superb administrator. Although the investigation ostensibly pointed to Mumaw's fitness for the presidency, it also was a referendum on Stauffer's own tenure as president. If Stauffer considered the flak against the school unfounded and frivolous, he may have thought that the investigation—which dredged up debris about his own presidency—would purify his legacy. If so, he succeeded, given that most of the charges were dropped and the general direction of the school was affirmed. Alternatively, given the widespread unrest, Stauffer may have wanted to seize the moment before certain critics initiated a conference-driven investigation *independent* of the trustees. Stauffer had astutely included the trustees on the investigation committee. An independent investigation might have rapped the college harder and led to a schism. If any or all of these motivations were true, Stauffer's ploy succeeded, to the dismay of the most vociferous critics.

The special conference that affirmed EMC ended on Thursday, January 18, 1951. The next evening, Stauffer, in his roles as a bishop and member of the RWC, reported the results to the faculty. Later that evening, EMC's Administration Committee (Stauffer, Mumaw, Lehman, and D. Ralph Hostetter) called an emergency meeting at the request of George Brunk II. The second-year professor asked if his brother-in-law J. Ward Shank could attend as a witness. The committee agreed. Brunk stated that he wanted to "terminate his services on the faculty immediately." He was "quite unhappy," because Stauffer's report to the faculty had portrayed "the entire investigation as useless and unnecessary." The critics who brought charges were depicted, in Brunk's eyes, "as a bunch of gripers, a bunch of belly-achers," and so the "charges evaporated." Furthermore, he maintained, Stauffer had not distinguished between "false charges" and those "not sustained." Both Mumaw and Lehman considered an immediate termination a breach of contract that would also stir gossip about Brunk, and in the end, he did not resign.[20]

The following Wednesday, J. L. Stauffer again addressed the faculty. This time he read a short report of the investigation's conclusions and clarified the different types of critics. "We can all rejoice," he said, because the investigation had not ended like the one that closed Goshen College. Moreover, he called EMC's investigation a good "clearinghouse" that would have the "wholesome effect" of improving church-college relations.[21]

In June 1951, George Brunk II resigned from his faculty position to engage in full-time evangelistic work.[22] That decision was made easier because, on June 3, George and his brother Lawrence started a spectacularly successful seven-week evangelistic tent revival in Lancaster, Pennsylvania. Thousands attended each evening. Attendance peaked at fifteen thousand on the final night. This and dozens of other tent revivals in Mennonite communities into the 1980s produced decisions for Christ and brought spiritual renewal to thousands of Mennonites and their neighbors.[23] Brunk's fruitful evangelistic campaigns could not have flourished had he stayed at EMC.

Forty years later, Mumaw insinuated that Brunk, with the support of friends, had aspired to the presidency in 1950, a claim confirmed by other sources. Mimicking Brunk's booming voice, Mumaw reported that someone came to him shortly after the investigation and declared, "Twenty charges and we couldn't make one of them stick, I just don't understand this." Asked if that was Brunk, Mumaw just smiled and mused, "We're pretty good friends now."[24]

On the floor of Virginia Conference in June 1951, conservative critics of EMU tried again to press their issues, but with no success. This time, in Mumaw's words, "a deliberate and stalwart majority" stood by EMC. For himself, Mumaw felt an "obligation to the Lord" and to the "conference whom we serve . . . to move on," regardless of the naysayers.[25] Still, his pain remained.

In March 1952, President Mumaw reached out to Bishop Truman Brunk, son of the late Bishop George R. Brunk, who had chaired the steering committee. Mumaw remained distressed, he confided to Brunk, that so many people had escaped without any consequence after submitting false accusations, stirring up strife, repeating gossip, disobeying the teachings of the conference and the Gospel, and committing other kindred sins. "Some of us who were falsely accused heard no apologies after the vindication," Mumaw mourned. "Will the wedge of estrangement between the college and conference remain? Will no one dare to tell the truth about EMC . . . to counterbalance the far spread rumors that embarrass us so frequently?"[26]

Despite all the pain, the investigation did clear the path for Mumaw's presidency. It avoided a serious schism, silenced the most conservative critics, clarified

The evangelistic tent revival led by brothers George Brunk II and Lawrence Brunk in Lancaster, Pennsylvania, 1951. Their slogan was "The Whole Gospel for the Whole World."

EMC's vision of Mennonite higher education, and gave the school more freedom to become a liberal arts college. In place of the preacher-farmer leaders of the first three decades, a new generation of professional educators now shouldered the task of shaping the school's growth in a changing church and modernizing society.

Will Mennonites Survive?

Anyone who had chuckled at A. D. Wenger's nostalgia for rural life when he told graduates to "go back to the farm" in 1935 was oblivious to the rural life movement that had been thriving in America since about 1915. Rather than looking back, Wenger was on the cusp of a crusade to resuscitate rural Mennonite communities. That call to action came from Guy F. Hershberger, a historian at Goshen College, in 1939. Hershberger held up the rural Mennonite community as an antidote to large-scale industrial-labor conflicts laced with hard-fisted power and violence.[27] Melvin Gingerich, a historian at Bethel College, soon joined Hershberger in the rural life campaign. Both men had grown up in Amish Mennonite communities in Iowa and held PhDs. These well-educated men—apparently longing for an idyllic Amish past—were urging Mennonites not to discard their plows, though the professors themselves had already done just that.

In their minds, Mennonite survival was at stake. Gingerich, in 1942, argued that "Mennonites are a rural people . . . who must preserve their rural life in order to survive." He cited studies showing that birth rates drop as people move to the city. "To escape possible extinction," Mennonites should stay on the farm, wrote Gingerich. Besides, "close-knit religious communities" are the best places to nurture "simplicity and nonresistance."[28] Bethel College professor J. Winfield Fretz, a farm boy from eastern Pennsylvania with a PhD in sociology, also joined the bandwagon. Hershberger, Gingerich, Fretz, and others convened the first Conference on Mennonite Cultural Problems in 1942 to address the scary scenario that "Mennonites as a cultural group [would] undoubtedly become extinct" if their assimilation into American society continued unabated.[29]

Hershberger argued that the "genius of Mennonitism" was its small religious communities that encapsulated a culture—a total way of life. Mennonite proponents of rural life pitted its virtues against urbanism, industrialism, and individualism. These forces, rather than theological liberalism, had become the new bogeyman threatening to exterminate the church. For Hershberger, Mennonites had always given their "most effective testimony" as a group, not as individuals.[30] The threat of Mennonite extinction fired enough passion to form the Mennonite Community Association in 1946. It published the *Mennonite Community*, a magazine edited by one of Hershberger's students, Grant Stoltzfus, an Amish Mennonite from eastern Pennsylvania. An EMS graduate and future EMC professor, Stoltzfus, who had married George and Katie Brunk's daughter Ruth in 1941, was engaged in Civilian Public Service in Maryland in 1943.[31]

But not all EMC students were enthralled by the call to rural life. In 1947, the *Journal* editor declared, "God has room in His plan for more occupations than

EMC's campus remained remarkably rural into the 1950s.

farming." The editorial was followed by five essays on Mennonites and the Big Apple, with titles such as "New York City—Queen of Commerce," "Churches of New York," and "Midnight on Manhattan."[32]

The high school had always offered one course in agriculture. It listed two in 1942 and then doubled the number to four in 1946 when it hired a full-time instructor. Dean Lehman hoped this move would "give boys a new vision of farming."[33] Agriculture got another bump up in 1952 when the college leased a local farm, sponsored a rural life week, and offered four courses in agriculture. After 1959, the college dropped agriculture but continued to offer rural sociology and Mennonite community courses taught by Grant Stoltzfus.[34] These courses taught students how to think about rural life but not how to live it.

Throughout the 1940s and 1950s, a social disruption rumbled across the Mennonite landscape as a steady stream of young people left the farm for college. A study of six thousand Mennonites in 1954 revealed that 50 percent of the men were farmers. Not all EMC students lived on farms, but in the mid-1950s, 85 percent of them came from rural areas and small towns.[35] No matter how many agricultural courses EMC offered, students had little appetite for farming. Though 54 percent of first-year students in the years 1951 to 1954 hailed from farms, only 3 percent had any interest in plowing. They came to EMC to pursue occupations in education (32 percent), medicine/nursing (18 percent), Christian service (16 percent), missions (6 percent), and various others.[36] Mennonite youth interested in farming stayed at home or enrolled at land-grant universities like Penn State, which offered full-fledged majors in agriculture.

The demise of the *Mennonite Community* magazine in 1954 marked the end of the rural life movement. It fizzled for several reasons. The pleas of Mennonite professors were no match for the Goliath of modernization that was revamping Mennonite occupations. Academic studies of rural communities, initiated by scholars, offered no compelling motivation to live in rural areas. Besides, the predictions of the doomsayers in the early 1940s were faltering. By 1955, the Mennonite Church was thriving and the number of college-age students was expected to grow in the next ten years to more than nine thousand.[37]

The rural life movement slowly shifted away from farming and toward an emphasis on community as a church-centered web of life—economic, social, cultural, and educational—that promised to perpetuate Mennonite peoplehood. This change inscribed the concept of community into Mennonite consciousness and identity in new ways. The word *community*—with its multitude of meanings—first appeared in EMC's statement of purpose in 1955, just as rural-based Mennonite communities were slowly dissolving.[38] The use of the word paralleled Benedict Anderson's notion of "imagined communities," which posits that people have a sense of being tied together with others across the country based on the traits, beliefs, and values they imagine they all share.[39] References to this imagined *community* gradually replaced words such as *church* and *brotherhood*, which had been generously sprinkled throughout EMS documents since 1917.

Before its demise, the Mennonite rural life movement supported an EMC project promoted by *Mennonite Community* editor Grant Stoltzfus. The Mennonite Community Association published *Mennonite Community Cookbook* in 1950. It was compiled by Mary Emma Showalter, who in 1957 would be the first woman on the faculty to earn a doctorate. With the help of 125 women in US and Canadian communities, Showalter gathered 5,000 recipes and selected 1,100 for the cookbook. The volume sold more than a half million copies, making it the all-time bestseller of any book published by an EMU faculty member. This grandmother of all Mennonite cookbooks, stocked in virtually every Mennonite home, testified to the common fare that helped bind the changing Mennonite community together, even as many youth fled the farm. Upon hearing plans for a revision of the book, one person snorted, "You mean you would mess with god herself?," alluding to the book's iconic stature in the last half of the twentieth century.[40]

Professionalizing Everything and Everyone

English professor Hubert Pellman called John R. Mumaw "[EMC's] first professional president because after he came, we had an agenda at faculty meetings."[41] The first four years of Mumaw's presidency (1948–1952) brought a burst of professional activity that reached far beyond agendas. The faculty conference that opened the 1951–1952 year featured four presentations on professional improvement.[42] EMC teachers, now turned professors, performed professional roles with specified privileges and duties. This required recalibrating the salary scale to academic degrees. Sabbaticals, tenure, retirement funds, and health insurance became part of the

Mary Emma Showalter in her kitchen, with *Mennonite Community Cookbook* on the shelf.

faculty package. The college established a "*professional* fund to attend *professional* meetings and purchase *professional* literature."[43]

Professor Irvin B. Horst, the new director of research, conducted seminars for the faculty exploring questions such as these: What is the difference between pure and applied research? Should we have a scientific attitude? Does doing research make better teachers?[44] For the first time, faculty members began attending the professional conferences of academic organizations: the National Council of English Teachers, the Classical Languages Association, the American Association of Physics Teachers, and the American Association for the Advancement of Science. Likewise, administrators began attending their own set of professional conferences. By 1958, EMC's thirty-four faculty members held ninety-one memberships in sixty-eight learned and professional societies. Seven faculty members held doctorates, and twenty-three held master's degrees plus additional study.[45]

EMC joined national organizations such as the American Association of Collegiate Registrars and Admission Officers and the Association of American Colleges. The college also began participating in the national College Sophomore Testing Program and other educational services. In another example of professional development, the college purchased copies of *How to Be a Good Small College* for faculty and board members.[46]

Since good small colleges hired consultants, EMC invited a University of Virginia professor to Harrisonburg to explain how to prepare a self-assessment for its first SACS application. Another way of learning how to operate a college was to scrutinize successful ones. Campus pastor B. Charles Hostetter did so in a visit to Wheaton College in Illinois. EMC staff also wrote to several colleges seeking advice on a range of issues, including how to remunerate faculty for out-of-class activities related to student clubs, committee work, and choral groups. In recognition of its status as a state-certified college, EMC began receiving invitations to attend inaugurals and celebrations at other colleges. Dean Lehman attended the festivities for the new president at Madison College in Harrisonburg.

Greater interaction with other colleges brought to campus a growing number of professional speakers and lecturers who did not have Mennonite connections or any religious affiliation. The new ties with other colleges and professional organizations had spun EMC into a new orbit of American higher education. Such intercollegiate ties, routine for most colleges, had not been the norm for EMC until Mumaw's presidency. Gone, apparently, were any worries about the historic Mennonite taboo on being yoked to secular organizations. EMC's new posture defied what President Stauffer had once told the president of Mary Baldwin College: "[EMS] *prohibits* inter-institutional cooperation of any kind" except with Mennonite schools.[47] The walls of the old fortress were crumbling, and crumbling quickly.

EMC's professional aspirations stimulated a new institutional self-awareness that produced a string of self-studies beginning with the Religious Welfare Survey from 1947 to 1949.[48] This massive examination of religion in every crevice of the campus was coordinated by the Mennonite Board of Education as a comparative research project with Hesston and Goshen Colleges.[49] The research effort inventoried dozens of religious activities and surveyed students and faculty. For example, 25 percent of the students rated the chapel services "excellent," and 33 percent gave the same score to Friday morning devotions.[50]

The process of collecting this cache of religious life data reflected modern thinking and methods. The project included "a survey of the objectives, degrees of success in spiritual life, promotion of Christian ideals, [and] devotion to Mennonite principles, [in the] *production of* workers for the church." With scientific scrutiny, the study measured and analyzed all aspects of religious life and quantified the results. The project produced EMC's first formal philosophy of Christian education. The study required faculty to establish clear objectives for all the religious activities and describe the "*techniques* designed to meet these *objectives* . . . and the *conditioning factors* which militate against achieving the goals."[51] Furthermore, faculty members were to list the "Religious Objectives and the Ways and the Means of Realizing Objectives" for all courses in the curriculum, both religious and nonreligious. One of the three religious objectives for analytical geometry, for example, was "to show that God is a God of numbers as well as of love."[52]

Two things jut out of the Religious Welfare study. First, the language and assumptions of modern, rational analysis underlaid the entire two-hundred-page document, attesting to the acceptance of a more scientific worldview by faculty and administrators. Second, religion—of all things—was placed under the microscope in this social laboratory. Religious faith was treated as an external object for study and analysis. For the first time in EMC's history, faculty and administrators stepped back and specified in a clear-minded way how religion was being taught and practiced at the school—a somewhat risky venture for any college hoping to preserve a venerated faith tradition.

The shift toward professionalism was also a shift of allegiance—a tilt away from Virginia Conference and the authority of ordained clergy with few academic credentials. Perplexed about how to rank faculty, the Administration Committee simply "followed the policy and standards of SACS."[53] Professional administrators and university-trained faculty were now taking charge of EMC. For advice, they turned to various higher education consortiums, scholarly societies, regional accreditation associations, and eventually to professional associations for accrediting academic programs such as nursing and social work.

Several factors drove the rapid professionalization. With the conclusion of the 1950 investigation, EMC was freer to move into new collegiate alliances, and a new cadre of university-trained faculty was eager to pursue professional development. Faculty members longing for change were suddenly allowed to flourish. More than these, the aspiration for SACS accreditation sped the embrace of professionalism. As EMC administrators and faculty developed new collegiate contacts, they eagerly adopted practices from other colleges and professional societies. EMC also benefited from widespread national efforts to professionalize higher education after World War II.

A Radio Reversal

Technology is arguably the primary torque of modernization.[54] Cautious about the impact of new technology on education, EMS always had to sort out the devices that it deemed would help or harm its mission. When the newly hired M. T. Brackbill arrived at the Harrisonburg train station in March 1919, H. N. Troyer drove him to campus in the "EMS jitney." The school, Brackbill exclaimed, "couldn't have gotten along without that flivver," a Model T Ford.[55] Although a visiting speaker once called cars a great curse for breaking down the hedge of separation from the world, EMS expressed no reservations about motor vehicles.

For the rest of its history, the school would readily embrace *utilitarian* technology—motor vehicles, electricity, telephones, hectographs, binoculars, and state-of-the-art equipment in science laboratories. In step with national trends, the college acquired its first computer, an IBM 1130, in 1968 thanks to a grant from the National Science Foundation. (Administrative computing consumed the machine's total capacity during the day, deferring all instructional work to the evenings.)[56] Leaders were more hesitant, however, to adopt technologies of *consumption* (such as radios, television, and films), which transmitted outside ideas and values to consumers, and technologies of *performance* (like musical instruments), which were designed for an audience. The lines among these three types of technology, which were never completely clear, would become quite murky with the rise of the Internet in the twenty-first century.

EMS banned radios in 1922, shortly after the first broadcast aired in the country. Uncertain if a "wireless" fit within EMS's stance on separatism, the faculty consulted the RWC. Bishop Brunk squashed it in a single sentence: "I vote BIG against one at the school."[57] Leaders feared that radios would become a pipeline to the voices of popular culture. The trustees even nixed a shortwave radio—constructed by a student to enable Professor Brackbill's new telescope to receive a daily signal from Arlington set to the exact celestial time—because they feared it would open the door to conventional radios.[58]

EMS's ban on the radio was buttressed by Virginia Conference's own taboo on radios. Beginning in 1936, church members who had radios were expelled, though this stirred so much acrimony and defection that the conference lifted the prohibition in 1944. President Stauffer, bishop of the Northern District, was embroiled in the radio conflict, which stiffened EMS's stance against the device.[59] Even so, the debate continued among students. Mocking the school's taboo on radios, a clique of boys enjoyed some chuckles when the Grand Old Opry radio show, at their request, dedicated two songs to J. L. Stauffer.

Beginning in 1948, radios were allowed on campus, but they were not permitted in dormitories. Nonetheless, several students had concocted homemade radios (with earphones to prevent detection) capable of receiving messages from Harrisonburg, which they kept in dormitory hideaways. This continued until radios were permitted in dormitories in 1955.[60] In the early years of his presidency, J. R. Mumaw received a record player–radio console from a friend. To avoid offending anyone, Mumaw removed the radio tube and only played recordings of religious music. When he traveled overnight, however, his mischievous daughters replaced the radio tube so that they could listen to their favorite programs.[61]

The Virginia radio saga took several ironic twists. Within eight years of the conference lifting the ban in 1944, a group of Virginia Mennonites started *The Mennonite Hour*, which grew into a national radio ministry. The format included a sermon by campus pastor B. Charles Hostetter and singing by students and faculty. *The Mennonite Hour* evolved from a 1950 foray into broadcasting by a male quartet of EMC students known as the Crusaders. The four managed to arrange free air time for a weekly fifteen-minute program on a local radio station. That same year, alumna Ruth Brunk Stoltzfus started *Heart to Heart*, a daily radio program for women. That a woman—the daughter of the bishop who voted a "BIG" no to the radio—had her own program airing on twenty-four stations in nineteen states by 1956 was a remarkable feat.[62]

In 1954, the college allowed students to organize a chorus to sing for radio programs.[63] That same year, a gift from the senior class prodded the college to establish its own ten-watt FM radio station. But WEMC's weak signal "could barely get off campus on a windy day," quipped Jim Bishop.[64] In 1957, the Promethean literary society presented a radio adaptation of the Dickens novel *A Tale of Two Cities* on WEMC with creative sound effects. Shocked constituents protested, abruptly ending dramatic shows on WEMC.[65] The station aimed to provide educational programming beyond the campus, enhance student education, and improve public relations—all the while providing "good listening" options for the public. It was the 124th educational radio station in the country and the first one in the state of

Virginia. WEMC could only air vocal programs and recordings, however, until instrumental music was permitted in 1962.[66]

In a turnabout, Bishop J. L. Stauffer was delighted that Virginia Conference had approved *Heart to Heart*, that the college had established WEMC, and that thirty-two US stations plus several in other countries were soon airing *The Mennonite Hour*. Stauffer prayed that these efforts would "contribute to the salvation of many unsaved" around the world.[67] Some thirty years after the greatly feared radio had been banned by EMS to keep the world at bay, it was converted into a tool for a worldwide Christian witness.

Victrolas, Movies, and Musical Instruments

In March 1947, J. L. Stauffer asked the RWC for permission to use a Victrola (record player) for a music appreciation course. He explained how the machine was similar to a Dictaphone but quite different from musical instruments like "a piano, organ, or orchestra." A month later, the five bishops on the RWC approved a Victrola as "laboratory equipment" for the music program. At the same meeting, they allowed EMC to purchase a "motion picture machine" similar to the long-used balopticon (forerunner of the overhead projector), which projected still images. The new projector for moving pictures was also labeled "laboratory equipment" and placed under strict supervision.[68] Obtaining conference approval seemed superfluous since the RWC (with five of Virginia's seven bishops) had already signed off and EMC's constitution did not prohibit these devices.

That ostensible approval, however, soon fizzled. Unfortunately for EMC administrators, the Victrola and the movie projector became entangled in a political storm in June 1947 when Virginia Conference lifted the ban on musical instruments for ministers. In that action, the conference declared itself "firmly opposed" to any use of musical instruments "in our schools." Surprisingly, many people viewed the record player as a musical instrument. So six months later, C. K. Lehman appealed to the RWC once again for permission to purchase a record player for music education. He contended that the record player was not a musical instrument, because many ordained ministers had owned one at the time instruments were forbidden in homes. The RWC did not have the gumption to fight this battle alone, so in June 1948, it bounced the issue back to the conference, which put the decision in limbo for five years.[69]

Meanwhile, as the 1950 investigation heated up, EMC's Administration Committee approved a work-around: faculty members could use a record player if they taught classes in their homes. In 1952, the trustee executive committee patiently masked its exasperation with the five-year hiatus in a lengthy plea to the RWC. For the third time, school officials argued that the record player was not a musical instrument but an educational device useful in various classes to learn bird calls, teach new languages, hear dialects, and learn the songs of African Americans and American Indians. Prodded by this plea, the conference approved the use of record players except in worship services.[70]

Recorders, by contrast, faced little resistance. They did not import foreign content as record players did but instead served the utilitarian purpose of preserving sermons, archiving conference proceedings, and recording dictation. Since the 1920s, teachers had been permitted to project photographs (from slides) on a screen in their classes. However, slides could not be projected in the chapel auditorium until the late 1940s. Both educational filmstrips shown by teachers and slides shown by non-Mennonite speakers required approval on a case-by-case basis.[71]

Since the 1920s, EMS had lambasted popular movies in its litany of worldly evils. Not surprisingly, motion pictures were the most controversial of media throughout the late 1940s and mid-1950s. The motion picture machine, which the RWC approved in 1947, was never used because of the confusion swirling around the Victrola. With the 1950 investigation and a dire conference statement in 1948 warning of the dangers of films, EMC administrators had no appetite to seek conference approval for films until 1956.[72]

That year Virginia Conference established the Audio-Visual Aids Committee to preview motion picture films for schools, churches, and social groups. The conference opposed watching films "purely [for] entertainment . . . [or] in worship services" and steamed against the "so-called gospel or religious movies," which it called a totally "inadequate substitute" for preaching. Virginia Conference also intensified its protest "against the commercial movies which use war, bloodshed, violence, sex, crime, romance, and heathen savagery to appeal to the depraved human nature."[73] Many Mennonite leaders worried that educational films would be the turnstile for watching Hollywood movies in theaters.

The film review process was tedious. Faculty members hoping to show a film had to obtain it and then receive approval by the three-member Audio-Visual Aids Committee plus a college administrator. In a single academic year, the committee met 57 times and spent 97 hours previewing 224 films. They approved 137. In a five-year period, the committee reviewed 853 films. But the small committee was no match for the avalanche of films flowing from the burgeoning movie industry. In 1961, the new conference-appointed Audiovisual *Advisory* Committee allowed EMC to judge which films were appropriate for instruction. Already in 1959, films were shown once a month on campus to a general student audience for educational purposes, and later, Saturday night films became a regular feature of social life on campus.[74]

Television was the last technology of consumption EMC resisted. Virginia Conference had warned about "the great threat of television" as early as 1949. Still smarting from the radio reversal, the conference decided to aggressively "build up a conscience" against television rather than threatening to expel members who owned one.[75] As a bishop, J. L. Stauffer had no interest in "making TV a test of membership and going through the mess we did with the radio."[76] On campus, the size of televisions made them more difficult than radios to conceal in dormitory hideaways. Nonetheless, two enterprising students acquired a used console television that was about four feet high with a nine-inch screen. They transported "the old trunk from home" on the freight elevator to the men's dormitory on the third floor of the administration building, where it resided happily for a time, though it was eventually seized.[77] After twenty years of resistance, the first approved television set appeared in the student center lounge in 1970.

EMC resisted the use of musical instruments for performance for nearly fifty years (1914–1962)—longer than any other technology. A draft constitution for the Alexandria Mennonite Institute intoned, "Music instruments shall not form any part of the equipment of the school." That sparse sentence remained embedded in the constitution until 1962, when the conference decreed that instruments could be used for "recreational activities and technical studies," but not for "artistic or professional use." As early as 1948, the college permitted students to play personal instruments in the recreation room.[78]

Why did the resistance persist for five decades? Sacred rituals, especially worship practices, are the last to crumble under the pressure of social change. Musical instruments were considered a threat to the quality and persistence of congregational singing. A cappella singing was an egalitarian exercise where all members, regardless of musical talent, could make a joyful noise to their Creator. Congregational singing fortified group solidarity and affirmed community. Apart from the fear that instruments would diminish vigorous singing was the concern that they spotlighted individual skill and performance. Besides, four-part a cappella singing had been tightly entwined with Swiss-German

Chorale performance without instrumental accompaniment in the basement chapel of the Ad Building, ca. 1942.

Mennonite identity since the late nineteenth century. Virginia Conference called it "[our] peculiar treasure." EMC music instructor J. Mark Stauffer was even more explicit when he named singing "our priceless heritage . . . that must be defended and promoted or else we will lose our identity in the vast sea of professional Christianity."[79]

An event in the fall of 1956 tested the musical boundaries. Some restless students formed a new literary society called the Prometheans. In Greek mythology, the god Prometheus called fire down from heaven, and the Prometheans hoped to fire things up a bit on campus. They rehearsed *The Legend of Sleepy Hollow*, a musical with piano accompaniment, at an off-campus home authorized by the college. Then, moving the piano from place to place, they presented the musical three times to packed audiences—twice at the *Mennonite Hour* studio and once in a local barn. The music faculty boycotted the performances, but to the delight of the Prometheans, the new campus pastor, Myron Augsburger, attended.[80]

Tired of shuffling pianos around off-campus sites, some members of the class of 1958 proposed buying a piano for their class gift, a suggestion that J. Mark Stauffer "less than graciously declined," according to one member.[81] This brash proposal struck at a long-standing tradition, the school's constitution, and the authority of Virginia Conference.[82] Agitation to accept instruments increased throughout the 1950s, with prospective music students enrolling at other schools, EMC students transferring to other colleges, students taking private lessons off-campus or enroll-ing in courses at Madison College, and some music graduates failing their teacher certification exams. At the same time, the college allowed literary societies to meet at off-campus locations so they could use pianos in their programs.

Because these issues incited so much student and faculty discontent, an all-day meeting was called in May 1962. Stakeholders from six college and conference groups debated the use of musical instruments. After that summit, Virginia Conference allowed instruments on campus for "recreation and technical studies." The decision sidelined instruments to "recreational" use in social settings, where they would not intrude on congregational singing. "Technical studies" meant using instruments for the study of theory, harmony, and ear training and for certification of public school music teachers.[83] The conference action enabled the college to accept a piano from a donor in 1962 for the lounge in the women's dormitory and one from the class of 1963 for the music department. College officials soon began interpreting "technical studies" broadly, leading to wider use of instruments on campus.

A Bold Spirit of Independence

In June 1958, President Mumaw told the faculty that a "spirit of independence . . . had invaded student opinion with serious proportions." Student writers in the

Weather Vane that year had spoken out against the "suppression of individualism" and claimed that "rugged individualism is the wellspring of the creative mind." Several years earlier, the *Weather Vane* had run a series of twenty short essays by M. T. Brackbill that highlighted individual personality traits.[84]

The students in the mid to late 1950s were the grandchildren of the founders' generation. These students, products of a different culture, were breathing the air of optimism that marked the Eisenhower years. They were daring, bold-minded youths, ready to criticize the dross of tradition that had accumulated over the years. Such students were less willing, for example, to continue that venerable ritual of Mennonite humility—kneeling for prayer—in chapel. Moreover, the college no longer used rituals of public confession to shame wayward students.[85] Displays of individual freedom on campus should not have come as a surprise, since Virginia Conference itself was combating individualism among its own ministers and lay members.[86]

For forty years, a cluster of words—*self-denial, dying to self, obedience, submission, humility,* and *loyalty*—had lined the texts that explained the school's purpose and seeped into student consciousness. These notions restricted self-expression somewhat and reinforced the authority of the community over the individual. Teacher D. W. Lehman had charged that all the aims of public education are "erroneous because they emphasize self and omit others." An early EMS catalog bemoaned that "popular education . . . tends to eliminate all restraint." The text explained that EMS disparaged disobedience, self-will, self-indulgence, and resisting authority.[87]

In a nod to communalism, solos—which showcased individual performance skills—were not permitted in literary programs and graduation exercises for many years.[88] Regulating attire and restricting individual photographs were two other ways of restraining individual expression. Seniors were not allowed to create their own yearbook because college officials thought this practice at Goshen College portrayed too much worldly behavior and individual achievement. Instead, the June 1923 issue of the EMS *Journal* was used to celebrate graduating seniors. It was the *Journal*'s first commencement issue and featured a group picture of the graduates. The next year, individual photos appeared alongside a brief description about each student. Constituent backlash was so strong that only group photos appeared for the next five years. Short depictions of the seniors were placed on different pages from the group portrait. When tiny individual photos did appear in 1930, they remained detached from biographical descriptions. Finally, in 1937, larger individual photos with biographical notes, the typical yearbook style, returned. Faculty members were not pictured individually until 1935. After the school became a college in 1947 and the *Shenandoah* became the official yearbook, restrictions on photos declined.

Personality and self—two new concepts that surfaced in the 1930s and 1940s—offered more positive views of the individual. In 1939, the *Journal* printed essays with tips for developing a pleasant personality. Several years later, an article titled "The Impelling Personality" explained that "the charming individual draws friends to himself like a magnet," and the author of "My Goals for a Christ-like Personality" underlined how personal habits can help project a beautiful and dynamic personality.[89]

Another string of essays focused on positive self-expression. One in 1933 emphasized self-control, self-mastery, self-reliance, self-discipline, and self-development. Ada M. Zimmerman, in her 1941 essay "Discover Your*self*," argued that "from the moment self-consciousness awakens, we have a self to discover, to understand, to use." The theme of the 1949–1950 student handbook was "Yours," with headlines proclaiming that EMC is "Yours for Relaxation," "Yours for Refinement," "Yours for Recreation," and so forth. A *Journal* essay titled "The Incomprehensible Self" offered additional evidence of the emerging focus on the self.[90] The growing use of *personality* and *self* in campus discourse encouraged individualism to blossom. Student handbooks in the 1930s and 1940s proclaimed that EMS exercised parental discipline. By the 1950s, all references to EMC playing the role of proxy parent had vanished.

When Virginia Conference dropped the ban on musical instruments for ministers in 1947, it left the use of instruments to "individual conscience." With those two words, Virginia Conference had transferred moral authority from the church to the individual.[91] This new-to-Virginia phrase paved the way for the rise of individualism and the decline of communalism at EMC. As early as 1949, a faculty committee had proposed replacing the school-prescribed dress code with the moral compass of individual conscience. EMC gradually shifted the moral heft of school regulations to individual students, giving them greater personal freedom and responsibility. By the early 1960s, the mantra of "self-denial, obedience, submission, loyalty" that had harnessed individualism throughout the founding era was fading rapidly.

A more robust sense of self was also linked to faith. A frequently repeated Bible verse emphasized self-actualization in these words: "*I can do all things* through Christ which strengtheneth me" (Phil. 4:13, emphasis added). For student Helen Good, this empowerment left "little room for complaints, little room for excuses, and little room for inactivity. The world is ours, and the strength to utilize our resources is available."[92] Flying out of the cocoon of communal restraint brought not only exuberance but also new choices and anxieties. Students longed to discover the Lord's will for their lifelong vocations. They assumed that God had a customized plan for each individual—an assumption that sometimes brought angst as they struggled to discern God's road map for their lives.

Since greater freedom brought greater responsibility to find and do the Lord's will, it also raised questions about the certainty of one's salvation. The perennial Mennonite teaching against eternal security troubled a new generation that had fewer traditions to guide it. Greater uncertainty prompted some to ask how they could be sure, beyond any doubt, that they were saved. President Mumaw offered certainty for any doubters in his book *Assurance of Salvation* and in a booklet for youth titled *Christian Assurance*. Meanwhile, former campus pastor and *Mennonite Hour* speaker B. Charles Hostetter, in *How to Gain Assurance of Your Salvation*, also tried to calm the anxieties of those fretting about their eternal passports.

A Big New Vision

In January 1947, nearly thirty years after Harold S. Bender had whisked Elizabeth Horsch away in his red roadster for an all-day outing in the Valley, he returned to EMC without romantic plans. This time, Bender, now the dean of Goshen Biblical Seminary, was at EMC to deliver "The Anabaptist Vision," a big idea that would transform Mennonite theology and EMU's ideology for the next seventy years.[93] Bender introduced three words—*Anabaptists, Anabaptism, discipleship*—that had rarely appeared in school documents, correspondence, courses, or campus conversation. Oblique references to Mennonite history typically included phrases such as "our Mennonite ancestors" or "our European forefathers" who had died for their faith in the foggy past. EMC leaders encouraged students to be disciples of Jesus, but the concept of discipleship was missing from school-related discourse in the founding era and even in Daniel Kauffman's books on Mennonite doctrine.[94]

Bender's talk refocused the Mennonite past with several simple ideas. Rather than talking about a "Mennonite vision," he invited his audience to picture the Anabaptists in Switzerland during the Protestant Reformation, which was under way in 1517. The Anabaptists stirred the ire of civic and religious leaders by baptizing adults rather than infants. This was a capital offense that brought severe persecution—torture, burning at the stake, and decapitation. The *Mennonite Quarterly Review* editor explained how core Anabaptist convictions differed from Catholic, Lutheran, and Calvinist views of Christianity. More important, Bender articulated why Anabaptist convictions mattered.

The Anabaptist vision stood on a tripod of discipleship, voluntary membership in a local church community, and an ethic of love, according to Bender.[95] Discipleship was the "first and fundamental" leg of the vision. As the essence of Christianity, discipleship involved "the transformation of the entire way of life of the *individual* believer and of a society . . . fashioned after the teachings and example of Christ." The key word for Anabaptists was not "faith" but "following" Christ (*nachfolge Christi*). The central theological question for them was, What does it mean to follow Jesus daily in life?

Voluntary adult membership in a church community was the second leg of the tripod. This concept of a voluntary community composed of adult-baptized believers was radically different, argued Bender, from the medieval state-supported mass church, whose members were baptized as infants by the fiat of custom and civil law. The Anabaptist-style church community was a counterculture that rubbed against the ways of the world and brought persecution and suffering. Yet in the midst of suffering, the Anabaptist vision espoused an "ethic of love and nonresistance." This third tenet applied to *all* human relationships and rejected "all warfare, strife, and violence."

This Anabaptist vision was simple, concise, and compelling. It was compelling because, in Bender's account, rather than being the scum of society, Anabaptists were wrestling with big ideas that were relevant for the entire Western world: "There can be no question but that the great principles of freedom of conscience, separation of church and state, and volunteerism in religion, so basic in American Protestantism and so essential to democracy, ultimately derive from the Anabaptists of the Reformation period." The Anabaptists, claimed Bender, were the first to clearly enunciate these principles and challenge the Christian world to put them into practice. Moreover, their convictions about religious pacifism predated the Quakers' by more than a century.

These claims were enough to give even humility-minded Mennonites a sense of pride that the convictions of their ancestors had shaped not only Protestant Christianity but Western democracy as well. Bender's story of Anabaptist beginnings legitimated current Mennonite endeavors. It also created a memory of the past—with a new self-understanding and confidence—that powered the school into the twenty-first century.

For his short talk at EMC in 1947, Bender pulled ideas from his presidential address to the American Society of Church History three years earlier at Columbia University.[96] Paradoxically, "The Anabaptist Vision" lecture that he had crafted for his professional colleagues was quickly consumed by his fellow Mennonites, who were tired of the sagging liberal-fundamental controversies and the endless millennial debates. The simplicity and clarity of Bender's new paradigm offered an escape from those timeworn controversies and the restrictions in Daniel Kauffman's books of doctrine.[97] The new ideas also eclipsed the discussions on nonconformity. The Anabaptist vision transcended those calcified categories of the Mennonite mind and bequeathed a fresh ideology—not one that Mennonites had brokered from outside theological traditions, but one that they could claim as their very own.

Because Bender summarized a large swath of history so succinctly, his formulation was vulnerable to criticism. His Swiss-centric story, for example, neglected other regions with multiplex Anabaptist visions, and his contention that all the early Anabaptists were pacifists was erroneous. Historical inaccuracies aside, Bender's narrative of the Anabaptist past invigorated mid-twentieth-century Mennonites.

Rather than turning to theology, biblical exegesis, ethnicity, or community studies, as Mennonite sociologists of his day were wont to do, Bender tapped the veracity of history to construct a new Mennonite identity.

Without doubt, "The Anabaptist Vision" was Bender's particular view of Anabaptist origins. For C. Henry Smith, longtime historian at Bluffton College, individual freedom was a key element of early Anabaptism. Bender had vigorously criticized Smith's accent on individualism in a review of Smith's *The Story of the Mennonites* (1941).[98] Smith responded that conscience was an individual matter, not a collective one.[99]

Yet ironically, Bender's Anabaptist vision dovetailed nicely with the rising individualism in Mennonite society. Discipleship rested on the idea of individual decision making, as did the concept of a voluntary church, which individuals chose to join by definition. The voluntary church community, in Bender's view, provided some communal accountability to harness hyperindividualism. Nonetheless, his framework rested upon the individual and choice—two key components of modernity. Underscoring the centrality of the church community also meshed with the interests of the emerging Mennonite community movement. Furthermore, this framework affirmed the long-standing Mennonite commitment to integrating faith with practice.

The Anabaptist vision was a perfect porridge for a new generation of Mennonites hungry for fresh ideas to guide them in the last half of the twentieth century. After EMC faculty members had a chance to digest Bender's vision, they began to use Anabaptist vocabulary in their talks and papers. The word *discipleship* began to appear in student handbooks. *The Cost of Discipleship*, written in 1937 by the German theologian Dietrich Bonhoeffer—who likely influenced Bender's thinking—was used in theology courses.[100] The faculty heard four presentations on discipleship at an annual faculty conference in 1958. President Mumaw proposed that discipleship should be integral to a philosophy of Mennonite Christian education.[101] Students read and discussed Bender's *Vision* in their classes and took courses on the Anabaptist Reformation and Christian discipleship. Years later, EMC would establish the Discipleship Center on the hill behind the administration building, and a circle of EMU donors known as Associates in Discipleship, founded in 1970, still existed in 2017.[102]

Stepping into the Larger Academic World

The capstone of John R. Mumaw's presidency was SACS accreditation, a prize that the college had eyed since 1932. With state certification in 1947 and the blessing of Virginia Conference in 1948, the college began a concerted effort for accreditation in 1951. Accreditation was crucial for the transfer of credits to other colleges, graduate school admission, teaching certification, recognition by foreign governments, and grant applications to industry, government, and private foundations.

Eleven faculty committees engaged in the six-year self-study. One committee discovered that five recently promoted faculty did not meet SACS standards, resulting in awkward demotions.[103] A SACS team conducted a site visit in the spring of 1958. Its otherwise positive report noted three deficiencies: a minuscule endowment, low faculty salaries, and a deficit of library books. Based on EMC's promises, SACS was willing to negotiate the deficiencies of salaries and books but not the endowment.

SACS required a $300,000 endowment to assure an annual yield of $15,000 for operations. To meet that goal, EMC proffered an annual stream of $15,000 from a "living endowment" pledged by donors, in addition to other gifts. SACS, however, rejected income from individuals. Orie O. Miller, Goshen alumnus and general secretary of MCC, then arranged to have Mennonite Mutual Aid guarantee to cover any shortfall between the annual SACS requirement and the school's gift income. Miller promised to personally reimburse Mennonite Mutual Aid for any payments to EMC. In December 1958, SACS rejected his plan. The $300,000 in hard cash was nonnegotiable.[104]

SACS agreed to reconsider the application a year later if the college could raise the cash. Although President Mumaw was on a five-month leave visiting alumni in Africa and Europe, a team led by the new academic dean, Ira Miller, designed an aggressive fund-raising plan. EMC's endowment of $9,000 stood far below the required $300,000 ($2.5 million in 2017 dollars). After the trustees signed off in February, the college had only eight months to hit the target by the November deadline. In the largest fund-raising blitz in its history, EMC deployed nearly seven hundred solicitors, captains, leaders, and regional chairpersons in fourteen constituent regions as far away as Nebraska, Oregon, Florida, and Alberta.

College students contributed about $11,000, which they had earned during fall breaks. Still, the day before the November deadline, the campaign was stalled at $275,000. Meanwhile, President Mumaw had traveled to the SACS office to present a progress report. Just thirty minutes before his presentation, he received a telephone call with good news: the US Steel Corporation had awarded EMC a $25,000 grant. That clinched EMC's long-sought goal. John Alger, chair of the trustees, credited the "efforts of the church and blessing of the Lord." To him, the achievement signaled greater "acceptance by our constituents and the educational world."[105]

December 1959 was a memorable month for John R. Mumaw. Shortly after receiving official word of the SACS accreditation, he learned that he and EMC professor Linden Wenger were the only nominees in the lot for a bishop ordination. Five days before Christmas, the presiding officials found the decisive slip of paper in Linden Wenger's hymnbook, freeing Mumaw from any new burdens. Mumaw also learned that his alma mater, Elizabethtown College, planned to award him an honorary doctorate. On February 3, 1960, Mumaw, in full academic regalia—which

THE WEATHER VANE

EMC

VOLUME IV   EASTERN MENNONITE COLLEGE, HARRISONBURG, VIRGINIA, DECEMBER 3, 1959   NUM

EMC ACCREDITE

College Secures Admission to Southern Association of College

Endowment Goal Is Surpassed with $25,000 U. S. Steel Gra

Distler Presents National Award

EMC received the $25,000 Quality Improvement Award from the United States Steel Foundation to push the college endowment fund to $304,000.

The announcement of the grant was made in Washington, D. C., by Theodore Distler, executive director of the Association of American Colleges. He said EMC was given the grant "because in the opinion of the committee, it gave evidence of excellent administration and noteworthy progress toward providing the kind of quality education that is the hallmark of the good small liberal arts college."

The selection was made by an awards committee of educators and representatives of industry approved by the Association of American Colleges. The committee carefully screened the applications of sixteen other unaccredited colleges from all over the U.S. before choosing EMC.

President Mumaw received the $25,000 check in Washington, D.C. In acknowledging the grant, he said,

President Mumaw receives the $25,000 check from A.A.C. representative Theodore Distler in Washington, Nov. 18.

Ira Miller's Call from Louisvil Breaks News of Accreditation

Dean Miller broke the news of EMC's accreditation in a call from Louisville at 11:15 this morning. The Southern A tion of Colleges received EMC as a provisional member in i 1-3 meeting at Louisville, Kentucky.

To receive the decision at the meeting were President M and Dean Miller. They reported directly by phone to E Martin at the president's office here. A chapel announcem formed the intent student body of the news..

EMC's accreditation ma climax of intense preparation ing the S.A. postponement of application in Dec., 1958. T areas of improvement inclu dowment fund, library enla teachers' salaries and teachir

President and Dean Attend SA Meeting

EMC accreditation was granted by the Southern Association of Colleges and Secondary Schools at Louisville, Ky. President Mumaw and Dean Miller represented EMC at the meeting.

The names of the newly accredited colleges were announced at the last session of the meeting, Dec. 3. Pre-

To celebrate the event a r tative group of students and will greet Mumaw and Mill tomorrow morning in their home. The reception group clude class executives and s

Program Announ
By Social Comm

President Mumaw accepts a grant enabling EMC to receive its first accreditation by the Southern Association of Colleges and Schools.

was still taboo at EMC—participated in a midterm commencement at the Elizabethtown Church of the Brethren. An overflow crowd of nearly nine hundred watched him receive an honorary doctor of the science of pedagogy degree for his national leadership in advancing small colleges and Christian higher education.[106]

In these two rituals—the ancient religious act of submission to the lot and the modern educational summit of awarding advanced degrees—Mumaw had gracefully straddled the worlds of Mennonite tradition and twentieth-century higher education. His educational leadership over the previous twelve years had built a bridge from a tottering fortress to a solid academy of higher education. As an institution, EMC was flexing its muscles and becoming a bureaucracy with all the earmarks of hierarchy, complexity, and specialization. It was stepping into a modern world marked by individualism, professionalism, scientific methods, technological imperatives, and a growing breach between secular and religious realms.

CHAPTER 7

The Ferment
of Freedom

Consider applicants on the basis of individual merit.
—Virginia Conference

Sit Wherever You Please

Beneath the joy of EMC's new accreditation, the campus roiled in breathless change.
The decade from 1955 to 1965 witnessed a spike in college enrollment from 296 to 604,
new ties to the collegiate world, looser coupling with Virginia Conference, transformations in student culture, and increased faculty activism. The changes persisted
throughout President Mumaw's tenure.

Freedom. Freedom. Freedom. That drumbeat remained constant amid the
upheaval. Freedom of individual expression. Freedom from the cuffs of tradition.
Freedom for intellectual exploration. The scent of freedom was exhilarating. Faculty
wanted more academic freedom and liberation from church control. Students pined
for less censorship and greater self-governance. The rise of the Freedom Riders in 1961
and the burgeoning civil rights movement pushed freedom into the national zeitgeist.

A new, more rambunctious generation of students was arriving on campus in the
late 1950s. Their demands for change and their clamor for freedom troubled President Mumaw, who described the students as having "an incessant *desire* and *demand*
for change . . . that seems revolutionary and altogether too rapid."[1] They voted,
for example, to replace the forty-five-year-old faculty-established assigned seating
system in the dining hall—designed to teach etiquette and refinement—with a
new "sit-wherever-you-please" system.[2] Mumaw blamed the riptide of change on
urbanization, commercialism, and secularization in American society.[3]

The president was also troubled by the students' growing *materialism*, which was
evinced by expensive record players, radios, elaborate wardrobes, and luxury acces-
sories; worldly dress; the immodesty of girls from conservative families; increased

selfishness expressed by students demanding certain dorm rooms; a pronounced independence, dislike of control, and unwillingness to submit to regulations; the desire for high-powered entertainment; persistent demands for "more athletics and more dramatics"; and greater tolerance for interdenominational and ecumenical activities, coupled with a dwindling love for the Mennonite Church and its distinctive witness. One student "even had leanings toward Buddhism," the president noted, although the majority of students did bring a sincere faith in Christ.[4]

Concern about these issues prompted a consultation of trustees, church leaders, college administrators, and faculty leaders that identified twelve pressing issues in 1959. These included determining who had final authority to make and change school policies, aligning school regulations with conference standards, controlling a spiraling interest in competitive sports, dealing with student demand for more theatrical activities, bolstering faculty convictions for plain garb, procuring loyal faculty with academic credentials, preventing conservative students from losing their convictions at EMC, and encouraging more students to become missionaries and church leaders.[5] One measure of the flux was the rate of constitutional revisions. After twenty-three years of stability, three revisions were made within fifteen years (1947–1963).

Confrontation: Not a Mennonite Tactic

The graduation of Peggy Webb Howard, the first African American student, in 1954 marked a big change. That milestone, however, was tarnished by the school's refusal to admit three students of color in the 1940s. Even at midcentury, Harrisonburg remained segregated. African Americans and whites were partitioned into separate neighborhoods, churches, schools, prisons, cemeteries, and baby wards in hospitals. Public drinking fountains and restrooms in Harrisonburg were marked "colored" and "white." Race divided public bathing areas, motels, restaurants, and seating on trains and buses. Intermarriage was illegal, and African American voting was stymied by poll taxes, literacy tests, and intimidation.

Institutional racism in Harrisonburg stretched far back into the nineteenth century. Well after the Civil War, the United States Supreme Court in 1896 (*Plessy v. Ferguson*) galvanized state and local laws to segregate all public facilities. The "separate but equal" philosophy of *Plessy* erected sharp barriers that codified and perpetuated white supremacy and ideas about African American inferiority. The jaws of these so-called Jim Crow laws remained clenched until 1954, when *Brown v. Board of Education* outlawed racial segregation in public schools. A decade later, the Civil Rights Act of 1964 and the Voting Rights Act of 1965 further dismantled segregation.

In the late 1940s, EMC men patronized a barbershop in downtown Harrisonburg where five African American barbers cut the hair of whites. One student sitting on a barber chair witnessed an African American man entering the door only to hear the African American manager yell at him to "get out of this white shop."[6]

The Jim Crow practices were tightly stitched into the seams of southern life—so tightly that it was difficult to imagine unraveling them. Even Mark Ethridge, the liberal editor of the *Louisville Courier Journal*, editorialized in the mid-1940s, "There is no power in the world—not even in all the mechanized armies of the earth, Allied and Axis—which could now force the Southern white people" to abandon segregation. It is cruel, he contended, to even tell African Americans that they can ever expect segregation to crumble.[7]

Mennonites born and raised in Virginia were reluctant to protest segregation. They had absorbed some of the racial norms as simply "the way things are." In 1954, a college-educated Mennonite school teacher explained, "A bit of the Southern attitude rubs off on us, perhaps as a result of our public school experience. One also tends to feel sympathetic to one's state and its part in the Civil War."[8] Besides, as a nonresistant, quiet-in-the-land, government-compliant people, Virginia Mennonites were not inclined to provocative protests. Grace Showalter, librarian of the Menno Simons Historical Library, explained that "confrontation as a way of combating society's ills was not a tactic of the Mennonite Church anywhere" at that time.[9]

Even so, Mennonites were not oblivious to the moral dimensions of segregation. In 1860, Rockingham County had about 420 slaveholders, most of whom owned two to nine slaves. "Uncle Pete" Hartman, born in 1846, was an early proponent of EMC (see chapter 3). The young Mennonite worked "a good many days on the farm" where the Ad Building was constructed in 1919, and he observed the slaveholder who owned that farm and the surrounding 640 acres cruelly mistreating his slaves. Hartman recalled, "The Mennonite Church stood foursquare against war and slavery."[10]

Indeed, Virginia Conference unequivocally declared in 1864 that "it is against our creed and discipline to own or traffic in slaves." Furthermore, in 1924, when struggling with how to welcome African American applicants for membership, the conference called racial prejudice "unscriptural," citing three New Testament injunctions against racial discrimination. The conference affirmed that "people of color" were welcome as members, but it opposed "close social relations" and marriage between "the colored and white races."[11]

Hypocrisy in the Holy of Holies

EMS alumnus Ernest Swartzentruber and his wife, Fannie, served as superintendent and matron of the Gay Street Mission from 1938 to 1945. This mission, started by EMS students in 1936, had four African American applicants for membership in the Mennonite Church by 1940. These requests created a crisis. Could African

American and white Mennonites mingle in the sacred rituals of baptism and communion? Conference leaders struggled with that question as they tried to establish an African American congregation led by whites. Acknowledging the southern attitude against interracial mixing, the conference cautiously adopted "a practical working policy . . . in the best interests for both colored and white."[12]

Echoing the "separate but equal" logic, Virginia Conference stipulated that the African American congregation would be "under a separate, but auxiliary organization." It also decreed that two Mennonite rituals would be segregated: the kiss of Christian salutation given at baptism and footwashing and the ritual of footwashing itself. A white bishop would baptize African Americans but not give them the kiss of Christian welcome at the conclusion of the ritual. Instead, an African American would give the kiss to the new African American member. The footwashing ritual would also be segregated, and the Gay Street Mission would use individual cups for communion instead of the traditional common cup. In short, there would be no mixed kissing, no mixed footwashing, and no drinking from the same cup.

This outcome trimmed the hedge of segregation by enabling African Americans and whites to worship together and hold membership in the same congregation. The conference struck this bargain to mollify members who opposed integration and to guide the white officials administering the rites. Yet the policy separated members by race in holy rituals involving physical touch, keeping African Americans second-class citizens in the inner sanctum of Mennonite life.

To the Swartzentrubers, the segregated rituals seemed hypocritical. Despite all the platitudes, racism remained intact even for those African American members who complied with Mennonite dress standards. For Fannie, the communion service in the fall of 1944 was a charade. It upset her so much that she bolted out of the service with a young daughter in tow and walked four miles home—leaving her husband to close the communion and drive home later.[13] Because of the ensuing hubbub, the mission board soon removed the Swartzentrubers from leadership. Shortly thereafter, the Gay Street congregation, under the leadership of EMS alumnus Ralph Shank, moved to a newly constructed building on Broad Street.

Watching this disturbance was Roberta Webb, a graduate of the Hampton Institute, a historic black college near Newport News. Webb, an able educator and community leader, had joined the congregation in 1943. A single parent with three daughters, she wore the traditional devotional head covering with strings, a plain cape-style dress, dark hose, and dark shoes. As a bona fide member of a white church, Webb was engaged in her own quiet protest of Jim Crow laws. This Jesus-loving, conservative-dressing Mennonite woman soon began pressing for her daughters to attend EMS.[14]

Cracking the Wall of Racism

EMS had faced the integration question before. In 1940, the faculty had refused to admit Thomas Stewart, a local African American. Worried that his presence would stoke animosity between "northern and southern students," the faculty advised him to take Bible correspondence courses, which he declined to do. To buttress their refusal, they noted that "the state of Virginia [had] ruled against the attendance of Whites and Blacks at the same public school." But that was a poor excuse. Private religious schools such as EMS were not bound by that law.[15]

Five years later, Roberta Webb's daughter Peggy applied for full-time admission. This time, the trustees reviewed the touchy issue. On May 14, 1945, the white men had a long discussion about "opening EMS to colored students." Capitulating to the "deeply set values . . . of the state and community," which Mennonites, as a small minority, "[couldn't] change at once," the trustees decided it was "unwise to admit such students." Nonetheless, they voiced their "heartfelt sympathy for our colored brethren and sisters with their educational problems," and they promised to open admissions at an opportune time.[16]

President Stauffer feared that admitting African American students would stir up "trouble" in the Mennonite and greater Harrisonburg community.[17] Mennonites, already scorned for refusing to fight in the war, did not want to incite more ill will. So Stauffer was likely surprised when Webb's rejection brought "trouble" to EMS's own front steps. Student Margaret Derstine recalled that Webb's turndown divided both students and faculty. "I will never forget a poster," she said, "placed near the front entrance of the old AD Building." The placard showed the president at the front door, blessing a graduate leaving for mission work in Africa, while the dean held the rear door shut to prevent an African American student from entering the school.[18]

With the EMS door locked, Peggy went to Hesston College, the two-year Mennonite school 1,200 miles away in Kansas, from which she graduated in 1947.[19] Roberta Webb's brother John observed, "They accept you in the church. . . . Yet, they won't accept your children at their college [EMS]."[20] Student Goldie Hummel and Tillie Yoder, a Sunday school teacher at the Gay Street Mission, met with President Stauffer to plead for integration. Stauffer explained that despite his personal sympathies for African American students, objections from local Mennonites made change impractical.[21] One prominent trustee and generous contributor, for example, had declared that African American students would not attend EMS as long as he was on the board, a statement he later recanted.[22]

Undeterred, Roberta Webb's second daughter, Ada, applied to EMS in the fall of 1947. Again, the answer was no. Consequently, Ada went to Chicago and took evening classes at Roosevelt College.[23] Yet the Mennonite conscience was uneasy. In January

1948, the trustees again debated "admitting colored students." Uncertain what to do, the trustees sent the delicate issue to Virginia Conference. In an executive session in June 1948, conference leaders directed college officials to "consider applicants on the basis of *individual merit*."[24] These two shocking words defied the Jim Crow laws and the racist views of some Mennonites.

In September 1948, part-time student Willis Johnson became the first African American to enroll at EMC. In January 1949, Ada Webb returned from Chicago to become EMC's first full-time African American student. Abram Hostetter, a Lancaster County student, recalled seeing Ada often sitting alone on the back bench of the chapel. Hostetter created a spectacle one day when he asked her if she would walk with him around the oval pathway on the grassy slope in front of the Ad Building. During the short break before the start of afternoon classes, courting couples and pairs of friends often walked side-by-side, forming a line on the path.

Ada accepted Abe's invitation. When the path turned back toward the Ad Building, they noticed that no one was following them and that many students were on the hill staring in amazement. Abe and Ada were likely the first mixed-race pair to appear in public at EMC.[25] This short walk was a scandalous example of exactly what so many Mennonites feared: integration at EMC would lead to mixed marriages.[26] One thirty-year-old local Mennonite Sunday school teacher opposed integration at EMC "because the problem of courtship and intermarriage would immediately arise. I think separate campuses might answer the problem."[27]

That fall (1949), Marjorie Thompson of Christiana, Pennsylvania, crossed a rigid racial barrier by being the first African American student to room in the EMC dormitory. (Many schools that had integrated in earlier years accepted African Americans as commuters but did not permit them to live in the dormitories.) EMC's first three African American students left after one semester for unknown reasons.

Another spectacle occurred five years after Ada Webb sat alone at the back of the chapel. After graduating from Hesston College, her sister Peggy returned to Harrisonburg and married John Howard. In 1952, Peggy Webb Howard entered EMC to study education and music. A gifted musician, she composed the music for the 1954 class song, "Conquering through Christ," written by her classmate Jay B. Landis. At the class-day program preceding commencement, Peggy walked onstage and led the assembly in singing the song. There she stood, nine years after being denied admittance, the first African American to graduate from EMC. Not a Mennonite, she led the song without wearing a head covering, which stirred more controversy than the color of her skin.[28]

Peggy Webb Howard graduated exactly three weeks after the Supreme Court desegregated public schools in 1954. A year later, Virginia Conference desegregated its communion rituals.[29] Although EMC had waffled on the race issue at first, its admission of

Ada Webb, the first full-time African American student, with classmates, spring 1949.

Willis Johnson in 1948 was six years ahead of the Supreme Court's desegregation order and seven years before Rosa Parks refused to leave a "white" seat on a Montgomery bus. EMC was the first undergraduate private school to integrate in the state of Virginia.[30]

Eleven years later, in 1959, EMC had five African American students, more than any other Virginia undergraduate institution except the University of Virginia, which had eighteen. That year, EMC and Bridgewater College, which had two, were the only private colleges in Virginia that had African Americans enrolled. And EMC was one of only eight integrated private colleges among dozens of schools in nine southern states.[31] In comparison with EMC's integration in 1948 and Bridgewater's in 1955, the College of William and Mary admitted its first African American undergraduate student in 1963, and Madison College followed in 1966.[32]

EMC's decision to integrate in 1948 outpaced the Southern Association of Colleges and Schools (SACS) by nine years. Although the Southern Association had hoped to integrate by 1960, the legal edict of *Brown v. Board of Education* prodded SACS to integrate by 1957. SACS had accredited black colleges for many years, but it refused to accept them as members or permit their representatives to attend the association's professional meetings. The decision to integrate in 1957 outraged some white member colleges, which remained segregated.[33]

The Virginia Conference directive to prioritize individual merit opened the school's doors to African Americans. By implication, EMC would consider other students without regard for religion, national origin, ethnicity, sex, disability, and sexual orientation. Those two simple words—individual merit—would reverberate through the halls of the school for the next seventy years.

Diversity and Selectivity

Meanwhile, Ira Miller, the new academic dean in 1956, was aggressively working to bolster the quality of EMC's academic program. If Mumaw was the first professional president, Miller was the first professional dean. His radar scanned far beyond Goshen College and SACS to the larger world of American higher education. He attended nine professional conferences in one year, instituted several testing programs to compare EMC students with national norms, and absorbed educational studies such as a 1959 Rockefeller report titled "The Pursuit of Excellence." Miller cited the relevance of a four-college study (Smith, Amherst, Mount Holyoke, and the University of Massachusetts) for several policies he initiated at EMC.

Miller wanted an instructional program with "creativity, imagination, elasticity, and experimentation," one that, he noted, might discard old habits, challenge conventional assumptions, and transcend traditional boundaries. He pressed for heterogeneity, telling the trustees that EMC should welcome a "diversity" of Mennonite students with various interests and social backgrounds. This was likely the first time the word *diversity* circulated in campus discourse.[34]

International students had already been adding some cultural spice to campus life. Dozens of Canadian Mennonites had attended the school since 1920. In 1947, three students from outside of North America arrived. Wai May Chan and Chee Tao Chan, both from China, were the first nonwhites to attend. The third student, Ivan Magal, was a Russian refugee who had been living in Belgium.[35] Within a year, the number of students from outside the United States grew rapidly. Of nearly eight hundred students in all EMC programs in 1948–1949, three were from Belgium, three from Germany, one from China, one from Holland, one from Korea, and thirty-four from Canada.[36] By 1957, some seventy-five students from seventeen nations outside North America had studied at EMC.[37] The school was particularly receptive to foreign students with Mennonite ties who were interested in a religious education. Beginning in the 1960s, numerous African students enrolled with the encouragement of Mennonite missionaries. President Mumaw was effusive about the contribution of foreign students to "international understanding" on campus.[38]

The number of non-Mennonite students grew slowly. In 1949–1950, there were four non-Mennonites in the student body.[39] Six years later, the faculty decided it had "a moral, missionary obligation" to educate non-Mennonites but decided to cap their number at 5 percent of the student body, exclusive of foreign students.[40] With the number of non-Mennonite students inching up in the early 1960s, EMC considered placing a surcharge on their tuition but decided against it because some non-Mennonite businesses and foundations were supporting the school financially.[41] By 1965, about forty non-Mennonite students, representing a dozen denominations, were on campus.[42]

Dean Miller wanted a student body that was at least 85 percent Mennonite. Yet Mennonites were not all alike. Church regulations across EMC's supporting conferences had become quite diverse. "How," asked Miller, "do we handle Mennonite diversity?" What should be done, for example, "with a female applicant with cut hair who does not wear a covering, which is typical in her home church?" How many different Mennonites and non-Mennonites could EMC admit "without harming the total campus atmosphere?"[43]

EMC also coped with another dimension of Mennonite diversity: academic ability. In the mid-1950s, the faculty asked, "When will we refuse to admit Mennonites on the basis of academic achievement?"[44] Should the gates of admission swing open for all Mennonites regardless of scholastic achievement? EMC's four-year graduation rate stood at a paltry 47 percent, which Miller attributed to the wide-open admissions. Is there a moral issue, debated the faculty, "in taking money from students" who will likely fail?[45] Both faculty and students were challenged by the intellectual disparity in the student body, with many weak ones dropping out and strong ones getting bored. Although EMC would not deny admission to anyone on the basis of religion, race, color, class, or nationality, it began rejecting some applicants on academic grounds and accepting others conditionally.[46] Several years later, the college used three exams plus high school records to measure academic aptitude and potential.[47] Sophomore Jim Halteman, for example, told his parents that he was pleased to rank in the 93–95 percentile of sophomores across the nation. But, he confessed, "I'll have to work harder because I should be getting all A's."[48]

Dean Miller paid careful attention to the performance of EMC students on the Graduate Record Exam and other national indicators that offered comparative benchmarks. He argued for higher admission standards and honors courses for the intellectual elite. Though 20 percent of EMC students ranked in the ninetieth percentile of the national School and College Ability Test, too many, in Miller's mind, had skidded below the median. In 1963, the faculty considered beginning an honors program and offering independent study options to better serve "our gifted students."[49] Independent study options were soon offered, but an honors program had to wait thirty years.

The Death of Indoctrination

Dean Miller buried EMC's forty-year philosophy of indoctrination with this rhetorical question: "Is it our primary duty to do the church's task of indoctrination?" For Miller, the answer was no. He thought an EMC education should aid students in developing deep convictions by "means other than mere indoctrination."[50] He wanted EMC educators to encourage students "to think soundly and critically . . . to evaluate carefully, independently, and skillfully." In his mind, "Too many people are living on inherited religious capital."[51]

For Harry Lefever, a young professor of sociology, a Mennonite college was an anomaly because it promoted voluntary choice in religion inside a little society dominated by people and policies committed to the Christian faith. EMC paradoxically spoon-fed students with ready-made answers yet encouraged them to make choices about religious faith, argued Lefever. In his opinion, voluntarism and choice should be especially *safeguarded* on a Mennonite campus; otherwise, indoctrination would prevail. This unconventional view turned the old idea of *safeguard* on its head. In the first four decades of its history, *safeguard* had meant protecting students from religious choice, not affirming it. Yet Lefever contended that to be faithful to its Anabaptist roots, EMC was compelled to safeguard voluntarism.[52]

The notion of voluntarism spurred discussions about student discipline in the 1955–1965 decade. Faculty and staff considered questions such as these: Should we allow students to discover their own needs for discipline? To what extent shall we superimpose our ideals and standards on students? Should students have more responsibility to control the conduct of other students? The faculty agreed that "regulations should be pared down to the absolute minimum things we can defend. We must allow people to make choices, and learn by making the wrong ones. We must strive to build within young people inner controls, self-discipline, self-direction, self-appraisal of conduct."[53]

In matters of attire and hairstyle, the faculty appealed to students to practice modesty and biblical simplicity. They urged women not to cut their hair: "We recognize that hairstyles are to some extent a matter of *individual choice* and the students need to be guided by their own convictions." The faculty affirmed, however, their responsibility to deny admission, to discipline, and to suspend those out of harmony with college standards.[54] Apart from its focus on individual responsibility, the college for the first time was setting its own standards with little reference to the church, because the diversity of dress standards, even within Virginia Conference, made alignment impossible.

Dean Miller supported greater student freedom. Reflecting on the 1963–1964 school year, he noted "an ever-increasing clamor for freedom of expression." Students that year wanted freedom to discuss and pass resolutions, distribute leaflets, circulate petitions, and act "on any matter which directly or indirectly concerns or affects them." Although a Faculty-Student Forum was initiated in 1957 to improve channels of communication, students yearned for their own organization. Miller proposed a "well-organized student government to regulate student-sponsored activities, organizations, publications, etc."[55] But his vision remained dormant until the Student Government Association (SGA) was formed in 1969.

Basketballs, Beatles, and the *Piranha*

For some students, freedom meant the liberty to compete in intercollegiate sports. In the mid-1950s, interschool competition remained off-limits because the EMC constitution forbade "all contest games with other schools." When the new student center and gymnasium opened in the spring of 1958, it sparked rivalries in the basketball games organized by the literary societies. These games were so exciting that administrators considered charging entrance fees to watch them. Still, students yearned for intercollegiate contests. Some traveled to other colleges to watch games and to occasionally compete illicitly against other teams.

Students were required to sign a pledge not to go off campus to movies or athletic events. Yet the college could do little to prevent it. One Friday night, after watching a basketball game at Bridgewater College, four students returned to campus after 11:00 p.m. to find the men's dormitory locked. All the windows except one were connected to the fire alarm. Trying to gain entrance, the tardy students threw pebbles up to that third floor window and it soon opened. The student resident of the room had promised the dormitory manager that he would never let anyone in the window. Nonetheless, the culprits climbed up the fire escape ladder and into the open window. Entering the room, they found the student lying on his bunk, face to the wall, with his hands over his ears, shouting, "Don't laugh and don't talk. I dare not know that any of you are going through the room."[56]

Athletes understandably wanted to play, not merely watch games. In the winter of 1956, six men and six "cheerleaders" drove two cars to Messiah College to play an illicit basketball game. The men wore army surplus shorts, since only sweatpants were permitted for the games sponsored by EMC's literary societies. They also wore green T-shirts with pinned-on numbers. Messiah held a modest lead throughout the first half. Midway through the third quarter, two EMC players fouled out, leaving only four on the court with the Messiah men up by twelve points. Three of the remaining EMC students soon had four fouls apiece, and the situation looked so pitiful that the Messiah fans started cheering for EMC. The four Mennonites chipped away at Messiah's lead and tied the score 90–90 with thirty seconds on the clock. Then the ball from a Messiah shot caromed off the rim into the hands of

Lowell Herr, who saw Josh Hiestand streaking toward the other end of the court. Herr threw a "Hail Mary pass that Hiestand caught to make a perfect left-handed layup."[57] With Messiah out of time, EMC eked out a 92–90 victory.

Back in Harrisonburg the next day, a student stood to offer the blessing on the noon meal in the dining hall. He then made a coded announcement designed to avoid recrimination by college officials. Using a musical metaphor, he explained, "Last evening, EMC played the Messiah and came out two beats ahead on the ninety-second score." After a brief silence, the students burst into a loud cheer.[58] Eight years later, an EMC basketball team played Messiah College officially for the first time.

In another under-the-table basketball game in the winter of 1958, a team of EMC men left campus in balmy weather and drove to Goshen, Indiana. Along the way, they crashed into a deer and veered into a deep snowdrift. The men nearly "froze to death until a Good Samaritan" rescued them, only to have the Goshen College Maple Leafs crush them on the court. At the end of the next chapel service, an eavesdropping student who had heard scuttlebutt about the game stood up and delivered a diatribe pronouncing woes on EMC for its many transgressions. He attributed the highway accident to God's wrathful judgment. C. K. Lehman finally silenced the "prophet" some ten minutes after the normal dismissal time.[59]

With escapades like these, student pressure for intercollegiate games accelerated. Caught between rising student demands and the constitution, President Mumaw sought a new interpretation of the prohibition against "contest games with other schools." What was the founders' intent? The meaning of this phrase, which had been clear for nearly forty years, was suddenly muddled. Did the rule really mean what it said? For some years now, college officials had allowed students to play sports against alumni and unofficial teams from other schools who came to EMC. Perhaps "contest games" meant league (conference) sports? Mumaw hinted that it did. Thus "games with other *schools*" was reinterpreted to mean "other *leagues*." This cleared the way for EMC to play teams from other schools without a rewrite of the constitution, as long as the games were not part of an organized athletic conference.[60] So a year after the illicit game at Goshen, EMC played its first sanctioned basketball game against the Maple Leafs.

Although freedom was in the air, a former student recalled that in the late 1950s, "the faculty valued conformity above almost everything else."[61] A peer criticism ritual encouraged that conformity. Students periodically received "crit slips," small slips of paper on which they could write and send anonymous feedback to any student on campus. "This ill-advised, faculty-sanctioned process," said an alumnus, "[allowed] students to express their feelings of admiration, resentment, grudge, or whatever, about other students without fear of being identified." Unpopular students could be devastated. It was one way of keeping students "in line."[62]

Until the early 1950s, the president and faculty held sway over the content of the student-run newspaper, the *Weather Vane*. Editor Daniel Hess, who had "many run-ins" with President Mumaw over his censorship of the paper, was grateful that faculty advisor Hubert Pellman helped get some controversial topics into print.[63] Still, the censorship spawned the first underground student newspaper. *Piranha*—that human-eating fish of the Amazon—splashed its tail in 1963–1964. The brainchild of five students (Dwayne Martin, Willard Gingerich, Ken Reed, Roy Martin, and Joe Lapp), the five-page mimeographed-and-stapled broadside sold for ten cents. It aimed to circumvent "the ever-present threat of censorship at EMC" and to fill the vacuum every other weekend when the *Weather Vane* was not published. *Piranha* contained a hodgepodge of poetry, opinion, satire, and raw humor. The paper argued for new ideas, constructive criticism, and rigorous intellectual work because "this is a college, not a playground."[64]

Essay titles included "Barnyard Intellectuals," "The Inadequacy of Capitalism," and "Don't Stifle the Stubble." The author of "Stubble" pointed to Abe Lincoln, Mitch Miller, Castro, Santa Claus, and "the old boys down at the bar" to support his argument that bearded men are happy men. *Piranha* also listed films at Madison College and theatrical performances in Harrisonburg and at Bridgewater College.

Student and later president Joe Lapp fishing in a mud puddle to protest potholes on campus walkways, 1964.

One lead article featured the Beatles, "THAT FANTASTIC FOURSOME, THE EXALTERS of the Mennonites and Amish, the glorifiers of simple attire . . . who are uniting the world behind nonconformity . . . with the cry 'a straight-cut [plain coat] for every American.'" In the midst of today's "ridiculous hairstyles," wrote Willard Gingerich, "the Beatles have turned the public eye to the simple FALLING-FREE hairstyle of the Amish."[65] Although students were tuned in to popular music, they were startled one morning to hear the Beatles singing "I Want to Hold Your Hand" in the staid dining hall. According to one student, "No one seem[ed] to know" how a Beatles album got mixed up with the religious ones that day.[66]

Some students in the late 1950s and early '60s pressed hard against school regulations. Most of those cited for violations and pranks were contrite and remained in school. But others, regardless of contrition, were expelled, some for drinking and some for attending a mixed-gender, all-night party held off campus. Most students, however, were "straight arrows," said one alumnus. "My friends find it hard to believe it when I tell them that I spent four years of undergraduate studies without ever seeing anyone smoke a cigarette or drink alcohol."[67]

Faculty Freedom

The faculty was also restless. In the late 1950s, college officials were still approving textbooks and films. Such censorship and a new batch of fresh-from-graduate-school instructors stirred concerns about academic freedom, which the faculty explored during the 1958–1959 school year.[68] Almost twenty-five years earlier, Bishop George R. Brunk had been the first to cite academic freedom as a threat for conservative schools like EMC.[69] President Mumaw contended that critical scrutiny of ideas, while helpful, must always be "compatible with Christian faith."[70] In 1962, Christian education professor A. Don Augsburger argued that on issues like racial integration, EMC faculty had more freedom to speak than in state schools, yet he reminded them that at a faith-anchored school, they were bound to some "voluntary restrictions around the pursuit of knowledge."[71]

President Mumaw outlined specific principles of academic freedom in 1963. He contended that EMC's commitment to a Christian interpretation of facts, "the truth of God," and a defense of the Mennonite way of life constrained academic freedom. For Mumaw, freedom of expression should raise no doubt about a faculty member's loyalty to the Word of God, the church, the trustees, and Virginia Conference.[72] Myron Augsburger, a new faculty member, was troubled by the negative tone of Mumaw's paper. Why not state positive guidelines, he suggested, rather than so many negative limitations?[73]

Dean Ira Miller argued for "free inquiry after truth [because] error flourishes wherever free inquiry" is stifled. Miller wanted "faculty members with originality and resourcefulness . . . teachers with imagination, ready to break loose from conventional procedure and move into untried fields." Such teachers, he warned, might question certain Mennonite practices.[74] The dean also noted that some EMC students were dismayed by the "shallowness, narrowness, and bias" of some faculty. This happened, opined Miller, because some faculty thought denominational commitments infringed on academic freedom. In his interviews with graduating seniors, the dean found that certain instructors "evade[d] questions rather than giv[ing] their honest-to-goodness convictions" because they feared the scrutiny of administrators, trustees, or the Religious Welfare Committee (RWC).[75]

Dean Miller advocated for faculty development and for hiring faculty with PhDs. Competent instructors, for him, were the prime requisite of a good liberal arts college. Yet he faced a serious question: How could the school attract qualified faculty who were willing to wear plain attire?[76] Bible instructors readily wore plain suits because they were ordained ministers. The problem was recruiting capable faculty in other departments. Faculty dress standards had always been covered by the blanket phrase "church-regulated attire."

By the early 1960s, some faculty men had two wardrobes: a plain outfit for campus and church life and a lapel coat and tie for professional conferences and out-of-state events. Some new faculty occasionally wore a tie to off-campus social events. Chemistry professor Henry "Hank" Weaver Jr. held the distinction of being the first professor to don a tie for a lecture. Home with the mumps in 1956, he wore a red bow tie to deliver a lecture to his class via shortwave radio.[77]

Faculty attire was a volatile issue in the 1963 revision of the constitution. Twenty-eight faculty members, including four women, petitioned the revision committee to "delete the constitutional requirements on regulation attire for faculty."[78] Struggling to placate strong conservative voices while providing flexibility, the revised constitution said the faculty should provide "positive leadership by personal example" and work to increase student convictions for nonconformity.[79] The vagueness and the shifting faculty sentiment provided an opening for one faculty member to take a daring step.

Professor Harold D. Lehman was the first to appear in a campus meeting wearing a tie and lapel coat. Son of longtime professor and bishop D. W. Lehman and nephew of C. K. Lehman, Harold had worked at EMC for nearly twenty years. He was scheduled to speak in a church-wide conference on campus. As a matter of courtesy, he informed his father in advance of his plans, but he did not tell President Mumaw. Before taking the stage, the participants gathered for a short prayer of blessing. When Mumaw saw the tie and coat, "he really went into shock," Lehman said, "[and] some people really talked me down."[80] A year later, in 1965, Virginia Conference reiterated its expectation that faculty members show "exemplary standards and practices of nonconformity." This vague plea, however, was powerless to stop the faculty from trading in their plain suits. Still, older faculty and administrators continued to wear them for many years.[81]

"I Fled to My Room"

As the faculty men discarded their plain suits, sometimes with glee, faculty women were still required to wear long hair, a devotional covering, and a cape—an additional piece of fabric over the front and back of the bodice to enhance modesty—on their dresses. For many young women considering faculty or staff appointments, the cape dress was burdensome as well as distressing. In the fall of 1962, Evelyn King, dean of women, invited Reta Halteman, a 1962 graduate, to consider serving as the dean of high school women. Halteman was enthused about the opportunity until she met with President Mumaw for her job interview.

She was surprised that he expected her to wear cape dresses. She had never worn them as a student and told him that she would not do so now because she could not afford them. As she became overcome with emotion and her nose began running, Halteman recalled, "[Mumaw] never offered me a tissue, but

Faculty and students view 1950 alumnus Warren Rohrer's woodcut portrait of Menno Simons, which he presented to the Menno Simons Historical Library in November 1961. Women's head coverings were gradually shrinking in size, but cut and flowing hair was not permitted. Sweaters were an acceptable substitute for cape dresses.

he did say, 'I'm sure the Lord will show you that this [wearing cape dresses] is the right decision.' I wanted to throw up!" Furthermore, as she later told her mother, "wearing a cape dress would be terribly humiliating; I have never worn any, I have no intentions of ever wearing any, and I have absolutely no convictions along that line." After the interview, Halteman said, "I fled to my room and cried and cried."[82]

Later that evening she spoke with Evelyn King and then confided to her mother, "Oh, Miss King is priceless! She was utterly understanding . . . finally she told me to lay it all before the Lord and forget about it for several days." But Halteman could not toss it aside. Up at 5:00 a.m. the next morning, she struck a deal with God in the women's prayer room: she would obtain a few cape dresses to wear at work, but she would not wear them all the time because that "would violate [her] conscience on stewardship." In going partway, she acknowledged, "My rebellion and will were sufficiently broken. Even in this, I shall have to suffer keenly next year."[83] Halteman's mother made her three dresses with capes that could be snapped off and on. She snapped on the capes for chapel and other public functions with conservative leaders, but not for other occasions.

This poignant tale has many threads. Here was the president—a powerful male representative of an organization and a minister trained in pastoral care, working under the stern eyes of religious conservatives—trying to explain to a twenty-one-year-old woman why she must obey, without any conviction, a decaying tradition that many women in her church no longer heeded. Twelve years earlier, when the president's own daughter Catherine had entered EMC, she had taken science courses hoping to become a nurse. "In truth and in secret," she said, "nursing appealed to me as a way to escape having to wear a cape dress," since nurses wore uniforms. After a traumatic experience in a temporary nursing job, she switched her major to home economics and ended up wearing cape dresses for another fifteen years.[84] When he spoke with Halteman, the president surely knew that cape-wearing would soon end. Yet at that moment, he had the hapless task of doing the bidding of the trustees and conference leaders.

Struggling against a powerful fifty-year tradition, Halteman survived by striking a compromise with God—one that required a willingness to suffer but validated her honor, integrity, and conscience. Her bargain turned a religious custom into an occupational uniform. Despite her enthusiasm for the job, she had to yield to and obey the communal order, suggesting that all the talk of freedom was still talk, at least for some people. This young woman had to fend for herself in the face of patriarchy, church authority, organizational clout, and gender inequity. Similar incidents occurred all too often in the twenty-year shift from EMC's paradigm of indoctrination-separation with its accent on submission to a still undefined model of moral education.

Dress Matters

As the church-prescribed standards of plain dress dissolved in the late 1950s, a curious thing happened: students employed the plain-dress principles to argue for academic regalia.[85] For several years, students had clamored to wear academic gowns at commencement. To prevent women from donning form-fitting, immodest, short dresses, commencement regulations required them to wear white dresses (cape not required) with a hem thirteen inches off the ground. Men were required to wear dark-colored suits (lapel or plain).

With EMC's long history of plain dress, the gown issue became more than a campus scuffle. Several regional church conferences discussed the gown question. Church and school leaders contended that the academic gown would lead to the academic cap, which would replace the devotional covering, usher in baseball and basketball uniforms, and tempt local church choirs and school touring choirs to wear gowns—all of which would violate the convictions of conservative students, reflect worldly academic fashions, trample stewardship principles of simplicity and frugality, and assist students trying to cover up immodest dresses.[86]

Aspiring to wear gowns at commencement for the first time, the class of 1963 conducted research on the history of regalia and compiled extensive arguments favoring it.[87] Their request was denied. But the class of 1964 mounted another campaign. To buttress their argument for gowns, the students appealed to the very principles used by school leaders to justify plain dress. Gowns, the students argued, would enhance uniformity, eliminate individual taste and personal expression, improve modesty since they hang closer to the floor than dresses, reflect good stewardship because renting a gown is cheaper than buying a new dress that might never be worn again, alleviate the annual conflict between the "subjects and the rulers," and align with faculty who had likely worn regalia at their university commencements. Had students seen President Mumaw don full regalia to receive his honorary doctorate at Elizabethtown College just three years earlier, they surely would have made him an exemplar for their cause. A 1964 editorial in the *Weather Vane* implored school officials to "Improve Modesty at Graduation" and avoid "a 108-member fashion show."[88]

The college and high school commencements were divided for the first time in 1964, making changes to the college ceremony easier. Conceding to student demands, officials finally permitted the class of 1964 to have a processional and recessional at commencement and to wear gowns. For those of a conservative

Typical commencement attire before academic regalia was permitted in 1964.

bent, the sight of graduates in academic gowns at EMC's culminating public ritual was a sure sign that worldliness had overtaken the school. Occasionally, students refused to wear regalia. "I refused to wear a cap and gown at my graduation at EMC in 1981," said one graduate, "out of conviction that it was worldly and unnecessary."[89]

Two strands of irony were woven throughout this change. First, students had used long-standing Mennonite values to overturn tradition. They had invoked the old shibboleths of uniformity, modesty, and simplicity to win the day. The same students who touted individualism and free expression had now argued for uniformity and the suppression of individual taste. Second, students and faculty who welcomed the new attire signaled their loyalty to the ceremonial norms of higher education instead of the threadbare standards of the church, a fact that did not escape the minds of conservative leaders. The shift in commencement attire reflected the growing separation between religion and academic life. Academic dress was fitting for academic occasions; churchly dress for religious occasions. Even so, dress still mattered—to everyone.

They Shrugged Their White Shoulders

In May 1962, Vincent and Rosemarie Harding visited EMC and area Mennonites at the bidding of the school's Peace Fellowship. The Hardings, the most visible African American Mennonite activists in the early 1960s, operated a Mennonite center in Atlanta to improve race relations. During their visit to campus, Vincent and Rosemarie discovered several disturbing things in the Harrisonburg area.[90] Nearly fifteen years after EMC had welcomed its first African American student, some Mennonites remained oblivious to racial injustice or refused to protest it. Some even practiced discrimination. It was one thing to accept African American students at EMC but an entirely different matter to protest racial injustice in the public square.

There were few accommodations for African Americans in the Harrisonburg area apart from two private "tourist homes." Otherwise, African Americans had to stay in Staunton or at Camp Lewis at Luray. One restaurant in Harrisonburg, Frank's, catered to black clientele (ca. 1941–1953).[91] But others, including the local Howard Johnson's, did not, as President Mumaw discovered firsthand when he took an African visitor there for lunch and the waiter refused to seat his friend. "It's either two or none," Mumaw told the waiter. The manager soon found them a private room.[92]

The Hardings learned that a Mennonite-owned motel refused dark-skinned people, even turning away the parents of an EMC student. Yet Mennonites had publicly protested a local merchant seeking a liquor license. The Hardings argued that racial segregation was as immoral as drunkenness, prostitution, and gambling—sins that Mennonites would readily condemn. Activists were especially annoyed that Mennonites who were aware of these incongruities simply shrugged their shoulders, saying, "What can we do about it? We're nonresistant, so we can't boycott, can't picket, can't sit in, etc."[93]

A cluster of students took up the challenge to address the evils of racism with essays in the *Weather Vane*. Eleven EMC students had already attended the Intercollegiate Peace Fellowship gathering at Fisk University in the spring of 1961 and had met with activists promoting nonviolent civil disobedience. *Weather Vane* editor Carroll Yoder, picking up on Vincent Harding's suggestion, urged students to protest segregated restaurants and motels, which refused to serve some of "our own students—our brothers in Christ."[94] Young People's Christian Association groups, traveling with African Americans, refused to eat at restaurants that barred them. One student writer, noting "the plurality of northerners on the EMC campus," urged his fellow Yankees to love not only African Americans but white southerners as well.[95]

Two African American students, Grandison Hill and Lee Roy Berry Jr., arrived on campus in fall 1962. Some of their experiences confirmed what the Hardings had found a few months earlier. Hill, a seventeen-year-old from Washington, DC, was sent to EMC by his upwardly mobile parents.[96] Already accepted at Howard University, his parents wanted him in a Christian school "without social distractions."

Because Hill had no connections to Mennonites or EMC, his pillow "was wet many a night." Chapels were different from his Methodist Church experiences, but the first time he heard a cappella singing, it made quite an impression. "The tears literally rolled down my face. I had to pinch my eyes to keep from making a scene. I was stunned how beautiful it was." The highlight of his day was the family-style meal with three men and three women randomly assigned to each table, a practice that would end two years later: "There was a rhythm and ritual to it, standing until all arrived, the saying of grace, the singing of a song, the passing of the bread to the right, the filling of water glasses. And then the pleasant conversation, getting acquainted around the table, each day learning to know a new set of students. By the end of the year, everyone on campus knew each other. And the food, like my parents promised, was always excellent."

One Saturday, when family-style meals were not served, Hill arrived in the cafeteria and sat at the first convenient table. The conversation stopped when a student diagonally across from him said, "You should be eating that meal on the back porch." Hill recalled, "I locked gazes with him, neither of us said a word. Eventually he looked away. I picked up my fork and continued eating." On another occasion, Hill was walking by a nonassigned table and heard someone say, "What the hell is he doing here?" It was also painful to hear a child call him a "n———r" in the presence of parents who said nothing.

Nonetheless, Hill found many welcoming and supportive students. One time, he accompanied several other students to a movie theater in Harrisonburg—a violation of school rules. After buying tickets, the manager told the other students, "*You* can sit in the regular seats, but *he* has to sit in the balcony." The other students decided to join him in the balcony. "About ten minutes later, the manager appeared upstairs saying there's an official from EMC downstairs looking for us. And he showed us a side door to exit. I knew he was lying, but we all left on the slim chance we'd be caught."

For Hill, the highlight of the year was his spiritual conversion: "It was here that I met the Lord. It was a combination of things that got me thinking. Everywhere I turned I'd find more evidence of the resurrection. The guys had an early morning prayer group. It wasn't a devotional thing as much as learning from Scripture, reading the stories in a deeper way and coming to my own conclusion—*He's real!*" At EMC, "[I met] many genuinely good people who did a lot to make me feel comfortable." Still longing to be with his "own people," however, he transferred in fall 1963 to Virginia Union University, a historically black Methodist school. Eventually, Hill worked for many years in Washington as a civil and criminal defense lawyer.

The other African American student, Lee Roy Berry Jr., came to EMC in 1962 at the behest of the pastor of a Mennonite mission in Sarasota, Florida.[97] For Berry, "a poor migrant boy," EMC was a different world in terms of both race and class. He roomed with Paul Zehr, a seminary student who the school hoped would help Berry succeed. Later that fall, Zehr and Berry went to Harrisonburg for a haircut in a shop with African American barbers. One of them cut Zehr's hair but refused to cut Berry's. In another instance of likely discrimination, Berry tried to donate blood for a classmate dying of leukemia at Rockingham Hospital but was told his blood was unacceptable.

Being selected in his junior year to play the role of Othello in the campus production of Shakespeare's play was a "significant climb and affirmation for me," recalled Berry. But another event that same year was not. On March 15, 1965, a week after deadly racial violence had erupted in Selma, Alabama, some EMC students, including Berry, listened to President Lyndon B. Johnson's address to the Congress. The president, borrowing a phrase from the civil rights movement, said, "We shall overcome." A short time later, Berry received an anonymous call from someone who told him to "eat s—t."

One of the most sensitive issues for Berry was dating white women. Virginia laws forbade interracial marriage, and many Mennonites stridently opposed it. Some feared that integration on campus would eventually lead to interracial marriages. Dean Ira Miller advised Berry not to stray far from campus with a date for safety reasons. When one of his roommates was married near Newport News, he invited Berry to be his best man, a role that would involve walking arm in arm with the maid of honor, who was white. The bride's father feared that such touching would provoke an incident at the reception. Berry graciously stepped aside as best man but still attended the wedding. While kneeling for prayer at his own interracial wedding to Beth Hostetler in 1969, Berry recalled, "I kept one eye open for fear that someone might shoot me, because of threats I had heard prior to our ceremony."

Lee Roy Berry Jr. graduated in 1966. For him, "EMC was a decent and good place. I appreciated it and I'm thankful for the support of teachers like Al Keim and John A. Lapp." He also credited some of his success to his surrogate family, the congregation in Sarasota, as well as to the generous Mennonite communities that provided him with work during the summers, in several different states. Berry later received a PhD and a law degree and taught at Goshen College.

A Flaming Cross

Professor John A. Lapp did not shrug his white shoulders when he saw a cross burning on his yard in June 1965 as three figures faded into the night. The day before, in Bogalusa, Louisiana, two black deputy sheriffs in a Ku Klux Klan stronghold had been gunned down. The next morning, in his post on the EMC Opinion Board in the Ad Building, Lapp drew a straight line from that attack to the cross-burning on his yard. Although the cross-burners remained anonymous, Lapp charged them with aligning themselves with the Ku Klux Klan, "the most heinous and barbarian organization in the world apart from the Nazis."[98]

Lapp actively promoted on-campus events that exposed students to the evils of systemic racism, and he was instrumental in organizing the Rockingham County Human Relations Council. He suspected that the cross-burning was a student prank.[99] Yet it might have been kindled by someone angered by his desegregation efforts in Harrisonburg. Regardless of the reason, cross-burning, for Lapp, was an "irreverent if not sacrilegious act." He chided the EMC community for arguing about far-off Russian communism instead of protesting vigilante justice and racial bigotry at home.[100]

As Vincent and Marie Harding discovered during their 1962 visit, some Mennonites on campus and off were reluctant to publicly protest racism. College officials stopped a faculty member from inviting a federal judge to give a public lecture on racial integration in 1958, because of "the quite tense integration problem."[101] Segregation sentiment had melted enough six years later for the college to host two prominent white activists—John Howard Griffin and Sarah Patton Boyle—for public lectures. Griffin, the author of *Black like Me*, described the discrimination he experienced during a six-week tour in the South after artificially coloring his skin black. Boyle, author of *The Desegregated Heart*, who grew up with deep commitments to segregation, described her radical turnabout.[102]

The Human Relations Council, which John A. Lapp, Samuel Horst, Harold D. Lehman, and other colleagues founded, included white and African American representatives from various churches. The council organized mixed-race committees to investigate segregation in restaurants, motels, and schools. "We had some doors slammed in our face," Lehman said. The council also held public mixed-race gatherings. One was a picnic at a public school. A menacing police car circled the block until the picnic ended. Harold D. Lehman credits the Human Relations Council for increasing integration in Harrisonburg without sparking any violence.[103] In addition to their local activities, Lapp and four EMC colleagues drove to Washington and participated in the two-hundred-thousand-person March on Washington for Jobs and Freedom in August 1963 and heard Martin Luther King Jr. give his "I Have a Dream" speech.[104]

In the 1950s and '60s, the Mennonite intelligentsia had resurrected a biblical concept—the lordship of Christ.[105] Historically, this phrase referred to an individual's total surrender of his or her life to Christ. It also supplied a moral logic to protest social ills, even those inscribed in law. The phrase soon slipped into parlance at EMC. Professor Ira Miller, for example, spoke about it in chapel in 1953.[106] Instead of pitting the church against the government, the "Jesus Is Lord" slogan declared that Christ is Lord of all creation and all social structures. It implied a single moral ethic to which not only Christians but also the state were accountable. And when governments enforced oppressive Jim Crow laws, Christians had a moral obligation to protest evil. This new paradigm placed a moral burden for greater civic responsibility on Mennonite shoulders. The civil rights movement nudged Mennonites to think more about earthly citizenship and less about being pilgrims and strangers in this world.

Organizational Tweaks

For nearly two decades, EMC held a secret, but held it rather loosely. Since the 1920s, the school had had three main divisions: Bible school, high school, and college. The Bible school was the cornerstone of EMC's identity. Dean C. K. Lehman, more than anyone, fed the growth of the Bible school. By 1948, EMC's Bible school offered a six-year bachelor of theology degree and a bachelor's degree in religious education. In 1960, the college began offering a postcollege three-year seminary-level bachelor of divinity degree.[107]

When Goshen College opened a seminary in 1944, J. L. Stauffer needled Dean Harold S. Bender that the seminary would become a "preacher factory." And J. Irvin Lehman, longtime instructor at EMC, chided Bender for making an "adroit move to a professional salaried ministry."[108] Mennonites in the East remained opposed to seminary-trained pastors. After 1970, the transition to full-time salaried pastors increased, but the rate of adoption varied by conference and congregation.

EMC's faculty, who wanted a conservative seminary to prepare leaders for church agencies and congregations, faced a dilemma: How could they develop one without using the word *seminary*? In the 1950s, that word would have ignited a furor, causing a delay if not killing the project. So administrators quietly developed the Bible school into a seminary without calling it one publicly. After a long debate in 1958, the trustees authorized the development of a "distinctive seminary."[109] How would it be distinctive? President Mumaw, in "A Philosophy of Bible School Training," said that it would emphasize service, discipleship, the lordship of Christ, and Anabaptist heritage.[110] Finally, in the 1964–1965 school catalog, the word *Seminary* replaced *Bible School*, revealing the secret. The president and the dean of the college also served as the president and the dean of the seminary.

While the Bible school was gaining prominence in the 1940s and '50s, the high school and college were moving apart. The high school received a part-time leader for the first time in 1941 when Professor D. Ralph Hostetter became its director. Over the next two decades, the two programs gradually diverged, with separate policies, library holdings, chapel services, student publications, and faculty meetings. In the late 1950s, the high school and college still shared dormitories, the dining hall, a chapel, and some classrooms, but beginning in 1958–1959, the high school had its own catalog. High school and college students mingled freely until the high school moved to a new building in January 1964. Even then, the high school used some of the college facilities—the cafeteria, gymnasium, classrooms, and available dormitory rooms—and it remained part of EMC's corporate structure until 1982.[111]

In another development, EMC established extension courses taught by local instructors at Mennonite high schools in Lancaster and Johnstown, Pennsylvania, in 1954. These courses offered professional development for teachers in Mennonite elementary and high schools in those areas.[112] The Lancaster extension flourished and, years later, offered graduate courses.

On still another front, the 1963 constitutional revision specified that the board consist of thirty-two trustees—double the number during the previous forty years. As before, sixteen were elected by Virginia Conference. Twelve of the new seats were filled by other conferences, and the other four were appointed by the trustees themselves. This change shifted authority away from Virginia Conference. Nonetheless, the trustee board was still expected to "perform its duties under the direction and authority" of the conference, which retained the right to dismiss "any trustee at any time."[113]

The 1963 constitution did not mention the church-wide Mennonite Board of Education (MBE), which had been a contentious issue in the 1920s and '30s. The MBE continued to provide arm's-length oversight of Goshen College and Hesston College by appointing their trustees and establishing some general policies. Although EMC collaborated informally with the MBE, the college still chose not to join it. President Mumaw was a close friend of Goshen College president Paul Mininger, and when Mininger traveled to Harrisonburg, he usually lodged at Mumaw's home. Faculty members from the two schools also collaborated on various church-wide projects. Thus, during Mumaw's presidency, Goshen College—that bastion of all things worldly and wrong for many years—ironically was becoming EMC's exemplar of a church-related liberal arts college.

Because of Mumaw's ability to deftly steer EMC forward in the midst of turbulent change, the trustees appointed him to a fourth four-year term (1962–1966).

In February 1963, they initiated an early search for the next president so that the appointee could prepare for educational administration. One candidate explained, "In those days you didn't apply. You just waited. If the Lord wanted you, he would call you. He knew your address."[114] In the fall of that year, an odd event occurred. Two brothers drove past each other on Route 11 south of Harrisonburg. The brother driving north had just completed an interview with the presidential search committee. The brother driving south was on his way to meet the committee at Belle Meade Restaurant. The three top candidates under consideration were alumni—Richard Detweiler, A. Don Augsburger, and A. Don's brother Myron Augsburger. Detweiler, a pastor in Franconia Conference, was the oldest. Myron Augsburger was the youngest. Both Augsburgers were faculty members.

On January 2, 1964, trustee chair John Alger announced that Myron Augsburger would succeed J. R. Mumaw in July 1966. The decision was difficult for both Mumaw and A. Don Augsburger, whom Mumaw had been mentoring for the position. A. Don Augsburger left EMC and later returned to teach in the seminary in 1970. Mumaw had hoped to have a seat on the Administration Committee for several years as J. L. Stauffer had done when Mumaw became president. But that never happened.[115]

In June 1964, while Mumaw was in Colorado attending a board meeting, he learned that his wife, Esther Mosemann Mumaw, had died suddenly. That event and the growing cross fire between conservatives in the conference and progressives on campus led Mumaw to request a sabbatical leave for the last year of his contract, 1965–1966. Thus Myron Augsburger took office in July 1965, a year earlier than planned. In June of that year, Mumaw married Evelyn King, who had served as dean of women since 1951. They promptly embarked on a ten-month assignment to consult with Mennonite churches in Japan, India, and Africa. Upon their return, Mumaw taught at Eastern Mennonite Seminary.[116]

Mumaw had served an unprecedented seventeen years as president (1948–1965). During his tenure, EMC was transformed from a small Bible school and junior college into a fully accredited liberal arts college. Mumaw's leadership thrust EMC into the modern world of higher education. In that world, he served a two-year stint as president of the Council for the Advancement of Small Colleges. Though still cognizant of its ties to Virginia Conference, EMC under Mumaw's guidance began flexing its muscles in robust ways as a more mature and independent school.

With grace, persistence, and a keen mind, President Mumaw wrote dozens of position papers and served on many church-wide boards and agencies. His era marked a pivotal shift away from the indoctrination-separation paradigm, with its communal language of loyalty, safeguarding, and obedience, to a new set of ideas—the Anabaptist vision, discipleship, the lordship of Christ, individual choice, community, and service. In one of his last chapel addresses, Mumaw spoke on "Education for Christian Discipleship."[117]

The progress-minded leader, who was almost sidelined by the 1950 investigation, had eventually been bypassed by turbocharged changes during the last years of his presidency. By the time Mumaw left office in 1965, he was seen by some younger faculty as a conservative who impeded progress. Upon hearing of Mumaw's cutting-edge initiatives in the 1950s, Professor Al Keim later mused, "That was a J. R. Mumaw we didn't know."[118] A 1959 graduate who remembered him as "rigid and authoritarian" later came to appreciate that Mumaw "needed to enforce strict rules on behalf of the church, no matter his opinion."[119]

By the early 1960s, the old symbols of nonconformity were disappearing so fast in Virginia Conference that it called a special two-day session in April 1965 to assess the damage. Conference leaders pleaded for "visible symbols of discipleship," a new phrase that was replacing the threadbare "nonconformity." Yet rhetoric was the only tool the conference had to cope with the rapid rise of individualism among its members and ministers.[120] Some conservatives in the conference still yearned for EMC to do with its organizational clout what the conference could not do with moral persuasion: stop the incessant change. This churning milieu awaited the arrival of the next president, Myron Shenk Augsburger.

CHAPTER 8

Engaging a Turbulent World

Can we have Menno and a Mercedes, Jesus and jewelry?
—Professor Omar Eby

A Community of Persuasion

If Virginia Conference was in a freefall over nonconformity, America was on its own precipice when Myron Augsburger took office in July 1965. President Lyndon B. Johnson had sent the first 3,500 troops to Vietnam in March, and that number soon mushroomed to 190,000. Alongside the sad Vietnam saga was the rising civil rights movement. As the first US Marines landed in Vietnam in March 1965, Martin Luther King Jr. led thousands of civil rights activists on a four-day march from Selma to Montgomery, Alabama. In August, President Johnson signed the Voting Rights Act of 1965 into law, guaranteeing African Americans the right to vote.

Besides these societal disruptions, thirty-five-year-old Augsburger—the youngest to occupy the president's office—found himself in a quandary as he sought to mediate student demands for change with constituent fears of the burgeoning hippie movement that scorned institutional authority. The social turbulence of the 1960s came in "like a flood," said EMU historian Hubert Pellman. For several years, "President Mumaw had been damming up the growing pressure on intercollegiate sports, music, drama, and plain clothing."[1] Now those issues—almost trivial beside the ones driving the antiwar and civil rights protests—were bursting over the dam.

Augsburger was bold, ambitious, and qualified. He knew the Mennonite world well. Growing up in Elida, Ohio, he spent late evenings as a teenager talking theology with his neighbor, former EMS president J. B. Smith. Beginning in 1947, Augsburger had eighteen years of intermittent ties with EMC as a student, campus pastor, and, since 1963, professor of theology. In 1950, Virginia Conference had ordained the twenty-year-old Augsburger as pastor of the Tuttle Avenue congregation in Sarasota, Florida. He served there briefly but soon received invitations to preach to larger audiences. Against the advice of President Mumaw—who thought the stain of Goshen would preclude any future service to EMC—Augsburger took his last year of seminary (1959–1960) at Goshen Biblical Seminary, where his views of Anabaptist theology were shaped by John Howard Yoder, a brilliant young Mennonite scholar.[2] When he was named president, Augsburger held a freshly minted doctorate in theology from Union Seminary in Richmond. His dissertation explored the life of Michael Sattler, a sixteenth-century Swiss Anabaptist martyr. In the ten years before he took office, Augsburger had conducted dozens of Billy Graham–style evangelistic campaigns across the United States and Canada. These city-wide interdenominational efforts linked him to a large network of evangelical leaders across the United States.

Acting more and more like a grown-up college, EMC held its first presidential inauguration on April 1966. Augsburger, followed by the faculty in full regalia, led the processional to the chapel, which was overflowing with guests. Hudson T. Armerding, president of Wheaton College, delivered the address, which was followed by Augsburger's own speech on "Education for Meaning."[3]

One lingering sign of institutional immaturity surfaced in the protocol for presidential spouses. When Esther Kniss Augsburger entered the chapel, she asked where she should sit. "Oh, anywhere you like," replied an usher. She found her new role challenging in other ways. A well-meaning relative of a former president told her, "You have to give up all your friends." Following that advice brought several "very lonely" years and gave her the impression that the president's wife mattered little except to "serve cookies and punch in the backyard" for hundreds of guests at commencement. After several exasperating years of baking and freezing cookies months in advance, she finally told her husband, "Please ask the trustees to have the college kitchen serve the snacks."[4]

The new president brought formidable strengths that enabled him to orchestrate major changes in campus life and the mission of the college. Unapologetically evangelical and decidedly Anabaptist, he held deep commitments to global missions, reconciliation, and Christian pacifism. His book *Invitation to Discipleship* came off the press just as he took office. Not surprisingly, Augsburger made discipleship and the lordship of Christ prominent ideas throughout his presidency. It was rare for him not to mention discipleship in his talks and writings. His bold vision for Christian higher education energized campus discourse and left the old debates about modernism, liberalism, Fundamentalism, millennialism, and plain dress in the dustbins of history.

Augsburger was articulate, poised, and persuasive. He typically spoke in the mandatory daily chapel once a week and usually held students' attention. Some of them took delight in counting how many times he used the word *perspective* in his chapel addresses. Alumni remember how he used words like *frontal*, *global*, and *dynamic* and emphasized a holistic view of evangelical outreach that integrated the spiritual, social, and economic needs of people. One student, a graduate of Lancaster Mennonite High School, had never heard the word *Anabaptist* until Augsburger used it in chapel in 1965. Another recalled, "He always made me feel so proud to be a Mennonite."[5]

Although EMC had relaxed its stringent indoctrination during the Mumaw years, Augsburger explicitly rejected it. In his inaugural address, he introduced a new *persuasion-engagement* paradigm when he declared, "The importance of the person calls us to interpretation rather than simple indoctrination. . . . Truth and value . . . cannot be indoctrinated."[6] In a later convocation address, he proclaimed that the college should be a "community of persuasion" where truth should never be "simply imposed." Rather, in the Anabaptist tradition, "persuasion . . . affirms the freedom of the individual . . . voluntarism in our tradition respects one's freedom to say no." He explained that "persuasion is an essential element of good teaching." For him, the Anabaptist tradition aimed "not simply at the head but at the will . . . to persuade persons to vital discipleship."[7] Augsburger was a great persuader. His emphasis on persuasion fit handily with the flowering emphasis on the *individual* and *choice* in both Mennonite and national culture.

"Opening Up, Letting Go, and Spilling Out"

If persuasion was the moral paradigm on campus, *engagement* was the stance toward the outside world. The days of sectarian separation and suspicion at EMC were gone. The new persuasion-engagement model reset EMC's view of the larger society. No longer a place to fear, the world was the prime site for Christian engagement, service, and mission. Augsburger argued that Christian education must have a "global perspective. We are beyond the time when any group can live comfortably within its own heritage and experience." The president wanted EMC to develop "informed disciples . . . with a mission to make Christian faith an option in the academic marketplace."[8] He brought speakers, consultants, and scholars from outside the Mennonite world to engage the campus community, calling them "a healthy mix who help to free us from provincialism and challenge us to rethink our own positions."[9]

Operating from an evangelical-Anabaptist perspective, Augsburger urged students and faculty to engage religious and evangelical leaders beyond the Mennonite orbit, as well as secular educators and politicians, hoping to convince them of the veracity of Anabaptist perspectives, especially on Christian peacemaking and reconciliation.[10] The president reached out to political leaders such as Senator Mark Hatfield from Oregon, with whom he had a close friendship. One of Augsburger's friends arranged for him to meet with Melvin Laird, President Nixon's secretary of defense (1969–1972), to discuss the Vietnam War. As their discussion concluded, Laird suggested that they pray for each other. *Time* magazine underscored Augsburger's national reputation in 1969 when it named him one of America's top ten preachers advocating social involvement.[11]

The Augsburger administration brought a stream of evangelical leaders, scholars (religious and secular), ambassadors, journalists, poets, musicians, and artists to campus. The annual lecture series in 1965–1966 sought to expand the global consciousness of students. The following year, "Urbanism as a Way of Life" was a theme of the series. Interterm seminars in three consecutive Januarys dealt with "Christian Discipleship in a Brave New World," "Peacemaking in a World of Revolution," and "Hunger." In an April 1969 teach-in, the college canceled classes and in various venues debated the question, Whose land is Palestine?

The new openness to the world was also showcased in a flurry of travel by faculty and students in the summer of 1967. The twenty-six-member Alleluia Singers took a five-week European tour that included singing at the Mennonite World Conference in Amsterdam. A dozen seminary students embarked on a six-week tour of the Holy Land and early sites of the Christian church. Several students spent a month in eastern Europe, three others were part of a six-week Latin American study tour in El Salvador, and seventeen of their peers were involved in a work-study seminar on urban life in New York City. These off-campus activities foreshadowed what one faculty member called a decade of "opening up, letting go, and spilling out."[12]

Augsburger worked earnestly to maintain EMC's mission in the midst of turbulent change. As he urged faculty and students to engage global issues and welcomed non-Mennonite perspectives on campus, he also promoted simplicity of life, radical discipleship, a community of voluntary believers, and unabashed confidence in Mennonite theology. Still, Augsburger seemed comfortable meeting with worldly power brokers and at ease with a middle-class lifestyle, all of which confounded his critics. Meanwhile, Mennonites themselves were becoming more affluent. Professor Omar Eby pondered whether this experiment of blending "secular, evangelical, and Anabaptist perspectives" would work: "Can we have Menno and a Mercedes, Jesus and jewelry?"[13]

The Arts and Sciences, Mennonite Style

EMC's first fully air-conditioned building, the $1.4 million Science Center, was dedicated on Founders Day, October 4, 1968. The facility was the culmination of President Mumaw's planning in the early 1960s. Its M. T. Brackbill Planetarium and D. Ralph Hostetter Museum of Natural History piqued considerable curiosity. Students were pleased to find pleasant lecture rooms and well-equipped laboratories with generous space. Despite its qualms about evolution, EMC had developed a strong science program over the years, with many students pursuing medicine and nursing as exemplary professions of Christian service.

Already in the 1920s, the *Journal* and the *Bulletin* promoted science. A premed track began in 1935 in the junior college curriculum.[14] By the late 1950s, EMC

Professor D. Ralph Hostetter presents a lecture in the old biology lab, 1926.

began touting its medical school acceptance rate and the number of doctors among its alumni. Sixty of the school's graduates (11 percent of all the men) in the 1959–1969 decade completed medical school.[15] Daniel Suter was the architect of EMC's stellar reputation for preparing premed students. A 1935 alumnus, he was the son of J. Early Suter, the first registrar at EMS, who in 1918 had urged the school to add non-Bible courses such as English, algebra, and Latin and had agreed to teach them without compensation. Daniel Suter, who eventually held degrees from Vanderbilt University and the Medical College of Virginia, began teaching at EMC in 1948. He soon chaired the biology department and became the premed advisor. Like many of his teaching colleagues, he was also a pastor.

Suter's reputation was legendary. He wrote more than three hundred letters of recommendation for students applying to professional schools. The acceptance rate of EMC graduates applying to medical, dental, and veterinary school exceeded 85 percent during Suter's thirty-five-year tenure. According to premed student lore, a Suter recommendation guaranteed acceptance at certain medical schools. Whether accurate or not, that perception motivated students to study science.[16]

Mid-twentieth-century Mennonite leaders urged women to consider nursing because the church needed 160 nurses a year to serve in church agencies, from children's homes to hospitals and schools in the United States and abroad. Alumna Dora Taylor told *Bulletin* readers that "Mennonite girls make good nurses because they are willing to serve unselfishly."[17] President Mumaw, Dean Miller, and Professor Suter, each of whom had a daughter who was a registered nurse, collaborated to launch EMC's nursing program.

To accommodate student interests, EMC offered a pre- and postnursing sequence of general education from 1949 to 1962 without any nursing faculty or nursing courses on campus. Following their prenursing courses at EMC, students obtained their

Registered Nursing diploma from a hospital-affiliated school. In 1949–1950, nine students were in the prenursing sequence and eleven registered nurses were enrolled in the postnursing curriculum, which led to a five-year BS in Nursing. After a four-year affiliation with Riverside Hospital in Newport News (1958–1962), EMC began to develop its own baccalaureate nursing curriculum and offered the degree in 1966.[18]

Vida Swartzentruber Huber, who began teaching nursing at EMC in 1966, chaired the department. It soon became a powerhouse on campus. The department received several federal grants to support its program and facilities. By 1975–1976, nursing was the most popular major, claiming 22 percent of all EMC majors—twice the number in biology. Together, nursing and biology (the latter heavy with premed students) commanded a third of the 967 students on campus.[19] Not surprisingly, nursing also had the largest departmental budget. With this number of students and dollars, Huber was arguably the most powerful department chair and woman on campus. EMC soon became recognized as a center of innovative nursing education.[20]

For three decades (1950–1980), the premed track and the nursing major were highly gendered. Reflecting national trends, men dominated the premed faculty and curriculum and women did the same in nursing. Medicine and nursing offered many EMC graduates paths to Christian service, both in church-related agencies and beyond.

Apart from medicine, theology, and education, EMC graduates entered other professional schools in the 1950s and '60s, though in fewer numbers. Donald Showalter, for example, broke new ground in 1962 when he entered law school, a long-discouraged occupation for Mennonites because of their nonresistance and rejection of litigation. Showalter became the first Mennonite lawyer in Rockingham County. Alongside his law practice, he taught business law at EMC and provided legal counsel to the college for some fifty years.[21]

President Augsburger was especially fond of the humanities. Shortly after taking office, he prodded the faculty to create a new general education sequence of ten Interdisciplinary Studies (IDS) courses in the humanities. After months of work, the exhausted curriculum committee was ready to scrap the whole project because of its complexity. The president, who met regularly with the committee, insisted that it meet again and cancelled a flight to Berlin to attend the next meeting.

The massive undertaking eliminated many courses and replaced them with interdisciplinary ones taught by teams of five faculty members from different fields. The Bible department eliminated twenty-one courses, and the history department pruned thirteen. In this seismic shift, the academic schedule also moved from two semesters to three terms per year.[22] Such a large number of required common courses was rare in academia. "Whenever I think of IDS, I think of work, work,

work," said its director, J. Herbert Martin.[23] The new core was implemented in the fall of 1968. Within two years, it shrank to a seven-course sequence.

Having all students take the same battery of core courses created a common bond of solidarity. It also provided a big target for student complaints. A *Weather Vane* editorial opined that a new curriculum was not enough: "Team teaching and core courses still depend on the quality of teachers for success."[24] Several students charged that "the very core of our liberal arts education epitomizes depersonalization. After all 225 of us sit down, we all take notes, and we all take our punch-card computerized test . . . maybe we are, after all, just part of a big machine? Did you ever get the feeling that you're learning a little bit of everything and a whole lot of nothing?"[25] Even so, transfer students rated IDS courses high and preferred them to the general education courses they had taken in other schools.[26] "As much as we complained about the IDS courses, they were among the most valuable ones I had here," recalled Fred Kniss.[27] Fifty years after its launch, Augsburger considered the IDS program one of his singular achievements.

Alongside IDS, another faculty debate raged: Should EMC adopt self-paced student learning across the curriculum? In the nursing department, chair Vida Huber and curriculum coordinator Beryl Brubaker had developed a modular, competency-based, self-paced curriculum without any courses (but with demonstration labs and clinical experience) in the late 1960s.[28] In the fall of 1971, Professor John H. Hess Jr., chair of psychology, introduced a different self-paced program called Personalized System of Instruction (PSI) in several courses.[29] Among its benefits were higher exam scores and better student retention. Within two years, Hess had converted all the psychology courses to PSI "to make learning less abrasive to both students and faculty."[30] Hess and Huber were a powerful duo who led the charge for using this innovative pedagogy across the curriculum. "It stirred a big debate," recalled Beryl Brubaker.[31]

After an eight-month period of study, a task force recommended adopting PSI as EMC's basic method of instruction. Critics, however, argued that PSI tested the things most easily measured, which were not necessarily the most important things to learn. Besides, some nursing students took seven years to complete the self-paced program because it offered little structure. Strong opposition prevented PSI from becoming the standard pedagogy.[32]

Sliding Drama under the Door

When J. R. Mumaw returned from his international trip in 1966, President Augsburger invited him to speak in chapel on a Monday morning. Over the weekend, students had removed the college motto, Thy Word Is Truth, which hung at the back of the stage, to make way for a drama production. Augsburger introduced the former president and was astonished when Mumaw walked up to the podium and said pointedly, "I see that, since I'm no longer president, the motto has been removed." Augsburger assured the former president that the school remained firmly committed to the motto despite an occasional shuffle for stage productions.[33]

President Augsburger thought art and drama were important for a Christian liberal arts college. Discontent about drama, simmering for more than fifteen years, was coming to a boil as he took office. Student Mary M. Troyer voiced the traditional view of drama in 1931 when she declared that theater scoffs at religion, exalts the wicked, and trifles with the sacredness of love. She concluded that Christians who visit "the immoral theater . . . will be defiled."[34] In the late 1940s, the faculty devised a set of regulations that required literary skits to have a purpose beyond mere entertainment. The guidelines prohibited costuming, "but you could drape something over a person like an Indian blanket," explained a faculty member.[35]

Apart from acting, the faculty objected to students attending operas and Shakespearean plays. The controversy intensified when some students attended an off-campus production of *Macbeth*. After extensive study by several committees, in 1955 the faculty adopted a new policy that permitted a limited use of drama.[36] Even so, the faculty remained divided and debate persisted. Literary societies, without official sanction, soon began producing full-length plays, with homespun costumes and props.

Jay B. Landis, English teacher in the high school, incorporated short dramas into some of his classes. In 1959, one of his literature classes enacted *The Barretts of Wimpole Street*. At the end of the semester, after an evening banquet, the class presented the play in the basement of the chapel. "The place was full," recalled Landis. "Parents came. It wasn't publicized, you know. It was just for the class. Students told their parents and they came." Professor Irvin B. Horst quipped that Landis had slid drama in under a closed door. "I always remembered that," Landis said. "I did sort of open the door."[37]

By the late '50s, an uneasy de facto policy had emerged. Although college officials forbade theatrical performances open to the public and offered no classes on acting, drama went underground on campus in student productions sponsored by literary societies. This awkward agreement worked for several reasons. It did not force a public division in faculty ranks. It enabled faculty sympathizers to work quietly behind the scenes with students. It also gave the college cover from conservative trustees and constituents. At the same time, the arrangement opened space for student creativity and gave students the opportunity to learn the rudiments of acting. Relegating theater to the shadows ironically boosted student interest in drama.

At Augsburger's urging, Jay B. Landis took several courses in drama during a sabbatical in Idaho in 1968. When he returned, he began advising student productions alongside teaching English. "Drama had already been creeping in," said Landis.

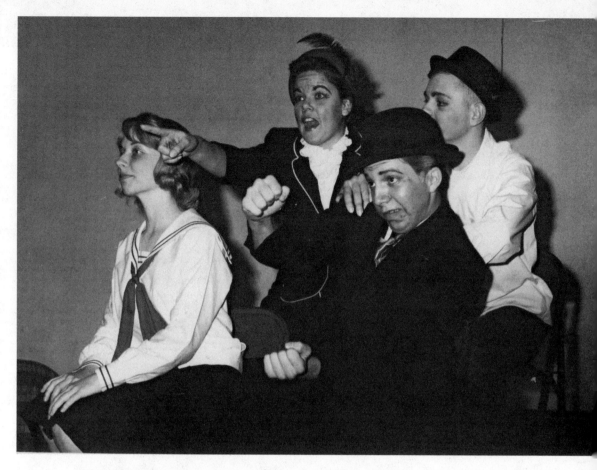

The Drama Guild's first production, *A Happy Journey from Trenton to Camden*, 1965. Left to right: Carolyn Mullet, Lois Martin, Gordon Yoder, Stephen Shriner.

"Students like Merle Good were directing and acting in the late '60s because none of the faculty knew how to do it, so the kids directed it themselves."[38] Student groups in the 1960s staged *The Diary of Anne Frank*, *The Boy with a Cart*, *Christ in the Concrete City*, *JB*, and *The Crucible*. Theater finally came out of the shadows in 1964–1965 when the Drama Guild was recognized as a legitimate student club. Claiming nearly a hundred members, it presented two or three major productions a year.[39]

"Our dream of a collegiate drama performance was realized in the Drama Guild's production of Jean Anouilh's modern version of *Antigone*," said student Karen Eby in November 1968. "With the demeanor of a professional, Merle Good nearly persuaded us of the validity of Creon's arguments. His variety of gestures and voice inflections kept the dialogue with Antigone intense and searching."[40] Some months later, the Drama Guild presented *Love Scenes*, with snippets from *The Taming of the Shrew*, *The Four Loves*, *The Glass Menagerie*, and *The Rainmaker*, all of which students arranged and directed. Chris Halverson, general producer, explained, "Eros love is shown the most in these dramas for it is the most talked about love in literature. We will try to represent all levels of love."[41]

In January 1969, several weeks before *Love Scenes* was performed, students—with instructor David Seitz directing an improvised orchestra—presented EMC's first-ever opera, *Solomon and Balkis*. Directed by senior English major Bob Hostetter, the performance received a positive review even though most of the participants "had never really seen a live professional operatic performance."[42] The Harrisonburg *Daily News-Record* captured a romantic photo of Solomon almost kissing Balkis in a dance routine. An incensed reader sent copies of the photo to church leaders in Lancaster, which sparked letters to the president calling the operatic dance terrible, shocking, shameful, immodest, and worldly.[43] Augsburger, however, had been assured that the opera would have no dancing or inappropriate things.[44] He explained to critics that "drama is difficult to handle," even with a faculty dramatics committee to advise student directors.[45] Although Augsburger wanted drama to flourish, strong objections from some constituents slowed the process.

Why did Mennonites resist drama? According to Jay B. Landis, the main objection was "impersonating someone else and losing your own identity. So it was equivalent to lying. You could read novels, I guess, but you couldn't act . . . couldn't become that person. It was a false impression." Besides, he said, "when you were acting you had to do things like kissing, smoking, and drinking, which were against rules. I had to fight through all that. Kids would come on stage and light up, even though they were told not to. This was Myron's hot potato. And I was supposed to solve all those issues!"[46] Critics also feared that staging drama would lead students to attend shows and movies. The 1955 faculty statement called for avoiding "the evils of indiscriminate dramatics," expensive costumes, and staging that violated the stewardship of time, money, and energy.[47] Moreover, said the faculty, EMC desired "to discourage anyone from entering a career in dramatics . . . [and hoped] to produce graduates dedicated to Christian service as missionaries, teachers, etc."[48]

Although drama enjoyed greater freedom under the Augsburger administration, it took a dozen years (until 1977) for the first course in dramatic arts to appear in the curriculum. The first instructor of theater, Barbra Graber, arrived in 1981, and a minor in theater came two years later.

"Leave Her as She Is"

Apart from that of presidential spouse, Esther Augsburger held other roles at various times—EMC student, James Madison College student, first EMC art graduate, founder of the art department in the high school, graduate student at James Madison, sculptor, and champion of art. She played a significant role in promoting art as a legitimate part of a conservative college whose tradition did not value it. Apart from Fraktur, quilts, and other types of folk art, rural Mennonites had little time for art.

By the mid-1930s, EMS was offering three art courses for elementary school teachers in the junior college curriculum. A decade later, as the school prepared for college status, its new Department of Language, Literature, and Fine Arts added an art laboratory. The laboratory and related courses emphasized arts and crafts.[49] When the Augsburgers arrived in 1965, the college was offering six art classes, half of which focused on art appreciation. The president recalled, "I brought the first *real* (professionally trained) art teacher to campus in the late '60s."[50]

Born in India to Mennonite missionary parents, Esther Augsburger began taking classes in music at EMC. "But Myron knew I loved art, and he kept saying, 'Your first love is art.'" She took an art course for elementary school teachers at EMC, yet she yearned to teach art in high school. So she took art courses at James Madison College, all the while worrying, "How can the church use an artist? And will my art be detrimental to Myron's ministry?" After finishing her art coursework at Madison, she transferred her credits to EMC, where she graduated as the first and only art major in 1972. She was the first person to walk across the stage at graduation. Myron handed the diploma to her and then kissed her as the audience applauded. The next graduate, a young woman, also paused for a kiss. "I didn't kiss her, but I should have," recalled the embarrassed president. "It could've started a whole new pattern."

Esther Augsburger founded the art department in the high school and taught there five years before pursuing a master's degree in art with a concentration in sculpture at James Madison. Her graduate exhibit, displayed at EMC, included a sculpture of an Anabaptist martyr woman who was nude from the waist up. Not wanting to offend conservative-minded people on or off campus, Augsburger had planned to drape the woman with a ragged cloth, although her mentor thought that would make the martyr even more risqué. Donald Jacobs, EMU grad and missionary in Africa, was visiting with the Augsburgers as Esther wrestled with how to complete the sculpture. Jacobs was moved to tears as he viewed the uncovered woman. "Leave her as she is," he told Esther. And she did.

Esther was flabbergasted to learn that her exhibit would coincide with the annual Ministers Week, when church leaders came to campus for worship and professional development. Should she remove the martyr from the exhibit? "Myron told me, 'It is part of your exhibit. Just leave it there.' I did and never heard one word of criticism." Shortly later she wrote "Why Nudity in Art?" for F*estival Quarterly,* a magazine devoted to "exploring the art, faith, and culture of Mennonite peoples." In the essay, she explained her struggle with the martyr and argued that "just as art needs no justification, the appropriate use of nudity in art needs none."[51]

Buoyed by Esther Augsburger's creative contributions and growing student interest, EMC began offering a full spectrum of art courses by 1975. Earlier, to support the growing interest in the arts, the college held an annual spring arts festival. The theme of the three-day event in April 1970 was "Mennonites in the Arts—Past and Present." Senior Shirley Hershey Showalter headed the festival, which drew several thousand people. She explained that "Mennonites sometimes feel as if we are culturally deprived. Our purpose is to show what art forms we really have."[52]

"Nay, We Will Have Varsity Sports"

Intense student pressure for intercollegiate athletics was building when Augsburger took office in July 1965. A constitutional revision in 1963 opened the door for intercollegiate sports and athletic conference membership by permitting "a limited number of extramural games," with administrative approval. This measured response revealed the persistent reservations of conservative constituents.

Augsburger, however, was sympathetic to intercollegiate sports. To pave the way for them, he convened a study conference on athletics in December 1965 to discuss the pros and cons of intercollegiate competition. This encouraged campus-wide discussion and reduced the immediate pressure for him to act.[53] Conference participants considered whether "athletics were scripturally justifiable" and sought to discern if athletics could offer venues for "Christian witness." Among other things, the conference suggested that men needed the outlet of intercollegiate athletics more than women; the latter could be satisfied with "a strong intramural program" and competitive games with women athletes from other schools on an annual sports day.[54]

Miriam Mumaw, daughter of the former president, overturned the assumption that women would be content with intramural sports. She began coaching intercollegiate women's varsity and junior varsity basketball while wearing a head covering and below-the-knee skirt. Mumaw's enthusiasm and expertise quickly boosted the popularity of women's sports.[55] The president endorsed a cheerleading program, with these provisos: that cheerleaders wear culottes, that the cheers not provide sensual entertainment, and that the program welcome all women, "not just the girl with short hair."[56] Augsburger hoped that EMC's physical education program would "avoid spectatoritis" and offer a Christian witness more than mere recognition of winners.[57]

Athletics and sports burgeoned in the first ten years of the Augsburger presidency. In his first year in office, men's soccer and basketball enjoyed their first season of intercollegiate competition.[58] During the next year (1966–1967), track, tennis, cross-country, and wrestling were added. Some students questioned the need for varsity sports in *Weather Vane* essays. James Wert, for example, wrote a parody, "Nay, We Will Have Varsity Sports," based on the biblical story in which the Hebrew people beg for a king, contrary to God's will (1 Sam. 8:20):

EMC men beat Davis and Elkins College 3–1 in EMC's first season of intercollegiate men's soccer, 1965.

Then all the students of EMC gathered themselves together, and came to the administration and said unto them, "Behold, EMC has come of age, and things are not as they once were. Now therefore make a varsity sports program like the other colleges." But the thing was evil in the eyes of the administration . . . [The leaders] said, "It will divert the energies of the student body into a pep club to feed the ego of the athletes. And behold, pagan ceremonies will be held to finance procuring of gorgeous robes for the cheerleaders. And the emphasis on sports shall sap your scholastic efforts . . ." Nevertheless, the people refused to obey the voice of the administration, and they said, "Nay, we will have varsity sports that we also may be like all the colleges, and that our varsity teams may bring glory upon us and make our hearts proud."[59]

The physical education program and intercollegiate sports grew quickly. Early on, Augsburger hired Roland Landes to build an intercollegiate program. Landes began to add more teams, and by 1970, the first varsity sports brochure was printed. A year later, the physical education department began offering a major. A camping, recreation, and youth ministries track was added in 1977.[60]

EMC was a founding member of the Interstate Athletic Conference, together with Shenandoah, Messiah, and Bridgewater Colleges. EMC joined the National Association of Intercollegiate Athletics in 1971, the National Christian College Athletic Association in 1972, the National Collegiate Athletic Association in 1974, and the Old Dominion Athletic Conference in 1976.

Athletic director Landes recalled that with Augsburger's support, intercollegiate athletics developed with a "free hand." For Landes, "the time was right—*everyone* was ready."[61] In 1980, the last year of Augsburger's presidency, the thirteen-person Task Force on Athletics produced an ambitious "blueprint" to upscale EMC athletics for the next decade.[62] Athletics and sports continued to flourish into the twenty-first century as many top EMU athletes received regional and national laurels for their achievements.[63]

Not Many Longhairs Here

The year 1969 brought a tumultuous mix of antiwar activities and student power demonstrations across the nation. The weeklong Woodstock Festival in mid-August attracted some four hundred thousand people to a six-hundred-acre dairy farm in New York. This event exemplified the free love–endorsing, drug-using, folk-singing, countercultural hippie generation. "The student revolt spreads," opined Ken Lehman in the *Weather Vane*. "Columbia, Berkeley, San Francisco State, etc., etc., have fallen. Cornell has fallen. Even Harvard falls. EMC will fall. Or will it? It can't happen here. Can it? No, of course not. We are a Christian College. We're a Mennonite college. We are a conservative college. We don't have many longhairs here."[64] EMC had a few long-haired aspiring radicals, a campus coffee shop, and Mennonite-style folk music—but there were no violent protests or sit-ins on campus. Still, one worried church leader from Lancaster asked the president if it was true that EMC had become a hippie settlement.[65]

Luke H. Wenger was the first student to voice concern about the Vietnam War publicly. In a *Weather Vane* essay in May 1962, he asked, "What are we getting into in Vietnam?" Student interest in the war was stirred by alumni who were serving in Vietnam with Mennonite relief and mission agencies. Everett and Margaret Metzler, for example, visited the campus in spring 1963, and a few weeks later, Luke S. Martin sent a letter to the *Weather Vane*. The stories they told encouraged junior Melvin Keim to see the Vietnam War through the lens of colonialism rather than those of communism or nationalism.[66]

While many EMC students remained oblivious to the national unrest, some marched, and others prayed for peace. Several student leaders returned their draft cards, and a few refused to register for the draft.[67] *Weather Vane* editor Stuart Showalter joined two hundred other college editors in signing letters to President Johnson questioning US policy in Vietnam.[68] Already in the spring of 1967, students held weekly peace vigils in front of Valley National Bank in Harrisonburg, where they received both rebuke and praise from onlookers. The roughest rebuke came from a band of teenage boys who challenged them and cut one of their placards in half.[69]

In January 1969, about two dozen EMC students walked in a peace march in Washington the day before President Nixon's inauguration and attended the

Sunday evening counterinaugural ball.[70] Two months later, EMC students joined some two hundred Mennonite and Brethren college students at an Intercollegiate Peace Fellowship gathering in Washington, where they heard speakers ranging from an avowed communist to President Augsburger talk about revolution.[71]

If the civil rights movement nudged a few Mennonites to protest racism, the Vietnam War created a crisis of conscience for many Mennonites because it shook the pillars of nonresistance. Unlike war protesters at other campuses, those at EMC always faced rebuttal and sometimes rebuke from fellow students—not because the critics supported the war but because they embraced traditional Mennonite commitments to nonresistance: Do not resist evil. Turn the other cheek. Pray for God-ordained government leaders. Do not tell the government what to do. Pay taxes and obey the laws. Live quiet and peaceful lives. These phrases had seeped into the minds of many EMC students beginning in childhood. But now the word *reconciliation*, which emerged from the civil rights movement and had a biblical ring, was increasingly used to replace *nonresistance*. The phrase *peace position* also came into vogue.[72]

The horrific war scenes flooding their television screens made peace-loving Mennonites squirm. Images of flaming napalm and burning bodies unsettled their nonresistant convictions. Nonresistance seemed to be an impotent response for a new generation of Anabaptists with a keen sense of American citizenship and a desire to protest the actions of their government. How could disciples of Jesus condone, by their silence and passivity, the evil wrought by their own government in Vietnam? And yet they also knew that their church discouraged protests against government policies and taught that civil disobedience completely violated its long-held conviction to obey the laws of the state.

In some ways, the growing emphasis on the lordship of Christ inadvertently supported civil disobedience. Some Mennonite scholars, as noted in chapter 7, contended that the lordship of Christ posited an ethical standard *above* all human authority, including government—not a parallel norm alongside the ethic of the state, as conceived by the traditional two-kingdom theology. It was but a short step to presume that the followers of Christ could call the government to the ethical norms of the gospel or, in everyday parlance, "tell the government what to do." And in a 1970 letter to President Nixon, Myron Augsburger did just that. On behalf of the EMC faculty and students, he urged Nixon to "promptly end our involvement in the Indo-China war [because] violence only begets violence, a just war is impossible, and friendship and love is the only cure for social and political ills."[73]

In the summer of 1969, at the church-wide General Conference in Turner, Oregon, thirteen long-haired draft resisters in ragged blue jeans confronted their elders. The group hoped that the church would support their civil disobedience—their refusal to cooperate with Selective Service. The request irked some church leaders because government-approved Alternative Service options had been intentionally designed to accommodate conscientious objectors (see chapter 5 for background). For draft resisters, that program was a moral compromise with militarism, akin to sleeping with the devil. They argued that a radical allegiance to Christ required absolute noncooperation with Selective Service—the jaws of the military-industrial complex. Two EMC faculty members, history professor John A. Lapp and seminary dean George Brunk II, played key roles in fashioning an agreement that both the resisters and the delegates eventually accepted. The "Turner statement" recognized "noncooperation as a legitimate witness" and pledged the support of church agencies to young men facing hardship because of their "costly discipleship."[74]

In September, two of the draft resisters, students at Goshen College, gave their account of the Turner conference at EMC. Both had destroyed their draft cards, yet Jon Lind and Devon Leu "did not come across as wild-eyed kooks," declared the *Weather Vane*.[75] The resisters praised Brunk for telling the five hundred conference delegates that he was convinced of the young men's sincerity. "If we can look past their hair," Brunk had said, "I think they have something to say to us."[76] Besides, Brunk was pleased that the event had spurred the "two generations to talk with each other."[77]

On October 15, 1969, EMC was the only college in Virginia to cancel classes for the national Vietnam War Moratorium Day, when colleges across the nation held rallies and teach-ins. EMC participated in the event "to educate and develop an awareness of the issues and symbolize our disagreement with the government's actions in Vietnam." President Augsburger explained that EMC had "more alumni working in Vietnam [in humanitarian service] than any other institution of higher learning."[78] Area residents were invited to campus to participate in the lectures, a student debate on draft resistance, a session for letter writing to government officials, and an evening "peace rally" with guitars, poems, and prayers. The newly formed Student Government Association (SGA) and the Peace Club organized the event and sponsored a half-page ad for it in the *Daily News-Record*.[79]

Some off-campus people were upset that EMC participated in the moratorium. A local citizen charged EMC students with "aiding and abetting America's enemies." EMC representatives were "peppered with biting questions" on local radio station WSVA's call-in show before the moratorium began.[80] President Augsburger received angry letters. One alumnus wrote, "A church supported college does not have the right to try to run the government. . . . Please stop soliciting donations . . . if you plan to become just another college with its Beatniks, Kookniks, and Nutniks."[81]

The *Weather Vane* reported that "student reaction to the moratorium ranged from enthusiasm to apathy." Peace Club president Duane Yoder estimated that 35 percent of the student body actively participated in the event. On the other side, some one hundred students opposed the moratorium because it violated their Christian principles.[82] For those on the sidelines, showing solidarity with noisy political protesters seemed inconsistent with their quiet willing-to-suffer nonresistance. Sometime later, Victor D. Obot, a physics major from Nigeria, captured the contradiction in his phrase "resistance of the nonresistant." He was disturbed not only by the public protests against the war but also by the "angry name-calling that goes on in the dormitories or the harsh, cruel character assassinations on the Opinion Board, or for that matter, the often-false gossip that goes around the campus daily."[83]

In March 1970, an FBI agent surprised Duane Shank in the hallway of his EMC dorm as he returned to his room after taking a shower. The agent verified Shank's identity, confirmed that he had refused to register for the draft, and then left. About a month later, as Shank was taking an exam in the chapel, a teacher tapped him on the arm and whispered that someone wanted to speak with him at the back. Leaving his books on his seat, Shank walked to the vestibule, where two FBI agents met him. They drove him thirty miles south to Waynesboro because the Harrisonburg jail lacked adequate security for federal prisoners. Within hours, EMC's dean of men, Jerry Shenk, cobbled together $500 for Shank's bail, drove to Waynesboro, and returned him to campus.[84]

Ruth Krady Lehman served as secretary to Lester C. Shank, the school's registrar. She had grown increasingly troubled with how easily EMC cooperated with the FBI's prosecution of draft resisters by allowing federal agents to access student files and use office space for interrogations. Lehman asked Shank, "Do you really think we ought to be allowing the FBI such free access to our files?" After checking with Dean Ira Miller, Shank reported that the two men thought EMC's cooperation was reasonable. Still, Lehman worried that she and the college were helping the government fight the Vietnam War. Her anxiety rose because her son Dan—grandson of violin-playing Bishop Daniel W. Lehman, a professor of education at EMC since 1921—was about to break the law, and she might find herself aiding her own son's arrest. On August 12, 1970, Dan Lehman returned his registration card to his draft board, saying, "To obey Christ and affirm life, I must refuse to cooperate with any system that affirms death. The Selective Service System is, I feel, an integral part of a violent system." He was prepared to move to Canada to avoid imprisonment, but his draft board never initiated prosecution.[85]

Young Mennonite draft resisters at EMC and Goshen College pointed to the early Anabaptists as exemplars of civil disobedience, even though the time and the context were different. A combination of theological justifications as well as the national draft resistance movement produced some fifty resisters in various Mennonite groups. Their actions prodded many Mennonites to ponder the ethical complications of civil disobedience for the first time in their generation.[86]

Almost a Miracle

In the spring of 1969, the national student power movement sparked the idea for creating the Student Government Association at EMC. That fall, negotiations between administrators and student leaders led to the formation of the SGA, with thirty representatives from the student body organized into an executive committee, a senate, several committees, and two judicial councils. In addition, school officials agreed to accept two student representatives on each of a dozen college committees and to allow the SGA president (Bruce Yoder) to be a voting member of the Administrative Council alongside six administrators and three faculty, beginning in January 1970. (The SGA president was also permitted to attend faculty meetings.)[87] A sense of optimism filled the air in the fall of 1969. Student Ben Gamber crowed that "students at Eastern Mennonite College have achieved that which college students all across the nation are clamoring for: a voice in college administration."[88] The vibrant student enthusiasm paved the way for what some campus observers would soon call a miracle.

Ten years after the college had raised endowment funds for Southern Association of Colleges and Schools (SACS) accreditation in December 1959, students orchestrated another fund-raising blitz. College officials hoped to construct a much-needed library that could accommodate 150,000 volumes and 550 patrons. The trustees required $400,000 in cash before proceeding with construction of the $1.4 million project. A pending federal grant of $389,000 for construction was set to expire in early December. Missing the deadline would have stalled the project for a long time.

Although the most successful alumni campaign in its history had just yielded $250,000, the college was still short $150,000 in October 1969.[89] Alumni director Ralph King explained that graduates "serving in war-torn areas" had little to give. There were eighteen alumni in Vietnam, eight in the Middle East, twelve in Biafra–Nigeria, and twenty-three in Honduras–El Salvador. Scores of others were serving in other countries. A student editorial, "Salvaging the Library," admitted that "EMC is not noted for having a 'rah-rah' type of school spirit, but perhaps with a little 'rah-rah' the new library can be salvaged."[90]

With alumni and constituent contributions waning, the college turned to students for help. At Thanksgiving break, students took home flyers asking for gifts before the December 9 deadline. One hundred sixteen students returned from the break with nearly $23,000. Following chapel on Wednesday, December 3, Augsburger led the college community in prayer to seek God's help. Late the next morning, campus pastor Truman H. Brunk Jr. proposed a weekend fund-raising marathon. After some brainstorming, two student leaders, Everett Ressler and Bruce Yoder, enthusiastically embraced the idea and began organizing students to raise $100,000.

Rebirth, a popular student folk group, performs in downtown Harrisonburg to raise funds for the library, 1969. Left to right: James Krabill, Elaine Warfel, Dean Clemmer.

Contributions came through gifts, work, an auction, and special projects. Students called their home congregations or attended services to ask for help. Sixty-seven congregations, some as distant as Arkansas, Minnesota, and Saskatchewan, contributed $25,000. Two college music groups, Optimists and Rebirth, garnered $360 as they performed on Harrisonburg's courthouse lawn, where one American Legion officer thought the singers were protesting the Vietnam War.[91] Students cleaned out a chicken house for $500, chopped wood for $1,000, and washed and waxed cars for as much as $200 a vehicle. The enthusiasm was contagious. "The dorms went crazy raising money," said Everett Ressler. "We even heard that women were charging admission to the bathrooms."[92]

The mood on Monday was exuberant as people brought items into the gym for the auction. When two auctioneers began hawking the items early that evening, a huge paper thermometer registered the $75,000 already raised that weekend. A large old dinner bell—from the farm where EMC founder L. J. Heatwole once lived—was on the auction.[93] Buyers bid on all sorts of valuable antiques, mementos, furniture, and even a handmade 1883 cello. Some two thousand people applauded wildly as the thermometer inched toward the $100,000 mark. At about two o'clock in the morning, President Augsburger auctioned off the bell, which the junior class bought for $800. With little sleep for forty-eight hours, students returned to their rooms exhausted but jubilant that the effort had overshot the goal by $11,000.

At the Tuesday morning chapel, the trustees sat on stage and officiated the program. They received a standing ovation from the students. And then—in what was surely an oddity in an era of rancorous student sit-ins demanding concessions from administrators—the trustees rose to their feet and gave the student body a sustained ovation. Librarian James O. Lehman called it a grassroots movement. "Students basically furnished the ideas, the enthusiasm, the leadership, and the muscle," he said. A responsive faculty, the local community, and the church at large helped to turn the unforgettable weekend into a "happening in unity." The new library opened eighteen months later, on June 30, 1971.[94]

Fascinated by this kind of student power, national wire services carried the story for two days in dozens of newspapers from the *New York Times* to the *Los Angeles Times*.[95] The Richmond *Times-Dispatch* declared that the library "will stand as a memorial to the 950 young men and women who showed that student power, when properly channeled, can indeed perform miracles."[96] James O. Lehman often called the new library "a miracle building" because it seemed so inexplicable. But skeptical professor G. Irvin Lehman demurred, noting that "everything had occurred within natural laws."[97]

The splendid cooperation among students, faculty, and administrators emerged from the trust developed during the birth of the SGA. But not everyone was happy about students attending faculty meetings. In 1970, Mary Emma Showalter Eby, speaking for herself and some other faculty members, told President Augsburger that the administration had "made a grave mistake in allowing a student to push his foot so far inside the door where institutional policy is determined." She refused to attend another faculty meeting where a student would "belittle the faculty . . . in a negative and know-it-all-manner." Besides, she resented that a student "sits in the highest administrative body [Administrative Council] where only three faculty are represented."[98]

The SGA spearheaded many actions regarding campus life in the following years: establishing Sunday hours for the library, reinstating the Opinion Board without a locked glass cover in the Ad Building, instigating teacher evaluations, actively protesting required chapel attendance, handling minor disciplinary cases through the SGA's judicial councils, developing the first student-written *Handbook*, and promoting revisions of policies relating to women's dorm hours, coed dorms, the bookstore, the cafeteria, and parking tickets. Even so, the SGA's power had limits. It was excluded from the decision to change EMC's moniker for sports teams from the Courtiers to the Royals, and it was denied voting seats on the board of trustees.[99] Nonetheless, the SGA signaled a new level of student involvement and influence in campus policies.

Spoiling a Sacred Spot

An event in 1971 kindled a new burst of student action. EMC's efforts to persuade students that discipleship—following Jesus in daily life—was the core of Christian faith proved, perhaps, to be too successful. In early January, the college announced that the Harman Family Foundation had given a grant of $45,000 for a prayer chapel in memory of Frank T. Harman, an alumnus and longtime trustee before his death in 1968. At the suggestion of the family, EMC planned to build the chapel on the crest of the hill behind the administration building. This beautiful spot with its spectacular views had served as a place for meditation, prayer, inspiration, and romance for more than fifty years. A *Weather Vane* editorial writer described the hill as a sacred spot—the site of "innumerable prayers, countless vesper services," the place where "scores of romances have flickered, grown, and died."[100]

President Augsburger announced the community's gratitude for the gift, but not everyone was grateful.[101] Within days of the announcement, 356 students and faculty had signed a petition asking that the gift be used to renovate the existing chapel or enlarge the gymnasium instead. "EMC students rose up in protest" and created what the *Weather Vane* called an imbroglio.[102] "Why," asked an editorial writer, "must we put four walls and a roof up there so we can pray without getting grass stains on our suits?"[103]

Dozens of alumni and friends of the college sent angry letters to the president saying that the chapel would scar a sacred spot with panoramic vistas of mountains to the east and west. One alumnus said that the building would "desecrate . . . a sacred place [and] insure our church's faster descent into hell."[104] Many of the letter writers thought the project clashed with EMC's commitment to radical discipleship and service to the needy.[105] An alumnus upset about spoiling nature wondered, "Will God, on Judgment Day . . . bless us for a gothic edifice" when the money could be used to help "black students in southern Virginia . . . or poor Mennonites" who cannot afford a college education?[106]

Blindsided by the harsh criticism, administrators and trustees paused to consider a name other than *chapel* for the building, since EMU already had a chapel. Some of the options included Retreat Center, Schleitheim Hall—after the town in Switzerland where a large gathering of early Anabaptist leaders met in 1527—and Discipleship Center. By May, the proposed prayer chapel was named the Discipleship Center. Sobered by the vitriolic tone of the protesters, officials stalled the project for two years despite a petition from 138 students and faculty urging them to proceed.[107]

To partially accommodate the critics, the trustees shifted the location of the building to the north end of the knoll, near the 1930s-era Vesper Heights Observatory.[108] After the center opened in 1974, it became a frequent site for small conferences, seminars, and other campus gatherings. Administrators had found legitimacy, or perhaps political shelter, in the word *discipleship*—which implied that the center's programs would promote following Jesus in daily life—the very word that had empowered many of the protesters in the first place.

Chapel: An Anabaptist Quandary

The new primacy of persuasion was tested by the long-standing policy that required attendance at daily chapel services. If Anabaptist theology emphasized voluntarism, students argued, the college should respect their personal decisions regarding chapel attendance. Otherwise the institution was coercing them. Augsburger contended that students had freely chosen to attend a Christian college, and with that choice came responsibilities determined by the community. "We respect your freedom to leave and go elsewhere," he said. "But if you choose to come here, we expect your participation."[109] Mandatory chapel attendance ignited vigorous debate in 1967, when four faculty and 125 students signed a petition (the first one in EMC's history) objecting to it. Noting that Christian discipleship is *voluntary* in Anabaptist theology, the petitioners contended that requiring chapel attendance was inconsistent, if not outright hypocritical.[110] A committee commissioned to study the issue, however, strongly endorsed mandatory attendance.

Twice in the 1969–1970 school year, the faculty discussed compulsory chapel attendance, and twice they failed to find a consensus. Early in 1970, the SGA also addressed the issue, pressing for flexibility. Late in the spring, President Augsburger and SGA leaders agreed, on a trial basis, to have three days of mandatory chapel (on Mondays, Wednesdays, and Fridays) and two voluntary ones.[111] That compromise became policy, but attendance on Tuesdays and Thursdays soon dwindled.[112]

Four years later, *Weather Vane* editor Mike Sarco was incensed by students' "lack of intellectual discipline" when fewer than one hundred came to hear philosophy professor Thomas Finger speak on faith and reason at a Thursday chapel. Sarco wrote, "We may rail against the inadequacies of compulsory chapel, its infringement on personal liberty, and its stifling effect on spontaneous expression, but when we face facts, we are forced to see that we need rules, standards, requirements, and deadlines in order to get anything significant accomplished."[113]

The question of compulsory chapel continued to simmer.[114] Students were especially annoyed that each absence above three reduced their grade point average by .25. The academic penalty ended in 1981–1982, the same year that students were required to attend only half of the chapels each term. By 1988, students reported their own attendance, and in the mid-1990s, chapels were held only three times a week.[115]

During 1974–1975, the college renovated the thirty-year-old chapel and turned it into EMC's first performing arts center. The renovation made the space more inviting for daily chapels, but poor acoustics sometimes plagued its use as a venue for vocal and instrumental music. The renovated facility's beauty and versatility was enhanced by the gift of a $50,000 organ, which exceeded the cost of the Discipleship Center.

Near the end of the spring 1977 semester, twelve students engineered their own memorable renovation of the chapel by devising a prank to turn all the pews backward. One prankster hid in the building before it was locked for the evening so the others could enter after midnight. The students removed the anchor bolts that secured the pews to the floor, turned the seats, and rebolted them to the floor. They drew a diagram of the process because they intended to confess their misdeed the next day and realign the pews.

The mischief-makers arrived at chapel the next morning amid surprise, confusion, and annoyance. The service was quickly moved outdoors, and President Augsburger announced that tampering with the pews had broken the manufacturer's twenty-year warranty, exposing the school to financial risk. After the service, one of the culprits asked the president if he had any idea who did this. Augsburger said, "No, but we think it's a pretty large group." After realizing that officials suspected the wrong group and that the broken warranty could result in fines, the culprits decided not to confess. Nonetheless, they sent their step-by-step procedure for reversing the benches to the maintenance staff, and some of them, along with other volunteers, helped realign the benches (which outlasted their warranty and remain in the chapel). College officials never identified the offenders.

About twenty-five years later, when he applied for the position of vice president for student life, Ken L. Nafziger confessed his complicity in the prank. After he took the position, former president Myron Augsburger told Nafziger, "You may find yourself feeling differently about pranks now in your new role."[116]

The Crisis of Mennonite Identity

In the late 1960s, Paul Peachey, an EMC alumnus and former professor, wrote an influential essay in the *Mennonite Quarterly Review* titled "Identity Crisis among American Mennonites." He argued that Mennonites "today are undergoing a deep crisis of identity [and] the cultural and psychic substance of Mennonite solidarity is rapidly dissolving." Peachey blamed the crisis on "the runaway pace of change in American life."[117] The speed of change, however, was but one of many forces prompting the existential questions, Who are we? What do we believe? And what exactly does it mean to be a Mennonite?

Mennonite identity, like all socially constructed group identities, was soft and pliable. The social scaffold that supported Mennonite identity in the first half of the twentieth century—rural life, cultural separatism, nonconformity, nonresistance, lay leadership, church authority, traditional gender roles—was collapsing. EMC students were uncertain if Mennonites were farmers or suburbanites, separatists or participants in political life, quiescent folks or activist peacemakers, plain-dressing or fashion conscious. Did Mennonites still forbid divorce, lawsuits, and television? The adjectives that had easily defined EMC's constituents for fifty years no longer fit. Since 1950, numerous tradition-minded groups—protesting the rapid Mennonite acculturation into modern society—had splintered into an assortment of new Mennonite groups.[118]

Shifting dress standards added to the identity crisis. The last residuals of plain dress—the devotional covering for women and the plain suit for men—declined rapidly in the first ten years of the Augsburger administration. The 1965–1966 student handbook devoted two pages to promoting clothing that reflected the scriptural principles of nonconformity, modesty, simplicity, moderation, and economy. Beyond advice, the handbook stipulated specific "safeguards from the devastating excesses of today's fashions," for both men and women. Although cape dresses were not named, Mennonite women were expected to wear long hair and a devotional covering in religious services, classes, and the dining hall and for off-campus worship and service activities. Sleeveless dresses, slacks, and shorts were prohibited. Plain suits were not mentioned for men, but short-sleeve shirts and shorts were taboo except for athletic events. Everyone was discouraged from wearing any type of jewelry, including rings.[119]

The following decade was especially hard for young women who were caught between their personal preferences and EMC's resistance to sleeveless dresses, slacks, short hair, and the decline of the devotional covering.[120] But that resistance soon waned. The 1975–1976 handbook intoned, "We should cultivate appreciation and respect for the *personal* preferences [of others]" because students were coming from diverse constituencies with a variety of dress styles. The lengthy attire code of bygone years shrank to four

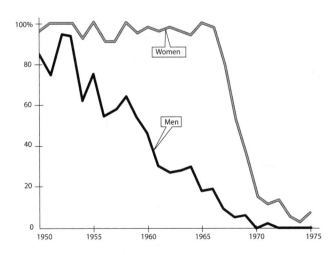

Decline of plain clothing among women and men students, 1950–1975. Plain dress is indicated by the wearing of the devotional covering by women and the plain suit by men in senior photos published in the EMC yearbook, *Shenandoah*, 1950–1975. Chart: Linda L. Eberly.

short statements: men should wear long pants and shirts; women should dress modestly in *their choice* of dresses, skirts and blouses, or slacks; shorts and culottes are acceptable for athletic activities; and sunbathing attire is restricted to sunbathing areas.[121]

The yearbook photos of graduating seniors from 1964 to 1974 confirm the decline of plain dress. The percentage of males wearing plain coats dropped from 31 to 0 percent, and the percentage of females wearing prayer coverings slid from 94 to 2 percent.[122] Over the same decade, the percentage of faculty men pictured in the yearbook wearing plain coats dropped from 100 to 2 percent, and the percentage of faculty women wearing coverings dipped from 100 to 16 percent.

In the summer of 1975, the faculty and staff women wrote a statement on attire that "avoids the extreme of legalism and the extreme of complete freedom." They agreed to wear attire that is "modest, neat, and appropriate for the occasion." The statement prompted a meeting of faculty representatives and the Religious Welfare Committee (RWC). At a follow-up session, the RWC "strongly" advised women not to wear slacks and urged the academic dean to counsel any deviant faculty.[123] Nonetheless, the covering remained the most delicate and difficult issue for women.

Because so many religious, gender, and identity markers were enshrined in the covering, women carried its composite burden longer than men wearing the plain suit. Specific Bible verses (1 Cor. 11:4–15) admonished women to wear the covering, whereas the plain suit was a Mennonite interpretation of a broad principle of nonconformity. Mennonites historically interpreted the Corinthian passage on the veil as a universal application regardless of cultural context. The core justification for the devotional covering was the traditional teaching on the submission of women to men—a patriarchal interpretation that benefited men. Women also struggled more with guilt when they removed this sacred sign, which their parents and church had taught them to wear as a symbol of reverence, submission, and obedience to biblical teaching. Unsurprisingly, the covering was the last visible symbol of Mennonite identity in the twentieth century.

The institutional standard-bearer also carried a burden. For twelve years, whenever he appeared in photos in college publications or at public events on or off campus, Augsburger wore a plain suit. That practice changed in the last three years of his presidency (1977–1980). He led the 1978 commencement processional wearing a regular lapel coat over a plain vest with a straight-cut stand-up collar. During those years, he sometimes wore a white turtleneck with a lapel coat. In the fall of 1978, he first appeared with a black tie and lapel coat while preaching in chapel.[124] By that time most male students, faculty, and trustees had shed their plain coats. When the symbolic figurehead of the college laid aside his plain coat, it signaled the end of a sixty-year struggle to use a church-school dress code to etch a boundary of separation from the world and to restrain self-expression. The era of collective

President Myron Augsburger watches Professor Harry Brunk cut the table-size campus cake to celebrate EMC's sixtieth anniversary, 1977. Brunk was one of the six charter students in 1917. The poster in the background lists the cake's ingredients, which included 50 pounds of flour, 98 pounds of sugar, 29 pounds of shortening, and 568 egg whites.

nonconformity had come to an end. Since the founding of the school, there had arguably been more debate and discord over attire than any other topic.

Still, not everyone was tossing plain clothing aside. Edsel Burdge had grown up in a non-Mennonite home in Franklin County, Pennsylvania. During his senior year (1980–1981), he attended a Mennonite church near campus that nurtured his conviction to wear a plain coat.[125] In later years, other students with conservative inclinations also wore plain attire out of heartfelt conviction.

In an ironic about-face, some members of the class of 1975 wanted to drop the practice of wearing academic regalia at commencement because of its expense—only eleven years after the class of 1964 had valiantly struggled for permission to wear it. Poking fun at President Augsburger's comments on "graduation raiment," a *Weather Vane* reporter wrote, "Next spake the wise orator Myronstrotle in a great flow of words: 'We need to be aggressively and frontally committed to significant involvement in contributing to a positive emphasis in the graduation exercises by maintaining mature dress in the context of brotherhood.'" The academic regalia stayed intact, but calls to eliminate it gave testimony to the churning tides of student opinion.[126]

If the identity crisis described by Paul Peachey troubled Mennonite adults, it also energized some of their offspring. Shirley Hershey Showalter, who graduated in 1970, was "very aware of the Vietnam War and very interested in peace." She joined the Peace Club on campus, participated in student peace vigils in Harrisonburg, and walked in a peace march in Washington. In her words, "It was an exhilarating time to be forming an adult Mennonite identity. I was always looking for new ways to be in the world but not of the world . . . as Mennonite pacifists were emerging from their sectarian and agrarian roots." On the opening day of her first job as a teacher in a Harrisonburg public school, she introduced herself to a group of students with these words: "I am a member of a religious group that for almost five hundred years has said that it is better to be killed than to kill." Choking up a bit as the words flowed out, she was overwhelmed as she recognized the weight of her new adult Mennonite identity.[127] For students like Showalter, the persuasion-engagement paradigm had worked its wonders. Nonetheless, Mennonite identity at EMC would remain in flux in the coming decades.

CHAPTER 9

Crisis, Retrenchment, Rejuvenation

The mood was pessimistic during these difficult years.
—Dean Albert Keim

The Doldrums of 1976–1986

For Mennonite Church youth in the 1950s and '60s, selecting a college was simple: live at home and commute to a nearby state school, or go to EMC, Goshen, or Hesston. Those well-worn ruts faded in the late 1970s and '80s for a host of reasons. Emerson L. Lesher's humorous book, *The Muppie Manual: The Mennonite Urban Professional's Handbook for Humility and Success (or, How to Be the Gentle in the City)*, explained two of them: Mennonite cultural assimilation and upward social mobility.[1] According to Lesher, Muppies were born between 1940 and 1960 to Mennonite parents and raised on a farm or in a rural area and then entered professional careers in an urban or suburban environment.

Muppies were savvy about college quality and wanted their children to attend prestigious schools. Increasingly, high school guidance counselors also advised students on selecting colleges. Moreover, non-Mennonite colleges were recruiting high-caliber students with tempting financial aid and scholarship offers. In comparison to many other colleges, the small Mennonite schools had limited program options. None offered majors in engineering or occupational therapy, for example. They also had fewer cocurricular programs and amenities. Already in 1964, Dean Ira Miller bemoaned the fact that Mennonite students were being "lured to prestige schools and private institutions with lucrative scholarships." EMC's director of athletics also lamented that good Mennonite athletes were going to other colleges because "they got better aid packages."[2]

Other factors also squeezed EMC's enrollment. The pool of college-age youth declined as the size of Mennonite families shrank.[3] Some students who attended

Mennonite high schools wanted to bolt from the first-grade-to-college ethnic escalator and study in a non-Mennonite environment. In addition, declining denominational loyalty in the Mennonite Church (as in other Protestant churches) eroded support for EMC. Thus, from 1976 to 1986, EMC's enrollment slipped from nearly 1,100 to 800 students.

Besides the competitive enrollment environment, the soaring inflation of the 1970s added stress to EMC's operations; it meant freezing budgets, cutting programs, releasing faculty, and canceling raises. Worst of all, a devastating fire struck the Ad Building in 1984. These challenges were exacerbated by an institutional budget tied to tuition and burdened by debt from building projects. A leadership change added to the uncertainty, as Myron Augsburger's presidency waned and, in 1980, gave way to a successor who remained off-campus for his first year.

All these factors led campus leaders to describe the decade of 1976–1986 with words like *difficult, frustration, crisis, malaise,* and *pessimism.* Already in the mid-1970s, Professor John H. Hess Jr. had claimed that EMC was "experiencing a crisis unique in its history, not just another difficult period."[4] Several years later, the crisis had deepened into retrenchment, and it wasn't until 1986 that the esprit de corps of the campus was rejuvenated. Amid these challenges, religious breezes from the broader society had been blowing over EMC since the 1960s.

Religious Crosscurrents

When Arnold Miller, a junior transfer student, arrived in the Maplewood men's dorm in the fall of 1965, he was surprised to hear his roommate speaking in tongues.[5] Miller had never met anyone who spoke in tongues, nor had he ever heard this spiritual utterance, described in 1 Corinthians 12–14. Miller soon discovered that other students also spoke in tongues. For them, this fire from heaven, this mystery language (glossolalia), confirmed the inner presence of God's divine Spirit. Some of them ran a storefront church three nights a week in Harrisonburg for "drifters, drunkards, and prostitutes."[6] A handful of students heard Pat Robertson (later presidential candidate and television show host) speak at the Full Gospel Businessmen's Fellowship at Belle Meade Restaurant south of Harrisonburg. After hearing Robertson's Pentecostal-style talk, Jim Halteman recalled, "We all had the strange feeling that maybe our Mennonitism is not the exclusive truth after all."[7]

Miller himself attended a large convention of the Full Gospel Businessmen's Fellowship in Washington, DC. Even so, as hard as he tried, Miller could not speak in tongues, the ecstatic language of piety. Why was he not blessed by the Holy Spirit? Was he not fully yielded to God? His only consolation was memories of times past when the Holy Ghost had deeply stirred his emotions. Still, his inability to speak the mysterious language troubled him.

One charismatic outburst on campus in fall 1971 was reminiscent of the Mast revival fifty years earlier. Some students marked a turning point in their spiritual pilgrimage when a chapel service erupted with "spiritual dynamite." It morphed into a seven-hour prayer and praise marathon that inspired more day- and night-long prayer and praise sessions, a renewed interest in Bible study and prayer groups, and a greater involvement in Young People's Christian Association (YPCA) activities.[8] Two *Weather Vane* writers claimed that the Holy Spirit was the most hotly discussed topic on campus that fall.[9] At the Consultation on the Person and Work of the Holy Spirit organized by the seminary in January 1972, theologians discussed the sudden rise of interest in the Holy Spirit.[10] As longstanding social practices and structures were tumbling in the Mennonite Church, many students turned inward for spiritual insight.

The charismatic stream of spirituality that stretched over two decades (1965–1985) in the Mennonite world was only one of six religious wells nourishing EMC students and faculty. The others were evangelicalism, customized spirituality, and three streams of Anabaptism: nonconformist, nonpolitical, and politically engaged.

When Jimmy Carter was elected president in 1976, pollster George Gallup Jr. declared it the "Year of the Evangelical." At about the same time, Preacher Jerry Falwell Sr., president of Liberty University (founded in 1971 in Lynchburg, Virginia), along with other leaders of the Christian Right launched the Moral Majority—a powerful political movement that promoted Republican causes. Baptist activists "entered politics with a vengeance during the 1970s and 1980s," said historian Mark Noll.[11] Meanwhile, the old stalwarts, Billy Graham and *Christianity Today*, continued to speak for less politically inclined evangelicals.

The Anabaptist engagement with American evangelicalism was quite different from earlier campus struggles between Fundamentalism and liberalism. For this go-round, Mennonites were not faced with a choice between two movements—Fundamentalism and liberalism; instead, they now engaged evangelicals from their own Anabaptist perspectives. President Augsburger, for example, sought to integrate Anabaptist and evangelical commitments. A collection of essays published in 1979, *Evangelicalism and Anabaptism*, edited by EMC alumnus C. Norman Kraus, parsed the distinctions and commonalities between these viewpoints and further energized campus discourse.

Amid the charismatic movement and the resurgence of American evangelicalism, some Christians left mainline denominations and customized their faith. One team of scholars identified an individualistic stream of spirituality they dubbed "Sheilaism" after a woman who had fashioned her own spirituality without any traditional religious content. Reflecting the rise of cultural individualism, more and more people were customizing their own personal spirituality and discarding denominational membership, beliefs, and labels.[12]

Three small streams were also emerging within Anabaptism itself. Some EMC students and faculty adhered to more traditional nonconformist Mennonite beliefs. Others embraced Harold Bender's nonpolitical Anabaptist vision. Still others, influenced by Mennonite ethicist John Howard Yoder's *The Politics of Jesus*, published in 1972, advocated a radical Anabaptist understanding of the church that had political consequences and addressed social justice and peacemaking.[13] These six streams of religious thought—charismatic, evangelical, customized spirituality, and the three strains of Anabaptism—shaped campus discourse in the 1970s and 1980s.

Growing the Seminary, Weaning the High School

In 1968, President Augsburger tapped George Brunk II to serve as dean of Eastern Mennonite Seminary (EMS). According to one observer, Augsburger was thinking it would be better to have Brunk under the Augsburger tent than outside of it.[14] Under Brunk's leadership (1968–1976), the seminary enjoyed steady growth. Adding to the Mennonite identity crisis, Brunk forecast a "ministerial crisis" because EMS was not graduating enough "men to serve the pastorates and pulpits of our denomination for tomorrow."[15] Mennonite congregations in the East were accepting professionally trained, salaried pastors so slowly that prospective seminarians had little incentive to invest in three years of postcollege study. Yet Brunk and other Mennonite leaders worried that the shift toward salaried pastors would soon accelerate and outpace the number of available seminary graduates. The seminary marked a milestone in 1977–1978 when its enrollment exceeded one hundred students, sixty-six of whom were full time. But only half of the twenty-three graduates that year were Mennonites.[16]

The rivalry with Goshen in EMC's DNA shaped the seminary's outlook. Professor Omar Eby described EMS's claim that it was not Goshen Biblical Seminary's "little kid sister" as "defensive chest-thumping." Some church leaders doubted that a small Mennonite denomination needed or could financially support two seminaries. To the contrary, Augsburger and Brunk II contended that EMS was "a unique program in its own right" that offered an alternative to Goshen. EMS was a more conservative theological school with a strong mission emphasis that would better serve Mennonite conferences in the East. Chester Wenger, chair of its board of overseers, said EMS was "unique with its emphasis on training servants of the congregations rather than scholars who do research, serve institutions, and write books."[17]

Following George Brunk II's retirement in 1976, the seminary's identity and mission continued to solidify. A year later, the seminary established its own board of

George Brunk II served as dean of Eastern Mennonite Seminary from 1968 to 1976.

overseers, which remained under the umbrella of the larger college structure. Richard Detweiler of Franconia Conference served as acting dean for a year. George R. Brunk III, the previous dean's son, then followed as acting dean for two years until he was named dean during the last year of Augsburger's presidency (1979–1980). The seminary thrived under Brunk's leadership with full-time equivalent (FTE) enrollment rising to eighty-three by 1993.

As EMC invested more energy in the seminary, it began to divest itself of the high school. During EMC's first three decades, the high school and college shared facilities, cocurricular activities, leadership, financial affairs, and a common public perception. Even in 1947, when EMC became a college, high school students still comprised 55 percent of enrollment.[18] But as the college grew and its identity gelled, the high school slipped into the shadows and lost its public identity. As the high school became more Virginia-centric, the college began attracting more students and financial support from outside the state.

A new building in 1963 helped sharpen the high school's identity, but at the cost of sizable debt. Its operating loss of nearly $70,000 in 1966–1967 was subsidized by the college. Some college faculty claimed that if the high school paid its own bills, each college professor would receive a salary increase of $1,000. Meanwhile, the high school enrollment was declining. Not surprisingly, some officials in the late 1960s considered closing the high school. "My hat's off to Myron Augsburger," said Sam Weaver, high school principal from 1969 to 1981. "He was the one with a vision to keep the high school alive."[19] During his tenure, Weaver facilitated a collaborative exit from the college. The high school formed an independent corporation in July 1982, ending sixty-five years of association with EMC.[20]

Revisions to EMC's constitution in 1970, 1975, and 1979 adjusted its governance structure during Augsburger's presidency.[21] These changes tilted the fulcrum of power away from Virginia Conference and toward other conferences and the board of trustees. The 1970 constitutional changes purged faculty expectations to exemplify nonconformity, uphold the Virginia Conference statement of faith, and expose errors of evolution and higher criticism. Now faculty were expected to commit to a biblical faith and promote "evangelical Christianity and historic Mennonitism as expressed in the Mennonite Church's 1963 Confession of Faith." In 1970, for the first time, "dedicated Christians of evangelical persuasion from other denominations" who supported Mennonite ideals could be "visiting teachers." Five years later, non-Mennonite faculty were upgraded to "fraternal teachers" but were not eligible for tenure.

By 1975, leaders from eight conferences—Lancaster, Franconia, Conservative, Washington-Franklin, Atlantic Coast, New York State Fellowship, Southeast Convention, and Virginia—comprised EMC's Constituent Conferences Committee.[22] This committee soon became EMC's primary point of reference for churchly advice and consultation. The thirty-two-member board of trustees elected seventeen members from nominees provided by the eight constituent conferences proportionate to their size. Virginia nominated five. The other fifteen trustees were selected and elected by the board itself.

During the Augsburger years, the influence of the venerable Religious Welfare Committee (RWC) gradually diminished into an advisory role for the president on issues such as women's attire, dance, hiring of non-Mennonite faculty, and review of the faith statements of applicants for faculty positions. In the 1979 constitutional revision, the Faith and Life Committee, composed of three persons nominated by the Constituent Conferences Committee and elected by Virginia Conference, replaced the RWC. The conference executive committee voted with the trustees to appoint the president, and the conference still authorized amendments to the constitution.[23]

Zigzags in Leadership

Ira Miller's worst year as dean was 1968–1969. He cited the new interdisciplinary studies program with its massive changes and team teaching, student unrest and dissent, the formation of the Student Government Association in spring 1969, and the generation gap. These issues prompted him to ask, "Who's in charge here?"[24] Then, in November 1969, as the library drive was under way, he told President Augsburger, "I am in utter confusion." Without consulting Miller, the trustees terminated his appointment as academic dean effective June 1970.[25] They also appointed a committee to review the dean's role and accept nominees for a new dean. If interested, Miller could apply. This felt like a slap in the face after fourteen years of diligent effort in the dean's office, not to mention a decade of previous work. A search committee, convened in late January, enumerated qualifications for the position and named potential candidates. Richard Detweiler, a former presidential candidate, was the only serious prospect. He declined an invitation, leaving the committee empty-handed. On March 6, President Augsburger made a final plea to Detweiler without success. Later that day, the trustees appointed Miller dean for a new two-year term.[26]

Leadership in the dean's office was unsteady from 1968 to 1977. Following Miller's retirement in 1972, Dan Yutzy, a sociologist from the State University of New York, held the office for four years. Besides his academic work, Yutzy was active in the Mennonite charismatic movement. He hosted a weekly prayer-and-praise meeting in his home, which was attended by dozens of students. His home was a setting, one observer noted, where many "fledgling charismatics found a sympathetic group where they could share their experiences" and learn some other dimensions of Christian faith.[27] Follow-up contacts with the students added to Yutzy's already busy schedule, as did his extensive travel to speaking engagements at charismatic-related events. He received so much flak for being off campus that the trustees asked him to curtail his travel. The faculty soon lost confidence in him for other reasons as well, and he left EMC in 1976.[28]

Instability in the dean's office during Augsburger's tenure gave him considerable control over the academic program. His busy speaking and fund-raising schedule, as well as his other external involvements, however, resulted in rough coordination and unattended details. Professor John H. Hess Jr. told the president that faculty frustration and the fear that some could not "match your rhetorical abilities or are intimidated by your 'aura'" led to calls for a faculty senate, which formed in 1972.[29] One faculty member recalled that Augsburger was "open to speak with you if you had problems or questions, but he operated his own thing. He didn't consult much and that frustrated people."[30] During his frequent travels, the president sometimes met promising scholars and invited them to consider teaching at EMC. Former faculty recount stories of how the president had encouraged individuals to go to graduate school or invited them to faculty positions, only to discover later that the academic department did not want them or that the job was no longer available.[31]

In 1975, a decade into Augsburger's presidency, administrative help arrived. The trustees hired Lee Yoder, principal of Christopher Dock Mennonite High School in eastern Pennsylvania to—in the words of one colleague—"harness Myron."[32] A deft manager, Yoder was named to the new post of vice president of administration, which had a broad scope of responsibility. In his first year, he faced a $180,000 operational deficit. At Yoder's prompting, the trustees mandated a cash reserve of 1.5 percent in the annual budget. After discovering that salary records were held in a manila folder in the president's desk and reflected little standardization, Yoder pushed for a salary schedule for all employees and faculty. In his opinion, EMC's administrative policies were pitifully behind the times. "Basic operational things were extremely sloppy; there was little accountability." One day, the president's assistant brought a box of files to Yoder and told him, "Now we have a personnel office. You are it."[33]

Yoder soon found out how difficult it was to rein in Augsburger's loose administrative style. Sixteen months after his appointment, he declined a second two-year term until administrative protocols could be clarified. Yoder was vexed by many issues—especially Augsburger's lack of consultation and tacit permission for staff and faculty to make end runs around deans and vice presidents. Yoder pointedly told Augsburger, "Somehow things at EMC must slow down!" Moreover, he said, "[Your] travel off-campus is a problem. We cannot adequately do staff work on-the-run, in brief capsules, nor in absenteeism. Something must change."[34] After some heart-to-heart conversations with the president and a realigned portfolio, Yoder accepted a second two-year contract effective July 1977.

Yoder had his own detractors. Some of the faculty considered his penchant for administration overzealous. One faculty member recalled, "He assigned every department a color of copy paper. His was pink, and he would issue pink statements to everybody. He also provided instructions on how to open your mail. You can imagine how that went down with the faculty."[35] Nonetheless, Yoder significantly streamlined EMC's administrative efficiency and tightened its financial accountability.

Corporate Sins

When Dan Yutzy left EMC abruptly in summer 1976, three faculty members—Willard Swartley, Jesse Byler, and Daniel Suter—were appointed associate deans for the next academic year. Swartley agreed to serve as associate dean of arts and humanities and as chair of an imploding music department. Within a year, four music faculty members had left, and one on leave was released, gutting the department except for newly hired John Fast.[36] The upheaval marred public relations as reports of the turmoil spilled into the *Weather Vane* and *Gospel Herald*.[37]

The roots of the conflict reached back to 1969, when forty-nine-year-old Earl Maust, the chair of the music department, was stricken with a fatal heart attack at the fall faculty conference.[38] His death brought several personnel changes and unrest in the department. The resulting meltdown had the usual ingredients of conflict-ridden academic departments: infighting, innuendo, misrepresentation, jealousy, mistrust, students siding with their favorite faculty, and antagonism toward the administration. A mix of other factors on campus thickened the brew—a budget squeeze, nepotism, salary discrepancies, rapid faculty turnover, muddled lines of authority, and weak academic leadership. They also included accusations of presidential favoritism, mistakes, and broken promises.

In addition to these woes, the very mission of the music department was contested during the mid-1970s. Participation in vocal music was part of EMC's history and ethos. It played an important role in EMC's public relations and ministry outreach, whether through choral groups on radio programs, musical productions at homecoming, or choirs singing in congregations. Music education, consistent with the midcentury emphasis, had aimed to prepare teachers for Christian schools. Also, President Augsburger had strongly urged the department to create a music major in church ministry so graduates could serve in congregations and larger arenas.[39] By the 1970s, however, some faculty wanted to focus on preparing students for professional performance, including training in instrumental music.[40]

To have a department paralyzed by discord was not unusual in the academic world. To have it happen at EMC, however, was especially excruciating because the school's corporate culture valued charity, grace, "brotherhood," and reconciliation. Participants described the conflict as sordid, cancerous, a Greek tragedy, chaotic and hopeless, and beyond repair—underscoring its disgrace of Christian virtues. Even students realized that the crisis had become "a major tragedy" and that cleaning house was "the only possible solution."[41] The three associate deans considered the quagmire beyond any hope of reconciliation. Swartley called it "a case of structural and corporate sin of immense proportions . . . with few innocent persons."[42]

Yet two things showed another side of EMC's corporate culture: the patient, persistent, and humane way that administrators pursued solutions and the president's public remorse. For two semesters, Associate Dean Swartley sought reconciliation in dozens of meetings and in three mediation sessions with the music faculty that were facilitated by a psychiatrist. Some faculty were offered a chance to reapply for a position within a year.[43]

A target of faculty criticism, President Augsburger apologized, in a chapel address, for his missteps. He began by listing failures "for which I carry deep pain and regret." He confessed, "I cannot tell you how deeply I felt about this and how disappointed I am that we have reached this impasse." He admitted that he had "failed in achieving the Christian affinities which should enrich our relationships and guide us in finding the answer of grace in our difficulties."[44] And he promised "to work together to build a strong music department with a highly qualified and competent faculty." The students applauded when he finished. For Swartley, the president's words were "a healing benediction to the episode."[45]

The painful saga underscored the complexity of balancing Anabaptist values of community and personal relationships with institutional structures and policies. The trustees' Academic Affairs Committee regretted that as a Christian community EMC was not "able to demonstrate reconciliation and brotherhood in a practical way." But it concluded that "reconciliation and job retention were separate issues."[46]

In May 1977, after twelve years in office, the president asked the three associate deans for advice on his administrative style. They encouraged him to be an on-campus president, even hinting that college relations and fund-raising were not the best use of his gifts. The deans recommended that departments and academic officers, not the president, should initiate searches for new faculty. They also urged him to show less favoritism to particular departments and to find more informal ways to interact with faculty.[47]

A year later, Albert N. Keim, the new academic dean, reported high morale in the music department and praised its new chair, Ken J. Nafziger, for "performing a major tour de force."[48] Keim, a history professor, served as dean for seven years. Raised Amish in Ohio, he brought intellectual depth, a penchant for philosophical reflection, and a determination to upgrade the academic caliber of the faculty. He was a breath of fresh air for faculty who longed for more direction in the dean's office but a cold wind for others. Keim made a bold move in his second year when he abolished faculty tenure and replaced it with five-year renewable contracts.[49] In his third year (1979–1980), which coincided with Augsburger's last year, Keim initiated the close of the physics major and the termination of tenured faculty members Robert Lehman and Ezra Byler. That May, Lehman appealed the decision to the faculty senate, which supported him. But a few days later, as the Augsburger presidency was ending, the trustees supported Keim and terminated Lehman.[50] Not surprisingly, some faculty charged Keim with unilateral decision making and excessive use of power. He acknowledged that the tenure issues were "the most difficult" of his three years as dean. He aimed to improve faculty quality and hoped that the long-term benefits would far outweigh the immediate costs of low faculty morale.[51] One apparent casualty was the eight-year-old faculty senate, which disbanded after losing its appeal of the Lehman case to the trustees.[52] The presidential transition took place in the summer of 1980 in this unsettled and chilly climate.

Balloons and Confetti

Augsburger's legacy was legendary. He wrote more than two dozen books and spoke at hundreds of engagements. The swath of his national and international influence bolstered EMC's stature and name recognition.[53] His openness to other religious traditions attracted many non-Mennonite students and faculty. During his fifteen-year tenure, the proportion of full-time, non-Mennonite students swelled from 7 to 37 percent. The number of non-Mennonite faculty, especially in nursing, also grew, requiring orientation seminars on Anabaptist beliefs and history. Under Augsburger's stabilizing leadership, the seminary's full-time enrollment increased sixfold during his tenure. The full-time equivalent enrollment for the combined college and seminary nearly doubled to 1,100 students.

Augsburger received high marks for cultivating strong relationships with EMC's constituent conferences in the East. He initiated a church evaluation team composed of thirteen representatives of constituent conferences and agencies. The representatives visited the campus in the spring and fall of 1975. Their lengthy, mostly positive report urged EMC to be authentically Anabaptist-Mennonite and not to imitate a fundamentalist school like Bob Jones University or a nondenominational evangelical one like Wheaton College.[54] Augsburger had hoped that the Mennonite Board of Education (MBE) would conduct similar assessments of all Mennonite colleges. In his view, the MBE had "become more of an institutional board running programs that did not engage faculty with a SACS [Southern Association of Colleges and Schools]-style church evaluation," which he thought had merit.[55]

Augsburger faithfully articulated an Anabaptist-Mennonite view of discipleship, Christian peacemaking, and reconciliation, as well as an enduring commitment to holistic, evangelical mission efforts. He took pleasure in a report that 41 percent of missionaries in church-wide mission agencies and 71 percent of the people deployed by Eastern Mennonite Missions had attended EMC.[56]

In tandem with his global vision, Augsburger enhanced EMC's reputation in the Harrisonburg community. Early in his tenure, Augsburger hosted civic and business leaders on campus for a conversation about EMC's role in the community.[57] Under his leadership, EMC solicited funds from a community organization for the first time in 1969.[58] "Before Myron came," recalled attorney Donald Showalter, "local professionals viewed EMC as a sectarian, isolated Bible college. They thought it was a place where women wore 'sin sifters' [prayer coverings] and men came only to find a spouse." According to Showalter, Augsburger changed those perceptions. He joined the Rotary Club and was elected to Valley National Bank's board.[59] In these ways, President Augsburger revamped EMC's reputation among the Shenandoah Valley's business and professional leaders.

In a joyful farewell in May 1980, the Student Government Association (SGA) feted Myron and Esther Augsburger in a surprise chapel program. The students invited the president to pull a rope dangling from the ceiling. At his tug, banners unraveled from on high, fire caps crackled, rice spewed over the audience, and balloons and confetti descended on everyone. After roaring its approval, the assembly sang "Take Thou My Hand, O Father," one of Augsburger's favorite hymns.[60]

As the search for a new president got under way, Richard C. Detweiler, the perennial choice, was offered the job. But once again, he declined, feeling that his primary calling was to pastoral leadership. After pursuing a short list of six candidates from a pool of fifty without success, the search committee pressed Detweiler to reconsider. He agreed to serve if he could live at home in Pennsylvania the first year (1980–1981) with limited presidential duties. The trustees accepted that arrangement and appointed Detweiler to his first regular four-year term, effective July 1981.[61] At the same time, the trustees elected a new chair—Joe Lapp, an attorney who lived near Detweiler in Lansdale, Pennsylvania. Lapp replaced Virginian Dewitt Heatwole, who had been a trustee for twenty-three years and had chaired the board during Augsburger's fifteen-year stint.

The fifty-five-year-old Detweiler, a graduate of EMC, was an esteemed church leader in Franconia Mennonite Conference. A skilled pastor, he held master of divinity and master of theology degrees from Princeton Theological Seminary. Detweiler was well known to the EMC community as a speaker, consultant, trustee, and the interim dean of EMS in 1976–1977. His gifts were in pastoral care, church administration, and leadership. He was unflappable, trustworthy, and measured.[62] The embodiment of humility, he accepted the office as a servant, called by the church. Like J. B. Smith, said one colleague, "Richard was a reluctant president."[63]

Mennonite Higher Education—in Crisis?

In April 1981, J. Lawrence Burkholder, president of Goshen College, gave the keynote address at Detweiler's inauguration. During the transition year of 1980–1981, Vice President Lee Yoder served as CEO in consultation with President Detweiler. Having already worked together at Christopher Dock High School in Pennsylvania, Yoder and Detweiler understood each other's temperament and ways of working. "Richard had the grace and Lee told the truth," said one colleague.[64] Pressing financial problems, a new capital campaign, and the long-simmering issues of dancing and EMC's relationship with the MBE awaited the new president's attention when he arrived on campus in July 1981.

By all accounts, President Detweiler had a rough ride that first year. His wife, Mary Jane, became ill, enrollment dropped by nearly sixty students, the operational budget ended in the red despite midyear freezes, and contributions were sluggish for the $3.1 million campaign to renovate the Ad Building. To aggravate matters, controversies over Bible department faculty and sexual orientation landed on Detweiler's desk in the spring of 1982.

Concerns about the Bible department's orthodoxy were not new. In 1972, the RWC recommended terminating instructor Harold H. Good for introducing his classes to historical criticism, which raised questions about the authorship of the Hebrew Bible and the synoptic Gospels and challenged the plenary inspiration of the Scriptures. EMS dean George Brunk II and seminary professor Herman Reitz were quite disturbed by Good's approach.[65] They were also "severely critical" of Willard Swartley, chair of the undergraduate Bible department in the 1970s, but did not force him out. They did scold him for exposing students to alternate interpretations of the virgin birth, multiple authors of the first five books of the Bible traditionally attributed to Moses, and various explanations of the Red Sea crossing. "I introduced views emerging from historical critical scholarship in my classes without clearly saying what I believed," explained Swartley.[66]

Another issue that annoyed Brunk was Swartley's use of the inductive method of Bible study, which had been growing among Mennonite scholars.[67] "The inductive method," said Swartley, "begins by reading the Scripture and asking what does it say, what does it mean?" This was quite different than the traditional deductive method that begins with a doctrinal belief and turns to Scripture to verify the belief. "I was viewed as a wolf in sheep's clothing since I did not begin with the doctrinal beliefs that reflected fundamentalism," Swartley said. "I was linked with an 'intruder' method of Bible study that fueled the criticism I received."[68]

In 1982, George Brunk II—retired but still operating on the old deductive paradigm—charged the Bible faculty with teaching heresy and questioning orthodox beliefs.[69] He asserted that textbooks riddled with theological errors were used by faculty and sold in the EMC bookstore. The year finally ended with a *Weather Vane* exposé of the fray.[70] Charges of heresy did not augur well for turning around enrollment, increasing contributions, and boosting confidence in the school. Regrettably, the spring dustup foreshadowed a roiling storm on the horizon.

About eight months later, in February 1983, Mennonite educational leaders trembled when seventy-two-year-old Brunk II published *A Crisis among Mennonites, in Education, in Publication*. Seventy-five-hundred copies of the booklet were distributed, and within a few weeks, five thousand copies of a revised and expanded edition were printed. In colorful, hyperbolic language, Brunk leveled a scathing critique of the Bible faculty at EMC and of books authored by Mennonite scholars at Goshen College and Associated Mennonite Biblical Seminaries (AMBS). His salvo was reminiscent of J. B. Smith's scolding of Goshen in the 1920s and his own father's unending criticism of liberalism. Brunk claimed that Bible faculty at EMC and the other two schools had succumbed to higher criticism—echoing Harold Lindsell's recent *Battle for the Bible*, which had ignited nationwide controversy in evangelical circles about biblical inerrancy.

Brunk claimed that "unsound teachers" were exposing students to biblical interpretations that eroded the *Truth* of doctrinal orthodoxy—creation, virgin birth, miracles, blood atonement for salvation, and the physical resurrection. He (and some students) also questioned the views of faculty members on homosexuality, premarital sex, and divorce. In the past, Brunk said, "indoctrination was not a bad word!" Now, he groused, some educators viewed "doctrinal erosion with indifference . . . as only a skin rash when in fact it is like blood poisoning." Instead of indoctrinating students in the truth, professors were using error-filled textbooks that raised questions in the minds of students. "Must one take the young to a house of prostitution to learn virtue or to drink liquor in a den of drunkards to learn the evils of strong drink?" Brunk asked. Worse yet, he claimed that while "this evil [was] doing its undercover work," constituents were assured "that all is well" in Mennonite colleges.[71] Shortly after publishing *Crisis* in 1983, Brunk circulated a paper titled "A Crisis in Education at Eastern Mennonite College."[72]

Mennonite leaders could not shrug off the criticism as a grouchy old man's lament. Brunk had a following, and he had credibility with conservative sectors of the church. Thousands of people had experienced spiritual renewal or personal salvation in his tent revivals. No theological slouch, Brunk held a doctorate in theology and had been dean of EMS for eight years (1968–1976). Moreover, he had his father's booming voice and the gift of incisive and persuasive language. He was able to articulate the concerns of many conservative-minded Mennonites who were dismayed by the changes churning in the church. Brunk soon received numerous invitations to speak at church gatherings and regional conferences that were sympathetic to his pleas.

President Detweiler had seen a prepublication draft of *Crisis*, so within days of its publication, he was prepared to defend his faculty. EMC distributed a concise, two-page statement explaining the theological stance of the Bible department, its methods of teaching, and the roster of teachers for the next year, which included the president. Not surprisingly, Detweiler received a barrage of letters from parents, pastors, conference leaders, and donors seeking information and asking for remedies. In late April 1983, the president sent a letter to the moderators of twelve regional conferences with a two-page statement titled "Developments in the Bible Department of Eastern Mennonite College." This updated the earlier statement and included the Bible and religion department's curriculum objectives.[73] Upon reading the letter, Brunk retorted, "I was shocked at your attempt to 'cover' for the teachers. . . . You come perilously close to misrepresentation and falsification. . . . You are sinning against the Lord and His church by defending those unsafe faculty members." Moreover, Brunk said that Detweiler reminded him of "another Richard [Nixon] of Watergate fame who resisted to the bitter end."[74]

The situation was more than awkward for George Brunk III, then dean of EMS. Serving on the staff of Brunk Revivals during the summers when he was a young adult, he had developed a lifelong appreciation for piety. Yet his mild temperament and diplomatic sensibilities were not the qualities for which his father was known. In response to a pastor's query about the crisis at EMC and EMS, Dean Brunk averred that there was no "crisis which demands extraordinary corrective measures on the part of the church. *To my knowledge* there is no doctrine of our faith that is in jeopardy."[75]

Mennonite leaders and the MBE sprang into damage control. They held meetings, sent letters, and wrote papers rebutting Brunk's views and his abrasive criticism of EMC.[76] The publication of *Crisis* fomented dissent at the Mennonite General Assembly in Bethlehem, Pennsylvania, in August 1983. At the assembly, Brunk II announced plans to form a para-church group, Fellowship of Concerned Mennonites (FCM), which organized a few months later. In its promotional pamphlet, the group described itself as a response to the "revolutionary changes over the last twenty years" in the church that it considered "contrary to the Scriptures."[77] By 1985, the crisis at EMC had subsided, but FCM continued to speak for many of the same conservatives who subscribed to the *Sword and Trumpet*.

In the heat of the controversy in May 1983, the Virginia Conference Council on Faith and Life issued "A Call for Trust and Discernment."[78] The council commended EMC for its philosophy of biblical education and its transparency in responding to the charges. Without naming George Brunk II, it lamented that some people had expressed their concerns outside church structures. With the council's affirmation of EMC's theological education, Virginia Conference thus marginalized and silenced the voice of its last patriarch.

One by one, the old Mennonite patriarchs of the twentieth century had died—George R. Brunk, Daniel Kauffman, J. L. Stauffer, and Harold S. Bender, with John E. Lapp soon to follow—and traditional authority yielded to professional and organizational authority. In his *Crisis*, Brunk II had straddled the midcentury shift of authority and had uttered the last protest of the patriarchs, at least within the progressive stream of Mennonite life.

Being Gay at EMC

A police raid in 1969 at the Stonewall Inn, a gay bar in Greenwich Village, heightened public consciousness about sexual orientation in North America. Seven years later, Martin Rock, a gay member of the Church of the Brethren, founded the Brethren Mennonite Council for Gay Concerns (BMC).[79] This initiative spurred a growing awareness of the presence of gay Mennonites among EMC students and faculty.[80]

The issue of sexual orientation first surfaced at EMC in a case of abuse in the fall of 1958. Monroe B. Wyse, the college controller (chief accountant), who also served as a class advisor and was admired by many students, had, according to a former student, become "too friendly with some of the boys."[81] Faculty and fellow administrators were uncertain how to respond when this became public. Although Wyse voluntarily submitted his resignation from the college, a solid majority of the male faculty voted against immediate dismissal. Following a psychiatric exam—which revealed a slight same-sex inclination—the trustee executive committee reassigned Wyse to a different role but continued his employment until June 30, 1959.[82] Ella May Miller, spouse of Spanish professor Samuel Miller, was upset that college authorities "had evaded their responsibilities" by continuing to employ the man for seven more months. Doing so, she said, "is a disgrace to our Lord . . . [and] stains the name of God."[83]

A quite different situation emerged in the late 1970s when a few students publicly identified as gay.[84] One of them described his pain in a 1977 letter to the editor of the *Weather Vane*. "I am a gay Mennonite Christian here for my second year at EMC," he wrote and then explained his long journey to affirm his identity. He withheld his name, saying, "I'm truly sorry I cannot sign this at this time. I yearn for the day when the light of Christ opens the many closed and bigoted minds here on campus."[85]

The campus ethos changed slowly. One morning in February 1982 when the *Weather Vane* copy editor, Kenny Boyers, opened the door to the editorial office in the Ad Building, he was shocked. The printer-ready galley proofs that the editors had carefully finished at 1:00 a.m. that morning lay in a small pile of ashes on the table. The fire left only some tiny flecks of ash in the hallway and the lingering smell of smoke. Editor Cathy Bomberger suspected that the arsonist was the author of an essay on sexuality that she had refused to publish because of the author's writing style. Later that morning, Dean Al Keim announced the burning in chapel.

Editor Bomberger discovered that the printer who had typeset the copy still had the text. Over the weekend, at Bomberger's home, the editors cobbled together a makeshift issue without photos. They copied, folded, and stapled a match to each *Weather Vane* before distributing them on campus.[86]

Some students had invited gay alumnus and BMC coordinator Martin Rock to campus to speak in classes and at a public forum in the Discipleship Center. The students were upset because President Detweiler and Dean Keim disinvited the guests and canceled the forum, which had been advertised on campus. Keim told the *Weather Vane*, "We'd be ruined for at least five years [if we explored this] most volatile issue." In lieu of the guest speakers, students led discussions in classes and showed the film *Some of Your Best Friends* one evening. "These events," according to one of the planners, "made our project a success by making homosexuality a campus-wide discussion."[87] All of this occurred just as the "Brunk Crisis" began to unfurl in 1982 before coming to a head a year later with the publication of *Crisis*.[88]

In 1984, college administrators again refused to permit gay persons to speak in a forum. After a lengthy debate, the SGA recommended that EMC "not discriminate against speakers, faculty or students on the basis of sexual orientation."[89] President Detweiler rejected the proposal because he believed that gay speakers would spawn "more polarized discrimination than it would help to alleviate" both on campus and among constituents.[90]

Three students responded directly to the president. Douglas Lehman, who had become acquainted with several gay people through a project for a course on peace and justice, was dismayed by Detweiler's argument. "How could you, one of my traditional pillar-of-the-church-models, reject faithfulness for pragmatism: a pragmatism which perpetuates discrimination? How would Jesus respond?" Lehman continued, "Your institutionalized discrimination is very discouraging to [gay people]. They are treated as not quite human and, at best, a lot more evil than the rest of us. They must suffer having their faith called into question before they can speak. In fact, they're not even allowed to speak." Lehman noted how challenges to racism in the South had triggered polarized reactions just as same-sex issues would on campus. "But, for *God's Sake* don't we have to stand for our morals?" Lehman said he was not trying to "make you [Detweiler] look stupid. . . . I care *a lot* about EMC. . . . You may think of me as too idealistic, but then how are Christians supposed to be?" In his response to Lehman, the president said he hoped to address the issue in ways that did not create new barriers but respected the welfare of both gay and straight students.[91]

Another student, Mary Jo Bowman, sent the president the text of a class presentation that challenged his rejection of the SGA proposal. She stood with those who challenged the church to recognize homosexuality as part of God's creation—a view she came to embrace after participating for several years in her Church of the Brethren congregation's controversy over this issue. She pressed the president to consider how EMC's de facto policy of discrimination against gay people fit with the school's liberal arts philosophy: "to broaden horizons, develop an inquiring mind . . . and supply a perspective for coping with, serving in, and speaking to a changing world."[92]

David Boshart, while taking a course titled "Biblical Theology of Peace and Justice," became convinced that God sided with the oppressed—whether in the Middle East, in Nicaragua, or on campus. He declared that "this campus oppresses homosexuals." He also recounted that a gay friend of his, "if found out, fears suspension and problems of job security because of EMC's stance." Moreover, he asked the president, "How can a school offer a Peace and Justice Program when the course content has to be censored?"[93]

EMC's commitments to radical discipleship and to peace and justice studies effectively prepared graduates to address injustice in the larger world. When applied to perceived oppression on campus, however, the rhetoric of radical discipleship encountered the political realities of a tradition-laden church and a slow-to-change college. Moreover, the deep differences on sexual orientation seemed intractable.

What one side considered sin and disobedience to the Bible, the other side considered God's good creation—making constructive discussions difficult and assuring that the issue would not be settled quickly or easily.

The Long Road to MBE Membership

In the midst of the Brunk controversy and the sexuality debate, President Detweiler was also managing EMC's connection with the Mennonite Board of Education. Dozens of discussions, debates, proposals, and counterproposals over some eighteen years (1966–1984) had helped thaw EMC's frosty view of the MBE.[94] Things had already begun warming in 1963 when EMC officially recognized the MBE for the first time and pledged to cooperate in "areas of overlapping interest."[95] Meanwhile, the MBE—one of five program agencies of the Mennonite Church—was fast becoming a small bureaucracy with paid staff, office space, and standardized policies. In 1966, Albert J. Meyer became the first executive secretary to receive a salary beyond a minimal honorarium. With these resources and the mandate of the church, the MBE tried to coordinate the mission of the three colleges and two seminaries affiliated with the Mennonite Church.

The MBE owned the property of Hesston College, Goshen College, and Goshen Biblical Seminary and controlled them by appointing their overseers and presidents. It also administered broad policies related to long-range planning, new academic programs, the proportion of Mennonite faculty and students, new construction, student recruitment, and fund-raising. These policies aimed to minimize program duplication among Mennonite schools. They also sought to reduce, or at least coordinate, competition for Mennonite dollars and students while assuring that the schools remained servants of the church.

The MBE staff and some church leaders feared that, over time, Mennonite colleges and seminaries would become powerful institutions more devoted to their own institutional success than to denominational constituents. With independent-minded faculty, loyal alumni, professional fund-raisers, and growing endowments, church-affiliated schools might easily be tempted to veer away from denominational priorities in order to survive in the ever-competitive market of higher education. Many Mennonite leaders hoped that the MBE would keep their colleges off the path to secularization that dozens, if not hundreds, of church-established colleges had trod.

EMC saw independence, not greater denominational affiliation, as the answer to secularization. Though EMC's presidents had participated in the church-wide Higher Education Council and collaborated on numerous projects with its sibling institutions, EMC had little interest in complying with the MBE's policies.[96] In the 1960s, church leaders in the East still considered Goshen College to be the bastion of liberal Mennonite scholarship. It was the place where young women cut their hair and students prized professional occupations more than mission work. Skeptics at EMC feared that—since the MBE's office was located adjacent to the Goshen campus and Al Meyer had a part-time appointment in the physics lab of Goshen College—a Goshen-centric bias would disadvantage EMC.[97] Even though EMC had plenty of bureaucratic earmarks of its own, the MBE template reflected the ghost of Fordism by imposing centralization, control, and standardization on Mennonite higher education. In short, the conflict pitted national Fordism against regional Fordism. What the MBE called coordination, EMC loyalists considered control.

The reorganization of the Mennonite Church into regions in 1971 inadvertently put more pressure on EMC to join the MBE. Soon after the reorganization, Meyer began attending EMC trustee meetings, gently but tenaciously guiding EMC under the wings of the MBE. During the eighteen-year discussion, EMC loyalists raised numerous objections to MBE control: EMC would lose its distinctive identity and its appeal to conservatives, MBE control would add a new layer of rules and regulations on top of EMC's own policies, centralization would hamper EMC's freedom to make quick decisions in its own interests, and church-wide coordination would take excessive time and impose a fee for the MBE's unwanted services. Some diehards claimed that "EMC was being sold to Goshen" and that EMC would "lose control." Others asked how "centralization" made any sense when the church was shifting "decision-making to local congregations."[98]

Even so, EMC needed the MBE. It was a vigorous advocate for Mennonite higher education. It coordinated programs and projects. It gathered information on potential students and tracked comparable institutional data. Most importantly, the MBE promoted the value of a Mennonite higher education through church channels and periodicals. EMC would gain legitimacy under the MBE as an adult institution in the Mennonite family. Moreover, EMC was facing enrollment pressures and funding shortages that an MBE affiliation might help assuage.

President Augsburger had welcomed collaboration with the MBE but not control. Though the first round of MBE discussions had opened in the second year of his presidency, it took thirteen years until a trial covenant was implemented in 1979–1980, the last year of his tenure.[99] This eventually led to a full-fledged agreement in February 1984 under President Detweiler, bringing Eastern Mennonite College and Seminary (EMC&S) fully under the MBE umbrella.[100] However, only three quarters of the EMC trustees approved the agreement. Trustee Chester Wenger, son of President A. D. Wenger, voted no. Wenger, who chaired the seminary overseers, feared that MBE control would not produce "a better future for EMC&S." Among other objections, he thought the proposed affiliation "seemed definitely out of step with the times," since central control was declining in the church.[101]

If the architects of central control could claim a victory for Fordism, it was a short one because it was out of sync with postmodern trends toward decentralization that would restructure the MBE in the early twenty-first century.

Dance: Vice or Artistic Expression?

Rose Stauffer, a junior liberal arts major, spoke for many EMC students in 1984 when she wrote a testimonial article in the *Weather Vane* in favor of dance in the arts. "For most of my life," she wrote, "I hardly knew dance existed beyond the obscurity of primitive tribal dancing in some faraway land, or the elitist, extravagant ballet in some faraway city." That innocence faded when Stauffer took a dance course at another college. Clad in a brand-new black leotard and tights, she found a new "avenue of self-expression, a way to communicate feelings and thoughts to others." Dance for her soon became, as she put it, "an art form, a gift, a niche that I am drawn to even though the discipline is sometimes painful."[102]

In the first half of the twentieth century, dance was one of a number of vices that most Mennonites and other evangelical churches shunned. In 1943, EMS's *Standards* included dance among other "strictly forbidden" things like liquor, profanity, gambling, cards, games of chance, theater, movies, pool rooms, and bowling. Twenty-five years later, a shorter taboo list still included dancing along with gambling, alcohol, and pornography.[103] The school could assume that any dancing that might occur would always be off campus. That assumption began dissolving by 1975 as dance-like activities began creeping into classes in the form of folk games, choreography, and rhythmic movements in drama and physical education. Trying to check them, President Augsburger argued that these could lead incrementally to dancing, with its excessive freedom, and to sexual immorality. For him, dancing was outside "the Mennonite lifestyle," and permitting it would hinder EMC's relationship with the church.[104] His views were consistent with those of most of EMC's constituents: in the early 1970s, nearly 80 percent of Mennonites in a national survey considered social dancing "always or somewhat" wrong.[105]

The president's admonition marked the beginning of a vigorous twenty-year discussion that finally ended in 1996, when the prohibition against dancing disappeared from the school handbook.[106] During this period, two task forces explored various types of dance and how they might fit with EMC's culture. The board of trustees and its student life committee visited the dance issue nearly a dozen times. The *Weather Vane* polled students several times, and the SGA lobbied for square dancing on campus. From all appearances, dancing animated such a long and lively discussion because it threatened traditional Mennonite identity and fostered worldly entanglements.

Peggy Landis, director of student life, offered a different explanation, which she summed up in two words: sexual intimacy. "The '70s were the days," she recalled in 2016, "when you couldn't even hold hands with a member of the opposite sex. You couldn't give free hugs or embrace others like we do all the time now."[107] The fear of sexual intimacy was the serpent lurking in the shadows.

When the SGA pressed for dancing in 1978, the president had "a wholesome interchange" with students and told the trustees "that the SGA was ready to drop the issue."[108] But the students rebounded a year later. This time an SGA poll revealed that 44 percent of the student body would be willing to risk attending a folk dance to promote a policy change.[109] Seniors Fred Kniss and Louise Otto cochaired the 1979 Spring Arts Festival. As part of the event, student planners arranged a square dance with a bluegrass band in the dining hall on Saturday night. They alerted the director of student life that he may want to miss the occasion. He winked and said, "Okay." Although everyone seemed to know about the "underground" dance, it surprisingly brought no backlash from administrators.[110]

Buoyed by their success, an ad hoc student committee developed a thoughtful rationale for allowing dancing at EMC, but the trustees were not persuaded.[111] Later in May 1979, the trustees approved a Statement of Commitment (a code of conduct for faculty, staff, and students) that included this phrase: "I will refrain from dancing as it does not advance the *unity* of the contemporary Mennonite Church."[112] Communalism thus trumped moral and biblical reasons for not dancing.

This logic hardly quelled student pressure. Early in his last year in office (1979–1980), Augsburger appointed a ten-member task force to explore the implications of dancing for Christians.[113] The group gathered dance policies from thirty other church-affiliated colleges. Six members researched and wrote papers on the relationship of dance to physical education, human sexuality, the Bible, cross-cultural practices, music, and the humanities. Without proposing a policy, the task force favored appropriate uses of dance at EMC.[114] A few weeks before leaving office, President Augsburger sent the report to the faculty and the trustees.

Due to the presidential transition, the issue of dancing lay in limbo for nearly four years despite occasional student pleas for square dancing.[115] In 1983, the SGA resurrected it with a student poll showing that nearly two-thirds of respondents would engage in social dancing if allowed, but one-third would be offended by it.[116] A new task force, appointed by President Detweiler and chaired by student life director Peggy Landis, again tackled the issue.[117] In December 1984, the trustees deleted the sentence in the handbook that prohibited dancing to preserve the unity of the church. They endorsed a new policy that restricted dance to "folk and ethnic dancing which foster wholesome group-oriented activity and broader cultural awareness." The policy also permitted integrating dance into instruction, artistic expression, celebrative worship, and other wholesome social activities.[118]

Peggy Landis reported mostly favorable reactions to the policy.[119] The first sanctioned square dance—a three-hour event in the gym, with 175 dancers—was held on March 30, 1985, six years after the first underground dance.[120] Though various types of dances were held after 1985, the new policy remained "official" until all references to dancing in the handbook disappeared in 1996. Details aside, EMC demonstrated a willingness to walk alongside the church as attitudes toward dance changed during this twenty-year period.

Rising from the Ashes

In 1983, R. Clair Sauder, treasurer of the board of trustees, declared that EMC was on the verge of its "most severe financial crisis" ever.[121] He was correct. Over two academic years (1983–1985), a string of disruptions made anxiety a campus staple. Enrollment had already been dipping, but the publication of Brunk's *Crisis* in the spring of 1983 and other factors sent it plummeting even further. Sauder's prediction came true as the 1983–1984 fiscal year ended with a $160,000 deficit. Despite meager resources, the college had committed to a $3.1 million renovation of the aging Ad Building. In June 1983, offices, classrooms, equipment, and furnishings had been relocated to other buildings to make way for the remodeling, which began that fall.[122] In the early morning of January 17, 1984, however, a fire of unknown origin devastated the building—stunning the community.

"Fire Guts Ad Building"

This headline announced the most dramatic event of those difficult years.[123] Retired professor Mary Emma Showalter Eby grieved the loss of her "dear old ad building," whose halls she had walked for fifty-four years. She mourned as she saw the smoking rubble of the "home" where she had lived three years as a dorm student and where she had studied with "the best scholars and beloved churchmen" who had shaped her "philosophy of life." Now the heart of EMC's campus jutted out of the hillside "like a deserted house, ravaged by fire, smoke, and water."[124]

The Cracker Box, touted as a fireproof building in 1920 with its masonry block and stucco walls, melted like cheese in the heat of the inferno. The flames destroyed the newly shingled roof that dozens of volunteers had recently installed. "How do you take a fire?" people asked President Detweiler. "With realism and hope," he replied.[125]

After sifting through several options, the trustees decided to demolish the burned-out structure and build a new campus center. The *Daily News-Record* correctly predicted that "EMC will rise stronger from the ashes of the fire."[126] A grassroots effort in Franconia Conference mimicked an old-fashioned barn raising as friends of

Burned-out shell of the Ad Building, January 17, 1984.

EMC donated a day's wages. Some 280 church leaders attending Ministers Week at the time of the fire gave a spontaneous $4,000 offering. Six college trustees, at the urging of fellow trustee Carl B. Harman, raised $1 million toward the new project. This included a matching gift that promised one dollar for every three raised, the largest gift ever given to EMC. Contractors and businesses provided equipment and services free of charge or at discounted rates. With a battalion of volunteers, Mennonite Disaster Service did the demolition work. Other volunteers gave endless hours to the construction of the new campus center.[127] When the insurance company balked at making payments for the burned-out building, President Detweiler refused to litigate a settlement, so the trustees authorized attorney Donald Showalter to seek whatever payment he could obtain. He successfully recovered a $1 million payment that was likely larger than what litigation would have achieved.[128]

Most remarkably, within nine months of the fire, contributions exceeded the $4.5 million goal for the center.[129] The three-story, fifty-thousand-square-foot building opened for the 1986–1987 academic year. The overwhelming generosity of EMC's extended family had turned the disaster into a symbol of strength and hope that became the heart and the hub of the campus for many years.

Keim's Legacy: The Global Village

By the early 1980s, the tread on the Interdisciplinary Studies (IDS) initiated by President Augsburger in the mid-'60s had worn thin. A new generation of faculty

Dedication of the new Campus Center, 1986. (Northlawn, a women's residence hall, is on the far right.)

wanted to revitalize EMC's general curriculum. Led by Dean Keim, the faculty radically redesigned the core requirements into a new program called Global Village. Marshall McLuhan had coined this phrase in the mid-'60s to capture the way modern communication had transformed the world into a village by linking far-flung places together. EMC's curricular architects envisioned the world "as a collection of many villages where humans share life, place, meaning, and a sense of belonging."[130] The EMC community was one *village* in a *world* of many villages. The Global Village core—consisting of one-third of the semester hours for graduation—would now be the common interdisciplinary curriculum for all students.

Under a rubric called Learning for Life, the Global Village had four components: From the Humanities, Through Faith, In the Village, and In the World. A sequence of courses for In the Village focused on the social and natural sciences. In the World required a semester-long, cross-cultural study term (typically international) or a cross-cultural experience of three weeks plus two cross-cultural courses on campus. The new core curriculum enlarged students' international exposure. In Keim's words, the Global Village concept "became a means to heighten awareness, enrich the learning experience, and prepare students for service which transcends the village [EMC] and the nation." In a reversal of the negative, over-against-the-world stance of EMC's first half century, Keim and his colleagues viewed the world as a laboratory for study—a place "that provides alternatives, new possibilities, and challenges."[131]

Many of the new generation of EMC faculty, including Keim, had served in international programs such as PAX and Voluntary Service in the Cold War era. Insights from those life-altering experiences motivated them to advocate for EMC's cross-cultural requirement. Keim introduced the Global Village curriculum in his last year in office (1983–1984). Despite a few hiccups, the implementation went well.[132] Amid the ashes of the Ad Building, the Global Village was a creative, bold venture that articulated EMC's mission in a way that would endure for more than twenty-five years.

As Keim left office, he was circumspect about the Global Village achievement: "Every generation enjoys the self-laudatory prospect of being the dramatic new cutting edge for the future; but the future has an unusual ability to be repetitive of the past. I hope EMC can be both creative and risk-taking while at the same time bringing stability, consequence, and a steady sense of direction to its ongoing programs."[133]

Keim's comment revealed his unconventional view of the school's relationship to the Mennonite Church. The college, he said, held an "exaggerated sensitivity toward church constituents." He despaired that "a critical sneeze in Ohio ricochets through our offices like a thunderclap." This kowtowing to the church, argued Keim, "drives us from the creative edge of our faith tradition to the complacent center . . . where we cannot do the intellectual questioning, the creative imagining, and the cultural pluralizing that we must do . . . to be a college in its true sense."[134] These were bold words for an Amish-raised boy from Ohio. Dean Keim was ahead of his time.

Restructuring: Terrible Taste, Great Cure

The generous financial outpouring that turned the Ad Building fire into a blessing did not stop the enrollment decline or the budgetary crisis. For help, EMC asked the Council of Independent Colleges to conduct an administrative audit. In September 1984, the presidents of Roanoke College and Gettysburg College spent several days on campus interviewing administrators, faculty, and students. They found "a strong and loyal residual spirit [and] a great reservoir of goodwill at EMC," despite the ongoing frustration.[135] If Augsburger was faulted for being too decisive and not consulting enough, Detweiler was the opposite: too much consulting and too indecisive. Explained a colleague, "We were in really bad financial straits and you put all that together and it was a blowup waiting to happen. People were competing for their budgets and we needed strong leadership."[136]

The consultants called for immediate and decisive actions by the president, noting that the "very caring nature of the institution" would make the decisions extremely painful. One of the consultants cited his mother's view of castor oil: "The taste is terrible, but the cure is great." The consultants recommended downsizing the college from one appropriate for a thousand students to one befitting a student body of eight hundred.[137] President Detweiler heard the message. Within ten days of receiving the consultants' report, he recommended staff and faculty reductions, which the trustees quickly approved. The consultants were correct. The taste was terrible. Family and friends of laid-off employees complained bitterly.

Lee F. Snyder, a one-year interim dean, found herself caught in the midst of the downsizing. Snyder had assumed her post in July 1984, a few weeks before the consultants' visit.[138] When the trustees mandated the downsizing, she realized her first major task involved cutting an equivalent of six FTE faculty positions, terminating six academic majors, merging departments, reducing some course requirements, and reallocating certain teaching loads. Outside the academic area, nearly five FTE administrative and staff positions were eliminated.[139] As a sacrificial interim lamb, she assumed that the trustees would likely "boot me out at the end of the year."[140] As the plans for shrinking the faculty became public, Detweiler praised Snyder's diplomatic skills, which gave good reason to extend her one-year contract. He told trustee chairman Joe Lapp, "Lee Snyder has already turned the faculty around in their attitudes and cooperation in our need to reduce program and personnel."[141] Even so, recalled Professor Jay B. Landis, "it was a very low period; morale was really bad until we got the new building."[142]

A Servant Leader in a Time of Crisis

Richard Detweiler took pleasure in occupying the new Campus Center during his last year in office (1986–1987). It was a well-deserved delight, delivered by the hands of fate at the end of a seven-year stint in a presidency spun about by economic and theological maelstroms. Although enrollment had dipped to a seven-year low in his last year, Detweiler was able to bestow on his successor not only the new Campus Center but also a remarkable uptick of one hundred more students in the fall of 1987. His passion for the church's mission had served as his compass throughout his presidency. That one-third of EMC's recent graduates were serving full time in church-related mission and service work energized his spirit in difficult times.[143]

Despite the whiplash of hard times, Detweiler was the epitome of a servant leader who extended empathy and respect to his severest critics. He preferred a low-cost hotel when he traveled on college business and occasionally paid his own lodging costs. He privately and voluntarily lowered his own salary during hard times. He quietly and faithfully carried the heavy burden of his institution's troubles, with joy and gratitude for God's grace and guidance. As Keim left the dean's office in 1984, he thanked Detweiler "for several years of good comradeship. Your wise counsel, patient perseverance, and good humor have been good for me."[144]

Throughout his presidency, Detweiler cared not only for the travails of the college but also for those of his wife, Mary Jane, who suffered a serious recurring illness with periodic hospital stays. All of these pressures took a toll on his body. Four years after leaving office, he died of pancreatic cancer at the age of sixty-six.

The Detweiler years saw a gradual shift in EMC's educational paradigm. Without Augsburger, the great persuader, the persuasion-engagement approach began to dissolve into a different educational philosophy that reflected Detweiler's pastoral style. Instead of persuasion, Detweiler built a bridge toward a stance of affirmation. In a paper on faith development in which he responded to his conservative critics, he frequently used the words *affirm*, *mutual affirmation*, and *faith affirmation*. His accent on affirmation and presence would eventually evolve into a new moral paradigm for EMU in the twenty-first century.

PART IV

Eastern Mennonite *University* and the Big Expansion, 1987–2017

CHAPTER 10

Justice, Mercy, and Peace
for a New Century

Maybe we should be a university.
—President Joe Lapp

No Bag of Miracles

As the search for a new president proceeded in 1985–1986, enrollment plummeted to a six-year low. Financial controller Donald Foth warned the presidential selection committee that Eastern Mennonite College and Seminary (EMC&S) was at a dire juncture in its history: "We need 200 more students enrolled ASAP and a president who recognizes the CRISIS."[1] The eight-person committee, appointed jointly by the Mennonite Board of Education (MBE) and the EMC&S trustees, interviewed five candidates from a pool of ninety-one but brought none to campus during the search.[2]

Then, in August 1986, the committee presented Joseph Lamar Lapp to the campus community as the school's seventh president.[3] He would take office in July 1987 after Richard Detweiler retired. Some were surprised that Lapp—an attorney and chair of the trustees who had little administrative experience and no advanced work in education—was selected. Others expected Lee Yoder, director of advancement and church relations, to get the position. When Lapp addressed the campus community in August, he confessed that he was as surprised as they were.

By selecting a layman, the committee upended a nearly seventy-year pattern of appointing ordained men whose ministerial credentials gave them religious authority, symbolized the school's close affiliation with the church, and assured constituents that the president would promote the interests of the church. That the trustees appointed a president who was not only a layman but also an attorney signaled a shift from churchly authority to professional competence. Until midcentury, Mennonites had strong reservations about members entering the legal profession. Particularly troublesome was the possibility that a Mennonite lawyer would engage in coercive litigation that might violate Jesus's teaching to turn the other cheek rather than retaliate. In the 1960s, it would have been inconceivable for a lawyer to lead the institution. Even in 1986, some constituents could not imagine it.

As an EMC student in the early '60s, Lapp was known as a fun-loving, innovative person with big ideas who helped launch the provocative underground paper *Piranha*.[4] In 1973, as a thirty-year-old, he was appointed the youngest trustee ever. The selection committee wanted an innovative leader with bold ideas. With EMC&S facing a financial predicament, the trustees were willing to take a risk in hiring an unconventional candidate.

Like his predecessor, Richard Detweiler, Joe Lapp hailed from Pennsylvania. He was married to Hannah Mack, a friend from first grade. After Hannah graduated from high school, Lapp's father hired her as a secretary in his home office—"perhaps to see if she would fit into the family," Lapp quipped later.[5] They were married prior to Lapp's junior year at EMC. With a BA degree in journalism and public relations from Temple University, Hannah served as an associate for public relations at EMC&S after Lapp's appointment. The Lapps had a daughter, Johanna.

When the president-elect addressed the EMC&S faculty and staff in August 1986, his vision included increasing enrollment, expanding contributions, and promoting the school more aggressively. He hoped the college would grow to one thousand undergraduates, the seminary to one hundred students, and the endowment to $10 million. He confessed, however, "I have no bag of miracles—or immediate cures for the present woes."[6] And he candidly recognized that trying to convert an attorney into a college president involved considerable risk.[7] In preparation for his new role, Lapp enrolled in the college management program at Carnegie Mellon University.

Some 1,500 people attended Lapp's inauguration in September 1987. The event had an "upbeat, EMC is going places" mood, offering hope that the sun rising over Massanutten Mountain would shine more brightly on the institution's future. After several presentations and a response by Lapp, his eighty-two-year-old father, Bishop John E. Lapp of Franconia Conference, offered "an eloquent benedictory prayer."[8]

From the outset, the new president was troubled by what he called "an insidious self-perception of inferiority that tend[ed] to permeate" the campus and constituents.[9] "Messiah College was growing and Goshen seemed to be doing fairly well, and yet we were struggling. It drove me nuts! It always seemed like everyone at EMC felt they were playing second fiddle to Goshen and other places. We had to find a way to turn things around."[10] During his first year, Lapp and his cabinet developed symbolic ways to help faculty and staff "recognize that EMC&S is better than people say or think."[11] More than a half dozen initiatives—including an

Inauguration of President Joseph L. Lapp, September 19, 1987. Left to right: Charles Gautsche, president of the MBE; Samuel Janzen, chair of the EMC trustees; Joseph L. Lapp; Hannah Lapp.

annual fiscal new year's breakfast party on July 1, a "Faculty Fling" to Washington, and the recognition of published scholarship—sought to celebrate the institution.[12]

The efforts appeared to pay off. By the end of Lapp's first year (1987–1988), EMC&S was one of ten colleges in the Council of Independent Colleges with "exceptionally high faculty morale." The institution met its contributions goal for the first time in eleven years, and the enrollment for fall 1988 looked promising. President Lapp joined the local Rotary Club as well as the board of the Community Mediation Center. He and Hannah also helped form the Harrisonburg/Rockingham Community Advisory Council. The president considered his first year "extremely successful."[13]

Seeds of Emancipation

Another boon to Lapp's early presidency was the expanding number of leadership roles filled by women. A new page had opened in EMC's history when in 1984 Lee F. Snyder accepted President Detweiler's invitation to become the interim academic dean. She was the first woman to hold a senior administrative role, and within a year, she was appointed dean.[14] When President Lapp appointed her vice president and academic dean in 1987, he described her as "well respected by faculty and staff" for her no-nonsense wit and gentle strength as a leader.[15] Snyder would later serve as acting president in the fall of 1993. Her leadership in the years leading up to and beyond 1994, when EMC&S became Eastern Mennonite University (EMU), paved the way for other women on campus. It also prepared her for the presidency of Bluffton College in 1996. Beryl Brubaker, EMU's first provost, recalled that "women really came into power in the Lapp era."[16]

It is worth recalling that men dominated EMU's power structure in its first half century (1917–1966). The school's founders understood that Scripture gave men spiritual authority to preach, teach, and lead in religious matters.[17] Faculty, staff, and students largely accepted the traditional gender roles depicted in the epistles as God-endorsed.

In this patriarchal environment, women did not teach Bible or theology courses. Men held senior administrative roles and filled all the seats on the board of trustees. They conducted all religious services at chapels, revival meetings, and the annual Short Bible Term. It was not until 1958 that college officials allowed faculty women to address the daily chapel.[18] Male speakers gave the commencement and baccalaureate addresses every year.[19] Women students rarely held leadership roles in campus life. The presidents of classes, literary societies, and the Young People's Christian Association were men. While women contributed to the *Journal*, *Weather Vane*, and *Shenandoah*, the lead editors were typically men until the mid-1960s.[20] With one exception, men authored the articles that appeared in the *Bulletin*, the school's public mouthpiece.[21] Men also presided over the alumni association for sixty-six years, from 1919 to 1985.[22]

Although EMU's early history reflected patriarchal gender roles, the school did provide significant opportunities for hundreds of young women to explore the world of education beyond the boundaries of their rural communities. In the first twenty-five years of the school, 55 percent of the graduates were women.[23] Still, men were more likely than women to receive encouragement to pursue professional careers or graduate school. One alumna in the 1940s recalled, "It seemed no one really cared *what* we planned to do, *where* we planned to go, or *why* we did or did not choose to make better use of the education we were getting." Those perceptions led to the first stirrings of feminism among students, and a handful of them started the Susan B. Anthony Society in the early 1940s. They held informal discussions in the lounge of the women's dormitory to talk about vocations, marriage, and their hopes for the future.[24]

The three women on the faculty in the 1930s—Dorothy Kemrer, Sadie Hartzler, and Ruth Stoltzfus—were single. The school paid single faculty about 85 percent of the wages earned by married faculty. During the Depression, the three women, all of whom worked full time, were reclassified as part time and paid two-thirds of their regular salary, which eliminated the equivalent of one full-time salary. Despite the salary cut, which did not apply to the men, Kemrer's and Stoltzfus's teaching load remained the same for at least two years. Even so, Stoltzfus explained, "In the beginning we had to make sacrifices [but] these things did not make us bitter; we were loyal."[25]

Well into the 1960s, single faculty, most of whom were women, received lower wages than married faculty, who were typically men. In 1942, a single person with a master's degree received $1,000 a year, whereas a married man received $1,200. This differential became a problem for Ruth Stoltzfus, who had left teaching when she married Paul Stauffer. Shortly after his untimely death, she returned to teaching, only to find that she was now classified as single. She protested that, as a widow, she still had a home to maintain and a mortgage to pay and did not have sideline incomes like most of the married male faculty. Nonetheless, the chairman of the board denied her appeal.[26]

Women faculty worked under the supervision of men throughout EMU's first half century. At faculty meetings, women could offer agenda items for discussion, and they had equal voting rights with men.[27] By tradition, women did not chair academic departments, but they sometimes provided leadership under the shadow of a man. Ruth Mininger Brackbill, a beloved teacher of English and American literature, held the longest tenure in the English department. Even so, Hubert Pellman, a new teacher, was appointed chair. He respected Brackbill's administrative skill and said, "We shared equally in all major department decisions."[28]

In the 1980s, Pellman identified Ada M. Zimmerman as "the seed of emancipation of women" at EMC. Hired in 1939 to teach psychology, she held a master's degree in education from George Peabody College. Unlike other women on the faculty, who let men take the lead, said Pellman, "Zimmerman was not awed by men; she felt she was their equal. You could talk to Ada Zimmerman just like you could talk to another man."[29] Within a year, the school appointed her to a newly created position: dean of women. In this role, she had no direct male supervision. In

Ada M. Zimmerman,
dean of women, 1940.

addition to her oversight of women's concerns, she also developed a variety of student services, including counseling, vocational planning, freshman orientation, and disciplinary procedures. Issues involving student discipline were no longer resolved by the faculty. Zimmerman founded what would eventually become the student life division of the school. Pellman explained, "She used her position as dean of women to test students, especially women. And there was, in this very act, the assumption that women could excel and grow just as much as men could. No one had denied this before, but no one had given much thought to it either."[30]

Cracking the Glass Ceiling

Mary Emma Showalter, author of the *Mennonite Community Cookbook* (1950), was the first woman on the faculty to receive a doctorate—an EdD in home economics in 1957. She was also the first woman to head an academic program. Under her leadership, the home economics major flourished and received state accreditation in the late 1950s.[31] Showalter was a leader among faculty women and, according to a male colleague, "the first woman who challenged men in faculty meetings."[32]

After Lois B. Bowman graduated from EMC in 1960, she received a fellowship for graduate study in German literature at Harvard University. The first alumna to receive a Harvard degree, she returned to EMC to teach in the fall of 1963. Although she had felt "very affirmed" as a student, she did not feel the same acceptance when she joined the faculty. "Women could not do anything without male supervision. Somehow women weren't quite as capable as men. Now I was competing with these poor, tender [male] egos."[33] At the time, faculty received a stipend for each child in addition to their base pay. Bowman's daughter was born soon after she began teaching. Expecting a stipend, she learned that because the school considered her husband—who was employed off campus—the family's main wage earner, she would not receive it.

Although after 1947 the salary schedule no longer distinguished between single and married faculty, the inequity persisted informally. Catherine R. Mumaw, who had received a PhD in 1967, discovered that she was paid only 80 percent of the salary of a married man with children. When she asked the president in 1972 about the discrepancy, he explained that faculty members with children received higher salaries.[34]

Professorial rank was another discrepancy. Ever since Eastern Mennonite School had become a college in 1947, it ranked faculty on the traditional four-step ladder: instructor, assistant professor, associate professor, and full professor. In 1971–1972, women constituted 29 percent of the faculty. However, 48 percent of them taught at the instructor level, compared with only 29 percent of the men.[35]

During the first ten years of the Augsburger presidency, the top two clusters of power were the Administration Committee and the Administrative Council. The committee typically consisted of four to six senior officials—at minimum, the academic dean, the seminary dean, the high school principal, and the president. The council included the Administration Committee, plus the registrar, business manager, campus pastor, director of student affairs, and one or more faculty leaders. No female professor sat on the Administrative Council until the fall of 1968. That year, English professor Anna Frey and two male professors joined the council alongside seven administrators.[36]

The presence of Frey on the Administrative Council in 1968–1969 represented a minuscule step of progress toward gender equity. Frey was the only woman occupying one of the fifteen seats of power on the committee and the council. Higher up the patriarchal ladder were thirty-two trustees, all men. This dominance of male power typified gender roles in the Mennonite Church, most small American colleges, and the broader society in the 1970s.

EMC was not isolated from the rising tide of feminism in American society. Betty Friedan published *The Feminine Mystique* in 1963 and formed the National Organization for Women in 1966. She inspired the nationwide Women's Strike for Equality in 1970 and the drive to establish an Equal Rights Amendment to the US Constitution. Within that context, a group of EMC faculty (women and men) gathered about once a month in 1971–1972 to discuss inequities in salaries and hiring procedures. At the end of that year, they shared their concerns with President Augsburger and other senior officials. Following the meeting, Professor Catherine R. Mumaw reported, "We decided to organize a faculty senate so we could convene the faculty without administrators present." Mumaw was elected president when the senate was established in 1972.[37] About two years later, the senate formed the Status of Women on Campus Committee to investigate concerns about gender-based salary discrimination. The committee compiled a list of eleven recommendations that raised consciousness and led to affirmative action in hiring.[38]

From 1970 to 1973, a group of students met with several faculty members to discuss feminist issues. "We talked mostly about the lack of women on the administration and faculty, but didn't do much about it," said one participant.[39] The glass ceiling was beginning to crack, however. In 1973, literature professor A. Grace Wenger became the first woman to join the board of trustees. A year later, Dorothy Shank joined the board and its executive committee by virtue of her appointment as principal of Eastern Mennonite High School. Twenty-four years after Shank's appointment, the trustees of EMU elected the first woman, Sheryl Wyse, as chair of the board (1998–2004). She was followed by Susan Godshall (2004–2010) and Kay Nussbaum (2015).[40]

Lee Snyder's appointment as interim academic dean in 1984 opened the door for other women to become senior-level administrators. In 1986, Peggy Landis

Lee F. Snyder, interim academic dean, 1984.

became the first woman appointed director of student life. For a span of thirty-two consecutive years—with one three-year break—Snyder and three other women (Marie Morris, Nancy Heisey, and Deirdre Smeltzer) served as academic deans.[41] Beryl Brubaker became EMU's first provost in 2000, and seventeen years later, Susan Schultz Huxman assumed the presidency. From 1998 to 2008, the proportion of faculty who were women grew from 39 to 59 percent. In 1998, 10 percent of the women faculty held the rank of professor, compared with 47 percent of the men. A decade later, that inequality had shrunk: 30 percent of the women and 34 percent of the men held full professorial status.[42]

Gender as a topic of study also stirred some interest. Sociologist John Eby, in response to student requests, proposed a course in women's studies that was offered in the fall of 1972, with sixteen students. A minor in gender studies, however, did not appear until forty years later, in 2013–2014. In 1982, alumna Shirley Hershey Showalter, assistant professor of English and history at Goshen College, delivered the keynote address at EMC's second annual conference on women and men. She told the audience that "the greatest crime against women through the centuries has not been the denial of property rights, voting rights, and equal pay. It has not even been physical rape and other forms of violence against women—though all of these are evil." For Showalter, the greatest crime against women was encouraging them "*not to change*, encouraging all females to remain infantile" rather than encouraging them "to take the kinds of risks that all human beings need in order to grow."[43]

Harvard graduate Lois B. Bowman, still wearing her devotional covering in 2015, summed up more than a half century of change at EMC since her graduation in 1960:

Table 2. First-Time Appointments and Accomplishments of Women

1928	Sadie Hartzler, librarian
1940	Ada M. Zimmerman, dean of women
1953	Grace Showalter, historical library and archives director
1957	Mary Emma Showalter, recipient of doctorate
1958	Mary Emma Showalter, head of an academic program (home economics)
1958	Mary Emma Showalter, full professor
1968	Anna Frey, Administrative Council member
1972	Catherine R. Mumaw, chair of the faculty senate
1973	A. Grace Wenger, trustee
1974	Dorothy Shank, trustee executive committee member
1984	Lee F. Snyder, interim academic dean
1984	Lee F. Snyder (interim dean) and Peggy Landis (interim director of student life), president's cabinet members
1984	Dorothy Jean Weaver, full-time faculty at the seminary
1985	Lee F. Snyder, academic dean
1985	Sadie Hartzler, namesake of Hartzler Library
1986	Peggy Landis, director of student life
1993	Lee F. Snyder, acting president
1994	Beryl Brubaker, vice president for enrollment management
1998	Sheryl Wyse, chair of the trustees
1999	Nancy Heisey, full-time faculty of Bible and religion at the college
2000	Beryl Brubaker, provost
2003	Beryl Brubaker, interim president
2007	Sara Wenger Shenk, vice president and dean of the seminary
2017	Susan Schultz Huxman, president

"Gender relations have changed considerably. Women are so much more vocal and take charge now. Men couldn't get by with condescending attitudes today as they did in the past."[44]

Will This Emu Fly?

If the trustees wanted a leader with bold ideas, President Lapp delivered on that expectation when he proposed that Eastern Mennonite College and Seminary become a university. The ensuing transformation into what became Eastern Mennonite University in 1994 was the signature accomplishment of Lapp's presidency, providing a scaffold for new programs to flourish for many years.

The concept of a university had been incubating since the seminary formed in 1965, and it continued as the college added other initiatives to its primary undergraduate mission. In 1976, at the initiative of alumnus Nelson Good and several students, the

Washington Study-Service Year (WSSY) was established in Washington, DC.[45] Initially, EMC administrators had been reluctant, but several students pressed hard for the program. "We threatened the administration that we [were] going to go elsewhere unless EMC started this program," said Phil Baker-Shenk, one of the nine students who participated in the program's first year. The students lived together in a house and interned in public and private agencies in metropolitan Washington in tandem with their academic courses. The program—renamed the Washington Community Scholars' Center in 2002—grew, with its durable mix of courses and internships. The urban setting offered a rich educational immersion with life-changing potential for small-town students. Rolando Santiago considered it the "most rich and stimulating year" of his life. For Dawn Longenecker, "It was an incredible year. . . . My whole life was transformed."[46]

Other expansions were added in the 1980s. In 1987, EMC&S established the Lark Leadership Education Program in Philadelphia in conjunction with the Center for Urban Theological Studies. This program provided college-level courses for African American Mennonite students and church leaders.[47] Back in Harrisonburg, some 590 students were enrolled in forty-six continuing education classes in 1987–1988.[48] Lancaster County, meanwhile, was finally ripe for Mennonite higher education. Although EMC had periodically offered courses at Lancaster Mennonite High School since the 1950s, a formal program had never emerged. At the invitation of an eastern Pennsylvania advisory group in 1986, a director was hired to organize a Pennsylvania extension with courses leading to an associate degree. The extension, approved by the Pennsylvania Department of Education, opened in 1989.[49] This outpost eventually grew into a sizable satellite of EMU. Finally, the cross-cultural requirement of EMC's Global Village curriculum produced dozens of international seminars and semester-long, life-changing experiences for hundreds of students.[50] All these activities and program initiatives were stretching the traditional college structure.

In 1989, college officials began brainstorming about a master's degree in counseling to add to the master's degree in church leadership already offered by the seminary along with its theological degrees. Plans were also under way for the college to create an Adult Degree Completion Program (ADCP), an intensive English program, an expansion of summer conferences, a master's in conflict analysis and transformation, and even an institute for conflict and peacebuilding. But where did such programs fit in the college structure? Did a master's in counseling, for example, belong under the college or the seminary? Lapp recalled, "I chuckled one day as I mentioned casually to some colleagues, 'Maybe we should be a university.'"[51]

The master's degree in counseling, eventually launched in 1993, became a tipping point toward university status. In November 1993, the trustees also approved a master's in conflict analysis and transformation and discussed a preliminary proposal for an institute for conflict and peacebuilding. For several years, these programs and other initiatives were housed within the Conflict Transformation Program (CTP).[52]

When Lapp first introduced the idea of a university to the trustees in March 1993, the chair of the board's academic committee—a professor at a large state university—laughed out loud. The board chair, a professor at a small liberal arts college, was also skeptical. Some days after the board meeting, however, the board chair called the president and confessed, "The university idea has grown on me. I like it, and I think we can do this." Lapp noted, "I knew then it was going to happen."[53]

The trustees encouraged senior administrators to explore the idea on campus in fall 1993, while Joe and Hannah Lapp led a student cross-cultural trip to the Middle East.[54] Students, faculty, and constituents weighed the pros and cons of becoming a university. The debates were sprinkled with humorous references to the Australian emu, a large flightless bird resembling an ostrich. The discussions also sparked serious and passionate responses. Critics thought it was ludicrous to describe small EMC&S as a university; proponents argued that the university concept reflected a vision of the future more than a description of the present.[55] All things considered,

e• mu (e′myoo) 1. a large, flightless, ratite bird, *Dromiceius novaeholandiae*, of Australia, resembling the ostrich, but smaller and having a feathered head and neck and rudimentary wings. 2. a small Mennonite liberal arts college in Harrisonburg, Virginia.

Weather Vane cartoon of the flightless Australian emu, March 4, 1993.

positive sentiments outweighed negative ones, and the trustees approved the make-over in March 1994.[56] At the same meeting, they approved the proposed ADCP and the Institute for Conflict and Peacebuilding. By late August, students and visitors arriving at the school saw directional signs to Eastern Mennonite University along interstate I-81—a sure signal that the Mennonite emu had taken flight.

By 2000, the ADCP was thriving, and the university was offering master's degrees in counseling, education, and business administration, along with graduate degrees in the seminary. The master's in conflict analysis and transformation was rapidly emerging as "EMU's signature graduate program." Already in 1996, a summer institute attended by international scholars and mediation practitioners had been "wildly successful." Moreover, the State Council for Higher Education, with a glowing endorsement, granted EMU the authority to confer degrees and employ new faculty in the Institute for Conflict and Peacebuilding.[57]

Student Life
Turmoil, Tragedy, Tenacity

Those were the words Peggy Landis used to describe the previous six weeks as she spoke to the trustees in mid-March 1991. As director of student life, she had the sensitive task of arranging grief counseling for distraught students as they processed four tragic events.[58]

Just two months earlier, on January 17, the US-led Operation Desert Storm had attacked Iraq to repel its invasion of Kuwait, leaving thousands dead and wounded. The war would continue through February. On Monday, January 21, EMC&S declared an "Emergency Sabbath," canceling all classes to allow students and faculty to engage in peace witness activities. Faculty and staff offered twelve workshops on the history of the Middle East conflict, war, and Christian peace witness. About two hundred students, faculty, and staff braved frigid temperatures to walk two miles to downtown Harrisonburg to mail hundreds of antiwar letters addressed to President George H. W. Bush and Iraqi government officials. They then assembled for a brief demonstration on the courthouse square. The college hosted a community-wide ecumenical worship service that evening.[59]

Four weeks later, tragedy struck the campus community. On February 17, the parents and younger sister of Steve Weaver, a rising senior, were stabbed to death by a family member. Eight days after that, EMC campus pastor Darrell Brubaker took his own life. And in early March, during spring break, first-year student Jeff Shoemaker died in his sleep from a heart malfunction.

The tragedies paralyzed the campus. The student life office organized extensive counseling services and safe places so grieving students could process their

EMC students and faculty pray at the Rockingham County Courthouse on January 21, 1991, during the Emergency Sabbath for the Persian Gulf War. Students also held protests and vigils in Harrisonburg during the Vietnam War. Photo: Cathy Kushner, *Daily News-Record* (Harrisonburg, VA).

emotions. Steve Weaver mused, "If there was a good place to be at a time like this, this was a good place to be." As tragedies are wont to do, these brought the community together in new and deeper ways. President Lapp proposed an annual festival and picnic on the front lawn of the campus center in mid-April to celebrate the blooming pear trees. One student recalled, "We began to have fun together again. I think the Pear Blossom Festival was a turning point."[60]

Growing into Professionalism

Thankfully, by 1991 the student life division had the resources and professional expertise to support students during times of tragedy and grief. Those benefits had not always been in place. The seeds of the student life program sown by Ada M. Zimmerman in 1940 had germinated slowly. Seventeen years later, the first part-time dean of students, Laban Peachey, directed the "Personnel Program," which handled Christian conduct, dress, orientation, housing, local transportation, testing, and records, among other things. Even so, developing and professionalizing the academic program held higher priority than did student life. For example, EMC's first application to the Southern Association of Colleges and Schools (SACS) for accreditation in 1959 allotted only eight of 391 pages to "extra-curricular activities," without mentioning anything akin to student affairs or student life.[61] The student life activities that grew slowly in the 1970s underwent rapid professionalization during the Lapp administration. Peggy Landis, director of student life (1986–1993), and her successor, Patricia Helton (1993–2001), drove the changes by introducing sexual assault policies, drug and alcohol abuse policies, multicultural programs, and student diversity initiatives typical in many colleges and universities.[62]

Lifestyle Commitment Encourages Responsibility

For many years, student life regulations appeared in a list of rules in the student handbook. That began to change in 1979 when the trustees adopted the "Statement of Commitment." This behavioral code applied to students, staff, and faculty. It underscored the primacy of community and explicitly stated, "The student, by enrolling, accepts responsibilities of membership in the college community." Expectations were couched in biblical language: "loving our neighbor as ourselves, seeking after righteousness, practicing justice, helping those in need, forgiving others, seeking forgiveness, and exercising freedom responsibly with loving regard for the sensitivity and weakness of others." The statement included an explicit commitment to reject "harmful discrimination based on racial, sexual, cultural or religious prejudices." Students also pledged to refrain from sexual immorality, gambling, dishonesty, abusive language, alcohol, tobacco, and illegal drugs.[63]

In 1994, the statement was renamed the Community Lifestyle Commitment (CLC).[64] In addition to referencing all levels of university life and refining some theological phrases, it stated, "Violations of these standards are regarded as a serious breach of integrity within the community." Like the earlier statement, it reminded students and employees that they were members of a religious community, not merely an educational one, and it repeated the warning against discrimination based on race and sex, as well as cultural or religious prejudice.

In Pursuit of Diversity

Already in 1949, the EMC faculty had thought about cultural diversity. While noting that their Mennonite "homogeneity was undoubtedly an asset," they feared it might hinder alumni seeking jobs in the larger society. In order to prepare their students for a "heterogeneous world," school officials considered ways to help them "sympathetically meet the variegated viewpoints, philosophies, religious faiths, and ways of life."[65] Although EMC was on the forefront of accepting African American students in the late 1940s, creating a congenial home for them was entirely different. Not only was EMC white, Christian, and Mennonite; its Swiss-German ethnicity ran deep.

Attempts to attract and keep ethnic minority students fluctuated over the years depending on their numbers on campus, administrative support, student life personnel, and the routine four-year turnover of student leadership. A black student union that formed in the late 1960s soon fizzled. A few years later, some students revived the union and promoted EMC to prospective students who were leery that racism might be rampant in a predominantly white, southern school with a German culture.[66] When Dean Al Keim attended the Mennonite Black Caucus Assembly in Philadelphia in July 1978, he was astonished to learn that Goshen had sixty "black minority students." He considered Goshen's "total monopoly on the education of black leaders" an egregious failure of EMC, given the many African American communities on the East Coast.[67]

Keim promptly created a task force to investigate how EMC could attract minority students. In May 1980, a campus protest prodded the task force to action. Sixty black and white students and some faculty marched around campus carrying signs to demonstrate their commitment to "break down the barriers that alienate us." The group demanded that the administration hire two minority professors, one international faculty member, and a full-time coordinator for a cross-cultural program.[68] By that fall, the cross-cultural program envisioned by Keim to promote racial integration on campus was operating. Abraham Davis Jr., hired as the first African American faculty member and the first director of multicultural services, also served as an advocate for African American students.

Dean Keim aimed to double EMC's twenty-five African American and Hispanic American students.[69] But progress was slow. Nine years after Davis's hiring, the number of minority students had dwindled from twenty-five to nineteen (2 percent of enrollment).[70] But by 1999–2000, the African American, Hispanic, Asian, and Native American students (8 percent) and the international students (9 percent) had lifted the number of nonwhite students to 17 percent across the university.[71]

Occasional incidents marred progress on racial diversity, but they also offered teachable moments. At one forum on racism, someone placed literature from the National Association for the Advancement of White People on a table with a note sympathetic to white supremacy. That event stoked campus-wide conversation on racism, including a statement by President Lapp. In chapel, he called the literature "an embarrassment to me which shamed this university because its message is antithetical to what we stand for." The president also reported that the university had earlier agreed to participate in the Damascus Road Project—a Mennonite Central Committee initiative to help organizations identify and correct systemic racism.[72]

Respect for the dignity and diversity of others was essential for a hospitable multicultural ethos. In 2001, the president's cabinet created a safety and behavioral expectations policy that explicitly forbade "any form of bigotry, harassment, intimidation, threat, destruction of personal property, name-calling or other forms of abuse whether written, spoken directly or implied." The policy stated that excuses such as "alcohol or other substance abuse, fatigue, ignorance or saying, 'it was just a joke'" were unacceptable. The policy also specified that gay and lesbian persons "have the same right to be treated with respect and dignity" as anyone else.[73] Sixty years after EMC had attempted to refine the dining etiquette of rural Mennonites, it now aimed to refine student habits of social respect—whether it was called political correctness, courtesy, or just old-fashioned decency.

Seminary: All about Formation

Lonnie Yoder, associate dean of Eastern Mennonite Seminary, was surprised to hear the executive director of the Association of Theological Schools (ATS) predict in 2015 that the future of theological education "is going to be all about formation." "We've been so far ahead of the curve on that," Yoder explained, "we can only strengthen what we already have."[74] Indeed, for some thirty years, the core of EMS's master of divinity program included a three-year sequence of spiritual formation courses—formation in personhood, ministry, and discipleship.[75] Advocates for this focus emphasized a process of integration that went well beyond absorbing academic information in courses. The classical discipline of *lectio divina* (divine reading) assumed that a given text could both illuminate and *form* the reader. Formation studies considered the spiritual development of the ministering person as important as the acquisition of theological knowledge and pastoral skills.

The accent on spiritual formation at EMS, alongside the focus on Anabaptist theology and peacemaking, owed much to the leadership of George Brunk III, who followed his father as dean (1977–1999). Brunk recruited Wendy J. Miller to teach in the fields of spiritual formation and direction. A key tenet of her teaching was the assumption that God takes the initiative in relating to humans. The task of the spiritual director was to assist in discerning and responding to that divine initiative through spiritual disciplines.[76] Under Miller's guidance, this curriculum evolved into a multifaceted ministry track. Increments included experiencing personal formation as disciples of Christ, discipling others through spiritual direction, supervising spiritual directors, and training supervisors. The two-week Summer Institute for Spiritual Formation provided another venue.

A colleague described Brunk III's leadership as "steady, sensitive, and diplomatic."[77] Institutional milestones during his tenure included accreditation by ATS in 1986 and construction of a new building in 1993. The seminary also developed master's degrees in religion and church leadership, launched a clinical pastoral education (CPE) program, and established the John S. Coffman Center for Evangelism and Church Growth. From as far back as the 1930s, the annual Ministers Week in January brought church leaders to campus. In 1983, planners added the subtitle "School for Leadership Training" to the name. The weeklong event offered Bible studies, workshops, and inspirational sessions for pastors, lay leaders, and seminary students. During Brunk's deanship, full-time equivalent (FTE) enrollment fluctuated from sixty-five to eighty. Nearly half of the students were affiliated with non-Mennonite denominations.[78] Adjunct faculty taught courses in Wesleyan history, doctrine, and polity, enabling United Methodist students to prepare for ministry in their denomination.

The enrollment of women accounted for the largest shift in the student body. Until the mid-1970s, one or two women attended EMS each year. By 1999, about 40 percent of the full-time students were women. Lonnie Yoder assessed EMS's strong commitment to spiritual formation as a draw for women considering theological training and ministry. This growth, at least among Mennonite women, reflected the rising number of opportunities for them to be ordained.

This situation created a quandary for seminary professor Nathan E. Yoder. In the late 1990s, he was leading the second-year formation in ministry course, which included a field placement. Yet he was not able to invite a woman contemplating ordination to preach in the congregation he pastored, Dayton Mennonite, because it opposed the ordination of women. "I wanted to support women and still honor the position taken by the congregation where I pastored," Yoder recalled. Eventually, he was able to wholeheartedly endorse the seminary's position of holding high the authority of Scripture and affirming women in ministry.[79]

Virginia Conference ordained its first woman in 1989—seventy-two-year-old Ruth Brunk Stoltzfus, daughter of George R. Brunk and speaker on the *Heart to Heart* radio program described in chapter 6. The move caused great consternation to her brother, George Brunk II.[80] The seventy-eight-year-old churchman was so troubled that he left Virginia Conference and founded Calvary Mennonite Fellowship as an independent congregation. Despite the seminary's encouragement of women in ministry, only one of its thirteen full-time, on-campus teaching faculty in 1999 was a woman—Dorothy Jean Weaver. Sara Wenger Shenk held administrative and teaching responsibilities, and Wendy J. Miller served as pastor to seminarians along with teaching.

As Dean Brunk left office in 1999, he reported reaccreditation by ATS for ten years, a $1.3 million grant from the Lilly Endowment, and a $110,000 gift from the

Arthur Vining Davis Foundations to underwrite startup costs for the clinical pastoral education program. Sara Wenger Shenk was appointed interim dean during 1999–2000 as the search for a new dean began.[81]

Dealing with Sexual Misconduct

News that Mennonite scholar John Howard Yoder was to offer a colloquium at EMS's School for Leadership Training (SLT) in January 1997 sparked a sharp reaction.[82] Yoder was one of the leading social ethicists of the twentieth century and arguably the best-known and most influential Mennonite in the world. If Harold S. Bender's Anabaptist vision shaped EMU's promotion of Anabaptism and discipleship in the 1950s and '60s, Yoder's *The Politics of Jesus* (1972) and his other books and essays had profoundly influenced many EMU faculty and students. He had drawn many scholars from outside the Mennonite world to Anabaptism, largely because of his claim that peacemaking and nonviolence are at the core of the Christian gospel.[83] From 1970 to 1984, he had served as professor at Associated Mennonite Biblical Seminaries in Elkhart, Indiana (and was president from 1970 to 1973), before being named professor of theology at the University of Notre Dame in 1985.

Reservations about Yoder's invitation to speak at EMS arose over concerns about his history of sexually violating women. His ministerial credentials had been suspended in June 1992 by the Indiana-Michigan Mennonite Conference.[84] Four years later, Indiana-Michigan officials reported progress in a discipline-accountability-therapy process and encouraged the church to use Yoder's "gifts of writing and teaching."[85] In the summer of 1996, EMS invited Yoder to lead a three-hour colloquium on Mennonite peacemaking at the beginning of the SLT, whose overall theme was "Pursuing Peace in the Congregation." Meanwhile, Barbra Graber, professor of theater, learned that Yoder had never apologized to his victims, publicly confessed remorse, or admitted he had sinned. On December 27, 1996, she wrote to seminary professor and ordained minister Duane Sider, director of the SLT and coordinator of Yoder's visit, protesting Yoder's participation and threatening public protests unless EMS disinvited him as Goshen College had done in 1986 and Bethel College had in 1994.[86]

Graber's letter prompted two hastily arranged meetings of a ten-person discernment group, which included her and Sider. The group faxed a letter to Yoder asking him for a public statement acknowledging and renouncing his wrongdoing. His response referred to his "testimony of repentance" and his gratitude "for the resources of forgiveness in the Christian community." But he blamed "institutional decisions [for] the persistence of the misperception that I had not repented or apologized." He also resolved that such offenses "will not recur."[87] Disappointed with the vagueness of his response, the discernment group was uncertain about what to do. They deferred the issue to the executive committee of the president's cabinet, since Lapp was traveling overseas. The three-person committee agreed unanimously to proceed with Yoder's invitation, send a statement of clarification to the campus community, and make his statement available as requested.[88] Yoder conducted the colloquium without incident to an overflowing crowd in the seminary chapel and flew back to Indiana the next day.[89] He died later that year of a heart attack in his office at Notre Dame, one day after his seventieth birthday.

If any self-righteousness lingered in the air after Yoder's visit, it dissipated quickly four months later when the EMU community learned that Duane Sider had, over several years, been involved in numerous extramarital affairs with women, some of whom were seminary students. Following a three-week investigation in June 1997, Sider, the husband of a faculty member and father of three children, resigned. The episode shocked and pained the university community.

Nearly twenty years later, in a scholarly exposé titled "'Defanging the Beast,'" Rachel Waltner Goossen revealed that John Howard Yoder's violation of women was much more horrific than EMS had realized in 1997.[90] Goossen unearthed extensive evidence that Yoder had sexually violated fifty to one hundred women in the United States and abroad while claiming he was doing theological experiments on how to defang the beast of sexual power. His "experiments" left a trail of traumatized victims. With theological language and twisted interpretations of Scripture, he justified his actions while refusing to confess his wrongdoings.

In March 2016, an art exhibit on campus revisited Yoder's abuse and the attempts of church agencies to conceal it. In some fifty evocative panels, EMU art professor Jerry Holsopple explored questions of lament and forgiveness in *7 × 7: Laments for an Age of Sexualized Power*. Holsopple explained that his project was "a response to the serial abuse by John Howard Yoder and the legacy of pain he left behind . . . [and] the many church leaders who gave preference to John Howard Yoder over the survivors." Holsopple used sandpaper to create the art. "I wanted the grit to rip the paint and ink, like residual pain, this can be raw." The exhibit felt especially raw to the EMU community because Luke Hartman, vice president of enrollment, had recently resigned in January (2016) following alleged sexual misconduct off campus.[91]

Y2K Bugs, Organizational Tremors, and a New Century

As the year 2000 approached, higher education officials across the country were vexed by the "Y2K bug." Consultants and IT departments on many campuses tried to assess, fix, and upgrade computers because only the last two digits of the four-digit year were coded. Some experts anticipated that at year's end, 1999 would turn over to 1900 instead of to 2000, causing a host of computers and computer-controlled devices to malfunction.[92] Happily, those fears were largely unfounded.

Apart from computer worries, EMU faced organizational uncertainties on campus and beyond. "We entered 2000 with low morale," said Beryl Brubaker, vice president for enrollment management. Although enrollment had been hovering around 1,200 FTE for several years, it required a scramble to meet enrollment targets. With EMU relying heavily on tuition fees for revenue, the growing programs and infrastructure prompted President Lapp to call the financial state "fragile."[93]

Staff transitions added to the pressure as undergraduate dean Bill Hawk and seminary dean George Brunk III both resigned in 1999 and the search for EMU's first provost got under way. The three searches for high-level administrators and unsettled questions about the university's structure fed anxiety. The stress rose even higher in June 2000 when the newly hired provost backed out of the assignment because of health concerns—just three weeks before his expected arrival. After hasty consultations, Beryl Brubaker agreed to begin a three-year term as provost on July 1, 2000, leaving the enrollment management position vacant. At about the same time, Professor Marie Morris became the new undergraduate dean, and Ervin Stutzman, bishop-moderator of Lancaster Conference, assumed the seminary deanship.[94]

In the midst of these transitions, sweeping changes were also under way in EMU's denominational constituency, which consumed an enormous amount of attention and added to the uncertainties. The Mennonite Church and the General Conference Mennonite Church, with which Bluffton (Ohio) and Bethel (Kansas) Colleges were affiliated, had been discussing a possible merger for a decade. This marriage of church bodies resulted in the new Mennonite Church USA (MC USA) and Mennonite Church Canada in February 2002.[95]

As a result, the MBE was replaced by the new Mennonite Education Agency (MEA) to coordinate all the educational efforts of MC USA, including the four colleges—Bethel, Bluffton, Goshen, and Hesston—and EMU. Although the changes appeared to strengthen school ties with the denomination, the merger actually weakened church control of EMU. Historically, the General Conference Mennonite Church had afforded Bluffton and Bethel more independence than the Mennonite Church colleges had enjoyed under the MBE. Likewise, the new MEA gave EMU more freedom.[96]

Beneath the surface of MC USA were two deep fissures. The first involved differences between the two merging denominations in their Mennonite ethnicity and ecclesiology. The Mennonite Church traced its roots to Switzerland and southern Germany, and its organizational pattern tended toward centralized authority. Many of the General Conference Mennonite Church members had Dutch-Russian roots and a less centralized ecclesial authority with stronger congregational autonomy.

Even deeper than these differences, however, was a *cultural-theological* rift that cut across both denominations. In 2000, Ervin Stutzman—dean of Eastern Mennonite Seminary and moderator-elect of the Mennonite Church—identified a growing polarity between religious *conservatives* and *liberals* on biblical interpretation, their view of salvation, their certainty of faith, the ordination of women, and homosexuality. The new struggles were all too reminiscent of the old fundamentalist-liberal debates swirling around EMU's origins. For Stutzman, "more differences emerged *within* the Mennonite Church" than between Mennonites and other Christians. He urged the president's cabinet to create forums for genuine dialogue on campus about these issues. The two crisscrossing cleavages of theology and culture would nevertheless fuel controversy, particularly around same-sex relationships, complicating the denominational merger as well as EMU's future.[97]

The university also had other serious growing pains at the turn of the century. The expanding graduate and ancillary programs that had been grafted onto the old college structure were straining interpersonal and organizational relations. These issues and the 1999 SACS review prompted a tedious and delicate discussion about how to structure the university.[98] The traditional undergraduate division, the seminary, and the graduate program were each guided by different policies and lines of accountability. In addition, inconsistencies abounded in the faculty handbooks, catalogs, financial aid policies, tuition rates, and decision making.[99] All of this created inequality, friction, and frustration.

Provost Brubaker was tasked with streamlining policies and accountability across the institution. The relationship of the thirty-five-year-old seminary to the new mix of graduate programs stirred heated controversy. Because the seminary was subsidized by the university, some faculty considered it a drag on other university programs. In fall 1998, Dean Hawk circulated a "modest proposal" to close the seminary because the new MC USA would be "too small to support two seminaries." The closure would generate $350,000 for the university (the amount critics said was subsidizing the seminary), and the university could then offer a graduate degree in religion and some seminary-related courses.[100] One seminary official called the complaint about subsidy downright "galling" because it was "far easier to raise money for the seminary than for the university," but the seminary was not permitted to do its own fund-raising. For one seminary leader, some of the sentiment seemed to reflect "widespread jealousy of the seminary's beautiful new building."[101] Still, the questions persisted: Should the seminary be closed, operated as a separate institution outside the university, or included within the university? Was the seminary an asset or liability to the university?

Interim seminary dean Sara Wenger Shenk was distressed by the spirit of Fordism that attempted to force the seminary into parity with four small graduate units.[102] "The seminary," she said, "has clearly been the most contentious issue. I am increasingly dismayed with how flawed the process has become." For her, the deliberations were driven by an "ideology of equity related to power and equal access to resources." She found the "unfair process too painful" to continue. From her perspective, the seminary could contribute more to the university if it had "a degree of autonomy that [kept it] distinct but encourage[d] it to contribute in vital ways to the whole community."[103]

Senior university officials considered the seminary an asset to EMU and a mutual benefit. Hoping to close the debate, President Lapp was candid and clear in the summer of 1999: "Our University mission is to maintain the Seminary as an integral part of the University. I believe the Seminary is essential to the well-being of the University and the University is essential to the well-being of the Seminary."[104] Even so, calls for the seminary to be self-supporting and autonomous continued until 2003.[105] Policy differences between the seminary, other graduate programs, and the undergraduate program required careful retooling and patience to satisfy all the stakeholders.

The university's growth created perceived inequities for all parties. In response to concerns that the five graduate entities would drain resources from the undergraduate program, the graduate programs were required to pay a 35 percent overhead. Leaders of the graduate programs considered those fees unfair since their programs were essential to the university's core mission. Some undergraduate faculty felt devalued because, although they generated the bulk of the university's revenue, they were treated as a single administrative unit alongside five different graduate programs. In addition, some undergraduate faculty resented that they had a lower status, larger classes, and less time for research than the graduate faculty.[106] Undergraduate dean Marie Morris described the situation as "perceived inequity, role confusion, and lack of symmetry and equal representation on the Academic Cabinet and the President's Cabinet."[107] Several practical issues remained as well: Could each graduate program have its own website? How many commencements were necessary?

To design a functional and satisfying university structure required at least five initiatives as the new millennium dawned: a structure committee, a strategic planning council, a task force on participatory decision making, a facilitator group to assist the flow of campus decision making, and a "philosophy of shared decision making."[108] In addition, Provost Brubaker led the charge to develop an equitable "policy on scholarship and practice" for faculty loads and professorial evaluation across all graduate departments.[109] Despite the organizational challenges, undergraduate and graduate faculty eventually worked collaboratively to fashion an educational paradigm for the maturing university.

The Limits of Dissent

The trustees startled the campus community in November 2002 by decreeing that faculty and staff who publicly advocated positions contrary to EMU's philosophy and its Community Lifestyle Commitment could jeopardize their jobs.[110] The statement came as a rising number of employees were publicly supporting same-sex marriage, which contradicted church and university policy. The declaration marked twenty years since same-sex controversies began at EMU in 1982.[111]

In July 1987, the Mennonite Church General Assembly, meeting at Purdue University, adopted "A Call to Affirmation, Confession, and Covenant regarding Human Sexuality." This so-called Purdue statement declared that biblical teaching "precludes premarital, extramarital, and homosexual genital activity."[112] Two years later, 90 percent of Mennonite Church members deemed homosexual acts "always wrong" and 78 percent opposed membership of noncelibate homosexuals in their congregation.[113] Throughout the 1990s, more than seven Mennonite Church agencies grappled with policies and practices related to homosexuality. The Mennonite Church and the General Conference Mennonite Church formed the joint Listening Committee for Homosexual Concerns, which engaged constituents in dialogue for several years. In 1991, the Mennonite Church urged its congregations to accept sexually abstaining homosexuals into church membership with love and grace—drawing a moral line between sexual orientation and practice.[114]

In the spring of 1989, *Weather Vane* editor Deborah Weaver wrote an editorial, "Breaking the Silence," in which she deplored "the disease of homophobia that infects our community." Among the examples she cited was a student's comment that "all homosexuals deserve to be shot." Weaver pleaded for "love and acceptance" to replace the "cruelty, pain, and suffering."[115] A year later, the student newspaper distributed a survey on homosexuality to one thousand faculty and students. The intent of the project was not to "prove" that homosexuality was right or wrong but to show that it "cannot be ignored."[116] The same issue of the paper included the story of an anonymous gay student who was afraid to "come out." As the controversy evolved over the next decade, the *Weather Vane* provided a lively forum for reporting campus events and discussions related to homosexuality.[117]

Two years after Weaver's editorial, EMC social work professor Titus Bender wrote an essay in *Dialogue*, the newsletter published by the Brethren Mennonite Council for Lesbian and Gay Concerns (BMC), linking the oppression of same-sex-oriented people, ethnic minorities, women, and the poor.[118] At homecoming that fall, some members of the class of 1951 signed a letter to the trustees asking for more tolerance and support of gay and lesbian members of the EMC community. In response, President Lapp reminded the alumni that students and employees affirm the Statement of Commitment, which said, "I . . . will refrain from sexual immorality [which] we *interpret* to mean any sexual activity—heterosexual or homosexual—outside of marriage."[119]

The debate erupted again in January 1994 during EMC's annual Spiritual Life Week. A team from Pastoral Care Ministries in Illinois spoke in chapel and promoted therapies to change sexual orientation. To Titus Bender's ears, one of the speakers made bigoted and demeaning comments that demonized all gays and lesbians, including EMC students in the audience. After listening for a while, Bender was so furious that he stood up and walked out. "My spirit wanted me to cry out, 'You're making obscene gestures at my friends right here in the sanctuary.' So I just slinked away."[120] Bender's walkout ignited more controversy on campus—some applauding his action and others chagrined by it. Monica Haines, an openly gay EMU student, was featured in a lengthy essay in the *Washington Blade*, the oldest LGBT newspaper in the United States. The piece was critical of the chapel speakers and quoted Haines on how tough it was to deal with some of her EMU peers "who believe gays are sinners."[121]

The president was in a quandary. Some faculty and staff were gay and lesbian, as were children of some employees.[122] He told two students who opposed accepting gays and lesbians, "I lean more towards open conversation [than using] a heavy hand as president to silence dissenting voices."[123] Lapp's stance irked some conservative constituents. Why, they wondered, should we ever debate sin? Responding to the critics of the Spiritual Life Week speakers, three officials of the nearby Mount Jackson Mennonite Church charged EMU with "liberal brainwashing." They were incensed that faculty member Gerald Hudson had purportedly called the guest speakers "bigots who brought violence, intolerance, and no love to campus."[124] Alumnus Gerald E. Martin, pastor of a Harrisonburg congregation, wrote a letter published in *Gospel Herald* expressing his dismay that a school whose motto is Thy Word Is Truth permits *any* discussion on the matter, since "there is no thing such as a practicing homosexual Christian."[125]

Shortly before the trustees met to consider becoming a university, President Lapp spent a sleepless night. The university issue did not worry him; he was troubled about the growing impasse on same-sex issues. So on the morning of March 22, 1994, he drafted a "2 AM letter"—a four-page epistle to the faculty and staff. Feeling slammed on all sides, he recounted the swirling debate about same-sex issues in society and church. He reminded readers that both he and EMC&S stood by the Mennonite Church's Purdue statement on human sexuality, which called Mennonites to "remain in loving dialogue." For him, "dissent was healthy" in a Christian academic community. Moreover, he continued, Anabaptists do not "silence dissent [or] silence opposing views with intimidating language." Lapp conceded that "dissent has its limits," but he did not specify what they were. He urged the community to communicate carefully and respectfully and to listen to opposing views.[126]

Eight months later, in November 1994, the trustees renamed and revised EMU's Statement of Commitment—the code of expected behavior that students and employees agreed to support. Now called the Community Lifestyle Commitment, it explicitly defined sexual immorality as "including premarital, extramarital, and homosexual practices."[127] This language maintained the Mennonite Church distinction between sexual orientation and practice. While the same-sex issue remained a hot topic on campus, it overheated so much across the Mennonite Church that in August 1995, *Gospel Herald* refused to print any more letters on the topic until tempers could chill, at least slightly.[128]

Five years later, on February 7, 2000, the *Mennonite Weekly Review* printed "A Welcoming Letter on Homosexuality" signed by some 650 North American Mennonites. The letter urged the church to "bless monogamous relationships of same-sex couples who affirm covenant vows." The letter, which was widely discussed on campus, had been signed by twelve EMU faculty and staff. The son of a faculty member was on the "welcoming committee" that organized the letter's publication. An on-campus "Friday support group," formed to support the letter signers, met weekly to discuss safety issues for same-sex-oriented students and employees.[129] One signatory said, "We've been in trouble with the administration ever since [signing the letter]."[130]

At the turn of the century, with the CLC defining same-sex covenanted relationships as immoral, EMU's de facto policy on same-sex relationships for employees was "don't ask, don't tell." Thus employees in such relationships lived in the shadows. In October 2001, the campus community learned what would happen when an employee living with a same-sex partner was unveiled. Sue Blauch—an alumna, longtime employee with a commendable work record, and regional director of development for the university—faced a difficult choice: resign or be fired for living with her same-sex partner. After several days of discussion with administrators and a legal agreement to extend her salary and some benefits for six months, she signed a letter of resignation on October 14.

Following Blauch's forced resignation, the Friday support group tripled in size to about sixty people. The *Weather Vane* was abuzz with critical commentary.[131] Angry letters from constituents arrived on the president's desk. Invoking images from the attack on the World Trade Center a few weeks earlier, one letter protested EMU's "continued terrorism against gays."[132] Amid the fray, President Lapp explained that he chose to "yield to the community"—meaning the church, EMU, the trustees, and the CLC.[133] Later, at an end-of-semester forum, Lapp explained that throughout his presidency he had agonized more over homosexuality than any other issue, because the differences seemed so irreconcilable, both in the church and on campus. He hoped that in the coming Christmas season EMU could find a way forward to "experience God's grace and truth and extend grace to each other."[134] A few months later, he announced his plans to retire after completing his fourth four-year term on June 30, 2003.

The issue flared up again in 2002. That May, Kathleen Temple, EMU instructor in biblical studies and a part-time pastor in a local Mennonite congregation, had relinquished her ordination credentials held by Virginia Conference. Although she was heterosexual and married, the conference had been pressuring her to lay aside her credentials because she actively supported gay and lesbian people. She agreed to relinquish her ordination but continued teaching in the Bible department and engaging in public advocacy on campus and in an off-campus program called the Open Door.[135]

In a September *Weather Vane* essay, biology professor Ken Roth wrote, "I don't believe homosexuality is a choice people make and I don't think the Bible condemns it as sin. Here comes the real kicker: I support covenant unions (weddings) of homosexual couples."[136] These words from a heterosexual faculty member sparked another flurry of opinion pieces in the student paper, provoking even President Lapp to write a letter. He reiterated EMU's ties to Mennonite Church USA and reviewed the agreement that faculty and staff had made when hired: to support the church's position and the CLC. Moreover, he continued, "academic freedom is not unlimited. . . . We uphold the church's positions . . . and only change when the church as a whole shifts position."[137]

On November 7, as the trustees were arriving on campus for their two-day fall meeting, the *Weather Vane* carried another essay by Ken Roth explaining why he wrote the previous one and defending his position: "I have stepped in a pile of do-do, there's no doubt about it. It stinks and we don't like to deal with it, but let's face it, do-do happens. The church must endure growing pains sometimes. With God's help, we will grow through our painful moments of disagreement."[138]

How could the trustees stop the bold, public outcry against church and university policy? The presidential transition was under way, and the future seemed unsettled and uncertain. In the end, the trustees clamped down on the dissent and warned that faculty and staff would jeopardize their employment if they "publicly advocated positions contrary to the university."[139] This November 2002 statement sent jitters through the faculty and spawned a whole new spate of essays in the *Weather Vane*. It would take a new president and at least a decade for the dust to settle. "I guess we were naïve," one senior official conceded later.[140] The struggle to find any accord on homosexuality was especially painful to members of the campus community who were devoted to justice in the wider world, even as same-sex justice seemed so elusive on campus.

Do Justice, Love Mercy, Walk Humbly

In February 1918, Preacher Benjamin Baer of Hagerstown, Maryland, spoke with fellow minister Denton Martin, who had just returned from the Special Bible Term at the newly opened Mennonite school in Virginia. Baer was dismayed to hear that Martin had seen a lot of pride at the school, even among its instructors. Baer considered pride a great sin, if not the greatest sin. "Pride and education are allies," he wrote afterward. But a "good solution" would be to "put education and humility together." Baer then quoted the Hebrew prophet Micah (Mic. 6:8): "All that's required of us is to 'do justly, and to love mercy, and walk humbly with thy God.'"[141]

Some eighty years later, EMU heeded Baer's advice by blending humility with education in a proposal to the Lilly Endowment on the theme of vocation. The university retrieved humility from its religious past and reached even further back to the prophet Micah for the title of the successful proposal: "Responding to God's Call: Do Justice, Love Mercy, Walk Humbly with God."[142] Completed just a few days before the September 11, 2001, attack on the World Trade Center, the proposal melded the venerable theme of humility, the recent Mennonite passion for justice, and the ancient words of the prophet. Within a year, the school's new vision statement declared, "We commit ourselves to do justice, love mercy, and walk humbly with God."[143]

These ideas captured a compelling vision like no other. *Walking together in the world* became EMU's educational paradigm for the twenty-first century. Do justice. Love mercy. Walk humbly with God. This vision diverged sharply from the older indoctrination-separation paradigm that readily fought for *the* truth and from the persuasion-engagement template. In the new accompaniment model, faculty did not try to indoctrinate or persuade students; they walked with them on *their* truth-seeking journey, empowering them to grow spiritually and vocationally.

Doing justice was activist. It reflected EMU's long transformation from a stance of nonresistance to one of justice and peacebuilding. Unlike EMU's nonresistant, world-avoiding past, doing justice looked outward. It assumed that the first step in peacemaking involved addressing social inequality and oppression. Sounding like the signature words of Jesus, *loving mercy* encapsulated the core of Jesus's kingdom-of-God message. The words rang a different chime than did the old calls for obedience and loyalty during the indoctrination era. Loving *mercy* while doing *justice* suspended two ideals in a delicate tension.

Walking humbly was one of the threads that tied EMU's twenty-first-century vision to its late-nineteenth-century Mennonite heritage. The phrase evoked an image of faculty traveling side by side with students on a mutual faith journey and collaborating in classes, advising, mentoring, and research. It also implied walking alongside others in the world—regardless of their social location—with a posture that repelled the ethnocentrisms of race, nationalism, culture, religion, and even Mennonite ethnicity. Humility encouraged empathy for the other, an open mind, and a casting aside of the arrogance of certainty. Accompanying others in God's presence was a journey—a sacred quest for truth—that enabled faculty and student sojourners to see the world as God did and hear the cries of those battered by injustice and oppression.

More than words in print, the Micah vision penetrated program and policy. It became the cornerstone of the Global Village curriculum. It was the organizing theme for the first-year seminar. It encouraged faculty and students to walk together in cross-cultural activities around the world. It also produced a new mentorship program titled "Enhancing Our Mentoring Culture."[144] In 2006, the Micah Think Tank received thirty-one proposals from students, faculty, and alumni to extend the theme into other areas of university life.[145] The proposals were then to be discussed at a weekend "fair" in March 2007.[146] Additionally, a fall faculty-staff conference explored the question "What does it mean to walk humbly with God?"

The question "What sets EMU nurses apart from others?" prompted the nursing department to adopt a "sacred covenant" model. The faculty encouraged students to view each patient's story as holy ground, where nurses "intersect with them in sacred space," said Professor Ann Graber Hershberger. "As nurses, we are privileged to be allowed into the most intimate points of people's lives when they are at their most vulnerable. Our view of nursing—as a vocation and a way of living out the daily call to do justice, love kindness, and walk humbly with God—is what sets EMU's nurses apart from others."[147] In a similar fashion, the vision for undergraduate teacher education also rested on Micah's prophetic text.

In 2010, the Global Village undergraduate general education curriculum was revised and renamed the EMU Core.[148] One of its four senior seminar courses was titled "Growing Identity while Walking Together." The hand-in-hand metaphor served to "help the class become a community of reflection, discernment, and support for each individual." A life wellness course in the 2016 EMU Core focused on creation care and stewardship of the body as it pertained to doing justice, loving mercy, and walking humbly with God.[149]

The Micah theme also seeped into the nonacademic regions of EMU's institutional culture. In 2011, the university received a gold rating from Leadership in Energy and Environmental Design (LEED) for its Cedarwood residence—the first residence hall in Virginia and one of thirty-three in the country to receive the honor. (Two other dorms later received the gold rating too.) "The sustainability emphasis of Cedarwood with EMU's mission reminds us to do justice, love mercy, and walk humbly with God, with each other, and with creation," said physical plant director Eldon Kurtz.[150]

The Micah mandate continued to guide EMU's vision as its centennial approached. When he welcomed new students in 2015, President Swartzendruber wrote, "Our faculty and staff will challenge you to take seriously our vision to do justice, love mercy, and walk humbly with God."[151]

CHAPTER 11

Progressive Vision, Changing Mission

EMU is like service on steroids.
—Professor Vi Dutcher

From Lawyer to Preacher

When the EMU community gathered on April 14, 2003, to celebrate the contributions of Joe and Hannah Lapp, Margaret "Speedy" Gehman, professor emerita of art, reminded Lapp that he was "in romper suits" when she began teaching at EMS in 1945. She commended him for his "commitment to EMU, to Christ, and [to] the church." Professor Carroll D. Yoder told Lapp, "You gave the faculty . . . the confidence to be who we are." Hannah Lapp was honored for always having "an eye and a heart for the needs and concerns of others" on campus and beyond.[1]

President Lapp served EMU for thirty years as a trustee and president. Among his achievements in sixteen years as president, converting the college into a university stands out. During those years, enrollment surpassed 1,500 students and the endowment increased nearly $12 million. In addition to enhancing EMU's stature in the professional and academic worlds, Lapp envisioned and led significant construction projects, notably the seminary building and the University Commons, which housed student services, a wellness center, and a state-of-the-art gymnasium.[2] The inception of graduate programs, the development of the Center for Justice and Peacebuilding, summer conferences, and the multiday Bach Festival that was initiated in 1992 and continues into 2017—all of these enhanced EMU's prominence as a Christian liberal arts university of distinction. Any naysayer doubts about an attorney leading the school vanished during Lapp's successful tenure.

The university turned to Iowa for his successor. Loren E. Swartzendruber was the first president born west of Ohio. Like Lapp, Swartzendruber followed an indirect route to his presidential post. After attending EMC for one year in 1968, he transferred to the University of Iowa School of Pharmacy to rejoin his high school sweetheart, Pat

Swartzendruber, who was studying nursing. They were married halfway through their sophomore year, which he confessed was "way too young." After completing four years of his five-year degree, Swartzendruber became restless in the field of pharmacy. "I came to a fork in the road theologically," he remembers, "and decided to enter seminary."[3]

Pat and Loren arrived at Eastern Mennonite Seminary in Harrisonburg in August 1973. "Our parents thought we'd lost it," he said. "I ended up thinking, what have I done? I just moved a three-week-old baby here, a thousand miles away from any grandparents, and we don't have a clue what to do." During his first semester, when EMS officials realized that Swartzendruber had not completed a college degree, they asked him to take some undergraduate courses. While in seminary, he worked part time for Myron Augsburger's interchurch evangelistic campaigns.[4] Later, Swartzendruber completed a doctor of ministry degree through Northern Baptist Theological Seminary in Illinois.

Swartzendruber's involvement in the church and in higher education provided strong preparation for his presidential role. They included five years as a pastor in eastern Pennsylvania, ten years as associate executive secretary for the Mennonite Board of Education, and ten years as president of Hesston College in Kansas. In his acceptance speech to the EMU community in February 2003, he made three promises: to act with the utmost integrity, not to take himself too seriously, and to do his best "to cultivate a community that knows great joy and hears much laughter. Because if we can't laugh together, we won't be able to cry together. And without both, we really aren't a community."[5]

After President Lapp retired, Provost Beryl Brubaker served as interim president until Swartzendruber took the helm in January 2004. In November 2003, she posed two questions to the trustees: Who are we, and who do we want to be? Those provocative questions about the university's identity and mission would drive campus discourse and planning for more than a decade.[6] Meanwhile, the rapid expansion of the university had outpaced the growth of revenue, forcing Brubaker to lead a difficult process of discerning institutional priorities.

Who Are We? Where Are We Going?

As Swartzendruber began his presidency in 2004, the university was wrestling with intense competition for students. According to EMU's internal research, the number of Mennonite applicants was declining as prospective students were going elsewhere for "greater prestige, lower cost, or proximity to home."[7] This pressure would persist into the university's centennial year. In 2000, about 60 percent of the undergraduate students were Mennonite, but by the fall of 2016, that proportion ebbed to 32 percent.[8] This fundamental shift in undergraduate enrollment produced three important initiatives: resetting priorities, refocusing the mission, and sorting out a

eymah Gbowee
MA in conflict transformation

Loren Swartzendruber
President

President Loren Swartzendruber listens as Leymah Gbowee, EMU alumna and Nobel Peace Laureate, speaks at a press conference during homecoming, 2011.

new institutional identity. In January 2005, EMU embarked on the first two, guided by two books: *Prioritizing Academic Programs and Services* by Robert Dickeson and *Quality with Soul* by Robert Benne. The third initiative on identity would follow in 2010.

"We expanded tremendously during the Lapp years," Provost Beryl Brubaker recalls, "but enrollment had dropped 10 percent in the last five years. That's why we prioritized. We overexpanded and then had to pull back. It wasn't a good time to be a provost."[9] Brubaker was struggling to live in the reality captured in Dickeson's memorable one-liner: "Most institutions can no longer afford to be what they've become."[10] EMU too would have to downsize to what it could afford.

The university appointed the Prioritization Steering Committee, which took on the painful process of evaluating programs to determine their viability. The committee declared, "We cannot afford to do all that we've been doing . . . and will need to discontinue certain programs based on mission, demand, quality, cost, and opportunity." Such talk sent jitters across campus. Which programs would be trimmed? Which ones completely cut? And which ones might get more funding?[11] The anxiety over priority-setting persisted so long that even five years later, one administrator confessed, "I never use the *P* word in public for fear of stirring panic."[12]

As prioritization was under way, campus educators also started reading *Quality with Soul*. In it, Benne (who spoke on campus in 2005 and again in 2011) analyzed how six premier colleges and universities had retained strong ties with their religious traditions. The campus conversation focused on EMU's mission and its linkage with the mission of Mennonite Church USA (MC USA). Coincidentally, the meaning of *mission* in MC USA discourse was evolving from foreign mission and evangelism to an emphasis on each congregation's local mission. The new missional language blended strategic planning concepts with Christian meanings of evangelistic outreach.[13] This blending helped legitimize EMU's mission as it shifted toward serving students outside the Mennonite world.

EMU's first formal mission statement appeared in 1980. As the institution's mission evolved, the statement underwent five revisions (in 1988, 1994, 1998, 2002, and 2008).[14] The statements had ever-changing subsections such as church accountability, intellectual development, social responsibility, values, vision, and mission. The original 1980 statement described EMU's mission as a call "to serve the Mennonite Church and the broader Christian community." Through the various revisions, the words *Christian, community,* and *peace* remained intact. The words *service* and *peacemaking* first appeared in the 1988 update; *peacebuilding* was added in 1998.

Two transformative revisions occurred in 2002 and 2008. The watershed 2002 statement rested solidly on the prophet Micah's admonition to "do justice, love mercy, and walk humbly with God."[15] But all references to the Mennonite Church, the broader Christian church, and evangelism vanished. New words—*justice, mercy, humility, Anabaptist,* and *discipleship*—populated the statement for the first time.

Although the 2008 update reasserted EMU's affiliation with MC USA, the statement declared for the first time that the university *"serves students of diverse religious and cultural backgrounds."*[16] Regardless of their origin, EMU invited "each person to follow Christ's call to bear witness to faith, serve with compassion, and walk boldly in the way of nonviolence and peace." After ninety years of serving primarily Mennonite students, EMU had pivoted to serving others. This significant shift gradually thinned Mennonite ranks to one-third of traditional undergraduates by 2016.

During Swartzendruber's presidency, EMU's mission acquired a progressive outlook. By 2010, the school offered, in its words, "an excellent liberal arts education in a progressive Christian environment."[17] The institution's strategic plan described EMU as "an explicitly Christian university that engages the full diversity of human experience and identity, facilitating progress and social change by addressing the most pressing problems in our world."[18] These themes reflected the university's moral paradigm of walking together in the world.

The idea that EMU would promote progressive social change was a turnabout from the world-shunning stance of its early premillennialist leaders. A senior official in 2016 exulted, "We proudly and unapologetically own a progressive agenda. This is who we are: a gift to the church."[19] This progressive view became apparent in the university's commitment to sustainability, academic freedom, diversity, LGBT issues, and social justice and peacebuilding. Linking a Christocentric theology to a progressive educational philosophy, EMU sought to carve out a distinctive mission in Christian higher education.

Trending Green before It Was Trendy

At about 5:30 a.m. on Friday, April 13, 2007, President Swartzendruber learned that a medevac helicopter was landing on campus to airlift someone who had fallen from the roof of the three-story Oakwood dormitory. He rushed over in the darkness to find preengineering student Michael Wiebe-Johnson being placed in the helicopter. Then, in the dim light of dawn, he saw a life-sized American bison dangling on a rope down the side of the dormitory, its head touching the bushes. Startled, Swartzendruber recognized it as the stuffed bison from the Science Center lobby. Several students had gained access to the Science Center during the night and transported the 275-pound bison on a pickup truck to Oakwood. Using a rope-and-pulley system, they lifted the bison to the edge of the roof. As Wiebe-Johnson tried to pull it onto the roof, he slipped and fell to the ground, where he lay unconscious.[20]

It was an unnerving morning for the president. A few days earlier, the British Broadcasting Corporation (BBC) had notified EMU that it wanted to compare the views of two Virginia universities (Liberty and EMU) on global warming, and this was the day they were coming to film Swartzendruber speaking on the subject. After assuring the chapel audience that the prospects for Michael Wiebe-Johnson's recovery were good, he noted the scientific evidence for global warming, contending that Christians hold a special responsibility to care for God's creation.

The BBC planned to air the story a few days after filming. That Monday, however, thirty-two students and faculty died in a campus shooting at Virginia Tech University. That tragedy dominated the news for days and scuttled the BBC story. About a month later, it was broadcast in Britain and scheduled for the United States, only to be upstaged by the sudden death of Jerry Falwell Sr., president of Liberty University.[21]

Ken L. Nafziger, vice president for student life and a conspirator in the chapel bench-turning prank in the 1970s, was ironically one of the first persons to show up at the bison accident. "Lessons I learned from the chapel prank were applied here," he said. "The bison pranksters were held accountable but not punished severely because it was innocuous and they had no malicious intent. Hopefully some of them will go on to be leaders in their churches and communities, with some sense of mercy for those who make mistakes that are unforeseen."[22]

While the prank was unpredictable, the theme of ecological stewardship was not. It ran deep and wide in EMU's culture. "We were into environmental sustainability long before it was cool," noted Provost Fred Kniss. Sustainability efforts began in the early '70s, and by 2005, EMU ranked third in energy efficiency of ninety schools surveyed by the Association of Higher Education Facilities Officers. That same year, the average energy cost per square foot at EMU was $1.04, less than half of that at comparable institutions.[23]

Sustainability was the cornerstone of EMU's application to the Southern Association of Colleges and Schools (SACS) for reaccreditation in 2010. The school submitted a Quality Enhancement Plan (QEP) with a detailed implementation proposal that SACS reviewed and approved. The project was titled "Peace with Creation: Environmental Sustainability from an Anabaptist Perspective." Faculty, staff, and students collaborated to select the QEP topic and to implement it through the Creation Care Council, which had representatives from all sectors of the campus.

The university offered a major and a minor in environmental sustainability, and it wove creation care into many of its curricular offerings, including its general education courses. Environmental themes marked other campus activities. For example, Emmi Itäranta's *Memory of Water*, the required reading for incoming students in 2016, highlighted unequal access to clean water. Implementation of the QEP included five desirable and measurable student learning outcomes. The program was so successful, so saturated with sustainability, that students complained of "green fatigue," which EMU reported to SACS along with plans for remediation in 2016.[24]

Table 3. Key Developments in Sustainability at EMU

Early 1970s	A group of faculty and students establishes Earthkeepers—a recycling effort that continued into 2017.
1976–1977	Physics professor Robert Lehman conducts research leading to significant reductions in campus energy consumption.
1986	The new Campus Center contains an innovative closed-loop heating and cooling system that will save about $4 million in its first decade.
2005	A major Lilly Endowment grant supports sustainability efforts.
2007	The Creation Care Council is founded, with representatives from all parts of campus.
2008	Trustees require all new buildings to meet Leadership in Energy and Environmental Design (LEED) Gold Standards.
2008	EMU's mission statement is revised with a clear focus on creation care.
2010	SACS approves "Peace with Creation: Environmental Sustainability from an Anabaptist Perspective," a Quality Enhancement Plan (QEP) for reaccreditation.
2010	A full-time sustainability coordinator is employed.
2010	Solar panels are installed on the roof of Hartzler Library, the largest solar array in Virginia.
2011	Thirty significant sustainability projects are under way across campus.
2016	The Center for Sustainable Climate Solutions is established at EMU with Goshen College and Mennonite Central Committee as founding partners.

Even so, thirty-five first-year students had enrolled in the environmental sustainability major that fall, which integrated biological and social science perspectives.

The initiatives bore fruit. First-year students and seniors performed above the mean on twenty questions pertaining to sustainability compared with cohorts from sixteen other colleges and universities in their Sustainability Education Consortium.[25] EMU consistently ranked in the top 20 percent of higher education institutions for recycling solid waste—paper, glass, cardboard, and plastics. The university's three-pronged effort—energy-saving facilities, curricular infusion, and habits of sustainability—made creation care integral and visible in campus culture. The on-campus efforts over several decades spurred many alumni to later engage in sustainability projects. Their initiatives were showcased in a special issue of *Crossroads* in spring 2011.

The Fuzzy Boundaries of Academic Freedom

Faculty anxiety followed the trustees' warning in November 2002 that employees who advocated positions contrary to the institution might lose their jobs.[26] Those worries sparked spirited conversations on and off campus. In early January, *The Mennonite* reported the trustees' ruling, and two weeks later, it published an editorial titled "Church Beliefs vs. Academic Freedom." The editorial noted that five EMU students had submitted a letter and a copy of a petition signed by two hundred students claiming that EMU's "restriction of academic freedom is harmful to the well-being of a church that values authenticity."[27]

At the request of President Lapp's cabinet, University Accord—a campus team charged with managing conflict through facilitation, mediation, and restorative justice—convened two meetings of staff and faculty to process their concerns about academic freedom.[28] As a result, the Listening and Facilitation Team (LiFT) was formed to guide communal discernment and determine how to proceed. It created a statement of clarifications and six concise steps of action.[29] Among other things, LiFT was the catalyst to reinstate the faculty senate, which had ended in 1980. The LiFT process also energized plans to update EMU's statement of academic freedom.

Since the senate had dissolved in 1980, the faculty had no organization in which to discuss faculty-related policies without administrators present. A faculty senate task force initiated discussions in 2004 about creating a new faculty senate.[30] With administrative support, the idea moved forward, and members of the faculty were elected to the senate from the faculty assembly. An organizational meeting was held in May 2006, and the faculty senate began functioning that fall. The senate gave faculty leaders a venue for processing issues and preparing proposals to take to the faculty assembly, which was composed of both faculty and administrators. Seminary professor Lonnie Yoder was elected president of the senate, signaling more harmonious relationships within the university structure and recognizing the seminary's significant role.[31]

Faculty concerns about academic freedom also fed new discussions about tenure policies. In 1953, tenure had been instituted at EMC for faculty who had given six years of satisfactory service. That policy was adjusted in 1966 to reduce the required years to four. Tenure was abolished, however, in 1979 and replaced by five-year renewable contracts.[32] In the years following the trustees' worrisome ruling in 2002, tenure discussions initiated by Provost Kniss and processed in the faculty senate led to a standard tenure policy in 2012, with post-tenure reviews.[33]

Uncertainty about academic freedom persisted after the November 2002 decree. For faculty and students, academic freedom allowed open expression of controversial ideas in the classroom, in research, in the performing arts, and in speaking and writing in the public square. Similarly, academic freedom protected colleges and universities from government censorship—and in the case of religious institutions, from their supporting ecclesial body. Even so, historian George Marsden calls academic freedom an elusive ideal, partly because its limits are often fuzzy.[34]

The faculty and trustees approved a revised statement in February 2005 that abhorred the cardinal sin of "*intellectual arrogance*," noted that EMU "attempts to keep scholarly pursuit and communal accountability in dynamic tension," and underscored the importance of "*sufficient humility*," and "*intellectual integrity*." The statement offered seven guidelines for "*responsible participation*" in public discourse, both on and off campus. Yet none of these would keep individuals like Bible and religion professor Kathleen Temple and biology professor Ken Roth from advocating for gay and lesbian rights as they did in 2002, contrary to the stance of EMU and the church. The revised academic freedom policy remained unclear on whether the university could in fact muzzle faculty members who actively promoted contrarian views. But it did give faculty members license to file a grievance if they thought their academic freedom was violated.[35]

The 2005 statement, however, did not address academic freedom for students. It would take a controversial student drama ten years later to focus that question and spur the faculty senate to initiate a revision of the policy.[36] In January 2015, administrators learned that theater major Christian Parks, a student leader with both the Black Student Union and Safe Space (for LGBTQ students and their allies), was planning to stage a public performance of *Corpus Christi* in late February for his senior project. Written by Terrence McNally, the 1998 play places the story of Jesus and his twelve disciples in present-day Texas and depicts the thirteen characters as gay. Judas betrays Jesus over sexual rivalries, and Jesus officiates at the marriage of two of the men. The provocative play had rarely been performed on a college or university campus for fear that it would incite threats of violence, as had happened at its first performance in New York and later at other theaters.[37]

When EMU officials learned of the planned production, they were disappointed that they had not been informed earlier. They wondered how they could, given the late hour, balance student academic freedom with any possible harm to campus safety the play might provoke. It was inevitable that some faculty, staff, and students, as well as EMU constituents and members of the Harrisonburg community, would consider the production sacrilegious, if not blasphemous. All of this unfolded as EMU was conducting a delicate public survey related to sexual orientation in its hiring policy.

The president's cabinet spent hours consulting with Parks, theater faculty, and campus leaders in search of a compromise. They considered a theatrical reading or a single private performance instead of the four public performances customary for senior projects. In the end, they agreed to stage two by-invitation-only performances. According to academic dean Deirdre Smeltzer, the performances would be for specific classes "so we could change this from a typical theater experience to an academic experience to generate conversation."[38]

The compromise was reached on a Monday. That Wednesday, Parks announced, "[I am] using my power as director to cancel my show because it became a dividing wall of hostility between administration and students."[39] Yet later that evening, officials learned that the play had been performed for supporters and their invitees, who filled the mainstage theater to show their support.

The imbroglio, reported widely on social media and in a national blog, divided the campus. On Thursday at noon, several dozen students demonstrated on campus in support of Parks.[40] Late that afternoon, a besieged President Swartzendruber called a town hall meeting in Lehman Auditorium for the campus community only. Rather than using the stage, Swartzendruber and Parks stood side-by-side on the floor at the front of the auditorium and offered their accounts of the complicated episode. The meeting included singing and opening and closing prayers. One faculty member found the gathering's tone of reconciliation very moving, saying as she left, "What's happening right here is what makes this community so unique. It's why I want to be here."[41] Yet backstage, the tangled story had layers of deception, hurt, and brokenness. A member of the president's cabinet who had served for five years ruefully remarked, "This was my worst week since I've been here."[42]

Nonetheless, the event inspired the community to rethink and clarify EMU's stance on academic freedom. In its policy revision in 2016, the university committed to maintaining a community of learning where faculty, staff, and students alike are "free to pursue truth in all disciplines and modes of inquiry and are protected from internal or external influences that would restrict them from responsible exercise of truth-seeking."[43]

The new policy, adapted from guidelines of the American Association of University Professors, included a set of procedures related to faculty, staff, and students.

It specified expectations and outlined avenues of action for times of controversy. When writing or speaking as citizens, employees would not face censorship but would be "expected to show appropriate restraint, show respect for others' opinions, and make every effort to indicate they are not speaking for the institution." As a servant of the church and the common good, EMU expected "academic freedom to be exercised responsibly in a spirit of civility, humility, respect, and care for the common good. When so exercised, academic freedom reflects and extends EMU's core Christian values of discipleship, community, and service." The procedures also clarified that the board of trustees would not be directly involved in dealing with risks, threats, or violations of academic freedom. Instead, the president would hold ultimate responsibility "to protect academic freedom within the university and to articulate it to the university's various publics."[44]

Reshaping Identity: Vanilla or Pistachio?

With fewer Mennonite students, EMU's undergraduate recruiting turned toward Virginia. The portion of undergraduate students from the state, irrespective of religion, doubled from about one-third in 2002 to two-thirds in 2016, giving EMU a much stronger regional character.[45] Attending a college closer to home reflected a national trend that was typical at other Mennonite colleges as well. One college official said, "Since 9/11, parents became more anxious and wanted to keep their students closer to home. Most students now go to a school within a hundred miles of their home."[46] Also, parents of athletes wanted to support their children's athletic events. Once-banned intercollegiate athletics, now flourishing at EMU, were essential to recruit students from the region.[47]

As EMU's undergraduate student body was becoming less Mennonite and more regional, its graduate programs were drawing larger numbers of students from outside the region who were attracted by advanced courses couched in an Anabaptist-Mennonite perspective. The two master's degrees in conflict transformation and restorative justice, for example, which highlighted Anabaptist-Mennonite identity, were enrolling a growing number of students from diverse religious backgrounds.

Missional language, then in vogue with MC USA, enabled EMU to sharpen its focus on recruiting students from "diverse religious and cultural backgrounds." But how could EMU most effectively attract such students? Should the word *Mennonite* appear at the front or the back of marketing materials, or should it even be dropped? The larger public sometimes confused Mennonites with Amish or with the Old Order horse-and-buggy Mennonites living south of Harrisonburg. One prospective graduate student came to the EMU campus expecting to find hitching posts.[48] Rather than highlighting *Mennonite*, should marketing materials emphasize *Christian* or underscore *Anabaptist*?[49]

Lady Royals Tia Byrd, Shakeerah Sykes, and Alicia Ygarza defend the EMU basket, spring 2015.

In a campus forum, enrollment managers proposed striking *Mennonite* from the marketing materials and reducing "other odd things about EMU to make it look less 'weird' and easier to recruit local Virginia students and mainstream evangelical Christian ones."[50] History professor Mark Metzler Sawin argued the reverse: "If EMU stops being distinctively Mennonite, we have no reason to exist. There are plenty of better-funded, better-situated Christian colleges and liberal arts colleges. If we try to be like them—to be just another mainstream, vanilla, Christian liberal arts school, I think we would, and perhaps should, fail. We aren't vanilla; we're pistachio. Most people prefer vanilla and chocolate, it's true, but those who prefer pistachio love it and will seek it out. To thrive we need to not lessen but increase our distinctiveness—we need to be more, not less, pistachio."[51]

Sawin also contended that vanilla-flavored marketing would set EMU on the trajectory taken by Quaker schools between 1925 and 1975 as they moved from distinctively Quaker institutions to very strong liberal arts schools with liberal justice-peace leanings but with no distinctive religious character and few Quaker students.[52] For him, Mennonite colleges were already on that path and would reach a similar state—unless they switched to pistachio branding soon.[53]

Seminary professor Mark Thiessen Nation hoped that EMU's distinctive identity would be "Christian in an *Anabaptist way* because any agnostic humanist could affirm peace, social justice, community, inclusiveness, and even creation care with their National Public Radio kind of civil religion." Beyond branding, Nation argued that without a deep and explicit anchor in Anabaptist-Mennonite understandings, EMU would eventually become "just another formerly church-related liberal arts college."[54]

After several years of "endless debates and going in circles," the enrollment and marketing team decided to accent EMU's uniqueness, not its generic traits. Still, according to marketing and communications director Andrea Wenger, some people on campus "thought the very concept of marketing was an evil or twisted thing." Others thought it was un-Mennonite because "it makes us proud of who we are."[55] Nonetheless, after completing the 2008 mission statement, EMU began a multiyear process of research and consultation to create a positional statement and sharpen the brand. That process produced the tagline "A Christian University like No Other" as a way of capturing the unique mix of things at EMU that made it distinctive. The tagline came into use in 2011–2012. "Some people have hated it; some loved it from the start. Some still hate it and some still love it," said Wenger. "Whether people like it or not, it gets us talking about what makes us unique and distinctive."[56]

The Conundrum of Diversity and Belonging

Community has been a sacrosanct word throughout EMU's history. For much of the twentieth century, most incoming students, staff, and faculty had been immersed in the social, ethnic, and religious waters that their church community called a "broth-erhood." Diversity on campus was largely a matter of blending different stripes of Mennonites with a few other-than-Mennonites. That near-homogeneity changed quickly in the twenty-first century, generating a vibrant diversity as students came from myriad cultural backgrounds and some forty different religious affiliations—or none at all.

Like most colleges and universities, EMU was actively promoting diversity, but for religious reasons. The 2016 Diversity Task Force explained why diversity mattered at EMU this way: "Diversity matters because: it reflects the best of who we claim to be, it aligns with the diversity in the kingdom of God, it challenges and expands our perspectives, it mattered to Jesus, and it reflects our commitment to do justice, love mercy, and walk humbly with God. Students and faculty who represent marginalized and oppressed people bring understandings that build empathy and strengthen our commitment to justice."[57]

Religious diversity brought challenges, especially for those outside the Christian tradition. For Ruayda Qadir, an Iraqi Muslim undergraduate in 2016, "EMU was very welcoming. I have not been discriminated [against] as we all work together. I've had warm smiles as I share that I'm a Muslim. My classmates, professors, and staff members ask many questions about my faith and seem surprised about how similar we are." Still, there were awkward times, especially those related to prayer. "I feel left out when a class or other group participates in a prayer to Jesus because Muslims pray to the one and only God. We love Jesus and the other prophets, but only pray toward God. I wish we could all pray to God for wishes and blessings and not include any of the prophets."[58]

Racial diversity brought a different set of issues. Melody M. Pannell, a biracial Mennonite from New York City, arrived at EMU in 1993 to study social work. Her African American father and Swiss-German Pennsylvania Dutch mother rooted her in two cultural traditions. As a student, she came to realize, through the advice of a mentor, that she needed EMU and EMU needed her. Pannell became active in many campus activities and served as president of the Black Student Union and copresident of the Student Government Association. She returned to EMU as director of multicultural services from 2003 to 2008 and convened the first reunion for the Black Student Union in 2005. In 2015, she joined the faculty as assistant professor of social work. Her success story, she acknowledged, "is an exception, not the normal experience of students of color at EMU."[59]

As a faculty member, Pannell has provided a voice for the growing number of students from diverse backgrounds. By 2016, nearly one-third of traditional undergraduates were international students (5 percent) or African American, Hispanic, Asian, or Native American (AHANA) students (24 percent).[60] The increase in these students gave the Black Student Union and the Latino Student Alliance enough members to flourish. "Embracing diversity can teach all of us," Pannell said. "Together we can engage, empower, and transform our Mennonite communities and create an inclusive fidelity of place that will be sustained, transform our society, and flourish into the future."[61]

Students, Mennonite and otherwise, came with different experiences and expectations than had earlier generations. "We have to work at creating a sense of community," explained Ken L. Nafziger, vice president for student life. "We can no longer take it for granted. We need to be intentional about creating it. More and more students are affected by *individualism*, and that's a fundamental shift."[62] Indeed, EMU's mission statement underscores community three times: "Our Christian *community* challenges students . . . our learning *community* marked by academic excellence . . . [our] enduring values of the Anabaptist tradition: Christian discipleship, *community*, service, and peacebuilding."[63]

At the 2015 convocation, Provost Fred Kniss articulated the tension: "The special quality of an EMU liberal arts education is that we combine the celebration of diversity with a shared sense of belonging in a community of learning. The conundrum of diversity and belonging, which we encounter in our everyday lives here at EMU, is at the heart of what we mean by a liberal arts education. Solving this conundrum is fundamental to achieving our ideal of being a Christian university *like no other*."[64]

As EMU neared the end of its first century, the student life division sought to create a meaningful campus ethos based on Ernest Boyer's six well-known principles

New friends Megan Weaver, Jolee Paden, Jasmine Miller, Oksana Kittrell, and Alexa Weeks wear T-shirts with the EMU seal and motto, fall 2015.

of community—purposeful, open, just, disciplined, caring, and celebrative.[65] Two of EMU's program components—the Community Lifestyle Commitment (CLC) and the use of restorative justice principles for student discipline—articulated some of the school's key values.

The CLC set common biblically based expectations and responsibilities for all faculty, staff, and students. The preamble referenced "principles that should guide our life together: loving God, loving neighbors, seeking righteousness, practicing justice, helping the needy, forgiving others, seeking forgiveness, and exercising freedom responsibly with loving regard for others."[66] The CLC spoke about stewardship of spirit and body, social responsibility with economic resources, and respect for the rights and property of others. Community members also pledged to avoid harmful and offensive acts toward others, including sexual harassment and abuse, violence, and abusive or demeaning language.

Some students signed the commitment without reading the text, just as they might check the "accept" box in a license agreement for software. They then appeared surprised if they were challenged for violating the CLC. Sometimes athletes recruited to play intercollegiate sports were surprised, if not offended, by EMU's custom of not observing the flag salute. "You have kids who show up here to play baseball and have no idea that we don't play the national anthem," one administrator said. "How do you tell them that? When they're signing up do you say, 'By the way, we don't play the anthem'? How do we help them fit in and have a sense of belonging? We hope they'll gradually develop a sense of respect for community even if they don't agree with everything at first."[67]

Restorative justice also became part of EMU's campus culture. This approach, first introduced on campus in 1999 and later expanded to include a full-time restorative justice coordinator for residence life, aims to avoid punitive measures for those who violate the CLC.[68] Instead, it invites the stakeholders involved in an incident into a circle for discussion focused on the harm, rather than on the broken rules, and seeks to restore ruptured relationships. Decision making about the outcome rests in the hands of the offender(s) and the harmed. The circle process is as important as the outcome.

Despite its virtues, the initiative began sagging because of its time demands and the refusal of some offenders to participate. In one prank, several students set off fire alarms in four dorms an hour apart. Student life staff urged the instigators to participate in a voluntary circle approach, but the offenders did not attend. As a result, they never heard how their actions harmed the police chief, the fire company, the resident director, and the campus technician who had to drive from his home several times during the night to turn off the alarms.[69] In some cases, offenders preferred receiving a penalty to spending so much time in meetings and facing the people they had harmed. Some who did participate reported being worn out by the process. In 2014–2015, restorative justice coordinator Jonathan D. Swartz conducted an assessment of the restorative justice program and recommended ways to clarify, simplify, and streamline it.[70]

Many faculty underscore the vitality of EMU's sense of community. Seminary professor Lonnie Yoder explained that seminarians from different religious traditions consistently vouch for the depth of community experience at EMU. "The word *community*," said Yoder, "is probably the most common word used around here in my twenty-four years of teaching."[71] Former provost Beryl Brubaker also underscored this EMU distinctive: "We care about the body. We care about the whole. We are committed to the whole. I love the annual faculty-staff conference. I love the way we sing together, the way we laugh together, the way we come together."[72]

Service on Steroids

Singing and service are two threads that tie 1917 and 2017 together. The word *serve* or one of its derivatives appears frequently in the founding documents, mission statements, catalogs, and other historical publications. It is the only word other than *Christian* that persisted from the earliest declarations of the school's purpose to the first line of the 2016–2017 mission statement: "*EMU educates students to serve and lead in a global context.*"[73] The statement goes on to laud four enduring values in the Anabaptist tradition: discipleship, community, service, and peacebuilding. It also invites students to accept the call of Jesus to "serve with compassion." Finally, the opening pages of the catalog state that EMU "reveres humble service guided by faith and knowledge" and prepares students for "service in the larger church and world."[74]

In EMU's early decades, Christian service permeated campus discourse and the many off-campus mission ventures of the Young People's Christian Association. The broad meaning of Christian service encompassed simple acts of kindness to friends and strangers, physical help to the needy, evangelistic services on street corners and in jails, volunteer work in local congregations, work in church agencies, and mission outreach in the United States and abroad. Since Mennonite conscientious objectors engaged in Civilian Public Service during World War II—and later served in PAX, I-W Service, Mennonite Voluntary Service, and Mennonite Central Committee (MCC)—the meaning of service at EMU expanded to include various sorts of social service.

In a 1989 report to SACS, university officials explained that EMU's strong service commitment, anchored in the school's Mennonite heritage, was "infused in the curriculum at all levels including general education."[75] By the late 1990s and early 2000s, many colleges and universities across the country promoted service learning, which combines reflection with service, an approach that EMU also embraced.[76]

Service is also part of the faculty folkways. Professor Vi Dutcher captured EMU's bent for service by comparing her previous work at another university to her EMU position: "For many years, the ethos here was like a church organization. You showed up for work early in the morning, and you worked until closing time or later. Where I came from . . . you only needed to show up to teach your classes and have your office hours. EMU is more communal. . . . EMU is like service on steroids."[77]

EMU's commitment to service was deeply rooted in the moral order of its sponsoring denomination. The theological roots of Mennonite understandings of service lay in Jesus's call to discipleship—following his example of loving and serving one's neighbor rather than being served. Service persisted as the one theme Mennonites could rally around in the last half of the twentieth century. Despite church squabbles and conflicting views of biblical interpretation, political participation, and cultural assimilation, Mennonites still collaborated in the international relief and development work of MCC, Mennonite Disaster Service, and other service efforts.

Bonnie Price Lofton, a journalist with Quaker roots and a former editor of *Crossroads*, identified EMU's habits of service in 2015: "Almost everyone who works here knows they could earn more money and rise higher in social rank if they worked elsewhere. . . . Almost everyone at EMU is here because they believe in its larger mission, however they may define that in their own mind, not for individualistic or egotistic reasons. . . . If the Mennonite ethos of EMU changes, we will lose that common sense of purpose that binds us together, that motivates us to work much harder, burdened by many more responsibilities than faculty and staff at better-endowed or state-supported schools."[78] That loyalty to a larger cause has motivated hundreds of EMU employees over the century—from cooks and maintenance staff to secretaries, and from teachers to administrators and trustees—to serve, often sacrificially, for the sake of the institution's greater cause.

The culture of service on campus is also revealed in the vocational directions of alumni. Well into the 1960s, the EMC Alumni Association typically reported how many alumni were teachers, ordained church leaders, missionaries, nurses, and doctors, reflecting the school's esteem for "service" occupations.[79] In 2013, self-reports of eighty-five members of the class of 1963 revealed that a preponderance of them worked in education, medicine, and international service.[80] Similarly, one-fourth of the class of 2000 was employed in church-related work six months after graduating.[81] In 2016, 54 percent of 10,700 alumni who reported their occupational endeavors listed health and medical services (21 percent), education (20 percent), and social and community services (13 percent).[82] These broad categories, however, miss the hundreds of alumni who served with domestic or international service agencies before pursuing graduate studies or a conventional career. Such labels also obscure EMU's more recent emphasis on the importance of service and servant leadership in whatever career a graduate might pursue, from business to fine arts.

Service was somewhat reinterpreted in EMU's cross-cultural program. "I rode a camel in the Negev desert. Planted trees on a farm in Palestine. I hiked the Jesus Trail. I saw Petra, the Roman Coliseum, I got my ears pierced in Istanbul, and I ate a gyro in Athens." With those words Mariah Martin described her 2015 cross-cultural semester, adding that it was "wonderfully life-altering and amazing." The experience now amplifies everything she sees, such as women suffering at the hands of the Islamic State and "the tears of Israelis and Palestinians as they clash again and again in the town of Hebron. I wrestle with empathy. . . . There is so much pain everywhere I can't turn it down."[83] If one purpose of cross-cultural courses was to create discomfort, the program was working.

One of the earmarks of EMU's academic program since 1982 has been a required cross-culture component during a semester or a summer. Its roots go back to 1965–1966, when Blair Seitz and Henry Rosenberger concocted their own cross-cultural adventure. On a whim, they dropped out of EMC and independently enrolled in the University of East Africa's Nairobi campus for their junior year. For Seitz, "It was the greatest year of my life. It changed my life forever." But without any reentry support, their return to EMU was emotionally traumatic.[84]

EMU student Lindsey Unruh with two friends in a primary school in Pimville, Soweto, South Africa. Harlan deBrun and Audra Baker led this 2007 cross-cultural experience.

EMU's earliest off-campus programs were language-focused summer courses in 1970 in Mexico and Quebec. A Europe winter term began in 1972–1973, and a Jerusalem term organized by the Bible department began in 1975. Some students were eager to study abroad. Mike Wenger, for example, switched to a Bible major because only those majors were eligible for the Jerusalem term. Due to their cost, the future of these programs was uncertain until cross-cultural credit became a graduation requirement in the Global Village curriculum in 1982.[85] After a two-day faculty meeting led by Dean Al Keim, four faculty—Vernon Jantzi, Ken J. Nafziger, Ann Graber Hershberger and Calvin Shenk—were charged with refining the faculty's rough ideas into a doable program.

At the outset, Professor Jantzi had argued, "The last thing we want in this program is service. We cannot put service in its name in any way. We don't want to reinforce the idea that we have the answers to other people's problems. We probably have something to offer, but we can't make that the core of our program."[86] Not wanting to reinforce Western ethnocentrism, the committee hoped that students would experience the raw fact that people in other cultures had something to teach them—something they could not learn in Harrisonburg. Jantzi admitted, however, that some types of service can fit into cross-cultural experiences.[87] By its centennial year, EMU had a thirty-five-year-old track record of creating cross-cultural discomfort for students as one of its distinctive undergraduate requirements.[88]

Cultivating Seeds of Peace

"My host took me out to a village campfire where the chiefs were sitting—a Muslim chief, a Christian chief, and an indigenous chief. They told me, 'We were engaged in genocide until three years ago when we all learned these techniques from your people, and now we are sharing this banquet.'" This was one of dozens of poignant stories that Bonnie Price Lofton heard as she visited some of the twelve peacebuilding institutes spawned by the alumni of EMU's Summer Peacebuilding Institute (SPI) that are scattered across the globe—from South Korea to South Africa, from the Philippines to Canada, and from Mozambique to India.[89] "The ripple effects of these peacebuilding initiatives are nothing short of amazing," said J. Daryl Byler, executive director of the Center for Justice and Peacebuilding (CJP), which operates the SPI. "Our graduates are changing the world through work in other venues too—consulting, working for NGOs (nongovernmental organizations), teaching in universities, and serving in government roles or with the United Nations. Others have promoted peacebuilding by becoming social entrepreneurs."[90]

The CJP story reaches back to 1978, when EMU—at the urging of Dean Al Keim—first offered a course on peace and justice co-taught by Bible professor Ray Gingerich and social work professor Titus Bender.[91] Several years later, in the mid-1980s, the idea for a program in conflict resolution germinated in Costa Rica, where sociologist Vernon Jantzi was investigating conflict provoked by government-forced land reform. At a social gathering, he inadvertently met John Paul Lederach, a Mennonite doctoral student studying Costa Rican modes of conflict transformation while also working with Mennonite Central Committee. Lederach was an early protégé of Adam Curle, a Quaker pioneer of faith-based peacemaking in postcolonial societies, including Nigeria and Pakistan.[92]

Jantzi and Lederach recognized the need to capture lessons emerging in the field and to prepare others to do the same kind of work. When Jantzi returned to EMC, he pressed the college to hire Lederach. Trying to address gender inequities at the time, EMC would hire only women for new positions. Dean Lee F. Snyder, however, was open to hiring Lederach if it could be done without adding a new position. Jantzi agreed to withdraw from half of his sociology teaching and fill a half-time vacancy in Spanish. This opened a half-time position for Lederach in sociology, and MCC agreed to cover Lederach's other half-time salary in conciliation work.[93]

Shortly after Lederach began teaching at EMC in 1990, he proposed the graduate Conflict Transformation Program (CTP). President Lapp, who had traveled to Nicaragua during the Contra War, was enthused about the proposal. The faculty voted it down, however, fearing that it would suck the best faculty out of the undergraduate program. Later they approved a revised proposal that required each CTP faculty member to teach at least one undergraduate course.[94]

The new program started as a 1994 summer gathering of "pioneers in peacebuilding" from around the world who traveled to Harrisonburg to share what they were doing and learning in their contexts. It was particularly oriented toward discovering from local people how best to promote peace in the midst of conflict. The emphasis on learning *from* practice and teaching others to *do* practice deeply influenced the CTP's pedagogy. This focus—reflecting the Anabaptist accent on discipleship in daily life—continued after the program was renamed the Center for Justice and Peacebuilding in 2004.

In the mid-1990s, few other universities had conflict resolution or peacemaking programs with a creative practice component. EMU had access to a loose global network of alumni and others working with MCC's international relief and development efforts. These colleagues, in turn, had ties with local leaders and agencies that had positive views of Mennonites' cultural sensitivity in their international service endeavors.

The CTP founders and funders were creative, innovative, and entrepreneurial.[95] "Our attitude was, we won't allow bureaucratic constraints to deter us," Vernon Jantzi recalled. "We were flexible, we took opportunities, we made things work. We did a lot of unusual things that changed some internal university policies."[96] This innovative spirit led some EMU faculty and administrators to think that the center not only worked outside the proverbial box but built its own box, apart from the university. Besides its entrepreneurial style, the center's rapid growth was bolstered by its laser focus on practice, its strong association with MCC, and its willingness to employ women in key positions.[97] By the end of its first decade, the CTP had engaged in projects in thirty-eight countries. Fifteen hundred participants from eighty-three countries had attended one of its annual summer programs. In addition, 170 alumni from fifty countries had received master's degrees in conflict transformation.[98]

The first non-Mennonite faculty member hired for a full-time position was Jayne Seminare Docherty—a Catholic, a longtime peace activist, and the daughter of a career military officer. Her arrival in 2001 coincided with the September 11 attacks. Coincidentally, that fall a Fulbright grant began to support a dozen international students each year for the two-year master's program in conflict transformation.[99] A new cohort each year came alternately from South Asia or the Middle East for the next six years. Thus, even as the world was being reshaped by conflicts often described as the Christian West versus the Islamic world, these cohorts of graduate students with diverse religious beliefs were engaging in spirited discussions about conflict transformation.

The CJP received a dramatic boost in visibility when alumna Leymah Gbowee (MA 2007) was awarded the Nobel Peace Prize in 2011. Over the years, the CJP has offered a variety of different programs. The SPI continues drawing students every May and June. The STAR (Strategies for Trauma Awareness and Resilience) training, which grew out of modules designed to address trauma following September 11, thrives as well. In 2016, the center added a master's degree in restorative justice, which grew out of the influential work of long-term CJP professor Howard Zehr, widely cited as the grandfather of restorative justice.[100] That same year, the Kellogg Foundation invited the center to join a multiyear initiative aimed at truth, reconciliation, and racial healing in the United States. Johonna Turner, the first full-time CJP faculty member of color, and Carl Stauffer, a rising leader of restorative justice programs, played key roles in the Kellogg partnership.[101]

"Our growing edge for the university's next century is bringing lessons in peacebuilding and justice advocacy learned abroad, home to the US," explained Docherty, the CJP's director of academic programs. Faculty and students will focus more on promoting racial, gender, and class justice in the United States and ponder ways to reduce the militarization of US society. As she noted, "There is no point building peace in other countries if the pyromaniacs are in Washington, New York, and the European capitals. We need to start at home."[102]

Since its origin, the center fomented some religious controversy on campus. Some faculty teaching religious studies, for example, thought its theological moorings were shallow. "Our peacemaking needs to have a stronger biblical foundation," contended one professor.[103] Another concurred, saying that peacebuilding should include "theological reflection and be faith-centered."[104] A representative of a Mennonite mission agency was disappointed that "Jesus" rarely appeared in CJP publications.[105] This tension grew when the university's undergraduate Justice, Peace, and Conflict Studies program migrated from the Bible and religion department to the department of applied social science, where it was redesigned as a program named Peacebuilding and Development.

The subtext of some of this critique was a debate over whether the Center for Justice and Peacebuilding should influence others toward the Christian faith tradition. Docherty described herself as a Mennonite-influenced Catholic akin to non-Christian graduates who were Mennonite-influenced Muslims, Hindus, and Buddhists, who discovered their own peace traditions without becoming Christian.[106] For Vernon Jantzi, however, the CJP's commitment to the way of Jesus was unequivocal: "We have a commitment to nonviolence, because if you read anything about Jesus's life, [you see that] he is committed to that. And we also interact with people who are committed to nonviolence but have a different ideological core than we do with Jesus."[107] This gentle witness is preserved in the current mission statement. The center remains committed

International participants in the Women's Peacebuilding Leadership Program sponsored by the Center for Justice and Peacebuilding, 2014.

to "educate a global community of peace builders through the integration of practice, theory, and research. . . . [Our] values are inextricably woven into our actions . . . consistent with EMU's grounding in Anabaptist theology and life." Those values and traditions "include *nonviolence*, *right relationships*, and a *just community*."[108]

The CJP has thus embraced faith-inspired peace and justice work while respecting the faith commitments of others who were similarly inspired by their own traditions. The center has sought to demonstrate that it is possible to work closely with those of other faiths and learn new peacebuilding insights from them. In fact, those who teach in the SPI each summer form a multifaith cluster within the SPI faculty.

The university's creation of the Center for Interfaith Engagement (CIE) in 2008 has extended the CJP's interfaith initiatives. The CIE was founded to promote respectful conversation and develop understanding, especially among Judaism and Christianity and Islam.[109] The center seeks funding for visiting scholars-in-residence who teach and facilitate events for a semester or a year. For example, in 2016–2017, Fulbright scholar Shafa Almirzanah, an Indonesian Muslim, taught several courses.[110] Some visiting scholars also participate in the CJP programs. The center has typically hosted an annual lecture or film series, supported the annual Interfaith Peace Camp for area youth, and promoted local interfaith gatherings.

Like the CJP, its activities have strengthened cross-religious understandings on campus and established a network of relationships outside the United States.

By the end of 2016, the CJP had 590 alumni with MAs or graduate certificates who were working in 78 countries. In addition, it counted 3,075 SPI alumni from 124 countries and more than 5,000 STAR alumni from 62 countries. With more than 78 Fulbright graduates, the CJP held the distinction of having the highest number of any conflict resolution program in the United States.[111] Against the odds, the CJP had become the flagship of EMU's national and global identity. Its contributions to peacebuilding and its hosting of dozens of international students and visitors every year had greatly enriched campus life while also promoting EMU's distinctive peacebuilding mission. Meanwhile, the university was struggling with its own issues of social justice.

A Deep and Difficult Divide

The week after his own inauguration in late March 2004, President Swartzendruber attended another at Mary Baldwin College. During the event, he received a call about a demonstration under way at EMU. Tracy King and Michael Shank, students in a course on ritual and peacebuilding, were leading a group of demonstrators carrying a rainbow flag that they then hung on the Campus Center. Several days later, they demonstrated again. The protesters told the *Weather Vane*, "We are displaying the Pride flag prominently to publicly declare our wish for a truly safe campus."[112] That same week, Kathleen Temple resigned as instructor in the Bible and religion department. Although still frustrated by disrespect shown to lesbian and gay people, she was pleased to see "rainbows coming out all over campus all of a sudden!"[113] Earlier that semester, the contract of a gay faculty member had not been renewed for job-related reasons.[114]

"Some Virginia Conference leaders were getting really nervous about how we were going to deal with homosexuality," Swartzendruber recalled. "And then we had this demonstration on campus which clearly, in my mind, was about testing me [as a new president]."[115] Several days later in a packed town hall meeting in Lehman Auditorium, Swartzendruber explained that EMU's "Safety and Behavioral Expectations" policy prohibited all types of social discrimination. He also pledged to support the efforts of the new vice president for student life, Ken L. Nafziger, to increase vigilance and promote a safe campus for gay and lesbian students.[116]

Without a safe campus environment, Nafziger had found it difficult to know how to advertise counseling services for gay and lesbian students. "Some of them thought we were attempting to change their orientation. But that wasn't true, even if it was perceived that way."[117] EMU also did not have an officially endorsed student organization for LGBTQ students at that time, although a private group met occasionally.

In 2004–2005, Nafziger honored his pledge by helping students gain official approval for Safe Space, an organization for LGBTQ students and their allies. Some faculty members displayed small "Safe Space" stickers on their office doors to invite students to talk. EMU's hiring policy, however, was still restrictive. Staff and faculty, who were not of one mind on LGBTQ issues, engaged in spirited discussions. Professors Ted Grimsrud and Mark Thiessen Nation, who held contrasting views on homosexuality, compiled a book of their counterpoint essays that provided a model of constructive dialogue for students and faculty.[118]

Questions about sexual orientation in the life of the church, debated since the mid-1980s, were still simmering. A national poll of MC USA churches in 2006 revealed that one-third of both members and pastors were willing to accept "practicing homosexuals" as members of their congregations.[119] Similarly, one-third of the credentialed leaders in a 2014 survey were willing to accept LGBTQ people as members without qualification.[120] These numbers, which varied by education, age, and region, revealed a significant wedge within the church.

Adding to the Brethren Mennonite Council's advocacy for LGBTQ people, a group of activists calling itself Pink Menno formed in 2008 and engaged in public demonstrations at the MC USA conventions in 2009, 2012, and 2015.[121] Many other Mennonites pushed back, defending the traditional stance on homosexuality. Some Mennonite district conferences expelled congregations and credentialed ministers over same-sex issues. The disquiet across the church persisted as EMU pondered how to resolve its exclusionary hiring practice.

Meanwhile, an avalanche of legal rulings on same-sex marriage was spreading across the country. In 2004—the year Swartzendruber assumed the presidency—Massachusetts became the first state to issue marriage licenses to same-sex couples. By October 2014, nineteen states allowed same-sex marriage, and eighteen months later, that number had risen to thirty-seven. On June 26, 2015, the US Supreme Court declared that gays and lesbians had a constitutional right to marriage.[122]

The changing legal climate fomented campus unrest. Swartzendruber recalled, "A few people were let go here over the years, not because they were gay, but for weak performance. Every time it happened, all havoc would break loose. The campus pressure on me to change just continued to grow and grow and grow." The calls for altering the hiring policy were persistent and persuasive.[123] Swartzendruber worried that the current policy that allowed the hiring of gay persons only if they were celibate would encumber the next president and might even become a litmus test for prospective candidates. The other Mennonite schools (Bethel, Bluffton, Goshen, and Hesston) were in a similar predicament, because none of them had inclusive hiring policies.

The president and the trustees had periodically discussed changing the university's policy. Finally, in November 2013, Swartzendruber, with the support of his cabinet and the trustees, approved a six-month public "listening process" to solicit feedback from EMU's constituents regarding its employment policy. "The trustees represented a full range of opinions," said the president. "They weren't sure about the outcome. But I had their support all along the way, which absolutely meant a lot."[124]

Although senior officials eventually chose the listening process as a way forward, they considered two other options first. One was to reinterpret the Community Lifestyle Commitment (which restricted sex to marriage) by using the new legal definition of marriage emerging in several states in 2013, which included same-sex covenants. Yet those who framed the CLC in 2001 had surely understood marriage to be exclusively heterosexual. A second option was to revise the CLC through a routine policy-revision process. Either of these options, while likely stirring unrest, might have prevented a prolonged public controversy.

The president preferred to name the proverbial elephant lurking in the room, discuss its features, and decide how to handle it. As one ranking official explained, "Swartzendruber wanted transparency. For him, integrity was more important than anything else. You should be transparent whenever possible. Tell people what you're doing and why."[125] The board's decision to begin a six-month listening process in early February 2014 generated media coverage in the Shenandoah Valley and in Mennonite media when it was announced that November.[126] Then, just as EMU was preparing to roll out a massive e-mail survey on February 5, an unexpected announcement fueled the same-sex debate across the Mennonite world.

In late January, the Mountain States Mennonite Conference decided to support plans by Denver's First Mennonite Church to license Theda Good—a graduate of Eastern Mennonite Seminary who was living with a partner in a same-sex covenant—as the first step toward ordination for her ministry.[127] This widely publicized announcement was a direct challenge to MC USA's authority to credential ministers. Church officials declared they would neither recognize the district conference's action nor accept Good's licensing. Despite repeated admonitions not to proceed to ordination in violation of denominational polity, both the district conference and Good signaled their intent to persist.[128]

This bold challenge, coming days before EMU would launch its listening process, conflated both events into a volatile controversy that sent seismic tremors across the Mennonite world. To conservative-minded Mennonites across the country, Good's licensing and EMU's openness to changing its policy were a double-barreled assault on traditional biblical teaching and Mennonite beliefs about marriage.

EMU's e-mail survey, sent to 22,800 stakeholders on and off campus in early February, yielded nearly 6,000 responses. Some 1,300 people expressed their views later in a public version of the survey available to interested parties outside the circle of stakeholders. In addition, 300 faculty, staff, and students participated in seventeen ninety-minute dialogue sessions. Two additional on-campus sessions addressed Christian perspectives on homosexuality, and undergraduates led a worship service and a prayer service focused on the discussion and upcoming decision.[129]

In Harrisonburg, Dean Welty—1964 alumnus and director of the Valley Family Forum, a ministry "dedicated to building faith, family, and freedom"—organized a blistering public attack on EMU. Welty's organization created a seven-point "Marriage Declaration for Eastern Mennonite University." The statement, signed by nearly four hundred people in the Harrisonburg area, reaffirmed traditional views of marriage.[130] Dozens of passionate stakeholders sent letters to President Swartzendruber, who patiently responded to each letter and phone call. One of his colleagues said the listening process "soaked up a lot of institutional energy and required 80 percent of the president's time over a two-year period. It took a toll on him."[131]

The results from the stakeholder survey revealed that some 70 percent of students, staff, and faculty supported hiring individuals in covenanted same-sex relationships, as did 50 percent of the external stakeholders (donors, alumni, and community members). Only 30 percent of parents were supportive, however. In general, younger and more educated respondents were more likely to affirm hiring people in same-sex relationships. Those most strongly opposed considered homosexuality a sin and thought the school was capitulating to popular culture. Advocates for change, however, argued that an inclusive policy expressed biblical values of love, acceptance, and social justice.[132]

University officials had planned to make a decision in late June 2014. But the turbulence across Mennonite Church USA over the ordination of LGBTQ persons complicated the timetable. When the trustees gathered in June, they learned that Bethel College had recently adopted an inclusive employment policy regarding sexual orientation and practice. The trustee board considered three options: uphold the current policy, revise it to accept individuals in same-sex covenants, or defer the decision a year until the next MC USA convention in June 2015.

Before acting, the president told the trustees that votes should be cast for the best interests of EMU: they did not represent particular regions or subgroups in the church. Swartzendruber noted that the listening process had alienated some of EMU's most traditional constituents, who were disgusted that the hiring policy was even being discussed. Regardless of the trustees' decision, some people would be sorely disappointed and pained.[133] After assessing all the factors, the board voted to defer action until July

2015 out of respect for EMU's relationship to MC USA's ongoing discernment. Until then, EMU would suspend any personnel actions related to these issues.

Although the next twelve months afforded a cooling-off time, a cloud of uneasiness hung over the campus as the community awaited the board's decision. Then a surprising announcement in late fall 2014 reenergized same-sex discussions on campus and across MC USA, even though it was not linked to EMU's decision. Ninety-six-year-old Chester Wenger—faithful EMU alumnus, teacher, trustee, chair of the seminary board, mission leader, ordained minister in Lancaster Conference, and the youngest son of EMU's second president, A. D. Wenger—wrote an open letter to the church. After reciting his long pedigree of church-related service, Wenger reported that he had happily conducted the private wedding ceremony of his gay son, a 1982 alumnus, and his son's committed partner of twenty-seven years. Some weeks later, Lancaster Conference retired Wenger's ministerial credentials in a graceful way. "I am at peace with their decision," Wenger declared afterward.[134]

A week after the US Supreme Court granted same-sex couples the right to marry in June 2015, MC USA held its convention in Kansas City. There, the church enacted two resolutions, "Forbearance" and "Membership Guidelines," designed to keep some semblance of unity amid the growing church-wide rift on same-sex issues. By articulating the polarities of freedom and mutual accountability, the resolutions aimed to allow space for ongoing conversation over the next four years.[135]

That outcome offered little guidance for EMU's trustees, who held a special session on July 16. By a majority vote, they revised the university's hiring and benefits policies to include employees in same-sex marriages. Earlier in 2015, Goshen College had expressed interest in joining EMU if it decided to revise its hiring policy. The two institutions released identical hiring policies the day of the decision. EMU's statement acknowledged the "deep divide" regarding the inclusion of LGBTQ individuals within MC USA and the broader Christian church.[136]

The vote was clouded by the knowledge that some constituents would celebrate the decision while others would deplore it. Some longtime donors vowed to never support EMU again. Other constituents pledged increased support. The long-term consequences for enrollment, charitable giving, and campus ethos were unpredictable. One thing was certain, however: the actions by EMU and Goshen sent ripples of concern among their 120 peer institutions in the Council for Christian Colleges and Universities (CCCU), none of whom hired people in same-sex covenants. The responses to EMU's and Goshen's actions threatened to splinter the CCCU if the two schools remained as members. Rather than fracture the organization that former EMU president Myron Augsburger had helped found and for which he later served as president and on whose board President Swartzendruber served, EMU and

Goshen voluntarily resigned their memberships. Nonetheless, their new employment policy stirred ongoing debate among the CCCU's constituent schools.[137]

On campus, the new employment policy created a dilemma for Eastern Mennonite Seminary: How could a seminary that served a denomination with a traditional teaching position on marriage also serve a university that employed people in same-sex marriages? Moreover, would EMS remain viable while the denominational networks and agencies that had traditionally supported it were in disarray? Among Mennonite conferences most likely to generate students for EMS in the past were Atlantic Coast, Franconia, Lancaster, Ohio, and Virginia. Many of these church bodies in 2016 had complicated relationships with MC USA over same-sex issues. Some were losing congregations, and the largest conference, Lancaster, had voted to leave MC USA.[138]

The words of Michael A. King, dean of the seminary and graduate programs, captured the feelings of many: "I pray that we're dreaming toward that far-off country of Hebrews 11, God's country. Here we name each other—even when tempted to declare each other enemies—mutual followers of Jesus, beloved children of God. Here we yearn toward what is so often still beyond the far horizon: making visible the power of the cross to reconcile us across our rifts and wrap us in the peace of Christ."[139]

Innovation and Reconciliation

As EMU's first century waned, its challenges were vast—as were its opportunities for innovation. Eastern Mennonite Seminary continued to provide training programs and graduate degrees for people pursuing ministry and leadership roles in the church, academy, and beyond. It offered a master of divinity degree, a master of arts in religion, and a master of arts in church leadership. In response to student interest and career flexibility, EMS also provided three dual degree options, combining the MDiv with a master's in counseling, conflict transformation, or business administration. About one-fourth of the one hundred students in 2016 were enrolled at EMU Lancaster.

The seminary emphasized peacebuilding, biblical studies, spiritual formation, and theology. It especially focused on training leaders for Mennonite Church USA and the United Methodist Church, but students came from other churches as well. A Mennonite faculty member described two full-time colleagues as "happy Anabaptists" in an "evangelical Anabaptist seminary."[140] Similarly, Dean King mused, "I've sometimes called EMS generously Anabaptist and richly ecumenical. Enrollment has held relatively steady on the ecumenical side particularly among Methodists. But current Mennonite numbers are down."[141] Some of that decline likely reflected the denomination-wide turmoil over same-sex issues and EMU's inclusive hiring policy, as well as downward enrollment trends at many seminaries.

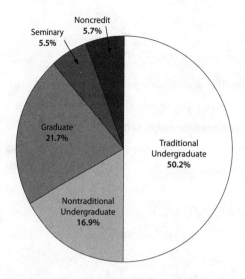

Distribution of university enrollment by degree program, fall 2016. Chart: Linda Eberly.

Note: Based on the combined headcount of 1,880 for the Harrisonburg and Lancaster programs. *Nontraditional Undergraduate* includes the Adult Degree Completion Program (ADCP) and the Study and Training for Effective Pastoral Ministry (STEP). *Graduate* includes the Center for Justice and Peacebuilding and all other graduate degree programs. *Noncredit* includes the Intensive English Program and Conflict Transformation Program. *Source:* Institutional Research Office.

The Lancaster extension grew significantly in the decade before the centennial. By fall 2016, some four hundred students were enrolled in graduate courses, undergraduate courses, and certificate programs designed for working adults. Program curriculum in Lancaster mirrored that in Harrisonburg with the exception of an undergraduate certificate program known as STEP (Study and Training for Effective Pastoral Ministry), which was coordinated with Lancaster Mennonite Conference. The RN to bachelor of science in nursing program accounted for approximately 60 percent of enrollment in Lancaster. The remaining enrollment was split between graduate teacher education and pastoral studies. The Lancaster programs were staffed by three full-time and several dozen part-time faculty.[142]

The word *innovation* most aptly describes EMU's programmatic changes in the centennial's final years. In 2014, the School of Graduate and Professional Studies was established to provide an umbrella for professional disciplines. Two years later, Vice President Michael A. King was appointed dean of both the seminary and graduate programs, further enhancing coordination. As the number of traditional undergraduates receded, graduate programs flourished with a panoply of master's degrees ranging from biomedicine to restorative justice, from education to health care management, as well as dual degrees such as the MDiv-MBA. A total of some twenty graduate degrees plus graduate certificates, online offerings, and nondegree programs were designed to meet student interests and ever-changing occupational markets.[143]

A new program of restorative justice education (RJE) exemplified EMU's innovative spirit and regional outreach. In 2014, the university launched the first program of RJE in the nation. Educators could pursue a graduate certificate or a concentration in a master of arts in education. Thirty educators from the Harrisonburg region formed the first cohort for the graduate certificate in fall 2015, and a year later, a cohort from the Harrisonburg City Public Schools began. The first cohort—principals, teachers, school counselors, district administrators, and behavioral specialists—completed their work in December 2016. "The level of collaboration, imagination, and support that these educators provided for one another was amazing and rewarding," said Professor Kathy Evans. "They really are transforming the field of education in the region and EMU is at the hub of that work."[144]

The burst of programs seemed new in some ways, yet it was consistent with a century of innovation. Beginning with the first Special Bible Term in Alexandria in 1915, EMU had created many educational options for students and constituents aside from its undergraduate program.

Although the growth of creative options augured well for the university's future, it also brought budgetary stress until the initiatives attracted enough students to sustain them. Throughout the course of its history, EMU experienced the recurring dilemma of too many good ideas and too few students—echoing the haunting words of Robert Dickeson: "Most institutions can no longer afford to be what they've become," or hope to be.[145]

Ironically, some of the new developments emerged in collaboration with EMU's old-time foe, Goshen—the very college EMU had been founded to combat. Besides the collaborative online MBA program (2014) and identical statements on inclusive hiring (2015), other signs of reconciliation appeared as EMU and Goshen, hand in hand, announced two significant programs in fall 2016. With a $1 million gift from Ray Martin, who studied at EMU and Goshen, the two schools founded the Center for Sustainable Climate Solutions, housed at EMU, with MCC as a third partner.[146]

In December 2016, with SACS approval, EMU and Goshen released collaborative plans to initiate the first doctorate offered by any MC USA institution of higher education.[147] A Doctor of Nursing Practice (DNP) degree—which promised to combine the rich resources of both schools' nursing departments—was set to begin as an online collaboration in January 2018. "Launching EMU's first doctoral program in 2018," said one senior official "is a great way to launch into our second century of preparing students to serve and lead in a global context."[148]

It was the kind of collaboration that Albert J. Meyer, former executive secretary of the Mennonite Board of Education, had hoped Mennonite colleges would foster. The vision of Fordism that Meyer was not fully able to implement in the 1970s and '80s now had happened for other reasons. Because of tight budgets, both EMU and Goshen were downsizing in fall 2016. A new generation of leaders, technological advances, and occupational opportunities—as well as economic, demographic, and market forces—prodded the old rivals to merge their resources to reach a larger student market in mutually beneficial ways.

As EMU stepped from its first century into an uncertain future, the wisdom of the late Dean Al Keim was particularly apropos: "Fear of the future, like disdain for the past, is an illness of the mind which distorts action in the present. It is in the providence of God to free us from both."[149]

Crossing Over

As EMU approached its centennial crossover, another presidential transition was under way. Loren Swartzendruber retired in June 2016, and Susan Schultz Huxman prepared to become EMU's ninth president in January 2017. Lee F. Snyder, former EMU academic dean and retired president of Bluffton University, served as interim president in fall 2016.

At Swartzendruber's farewell ceremony, Nancy Heisey, professor of Bible and religion, lauded Swartzendruber's "refusal to see a conflict between his love for the church and the work of the academy." He had served "with dignity, precision, and grace" while remaining calm in the face of controversy.[150] The board of trustees applauded his thirteen years of "quality leadership, excellence, dedication, and distinction." They noted his gift for empowering faculty and staff to pursue EMU's mission with hope and collaboration and his courageous leadership in making EMU a more diverse and inclusive community. During his tenure, some four thousand students had graduated. Student enrollment increased by 30 percent to 1,880, and philanthropic support to the university totaled $65 million. Core academic programs were enhanced, graduate programs were added, and online educational opportunities multiplied. With his leadership and support, EMU initiated a major commitment to ecological sustainability, both in curricular content and in campus facilities, garnering national recognition.

The trustees also recognized Pat Swartzendruber for her active role in promoting EMU's mission through her involvement with students, alumni, donors, parents, and area leaders. She was honored for her wise counsel, enthusiasm, and compassion, as well as her gracious hospitality to the campus community and to its many visitors.[151]

Susan Schultz Huxman was serving as president of Conrad Grebel University College in Waterloo, Ontario, when she was invited to EMU. Prior to the Conrad Grebel appointment, she had directed the Elliott School of Communication at Wichita State University in Kansas. Huxman earned an MA and PhD in communication studies from the University of Kansas. A graduate of Bethel College in North Newton, Kansas, she served on the Mennonite Education Agency from 2001 to 2007. She was married to Jesse Huxman, a communications professional, and they had three adult children.

Huxman's appointment on the cusp of EMU's second century set several significant precedents: She was the first woman to assume the presidency and the first president affiliated with the former General Conference Mennonite Church

President-elect Susan Schultz Huxman speaks in chapel during a campus visit, April 2016.

(before it became part of MC USA). She was the first president with a PhD who had ascended the faculty ranks to full professor and was the first second-generation Mennonite college president of any MC USA school. Her father, Harold J. Schultz, had served Bethel College for twenty years (1971–1991). Born and raised in Florida, she was the first president raised outside a region heavily populated by Mennonites. She and Joe Lapp were the only two nonordained presidents. Moreover, Huxman and Swartzendruber were the only two who had previous presidential experience.

Optimistic about leading EMU into its second century, Huxman said, "As an academic and passionate ambassador of Mennonite education, I see EMU as a real gift to the church and our world today as it prepares students to serve and lead."[152] It seemed only fitting that the symbolic circle of Mennonite higher education was widening. Three of EMU's alumna had earlier assumed presidencies at other Mennonite institutions of higher education—Lee F. Snyder at Bluffton University (1996–2006), Shirley Hershey Showalter at Goshen College (1996–2004), and Sara Wenger Shenk at Anabaptist Mennonite Biblical Seminary (2010–). That an alumna of Bethel College—which EMU founders considered even more "worldly" than Goshen College—would take the helm of the eastern school that had eschewed all things western in its early years spoke volumes about the changes that had unfolded across a century.

PART V

The Transformation of Countercultural Education, 1917–2017

CHAPTER 12

An Experiment like No Other

The past is never dead. It's not even past.
—William Faulkner

A Big Experiment

When Mary Nafzinger left Michigan in October 1917 to go to the new Mennonite school in Virginia, she found a large, rickety white house in Assembly Park. Here she would live and attend her classes. Five other students registered with her, and a few more arrived in the following weeks. Nafzinger could not have imagined that a century later Ruayda Qadir, an Iraqi student in the class of 2018, would find nearly 1,900 students from diverse ethnic and national backgrounds pursuing studies in dozens of academic disciplines. Nor could Qadir grasp how a student like Nafzinger might have felt at a tiny school offering Bible classes and high school courses taught by five plain-dressed teachers. Neither woman knew that she was part of a century-long development that two scholars called "holy experiments" in Christian higher education.[1] In 1916, C. H. Brunk, chairman of Eastern Mennonite School's trustees, likewise called the birth of his institution "an experiment."[2] Several other founders expressed the same sentiment. They were not thinking of a tightly controlled clinical trial. They had in mind a high-stakes venture that would test this idea: Could Mennonites establish a school that would serve the church and remain its servant as it grew into adulthood?

Thirty years later, physics professor M. T. Brackbill spoke in chapel about EMS's risky venture. He told the students that "an experiment in engineering may fail and no souls would be lost," but an experiment in religion would have eternal consequences. Brackbill recalled that when EMS began, many Mennonites thought that "higher education had been the ruin of every conservative church that tried it. It was impossible. It was hopeless." But a few eastern leaders "were not convinced that it was hopeless; they had a scientific attitude toward the problem" and were willing to tackle it.

Brackbill concluded his talk by paraphrasing President Lincoln: "A score and a half years ago, our Mennonite Church fathers established here on this campus a new school, conceived in a courageous faith, and dedicated to the conviction that higher education is compatible with Mennonite beliefs and practices and will not destroy them. And we are now engaged and have been engaged in an experiment to prove whether this school, or any school so conceived and so dedicated, can long succeed."

Still following Lincoln, he pressed for a new commitment: "It is for us to take increased devotion to the cause, and to highly resolve that those who dreamed and founded shall not have dreamed and founded in vain, but that Eastern Mennonite School shall, under God, have a new birth of zeal and loyalty, that the distinctive features of the Mennonite Church . . . which make her different shall not perish from off the earth."[3] It was not surprising that a professor of physics would use the metaphor of an experiment to describe the school's fate. But it did demonstrate how science had shaped how he thought about a religious problem. The laboratory metaphor persisted into the university era, when President Joe Lapp also described EMU's journey as a "grand experiment" in the history of church-related colleges.[4]

In broad strokes, the experiment had four possible outcomes. First, the school might gradually succumb to secularism, lose its Christian commitment, and sever meaningful church ties. Second, EMU might relax its Christian commitments even as it held onto a symbolic denominational identity. Third, the school might maintain a Mennonite affiliation and Christian commitment that reflected or revised the founders' vision. Finally, EMU might drop its denominational affiliation yet retain a robust Christian identity amid a spectrum of theological perspectives. These outcomes are not necessarily mutually exclusive.

The Myth of a Unified Mission

In 2007, the EMU publication *Crossroads* noted some changes over the university's history. "But one thing has not changed," it asserted. "EMU's mission remains largely the same as it was when it was founded ninety years ago."[5] That statement begs the question of the nature of the original mission. Institutions sometimes find legitimation for their contemporary mission by purporting to uphold the vision of the founders. The notion that the founders of EMS had a single unified vision, however, is largely a myth. It's even more fanciful to think that EMU has faithfully pursued that mythical mission for a century.

Documents produced during the founding era (1913–1924) lay out at least seven mission statements with commonalities and differences.[6] The statements make one thing clear: the founders hoped to indoctrinate Mennonite youth to become loyal, conservative Mennonites who would help save the church from liberalism.

To achieve that mission, a handful of educational entrepreneurs, without official church endorsement, established a conservative Bible school and high school as an alternative to Goshen College. The founders hoped the new school would serve the church and eventually be controlled by it.

L. J. Heatwole was the likely author of the school's first published vision statement, which appeared in the initial catalog: "The Eastern Mennonite School is intended as a *safeguard* for the student life of the young people of the Mennonite Church and *others* who may be in sympathy with the principles that the institution upholds—in the acquirement of a *general education* amid Christian and ennobling influences; preparing them for *Christian service*, or the profession of *teaching*, and general *usefulness* in life."[7] The school also promised to prepare students for strengthening singing in local congregations.

After appearing in the 1917–1918 catalog, the statement was replaced a year later by a lengthy theological vision, probably written by President J. B. Smith. It said the school's "*chief purpose* is to supply the needs of the church with loyal and competent workers, ready to go forth with a profound conviction for the tenets of the denomination and the plain teaching of God's Word."[8] It noted that "the acquisition of knowledge has value *only* as it contributes to the necessary comforts of life, to the salvation of souls, to the upbuilding of the church and to the glory of God." The school hoped to supply workers for the church because "*the church needs many workers and a few scholars.*"[9] Four years later, under President A. D. Wenger, the mission was again revised: "It is our *aim and purpose* not only to save young people [from leaving the church] while they are getting an education, but to give them a good knowledge of God's Word and to strengthen them in their moral and spiritual life, thus fitting them to be staunch defenders of the faith as well as consecrated workers in the Lord's great harvest field."[10]

Several common themes in the early visions include nurturing Christian faith, keeping the Bible central in the curriculum, indoctrinating youth in the church's distinctive doctrines and peculiar practices, and preparing youth for vocations, everyday life, mission work, rural life, and service in the Mennonite Church. These ideas continued to evolve throughout the century, making it even riskier to draw a straight line from 1913 to 2017. One EMU professor suggested in 2016 that "being faithful to the way of Jesus" is the primary link between EMU's past and present.[11] However, that phrase harkened back to Harold Bender's Anabaptist vision of the 1940s, not to the founders' doctrine-heavy theology.

While it is tempting to realign the founders' visions with the present-day mission, to do so obscures the sweeping changes of the twentieth century. The founders had no experience building institutions of any kind. They were visionaries who did what they deemed best for the church despite meager financial resources and lack of official church support. Not until 1924, twelve years after the school movement began in Denbigh and seven years after classes began in Harrisonburg, did Virginia Conference assume control of the school.

In 1921, EMS sought state accreditation for its high school. That small step began a gradual accession to outside influence, and sometimes to control, from nonchurch entities: the alumni association, donors, college and seminary accreditation bodies, consultants, government regulatory bodies, philanthropic foundations, professional and scholarly associations, and other institutions recruiting the same students. As a result, by 2017, EMU's external environment was much more complex than in its early days. Likewise, the Mennonite world in 2017 was far more variegated—with Mennonite Church USA (MC USA) plus some fifty smaller Mennonite affiliations nationwide showing a wide diversity of theology, ethnicity, language, and culture—than the early twentieth-century Mennonite landscape.[12]

Just as the founders sought to implement their mission for their time, so do the contemporary administrators, faculty, and trustees of EMU work to realize their vision in a very different twenty-first-century world: "EMU educates students to serve and lead in a global context. Our Christian community challenges students to pursue their life calling through scholarly inquiry, artistic creation, guided practice, and life-changing cross-cultural encounter. We invite each person to follow Christ's call to bear witness to faith, serve with compassion, and walk boldly in the way of nonviolence and peace."[13]

Wrestling with Modernity

Unlike a tightly controlled laboratory trial, the EMU experiment unfolded as the forces of modernity wrought enormous changes in the Mennonite Church, American society, and American higher education after 1917. The rapid modernization of twentieth-century America transformed Mennonites from rural sectarians into a largely suburban, middle-class people. At the same time, the broader social world underwent a transformation of its own. Social analysts began using terms like *postmodern* and *late modern* to characterize the late twentieth century. Sociologist Zygmunt Bauman depicted the shift as a metamorphosis from *solid* to *liquid* modernity.[14] For him, the rigid boundaries of the early twentieth century related to race, gender, ethnicity, and religion began to melt, as did the lines separating work and leisure, production and consumption, and time and distance. In the twenty-first century, solid distinctions are slowly dissolving into more fluid, amorphous forms in the online world of virtual reality, where truth and fiction, purity and pornography, become blurred.

As Eastern Mennonite School transitioned to Eastern Mennonite College, it gradually began adopting some cultural practices it had shunned for years. Mainstream values and practices, especially those borrowed from American higher education, were assimilated over time. As noted in previous chapters, the metamorphosis at EMU reflected many of the themes that accompany worldwide modernization—technology, individuation, choice, specialization, bureaucracy, and incessant planning for the future.

In the early 1980s, EMU rode the wave of campus-wide computerization.[15] By 2010, members of the campus community used software to collaborate, manage courses, host streaming media, share documents, and scrutinize academic integrity. In 2015, an Iowa farmer used a handheld device to join colleagues in one of the university's online business courses while harvesting grain with his GPS-driven combine.[16]

Another change entailed a shift in deep-seated Mennonite values as EMU transitioned from a communal moral order to one that affirmed individual choice and achievement. Ever since 1948, when Virginia Conference insisted that students be admitted on the basis of individual merit, individualism continued to blossom. Choice also grew rapidly as EMU moved from assigned seating to free-choice seating in the dining hall, from compulsory to voluntary chapel attendance, and from mandatory dress standards to none. Nonetheless, EMU's strong accent on community and the Community Lifestyle Commitment helped to curb individualism.

Specialization increased as well, especially after the 1950s, with ever-sharper distinctions of faculty expertise, professional credentials, roles, and functions, along with the proliferation of some forty undergraduate majors and numerous minors. The university's organizational structure shifted from a familial church "brotherhood" to a complex organization with the usual traits of bureaucracy. Except for military recruiters, the politically shy school accepted federal and state educational initiatives as they expanded in the twentieth century. EMU participated in Social Security and accepted federal grants and student financial aid that often carried restrictions.

If failing to plan for the future is a cardinal "sin" of modern life, EMU had reason to strut a bit. Already in the late 1970s, its data-driven Analytic Studies Group was forecasting future trends, and by 1989, EMU was engaged in a "continuous and increasingly comprehensive process of strategic planning and evaluation . . . with a two-year strategic planning and evaluation cycle."[17]

Three significant transformations involved race, gender, and sexual orientation. Among private colleges in Virginia, EMC led the way on racial integration in 1948. The rise of women in leadership at EMC in the 1970s and '80s was mostly on par with other small private colleges. However, its nondiscriminatory hiring policy with regard to sexual orientation in 2015 set EMU apart from its 120 fellow institutions in the Council of Christian Colleges and Universities.

Finally, the centennial journey witnessed the transformation of a school that was aloof from the world to one that actively engaged it. In its first quarter century, EMS sought to protect students from the wiles of secular society by rejecting "worldly" things—radio, dancing, drama, musical instruments, intercollegiate sports, and fashionable dress. By 1982, President Detweiler was calling for a new Mennonite "worldview [to fit] our transition as a church from *separation* to *involvement* as disciples of Jesus in the world."[18] Echoing that point in sharper language in 2015, one school official said, "We want to engage the world. We don't want boundaries between us and the world. We are intentionally tearing them down."[19] By then, an EMU student—with a swipe of a finger on a handheld device—could explore the world out there so feared by school officials and church leaders in its first half century. That world could now enter any crevice of the campus willy-nilly.

EMU's commitment to a Christian worldview was one realm in which the school did not acquiesce to secularization. However, the meaning of Christian faith and practice changed significantly at EMU over the years. The tilt toward individual choice and world engagement, for example, turned EMU's educational paradigm from *indoctrinating* students in the truth to *walking together with them* in a search for truth. Some interesting transformations of language and ideas accompanied the educational change.

Tinkering with Words and Ideas

"Last year's words belong to last year's language. And next year's words await another voice," said T. S. Eliot.[20] As a flag points to national identity, words signify concepts and ideas. Changes in language reflect ideological transitions. This was true of the shifting landscape of ideas in EMU's history.

As the college and seminary assimilated into mainstream culture, certain ideas were shelved and others were added. Words such as *obedience, devil, nonconformity, church standards, self-denial, loyalty, sacrifice, pride, indoctrination, doctrine, safeguard,* and *separation from the world* dropped from conversation. Their disappearance signaled the passing of EMS's early philosophy. As old ideas were discarded, a new vocabulary entered campus discourse: *discipleship, Anabaptist, individual conscience, self, diversity, persuasion, choice, global,* and *social justice.* Some of these terms originated in popular culture and others within Mennonite life. Regardless of their origin, they reflected a new ideological outlook.

Besides dropping and adding vocabulary, four types of symbolic transformations occurred in EMU's collective mind: reversal, renovation, reproduction, and fusion.[21] Some once-honored words did not merely fall away. Instead, in a *symbolic reversal,* they turned into bad words because they contradicted EMU's moral philosophy in its second half century. Such words included *indoctrination, safeguard,* and *obedience.* Other older words that conveyed the ideas of loyalty, sacrifice, and doctrine mostly dropped out of use, but they were not offensive if used occasionally in the twenty-first century.

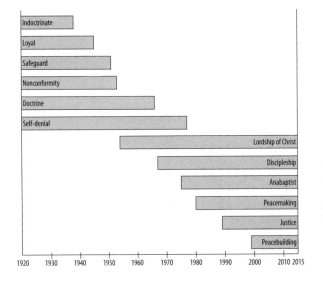

Changing patterns of vocabulary showing last and first appearance of words. *Sources*: Mission, vision, and philosophy statements in undergraduate catalogs, 1920–2015. Chart: Linda L. Eberly.

Some ideas underwent more subtle transformations. The term *world* experienced a *symbolic renovation* as it accrued new meanings, analogous to an old house acquiring a new interior. For the founders, the "world" was a source of much evil—something to fear, to avoid, to shun. As A. D. Wenger said, "The Eastern Mennonite School may be counted on to oppose . . . entanglements in worldly commercialism and political issues—in short, a full separation from the world."[22] The negative meanings of *world* were largely eradicated in EMU's second half century. No longer shunned, the world was renovated into a laboratory for study, which EMC embraced as "our world." At the same time, not everything in the world was positive. Students and faculty were still expected to make discerning choices about their involvement in it.

Similarly, the word *service* experienced symbolic renovation. Prior to Civilian Public Service (CPS) in the mid-1940s, Christian service at EMS meant some form of evangelistic outreach: street-corner meetings, tract distribution, or prison visitation. In CPS, service expanded beyond soul winning to include socially oriented activities such as fighting forest fires or caring for the mentally ill. For Mennonites, CPS also underscored the distinction between Christian service and military service. Service later became aligned with vocation as students entered professions in social work, education, and medicine. By the twenty-first century, the term *service* evoked such a wide range of meanings—from unpaid sacrificial service to customer service, from Christian service to highly paid professional services—that it risked becoming bland.

Although the word *discipleship* rarely entered campus discourse in the 1920s and '30s, by midcentury it was widely used, highly durable, and eventually asked to carry considerable freight.[23] The public statement of EMU's philosophy in 2015–2016, for example, said, "Discipleship—which includes personal devotion to Christ, simplicity of life, peacebuilding (which expresses itself in reconciliation, active pursuit of justice and nonparticipation in the military), evangelism and Christian service—is the mark of an authentic Christian life."[24] These examples provide practical applications of discipleship, yet such an expansive definition threatens to jeopardize its original meaning of following Jesus in daily life.

In another case of symbolic renovation, the term *Anabaptist* began to circulate in the late 1940s. During the last quarter of the twentieth century, it became the single most powerful label signifying EMU's identity and theological orientation. The word *Anabaptist* pointed to a radical, spiritual, theological tradition rather than a denomination. This tradition was countercultural and emphasized the centrality of Christian peacemaking. "Anabaptism is a broader theological and philosophical umbrella that doesn't evoke the sense of a tight Mennonite community with impermeable boundaries," explained one administrator.[25] Like *discipleship*, it became quite elastic—stretching over a multitude of meanings. As a noun, it could refer to a sixteenth-century martyr or to his or her spiritual descendant, and as an adjective, it could modify contemporary words like *faith*, *peacemaking*, *hermeneutic*, *community*, *service*, *orientation*, and *heritage*. "Whate'er we construe, to be good and true, we name the word Anabaptist," quipped Theron Schlabach. Such elasticity threatened to dilute some of the word's rich spiritual meanings.[26]

Not surprisingly, the word *Goshen* also experienced many symbolic iterations of meaning by the end of EMU's centennial—from enemy to exemplar, and from rival to collaborator.

The two pillars of early twentieth-century Mennonite doctrine—*nonconformity* and *nonresistance*—dropped out of usage after spawning offspring through *symbolic reproduction*. For early school officials, nonconformity involved a wide rejection of popular culture on campus. Soon, however, it became code for plain dress regulations. Already in the mid-1960s, terms like *modesty*, *simplicity*, *a simple lifestyle*, and *countercultural* were intermingled with *nonconformity* until they replaced it in the '70s. The term *countercultural* signaled selective participation in popular culture and a critical attitude toward mass consumption, leisure, materialism, and affluence. EMC professor Conrad Brunk, in his 1970 baccalaureate address, argued for a "new nonconformity," an active and "noisy" nonconformity that spoke out "against injustice, hate, violence, and plastic values."[27] The symbolic reproduction of nonconformity also shifted from a *collective* practice to an *individual* one. Self-defined countercultural living, however, was more erratic than the communal version with its shared practices.

Nonresistance, which as a term also faded from use, generated a large number of heirs, including *reconciliation*, *peace position*, *Christian pacifism*, *nonviolence*, *peacemaking*, and *peacebuilding*. Although still in the same semantic family, *nonviolent resistance* and *activist peacemaking* were quite different from, almost contradictory to, historic nonresistance. Like nonconformity, nonresistance as it pertained to military service also became a matter of individual conscience rather than church regulation. Members of Virginia Conference who entered the military during World War II, for example, automatically lost their church membership. But that was no longer the case in 2017.

The word *Mennonite* was the cornerstone of the school's name and of its supporting denomination. The word was derived from Menno Simons, who influenced scattered Anabaptist groups in the sixteenth century. With denominational identity and loyalty declining since the 1980s, the term took on more of a cultural rather than theological connotation in the public mind and lost some of its historical cachet. Meanwhile, the word *Anabaptism*, inspired by Bender's "Anabaptist Vision," growing research on sixteenth-century Anabaptist history, and rising respect for Anabaptist theology in the larger Christian world, took on increasing influence, prominence, and prestige. Those meanings empowered young activists and attracted outside scholars and theologians who identified as Anabaptist regardless of their church affiliation.[28]

Despite how well-worn it seemed, the word *Mennonite* could not be discarded without great peril. That predicament produced a *symbolic fusion* by creating the hyphenated term *Anabaptist-Mennonite*. "Anabaptism" was part of campus discourse since the late 1940s, though it did not appear in the front matter of the catalog until 1975, with a fleeting reference to the "Anabaptist tradition." Thirteen years later, the trustees approved a philosophy statement that included two instances of *Anabaptist-Mennonite*.[29] Since then, its use has spread. By 2015, the term appeared frequently in the undergraduate catalog as *Anabaptist-Mennonite tradition*, *Anabaptist-Mennonite faith*, and *Anabaptist-Mennonite biblical faith*, along with occasional references to Mennonites and Anabaptists.[30] It even occurred in the 2012 name change of EMS's sister seminary in Indiana—from Associated Mennonite Biblical Seminary to Anabaptist Mennonite Biblical Seminary.

Institutional Discipleship? Or Verbal Blather?

"Our problem at EMC is how to combine the imperatives of Christian brotherhood—notably compassion and candor—with the realities and demands of institutional power."[31] With those words in 1972, Professor Al Keim pinpointed a small experiment inside the bigger experiment. Could Mennonites operate a complex organization on Anabaptist principles? The American theologian and ethicist Reinhold Niebuhr, in his 1947 book *Moral Man and Immoral Society*, argued that people are more prone to evil as members of a group than as individuals. This idea posed a question for EMU: Would Mennonites also slip into sin when operating a complex organization? Put another way, could morally upright Mennonites create a just and fair organization?

Three factors intensified this dilemma for EMU: its radical Anabaptist history, the informal familial-tribal-brotherhood ethos of its early decades, and since the mid-1970s, its outspoken advocacy for social justice. Should a complex organization informed by Anabaptist-Mennonite principles operate differently than a secular one? Would Anabaptists, more concerned with personal discipleship than with doctrinal beliefs, be able to establish the just and fair policies that Keim dubbed "institutional discipleship"?[32]

Professor Keim contended that EMC as an organization was a Christian body that mixed Christian and secular functions, reminiscent of the Middle Ages. "Like the medieval papacy, the college administration exercises both spiritual and worldly sanctions. The faculty functions much like the medieval clergy, purveying truth and guarding the gates to paradise. And the students, like their peasant counterparts of the Middle Ages, are at least ostensibly Christian."[33]

Keim doubted "that the Anabaptist model is viable for a large and complex community such as EMC."[34] Anabaptism insisted on the *separation* of spiritual and secular power; faith was to be unmediated and voluntary. And yet the college president and his colleagues were both preachers and governors. They exercised administrative authority but couched it in the ideals and language of Anabaptist community. Required to hold Anabaptist beliefs, the faculty also held advanced degrees in secular fields. And students were required to attend chapel under the threat of losing GPA points.

When the faculty council denied the *Weather Vane* access to the minutes of faculty committees because it feared editors and reporters would use the minutes indiscriminately, editor Ben Gamber was outraged. He charged that the denial "runs contrary to all the rhetoric that comes from behind the chapel podium: 'we are a brotherhood, a community.' Your action means: 'We don't trust the students any further than we can see them.' Now what kind of a brotherhood is that? . . . Either make the action consistent with the rhetoric, or else stop the verbal blather and own up to the way things really are."[35]

Institutional and individual interests collide when an organization lays off people for its survival. Was EMS justified in shrinking the salaries of the three single women, but none of the married men, in order to rescue the school from collapse during the Great Depression? Similarly, in the 1980s, was EMC right to eliminate some academic majors and lay off employees to alleviate a financial crisis? A family member of an older woman forced to retire early appealed to President Detweiler: "Does EMC not have a more brother-sister-hood way of thanking such a loyal servant . . . who labored sacrificially through thick and thin?"[36]

Despite its bureaucratic traits, EMU retained a pliable organizational structure that encouraged participatory decision making. Former provost Beryl Brubaker noted, "EMU doesn't fire people. We at least have some conversation before we request a resignation."[37] EMU has not recognized a teacher of the year because the faculty did not want to elevate one person. "We have a very flat egalitarian institutional structure," said an official who had worked in a large university. "It can be inefficient sometimes because everyone wants to contribute something. People are on a first-name basis. They like each other and are generally polite. But there's also a dark side that we sometimes call whack-a-mole. If anyone sticks their head up too high, they might get whacked."[38]

Searching for EMU's Soul

German sociologist Max Weber famously called the modern world disenchanted—with little space for mystery, myth, or magic. By contrast, traditional societies reminded him of enchanted gardens. The rise of the Enlightenment with its Age of Reason privileged scientific discovery over religious belief and reason over revelation. Enlightenment philosophers spurned the notion of a transcendent God and relied on human reason to explain how the world worked. The spreading secularization shrank the influence of religion and diminished the sense of magic in the world.[39]

As noted in chapter 1, many of the colleges founded in the nineteenth century had a religious vision and ethos that gradually waned in the twentieth century. Foremost among scholars who have tracked the secularization of higher education is George Marsden. His magisterial work, *The Soul of the American University*, traces the demise of religion in seven of America's most influential universities, including Harvard, Yale, and Chicago. James T. Burtchaell's influential book *The Dying of the Light* documents a similar decline in seventeen institutions affiliated with seven different religious traditions. These studies show the pervasive influence of secularization and illustrate why EMU's founders properly called their project an experiment. The search for EMU's soul revolves around three identity-related questions: Does the declaration "Thy Word Is Truth" still hold? Is EMU still Christian? And is EMU still Mennonite?

Is Thy Word (Still) Truth?

Even in a disenchanted world, many institutions of higher education, Christian or not, embrace the pursuit of truth in their missions. Christian colleges, however, make a particular faith claim: the Christian worldview provides a prism for assessing all other truth claims. In his 2016 review of the ruckus over academic freedom related to same-sex relationships and other topics in Christian higher education, William Ringenberg contends that all those disputes distill down to the question of truth. "Freedom is not an end in itself. Truth is," Ringenberg says. "Fear bad theology or bad science or bad sociology. Fear missing the truth. [But] do not fear the truth." EMU's *mode* of truth-seeking gradually changed from indoctrination to a collaborative journey, resonating with what Ringenberg calls "truth-seeking in community."[40]

Christian colleges and universities are crucibles for competing truth claims. EMU wrestled with its own set of competing queries: Could a Mennonite liberal arts college, open to different perspectives and worldviews, preserve and perpetuate a denominational heritage? Was it feasible for a Mennonite college that affirmed a Christian worldview to offer a genuine liberal arts experience? Could faculty trained in specialized disciplines in secular universities transmit a religious heritage?

For President Lapp, the Christian university "stretche[d] between the questions we cannot answer and the certainty of faith." He also acknowledged "the tension between ambiguity and certainty."[41] By nature, the liberal arts encourage free inquiry, critical thinking, intellectual exploration, artistic expression, and unfettered investigation; still, those traits are constrained by some version of rationalism. Similarly, scientific scrutiny involves empirical evidence and questioning, while religious faith rests on belief and revelation.[42] Religion promotes certainty, offers meaning, and provides answers to life's troubling questions. Yet the search for truth often leads to uncertainty, paradox, and ambiguity.

One student found his way through the tangle of faith and science at EMC in the 1940s. Growing up on a small Depression-era farm, Carl S. Keener found the wildflowers in the pastures he roamed and the stars he saw at night quite fascinating. As a thirteen-year-old, he began corresponding with EMC professor M. T. Brackbill. In a postcard response, Brackbill assured the curious boy, "It won't hurt you to read things that make you stretch your mind." Before arriving at EMC in 1949, the precocious eighteen-year-old had already read C. K. Lehman's *The Inadequacy of Evolution*, in which Lehman asserted that the species were "fixed" by creation, and that biological "life [is] not in a state of flux."[43] Like EMC as an institution, Keener initially accepted this worldview. But in his junior year, a small book on flowers and plant taxonomy "blew apart [his] firm view that all species were fixed during the six-day creation." It was "an instantaneous cognitive shift," Keener recalled. "I jumped up and ran out of the library and down the stairs to tell a friend that at least parts of evolution are true!"[44]

Stranded between its staunch opposition to evolution and its commitment to build a strong science department, EMC faced a dilemma: How does one reconcile the competing claims of Christian faith and science? Remarkably, when compared with other long-running and sometimes contentious disputes over millennialism, higher criticism, Fundamentalism, race, gender, dancing, and sexuality, the faith-science issue never stirred a public skirmish. Periodically over the decades, the natural science faculty quietly addressed the tension within their department. In a 2008 paper, for example, they confessed, "By faith we believe God originated the cosmos, but we remain undogmatic on the specifics of God's methodology. . . . God continually creates and sustains the cosmos [but] we do not insist that our students adopt any specific point of view about this blending." The faculty would teach and model the way Christian scholars integrate their faith and their scientific knowledge, and they would ask the students to do the same. In a capstone course titled "Faith, Science, and Ethics," senior-level students would write a reflective paper describing how their worldview influenced their scientific work.[45]

Apart from faith-science issues, a deeper question involved the perennial quest for truth underscored by EMU's motto, Thy Word Is Truth, and the school's early declarations of immutable truth. Dogmatic certainty began to waver as EMS prepared to become a liberal arts college. One of the titles proposed for an official history of EMU's first half century was *Thy Word Is Truth*. For unknown reasons, the faculty objected. Instead, a gold-colored college seal with the school's motto inscribed in it appeared on the book's blue cloth cover.[46] Although the university's bylaws stipulate the motto's use, its appearance on catalogs, publications, and stationery began to fade after 1980. In a surprising renaissance in the fall of 2014, first-year students saw the seal on their orientation packets, on the back of the blue T-shirts worn by the orientation staff, and on the blue coffee mugs they received from President Swartzendruber.[47]

The motto's durability likely derives in part from its multiple meanings, which Dean C. K. Lehman noted when it was adopted in 1928 (see chapter 4).[48] In 1962, the EMC faculty pondered whether the motto pointed to one central reality or to many.[49] Some people understood *Word* to refer to the Bible, and others thought it meant Jesus. Other observers have noted that the phrase claims that Thy Word *Is* Truth but leaves open the claim that it is *the* truth. For President Lapp, the motto referred to Jesus—the Word made flesh.[50] One retired professor of literature captured an idea that explains not only why the motto endured but also why it finds smooth sailing in the murky waters of liquid modernity: "We can interpret it any way we want, because that is what we do when we read anything."[51]

Is EMU Still Christian?

Some scholars have studied "survivor" colleges and universities—those that remain, in Max Weber's terminology, "enchanted" by retaining strong religious identities within a secular world. Robert Benne researched how six premier schools have remained coupled with their religious traditions.[52] Another investigation of fourteen colleges and universities from seven different Christian heritages examined the same question.[53] Although the stories, contexts, and religious traditions of each school are distinct, the researchers asked, How robust was the institution's *commitment to a Christian identity*? And how strong were the school's *ties to its denomination*, religious order, or religious constituents?

Those two issues were prominent in the founders' thinking. EMS catalogs in the first two decades highlighted its *Christian* commitment, *denominational* affiliation, and beautiful *location*. The physical splendor of the Shenandoah Valley remained, but the twenty-first century brought new questions about where EMU stood on the intersection of Christian faith and denominational allegiance.

To assess the *Christian* dimension, scholars like Benne typically examine an institution's mission or vision statement, required courses in religion, chapel attendance, religion departments, faculty commitments to religion, and campus ethos. An abundance of evidence suggests that EMU remains an enchanted garden of higher education. The first line of EMU's 2016–2017 catalog declares that it is a "Christian university like no other." Statements of mission, vision, and values explicitly underscore the university's Christian identity, along with phrases like *our Christian community*, *Christ's call*, *Christian faith*, and *Christian discipleship*, which unapologetically anchor its public identity in Christian faith.

EMU's course requirements are also tied to its mission statement. Among the thirty-eight credits in the EMU Core, students are required to take at least eight Christian Faith credits, including one course on Anabaptist-biblical perspectives and another on Christian identity and witness. The eight credits do not adequately reflect the pervasive influence of religion across the curriculum, because faculty seek to integrate Christian perspectives into nonreligion courses as well. Even so, EMU's Bible and religion department of seven faculty is substantial for a university with fewer than a thousand undergraduate students. The department offers five majors as well as several minors.

Chapel services, held twice a week, are not required, but students are expected to attend at least one each week. Attendance ranges from several dozen to several hundred, depending on the program. That required chapel attendance ended in the mid-2000s may reflect the Anabaptist emphasis on voluntarism, or on praxis rather than dogma. On the other hand, it may signal some incipient secularization.[54]

EMU's Christian commitment is also reflected in its hiring practices. All candidates who apply for tenure-track positions across the university write essays about their spiritual journeys. The essays address how their Christian commitments shape their worldview, daily faith, and participation in church life. Moreover, candidates indicate their willingness to support EMU's philosophy, mission, and Community Lifestyle Commitment (CLC), as well as the *Confession of Faith in a Mennonite Perspective*.

Researchers like Benne emphasize the importance of campus ethos and institutional culture as indicators of religious vitality. This includes religious-oriented activities, rituals with religious content, and public discourse on religion in student newspapers and public events. Such elements of Christian commitment abound at EMU in religiously oriented student clubs and public events. The preamble to the CLC invokes the lordship of Jesus Christ and the Scriptures as its source of legitimacy. Prayers or brief devotionals open the meetings of some academic departments, the faculty senate, and the president's cabinet. Moreover, worship is a hallmark of the fall faculty-staff conference. These rituals remind everyone that they are members of an "enchanted" university. While mission statements, course credits, and rituals can rightly be suspected of marketing spin, there is little evidence to challenge EMU's claim of being a Christian university. But what *kind* of Christian university? We will explore that question later in this chapter.

Institutions of higher learning with a prominent commitment to Christian faith carry an extra burden. In addition to the typical academic and campus life challenges, they must devote considerable energy to religious issues. These loom large in a Christian setting because they evoke moral and religious sentiments. Historically, practices reflecting religious beliefs provoked the most public debate at EMU: drama, dancing, instrumental music, intercollegiate athletics, and same-sex relationships. Academic controversies rarely last as long or generate as much heat as religious and moral ones. To this day, a moral lapse such as adultery, not worth a raised eyebrow in a secular school, creates a stir at EMU because employees have pledged to support the CLC and are seen as exemplars for student behavior.

"Why," asked an exasperated trustee, "do we spend so much time arguing about theological issues? Are we a debate society?"[55] The rhetorical answer is this: because those issues matter so much in a faith-centered institution. The same-sex employment controversy of 2014–2015, which might have been dispatched quietly in the human resources office of a secular school, sparked intense controversy because of its intractable theological questions. Likewise, the *Corpus Christi* imbroglio in 2015 kindled a fire because important religious issues were entangled with administrative protocol.

By the beginning of the twenty-first century, the veracity of a Christian faith claim sounded more scandalous than ever. Ironically, it made EMU's motto, Thy Word Is Truth, seem more countercultural in 2017 than it was in 1917, when Christian worldviews were more widely accepted. The unambiguous claim to be "a Christian university like no other" in 2017 was a stark statement of nonconformity—if not an offensive one—in a world of higher education engulfed in unbelief. Yet two contemporary realities tempered the offense: the reenchantment of the world and new insights into how reality is socially constructed.

Max Weber's grand secularization narrative was breaking apart by the mid-twentieth century. Scholars were citing evidence that the world remained enchanted with new secular forms of "religion," the persistence of traditional religions, and novel expressions of spirituality quite different from conventional religious beliefs and practices.[56] Besides, growing evidence underscored how an individual's worldview was constructed and shaped by his or her social location in ethnicity, race, gender, class, and religion.[57] The wider acceptance of social constructivism granted a seat of respect to everyone at the twenty-first-century table, whether atheist, feminist, Marxist, Hindu, or Christian. Thus, while a Christian university might seem peculiar, it still has as legitimate a seat at the table as any other worldview.

Is EMU Still Mennonite?

The strength of a school's *denominational* affiliation involves people, money, and governance. Does the institution have a critical mass of students, staff, and faculty who are affiliated with the sponsoring denomination? How significant is the ecclesial body's influence on governance and financial support?

As noted in chapter 11, the proportion of Mennonite students in EMU's traditional undergraduate program has declined steadily in the last twenty-five years, dropping from 72 percent in 1990 to 32 percent in 2016. Between 2010 and 2016, Mennonites slipped from one-half to one-third of the student body.[58] In part, this reflected a marketing strategy to recruit regional students regardless of religious affiliation in order to increase undergraduate enrollment. It is not clear whether regional students were drawn to EMU because of its geographical convenience, religious identity, sports program, academic offerings, or other qualities. Nonetheless, changes in the religious background of students will produce long-term consequences for alumni membership, fund-raising, and other forms of support. If the decline in Mennonite students continues, the religious ethos of the student body will also surely change.

The proportion of Mennonites among tenured faculty remained steady at 78 percent in the five-year period from 2009 to 2014.[59] But figures can mislead. Some faculty affiliated with non-Mennonite churches were more enthused about an Anabaptist-Mennonite university than were some lifelong Mennonites. One faculty member, the granddaughter of a former president, was more animated about Anabaptist values than membership in a Mennonite church.

The number of EMU alumni on the faculty was another indicator of critical mass. In 2015, one-third of the undergraduate faculty had received their baccalaureate or master's degree from EMU.[60] While this might suggest provincialism, it also meant a sizable segment of the faculty held a deep memory of institutional history and a hearty commitment to EMU's values.

Governance policies also strengthen denominational ties. Virginia Conference, guardian of EMU from 1924 to 1984, no longer has official jurisdiction over the university. Still, many staff and faculty continue to participate in Virginia Conference congregations and activities. At the national level, the Mennonite Education

Agency (MEA) coordinates the five Mennonite colleges (Bethel, Bluffton, EMU, Goshen, Hesston), linking them to Mennonite Church USA.

The MEA has a separate Statement of Arrangements (SOA) with each Mennonite college, and each college has its own bylaws.[61] While EMU holds legal title to its property, at least three quarters of the EMU trustees are appointed by the MEA. The rest are appointed by the board of trustees itself. Except for two who are selected for their expertise, trustees must be members of MC USA congregations or of related denominations.[62] MEA and EMU's trustees jointly approve presidential searches and appoint the president. EMU's trustees approve faculty appointments within the SOA guidelines, which stipulate that 75 percent of tenure-track faculty hold membership in MC USA congregations or related denominations.[63]

The MEA plays an important role in prodding the Mennonite colleges to remain in conversation with each other. "It is very helpful," said one EMU official, "in managing common financial investments, pooling health insurance, and encouraging us to collaborate." One example is a collaborative MBA program offered by EMU, Bluffton, and Goshen. Another is a collaborative undergraduate sociology major. These programs are largely online courses that involve teleconferencing at the three schools.[64] Such willingness to collaborate more and compete less, noted one observer, relates somewhat to the growing regional orientation of Mennonite colleges.[65]

As for financial support, nearly 60 percent of all contributions to EMU come from individuals (alumni, parents, and friends) who are either current or past members of Mennonite congregations. Mennonite Church organizations contribute about 5 percent of the financial gifts. Altogether, about two-thirds of EMU's philanthropic support is given by people and organizations linked to MC USA or Mennonite-affiliated entities.[66]

These indicators attest to a vibrant ongoing relationship with EMU's sponsoring denomination. Even so, at the threshold of the university's second century, challenges remain. If power follows revenue, the MEA's authority is somewhat tenuous. The bulk of its income originates from a required fee contributed by the organizations it coordinates. (EMU's annual fee is about $82,000.) Some MEA policies, such as those pertaining to the proportion of Mennonite faculty, "are difficult to enforce," said a former Goshen College president. "Fordism never really worked."[67] Thus the MEA and the Mennonite institutions of higher education are essentially bound together by a goodwill agreement to remain in conversation about collaboration.

Following the 2002 merger that gave birth to MC USA, denominational membership declined as some congregations and conferences withdrew over theological and cultural differences. From a premerger high of 120,000 in 2000, membership slid to 79,000 by 2016.[68] Although MC USA is EMU's sponsoring body, denominational strife over same-sex issues and EMU's employment decision in 2015 weakened the school's ties to the church. This increased the need for more students and a wider circle of supporters who are enthused about promoting an Anabaptist-oriented university.

Robert Benne contends that more than anything else, a Christian college or university needs a strong core of faculty and administrators who are passionate about the institution's religious vision and mission irrespective of their church affiliation.[69] If EMU's denominational ties decline, it will need a stalwart team of faculty and administrators who are passionate about an Anabaptist worldview for it to flourish as a Christian university engaged in countercultural education.

A Third Way

Every college or university aims to distinguish itself in its branding. But what kind of Christian university is EMU, and how is it unique? That question has been asked repeatedly over the years. In an entire issue of *Crossroads* devoted to EMU's distinctives, one essay was titled "Why EMU Is Not Harvard or Duke (and Why We Feel Fine about It)."[70]

When a congregation criticized EMC&S for being too liberal in 1994, communications director Steve Shenk told President Lapp, "I was raised to believe that the Anabaptist-Mennonite way is neither mainline-liberal nor conservative-evangelical. . . . EMC&S offers a *third way*."[71] This notion emerged from a book on the sixteenth-century Anabaptists titled *Anabaptism: Neither Catholic nor Protestant*.[72] Harold Bender's *Anabaptist Vision*, which offered an alternative to the liberal and fundamentalist camps in the early twentieth century, also reflected a third-way option. Another rendition appeared in Paul M. Lederach's 1980 book *A Third Way: Conversations about Anabaptist/Mennonite Faith*. An interactive website of MC USA is also named Third Way; it introduces the public to Anabaptist-Mennonite faith and thus continues to illustrate attachment to this identity in 2017. While the phrase carries some potential for smugness, it has nevertheless become shorthand for a unique worldview that Anabaptists have come to represent.[73]

Thus it is not surprising to find EMU aspiring to become "the premier Christian university offering a *third way*." With these words in the 2015–2020 strategic plan, institutional visionaries argued that "EMU's rootedness in the Anabaptist-Mennonite faith tradition—emphasizing the ethical practice of Christian faith and the search for peace and justice in this world—provides a rich base from which such a third way can develop and progress."[74] Their use of third-way language focused on EMU's identity *inside* the orbit of Christian higher education.

In the words of one senior official, "*Anabaptist* articulates the third-way niche that we're trying to fill. We want to have an intentional, faith-based, Christian engagement with the world. And Anabaptism captures that third way, that Jesus-based engagement with the world. That's what distinguishes us from Wheaton and Calvin, and also from the Methodist and United Church of Christ colleges that have kind of drifted away from their churches."[75] For EMU, the third-way vision offers an alternative to the strident religious conservatism of some Christian colleges and the ambivalent liberal progressivism of others.

EMU's pursuit of an alternative path became clear in 2015 when Jerry Falwell Jr., president of Liberty University, urged his students to purchase guns and take a free on-campus course on gun safety. President Swartzendruber quickly spoke out, saying that EMU "does not support or condone such practices." He found it distressing that the views and actions of Christian leaders like Falwell might encourage "even more violence."[76] That same year, EMU's decision to extend employment to noncelibate LGBTQ staff and faculty threatened to split the Council for Christian Colleges and Universities (CCCU). To prevent that from occurring, EMU and Goshen College chose to withdraw from the CCCU, setting them apart from the 120 other CCCU members that had restrictive employment policies.

Introducing the culture of a third-way Christian university to students from diverse cultural and religious backgrounds is a challenge. One professor noted, "Some students are accustomed to having the 'Star Spangled Banner,' flag-waving, and maybe the Pledge of Allegiance at school sporting events. EMU doesn't do any of that at our games. At first, some students find us disrespectful, because these are powerful symbols. So I explain to them why we are different. And we talk about the Mennonite peace position to help them understand our perspective."[77]

If any new students were confused about what it meant to attend such a university in the fall of 2016, they may have caught a hint as Provost Fred Kniss spoke at the matriculation ceremony. Kniss reminded the students, "Over the course of this summer, societies around the world have been bombarded almost continuously by horrific acts of physical and emotional violence—violence against African Americans, against members of the LGBTQ community, against immigrants and refugees, against Muslims, against Christians, against Democrats, against Republicans." In the midst of such malice, he explained, "EMU strives to provide an alternative—a community of learning where differences are valued, where respectful debate is encouraged, and where we collaborate across our differences in order to constructively confront the very real challenges we face as a human species."

The provost's next words may have surprised any student who had scoffed at these ideas as just politically correct pabulum. "Most importantly for EMU, 'a Christian university like no other,' the soul of our university is animated by the love of Jesus. The love of Jesus has a dual impact on our learning. First, in Jesus, we meet the God who is love, and we begin to comprehend the nature of God's love for us, for creation, and especially for those on the margins. Second, as we reflect the love of Jesus in our own lives, we are moved to take the risk of reaching across our boundaries to engage those on our own margins."

Kniss then reminded them that ever since the sixteenth century, Anabaptist-Mennonite Christians have contended "that we can see and experience the love of God best and most concretely in the life and teachings of Jesus, and that as Christians we express God's love by following the way of Jesus. This core theological claim is our university's distinctive character within the broad liberal arts stream, and even distinguishes us from many other Christian liberal arts universities."

In closing, Provost Kniss urged them to heed EMU's vision, which he said, "[challenges] us to commit ourselves to offering healing and hope in our diverse world by doing justice, loving mercy, and walking humbly with God. As we live into that vision, we follow Jesus' call to bear witness to truth, serve with compassion, and walk boldly in the way of nonviolence and peace."[78]

When faculty and staff convened on August 17, 2016, for their annual gathering, the setting aptly marked EMU's century-long commitment to the call of Jesus. They met at Park View Mennonite Church, about five blocks north of the long-gone White House, where the first Special Bible Term in Harrisonburg had opened in January 1916.

In that early venue, Bishop L. J. Heatwole had finally seen his efforts to start a school in the East come to fruition. He was profoundly moved by the beauty of the singing. It seemed "so perfect" with the lovely voices of the sopranos, the "rich and soothing tones" from the altos, the soaring notes of the tenors, and "the deep, resounding voices of the basses." Echoing through the woods, "the singing seemed so rapturous and so inspiring as to give the old building . . . a veneration and a sanctity that must continue."[79] The White House eventually fell, but the venerable singing, the very soul of the school, survived.

In the sanctuary of the Park View church, unison and four-part singing carried the century-old tradition forward, now joined by piano, flute, and drums. Staff and faculty celebrated the cultural diversity of the world church and of EMU itself. The moving songs of praise that had opened the school's first century—an evocative tradition that bound everyone together—had endured. "The singing really built community for me," Professor Vi Dutcher recalled. "I was back together with these people whom I can actually say I love. I don't just work with them; I love them."[80]

Acknowledgments

Community is a core value in the history and culture of Eastern Mennonite University. This book reflects that communal spirit. My trail of gratitude to those who have generously supported this project begins at the Young Center for Anabaptist and Pietist Studies at Elizabethtown College, my academic home. Young Center director Jeff Bach and my wonderful colleagues at the center have supported my efforts on this project over the past seven years. Cynthia Nolt, my longtime colleague, deserves a paragraph of her own for her superb research and editorial skills and meticulous attention to detail. With tact and patience, she frequently saved me from authorial embarrassment. Young Center student assistants Samantha M. Kick, Katherine Frances Rozman, and Crystal Uminski performed a host of research tasks with enthusiasm and delight.

At Eastern Mennonite University, archivist Nathan E. Yoder, who in 2011 first proposed that I undertake this project, was a bounteous source of knowledge of EMU's past, Mennonite Church history, and theological issues. His knack for finding obscure documents in the archives was remarkable. Yoder's written summaries of particular topics and their chronological development saved me enormous time. I also benefited immensely from the kind assistance and expertise of EMU's library directors, Beryl Brubaker and (after 2015) Marci Frederick, and Special Collections librarian Simone Horst. The university's professional library staff and work-study students—including Thane Hostetler, who devoted two summers to the project—dedicated countless hours to researching, processing, scanning, and transcribing materials. The library staff always welcomed my visits with warm hospitality and robust coffee. The staff and faculty in other EMU departments also kindly obliged my frequent requests for help.

Jo Anne Kraus graciously shared her research and knowledge of the history of the Warwick River Mennonite settlement near Newport News, Virginia. James Rush and Harold D. Lehman deserve special thanks for explaining the history of Assembly Park and the physical layout of the early campus. An EMU advisory committee of Michael A. King, Fred Kniss, Mark Metzler Sawin, Andrea Wenger, Nathan E. Yoder, and Twila Yoder provided overall guidance for the project. I was most honored that they granted me broad latitude to select topics and craft the narrative without any restraints or censorship.

I benefited from constructive criticism and helpful suggestions from three scholarly reviewers selected by Penn State University Press. In addition, the following people offered incisive reactions and corrections on selected chapters or on the entire manuscript: Beryl Brubaker, Edsel Burdge, Marci Frederick, Simone Horst, Susan Schultz Huxman, Michael A. King, Fred Kniss, Mark Metzler Sawin, Shirley Hershey Showalter, Lee F. Snyder, Mary Sprunger, Loren Swartzendruber, Andrea Wenger, and Nathan E. Yoder. I was especially fortunate to have conversation partners who thoroughly critiqued certain sections and topics of the narrative and engaged in helpful give-and-take: Beryl Brubaker, Marci Frederick, Simone Horst, Mark Metzler Sawin, Sara Wenger Shenk, Shirley Hershey Showalter, Steven M. Nolt, and Nathan E. Yoder. Some of their suggestions appear in the text without credit. Advice from this community of readers has greatly enhanced the narrative. Even so, I hold responsibility for the final version of the text.

Natasha Sawatsky-Kingsley scoured pertinent sources at Mennonite Church USA Archives and transcribed some of my interviews. The perceptive eyes and editorial acumen of Cynthia Nolt and Byron Rempel-Burkholder refined and polished every line of every chapter. I was fortunate to collaborate with such highly skilled editors.

Some three dozen people knowledgeable about different aspects of EMU's past granted me lengthy face-to-face interviews. These included Ruth Stauffer Alger, Robert Alger, A. Don Augsburger, Esther K. Augsburger, Myron S. Augsburger, Lee Roy Berry, Doris Good Bomberger, James Bomberger, Lois B. Bowman, Beryl Brubaker, Edsel Burdge, Vi Dutcher, Vernon Jantzi, Fred Kniss, C. Norman Kraus, Jay B. Landis, Peggy Heatwole Landis, Joseph L. Lapp, John A. Lapp, Harold D. Lehman, Bonnie Price Lofton, Catherine R. Mumaw, Kenneth L. Nafziger, Mark Thiessen Nation, Hubert Pellman, Mildred Kauffman Pellman, Theron Schlabach, N. Gerald Shenk, Donald E. Showalter, James Stauffer, Loren Swartzendruber, Samuel O. Weaver, Chester L. Wenger, Sara Jane Weaver Wenger, Andrea Wenger, Lee Yoder, Lonnie Yoder, and Nathan E. Yoder. In addition, several dozen alumni, current staff, and some scholars unaffiliated with EMU provided information in person, via e-mail, and by phone. I appreciate the wisdom, perspective, and gracious gift of time that these people shared.

It was a pleasure to work with Penn State University Press acquisitions editor Kathryn B. Yahner and her professional colleagues, who smoothly navigated all the twists and turns of publication to produce a well-designed and beautiful book.

Appendix A

Chronology of Key Events

1912	Eastern school advocates meet in Denbigh, VA (Dec.)
1915	Special Bible Term at Hayfield Mansion, Alexandria, VA (Jan.)
1916	Special Bible Term at Assembly Park, Harrisonburg, VA (Jan.)
1917	Special Bible Term at Assembly Park (Jan.)
1917	Purchase of Assembly Park (Apr.)
1917	First six students register at Eastern Mennonite School (Oct. 10)
1917	J. B. Smith assumes office as first president (Oct. 22)
1919	Administration Building, the "Cracker Box," constructed
1921	Commonwealth of Virginia accredits EMS high school programs
1922	A. D. Wenger assumes office as second president
1926	Administration Building's south annex (chapel, dining room) constructed
1930	Commonwealth of Virginia accredits EMS as junior college
1935	J. L. Stauffer assumes office as third president
1939	*Weather Vane* begins publication
1941	Administration Building's north annex (library, science room) constructed
1943	Chapel constructed (named Lehman Auditorium in 1976)
1947	Eastern Mennonite School renamed Eastern Mennonite College
1947	Commonwealth of Virginia accredits EMC as a four-year college
1948	John R. Mumaw assumes office as fourth president
1948	Willis Johnson, EMC's first African American student, admitted
1950–1951	Virginia Mennonite Conference investigates EMC for liberalism
1959	Southern Association of Colleges and Schools accredits EMC
1964	High school building constructed
1964	Eastern Mennonite Seminary begins
1965	Myron Augsburger assumes office as fifth president
1967	Science Center constructed
1969	Student Government Association formed
1969	Students initiate fund drive for new library building

(continued)

1972	First overseas cross-cultural study term
1976	EMC admitted into Old Dominion Athletic Conference
1976–1977	Washington Study-Service Year begins (renamed Washington Community Scholars' Center in 2002)
1980	Richard Detweiler assumes office as sixth president
1982	Eastern Mennonite High School legally separates from EMC
1984	Administration Building burns (Jan.)
1984	EMC&S becomes accountable to Mennonite Board of Education
1986	Association of Theological Schools accredits the seminary
1986	New Campus Center dedicated
1987	Joseph Lapp assumes office as seventh president
1989	Lancaster satellite program established
1993	Master's in counseling offered as first nontheological graduate degree
1993	Bach Festival inaugurated
1993	Seminary building constructed
1994	Eastern Mennonite College renamed Eastern Mennonite University
1994	Adult Degree Completion Program begins
1994	Conflict Transformation Program (later, Center for Justice and Peacebuilding) established
2000	University Commons constructed
2000	Beryl Brubaker appointed first provost
2002	EMU becomes accountable to Mennonite Education Agency
2004	Loren Swartzendruber assumes office as eighth president
2009	Fred Kniss becomes provost
2014	School of Graduate and Professional Studies organized
2017	Susan Schultz Huxman assumes office as ninth president

Appendix B

EMU Annual Enrollment, 1917–1950

	High School	College	Other	Total
1917–1918	19	0	58	77
1918–1919	38	0	81	119
1919–1920	77	0	237	314
1920–1921	87	4	125	216
1921–1922	105	14	148	267
1922–1923	98	16	112	226
1923–1924	81	10	130	221
1924–1925	96	20	183	299
1925–1926	116	20	102	238
1926–1927	136	25	80	241
1927–1928	133	24	296	453
1928–1929	129	26	288	443
1929–1930	115	34	282	431
1930–1931	109	39	229	377
1931–1932	121	37	107	265
1932–1933	121	40	173	334
1933–1934	89	42	213	344
1934–1935	111	45	172	328
1935–1936	117	42	190	349
1936–1937	134	38	186	358
1937–1938	142	50	162	354
1938–1939	141	40	121	302
1939–1940	188	54	95	337
1940–1941	206	55	99	360
1941–1942	256	78	112	446
1942–1943	206	82	113	401
1943–1944	242	90	186	518
1944–1945	272	91	248	611
1945–1946	286	133	235	654
1946–1947	281	153	206	640
1947–1948	251	206	274	731

(continued)

	High School	College	Other	Total
1948–1949	254	258	293	805
1949–1950	192	254	246	692
Totals	**4,949**	**2,020**	**5,782**	**12,751**

Note: The table portrays full school-year enrollment, including part-time and special students, but not including those enrolled in summer school or extension courses. High school and college levels include Bible school registration. Other includes Special Bible Term and correspondence courses.

Sources: President's Annual Report in *Bulletin*; Pellman, *EMC*, 269.

Appendix C

EMU Annual Enrollment, 1950–2017

	Undergraduate	Graduate	Total
1950–1951	238	8	246
1951–1952	210	7	217
1952–1953	235	6	241
1953–1954	229	10	239
1954–1955	288	10	298
1955–1956	340	13	353
1956–1957	373	5	378
1957–1958	395	4	399
1958–1959	453	9	462
1959–1960	430	5	435
1960–1961	481	13	494
1961–1962	502	10	512
1962–1963	519	8	527
1963–1964	568	10	578
1964–1965	567	8	575
1965–1966	608	9	617
1966–1967	728	8	736
1967–1968	786	10	796
1968–1969	830	21	851
1969–1970	901	20	921
1970–1971	909	28	937
1971–1972	938	40	978
1972–1973	885	35	920
1973–1974	912	45	957
1974–1975	860	52	912
1975–1976	936	52	988
1976–1977	965	50	1,015
1977–1978	1,024	72	1,096
1978–1979	1,025	57	1,082
1979–1980	1,010	78	1,088
1980–1981	1,036	64	1,100

(continued)

	Undergraduate	Graduate	Total
1981–1982	979	62	1,041
1982–1983	919	50	969
1983–1984	858	55	913
1984–1985	824	54	878
1985–1986	789	53	842
1986–1987	747	55	802
1987–1988	834	77	911
1988–1989	932	64	996
1989–1990	906	74	980
1990–1991	921	70	991
1991–1992	930	87	1,017
1992–1993	911	75	986
1993–1994	920	97	1,017
1994–1995	953	106	1,059
1995–1996	964	111	1,075
1996–1997	991	136	1,127
1997–1998	991	135	1,126
1998–1999	1,066	132	1,198
1999–2000	1,081	140	1,221
2000–2001	1,073	164	1,237
2001–2002	1,064	171	1,235
2002–2003	1,048	179	1,227
2003–2004	1,019	197	1,216
2004–2005	1,031	208	1,239
2005–2006	1,014	235	1,249
2006–2007	1,038	215	1,253
2007–2008	1,025	211	1,236
2008–2009	954	205	1,159
2009–2010	1,020	223	1,243
2010–2011	1,043	228	1,271
2011–2012	1,030	223	1,253
2012–2013	1,086	212	1,298
2013–2014	1,145	232	1,377
2014–2015	1,159	245	1,404
2015–2016	1,136	329	1,465
2016–2017	1,159	300	1,459

Note: Undergraduate includes nontraditional Adult Degree Completion Programs. Graduate includes Eastern Mennonite Seminary, Center for Justice and Peacebuilding, and other graduate programs. Full-time *headcount* data are reported from 1950–1951 to 1970–1971. Full-time *equivalent* data are reported from 1971–1972 to 2016–2017. The table includes enrollment for the Harrisonburg and Lancaster programs. It does not include high school enrollment or noncredit courses such as the Intensive English Program.

Source: EMU Registrar's Office.

Abbreviations for Manuscript Collections and Depositories

(Note: Eastern Mennonite University Archives are located in Harrisonburg, VA.)

ADW	Amos D. Wenger Presidential Records, Eastern Mennonite University Archives
AGH	Abram G. Heishman Collection, Eastern Mennonite University Archives
ANK	Albert N. Keim Deans Records, Eastern Mennonite University Archives
CKL	Chester K. Lehman Collection, Eastern Mennonite University Archives
DK	Daniel Kauffman Papers, Mennonite Church USA Archives, Elkhart, IN
DWL	Daniel W. Lehman Collection, Virginia Mennonite Conference Archives, Harrisonburg, VA
EGG	Ernest G. Gehman Collection, Eastern Mennonite University Archives
EMUA	Eastern Mennonite University Archives
GRB1	George R. Brunk I (George Reuben, 1871–1938) Collection, Virginia Mennonite Conference Archives, Harrisonburg, VA
GRB2	George R. Brunk I (George Reuben, 1871–1938) Collection, Eastern Mennonite University Archives
HSB	Harold S. Bender Papers, Goshen College Archives, Goshen, IN
IEM	Ira E. Miller Collection, Eastern Mennonite University Archives
JBS	Jacob B. Smith Presidential Records, Eastern Mennonite University Archives
JEH	J. E. Hartzler Papers, Goshen College Archives, Goshen, IN
JJW	John J. Wenger Collection, Eastern Mennonite University Archives
JLL	Joseph L. Lapp Presidential Records, Eastern Mennonite University Archives
JLS	John L. Stauffer Presidential Records, Eastern Mennonite University Archives
JRM	John R. Mumaw Presidential Records, Eastern Mennonite University Archives
JRMCOLL	John R. Mumaw Collection, Eastern Mennonite University Archives
KCR	Kraybill Centennial Research Collection, Eastern Mennonite University Archives

(continued)

LJH	Lewis J. Heatwole Collection, Virginia Mennonite Conference Archives, Harrisonburg, VA
LMHSA	Lancaster Mennonite Historical Society Archives, Lancaster, PA
LMY	Lee M. Yoder Administrative Records, Eastern Mennonite University Archives
MBE*	Mennonite Board of Education Collection, Mennonite Church USA Archives, Elkhart, IN
MGC	Mennonite General Conference Collection, Mennonite Church USA Archives, Elkhart, IN
MHACVA	Mennonite Historical Association of the Cumberland Valley Archives, Chambersburg, PA
MSA	Myron S. Augsburger Presidential Records, Eastern Mennonite University Archives
MSHL	Menno Simons Historical Library, Eastern Mennonite University, Harrisonburg, VA
MTB	Maurice T. Brackbill Collection, Eastern Mennonite University Archives
OOM	Orie O. Miller Papers, Mennonite Church USA Archives, Elkhart, IN
RCD	Richard C. Detweiler Presidential Records, Eastern Mennonite University Archives
RWC	Religious Welfare Committee, Eastern Mennonite University Archives
SCY	Sanford C. Yoder Papers, Goshen College Archives, Goshen, IN
SHR	Samuel H. Rhodes Collection, Virginia Mennonite Conference Archives, Harrisonburg, VA
TFD	Task Force on Dance, Eastern Mennonite University Archives
VMCA	Virginia Mennonite Conference Archives, Harrisonburg, VA
WMS	Willard M. Swartley Deans Records, Eastern Mennonite University Archives

*Some records in this collection may be housed at the Goshen College Archives.

***

Minutes, Reports, and Documents Cited without a Depository

(All are housed in the Eastern Mennonite University Archives)

Administration Committee minutes

Administrative Council minutes

Charter

Committee on Administration minutes

Constitution

Dean's Reports

Eastern Mennonite Seminary (EMS) Dean's Reports

Faculty minutes

Faculty senate minutes

Faculty status committee minutes

General Board minutes

Micah Think Tank minutes

Opinion Board documents

President's cabinet minutes

President's Reports

RWC (Religious Welfare Committee) minutes

SACS (Southern Association of Colleges and Schools) accreditation reports and
materials

Standards Committee minutes

Trustee minutes

Trustees Academic Affairs Committee minutes

University Graduate Council minutes

***

EMU Publications

(All EMU publications are cited in the notes only, not in the bibliography)

Bulletin	Quarterly periodical for students, friends, and alumni (1920–1994)
Catalog	Undergraduate catalog
Crossroads	Alumni magazine (1994–)
EMC	*Eastern Mennonite College, 1917–1967: A History*, by Hubert R. Pellman
Factbook	Annual compilation of institutional data (1976–)
Handbook	Student policy booklet
Journal	Monthly periodical written by students for friends and alumni (1923–1956)
PeaceBuilder	Publication of the Center for Justice and Peacebuilding (2005–)
The Seminarian	Newsletter of Eastern Mennonite Seminary (1970–1997)
Shenandoah	Student yearbook (1947–)
Standards	Student behavioral expectations booklet
Weather Vane	Student newspaper (1939–)

***

Abbreviations in Bibliography

GH	*Gospel Herald*
MQR	*Mennonite Quarterly Review*
ST	*Sword and Trumpet*

Notes

PREFACE

1. Twila Yoder, e-mail message to author, June 8, 2015.
2. Gbowee tells the story of the protest in her book, *Mighty Be Our Powers*, and in the documentary film *Pray the Devil Back to Hell*.
3. Berger, *Facing Up to Modernity*, 61.
4. Juhnke, *Vision, Doctrine, War*, 164, 304; Sprunger, *Bethel College*, 16–17; Bush, *Dancing with the Kobzar*, 25–38, 64–70. Although Bethel College was chartered in 1887, the first classes were held in 1893.
5. *Family Almanac 1910*, 56. The membership count does not include the three Amish-Mennonite conferences and two Canadian conferences.
6. Heatwole to "Dear Brother [unnamed]," Jan. 5, 1915, B3, F14, LJH. Slight editing for stylistic reasons.
7. Gleason, *Contending with Modernity*.

CHAPTER I
EPIGRAPH: Hartzler and Kauffman, *Mennonite Church History*, 358.

1. Unless otherwise noted, the sources for this section are A. D. Wenger, "Tour to Foreign Lands Diary," books 1 and 2, B1, F1, ADW, and A. D. Wenger, *Around the World*. For other accounts of Wenger's trip, see Ruth, *The Earth Is the Lord's*, 754–59, and Charles, "Innocents Abroad," 3–5.
2. George Lambert, whose Mennonite Church membership was brief (1896–1911), had written *Around the Globe and through Bible Lands* based on his trip in 1894–1895. Lambert "almost single-handedly created the momentum for a mission in India, indeed for all overseas Mennonite missions," according to John A. Lapp in *The Mennonite Church in India*, 27–28.
3. Emphasis added.
4. Sara Wenger Shenk, one of Wenger's granddaughters, reflects on Wenger's trip in *Thank You for Asking*, 33–43.
5. Unless otherwise noted, the sources for quotations in this section are Wenger's

unpublished thirteen-page autobiography prepared for his biographer, J. C. Wenger, n.d., ca. 1932, B1, F1, ADW; and John C. Wenger, "Biography of Amos Daniel Wenger until 1933," with handwritten corrections by A. D. Wenger, B1, F1, ADW. Additional sources include Wenger and Kratz, *A. D. Wenger*; Lehman and Cressman, *A. D. & Annie*; M. Wenger, "Ripe Harvest"; and Ruth, *The Earth Is the Lord's*, 754–59.
6. Lehman and Nolt, *Mennonites, Amish, and the Civil War*, 197–212. Other sources for this paragraph are Hartman, *Reminiscences of the Civil War*; L. J. Heatwole, *Mennonite Handbook of Information*, 87–89; and R. J. Heatwole, "Reminiscences of War Days."
7. Wayland, *Bridgewater College*, 1–16.
8. Grove, *L. J. Heatwole*, 151–55; L. J. Heatwole, "A Leave-Taking Sermon," *Journal*, Jan. 1929, 4.
9. Ruth, *The Earth Is the Lord's*, 724.
10. L. J. Heatwole, "The Mennonite Church," 16 (emphasis added). Personal evangelism was also called "direct Gospel work" because it was directed toward individuals.
11. For more on Coffman, see B. Coffman, *His Name Was John*; Steiner, *John S. Coffman*; and *Centennial Memorial of J. S. Coffman*.
12. Wenger and Kratz, *A. D. Wenger*, 14; M. Wenger, "Ripe Harvest," 13.
13. Lehman and Cressman trace the courtship and correspondence in *A. D. & Annie*, 35–38.
14. Historically called "casting lots," this ritual appears in Proverbs 16:33 and was used to select a replacement for Judas in Acts 1:24.
15. Heatwole described his lack of confidence in the lot on December 10, 1895, in a preparatory sermon for the ordination of two ministers. Dissension over those ordinations was one element that stirred unrest in Virginia Conference from 1895 to 1902, resulting in the formation of the Old Order Mennonite Church. Harry Brunk, in *History of Mennonites*, offers a detailed account of the unrest (1:443–518) and excerpts from Heatwole's sermon (1:451–60). See also

Kraybill and Hurd, *Horse-and-Buggy Mennonites*, 22–23.

16. For accounts of L. J. Heatwole's ordination and his homiletic skills, see Grove, *L. J. Heatwole*, 121–24; and H. Brunk, *History of Mennonites*, 1:342, 451.

17. L. J. Heatwole diaries, 1887, 189, B31, LJH.

18. Quoted in Grove, *L. J. Heatwole*, 122–23.

19. L. J. Heatwole diaries, 1887, 196–97, B31, LJH.

20. H. Brunk, *History of Mennonites*, 1:342.

21. Throughout his book *Peace, Faith, Nation*, Theron Schlabach highlights humility in nineteenth-century Mennonite spirituality.

22. The German phrase *Die Stillen im Lande* refers to Psalm 35:20. The "quiet in the land" label, first used in Europe to refer to German Pietists, mystics, and various separatist groups, was later applied to Anabaptist groups. Joe Springer, e-mail message to Steven Nolt, 2009, KCR.

23. L. J. Heatwole, *Mennonite Handbook of Information*, 67–70.

24. Sawatsky and Holland, *Limits of Perfection*, and Kaufman, *Nonresistance and Responsibility*, address these issues.

25. Denlinger, *Glimpses Past*, 81–91, provides many examples of nonconformity practices from the pages of *Herald of Truth, Gospel Witness,* and *Gospel Herald* between 1870 and 1922.

26. L. J. Heatwole, "The Mennonite Church," 12.

27. L. J. Heatwole, "The Virginia Conference."

28. H. Brunk, *History of Mennonites*, 1:299; *Minutes of the Virginia Conference*, 1:29.

29. *Minutes of the Virginia Conference*, 1:24–35.

30. Juhnke, *Vision, Doctrine, War*, 21–22.

31. The period 1870–1900 is sometimes referred to as the Gilded Age and the years 1890–1920 as the Progressive Era. No sharp demarcations divide these time periods.

32. B2, F6, ADW.

33. Sobek, "New Statistics on the US Labor Force, 1850–1990," 71; Haines, "Population of the United States," 156.

34. Hounshell, *Mass Production*.

35. Hirschman and Mogford, "Immigration and the American Industrial Revolution."

36. Lears, *Rebirth of a Nation*, 45–46, 197.

37. Evans, "Social Gospel."

38. O'Neill, "Higher Criticism."

39. Hounshell, *Mass Production*, 217–61; Harvey, *Condition of Postmodernity*, 125–40.

40. *Report of Preliminary General Conference Meeting*, 1897, KCR.

41. Ibid.

42. D. Kauffman, "A General Conference."

43. *Report of Preliminary General Conference Meeting*, 1897, KCR.

44. L. J. Heatwole, *Mennonite Handbook of Information*, 126.

45. *Minutes of General Conference*, 1898, KCR.

46. Theron Schlabach, in *Peace, Faith, Nation*, 295–321, summarizes the Great Transformation, which he calls a "quickening."

47. D. Kauffman, "A General Conference."

48. Daniel Kauffman to N. E. Byers, Feb. 6, 1908, B1, F24, MBE-Goshen, MBE (emphasis added).

49. See Gollner, "How Mennonites Became White."

50. L. J. Heatwole, *Mennonite Handbook of Information*, 144–45; Schlabach, *Gospel versus Gospel*, 28–47.

51. D. Miller, "Progress of the Mennonite Church," 10–12.

52. Shoemaker, Shetler, and Weaver, *Christian Worker's Manual*.

53. D. Kauffman, "A General Conference."

54. Kolb, Editorial Notes, 65.

55. Weber, *Theory of Social and Economic Organization*, 324–58; Kalberg, "Max Weber's Types of Rationality."

56. Ruth, *The Earth Is the Lord's*, 744.

57. A chapter in Daniel Kauffman's *Bible Doctrine* is titled "Personal Work."

58. Ruth, *The Earth Is the Lord's*, 788–90 (quotation revised); Graybill, Landis, and Sauder, *Noah H. Mack*, 112–15.

59. D. Kauffman, *Briefly Stated*, 23–26.

60. D. Kauffman, *A Talk with Church Members*, 91–106.

61. Siegrist, *Mennonite Women of Lancaster County*, 43–55.

62. Ley, *Fashion for Everyone*, 1–11; Hounshell, *Mass Production*, 67–123; Peterson, *Clothing through American History*, 1:14–33.

63. In the late nineteenth century, the Old Order Amish and the Old Order Mennonites wore distinctive plain clothing, but it was not highly codified. See Gingerich, *Mennonite Attire*.

64. D. Kauffman, *Briefly Stated*, 34–36.

65. Juhnke, *Vision, Doctrine, War*, 164. The three groups were the General Conference Mennonite Church, the Mennonite Church, and the Mennonite Brethren.

66. Hartzler and Kauffman, *Mennonite Church History*, 358–59.

67. L. J. Heatwole, *Mennonite Handbook of Information*, 61. The loss of Mennonite youth through attendance at non-Mennonite schools—often called "the school problem"—was a frequent lament of church leaders and laypeople at the turn of the century. For examples, see S. Wenger, "Observations of Goshen College"; A. D. Wenger, *Who Should Educate Our Children?*; A. D. Wenger,

"The Mennonites a Prey of Others"; and H. Bender, *Mennonite Sunday School*.

68. Marsden, *Soul of the American University*, 3–5; Marsden and Longfield, *Secularization of the Academy*, 46–63.

69. For developments in this period, I lean heavily on Mark Noll's splendid essay "The Christian Colleges and American Intellectual Traditions."

70. Sack, *History of Higher Education in Pennsylvania*, vol. 1.

71. C. Heatwole, *History of Education in Virginia*; Bell, *Church, the State, and Education in Virginia*.

72. Durnbaugh, *Brethren Encyclopedia*, vol. 1, s.v. "higher education"; Durnbaugh, *Fruit of the Vine*, 252–62.

73. For histories of Bridgewater College, see P. Bowman, *Brethren Education*, and Wayland, *Bridgewater College*.

74. Kaylor, *Truth Sets Free*; Schlosser, *History of Elizabethtown College*; Williamson, *Uniting Work and Spirit*.

75. Sider, *Messiah College*.

76. Sprunger, *Bethel College*; Bush, *Dancing with the Kobzar*.

77. S. Miller, *Culture for Service*; Umble, *Goshen College*; J. S. Hartzler, "Elkhart Institute," n.d., B8, F8, Goshen College Archives.

78. J. Coffman, "Spirit of Progress," 127.

79. M. Miller, *Pillar of Cloud*; Sharp, *School on the Prairie*.

80. N. E. Byers to A. D. Wenger, Apr. 27, 1903, B4, F5, ADW.

CHAPTER 2

EPIGRAPH: "Special Meeting of the Provisional Board, Hayfield Mansion, Alexandria, Virginia," July 17, 1913, B3, F2, LJH.

1. Unless otherwise noted, sources for this section draw from Lehman and Cressman, *A. D. & Annie*, 155–63.

2. On Mennonite colonization in the United States in the early twentieth century, see H. Brunk, *History of Mennonites*, 1:430–42. The history of the Denbigh settlement is sketched by Jo Anne Kraus in "Holy Experiment" and Harry Brunk in *History of Mennonites*, 2:278–302. In 1958, Denbigh was consolidated as a neighborhood on the north side of Newport News. The city's 2015 population was 183,000.

3. Harry Brunk, in *History of Mennonites*, 2:303–21, and Lehman and Cressman, in *A. D. & Annie*, 207–60, tell the Fentress story.

4. Norfolk (population 246,392 in 2015), located at the core of the Hampton Roads metropolitan area, is a strategic military and transportation center. It is home to the largest navy base in the world and one of NATO's two strategic command headquarters.

5. Chester Wenger, interview by author, June 20, 2013.

6. Biographical sources for George R. Brunk's early life include J. C. Wenger, *Faithfully, Geo. R.*; George R. Brunk, "Life Notes" (handwritten autobiographical reflections), B1, F6, GRB1; Brunk to Harry Diener, Dec. 5, 1931, B1, F24, GRB1; J. Kraus, "Holy Experiment," chaps. 1–4; and J. Kraus, research notes, 2010, KCR.

7. J. Kraus, "Holy Experiment," chap. 5.

8. J. C. Wenger, *Faithfully, Geo. R.*, 19–24; Stoltzfus, *A Way Was Opened*, 28–30.

9. J. C. Wenger, *Faithfully, Geo. R.*, 24.

10. George R. Brunk, "Life Notes," B1, F6, GRB1.

11. In May 1895, Virginia Conference agreed that "a series of meetings could be held occasionally where there are no resident ministers or where the church is weak or on the decline." *Minutes of the Virginia Conference*, 1:45.

12. J. C. Wenger, *Faithfully, Geo. R.*, 32–33.

13. George R. Brunk, autobiographical account to Ernest G. Gehman, n.d., ca. 1930, transcription by Simone Horst, B3, F32, EGG. For a description of the troubles leading to the Old Order division, see H. Brunk, *History of Mennonites*, 1:443–518. The Virginia Old Order division was one of a series in different states that began in Indiana in 1872 described by Kraybill and Hurd, *Horse-and-Buggy Mennonites*, 10–25. See also Hostetler, "Formation of the Old Orders."

14. George R. Brunk, autobiographical account to Ernest G. Gehman, B3, F32, EGG.

15. George R. Brunk, "OPPOSERS # 4," KCR.

16. J. C. Wenger, *Faithfully, Geo. R.*, 63.

17. H. Brunk, *History of Mennonites*, 2:311.

18. Ibid., 2:285–89; J. Kraus, "Holy Experiment," chap. 5.

19. H. Brunk, *History of Mennonites*, 1:360–61.

20. George R. Brunk, "OPPOSERS # 4," KCR.

21. George R. Brunk, autobiographical account to Ernest G. Gehman, B3, F32, EGG (exclamation points in original). Brunk criticized Goshen College for promoting pride and a liberal theology.

22. Nathan E. Yoder, EMU archivist, prepared an extensive document, "Chronology of EMU Board-Related Activity/Documents to September 1917," Trustees Records Group, EMUA. This annotated chronology traces the development of EMU at Denbigh, Alexandria, and Harrisonburg. The minutes of the first eleven meetings at Denbigh (Dec. 18, 1912, through May 15, 1913) are

written in a composition book titled "Warwick Mennonite Institute," B5, F4, GRB1. The newly formed General Board first met on February 26, 1913, with seven successive meetings. The eighth one was held in Denbigh on June 17, 1913, to consider the Alexandria proposal. An abbreviated record of the meetings is provided by George R. Brunk, "Beginnings of the E.M.S.," *Journal*, May 1929, 3–4. See also Pellman, *EMC*, 16–19; and J. Kraus, "Holy Experiment," chap. 5. Unless otherwise cited, the minutes recorded in "Warwick Mennonite Institute" are the source for this section.

23. Beginning at Denbigh in February 1913, the General Board of Eastern Mennonite School was composed of all the officials on various committees and minor boards, including the faculty committee, managing board, board of trustees (responsible for buildings and grounds), constitution committee, finance committee, auditing committee, and others. The term *General Board* and the number and function of subcommittees remained in flux until 1923, when the General Board became the Board of Trustees of Eastern Mennonite School. Until 1923, a subcommittee of the General Board (sometimes called "the trustee committee" and other times called "the board of trustees") functioned at times as a de facto executive committee of the General Board. To complicate matters even more, a charter adopted in 1917 established the corporate name "Trustees of Eastern Mennonite School, Inc." This group of six trustees from the Harrisonburg area, operating without an official constitution, was known as "the Trustee Board." It functioned fairly independently of the General Board, which held a perfunctory annual meeting until 1923, when a constitution was approved. The new constitution dismantled both the trustee board and the General Board and replaced them with a single board of trustees of sixteen men (from Maryland, Pennsylvania, and Virginia) elected by Virginia Conference.

24. The 1632 Dordrecht Confession of Faith was in use in most Mennonite Church settings in 1913.

25. The Warwick Mennonite Institute minutes reported that two-thirds of the household heads of the congregation approved the new site. However, a flyer titled "Preliminary Meeting" (in KCR) says the congregation was "unanimous" in supporting the site.

26. Pellman, *EMC*, 18.

27. George R. Brunk, autobiographical account to Ernest G. Gehman, B3, F32, EGG;

Pellman, *EMC*, 19–29; [Hubert Pellman], "The Story of the Hayfield Proposition," n.d., KCR. (Pellman confirmed his authorship in an interview by the author, Oct. 12, 2012.)

28. Daniel Shenk to A. D. Wenger, June 23, 1913, B3, F4, ADW; Bonnie Price Lofton, "90 Years," *Crossroads*, Summer 2007, 2–30.

29. Brunk to J. J. Wenger, Mar. 6, 1914, B1, F10, JJW; Brunk to J. J. Wenger, Mar. 15, 1914, B1, F10, JJW.

30. The number of acres and the asking price per acre varies somewhat among different proposals.

31. Shenk to A. D. Wenger, June 23, 1913, B3, F4, ADW.

32. *Washington Times*, July 14, 1913, 4; *Washington Herald*, July 15, 1913, 7.

33. Shenk to Daniel Kauffman, July 21, 1913, B1, College Correspondence 1913, DK; Shenk to L. J. Heatwole, July 6, 1914, B3, F24, LJH.

34. Daniel Shenk and George R. Brunk accompanied the committee of three.

35. "Special Meeting of the Provisional Board, Hayfield Mansion, Alexandria, Virginia," July 17, 1913, B3, F2, LJH. See also L. J. Heatwole to "Dear Brother [unnamed]," July 17, 1913, B3, F2, LJH.

36. "Propositions and Statements Advocating a New Location for an Eastern School," two-page document signed by the three members of the committee, B1, F4, JJW; "Special Meeting of the Provisional Board, Hayfield Mansion, Alexandria, Virginia," July 17, 1913, KCR.

37. "Propositions and Statements Advocating a New Location for an Eastern School," B1, F4, JJW.

38. William Wenger, "Memory of George R. Brunk," B1, F1, JJW. Internal and circumstantial evidence suggests that J. J. Wenger likely wrote this document using "William" as a pseudonym.

39. *Minutes of the Virginia Conference*, 1:107.

40. There is no record of how many members of the General Board attended this meeting, nor of the ninth or tenth meetings, apart from passing references by George R. Brunk in "Beginnings of the E.M.S.," *Journal*, May 1929, 3–4; and "Resolutions Passed at the Eleventh Preliminary Meeting of the General Board of the Warwick Mennonite Institute," Nov. 12, 1913, B1, F3, JJW.

41. Shetler declined in early November. Brunk to J. J. Wenger, Nov. 11, 1913, B1, F10, JJW; Brunk to Garber, Nov. 25, [1913], B5, F3, GRB1.

42. From the outset, J. J. Wenger was a member of the finance committee of the General Board. J. M. Shank to J. J. Wenger, Dec.

30, 1912, B1, F25, JJW; David Garber to J. J. Wenger, Apr. 18, 1913, B1, F14, JJW.

43. Garber to J. J. Wenger, Apr. 18, 1913, B1, F14, JJW.

44. Brunk to Chris Garber, Nov. 25, [1913], B5, F3, GRB1.

45. Ibid. (emphasis in the original).

46. Paul E. Whitmer to Daniel Kauffman, Oct. 6, 1920, B1, Corres. Oct.–Dec. 1920, DK.

47. William Wenger, "Memory of George R. Brunk," B1, F1, JJW (emphasis added).

48. Minutes of School Meeting Held at Maugansville, MD, February 17 and 18, 1914, KCR; [Loucks], "Report of School Meeting"; Order of Business, Maugansville, MD, Feb. 17, 1914, B1, F3, JJW; Constitution and Bylaws of the Alexandria Mennonite Institute (unpublished draft), n.d., B3, F4, ADW.

49. Trustee Committee Written Offer, Feb. 20, 1914, B1, F4, JJW.

50. J. J. Wenger to unidentified recipient, Feb. 24, 1914, B1, F4, JJW.

51. Report of Arbitrating Committee, n.d., B1, F4, JJW.

52. Heatwole to J. J. Wenger, June 2, 1914, B1, F-Misc. Correspondence, JJW.

53. Garber to L. J. Heatwole, June 4, 1914, B3, F18, LJH.

54. J. J. Wenger to unidentified recipient, [July 28, 1914], B1, F4, JJW; Statement of Confession, signed by Chris Garber, July 28, 1914, B1, F4, JJW.

55. Trustee committee to David Garber, July 31, 1914, B1, F4, JJW; Article of Agreement [between Garber and Wenger], n.d., ca. July 28, 1914, B1, F4, JJW.

56. J. J. Wenger to unidentified recipient, [July 28, 1914], B1, F4, JJW.

57. Heatwole to General Board, June 18, 1914, B1, F3, JJW; Heatwole to General Board, July 10, 1914, B3, F4, ADW; Heatwole to General Board, Sept. 21, 1914, B1, F3, JJW; Report of General Board Meeting, Oct. 9, 1914, KCR.

58. Sources for this section include several student reports and diaries: J. Irvin Lehman, *Spots on My Trousers*, 29–30; J. Irvin Lehman, "Special Bible Term at Hayfield," *Journal*, Mar. 1934, 1–2, 15; J. Irvin Lehman, diary, 1914 and 1915, B1, F1, J. Irvin Lehman Collection, MHACVA; Clarence S. Shank, diary, 1915, B1, F2, His-Mss 1–5, MHACVA; [J. J. Wenger], "Seventeen Points on EMS Early Days," B1, F8, JJW; *Special Bible Term at Hayfield Mansion, Jan. 12th to Feb. 9th, 1915* (flyer), B1, F7, JJW; "Students at the Special Bible Term," B1, F7, JJW; Pellman, *EMC*, 23–25.

59. Emphasis added.

60. In a letter describing the management for the Bible term, Heatwole wrote, "I suppose I will have to serve as acting president until we can organize." Heatwole to J. J. Wenger, Nov. 18, 1914, B1, F18, LJH.

61. Pellman, *EMC*, 24.

62. Ibid., 25 (emphasis added).

63. J. Irvin Lehman, diary, 1915, B1, F1, J. Irvin Lehman Collection, MHACVA; [Minutes of] Meeting of the General Board, Feb. 6, 1915, KCR.

64. [Loucks] to George R. Brunk, Mar. 4, 1914, B1, F17, JJW.

65. Cited in Pellman, *EMC*, 26.

66. Pellman, *EMC*, 27 (emphasis in the original).

67. Ibid.; Brunk to J. J. Wenger, June 17, 1915, B1, F11, JJW (emphasis in the original).

68. Wenger to L. J. Heatwole, July 6, 1915, B3, F4, ADW.

69. "Alexandria Mennonite School," May 3, 1915, B1, F4, JJW.

70. Daniel Kauffman, "The Eastern School Proposition," B3, F4, LJH.

71. Article of Agreement [between Garber and Wenger], n.d., ca. July 28, 1914, B1, F4, JJW.

72. David Garber to J. J. Wenger, Sept. 10, 1915, B1, F14, JJW.

73. The following correspondence illustrates the ongoing controversy between Chris Garber and J. J. Wenger: David Garber to James M. Duncan, Jan. 31, 1916, B1, F14, JJW; David Garber to Chris Garber, Jan. 31, 1916, B1, F14, JJW; J. J. Wenger to Chris Garber, Jan. 31, 1916, B1, F13, JJW (Wenger asks Garber's forgiveness for suing him); Chris Garber to David Garber, Feb. 1, 1916, B1, F13, JJW (Chris Garber says he has hired a lawyer and has no plans to repay J. J. Wenger until his other debts are paid); J. J. Wenger to H. Noel Garner, Feb. 28, 1916, B1, F17, JJW (Wenger explains to Garner, "I never caused [Garber] to lose one cent. . . . I was trying to help him out of the heavy [financial] burden"). The flow of correspondence related to the Garber–Wenger conflict continued at least through August 1918: Peter Garber to J. J. Wenger, Aug. 12, 1918, B1, F16, JJW.

74. George R. Brunk to J. J. Wenger, Mar. 6, 1914, B1, F10, JJW.

75. Thomas Cover to J. J. Wenger, Oct. 8, 1915, B1, F12, JJW; Thomas Cover to J. J. Wenger, Oct. 13, 1915, B1, F12, JJW; Thomas Cover to J. J. Wenger, Oct. 16, 1915, B1, F12, JJW; [Hubert Pellman], "The Story of the Hayfield Proposition," n.d., 3, KCR.

76. Wenger to J. J. Wenger, n.d., B1, F26, JJW.

77. George R. Brunk to J. J. Wenger, Mar. 6, 1914, B1, F10, JJW.

78. S. Miller, *Culture for Service*, 60–61; George R. Brunk, autobiographical account to Ernest G. Gehman, B3, F32, EGG.

79. J. C. Wenger, *Faithfully, Geo. R.*, 201–4.
80. Cited in Pellman, *EMC*, 21.
81. Chester Wenger, interview by author, June 20, 2013.
82. Brunk to Wenger, Mar. 13, 1915, cited in Pellman, *EMC*, 26 (emphasis in the original).
83. L. J. Heatwole to Marion Charlton, Apr. 2, 1914, B3, F11, LJH; Daniel Kauffman to Heatwole, Apr. 13, 1914, B3, F20, LJH; Heatwole to Charlton, Apr. 15, 1914, B3, F11, LJH; Heatwole to J. J. Wenger, June 2, 1914, B3, F26, LJH; David Garber to Heatwole, June 4, 1914, B3, F18, LJH; Daniel Shenk to Heatwole, June 9, 1914, B3, F24, LJH; and Daniel Shenk to Heatwole, July 6, 1914, B3, F24, LJH.
84. L. J. Heatwole to Daniel Kauffman, Apr. 10, 1914, B3, F20, LJH.
85. George R. Brunk to Chris Garber, Nov. 25, 1913, B5, F3, GRB1.
86. Both A. D. Wenger and Aaron Loucks preferred Hagerstown. A. D. Wenger to J. J. Wenger, Sept. 14, 1914, B1, F26, JJW; Aaron Loucks to J. J. Wenger, Dec. 4, 1915, B1, F24, JJW.
87. Daniel Kauffman to L. J. Heatwole, Apr. 13, 1914, B3, F20, LJH.
88. L. J. Heatwole to J. J. Wenger, June 18, 1914, B1, F3, JJW; L. J. Heatwole to J. J. Wenger, May 30, 1914, B3, F26, LJH.
89. Photo and flyer in B3, F10, LJH; J. J. Wenger to George R. Brunk, June 23, 1914, B3, F26, LJH.
90. L. J. Heatwole to J. J. Wenger, May 20, 1914, B1, F17, JJW; Heatwole to board of trustees, June 18, 1914, B1, F3, JJW; Report of Committee to Board of Trustees Regarding Visit to Waterlick Sulfur Springs Property, n.d., B3, F3, LJH; Pellman, *EMC*, 29.
91. Heatwole to General Board, Nov. 19, 1915, B3, F4, LJH.
92. "Record of Meeting," trustee minutes, Dec. 4, 1915; Article of Agreement [with Funkhouser], Dec. 20, 1915, B1, F5, JJW.
93. Heatwole to Wenger, Dec. 28, 1915, B3, F4, ADW; "Special Bible Term at Assembly Park, January 19 to February 25, 1916," B1, F7, JJW.
94. Heatwole to A. D. Wenger, n.d., ca. Dec. 22, 1915, B3, F4, ADW; Pellman, *EMC*, 29.
95. L. J. Heatwole, "Short Term Bible Course," 655–56.
96. Tradition has established October 1917 as the beginning of EMU, despite the fact that the first Special Bible Term classes were held in Alexandria in January 1915 and in Harrisonburg in January 1916 and again in January 1917. This is likely because October 1917 signaled the beginning of the first full-length school year.
97. *Church and Sunday School Hymnal*, #277.
98. Ibid., #410.
99. L. J. Heatwole, "The First Day at Eastern Mennonite School," *Journal*, Jan. 1928, 4.

CHAPTER 3

EPIGRAPH: C. H. Brunk to L. J. Heatwole, June 19, 1916, B3, F4, ADW.
1. L. J. Heatwole, Announcement.
2. Trustee minutes, Apr. 19, 1917.
3. Shetler, *Preacher of the People*, 9.
4. Homan, *Great War*, 57–80.
5. Fry and Hartzler, "Change of Place."
6. L. J. Heatwole, "The First Day at Eastern Mennonite School," *Journal*, Jan. 1928, 4; "Mennonites Establish Institute at Park," *Daily News-Record* (Harrisonburg, VA), Jan. 22, 1916.
7. Funkhouser to Heatwole, Feb. 12, 1916, B1, F-Misc., LJH.
8. The other four sites that were not chosen were Waterman, Burkholder Spring, Raleigh Pike, and Dayton. Trustee minutes, May 17, 1916, Sept. 21, 1916, and Oct. 26, 1916; C. H. Brunk to L. J. Heatwole, June 19, 1916, B3, F4, ADW; L. J. Heatwole to Daniel Kauffman, June 20, 1916, B3, F4, ADW.
9. C. H. Brunk to A. P. Funkhouser, Oct. 20, 1916, B1, F4, AGH.
10. Funkhouser to Brunk, Oct. 24, 1916, B1, F4, AGH.
11. On January 3, 1917, the General Board authorized Harrisonburg area men to convey the property, perform other duties set forth in a charter (executed April 19, 1917), and serve as trustees. The six men on this newly created local board were J. S. Martin, D. R. Martin, Joseph Shank, C. H. Brunk, A. G. Heishman, and L. J. Heatwole. Heishman was secretary of both the General Board and the local board. Because Heatwole served as chair of the General Board, C. H. Brunk was elected chair of the local board, which served as a de facto executive committee for the General Board. Heatwole and Heishman were the primary links to the General Board, which met once a year. The six local trustees met frequently to manage the school's affairs. Most remarkably, the 1917 charter did not mention the church-wide Mennonite Board of Education, the General Board of Eastern Mennonite School (which had guided the project since February 1913), Virginia Conference, or any local Mennonite congregation. A revised charter in 1923 empowered a new board of trustees to establish a constitution and bylaws, which were adopted in 1924. Trustee minutes, Jan. 3, 1917, Apr. 19, 1917, Apr. 24, 1920, May 22, 1920, Aug. 21,

1920, Feb. 26, 1921, June 14, 1921, and June 13, 1922.

12. Brunk to the General Board, Nov. 15, 1916, B1, F5, AGH (emphasis added).

13. Faculty minutes, Mar. 11, 1927; trustee minutes, Mar. 14, 1927. The Plain of Sharon is a fertile area in Palestine known for its flowers, and Olivet refers to the Mount of Olives in Jerusalem.

14. A. G. Heishman, Announcement.

15. Pellman, *EMC*, 49.

16. Kauffman to Smith, Sept. 19, 1917, B2, F-Kauffman, JBS. In February of 1917, Smith had circulated a proposal to establish a Bible school in Ohio but received little church-wide enthusiasm for the project. Smith wrote a long letter to Mennonite Board of Education treasurer S. C. Yoder explaining his proposal. He had visited supporters in several adjoining counties and anticipated a six-month Bible school that would open on October 1, 1917. (See Daniel Kauffman to J. B. Smith, Feb. 15, 1917, B2, F-Kauffman, JBS; D. J. Johns to J. B. Smith, Mar. 17, 1917, B2, F-Goshen College, JBS; S. C. Yoder to J. B. Smith, July 14, 1917, B1, F18, SCY; and J. B. Smith to S. C. Yoder, July 18, 1917, B1, F18, SCY.)

17. Trustee minutes, Oct. 22, 1917. The term *president* was not used until A. D. Wenger's title was changed from "principal" to "president" when development of the junior college began in 1928. Use of the term *president* for all the chief administrators in this text complies with the popular usage of the term in later institutional references to both Smith and Wenger.

18. J. B. Smith, "Education of, and for, Our Young People," pts. 1 and 2; Smith, "Educational Problem"; Smith, "God of Modernism."

19. Former EMC administrator and friend of Smith, interview by author, July 23, 2014.

20. The tollgate was removed in 1919 or 1920. Pellman, *EMC*, 48.

21. Pellman, *EMC*, 48.

22. Brereton, *Training God's Army*; H. Bender, "Bible Institute"; H. Bender, "Bible School."

23. *Catalog 1918–1919*, 15; *Catalog 1926–1927*, 12.

24. H. Pellman interview with J. Early Suter, Feb. 1966, cited in Pellman, *EMC*, 35.

25. Faculty minutes, Mar. 6, 1918.

26. M. T. Brackbill, "First Impressions and Experiences," *Journal*, Nov. 1937, 7; M. T. Brackbill, "And Now for Another Twenty-Five Years," *Journal*, Jan. 1948, 3–4; M. T. Brackbill, diary entry, Mar. 10, 1919, B4, F-Diary 1919–1921, MTB; M. T. Brackbill, diary entry, Mar. 29, 1919, B4,

27. F-Diary 1919–1921, MTB (emphasis in the original).

27. Pellman, *EMC*, 38.

28. Faculty minutes, Jan. 19, 1919; trustee minutes, Feb. 8, 1919; General Board minutes, Feb. 14, 1919; trustee minutes, Feb. 20, 1919.

29. General Board minutes, Feb. 14, 1919.

30. J. B. Smith, *The Eastern Mennonite School: A Plea for Church-Wide Interest and Support*, n.d., B1, F12a, JBS.

31. Faculty minutes, Mar. 10, 1919, Mar. 22, 1919, and Apr. 26, 1919. Smith's endowment fund proposal does not appear in the trustee minutes.

32. Wenger to Smith, Feb. 25, 1919, B2, F-Wenger, JBS.

33. H. N. Troyer, "The First Commencement," *Journal*, Jan. 1928, 11–12.

34. Edward Byers to J. B. Smith, Apr. 9, 1919, B1, F-1917–1922, JBS. This letter implies that Smith had initiated the conversation with the property owner, Edward Byers.

35. Trustee minutes, Apr. 30, 1919.

36. Cited in Pellman, *EMC*, 64 (emphasis in the original).

37. Trustee minutes, May 14, 1919 (emphasis added).

38. Background on John Kurtz and Elizabeth Lehman is from Lehman and Cressman, *A. D. & Annie*, 115–24. Kurtz's near-death experience is described in detail by M. T. Brackbill in his diary, Feb. 8–24, 1920, B4, F-Diary 1919–1921, MTB.

39. H. N. Troyer, "Memories of Early Years," Jan. 16, 1952, B3, F1, ADW.

40. Mary C. Shenk, "Memories of Early Years," Jan. 1952, B3, F1, ADW.

41. M. T. Brackbill, diary entries, Jan. 9 and 26, 1920, B4, F-Diary 1919–1921, MTB.

42. Originally, Northlawn was styled as two words: North Lawn.

43. Keim, *Harold S. Bender*, 72–73.

44. C. K. Lehman, "The Junior College," *Bulletin*, Feb. 1926, 4; *Catalog 1920–1921*, 7.

45. Ruth Smith Brunk, "Memories of Early Years," Jan. 22, 1952, B3, F1, ADW. Ruth Smith Brunk was the first EMS high school graduate who completed all four years of high school at EMS.

46. Paul Huddle, "Memories of Early Years," Jan. 9, 1952, B3, F1, ADW.

47. C. F. Derstine, "Memories of Early Years," Jan. 1952, B3, F1, ADW.

48. Ibid.

49. C. K. Lehman to A. D. Wenger, Dec. 12, 1920, B4, F16, ADW.

50. George R. Brunk to Smith, Dec. 6, 1921, B1, F-Brunk, JBS; Smith to S. C. Yoder, Feb. 22, 1922, B1, F18, SCY.

51. Smith to S. C. Yoder, Feb. 11, 1922, B1, F18, SCY (emphasis in the original); David Garber to Smith, June 4, 1921, B1, F-1917–1922, JBS; Kauffman to Smith, Mar. 16, 1918, B2, F-Misc., JBS.

52. Committee report, Sept. 14, 1921, B1, F10, JLS.

53. Ibid.

54. Brunk to Smith, Dec. 6, 1921, B1, F-Brunk, JBS.

55. Ibid. At a later time, Smith wrote his account of the event as a postscript on Brunk's letter.

56. Brunk to Smith, Dec. 15, 1921, B2, F35, GRB1. Brunk mentions Smith's letter of rebuttal in this reply.

57. George R. Brunk, *Musical Instruments*, n.d., KCR.

58. Wenger to Brunk, Feb. 14, 1922, B2, F39, GRB1.

59. Brunk to Wenger, Jan. 4, 1922, B2, F39, GRB1 (emphasis in the original).

60. Wenger to Brunk, Feb. 14, 1922, B2, F39, GRB1.

61. Bender to Smith with blind copy and note to S. C. Yoder, Mar. 27, 1922, B1, F18, SCY.

62. "Retrospect 1921–1922," *Bulletin*, Midsummer 1922, 4.

63. C. K. Lehman to A. D. Wenger, July 27, 1922, B4, F16, ADW.

64. Smith to S. C. Yoder, Mar. 18, 1922, B1, F18, SCY.

65. Wenger to George R. Brunk, Feb. 14, 1922, B2, F39, GRB1.

66. Trustee minutes, Feb. 25, 1922; faculty minutes, Apr. 29, 1927; trustee minutes, May 25, 1928.

67. Charter 1923; Constitution 1924.

68. A. D. Wenger, *Who Should Educate Our Children?*, 11 (emphasis in the original). See also A. D. Wenger, "The Mennonites a Prey of Others."

69. C. K. Lehman, "The Junior College," *Bulletin*, Feb. 1926, 6.

70. Ibid., 3–4; Special Occasions Report, *Journal*, Mar. 1926, 18.

71. M. T. Brackbill, "Term Address," *Journal*, Jan. 1924, 8.

72. C. K. Lehman, "The Eastern Mennonite School," *Bulletin*, Feb. 1923, 7; C. K. Lehman, "The Junior College," *Bulletin*, Aug. 1923, 5–9; faculty minutes, Sept. 11, 1923; trustee minutes, June 2, 1930.

73. Report of the President, *Bulletin*, July 1932, 1; Report of Alumni Association, *Journal*, July–Aug. 1932, 12.

74. H. Lehman, "To the Country Schoolhouse," 58.

75. Pellman, *EMC*, 61.

76. David Alderfer, "The Songs We Used to Sing," *Journal*, Feb. 1931, 12–14.

77. Pellman, *EMC*, 63 (emphasis added).

78. Gertrude Nissley, "An Example of Social Progress," *Journal*, Mar. 1925, 6–7.

79. Editorial, *Journal*, May 1926, 1.

80. Emma Z. Horst, "Memories of Early Years," Jan. 1952, B3, F1, ADW.

81. Former student, interview by author, Nov. 5, 2014.

82. Laura Slabaugh, "Memories of Early Years," Jan. 17, 1952, B3, F1, ADW (emphasis in the original).

83. N. E. Miller, "Looking In," *Bulletin*, Feb. 1928, 3.

84. "YPCA," *Journal*, July–Aug. 1929, 20.

85. Report of Alumni Association, *Journal*, July–Aug. 1928, 22.

86. Elizabeth Gish, "Phases of Christian Humility," pts. 1 and 2, *Journal*, Oct. 1923, 9; Nov. 1923, 5.

87. *Catalog 1918–1919*, 14; *Catalog 1935–1936*, 31.

88. D. W. Lehman, "Worthy and Unworthy Aims in Education," *Bulletin*, Jan. 1929, 3.

89. Faculty minutes, Dec. 14, 1928; Pellman, *EMC*, 121–22.

90. Faculty minutes, Feb. 15, 1921, Jan. 10, 1923, May 14, 1925, and Dec. 14, 1926.

91. N. Yoder, "Mennonite Fundamentalism," 203–4; Burdge and Horst, *Building on the Gospel Foundation*, 434–35.

92. A. D. Wenger, President's Message, *Journal*, Commencement Number 1935, 10.

93. Charter 1917, 2.

94. *Catalog 1920–1921*, 19–21, 52–53.

95. J. Mumaw, "Mennonite Witness," 76–79.

96. C. K. Lehman and Daniel Kauffman, also ideological architects of the school, rarely used the spiritual warfare metaphor, likely because they were not ardent premillennialists. See Victor Turner's discussion of root metaphor and root paradigm in *Dramas, Fields, and Metaphors*, 24–32. The root metaphor is somewhat analogous to Pierre Bourdieu's concept of *habitus*. Bourdieu and Wacquant, *Invitation to Reflexive Sociology*, 115–27.

97. C. K. Lehman, "The Junior College," *Bulletin*, Aug. 1923, 9.

98. Minutes of the Warwick School Advocates, Dec. 26, 1912; Charter 1917, 1; Constitution 1924, 4; Constitution 1947, 5; Constitution 1952, 5; Constitution 1963. Emphases added in this paragraph.

99. A. D. Wenger, *Who Should Educate Our Children?*, 2–3.

100. D. W. Lehman, "What Is Wrong with the Modern State High School?; or, The 'Scum' of High School Experiences," pts. 1 and 2, *Bulletin*, Mar. 1929, 1–3; Apr. 1929, 1–3.

101. With the exception of the four years 1922 to 1925, the term *loyalty* appeared at least once

in the catalog's mission statement every year from 1918 to 1945. That loyalty was more than a Mennonite concern is evinced by Harvard professor Josiah Royce's publication of *The Philosophy of Loyalty* in 1916.

102. Faculty minutes, Mar. 1, 1927.

103. Faculty minutes, Oct. 16, 1931.

104. D. W. Lehman, "Worthy and Unworthy Aims in Education," *Bulletin*, Jan. 1929, 3; George R. Brunk, "The Drift," 7.

105. The Christian salutation of a holy kiss, practiced in Mennonite Church congregations at the time, was supported by numerous New Testament verses: Acts 20:37, Rom. 16:16, 1 Cor. 16:20, 2 Cor. 13:12, 1 Thess. 5:26, and 1 Peter 5:14. Daniel Kauffman describes the reason and meaning of this practice in *Bible Doctrine*, 428–32.

106. Steven Nolt, e-mail message to author, Oct. 24, 2016.

107. Faculty minutes, Feb. 22, 1922; Wenger to Brunk, Oct. 4, 1932, B2, F39, GRB1; "Is It True?," *Bulletin*, Apr. 1929, 3; John R. Mumaw, "The Alumni Association," *Journal*, Nov. 1937, 38.

108. "Distribution of Student Enrollment," *Bulletin*, Mar. 1936, 2.

109. *Catalog 1920–1921*, 7.

110. Faculty minutes, May 3, 1929.

111. C. K. Lehman, "The Eastern Mennonite School," *Bulletin*, Feb. 1923, 5 (emphasis added).

CHAPTER 4

EPIGRAPH: Mosemann, "Fundamentalism versus Modernism," 20.

1. Marsden, *Fundamentalism and American Culture*, 139.

2. Smith to the MBE, Feb. 18, 1918, B23, F16, JEH. The EMS endorsement appears in trustee minutes, Feb. 15, 1918.

3. Smith to the MBE, Feb. 18, 1918, B23, F16, JEH.

4. Kauffman, "Christianity's Greatest Foe," 1 (emphasis in the original).

5. L. J. Heatwole, *Mennonite Handbook of Information*, 35. See also Horsch, *Modern Religious Liberalism*.

6. Mosemann, "Fundamentalism versus Modernism," 20 (emphasis in the original).

7. Kauffman, *Conservative Viewpoint*, 9–12; Kauffman, "Modernism," 250.

8. Kauffman, *Conservative Viewpoint*, 9–12.

9. A. D. Wenger, President's Message, *Journal*, Commencement Number 1935, 10 (emphasis added).

10. George R. Brunk, "The Drift," 2.

11. A. D. Wenger, *Who Should Educate Our Children?*, 8.

12. Smith to the MBE, Feb. 18, 1918, B23, F16, JEH.

13. Sutton, *American Apocalypse*, 107. I have benefited from four scholars' research on Fundamentalism and Mennonites: C. Norman Kraus, "American Mennonites and the Bible"; Nathan E. Yoder, "Mennonite Fundamentalism"; Rodney J. Sawatsky, *History and Ideology*; James C. Juhnke, *Vision, Doctrine, War*, chaps. 6 and 9.

14. Sutton, *American Apocalypse*, 82–90.

15. Unsigned review of *The Fundamentals* in *Gospel Herald*.

16. "The Fundamental of Fundamentals"; "Once in a While"; "No Middle Ground"; "Modernism vs. Fundamentalism"; "Fundamentalism versus Modernism"; "Modernism versus Orthodoxy"; Riley, "Fundamentalists and Modernists Compared"; "Bryan on Evolution."

17. Marsden, *Fundamentalism and American Culture*, 56–57; Barr, *Fundamentalism*, 1–2, 40, 72–73; Trollinger and Trollinger Jr., introduction to *Righting America at the Creation Museum*.

18. Smith, "The Bible," 111; C. Kraus, "American Mennonites and the Bible," 321.

19. *Minutes of the Virginia Conference*, 1:120–24.

20. Ibid., 1:124–32.

21. Brunk to Smith, Sept. 27, 1919, B1, F-Brunk, JBS; George R. Brunk, "Origin of the General Conference Fundamentals."

22. *Minutes of the Virginia Conference*, 1:124–32 (emphasis added).

23. *Mennonite General Conference, Held Near Garden City, Mo., Aug. 24–26, 1921*, B2, F3, MGC. The statement is available at *Global Anabaptist Mennonite Encyclopedia Online*, s.v. "Christian Fundamentals (Mennonite Church, 1921)," last modified Aug. 20, 2013, http://www.gameo.org/index.php?title=Christian_Fundamentals_(Mennonite_Church,_1921).

24. *Catalog 1938–1939*, 14; *Catalog 1939–1940*, 12; *Catalog 1946–1947*, 14; faculty minutes, Oct. 4, 1920, and Sept. 18, 1922.

25. *Catalog 1961–1962*, 19.

26. C. Kraus, "American Mennonites and the Bible," 313–18.

27. The text is available at *Global Anabaptist Mennonite Encyclopedia Online*, s.v. "Dordrecht Confession of Faith (Mennonite, 1632)," last modified Jan. 16, 2017, http://gameo.org/index.php?title=Dordrecht_Confession_of_Faith_(Mennonite,_1632).

28. L. J. Heatwole, *Mennonite Handbook of Information*, 36; George R. Brunk, "Origin of the General Conference Fundamentals"; J. C. Wenger, *Doctrines of the Mennonites*, 86.

29. *Catalog 1918–1919*, 8.

30. Constitution 1924.

31. Ibid.

32. Stauffer, "Fundamentals and Fundamentalists." Theron F. Schlabach also distinguishes between generic fundamentalists (small *f*) and ideological Fundamentalists (large *F*); see *War, Peace, and Social Conscience*, 22.

33. Sutton, *American Apocalypse*, 119–20; Ammerman, *Bible Believers*, 3–4.

34. EMU history professor Mark Metzler Sawin, in personal communication with the author (Oct. 3, 2016), notes that these two issues pertain more to dispensationalism than to Fundamentalism.

35. Wenger, "Gospel Church Unity," 1931, 6–7, B2, F39, GRB1.

36. George R. Brunk, "Faulty Fundamentalists," 13 (emphasis added).

37. Ibid. (emphasis in the original).

38. George R. Brunk, Editorial, 1.

39. George R. Brunk, "A Fractional Gospel," 8.

40. Juhnke, *Vision, Doctrine, War*, 258–59.

41. J. Coffman, *Outlines and Notes*, 3–5, 50–59; H. Bender, "History of Millennial Theories," 57–59; Ruth, *The Earth Is the Lord's*, 743–44. The reference to meeting Jesus in the air is based on 1 Thess. 4:13–17.

42. Sutton, *American Apocalypse*, 8–46, provides a concise history of premillennialism.

43. Kauffman, "Millennium"; Lapp, "Amillennialism"; J. C. Wenger, "Chiliasm"; Stauffer, "Premillennialism"; Stauffer, *The Coming of the Lord*.

44. C. K. Lehman, "Interpretation of Prophecy."

45. This rapture sequence is one of three variations (pretribulation rapture, midtribulation rapture, posttribulation rapture), all hotly debated within an overarching premillennialism. See Marsden, *Fundamentalism and American Culture*, 52, 93, 241n17.

46. This is the assessment of Marsden in *Fundamentalism and American Culture*, 269n9.

47. Sutton, *American Apocalypse*, 9.

48. Ibid., 346–48; http://www.leftbehindmovie.com/.

49. Nathan E. Yoder traces the interaction between Mennonites and dispensational premillennialism in "Mennonite Fundamentalism," 216–24.

50. Stauffer, *The Coming of the Lord*; H. Bender, "History of Millennial Theories," 57.

51. H. Bender, "History of Millennial Theories," 57–59.

52. The pessimism/optimism dichotomy was not inherent in early pre- and postmillennial interpretations, but it was assumed by 1900. Steven Nolt, interview by author, Nov. 11, 2016.

53. George R. Brunk, "Keeping the Faith," 85. (The article is a reprint of his sermon to the General Conference in 1929.)

54. Marsden, *Fundamentalism and American Culture*, 7, 111–12; Steven Nolt, interview by author, Nov. 11, 2016.

55. Sutton, *American Apocalypse*, 28; C. Kraus, *Dispensationalism in America*, 111–30.

56. J. Mumaw, "Dispensationalism"; Stauffer, "Fundamentals and Fundamentalists."

57. Brunk to John H. Mosemann and Noah Mack, Feb. 26, 1929, B5, F5, GRB1; George R. Brunk, "Scofield Errors," 5.

58. Scofield, *Scofield Reference Bible*, iii.

59. *Minutes of the Virginia Conference*, 1:204–5.

60. Stauffer to W. W. Hege, Oct. 19, 1916, B14, F-General Corr., JLS.

61. "Conference Report," 614. Burdge and Horst provide an in-depth discussion of the premillennial controversy in the larger Mennonite Church context in *Building on the Gospel Foundation*, 473–79.

62. Ruth, *The Earth Is the Lord's*, 743–46, 906–8; Hostetler, *American Mennonites*, 210, 223–34.

63. Stauffer to W. W. Hege, Oct. 19, 1916, B14, F-General Corr., JLS.

64. Sutton, *American Apocalypse*, 21–22; Marsden, *Fundamentalism and American Culture*, 199–205; Boyer, *When Time Shall Be No More*, 270–71.

65. Stauffer to RWC, June 30, 1941, B1, F30, SHR.

66. Stauffer, *The Coming of the Lord*, 9.

67. Paul Boyer, *When Time Shall Be No More*, 300–301, notes the link between premillennialism and mission efforts.

68. Smith to the MBE, Feb. 18, 1918, B23, F16, JEH; Bush, *Dancing with the Kobzar*, 59–94.

69. Daniel Kauffman to J. B. Smith, Mar. 16, 1918, B2, F-Misc. Corr., JBS.

70. Trustee minutes, Feb. 14, 1919.

71. H. N. Troyer, "EMS Learning to Walk" (unpublished draft), 1952, B3, F1, ADW.

72. Stauffer to Daniel Kauffman and Orie Miller, May 6, 1935, B6, F38, JLS. This letter summarizes EMS critiques of relations between Goshen and the MBE.

73. Natasha Sawatsky-Kingsley, "Mennonite Board of Education Officers and Members, 1905–1930," Jan. 13, 2014, KCR.

74. "EMS–Goshen Conflict 1915–1935," excerpts from one hundred letters and documents, KCR.

75. Byers to Brunk, Mar. 15, 1906, B2, F48, GRB1; Brunk to Byers, Mar. 21, 1906, B2, F48, GRB1.

76. Brunk to Jonas Culler, Sept. 5, 1916, B3, F10, GRB1 (emphasis in the original); Brunk to George Lapp, Apr. 20, 1918, B1, F-Brunk, JBS (emphasis in the original).

77. "Synopsis of Inaugural Address," *Goshen College Record*, Nov. 1913, 8.

78. MBE minutes, Aug. 16, 1915, and Oct. 25, 1916, B1, F-Minutes 1905–19, MBE-Minutes, MBE; George R. Brunk, "Report of Trial at Goshen," n.d., B3, F10, GRB1.

79. George R. Brunk, "Account, in Detail, of a Visit Made to the Warwick River Mennonite Congregation, July 21, 1916, by J. E. Hartzler," n.d., B3, F10, GRB1.

80. MBE minutes, Aug. 16, 1915, and Oct. 25, 1916, B1, F-Minutes 1905–19, MBE-Minutes, MBE; George R. Brunk, "Report of Trial at Goshen," n.d., B3, F10, GRB1.

81. "To Whom This May Concern," Sept. 5, 1916, B2, F6, JBS.

82. Smith to the MBE, Feb. 18, 1918, B23, F16, JEH.

83. Ibid.

84. Ibid. (emphasis added).

85. Smith, "Unsound Books in Goshen College Library Recommended for Removal by J. B. Smith," n.d., B6, F3, JBS. (The list of books was likely compiled in late 1918; it is referenced in a letter from Daniel Kauffman to J. B. Smith, Jan. 1, 1919, B2, F-Misc. Corr., JBS.)

86. J. M. Kreider to J. B. Smith, May 5, 1922, B1, F-1922–1930, JBS.

87. J. L. Stauffer to H. N. Troyer, Aug. 2, 1919, B2, F-Misc. Corr., JBS; Stauffer to Troyer, July 26, 1919, B2, F-Misc. Corr., JBS.

88. Bender to Stauffer, Mar. 1, 1920, B3, F8, HSB; Stauffer to Bender, Mar. 19, 1920, B3, F8, HSB.

89. Bender to Stauffer, May 18, 1920, B3, F8, HSB.

90. Stauffer to Bender, Mar. 19, 1920, B3, F8, HSB (emphasis in the original). See also Stauffer to Bender, May 31, 1920, B3, F8, HSB.

91. This estimate of the number of liberals is found in one version of the statement but not in a revised one. The two versions of the undated statement "Shall the Old Landmarks Stand?" are in B2, F35, GRB1, and B12, F13, JLS. For correspondence pertaining to the statement, see [J. B. Smith] to Brunk, Feb. 27, 1920, B2, F35, GRB1; J. B. Smith to George S. Keener, July 2, 1920, B1, F-1917–1922, JBS; and Burdge and Horst, *Building on the Gospel Foundation*, 476.

92. Smith to the MBE, July 16, 1921, B1, F18, SCY (emphasis in the original).

93. S. Miller, *Culture for Service*, 82–86; Goshen College Alumni Association letter, Aug. 16, 1923, B5, F6, EGG. Sources frequently use "Old Goshen" and "New Goshen" to refer to Goshen College before and after the closing.

94. Smith to S. C. Yoder, Mar. 27, 1923, B1, F18, SCY.

95. George R. Brunk, "Virginia Conference Vigilance," 5.

96. S. Miller, *Culture for Service*, 82–86.

97. Noah Oyer to Chester [C. K.] Lehman, Aug. 18, 1925, B4, F27, ADW.

98. Lehman to A. D. Wenger, Aug. 19, 1925, B3, F5, ADW.

99. Ibid.

100. Wenger to D. H. Bender, Sept. 8, 1925, B4, F2, ADW; Wenger to A. Yoder, Feb. 11, 1932, B3, F7, ADW.

101. A. D. Wenger to D. H. Bender, Oct. 22, 1925, B4, F2, ADW. The special meeting included the Religious Welfare Committee and the trustees' executive committee.

102. A. D. Wenger to John H. Mosemann, Oct. 3, 1927, B4, F26, ADW.

103. Wenger to John H. Mosemann, Nov. 14, 1932, B4, F26, ADW.

104. Wenger to Brunk, Mar. 10, 1933, B2, F39, GRB1.

105. Trustee minutes, May 1, 1929.

106. Wenger to John H. Mosemann, Oct. 3, 1927, B4, F26, ADW.

107. Wenger to Yoder, Oct. 16, 1930, B4, F36, ADW.

108. Yoder to Stauffer, Oct. 8, 1930, B6, F9b, JLS.

109. Wenger to D. H. Bender, Oct. 22, 1925, B4, F2, ADW.

110. A. D. Wenger, "Gospel Church Unity," 5–67, 1931, B2, F39, GRB1.

111. A. D. Wenger to D. H. Bender, Mar. 14, 1927, B3, F8, ADW.

112. H. Bender, Editorial.

113. George R. Brunk, Introduction.

114. Bender to J. L. Stauffer, Oct. 2, 1928, B6, F9b, JLS.

115. Lehman to H. S. Bender, Oct. 29, 1929, B1, F10, HSB.

116. A. D. Wenger to H. S. Bender, Feb. 23, 1933, B3, F8, ADW.

117. Smith, "A Statement of Facts . . . ," n.d., B3, F27, LJH; S. Miller, *Culture for Service*, 143–45.

118. Bender to John Horsch, Mar. 3, 1931, B6, F1, HSB; Bender to John Horsch, Mar. 26, 1931, B6, F1, HSB; Bender to George R. Brunk, Mar. 12, 1931, B4, F-GRB, HSB.

119. John H. Mosemann, "Arguments Favoring the J. B. Smith Exposure," n.d., B6, F9a, JLS; [J. B. Smith], untitled list of fifteen reasons to write another letter, n.d., B6, F9a, JLS.

120. John Horsch to H. S. Bender, Mar. 14, 1931, B6, F1, HSB; H. S. Bender to John Horsch, Mar. 26, 1931, B6, F1, HSB.

121. Lehman to the MBE, Feb. 1, 1932, B6, F38, JLS.
122. Lehman to the MBE executive committee, Dec. 28, 1932, B3, F7, ADW.
123. "Concerning an Appeal to the Mennonite Board of Education," undated petition containing forty signatures, B1, F37, MBE-Secretary's Records, MBE.
124. Bender to Lehman, Feb. 14, 1932, B7, F5, HSB.
125. Bender to Wenger, Feb. 13, 1932, B6, F9b, JLS.
126. Wenger to Bender (unsent letter), Feb. 23, 1933, B3, F8, ADW; A. D. Wenger to Bender, Feb. 24, 1933, B3, F8, ADW.
127. Gehman, untitled poem, n.d., ca. 1931, B7, F8, EGG (emphasis in the original).
128. Stauffer to the MBE executive committee, Feb. 3, 1934, B6, F38, JLS.
129. A. D. Wenger to John H. Mosemann, Oct. 3, 1927, B4, F26, ADW.
130. C. K. Lehman to A. D. Wenger, Aug. 19, 1925, B3, F5, ADW.
131. Harold S. Bender to C. K. Lehman, Mar. 28, 1934, B7, F5, HSB.
132. A. D. Wenger to John H. Mosemann, Nov. 14, 1932, B4, F26, ADW.
133. Faculty minutes, Jan. 28, 1927, and Feb. 4, 1927; D. H. Bender to A. D. Wenger, May 6, 1927, B4, F2, ADW.
134. Wenger to George R. Brunk, Dec. 1, 1932, B1, F4, ADW.
135. Wenger to S. C. Yoder, Oct. 16, 1930, B4, F36, ADW.
136. Wenger to Daniel Kauffman, May 4, 1927, B4, F14, ADW.
137. Wenger to D. H. Bender, Sept. 8, 1925, B4, F2, ADW.
138. Wenger to Yoder, Oct. 16, 1930, B4, F36, ADW.
139. Wenger to D. H. Bender, Oct. 22, 1925, B4, F2, ADW.
140. Wenger to Brunk, Mar. 10, 1933, B2, F39, GRB1 (emphasis added).
141. Wenger to Mosemann, Oct. 3, 1927, B4, F26, ADW.
142. Wenger to Daniel Kauffman, May 4, 1927, B4, F14, ADW.
143. Brunk to A. D. Wenger, Nov. 28, 1932, B2, F39, GRB1.
144. Wenger to Brunk, Dec. 1, 1932, B1, F4, ADW.
145. Wenger to John H. Mosemann, Nov. 14, 1932, B4, F26, ADW.
146. Sawatsky, *History and Ideology*, 60.
147. *Mennonite Yearbook and Directory 1925*, 39–57.
148. Stauffer to Bender, May 31, 1920, B3, F8, HSB; J. B. Smith to George S. Keener, July 2, 1920, B1, F-1917–1922, JBS; Burdge

and Horst, *Building on the Gospel Foundation*, 476.
149. Smith to the MBE executive committee, July 16, 1921, B1, F18, SCY; Stauffer to Daniel Kauffman and Orie Miller, May 6, 1935, B6, F38, JLS; Wenger to George R. Brunk, Aug. 6, 1931, B2, F39, GRB1.
150. These themes frequently appear in 1929, the first year the *Sword and Trumpet* was published.
151. Bender to Stauffer, May 18, 1920, B3, F8, HSB.
152. Brunk to Harold S. Bender, June 16, 1920, B1, F5, HSB (emphasis in the original).
153. Ibid. See also George R. Brunk, "The Drift," 1–4.
154. Brunk to J. B. Smith, A. D. Wenger, and Daniel Kauffman, Dec. 17, 1918, B2, F22, GRB1.
155. Yoder to J. L. Stauffer, Dec. 12, 1930, B6, F9b, JLS.
156. Marsden, *Fundamentalism and American Culture*, 102–23, 164–84.
157. 2 Tim. 3:13. See also 1 Tim. 4:1–2, Eph. 4:13–16, Acts 20:19–31, and Matt. 10:24. Clayton Derstine's *The Great Apostasy* offers a Mennonite view of this belief in 1919.
158. A. D. Wenger, "Gospel Church Unity" (unpublished manuscript), 7–8, 1931, B2, F39, GRB1.
159. C. K. Lehman, "Thy Word Is Truth," *Journal*, Sept.–Oct. 1928, 8–11.

CHAPTER 5

EPIGRAPH: Brunk to A. D. Wenger, Jan. 22, 1935, B4, F4, ADW (lightly edited for style; emphasis in the original).
1. George Smoker, "Depression," *Journal*, Sept.–Oct. 1931, 20–21.
2. Catherine R. Mumaw, interview by author, July 12, 2013.
3. Trustee minutes, Apr. 8, 1931, Mar. 2, 1932, and Apr. 5, 1932.
4. Mildred Kauffman Pellman, interview by author, Oct. 12, 2012.
5. "Report of Business Manager," *Bulletin*, July 1930, 7, and Aug. 1931, 4.
6. "128 Students Enrolled to Date," *Bulletin*, Sept. 1933, 1.
7. Chester Wenger, interview by author, June 20, 2013.
8. "Student Self-Help," *Bulletin*, Aug. 1933, 4; Pellman, *EMC*, 104, 257n42; Lehman and Cressman, *A. D. & Annie*, 327–28; Chester Wenger, interview by author, June 20, 2013.
9. Trustee minutes, Sept. 22, 1932.
10. E. Wenger, *The Weaverland Mennonites*, 110–11; "A Chronology of Events Related to EMS in Lancaster County, 1908–1933," KCR.

11. Heatwole to Weaver, Sept. 26, 1923, B3, F9, LJH; Weaver to Heatwole, Sept. 28, 1923, B3, F15, LJH; John Mosemann to A. D. Wenger, Mar. 3, 1927, B4, F26, ADW (emphasis in the original).

12. Minutes of the bishop board of Lancaster Mennonite Conference, June 9, 1927, LMHSA.

13. Shenk to John Mosemann, Nov. 10, 1928, B4, F26, ADW.

14. Minutes of the bishop board of Lancaster Mennonite Conference, Oct. 18, 1933, LMHSA; Mack, "Situation in American Mennonitism." Mack, one of EMS's strongest advocates in Lancaster, included a critique of Goshen College and a positive assessment of EMS in his essay decrying liberalism.

15. Sara Weaver Wenger, interview by author, June 20, 2013.

16. Theron Schlabach, e-mail message to author, Oct. 19, 2013.

17. G. Showalter, "The Virginia Mennonite," 2–3.

18. Wenger to Hess, Mar. 7, 1933, B3, F8, ADW.

19. Wenger to Brunk, Oct. 29, 1934, B2, F39, GRB2. (Wenger recounts to Brunk what Heishman told him about the plan.)

20. Brunk to L. Shank and S. H. Rhodes, Sept. 24, 1934, B4, F4, ADW.

21. Brunk to Wenger, Sept. 24, 1934, B4, F4, ADW.

22. Heishman to Brunk, Sept. 29, 1934, B2, F39, GRB2.

23. Brunk to A. D. Wenger, Dec. 29, 1930, B2, F39, GRB2.

24. Brunk to Wenger, Feb. 13, 1930, B4, F4, ADW (emphasis added); Brunk to Wenger, Dec. 29, 1930, B2, F39, GRB2.

25. Brunk to Wenger, Apr. 29, 1931, B2, F39, GRB2.

26. Wenger to Brunk, May 2, 1931, B4, F4, ADW; Wenger to Brunk, Dec. 1, 1932, B4, F4, ADW; Wenger to Brunk, Dec. 5, 1934, B4, F4, ADW.

27. George R. Brunk, "Relation of Faith and Works," and Rightly Dividing the Scriptures; Nathan E. Yoder, "Notes on George R. Brunk's View of Calvinism," June 25, 2014, KCR; N. Yoder, "Mennonite Fundamentalism," chap. 4; "Calvinism," faculty questionnaire, n.d., B6, F-College Materials Misc., JLS.

28. Wenger to Brunk, Dec. 5, 1934, B4, F4, ADW; Brunk to Wenger, Jan. 22, 1935, B4, F4, ADW (emphasis in the original).

29. George R. Brunk, "Serving Our Generation," Journal, July–Aug. 1935, 1–6.

30. The traditional preparatory service before communion required members to pledge that they were at peace with other members.

31. Wenger to Brunk, Feb. 25, 1935, B2, F39, GRB2; Wenger to RWC, Apr. 12, 1935, B4, F16, ADW.

32. Wenger to Brunk, Feb. 25, 1935, B2, F39, GRB2; Wenger to RWC, Apr. 12, 1935, B4, F16, ADW.

33. Trustee minutes, Mar. 1, 1935, Mar. 25, 1935, and June 1, 1935.

34. Faculty minutes, Feb. 22, 1935; C. K. Lehman, "A Forward Step in the Bible School," Bulletin, May 1935, 1–3.

35. Trustee minutes (executive committee meeting jointly with the faculty), Sept. 10, 1935.

36. Faculty minutes, June 7, 1935.

37. Chester Wenger, interview by author, June 20, 2013; Lehman and Cressman, A. D. & Annie, 34–36. Family members surmise that Wenger likely died of a heart attack.

38. J. C. Wenger, Faithfully, Geo. R., 206–7.

39. Stoltzfus, A Way Was Opened, 49.

40. L. J. Heatwole died December 26, 1932. Grove, L. J. Heatwole, 205.

41. Ernest G. Gehman, "Dirge," Journal, Nov. 1935, 22–23. The poem has fourteen stanzas. The November 1935 issue of the Journal also contains A. D. Wenger memorial essays.

42. Trustee minutes, Oct. 7, 1935, Nov. 11, 1935, and Nov. 21, 1936.

43. Stauffer wrote a widely distributed booklet, The Eternal Security Teaching, which he self-published in 1933.

44. Biographical sources include Stauffer to L. J. Heatwole, Sept. 5, 1918, B1, F2, JLS; Dorothy Kemrer, "Biographies," Journal, Mar. 1923, 6; and L. Wenger, "J. L. Stauffer (1888–1959)."

45. James Stauffer, interview by author, Nov. 5, 2014.

46. Ruth Stauffer Alger, interview by author, Nov. 5, 2014; James Stauffer, interview by author, Nov. 5, 2014.

47. Administration Committee minutes, Nov. 22, 1948.

48. Handbook 1941–1942, 74–75; Handbook 1946–1947, 20–22.

49. Science teacher D. Ralph Hostetter was on the Administration Committee because he was the director of the high school. Likewise, President Stauffer and Dean Lehman also taught alongside their administrative duties.

50. Administration Committee to RWC, July 18, 1946, B1, F29, SHR.

51. YPCA Opportunities, Journal, Sept.–Oct. 1931, 3–4.

52. YPCA Rural Mission Work, *Journal*, Feb. 1932, 3.
53. Aaron King, "The Iron Gate Prison Camp," *Journal*, Apr. 1949, 6.
54. Ruth Mininger, *Journal*, Dec. 1931, 21–24; "Sharonean Literary Notes," *Journal*, July–Aug. 1932, 6.
55. Mike Martin, "Y-Churches Take Mennonite Faith into Community," *Weather Vane*, Oct. 1, 1992, 6; "The Missions in Harrisonburg," *Bulletin*, Feb. 1937, 1–2; Earl Delp, "Mission Work in Harrisonburg," *Journal*, Sept.–Oct. 1936, 15–16; "Working with Christ for the YPCA," *Journal*, Dec. 1936, 17; Sadie Hartzler, "The Growth of the YPCA," *Journal*, Nov. 1937, 30–32.
56. W. Ray Wenger, "City Worker's Band No 2," *Journal*, Dec. 1937, 11–12.
57. The name of the mission was emblazoned on the sign above the building's entrance.
58. H. Brunk, *History of Mennonites*, 2:450.
59. James Lehman, *Lindale's Song*, 126; *Minutes of the Virginia Conference*, 1:226; Swartzentruber, "History of the Colored Mission," 1.
60. Mike Martin, "Y-Churches Take Mennonite Faith into Community," *Weather Vane*, Oct. 1, 1992, 6.
61. "The Missions in Harrisonburg," *Bulletin*, Feb. 1937, 1–2.
62. Ruth, *The Earth Is the Lord's*, 925–26.
63. "Breezes from the Weather Vane," *Journal*, July–Aug. 1940, 28.
64. Mahlon M. Hess, "Working for Christ with the YPCA," *Journal*, July–Aug. 1940, 22–23.
65. E. Warren Rohrer, "The Ambassador Tour," *Journal*, Sept.–Oct. 1948, 4–6.
66. Sara Weaver Wenger, interview by author, June 20, 2013.
67. J. L. Stauffer, "A Message from Our President," *Journal*, May 1940, 4–5.
68. Richard Detweiler, "Annual Report of the President of YPCA, 1947–48," *Bulletin*, June 1948, 1–7.
69. Lehman to RWC, June 10, 1941, B1, F-1941, RWC.
70. J. L. Stauffer to RWC, June 30, 1941, B1, F-1941, RWC.
71. College students millennial survey results, Jan. 1943, B1, F9, JLS.
72. Tensions dissipated after a church-wide conference in 1952, recorded in the nineteen chapters of *Prophecy Conference*. Lehman summarized his views on millennialism in a long treatise that was published posthumously in 2016 as *The Last Things in the Teaching of the Bible*.
73. Hubert Pellman, interview by author, Oct. 13, 2012.
74. Simone Horst, e-mail message to author, Aug. 14, 2015.
75. Harold D. Lehman, interview by author, July 13, 2013; Campus Throbs, *Journal*, Nov. 1943, 9.
76. Keim and Stoltzfus, *The Politics of Conscience*, 56–126; Schlabach, *War, Peace, and Social Conscience*, 87–116.
77. Of the 175 inductees who were *not* deferred, 59 percent entered CPS and 37 percent signed up for military combat. Calculations were derived from Guy F. Hershberger, *The Mennonite Church in the Second World War*, 40–41. Steven Nolt and Theron Schlabach note the important distinction between draftees and inductees in "The Facts about Nonresistance."
78. Gingerich, *Service for Peace*, 95, 452.
79. Keim, *The CPS Story*, 31.
80. Report of Theological Student Enrollments to Selective Service, Mar. 1947, B26, F22, JRM.
81. C. K. Lehman, "To Whom It May Concern," Sept. 17, 1941, B26, F15, JRM; C. K. Lehman, "Deferment Problems," *Bulletin*, July 1944, 2–3.
82. *Minutes of the Virginia Conference*, 1:283.
83. Peachey, "A Hippocratic Mid-life Course Change."
84. Irvin B. Horst, "EMS Alumni in Civilian Public Service," *Journal*, Jan. 1944, 25–27.
85. C. K. Lehman, "EMS Invites Civilian Public Service Men," *Bulletin*, Jan. 1946, 3, 8; Pellman, *EMC*, 133.
86. Juhnke, "Mennonite Benevolence."
87. Andrew Jenner and Bonnie Price Lofton, "Striving for Love amid Filth and Abuse: Why EMU Has a Heart for Mental Health Care," *Crossroads*, Fall/Winter/Spring 2011–2012, 2–11.
88. Council minutes, Aug. 23–25, 1945, and Jan. 8, 1946, B6, F6a, JLS; J. L. Stauffer to Lloyd L. Ramseyer (president of Bluffton College), Oct. 7, 1946, B6, F6b, JLS. Formed in the 1940s to coordinate Mennonite collegiate involvements with CPS, the council included Bluffton and Bethel Colleges as well as Messiah College and Tabor College.
89. J. L. Stauffer to "The Faculty Sisters," Spring 1947, B1, F12, Standards Committee.
90. Dress Committee minutes, Jan. 27, 1948, B1, F13, Standards Committee.
91. Dress Committee minutes, Jan. 13, 1948, B1, F13, Standards Committee.
92. Zimmerman to College Women, May 21, 1948, B1, F10, Standards Committee.
93. Stauffer to "The Faculty Sisters," Dec. 12, 1942, B1, F9, Standards Committee.
94. *Catalog 1924–1925*, 22–23; *Standards 1943–1944*, 13–14.
95. *Standards 1943–1944*, 14 (emphasis added).

96. J. L. Stauffer to Women's Dress Committee, Nov. 13, 1947, B1, F12, Standards Committee.

97. Dress Committee minutes, Dec. 9, 1947, and Jan. 20, 1948, B1, F13, Standards Committee.

98. Lois B. Bowman, interview by author, Mar. 4, 2015.

99. Ada M. Zimmerman to College Women, May 21, 1948, B1, F10, Standards Committee.

100. Edsel Burdge, interview by author, Nov. 13, 2014.

101. Men's Attire Committee minutes, May 10, 1948, B30, F19, JRM.

102. *Standards 1948–1949*, 14–15. (The 1948–1949 academic year was the first to have two different *Standards* booklets, one for the college and one for the high school.)

103. Chester Wenger, interview by author, June 20, 2013.

104. Statement at the first meeting of Men's Attire Committee, n.d., ca. Feb. or Mar. 1948, B1, F15, Standards Committee.

105. C. Norman Kraus, interview by author, Oct. 10, 2013.

106. Men's Attire Committee to members of the faculty, [Fall 1949?], B30, F19, JRM (emphasis added).

107. Dress Committee minutes, Dec. 11, 1947, and Jan. 13, 1948, B1, F13, Standards Committee.

108. Former student, interview by author, Mar. 4, 2015.

109. Sarah Kehrberg, "Dressing Girls."

110. Ada M. Zimmerman to College Women, May 21, 1948, B1, F10, Standards Committee (emphasis added).

111. Edith Showalter, "The Necessity for Regulation of Attire in the Mennonite Church," *Journal*, May 1939, 3–5, 17–20.

112. Stauffer to EMC faculty, Aug. 18, 1947, B2, F-Misc. Papers 1940s, JLS (emphasis added).

113. *Catalog 1918–1919*, 17–18.

114. Women's Dress Committee minutes, Apr. 6, 1948, B1, F14, Standards Committee (emphasis added).

115. C. Norman Kraus, interview by author, Oct. 10, 2013 (emphasis added).

116. Theron Schlabach, e-mail message to author, Oct. 19, 2013.

117. Emma Shenk, "Personal Appearance," *Journal*, May 8, 1938, 5; Daniel Hertzler, "The Well-Groomed Christian Gentleman," *Journal*, Sept.–Oct. 1948, 15–16; Grant M. Stoltzfus, Editorial, *Journal*, Dec. 1937, 1–2.

118. Esther Huber, "Marks of a Gentleman," and Robert Martin, "Marks of a Lady," *Journal*, July–Aug. 1939, 2–3, 4–5.

119. *Handbook 1949–1950*, 33.

120. Theron Schlabach, e-mail message to author, Oct. 19, 2013.

121. Daniel Hertzler, "The Well-Groomed Christian Gentleman," *Journal*, Sept.–Oct. 1948, 15–16.

122. "General Standards," n.d., B6, F1f, JLS.

123. Fretz to Stauffer, Dec. 11, 1945, B2, F13, JLS.

124. *Catalog 1918–1919*, 17–18.

125. Hubert Pellman, interview by author, Oct. 12, 2012.

126. Ibid.

127. *Standards 1943–1944*, 11–12.

128. Anna May Wenger to Annie Wenger, June 18, 1926, cited in Lehman and Cressman, *A. D. & Annie*, 331.

129. *Standards 1943–1944*, 3, 6.

130. Theron Schlabach, e-mail message to author, Oct. 19, 2013.

131. *Catalog 1950–1951*, 160–61.

132. Silas Hertzler, "Attendance at Mennonite Secondary Schools and Colleges, 1949–50," 50. Enrollment figures do not include students attending under special conditions or those enrolled in summer school or correspondence courses.

133. Faculty minutes, Feb. 23, 1948.

134. C. K. Lehman, "A Look Forward," *Bulletin*, July 1944, 3; C. K. Lehman, "History of the College Department," *Bulletin*, Aug. 1947, 1–2.

135. *Minutes of the Virginia Conference*, 1:290, 297.

136. Constitution 1947.

137. "Eastern Mennonite College Approved by Virginia State Board of Education," *Bulletin*, Dec. 1947, 1–2.

138. *Minutes of the Virginia Conference*, 1:164–65, 297–98; Lehman and Cressman, *A. D. & Annie*, 128–29, 138–41; Catherine R. Mumaw, interview by author, July 12, 2013; Harold D. Lehman, interview by author, July 13, 2013.

139. M. J. Brunk, "Where Does Eastern Mennonite School Stand?," *Bulletin*, Jan. 1945; D. W. Lehman, "Where Does Eastern Mennonite School Stand?," *Bulletin*, Feb. 1945; Ada Zimmerman, "Where Does Eastern Mennonite School Stand?," *Bulletin*, Mar. 1945.

140. "Complaints," 1945, B2, F1, RWC; "S. H. Rhodes Complaints, Jan. 8, 1945, to J. L. S," B2, F1, RWC; "Jan. 8, 1945, and Feb. 1945 Complaints to J. L. Stauffer," B2, F1, RWC.

141. Kurtz to S. H. Rhodes, Jan. 23, 1945, B1, F29, SHR.

142. Garber to RWC, n.d., ca. Feb. 20, 1945, B1, F29, SHR.

143. RWC minutes, Feb. 21, 1945, Mar. 12, 1945, Apr. 16, 1945, and Aug. 15, 1945.

144. James Lehman, *Lindale's Song*, 170–72.

145. Trustee minutes, Jan. 10, 1948, Dec. 13, 1948, Dec. 13, 1949, Dec. 22, 1949, and Jan. 30, 1950.

146. J. Mumaw, "My Faith Story"; A. Don Augsburger, interview by author, May 28, 2014;

Hubert Pellman, interview by author, Oct. 12, 2012.

147. Faculty minutes, Feb. 15, 1921; J. Mumaw, "My Faith Story"; [John R. Mumaw], Editorial, *Bulletin*, Jan. 1933, 1–2; Catherine R. Mumaw, interview by author, July 12, 2013; Hubert Pellman, interview by author, Oct. 12, 2012.

148. Pellman, *EMC*, 179; *John R., Esther F., and Evelyn K. Mumaw: Celebration of Ministry*, Nov. 14, 2009, KCR. In the 1960s, John Mumaw's first wife, Esther, died, and he married Evelyn.

CHAPTER 6

EPIGRAPH: Ada Zimmerman, "Discover Yourself," *Journal*, Sept.–Oct. 1941, 1.

1. Report of the Meeting Related to the Civilian Public Service Program, Mar. 17, 1942, B5, F3, EGG; Sharp, *My Calling to Fulfill*, 222–28.

2. *Minutes of the Virginia Conference*, 1:323; "Virginia Mennonite Conference Investigation of Eastern Mennonite College, 1950–1951, an Archival Calendar," EMUA; Pellman, *EMC*, 180–83.

3. J. R. Mumaw to Truman Brunk, Mar. 10, 1952, B14, F-Investigation Papers 1950, JRMcoll.

4. Based on an undated and untitled thirteen-page summary of the testimony, hereafter called "Hearing Testimony," B6, F14c, JLS. The document contains the names of the presenters and of the three steering committee members: Bishop Truman Brunk (moderator of the conference), Bishop Joseph Driver (conference appointee to the RWC), and Deacon John Alger (chair of the trustees).

5. Historian Nathan E. Yoder distinguishes the founding, transitional, and contending generations of leadership at EMC and Virginia Conference during the years 1917 to 1950 in "Generational Transition," 2015, KCR.

6. "Hearing Testimony," B6, F14c, JLS (emphasis added). Unless otherwise cited, quotations in this section come from this document.

7. Trustee minutes, Jan. 29–30, 1950.

8. [C. K. Lehman], "Looking Forward to Further Accreditation," n.d., ca. 1949, B7, F-EMC Investigation, CKL.

9. *Minutes of the Virginia Conference*, 1:302, 312.

10. Mumaw, "On the Use of Titles," 1942, B6, F1d, JLS; Pellman, *EMC*, 141.

11. *Report of the Special Session of the Mennonite General Conference*, Aug. 15–18, 1944, MSHL.

12. H. Shenk, "Can a Church School Promote the Simple Faith?"

13. Steering committee to "Dear Brother [J. R. Mumaw]," Aug. 2, 1950, B14, F-Investigation Papers 1950, JRMcoll; J. R. Mumaw, "Reply to Accusations Brought to Committee Investigating Reported Irregularities at EMC," Aug. 22, 1950, B14, F-Investigation Papers 1950, JRMcoll.

14. Steering committee to "Dear Brother [C. K. Lehman]," Aug. 2, 1950, B7, F39, CKL. Lehman's undated, ten-page response is attached to the letter.

15. Ibid.

16. *Minutes of the Virginia Conference*, 2:7–8. For a preliminary and a final report of the investigation, see Minutes of the investigation committee, Nov. 7, 1950, B6, F14i, JLS, and "Consideration of matters of policy. . . . ," untitled report to the special conference, Jan. 17, 1951, B6, F14j, JLS.

17. Memorandum of the subcommittee on administration regarding the services of Milton Brackbill for 1951, B7, F-EMC investigation, CKL; "Action Regarding Milton Brackbill," n.d., Steering Committee recommendation, B14, F-Investigation Papers 1950, JRMcoll.

18. J. Irvin Lehman, *Spots on My Trousers*, 62–63.

19. *Minutes of the Virginia Conference*, 2:14; Constitution 1952.

20. Administration Committee minutes, Jan. 19, 1951.

21. Stauffer, "To the EMC Faculty," B6, F14k, JLS.

22. Administration Committee minutes, June 29, 1951.

23. James Lehman, *Mennonite Tent Revivals*, 1–10; *Global Anabaptist Mennonite Encyclopedia Online*, s.v. "Brunk Brothers Revival Campaign," by Harold S. Bender and Sam Steiner, last modified Aug. 26, 2016, http://gameo.org/index.php?title=Brunk _Brothers_Revival_Campaign.

24. Mumaw colleague, interview by author, Mar. 4, 2015; C. Norman Kraus, interview by author, Oct. 10, 2013; Catherine R. Mumaw, interview by author, July 12, 2013; Peggy Shenk, e-mail message to author, Jan. 21, 2016; Pellman, *EMC*, 180.

25. Mumaw, untitled document, n.d., ca. June 15, 1951, B14, F-Investigation Papers 1950, JRMcoll.

26. J. R. Mumaw to Truman Brunk, Mar. 10, 1952, B14, F-Investigation Papers 1950, JRMcoll.

27. Schlabach, *War, Peace, and Social Conscience*, 165–216.

28. Gingerich, "Is There a Need for a Mennonite Rural Life Publication?," 60–61.

29. Fretz, "Explanatory Remarks," v–vi.
30. Hershberger, "Suggestions for Improving the Small Christian Community," 52, 56.
31. Schlabach, *War, Peace, and Social Conscience*, 191–203; Stoltzfus, *A Way Was Opened*, 54–59.
32. Gordon Shantz, "Let's Talk It Over," Editorial, *Journal*, Feb. 1947, 2.
33. Maurice E. Lehman, "The Curriculum of Agriculture at EMS," *Bulletin*, Aug. 1945, 2–4; C. K. Lehman, "The 1945–46 Session," *Bulletin*, Aug. 1945, 1.
34. *Catalog 1945–1946* through *Catalog 1958–1959*; Pellman, *EMC*, 203.
35. "A Study on Mennonite Higher Education," 1957, 113, EMUA; SACS Self-Survey Report 1958, 299.
36. President's Report, 1951–1952 through 1954–1955.
37. "A Study on Mennonite Higher Education," 1957, 109, EMUA.
38. *Catalog 1954–1955*, 23.
39. Anderson, *Imagined Communities*.
40. M. Showalter, *Mennonite Community Cookbook*; Catherine R. Mumaw, "A Tribute to Mary Emma Showalter Eby, 1913–2003," May 11, 2003, KCR; Davis, "The Woman behind *Mennonite Community Cookbook*."
41. Hubert Pellman, interview by author, Oct. 12, 2012.
42. Unless otherwise specified, sources for this section appear in Administration Committee minutes, 1948–1955.
43. Emphasis added.
44. Faculty minutes, Sept. 25, 1956.
45. SACS Self-Survey Report 1958, 148–49, 144.
46. Faculty minutes, Oct. 2, 1957.
47. Stauffer to Kenneth L. Smoke, Jan. 12, 1937, B2, F8, JLS (emphasis added).
48. Other studies included the Study on Mennonite Higher Education, 1957, and the SACS Self-Survey Report 1958, both of which can be found in the EMU Archives.
49. Report of the Religious Welfare Survey Committee 1948–1949, EMUA; Religious Welfare Survey 1947–1951, EMUA.
50. Report of the Religious Welfare Survey Committee 1948–1949, 16, 22, EMUA.
51. Ibid., 1–2, 66 (emphasis added).
52. Ibid., Exhibit G, 54.
53. Administration Committee minutes, Feb. 11, 1952.
54. This is not an argument for technological determinism. Many forces shape modernization, and their relative influence is difficult to measure, as is the extent to which they are a cause or an effect. Sociocultural factors mediate the influence of technology, yet it remains a potent force of modernization.
55. Maurice T. Brackbill, "First Impressions and Experiences," *Journal*, Nov. 1937, 8.
56. "History of Computer Services at Eastern Mennonite College," attachment to Al Keim memo to Lee Yoder, Aug. 7, 1978, B2, F9, LMY.
57. Faculty minutes, Oct. 30, 1922; Brunk to A. D. Wenger, n.d., B2, F39, GRB2 (emphasis in the original).
58. J. L. Stauffer to J. R. Driver, Dec. 6, 1938, B1, F-1938, RWC; trustee minutes, Nov. 1, 1939.
59. *Minutes of the Virginia Conference*, 1:180, 213–14, 269–70, 274–75; H. Brunk, *History of Mennonites*, 2:437–43.
60. *Standards 1948–1949*, 7; *Handbook 1955–1956*, 21; Administration Committee minutes, Mar. 4, 1948.
61. Catherine R. Mumaw, interview by author, July 12, 2013.
62. Pellman, *EMC*, 210–11, 214; Pellman, *Mennonite Broadcasts*, 9–13, 22–23; Stoltzfus, *A Way Was Opened*, 83–87.
63. Trustee minutes, June 1, 1954; Administration Committee minutes, Nov. 23, 1954.
64. Kara Lofton, "Centennial Stories: WEMC, Virginia's First Noncommercial Radio Station," Eastern Mennonite University, Dec. 1, 2015, http://emu.edu/now/news/2015/12/centennial-stories-wemc-virginias-first-noncommercial-radio-station-was-founded-on-campus-in-1954/.
65. J. Daniel Hess, e-mail message to author, Jan. 6, 2016.
66. Broadcasting Committee minutes, Jan. 12, 1956, B17, F34, MSA; Terry Cowan, memo to Myron Augsburger, n.d., B17, F34, MSA; Lloyd Kauffman, "Survey of Background Music Related to WEMC" (term paper), May 22, 1970, B17, F34, MSA; Kara Lofton, "Centennial Stories: WEMC, Virginia's First Noncommercial Radio Station," Eastern Mennonite University, Dec. 1, 2015, http://emu.edu/now/news/2015/12/centennial-stories-wemc-virginias-first-noncommercial-radio-station-was-founded-on-campus-in-1954/.
67. J. L. Stauffer, "1953–1954 Report of Radio Committee to Virginia Conference," July 29, 1954, B5, F18, EGG.
68. Stauffer to RWC, Mar. 4, 1947, B1, F29, SHR; RWC minutes, Apr. 5, 1947.
69. Lehman to RWC, Dec. 5, 1947, B1, F29, SHR; *Minutes of the Virginia Conference*, 1:301.
70. Trustees' executive committee to RWC, Feb. 27, 1952, B1, F29, SHR; *Minutes of the Virginia Conference*, 2:13.
71. Administration Committee minutes, Jan. 27, 1948, and Nov. 18, 1950.

72. Report of the Committee on Teaching Aids, Jan. 30, 1950, B6, F1h, JLS; Trustee minutes, Jan. 30, 1950; *Minutes of the Virginia Conference*, 1:305.

73. *Minutes of the Virginia Conference*, 2:47.

74. *Minutes of the Virginia Conference*, 2:104–5; Previewing Committee Report, 1956–1961, B2, F28, DWL; Pellman, *EMC*, 197.

75. *Minutes of the Virginia Conference*, 1:309, and 2:4, 18.

76. Son-in-law of J. L. Stauffer, interview by author, Nov. 5, 2014.

77. Richard Stoltzfus, e-mail message to author, Jan. 19, 2016; John Rutt, e-mail message to author, Jan. 19, 2016; Joe Longacher, e-mail message to author, Jan. 8, 2016.

78. Draft constitution, Alexandria Mennonite Institute, Feb. 18, 1914, B3, F4, ADW; *Minutes of the Virginia Conference*, 2:115; *Standards 1948–1949*, 7.

79. *Minutes of the Virginia Conference*, 1:296; J. Mark Stauffer, "The Problem of Instrumental Music," *Journal*, Oct. 1943, 19–20; *Minutes of the Virginia Conference*, 1:164–65, 298.

80. Administration Committee minutes, Nov. 22, 1957; J. Daniel Hess, "Fire from Heaven," Jan. 7, 2016, https://jdanielhessblog .wordpress.com/2016/01/07/fire-from -heaven/; J. Daniel Hess, e-mail message to author, Jan. 6, 2016.

81. John Spicher, e-mail message to author, Jan. 7, 2016; Urbane Peachey, e-mail message to author, Feb. 1, 2016.

82. Minutes of a meeting of faculty, RWC, and executive committee of Virginia Conference, June 3, 1958, 1, B2, F11, RWC; Administration Committee minutes, Feb. 24, 1958.

83. Administration Committee minutes, Nov. 22, 1957; minutes of joint meeting, May 3, 1962, B2, F15, RWC; RWC minutes, Jan. 7, 1964.

84. Robert Showalter, "Too Normal," Editorial, *Weather Vane*, Nov. 8, 1957, 2; Reverberations, *Weather Vane*, Nov. 22, 1957, 2; M. T. Brackbill, "Personalgrams," *Weather Vane*, Sept. 30, 1954, through Apr. 21, 1955. The *Weather Vane* began publication as a campus student newspaper in 1939. The *Journal* continued publication until it merged with the *Weather Vane* in 1956.

85. Faculty minutes, Mar. 26, 1952.

86. Minutes of a meeting of faculty, RWC, and executive committee of Virginia Conference, June 3, 1958, 14–15, B2, F11, RWC.

87. D. W. Lehman, "Worthy and Unworthy Aims in Education," *Bulletin*, Jan. 1929, 3; *Catalog 1918–1919*, 14.

88. Faculty minutes, Apr. 27, 1928.

89. "Personality," *Journal*, Sept.–Oct. 1939, 2; D. W. Lehman, "Personality," *Journal*, Oct. 1939, 22–24; "Personality," *Journal*, Nov. 1939, 24–25; Miriam Barge, "The Impelling Personality," *Journal*, Apr. 1946, 12–13; Mabel Erb, "My Goal for a Christlike Personality," *Journal*, Oct. 1948, 3–4.

90. J. R. Mumaw, "Issues of Life," *Journal*, Mar. 1933, 1–3, 30; Ada Zimmerman, "Discover Yourself," *Journal*, Sept.–Oct. 1941, 1 (emphasis added); *Handbook 1949–1950*; James R. Hess, "The Incomprehensible Self," *Journal*, July–Aug. 1948, 7–8.

91. *Minutes of the Virginia Conference*, 1:298 (emphasis added); Men's Attire Committee to members of the faculty, [Fall 1949?], B30, F19, JRM. Although "individual conscience" was a new phrase for EMC and Virginia Conference, it had been widely used early in the twentieth century by General Conference historians such as C. Henry Smith and J. E. Hartzler.

92. Helen Good, "Let's Talk It Over," *Journal*, Aug.–Sept. 1945, 2.

93. Gordon Shantz, "Dean Bender Visits the School," *Journal*, Feb. 1947, 10.

94. One exception is found in the sentence "Jesus requires full obedience for discipleship," in A. D. Wenger, "Our Position on Distinctive Doctrines," *Bulletin*, Apr. 1924, 9. Ironically, Charles Sheldon's novel *In His Steps*, read by some students in the 1920s and 1930s, frequently mentions discipleship.

95. Unless otherwise cited, sources in this section are from H. Bender, *Anabaptist Vision* (all emphasis added).

96. Keim, *Harold S. Bender*, 306–31.

97. Leonard Gross called the first half of the twentieth century preceding "The Anabaptist Vision" the doctrinal era of the Mennonite church due to the influence of Daniel Kauffman's writings on doctrine. See Gross, "The Doctrinal Era."

98. Keim, *Harold S. Bender*, 315; Bender and Correll, "C. Henry Smith's *The Story of the Mennonites*," 273.

99. For a nuanced discussion of Smith's view of individual conscience in Anabaptism, see Bush, *Peace, Progress, and the Professor*, 327–32.

100. Myron Augsburger, interview by author, July 23, 2014.

101. "1958 Faculty Conference [Schedule] for August. 26–29, 1958," B1, F13, Committee on Admin. 1943–1959, EMUA; *Handbook 1955–1956*; *Handbook 1956–1957*; J. R. Mumaw, "Christian Education for Christian Discipleship," n.d., B16, F22, MSA.

102. Richard L. Benner, "Associates in Discipleship," *Bulletin*, Apr. 1971, 27.

103. Trustee minutes, Jan. 27, 1959.

104. Trustee minutes, Dec. 3 and 15, 1958; Gordon Sweet to Ira Miller, Dec. 9, 1958, B6, F10, JLS; John Mumaw to Orie O. Miller, Oct. 29, 1957, B3, F1, OOM; Orie O. Miller to Mennonite Mutual Aid board of directors, Nov. 2, 1957, B3, F1, OOM; SACS Self-Survey Report 1958, 56–57.

105. Trustee minutes, Dec. 15, 1959, Nov. 3, 1959, Apr. 3, 1959, and Feb. 24, 1959; The President's Report, *Bulletin*, Sept. 1960, 9–10; Pellman, *EMC*, 183–84, 193.

106. "Overflow Audience," *The Etownian*, Feb. 6, 1960, 1, 3; citation of achievements presented to John R. Mumaw, Feb. 3, 1960, Hess Archives, Elizabethtown College.

CHAPTER 7

EPIGRAPH: Trustee minutes, Jan. 10, 1948; *Minutes of the Virginia Conference*, 1:303 (emphasis added).

1. President's Report, 1958–1959.
2. Susan Martin, "Dining Rituals on Review," *Weather Vane*, Mar. 19, 1964, 3.
3. J. R. Mumaw, "The Youth We Serve," Mar. 1962, 2–3, B16, F21, MSA.
4. Ibid. (emphasis added).
5. Report of the Findings Committee, [after] a meeting of trustees, RWC, college administrators, and faculty leaders on June 27, 1959, B21, F11, JRM.
6. Abram Hostetter, interview by author, Jan. 28, 2016.
7. The *UVA Quarterly Review* quoted Ethridge in 1942, according to C. Norman Kraus, e-mail message to author, Jan. 25, 2016. Background sources on race: Mark Metzler Sawin, Notes of Chapel Talk, Jan. 17, 2014, KCR; H. Brunk, *History of Mennonites*, 2:389–91; James Lehman, *Lindale's Song*, 125–30; Shearer, *Daily Demonstrators*, 33–47; Mike Martin, "Y-Churches Take Mennonite Faith into Community," *Weather Vane*, Oct. 1, 1992, 6, 8–9; Bonnie Lofton, "Checkered Past, Colorful Present," *Crossroads*, Spring 2007, 6–10.
8. Audrey Shank, "Racial Attitudes of the Zion Congregation," 1954, 2, Term Paper file, MSHL.
9. Bechler, *Black Mennonite Church*, 73.
10. 1860 census reported in *African-American Heritage Sites: Stories of People and Places in Harrisonburg and Rockingham County, Virginia*, compiled by Rosemarie Palmer, Jan. 2006, Harrisonburg Tourism and Visitors Services, KCR.
11. *Minutes of the Virginia Conference*, 1:6, 151–52.
12. Ibid., 257.
13. Shearer, *Daily Demonstrators*, 33–47.
14. Ibid.; Bonnie Lofton, "Checkered Past, Colorful Present," *Crossroads*, Spring 2007, 6–10.

15. Pellman, *EMC*, 133; faculty minutes, Sept. 4, 1940.
16. Trustee minutes, May 14, 1945.
17. J. L. Stauffer to Milo Kauffman, Apr. 16, 1945; Milo Kauffman to J. L. Stauffer, Apr. 9, 1945, B2, F-College Correspondence Miscellaneous, 1943–1946, JLS.
18. E-mail exchange between Bonnie Lofton and Margaret Derstine, Apr. 26, 2007, vertical file: Mennonites and Race, MSHL.
19. Sharp, *School on the Prairie*, 231.
20. Roberta Webb and Janet Eaton, "Personal Copy of Mrs. Roberta Webb's Story," Nov. 10, 1981, MSHL. See also Roberta Webb to Rosalie Wyse, Dec. 5, 1947, Papers of the Virginia Mennonite Board of Missions, MSHL; and Harold Huber's papers, Broad Street Mennonite Church, VMCA.
21. Shearer, *Daily Demonstrators*, 237–38.
22. James Lehman, *Lindale's Song*, 283n13.
23. Shearer, *Daily Demonstrators*, 10, 44–45.
24. Trustee minutes, Jan. 10, 1948; *Minutes of the Virginia Conference*, 1:303 (emphasis added).
25. Abram Hostetter, interview by author, Jan. 28, 2016.
26. This fear was articulated by numerous members of the Zion Mennonite congregation in 1954, as reported in Audrey Shank, "Racial Attitudes of the Zion Congregation," 1954, 2, Term Paper file, MSHL.
27. Ibid.
28. Jay B. Landis, e-mail messages to author, Jan. 26, 2016, and Feb. 4, 2016; "50 Years since Integration," *Crossroads*, Spring 2007, 6; Bonnie Lofton, "Checkered Past, Colorful Present," *Crossroads*, Spring 2007, 7–10; *Shenandoah 1954*. Peggy Webb Howard stayed in contact with friends and faculty at EMC after she moved to Texas. She attended a class reunion in the 1990s and spoke to students about her experience as a student of color. Her sister Ada became a nurse after graduating from a school in Colorado.
29. *Minutes of the Virginia Conference*, 2:35.
30. Guzman, *1952 Negro Year Book*, 241–42.
31. Allan Jones, "Negroes Attend 6 State Colleges," *The Richmond Times Dispatch*, Nov. 29, 1959, MSHL; Pettigrew, "Our Caste-Ridden Protestant Campuses"; Mark Newman, *Getting Right with God*, 180–81.
32. Steve Longenecker, e-mail message to author, Feb. 11, 2016; P. Bowman, *Brethren Education*, 317; Bailey Kirkpatrick, "The College's History of Racial Integration," *The Flat Hat*, Sept. 29, 2014, http://flathatnews.com/2014/09/29/the-colleges-history-of-racial-integration/.
33. James Miller, *A Centennial History*, 138–44.

34. Dean's Report, 1962–1963.
35. *Catalog 1948–1949*, 125, 129, 132–33.
36. *Catalog 1949–1950*, 157.
37. SACS Self-Survey Report 1958, 300.
38. President's Report, Aug. 1, 1958.
39. Report of the Religious Welfare Survey Committee, 59.
40. Faculty minutes, May 22, 1956.
41. Minutes of conjoint meeting of faculty, trustees, and the RWC, June 5, 1962, B2, F15, RWC.
42. Blair Seitz, "Non-Mennonite Students Speak Out," *Weather Vane*, Apr. 2, 1965.
43. Minutes of conjoint meeting of faculty, trustees, and the RWC, June 5, 1962, B2, F15, RWC.
44. Faculty minutes, May 8, 1956.
45. Dean's Report, 1958–1959; minutes of conjoint meeting of faculty, trustees, and the RWC, June 5, 1962, B2, F15, RWC.
46. Faculty minutes, May 22, 1956.
47. Minutes of conjoint meeting of faculty, trustees, and the RWC, June 5, 1962, B2, F15, RWC.
48. Jim Halteman to his parents, May 14, 1964, Letters 1962–1964, 256, EMUA.
49. Faculty minutes, Jan. 29, 1963.
50. Dean's Report, 1960–1961; Dean's Report, 1963–1964.
51. Ira Miller, notes handwritten on faculty minutes, Dec. 12, 1951.
52. Harry G. Lefever, "Toward a Philosophy of Education," n.d., ca. 1964, B2, F17, RWC.
53. Faculty minutes, Feb. 17, 1959.
54. "Guidelines for Counseling and Discipline at EMC," May 3, 1963, B12, F26, MSA.
55. Dean's Report, 1963–1964.
56. Lowell Herr, e-mail message to author, Feb. 2, 2016.
57. Ibid.
58. Ibid.
59. Ibid.; Duane Kauffman, e-mail message to author, Feb. 3, 2016; Administration Committee minutes, Mar. 4, 1959.
60. Minutes of a meeting of faculty, RWC, and executive committee of Virginia Conference, June 3, 1958, 8–9, B2, F11, RWC.
61. Ernest Kraybill, e-mail message to author, Feb. 2, 2016.
62. Ibid.
63. Daniel Hess, e-mail message to author, Jan. 18, 2016.
64. Herman R. Reitz, n.d., ca. 1963, B1, F4, Opinion Board.
65. Excerpts from *Piranha* issues, Feb. 14 through May 22, 1964, Unofficial EMU Publications, EMUA (emphasis in the original).
66. "EMC Has Beatles for Breakfast," news story from the Harrisonburg *Daily News-Record* posted by Ellen Shenk, n.d., B1, F4, Opinion Board.
67. Lowell Herr, e-mail message to author, Feb. 2, 2016.
68. Faculty minutes, May 26, 1958.
69. George R. Brunk, "The Church-School Problem," *Bulletin*, Sept. 1934, 3–4; George R. Brunk, Editorial Message.
70. President's Report, 1958–1959.
71. A. Don Augsburger, "Introducing the Implications of Academic Freedom on a Church College Campus," 1962, B2, F15, RWC.
72. John R. Mumaw, "Principles of Academic Freedom at Eastern Mennonite College," 1963, B12, F29, MSA.
73. Faculty conference notes, Sept. 1963, B16, F50, MSA.
74. Dean's Report, 1960–1961.
75. Dean's Report, 1961–1962.
76. Dean's Report, 1958–1959.
77. J. Daniel Hess, e-mail message to author, Jan. 6, 2016.
78. "To the Constitutional Revision Committee," Nov. 17, 1962, B1, F-Constitutional Revision Committee, 1962–1963, Constitution series, EMUA.
79. Constitution 1963.
80. Harold D. Lehman, interview by author, July 13, 2013.
81. *Minutes of the Virginia Conference*, 2:154.
82. Reta Halteman to her parents, Mar. 10, 1962, Letters 1962–1964, 21–22, EMUA.
83. Ibid.; Reta Halteman Finger, e-mail message to author, Feb. 25, 2016.
84. C. Mumaw, "Touched by the World," 293.
85. Faculty minutes, Nov. 4, 1958.
86. Geraldine Wilcox, "Graduation Attire," attachment to Administration Committee minutes, Mar. 19, 1963.
87. Ibid.; "Statement Regarding Graduation Robes," attachment to Administration Committee minutes, Apr. 25, 1962; minutes of joint meeting of trustees and faculty, June 9, 1964, B1, F17, RWC.
88. "Improve Modesty at Graduation," Editorial, *Weather Vane*, Apr. 24, 1964, 2.
89. Edsel Burdge, personal communication with the author, July 27, 2017.
90. Vincent and Rosemarie Harding, "Reflections on a Visit to Virginia," Nov. 9, 1962, 1, vertical file: Mennonites and Race, MSHL.
91. *The Travelers' Green Book*, published for African American travelers from 1936 to 1966, provided information on accessible lodging and restaurants, including those in the Harrisonburg area. For the kinds of establishments available to the Hardings during their visit, see *Green Book 1962*, New York Public Library Digital Collections, New York

Public Library, http://digitalcollections
.nypl.org/items/786175a0-942e-0132-97b0
-58d385a7bbd0.

92. Catherine R. Mumaw, interview by author,
July 12, 2013.

93. Vincent and Rosemarie Harding, "Reflections on a Visit to Virginia," Nov. 9, 1962, 1,
vertical file: Mennonites and Race, MSHL.

94. S. David Garber, "Of One Blood," *Weather
Vane*, Oct. 10, 1958, 2; J. Mark Brubaker,
"Black and White and Maybe Red,"
Weather Vane, Feb. 6, 1959, 5; "IPF Convenes
at Fisk University," *Weather Vane*, Apr. 14,
1961, 1; Carroll Yoder, "Committed to Class
Conformity," *Weather Vane*, May 25, 1962, 2.

95. Richard Lichty, "Love and Race Relations,"
Weather Vane, Apr. 28, 1961, 2.

96. Paul Souder and Bonnie Price Lofton,
"Much Pain, One Big Gain, from Being
an African American Student at EMU in
1962–63," Eastern Mennonite University,
last modified Feb. 11, 2014, http://emu.edu/
now/news/2014/01/much-pain-one-big
-gain-from-being-an-african-american
-student-at-emu-in-1962-63/. This article is
the source for Hill's story.

97. Lee Roy Berry Jr., interview by author, Nov.
17, 2016. This interview is the source for Berry's story.

98. John A. Lapp, June 4, 1965, B1, F4, Opinion
Board.

99. As late as July 2015, Lapp did not know who
had burned the cross. However, according
to Jim Wert in an e-mail message to the
author, Dec. 4, 2014 (and verified by Herb
Kraybill in an interview by the author,
May 1, 2016), three male first-year EMC
students did it as a prank at the urging of
upperclassman Walt Hackman.

100. John A. Lapp, June 4, 1965, B1, F4, Opinion
Board.

101. Administration Committee minutes, Sept.
30, 1958.

102. Elsianne Hess, "John Howard Griffin to
Lecture on Race Crisis Tonight," *Weather
Vane*, Mar. 6, 1964, 1; "Mrs. Boyle, Griffin
Join Forces to Expose System of Racism,"
Weather Vane, Mar. 19, 1964, 1, 3.

103. Harold D. Lehman, interview by author,
July 13, 2013.

104. John A. Lapp, "We Joined the Washington
Freedom March," *Weather Vane*, Sept. 27,
1963, 2; Katrina Wert, "EMC Faculty Fight
for Civil Rights," *Weather Vane*, Oct. 1, 1992,
10.

105. The phrase appears in "A Declaration of
Christian Faith and Commitment," pro-
duced by a study conference sponsored by
MCC, Nov. 9–12, 1950, KCR. John Howard
Yoder developed the political implications

in *The Christian Witness to the State*, 8–14.
See also Driedger and Kraybill, *Mennonite
Peacemaking*, 84–91, and Stutzman, *From
Nonresistance to Justice*, 133–57.

106. Faculty minutes, Apr. 29, 1953.

107. Dean's Report, 1955–1956.

108. Stauffer to Bender, July 1, 1944, B23, F5,
HSB; Bender to Lehman (quoting Leh-
man), July 25, 1944, B19, F5, HSB.

109. Trustee minutes, Jan. 31, 1958.

110. John R. Mumaw, "A Philosophy of Bible
School Training," Exhibit II, trustee minutes, Jan. 8, 1960.

111. Pellman, *EMC*, 223–24.

112. President's Report, 1954–1955; SACS Self-
Survey Report 1958, 61.

113. Constitution 1963.

114. EMC presidential candidate, interview by
author, May 28, 2014.

115. Ibid.

116. *Global Anabaptist Mennonite Encyclopedia Online*, s.v. "Mumaw, John Rudy
(1904–1993)," by Hubert R. Pellman, last
modified Sept. 15, 2016, http://gameo.org/
index.php?title=Mumaw,_John_Rudy_
(1904-1993); Pellman, *EMC*, 236–37; *John R.,
Esther F., and Evelyn K. Mumaw: Celebration of Ministry*, Nov. 14, 2009, KCR.

117. Betty Lois Wenger, "President Addresses
College on Training for Discipleship,"
Weather Vane, Sept. 27, 1963, 5.

118. Nathan E. Yoder, interview by author, Dec.
4, 2015.

119. Joe Longacher, e-mail message to author,
Feb. 15, 2016.

120. *Minutes of the Virginia Conference*, 2:153–55.

CHAPTER 8

EPIGRAPH: Omar Eby, "The Restless Decade:
1967–77," *Bulletin*, Dec. 1977, 2.

1. Hubert Pellman, interview by author, Oct.
12, 2012.

2. Myron Augsburger, interview by author,
July 23, 2014.

3. Myron Augsburger, "Education for Meaning," *Bulletin*, June 1966, 4.

4. Esther Augsburger, interview by author,
July 23, 2014.

5. Alumni, personal communication with the
author.

6. Myron Augsburger, "Education for Meaning," *Bulletin*, June 1966, 4.

7. Myron Augsburger, "The College, a Community of Persuasion," Sept. 1967, B12, F23,
MSA.

8. President's Report, 1968–1969.

9. Omar Eby, "The Restless Decade: 1967–77,"
Bulletin, Dec. 1977, 3.

10. Manzullo-Thomas, "Prophet and President," 136–42.

11. Myron Augsburger, interview by author, July 23, 2014; "Preachers of an Active Gospel," 60.

12. Omar Eby, "The Restless Decade: 1967–77," *Bulletin*, Dec. 1977, 2.

13. Ibid., 3.

14. Faculty minutes, Feb. 22, 1935.

15. Stuart Showalter, "Support for the Church's Mission," *Bulletin*, Dec. 1969, 16.

16. "Dr. Suter, Model Teacher," *Crossroads*, Summer 2008, 26–27; "Suter Sent Hundreds into Health Careers," *Crossroads*, Spring 2007, 29.

17. Dora Taylor, "Nursing Education," *Bulletin*, Jan. 1950, 1.

18. Arlene G. Wiens, "Innovative Nursing Education: A History of Nursing at Eastern Mennonite College," 1988, 30, MSHL; Pellman, *EMC*, 203.

19. *Factbook 1976*, E.6, D.1.

20. Arlene G. Wiens, "Innovative Nursing Education: A History of Nursing at Eastern Mennonite College," 1988, 48, MSHL.

21. Donald Showalter, interview by author, June 1, 2016.

22. "The Core Curriculum: Focus for the Future," *Bulletin*, July 1969, 1–4.

23. Omar Eby, "The Restless Decade: 1967–77," *Bulletin*, Dec. 1977, 4.

24. "More than Curriculum," *Weather Vane*, Mar. 8, 1968, 2.

25. "The 'Curriculum for Tomorrow'—Today," B17, F16, MSA.

26. Omar Eby, "The Restless Decade: 1967–77," *Bulletin*, Dec. 1977, 5.

27. Fred Kniss, interview by author, June 1, 2016.

28. Beryl Brubaker, interview by author, Aug. 5, 2016, and Aug. 26, 2016.

29. Chuck Kauffman, "Students Study at Own Rate in Psych," *Weather Vane*, Jan. 29, 1971, 1.

30. Omar Eby, "The Restless Decade: 1967–77," *Bulletin*, Dec. 1977, 5.

31. Beryl Brubaker, interview by author, Aug. 5, 2016.

32. Omar Eby, "The Restless Decade: 1967–77," *Bulletin*, Dec. 1977, 5.

33. Myron Augsburger, interview by author, July 23, 2014.

34. Mary M. Troyer, "Doubtful Amusements," *Journal*, July–Aug. 1931, 11, 13.

35. Jay B. Landis, interview by author, Mar. 3, 2016.

36. "Proposed Principles and Standards Related to the Use of Dramatics at Eastern Mennonite College," approved by the faculty on Nov. 23, 1955, B6, F8, JLS.

37. Jay B. Landis, interview by author, Mar. 3, 2016; Pellman, *EMC*, 216–17.

38. Jay B. Landis, interview by author, Mar. 3, 2016.

39. *Catalog 1968–1969*.

40. Karen Eby, "*Antigone* Demonstrates Dramatic Sensitivity," *Weather Vane*, Nov. 22, 1968, 3.

41. "Guild Will Present Love Scenes," *Weather Vane*, Feb. 21, 1969, 1.

42. Jerry E. Shenk, "Amusing Opera Succeeds with Surprising Quality," *Weather Vane*, Feb. 7, 1969, 3; "Hostetter Directs MENC Opera," *Weather Vane*, Jan. 24, 1969, 1.

43. Mahlon M. Horst to Augsburger, n.d., B16, F54, MSA; unknown writer to "Mr. Krall," Feb. 6, 1969, B16, F54, MSA.

44. Augsburger to Earl Delp, Feb. 13, 1969, B16, F54, MSA; Augsburger to Mahlon M. Horst, Feb. 10, 1969, B16, F54, MSA.

45. Augsburger to Russell Baer, July 24, 1969, B16, F54, MSA.

46. Jay B. Landis, interview by author, Mar. 3, 2016.

47. "Proposed Principles and Standards Related to the Use of Dramatics at Eastern Mennonite College," approved by the faculty on Nov. 23, 1955, B6, F8, JLS.

48. Summary Report of the Committee on Limitations of Dramatics, n.d., ca. 1955, KCR.

49. Ruth Kurtz, "Introducing the Art Laboratory," *Journal*, Nov. 1945, 14; Anna Frey, "Arts and Crafts at EMC," *Journal*, July–Aug. 1948, 13–14.

50. Unless otherwise cited, quotations in this section are from interviews of Myron and Esther Augsburger by author, July 23, 2014 (emphasis added).

51. Esther K. Augsburger, "Why Nudity in Art," 16–17.

52. Fern Miller, "Mennonites in the Arts," *Bulletin*, Feb. 1970, 12–13. (Hershey married Stuart Showalter after her junior year at EMC.)

53. Myron Augsburger, interview by author, July 23, 2014.

54. Study Conference on Athletics and Recreation, Minutes of the Proceedings, Dec. 13–14, 1965, B17, F35, MSA.

55. Lester R. Zook, "Exercise and Athletics at Eastern Mennonite College," Dec. 6, 1988, 23, MSHL.

56. Augsburger to Miriam Mumaw, Oct. 14, 1966, B17, F35, MSA.

57. Myron Augsburger, "Our Philosophy of Physical Education," B17, F35, MSA.

58. *Shenandoah 1966*.

59. James Wert, "Nay, We Will Have Varsity Sports," *Weather Vane*, May 19, 1967, 2.

60. *Catalog 1971–1973*; Gretchen H. Maust, "Physical Education: A Progress Report," *Bulletin*, Dec. 1978, 6–7.

61. Lester R. Zook, "Exercise and Athletics at Eastern Mennonite College," Dec. 6, 1988, 28, MSHL (emphasis in the original).

62. Task Force on Athletics: Blueprint, June 1980, B8, F21, ANK.

63. *Crossroads*, Fall/Winter 2009–2010. The entire issue is devoted to the history of sports.

64. Ken Lehman, "It Can't Happen Here," *Weather Vane*, May 2, 1969, 2.

65. Jacob Stahl to Myron Augsburger, Apr. 30, 1969, B16, F54, MSA.

66. Luke H. Wenger, "Direction: US Faces Undeclared War in Vietnam Guerrilla Action," *Weather Vane*, May 11, 1962, 2; "Saigon Trembles with Fear; Metzler Enlightens Inhabitants," *Weather Vane*, Mar. 1, 1963, 3; Melvin Keim, "As Congs Plague Regime, Discord Goes on in Vietnam," *Weather Vane*, Oct. 11, 1963, 2; Jason Sprunger, "Pacifism, Nonresistance and Protests: The Eastern Mennonite College Student Response to the Vietnam War, 1962–1972," 2011, Term Paper file, MSHL.

67. Steve Shenk, "Senior Quits Draft System, Attacks SSS," *Weather Vane*, May 7, 1971, 5.

68. "Editor Endorses Johnson Letter," *Weather Vane*, Feb. 24, 1967, 3.

69. Shirley Hershey, "Peace Vigils Result in Increasing Controversy," *Weather Vane*, Feb. 24, 1967, 3.

70. Mel Lehman, "EMC Students View Inaugural Activities," *Weather Vane*, Jan. 24, 1969, 1; Mel Lehman, "The March, the Ball, the Man," *Weather Vane*, Jan. 24, 1969, 6.

71. "IPF Conference Considers 'Peacemaker in Revolution,'" *Weather Vane*, Apr. 4, 1969, 3.

72. For examples of *reconciliation* and *peace position*, see the first page of each college catalog from 1975 through 1982.

73. Augsburger to Nixon with copies to Sen. Mark O. Hatfield and Sen. Harry F. Byrd, May 8, 1970, attachment to trustee minutes, June 4, 1970.

74. Miller and Shenk, *Path of Most Resistance*, 44–52, 234.

75. "Mennonite Resistance," *Weather Vane*, Oct. 3, 1969, 2.

76. "Resisters Tell Story of Oregon Resolution," *Weather Vane*, Oct. 3, 1969, 4.

77. Phil Ropp, "Church Decides to Support Mennonite Draft Resistance," *Weather Vane*, Oct. 3, 1969, 4.

78. "EMC Participates in Vietnam Moratorium Day," *Weather Vane*, Oct. 17, 1969, 1. Union Theological Seminary in Richmond also canceled classes.

79. "An Appeal for Peace," Oct. 15, 1969, B12, F3, MSA; "EMC's Observance of the October 15 Moratorium," Nov. 6, 1969, B12, F3, MSA.

80. Fern Miller, "Programs and Prayers for Peace," *Bulletin*, Dec. 1969, 11.

81. Leonard Brydge to Augsburger, Oct. 15, 1969, B16, F54, MSA.

82. "EMC Participates in Vietnam Moratorium Day," *Weather Vane*, Oct. 17, 1969, 1.

83. Victor D. Obot, "Resistance of the Nonresistant," *Weather Vane*, Feb. 23, 1973, 2.

84. Miller and Shenk, *Path of Most Resistance*, 27–29.

85. Ibid., 156–58.

86. Ibid., 13.

87. Ben Gamber, "SGA Constitution Undergoes Changes," *Weather Vane* Sept. 19, 1969, 2; Ben Gamber, "Students Gain Positions and Faculty Committees," *Weather Vane*, Nov. 14, 1969, 4; Jim Krabill, "Students Gain Representation in Ad. Council," *Weather Vane*, Jan. 16, 1970, 1.

88. Ben Gamber, "Students Gain Positions and Faculty Committees," *Weather Vane*, Nov. 14, 1969, 4.

89. "Board to Decide the Fate of New Library," *Weather Vane*, Oct. 17, 1969, 1; Wilmer Otto, "Board Postpones Decision on Library," *Weather Vane*, Nov. 14, 1969, 1.

90. "Salvaging the Library," *Weather Vane*, Oct. 17, 1969, 2.

91. Wilmer Otto, "Students Unite in Massive Fund Drive to Build New Library," *Weather Vane* Dec. 12, 1969, 1.

92. "The Bell Tolls for Unity," *Bulletin*, Dec. 1969, 2–3.

93. Jeanette Noll, "Old Bell Becomes Symbol of Unity," *Weather Vane*, Jan. 16, 1970, 5.

94. James O. Lehman, "Library Happening," n.d., MSHL.

95. Omar Eby, "The Restless Decade: 1967–77," *Bulletin*, Dec. 1977, 4.

96. "The Bell Tolls for Unity," *Bulletin*, Dec. 1969, 2–3; James O. Lehman, "The Library Happening at Eastern Mennonite College: A Modern-Day Miracle in Three Acts," *Bulletin*, Oct. 1971, 2.

97. Ben Gamber, "Participants Evaluate Library Drive," *Weather Vane*, Oct. 22, 1971, 4.

98. Mary Emma Showalter Eby to Myron Augsburger, Jan. 23, 1970, B16, F55, MSA.

99. Ken Schildt, "School Nickname Creates Conflict," *Weather Vane*, Feb. 26, 1970, 4; Wilmer Otto, "Students Show Disagreement on Method of Choosing Name," *Weather Vane*, Feb. 26, 1970, 3; John Otto, "The Case for Student Power," *Weather Vane*, Feb. 26, 1971, 2.

100. John Otto, "Improving God's Work," *Weather Vane*, Jan. 15, 1971, 2.

101. News release, Jan. 6, 1971, B17, F41, MSA.

102. Petition, B17, F41, MSA; John Otto, "More on the Imbroglio," *Weather Vane*, Jan. 29, 1971, 2.
103. John Otto, "Improving God's Work," *Weather Vane*, Jan. 15, 1971, 2.
104. J. Clair Buckwalter to EMC Administration, B17, F41, MSA.
105. Chester Kauffman, Dennis Peachey, and Wilma Stoltzfus, "To Whom It May Concern," Jan. 28, 1971, B17, F41, MSA.
106. John Metzler to Myron Augsburger, Jan. 28, 1971, B17, F41, MSA.
107. Trustee minutes, Mar. 12, 1971; Discipleship Center petition, Sept. 28, 1971, B17, F41, MSA; Planning Committee for the Discipleship Center minutes, May 21, 1971, B17, F41, MSA; "Schleitheim Hall," n.d., B17, F41, MSA; trustee minutes, Nov. 6, 1973; "Discipleship Center Will Facilitate Small Groups," *Bulletin*, Feb. 1974, 5.
108. "1960–1990: Adding Beauty to Function," *Crossroads*, Summer 2007, 18.
109. Myron Augsburger, "The College, a Community of Persuasion," Sept. 1967, B12, F23, MSA.
110. Untitled petition, [1967], B16, F76, MSA.
111. Chapel Study Committee Report, Apr. 27, 1967, B16, F76, MSA; Truman H. Brunk Jr. to Administrative Council, Feb. 27, 1970, B16, F55, MSA.
112. Omar Eby, "The Restless Decade: 1967–77," *Bulletin*, Dec. 1977, 7.
113. Mike Sarco, "Priorities Again," *Weather Vane*, Apr. 12, 1974, 2.
114. *Handbook 1971–1972*, 4; Religious Life Committee to Committee on Administration, Jan. 5, 1973 B2, F23, RWC; Myron Augsburger, "Philosophy of Chapel," attachment to Administrative Council minutes, Dec. 9, 1975, B16, F55, MSA.
115. *Handbook 1981–1982*, 16–17; *Handbook 1988–1989*, 6; *Catalog 1995–1997*.
116. Ken L. Nafziger, interview by author, Mar. 2, 2015.
117. Peachey, "Identity Crisis among American Mennonites," 243.
118. Scott, *Old Order and Conservative Mennonite Groups*, 162–63.
119. *Handbook 1965–1966*, 8–9.
120. Enns, "Standards of Nonconformity"; Miriam L. Weaver, memo to Committee on Administration, Regarding: Slacks Issue, Oct. 12, 1971, B16, F66, MSA.
121. *Handbook 1975–1976*, 9 (emphasis added).
122. *Shenandoah 1950–1975*. Plain dress decline tallied and prepared by Simone Horst, KCR.
123. RWC minutes, Sept. 19, 1975, and Oct. 17, 1975.
124. In the *Catalog 1975–1977* photo, Augsburger wore a lapel coat and no tie, but in the next three catalogs, he wore a plain coat.

Photos of his changing attire appear in *Bulletin*, Aug. 1978, 3; *Bulletin*, Aug. 1979, 4; *Bulletin*, Oct. 1978, 2; and *Bulletin*, Apr. 1979, 16.
125. Edsel Burdge, interview by author, Nov. 13, 2014.
126. Melody Miller, "The Clothing of the Multitude," *Weather Vane*, Apr. 4, 1975, 6.
127. Showalter, e-mail message to author, Oct. 10, 2015.

CHAPTER 9
EPIGRAPH: Dean's Report, 1977–1978.
1. *Muppie* played off of the popular 1980s term *Yuppie* (young urban professional).
2. Dean's Report, 1963–1964; Gretchen H. Maust, "Physical Education: A Progress Report," *Bulletin*, Dec. 1978, 7.
3. M. Yoder, "Findings from the 1982 Mennonite Census."
4. Dean's Report, 1977–1978; Dean's Report, 1984–1985; Hess to Augsburger, n.d., ca. 1974, B17, F26, MSA.
5. Miller is a pseudonym for the author.
6. "Storefront Meets Needs of North Main Street Drifters," *Weather Vane*, May 13, 1966, 2, 4.
7. Jim Halteman to his parents, May 4, 1964, Letters 1962–1964, 252, EMUA.
8. Omar Eby, "The Restless Decade: 1967–77," *Bulletin*, Dec. 1977, 2; Eldon Kurtz, "Prayer Groups at EMC: Their Nature and Significance," Feb. 27, 1976, MSHL.
9. James Penner and Herman Bontrager, "Church Discusses, Experiences Spirit," *Weather Vane*, Oct. 8, 1971, 2; Carolyn Yoder, "Students, Faculty Encourage Campus to Carry on Revival All Year," *Weather Vane*, Oct. 22, 1971, 7.
10. Merle Stoltzfus, "Uncertainties in the Midst of Revival," *Bulletin*, Apr. 1972, 5–6. See George R. Brunk II, *Encounter with the Holy Spirit*, for the papers from the consultation. Other sources that reflect the new emphasis on the Holy Spirit include RWC minutes, Apr. 28, 1964, and May 25, 1964, and A. Don Augsburger, "The Christian and the Spirit's Gift of Tongues," Jan. 1970, B16, F15, MSA.
11. Noll, *American Evangelical Christianity*, 23.
12. Bellah et al., *Habits of the Heart*, 221–35; Wuthnow, *Restructuring of American Religion*, 71–99.
13. For an assessment of Yoder's impact, see Burkholder, *Continuity and Change*.
14. Sam Weaver, interview by author, July 14, 2013.
15. George R. Brunk II, "Wanted: Men for the Ministry," *Bulletin*, May 1969, 1.
16. George R. Brunk III, "Seminary Year Sets Records," *Bulletin*, Oct. 1978, 12; *Factbook 1978*, C.11.

17. All quotes are in Omar Eby, "Seminary Grows, Examines Its Mission," *Bulletin*, Dec. 1977, 12.

18. *Catalog 1948–1949.*

19. Omar Eby, "High School Gains Own Identity," *Bulletin*, Dec. 1977, 14–15; Sam Weaver, "Report to Virginia Conference: Study Committee on Relationships between EMC and EMHS," Jan. 7, 1977, KCR; Sam Weaver, interview by author, July 14, 2013.

20. Trustee minutes, Feb. 18–19, 1982, and Aug. 19–20, 1982.

21. Constitution 1970, 1975, 1979. Minor constitutional revisions also occurred in 1972 and 1976. For an overview of the issues at stake in the 1970 revision, see the May 12, 1970, minutes, Constitutional Revision Committee, Constitution series, EMUA.

22. A reorganization of the Mennonite Church in 1971 created the General Assembly, which replaced the General Conference. Most of EMC's constituent conferences were part of Region Five in the East.

23. Linden M. Wenger to Lloyd Weaver Jr., Sept. 3, 1975, B2, F26, RWC; Constitution 1979.

24. Dean's Report, 1968–1969.

25. Miller to Augsburger, Nov. 17, 1969, B16, F57, MSA; trustee minutes, Nov. 7, 1969.

26. Dean Selection Committee minutes, Jan. 28, 1970, B16, F57, MSA; Detweiler to Augsburger, Feb. 26, 1970, and Mar. 17, 1970, B16, F57, MSA; trustee minutes, Mar. 6, 1970.

27. Eldon Kurtz, "Prayer Groups at EMC: Their Nature and Significance," Feb. 27, 1976, 11–12, MSHL.

28. Trustee minutes, Aug. 16, 1974; Lee Yoder, interview by author, Nov. 6, 2014; Harold D. Lehman, interview by author, July 13, 2013; "Re-appointment of Daniel Yutzy As Dean," attachment to faculty senate minutes, [Jan. 1974?]. The Religious Welfare Committee had "strong feelings" that Yutzy should be retained. RWC minutes, Jan. 21, 1976.

29. John H. Hess to Augsburger, n.d., ca. 1974, B17, F26, MSA.

30. Retired faculty member, interview by author, Mar. 3, 2016.

31. Augsburger to Dan Yutzy, June 21, 1973, B1, F-Wilbur Maust, Music Department, EMUA.

32. Retired faculty member, interview by author, Mar. 3, 2016.

33. Lee Yoder, interview by author, Nov. 6, 2014.

34. Yoder to Augsburger, Nov. 10, 1976, and Dec. 14, 1976, B2, F5, LMY.

35. Retired faculty member, interview by author, Mar. 3, 2016.

36. Wilbur Maust, Amos Burkholder, Lowell Byler (chair), and Miriam Byler resigned. Carol Weaver, on leave, was not invited to return. Music professor Roy Roth was teaching music at the seminary.

37. Mark Young, "Mast, Burkholder Resign," *Weather Vane*, Dec. 10, 1976, 1; Paul Souder, "Bylers Leave Music Department," *Weather Vane*, Apr. 29, 1977, 1–2; "Two EMC Music Teachers Resign."

38. Myron Augsburger to trustees, Sept. 8, 1969, B1, F-Earl Maust, Music Department, EMUA; "Service at EMC: His [Earl Maust's] Contribution to Christ," *Bulletin*, Oct. 1969, 3.

39. Augsburger to Earl Maust, Oct. 23, 1968, B1, F-Earl Maust, Music Department, EMUA; Augsburger to Wilbur Maust, June 21, 1973, B1, F-Wilbur Maust, Music Department, EMUA.

40. Nathan E. Yoder, "Music Department Themes, Developments, and Issues," July 1, 2016, KCR.

41. Trustees Academic Affairs Committee minutes, May 12, 1977.

42. Willard Swartley, "What Happened in the Music Department, 1973–1977?," Apr.–May 1977, 7, B1, F15, WMS.

43. Ibid., 5–6.

44. Myron Augsburger, "Memorandum of Understanding with Respect to the Music Department," May 1977, B1, F15, WMS. This document served as the president's notes for the chapel address.

45. Trustees Academic Affairs Committee minutes, May 12, 1977.

46. Ibid.

47. Willard Swartley, Daniel Suter, and Jesse Byler to Augsburger, June 9, 1977, B1, F10, WMS.

48. Dean's Report, 1977–1978, 14.

49. Dean's Report, 1979–1980.

50. Faculty senate minutes, May 12, 1980; trustee minutes, May 23, 1980.

51. Dean's Report, 1979–1980.

52. Faculty senate minutes, May 15, 1980.

53. In the sphere of Christian higher education, Augsburger helped found the Christian College Consortium in 1972 and the Coalition (later, Council) for Christian Colleges and Universities (CCCU) in 1976. He served as president of the CCCU from 1988 to 1994.

54. Report of the Church Evaluation Team to Eastern Mennonite College, 1975, 11, KCR; "Church Team Submits Report," *Bulletin*, Apr. 1976, 2–3.

55. Myron Augsburger, interview by author, July 23, 2014.

56. Stuart Showalter, "Support for the Church's Mission," *Bulletin*, Dec. 1969, 16.

57. SACS Self-Study Report 1969, viii–x; "Harrisonburg Businessmen Launch Fund Drive for Library," *Weather Vane*, Feb. 13, 1970, 2.

58. Richard Benner, "Signs of the Times," *Bulletin*, Feb. 1970, 6.

59. Donald Showalter, interview by author, June 1, 2016.

60. "Myron and Esther Augsburger: Tributes Given for Fifteen Years of Service," *Bulletin*, July–Sept. 1980, 2–3.

61. Presidential search committee to faculty and staff, May 23, 1979, B1, F27, JLL; trustee minutes, Feb. 7–8, 1980.

62. Samples of Detweiler's vision for the college appear in Detweiler, "Personal Greetings and Priorities," *Bulletin*, July–Sept. 1980, 16; Detweiler, "Vision for Mission Is Foremost," *Bulletin*, Oct.–Dec. 1980, 10; and Detweiler, "The Rediscovery of Sacrifice," *Bulletin*, Apr.–June 1981, 15.

63. Former administrator, interview by author, Nov. 6, 2014.

64. Sam Weaver, interview by author, July 14, 2013.

65. Nineteen people (including RWC members, Bible faculty, seminary faculty, faculty status committee, the dean, and the president) interrogated Good about his views and pedagogy. RWC minutes, Apr. 21, 1972, and May 26, 1972.

66. Willard Swartley, e-mail message to author, Nov. 12, 2016.

67. Nolt, "An Evangelical Encounter"; Steven Nolt, interview by author, Nov. 11, 2016.

68. Willard Swartley, e-mail message to author, Nov. 12, 2016.

69. Brunk II to Ray Gingerich, Feb. 3, 1982; Roger Hershberger to Detweiler, Mar. 29, 1982; Kenneth Zehr to Detweiler, Mar. 20, 1982; Detweiler to Zehr, Apr. 6, 1982; Marlin Ebersole to Adam Martin with copy to Detweiler, Apr. 19, 1982; Byron Shenk to students of EMC, Apr. 15, 1982; "Statement of Concerns by Eleven Students," n.d., ca. late Apr. 1982; George Brunk II to Detweiler, Apr. 29, 1982. All documents in B6, F5, RCD.

70. Steve King, "Biblical Interpretation Sparks Controversy," *Weather Vane*, May 7, 1982, 5.

71. George R. Brunk II, *A Crisis among Mennonites*, 2, 10–11.

72. George Brunk II, "A Crisis in Education at Eastern Mennonite College," Mar. 1983, B6, F7, RCD.

73. "Background on Critique of Bible Course Textbooks," Feb. 24, 1983, B5, F2, RCD; Detweiler to Conference Moderators (with attachments), Apr. 28, 1983, B6, F10, RCD.

74. Brunk II to Detweiler, Apr. 1, 1983, B6, F18, RCD.

75. George Brunk III to Albert Slabach, Mar. 28, 1983, B6, F18, RCD (emphasis in the original).

76. These are a few examples of strong pushback by Mennonite leaders: Virginia Conference leaders, "A Call for Trust and Discernment," May 26, 1983, B1, F11, JLL; Franconia Conference leaders to pastors, June 6, 1983, B6, F12, RCD; executive committee of the Mennonite Church to the Mennonite Church General Board, July 6, 1983, B5, F2, RCD; James Longacre et al., "A Summary of the Issues and Concerns Identified by George Brunk II," Aug. 1, 1983, B5, F2, RCD.

77. "Introducing the Fellowship of Concerned Mennonites," n.d., KCR.

78. "A Call for Trust and Discernment," May 26, 1983, B1, F11, JLL.

79. Rock had been employed by Mennonite Central Committee but was dismissed after his sexual orientation became known. The Brethren Mennonite Council for Gay Concerns was renamed the Brethren Mennonite Council for Lesbian and Gay Concerns in 1986 and renamed the Brethren Mennonite Council for Lesbian, Gay, Bisexual, and Transgender Interests in 2002.

80. Nathan E. Yoder, "Historical Sketch (1969–2015): Mennonites and Conversation about Homosexuality with Particular Attention to Developments at EMU," KCR.

81. Former student, e-mail message to author, Feb. 2, 2016. Each class had a faculty or staff advisor as liaison between the class and the college.

82. RWC to Ella May Miller, Nov. 15, 1958, B6, F10a, JLS; executive committee minutes, Dec. 15, 1958, B6, F10a, JLS; Ira Miller to J. C. Wenger, Mar. 5, 1959, B1, F-Mennonite General Conference, IEM.

83. E. Miller to RWC, Nov. 12, 1958, B6, F10a, JLS.

84. Former student, interview by author, June 1, 2016.

85. "Out of the Closet," *Weather Vane*, Dec. 14, 1977, 2.

86. Catherine B. Custalow, interview by author, June 15, 2015.

87. Mike Martin, "Homosexuality a Burning Issue in 1982," *Weather Vane*, Mar. 3, 1994, 6.

88. Luke Hurst, "Dean Censors Homosexuality Forum," *Weather Vane*, Feb. 19, 1982, 7; Steve King, "Biblical Interpretation Sparks Controversy," *Weather Vane*, May 7, 1982, 5;

Scott Eldridge, "On Maintaining Balance," *Weather Vane*, May 20, 1982, 2.

89. J. Roger Kurtz, "SGA Passes Recommendation," *Weather Vane*, Oct. 12, 1984, 1.

90. Detweiler to John Swartzentruber, Oct. 24, 1984, B1, F9, JLL.

91. Lehman to Detweiler, Oct. 25, 1984, B22, F26, JLL; Detweiler to Lehman, Nov. 21, 1984, B22, F26, JLL (emphasis in the original).

92. Bowman to Detweiler, Nov. 11, 1984, B22, F26, JLL; *Catalog 1983–1984*, 9.

93. Boshart to Detweiler, Dec. 6, 1984, B22, F26, JLL.

94. Highlights of the discussions are recorded in trustee minutes of Nov. 11, 1966, May 24, 1974, Aug. 16, 1974, May 23, 1975, Nov. 14, 1975, May 21, 1976, Aug. 20, 1976, Nov. 12, 1976, Feb. 18, 1977, Aug. 19, 1977, Nov. 18, 1977, Feb. 17, 1978, May 18–19, 1978, Aug. 25, 1978, Feb. 18–19, 1982, and Feb. 16–17, 1984. Proposals and position papers are attached to trustee minutes of Aug. 16, 1974, May 25, 1975, and Feb. 17, 1982, and to Richard Detweiler and Lee Yoder, memo to executive committee, Apr. 22, 1982, B1, F12, JLL.

95. Constitution 1963.

96. Myron Augsburger to Higher Education Council, Nov. 14, 1972, B17, F15, MSA. The council dissolved in 1972.

97. Orv Yoder, e-mail message to author, June 24, 2016. Until the mid-1970s, the MBE offices were located in the Mennonite Church Archives and Historical Library, attached to the Goshen Biblical Seminary building on the edge of the Goshen College campus.

98. Trustee minutes, Feb. 18, 1977.

99. Attachment to trustee minutes, Feb. 17, 1978. The covenant took effect in July 1979.

100. Trustee minutes, Feb. 16–17, 1984. Under the agreement, title to the property was held by EMC&S as a subsidiary corporation of the MBE.

101. Wenger to Richard Detweiler, Jan. 10, 1984, B1, F9, JLL.

102. Rose Stauffer, "Finding a Place for Dance," *Weather Vane*, Feb. 20, 1984, 2.

103. *Standards 1943–1944*, 9; *Handbook 1968–1969*, 5.

104. Myron Augsburger, "Philosophy Concerning Dancing," 1975, B16, F55, MSA.

105. Church member profile of four Mennonite denominations and the Brethren in Christ in 1972, KCR.

106. Nathan E. Yoder, "Chronology of Dance at EMU," B1, F1, KCR.

107. Peggy Heatwole Landis, interview by author, Mar. 3, 2016.

108. Trustee minutes, Feb. 16, 1978.

109. Jim Shenk, "Student Government Analyzes Survey," *Weather Vane*, Mar. 16, 1979.

110. Former student, interview by author, June 2, 2015.

111. Student Ad Hoc Committee on Dance, Rationale Abstract, 1979, B1, F4, TFD.

112. Trustee minutes, May 18, 1979 (emphasis added).

113. Augsburger, memo to Beryl Brubaker, Aug. 8, 1979, B1, F5, TFD.

114. Task Force on Dance, "Dance," Mar. 21, 1980, B1, F14, TFD.

115. Al Keim to Lanny Millette and John Landes, Nov. 26, 1980, B1, F15, TFD.

116. "SGA Proposes a Change in Dancing Policy," *Weather Vane*, Dec. 2, 1983, 1; student poll, B1, F17, TFD.

117. Trustee Student Life Committee minutes, Feb. 16, 1984; Peggy Landis, "History of Dance Policy at EMC," Oct. 30, 1984, B1, F25, TFD.

118. Trustee minutes, Dec. 3, 1984. The policy was one part of a larger statement accepted by the dance policy committee on July 10, 1984, B1, F24, TFD.

119. "New Dance Policy," *Weather Vane*, Jan. 18, 1985, 3.

120. "First Square Dance Held," *Weather Vane*, Mar. 1, 1985, 3; Harold K. Shenk to EMC trustees, Apr. 10, 1985, B1, F31, TFD.

121. Sauder to executive committee, Oct. 27, 1983, B1, F10, JLL.

122. Mary Jane King, "Breaking Ground," *Bulletin*, Fall 1983, 10–11.

123. "Fire Guts Ad Building," *Bulletin*, Spring 1984, 12.

124. Mary Emma Showalter Eby, "Dear Old Ad Building," *Bulletin*, Spring 1984, 13.

125. Richard Detweiler, "Aftermath: Realism, Hope," *Bulletin*, Spring 1984, 16.

126. Ibid. (Detweiler quotes the paper's editorial in his essay.)

127. "Disaster Spawns Community Effort, Engenders a New Beginning," *Lawyers Title News*, Nov.–Dec. 1985, 8–9, 21.

128. Donald Showalter, interview by author, June 1, 2016; trustee minutes, Dec. 3, 1984.

129. Trustee minutes, Oct. 30, 1984.

130. *Catalog 1985–1987*, 29–39; Albert Keim, "Global Village: New Curriculum," *Bulletin*, Fall 1982, 6; Dean's Report, 1981–1982.

131. Rachel Keshishian, "Albert Keim: Cross-Cultural Visionary," *Crossroads*, Summer 2012, 7.

132. "Significant Developments: Academic Program," *Bulletin*, Fall 1984, 4.

133. Dean's Report, 1983–1984, 5.

134. Dean's Report, 1982–1983, 4.

135. Albert Meyer to Richard Detweiler, Sept. 17, 1984, B12, F4, JLL; Richard Detweiler, "Report of Consultants' Visit," Sept. 12–13, 1984, B12, F4, JLL; Charles Glassick and Norman Fintel, "Eastern Mennonite College Visit," Sept. 12–13, 1984, B12, F4, JLL.
136. President's cabinet member, interview by author, Mar. 3, 2016.
137. Charles Glassick and Norman Fintel, "Eastern Mennonite College Visit," Sept. 12–13, 1984, B12, F4, JLL; Detweiler to trustees, Oct. 10, 1984, B1, F9, JLL; Richard Detweiler and Lee Snyder to faculty and staff, Nov. 1, 1984, B4, F25, RCD.
138. "Significant Developments: College Dean Appointed," Bulletin, Fall 1984, 4.
139. Exhibit I–II, trustee minutes, Oct. 30, 1984.
140. Snyder, personal communication with the author, July 14, 2016.
141. Detweiler to Lapp, n.d., B12, F5, JLL.
142. Jay B. Landis, interview by author, Mar. 3, 2016.
143. 1981 Graduates of Eastern Mennonite College, B1, F12, JLL.
144. Dean's Report, 1983–1984, 5.

CHAPTER 10

EPIGRAPH: Lapp, "Leading against Giants," seminary chapel address, Feb. 21, 1995, B4, F101, JLL.
1. Foth to Vernon Jantzi, Jan. 10, 1986, B1, F6, JLL (emphasis in the original).
2. Joe Lapp was one of the five candidates interviewed. Report of the Presidential Selection Committee to the Board of Trustees, July 30, 1986, B1, F29, JLL.
3. MBE news release, Aug. 9, 1986, B1, F30, JLL.
4. Kathy Lehigh, "Joe Is a Man of Ideas," Weather Vane, May 13, 1966, 3–4.
5. Joe Lapp, interview by author, Nov. 6, 2014.
6. Joe Lapp, "Comments to EMC&S Faculty and Staff Meeting," Aug. 12, 1986, B1, F30, JLL.
7. President's Report, 1987–1988.
8. "Inauguration, 1987," Bulletin, Fall 1987, 2–5.
9. President's Report, 1987–1988.
10. Joe Lapp, interview by author, Nov. 6, 2014.
11. Ibid.
12. President's Report, 1987–1988.
13. Ibid.
14. Trustee minutes, June 5–6, 1985.
15. President's Report, 1987–1988.
16. Beryl Brubaker, interview by author, Nov. 5, 2014.
17. For example, see 1 Cor. 11:1–16 and 1 Tim. 2:12.
18. Minutes of Committee on Administration, Nov. 1, 1958.
19. Pellman, EMC, 270–71.

20. Ibid., 271–73; tabulation of lead editors of Journal, Weather Vane, and Shenandoah, KCR. The exceptions to male editorial dominance before 1967 included these: The Journal had a woman editor in 1950, 1951, 1955, and 1956. The Weather Vane, which began replacing the Journal in 1939, had a woman editor in 1946, 1950, 1951, and 1952. The student yearbook, Shenandoah (the commencement issue of the Journal from 1923 to 1946 and then a yearbook in its own right), had a woman editor only twice in the forty-four years from 1923 to 1966: two men and two women edited the 1951 volume, and a woman edited the 1961 volume.
21. A. Grace Wenger, "Our Need of the Devotional Life," Bulletin, Oct. 1945, 1–2.
22. Eastern Mennonite College & Seminary Alumni Directory, vii.
23. Ibid., 170–71.
24. Ruth K. Lehman, "'The One Thing Lacking . . .'; or, The Status of Women Faculty at Eastern Mennonite College, 1917 to 1980" (bachelor's thesis, James Madison University, 1981), 80, MSHL (emphasis in the original).
25. Ibid., 59; Ruth K. Lehman, "How Three Women Helped Save the School," Bulletin, Spring 1983, 4–5, 13. See also Evelyn King, "A Study of the Status of Unmarried Women Graduates of Eastern Mennonite College" (master's thesis, 1962), MSHL. Some of the findings were later published in Evelyn King Mumaw, Woman Alone.
26. Ruth K. Lehman, "'The One Thing Lacking,'" 74.
27. Ibid., 56.
28. Pellman interview, June 10, 1981, cited in Ruth K. Lehman, "'The One Thing Lacking,'" 85.
29. Ibid., 84; Hubert Pellman, "Ada Zimmerman, New Air of Professionalism," Bulletin, Spring 1983, 7.
30. Pellman interview, June 10, 1981, cited in Ruth K. Lehman, "'The One Thing Lacking,'" 83.
31. Catherine R. Mumaw, "A Tribute to Mary Emma Showalter Eby, 1913–2003," May 11, 2003, KCR. Showalter added the name Eby when she married Ira Eby in 1960.
32. John Lapp, interview by author, July 21, 2015.
33. Lois B. Bowman, interview by author, Mar. 4, 2015.
34. Catherine R. Mumaw, interview by author, July 12, 2013.
35. Factbook 1971–1972. Differences in advanced degrees likely influenced the male/female discrepancy in rank.
36. Catalog 1968–1969. During the previous year (1967–1968), librarians Margaret Shenk and

Grace Showalter met with the Administrative Council, likely to assist with planning the new library.

37. Catherine R. Mumaw, interview by author, July 12, 2013.

38. Susan Moyer, "Committee Studies Sex Discrimination," *Weather Vane*, May 16, 1975, 6.

39. Beryl Brubaker, interview by author, Nov. 5, 2014. For student unrest related to feminism and dress in the early 1970s, see Rebekah Enns, "Standards of Nonconformity."

40. Annual catalogs. The catalogs provide a listing of board members and their roles on the board.

41. Bill Hawk served as dean for three years, 1997–1999.

42. *Factbook 1998*; *Factbook 2008*.

43. Shirley Hershey Showalter, "The Moment of Change Is the Only Poem," *Bulletin*, July 1983, 4–5 (emphasis added).

44. Lois B. Bowman, interview by author, Mar. 4, 2015.

45. Dean's Report, 1976–1977.

46. Andrew Jenner, "They Don't Come Back the Same: Washington Community Scholars' Center," *Crossroads*, Fall/Winter 2012–2013, 8–9.

47. SACS Self-Study Report 1989, 3.32–3.33.

48. Ibid., 3.28.

49. Ibid., 3.30–3.32; J. Richard Thomas to Richard Detweiler, Nov. 13, 1986, Exhibit I, trustee minutes, Nov. 19–20, 1986; "Discussion Model for Accredited Education in Pennsylvania," Exhibit I, trustee minutes, Aug. 14–15, 1987.

50. SACS Self-Study Report 1989, 3.28–3.29.

51. Lapp, "Leading against Giants," seminary chapel address, Feb. 21, 1995, B4, F101, JLL.

52. The names of these programs evolved. They were broadly under the rubric of the Conflict Transformation Program (CTP) until 2005, when a new umbrella term—the Center for Justice and Peacebuilding (CJP)—covered three distinct components: the master's program in conflict transformation, the Practice Institute, and the Summer Peacebuilding Institute. *PeaceBuilder*, Summer/Fall 2005, 2.

53. Joe Lapp, interview by author, Nov. 6, 2014.

54. Trustee minutes, July 9–10, 1993.

55. The campus discussion appears in several issues of the *Weather Vane*: Jessica King, "EMU?!!!: Name Change Debated," Mar. 4, 1993; Peter Kraybill, "Student Forum on EMC Name Change Slated," Nov. 4, 1993.

56. Trustee minutes, Mar. 21–22, 1994; Bob Brenneman, "A Dream Becomes Reality," *Weather Vane*, Mar. 24, 1994; Jim Bishop, "Campus Celebrates a New Name," *Weather Vane*, Sept. 8, 1994.

57. Dean's Report, 1996–1997.

58. Trustee minutes, Mar. 11–12, 1991.

59. "An Emergency Sabbath: Prayers and Action for Peace," *Bulletin*, Spring 1991, 5–6. Grant Miller describes the wider Mennonite church response to the war in "A Peace Witness Transformed."

60. Quotations cited in Melody M. Davis, "A Gathered Place to Share Grief," *Bulletin*, Summer 1991, 3–4.

61. *Catalog 1957–1958*; SACS Self-Survey Report 1958, 172–79.

62. Trustee minutes, Mar. 22–23, 1993. The trustees approved lengthy policies and procedures on sexual harassment and substance abuse.

63. Exhibit I, trustee minutes, May 18, 1979.

64. Trustee minutes, Nov. 18, 1994.

65. Progress report of the Religious Welfare Survey at Eastern Mennonite College, 1947–1951, section titled "Actions of the Committee," Nov. 4, 1947–May 5, 1949, 66–67, EMUA.

66. Lanny Millette, "Black Students Revive Union," *Weather Vane*, Feb. 7, 1975, 3.

67. Al Keim, memo to Myron Augsburger et al., July 18, 1978, B2, F9, LMY.

68. John Wert, "Students Rally for Equal Rights," *Weather Vane*, May 9, 1980, 1.

69. "Task Force Proposal for Cross-Cultural Educational Programming," revised July 12, 1979, EMUA; Al Keim, memo to board of trustees on Nov. 13, 1980, Exhibit III, trustee minutes, Nov. 14, 1980.

70. SACS Self-Study Report 1989, 6.7.

71. *Factbook 2001–2002*, 1.13, 4.6.

72. Melody Pannell, "Racist Propaganda Prompts Discussion," *Weather Vane*, Feb. 22, 1996, 5.

73. Statement adopted by president's cabinet, July 16, 2001, KCR.

74. Lonnie Yoder, interview by author, Mar. 3, 2015.

75. *Eastern Mennonite Seminary Catalog 1983–1985*.

76. Wendy J. Miller, "So What's This *Spirituality* Thing All About," *The Seminarian*, Dec. 1997, 1–2.

77. Gerald Shenk, interview by author, Oct. 30, 2012.

78. *Factbook 2001–2002*.

79. Nathan E. Yoder, interview by author, Mar. 6, 2015.

80. Stoltzfus, *A Way Was Opened*, 325–47.

81. EMS Dean's Reports, 1998–1999, and 1999–2000.

82. "Peace Is 1997 SLT Theme," *The Seminarian*, Dec. 1996, 2.

83. Roth, *Engaging Anabaptism*. For an assessment of Yoder's theological works and significance, see Mark Thiessen Nation, *John Howard Yoder*.

84. Indiana-Michigan Conference, news release, June 1992, B21, F68, JLL.
85. "Disciplinary Process with John Howard Yoder Draws to a Close," Indiana-Michigan Conference, news release, June 1996, B21, F68, JLL; Goossen, "'Defanging the Beast,'" 14.
86. Graber to Sider, Dec. 27, 1996, B21, F68, JLL.
87. Duane Sider and George Brunk III to Yoder, Jan. 10, 1997, B21, F68, JLL; Yoder to George Brunk III, Jan. 14, 1997, B21, F68, JLL.
88. Executive committee of the president's cabinet to EMU community, Jan. 16, 1997, B21, F68, JLL.
89. In a question period after his presentation, Yoder repeated some of the vague language in his January 14, 1997, letter to George Brunk III, as reported in the student paper: "Seminary Features Yoder, Theologian's Return Raises Questions," *Weather Vane*, Jan. 23, 1997, 1, 6.
90. Goossen, "'Defanging the Beast.'" For candid reflections on Yoder's sexual misconduct, see Mark Thiessen Nation, "Sexual Abuse, Hypocrisy & the Call to Be a Community of Shalom: Living with Two Legacies of John Howard Yoder" (unpublished paper), Fall 2016, KCR.
91. Jerry Holsopple, *7 × 7 Laments*. Other developments in the Hartman story that became known after March 2016 were released in an EMU report, "Findings and Recommendations from the Independent Investigation by D. Stafford & Associates," Nov. 28, 2016, http://emu.edu/cms-links/president/docs/DSA_Report.pdf.
92. Joe Lapp, "Foundations for the New Century," convocation address, Jan. 6, 1999, B4, F76, JLL. The phrase "Y2K" referred to Year Two Kilo (Thousand), the beginning of the twenty-first century.
93. President's Report, 2001–2002.
94. President's Report, 2000–2001.
95. Kraybill, *Concise Encyclopedia*, 95–96, 134.
96. Fred Kniss, interview by author, Oct. 14, 2016.
97. Stutzman to president's cabinet, attachment to the agenda for the cabinet's Sept. 4, 2000, meeting, Aug. 30, 2000 (emphasis in the original). Stutzman's argument reflected Robert Wuthnow's in *The Struggle for America's Soul*, 19–38.
98. SACS Strategic Self-Study 1999, 44–66.
99. Ibid., 4–5.
100. William J. Hawk, "A Modest Proposal to Relocate the Seminary at Eastern Mennonite University," Oct. 6, 1998, KCR.
101. Former seminary official, e-mail message to author, Sept. 8, 2016.
102. The four graduate programs were conflict transformation, counseling, education, and business administration.
103. Shenk to Joe Lapp, Apr. 20, 1999, and Shenk to the structure committee, Apr. 15, 1999, B5, F31, JLL.
104. Joe Lapp, excerpt from report to Virginia Mennonite Conference Assembly, July 16, 1999, KCR.
105. University Graduate Council minutes, Jan. 16, 2003.
106. University Graduate Council minutes, Oct. 24, 2001, Oct. 10, 2001, and Jan. 16, 2003.
107. Morris to Joe Lapp, May 7, 2001, B6, F20, JLL.
108. Documentation for the initiatives: Structure Committee, B5, F31, JLL; Strategic Planning Council, B5, F45, JLL; Task Force on Participatory Decision-Making, B3, F42, JLL; Facilitator Group, B3, F43, JLL; Philosophical Statement on Decision-Making, B3, F42, JLL.
109. "Eastern Mennonite University Policy on Scholarship and Practice," attachment to University Graduate Council minutes, Feb. 20, 2002.
110. Trustee minutes, Nov. 8–9, 2002.
111. Nathan E. Yoder, "Historical Sketch of Mennonites and Conversation about Homosexuality (June 1969–July 2015)," KCR. This document, with its attention to developments at EMU, provided a framework for this section.
112. The statement appears as Exhibit A in Proceedings of the Mennonite Church General Assembly, July 7–12, 1987, B22a, F1, JLL.
113. Kaufman and Driedger, *The Mennonite Mosaic*, 192, 198.
114. Summary Statements by General Board on Homosexuality, July 29, 1991, B22a, F1, JLL.
115. Deborah Weaver, "Breaking the Silence," *Weather Vane*, Mar. 22, 1989, 2.
116. Jenni Leister and Steve Weaver, "Survey Links Reading, Attitude on Homosexuals," *Weather Vane*, Apr. 11, 1990, 4–5.
117. For sample essays, see the following issues: Sept. 26, 1991, Nov. 21, 1991, and Feb. 4, 1993.
118. Titus Bender, "Common Threads of Racism, Sexism, Classism, and Heterosexism," *Dialogue* 13, no. 2 (Aug. 1991): 4–5.
119. Joe Lapp to select members of the class of 1951, Dec. 11, 1991, B22a, F3, JLL (emphasis added).
120. Bender to Sam Weaver, Jan. 30, 1994, B16, F19a, JLL.
121. Sheila Walsh, "Bringing Balance to the Campus," *Washington Blade*, Feb. 4, 1994, B22a, F4, JLL.
122. Former faculty member, interview by author, Mar. 3, 2016.
123. Lapp to Jennifer Field and Allison Loucks, Mar. 8, 1994, B22a, F4, JLL.

124. Jeff Earman, David Miller, and Loren Lehman to Joe Lapp, Feb. 24, 1994, B17, F24, JLL.

125. Gerald E. Martin to *Gospel Herald*, Mar. 1, 1994, B22a, F4, JLL (emphasis added).

126. Lapp to faculty and staff, Mar. 16, 1994, B2, F20, JLL.

127. Trustee minutes, Nov. 18, 1994.

128. *Gospel Herald*, Aug. 29, 1995.

129. Former faculty member, interview by author, Mar. 3, 2016.

130. Amanda Jantzi, "Faculty and Staff Take Issue with Forced Resignation," *Weather Vane*, Dec. 6, 2001, 1.

131. Ibid.

132. Grace Shenk Lynch to Joe Lapp, Nov. 6, 2001, B16, F20, JLL.

133. Lapp to Charles B. Shenk, Dec. 5, 2001, B16, F20, JLL.

134. Lapp to faculty and staff, Dec. 14, 2001, B2, F25, JLL.

135. Kelly M. Miller, "Behind Mennonite Same-Sex Sexuality Debates: Kathleen Temple in Virginia Mennonite Conference, 1998–2002" (senior history thesis, Goshen College, 2001), KCR.

136. Ken Roth, "Ken's 'Coming Out,'" *Weather Vane*, Sept. 26, 2002.

137. Joseph Lapp, "Lapp on Academic Freedom at EMU," *Weather Vane*, Oct. 25, 2002.

138. Ken Roth, "We Cannot Avoid the Issue," *Weather Vane*, Nov. 7, 2002.

139. Trustee minutes, Nov. 8–9, 2002.

140. Former administrator, interview by author, Nov. 5, 2014.

141. Benjamin M. Bear to Isaac M. Baer, Feb. 10, 1918, F21, Isaac M. Baer Collection, MHACVA.

142. "A Proposal to the Lilly Endowment on Theological Exploration of Vocation," Aug. 29, 2001, KCR.

143. *Catalog 2002–2003*; Nancy Heisey, e-mail message to author, Aug. 15, 2016. This philosophical orientation recalled President Richard Detweiler's emphasis on affirmation and presence. It also drew from faculty member Ann Graber Hershberger's research on empowerment (see "Empowerment: Concept Analysis and Application to Christian Nursing Education" [unpublished paper], Nov. 20, 1992, KCR) and from similar notions proposed by the nursing faculty in seeking to distinguish the theological basis of their education of nurses. The Micah phrase itself emerged in discussions of the General Education Committee for the 1999 SACS review and then was used in the Lilly Endowment proposal.

144. "Lilly Grant Report for Year Two," July 2004, KCR.

145. The Micah Think Tank was an ad hoc group that met over several months in 2006 to brainstorm possible ways to incorporate the Micah theme into the academic program and campus life.

146. Micah Think Tank minutes, Dec. 14, 2006.

147. Ann Graber Hershberger, interview by author, Aug. 15, 2016.

148. Nancy Heisey, e-mail message to author, Aug. 18, 2016. One reason for the revision was to reflect a deeper understanding of the imperative to "do justice."

149. *Catalog 2015–2016*, 35.

150. Mike Zucconi, "LEED-Certified Dorm Sets College Precedent," EMU News, Sept. 16, 2011, http://emu.edu/now/news/2011/09/leed-certified-dorm-sets-college-precedent.

151. *Catalog 2015–2016*, 1.

CHAPTER 11

EPIGRAPH: Vi Dutcher, interview by author, Apr. 29, 2014.

1. "EMU Salutes Servant Leadership of Joe and Hannah Lapp," *Crossroads*, Summer 2003, 19.

2. "Resolution of Appreciation for Joseph L. Lapp," trustee minutes, June 28, 2003.

3. Loren Swartzendruber, interview by author, June 3, 2015.

4. Ibid.

5. "EMU Names Next President," *Crossroads*, Summer 2003, 19.

6. Trustee minutes, Nov. 7–8, 2003; Beryl Brubaker, "Interim President's Oral Report to Board of Trustees," Nov. 7, 2003, KCR.

7. SACS Strategic Self-Study 1999, 5.

8. EMU Enrollment & Mennonite Student Data: Fall 2000 and Fall 2016, Institutional Research Office, KCR. The category "Mennonite" includes MC USA, the Brethren in Christ, Mennonite Brethren, and other Anabaptist groups in the Mennonite Central Committee constituency.

9. Beryl Brubaker, interview by author, Nov. 5, 2014.

10. Dickeson, *Prioritizing Academic Programs*, 29.

11. "Prioritization Steering Committee Final Recommendations," Feb. 16, 2006, KCR.

12. Senior official, interview by author, June 2, 2015.

13. "Purposeful Plan: A Vision for Mennonite Church USA," Mennonite Church USA, http://mennoniteusa.org/resources/purposeful-plan/.

14. The mission statement appears in each annual catalog.

15. Micah 6:8, adapted from several translations.

16. The statement, approved by the trustees in 2008, first appeared in *Catalog 2009–2010*, 7 (emphasis added).

17. President's cabinet minutes, Jan. 16, 2010.

18. Trustee minutes, June 21, 2014.

19. Member of president's cabinet, interview by author, Oct. 14, 2016.
20. Loren Swartzendruber, e-mail message to author, Oct. 15, 2016; Jim Bishop, "Injured Student Now in Stable Condition," Eastern Mennonite University, April 15, 2007, http://emu.edu/now/news/2007/04/injured-student-now-in-stable-condition/.
21. Loren Swartzendruber, "Global Warming," chapel address, April 13, 2007, KCR. The BBC program never aired in the United States, but it is available at http://news.bbc.co.uk/2/hi/6648265.stm.
22. Ken L. Nafziger, e-mail message to author, Dec. 14, 2016.
23. Unless otherwise cited, sources for this section include "Sustainability and Creation Care at EMU," Eastern Mennonite University, https://www.emu.edu/sustainability/; Quality Enhancement Plan, SACS Reaffirmation of Accreditation, 2010; "Leading the Way in Energy Efficiency," Crossroads, Summer 2007, 33; and "Sustainability," special issue, Crossroads, Spring 2011.
24. SACS Fifth-Year Interim Report, 2016, 55–66.
25. National Survey of Student Engagement, 2015 Sustainability Education Consortium Report, Institutional Research Office.
26. Trustee minutes, Nov. 8–9, 2002.
27. Thomas, "Church Beliefs vs. Academic Freedom," 32.
28. Lapp to faculty, staff, and students, Feb. 10, 2003, B2, F25, JLL; "Faith, Student Life, and Enrollment Committee," trustee minutes, Mar. 24, 2000.
29. LiFT to Lapp and cabinet, "Executive Summary on Statement of Clarifications," "Explanation of LiFT Web-Vote," and "Statement of Clarifications," all attachments to president's cabinet minutes, May 5, 2003.
30. Beryl Brubaker, e-mail messages to faculty and staff, Oct. 28, 2004, Nov. 22, 2004, Feb. 2, 2005, and Apr. 11, 2005, KCR.
31. Faculty senate minutes, May 23, 2006 (these minutes provide a rich record of faculty concerns and dreams for EMU); faculty senate minutes, Aug. 23, 2006.
32. "Policy of Tenure for the Faculty of EMC," Feb. 16, 1953, B6, F-Coll. Misc., JLS; "Policy of Tenure for the Faculty of EMC," Oct. 1966, B17, F18, MSA; Nathan E. Yoder, "Tenure Timeline: 1953–1980," EMUA.
33. Faculty senate minutes, Jan. 13, 2012, and Feb. 20, 2012.
34. Marsden, Soul of the American University, 292. See also Kevin Carey, "Academic Freedom Has Limits," and William Ringenberg,

The Christian College and the Meaning of Academic Freedom.
35. "Academic Freedom Policy and Addendum," approved by the board of trustees on Feb. 17, 2005, KCR (emphasis in the original).
36. Faculty senate minutes, Mar. 16, 2015.
37. The play was performed at Temple University in 1999, Florida Atlantic University in 2001, and Indiana University–Purdue University Fort Wayne in 2001.
38. Katrina Poplett, "Parks Cancels 'Corpus Christi' amid Controversy," Weather Vane, Feb. 19, 2015, 1.
39. Ibid.
40. Howard Sherman, "Religion and Theatre Education Clash over McNally's 'Corpus Christi' at a Virginia University," Feb. 25, 2015, http://www.hesherman.com/2015/02/25/religion-and-theatre-education-clash-over-mcnallys-corpus-christi-at-a-virginia-university/; Harrison Horst, "Protest Brings Students Together for 'Corpus Christi,'" Weather Vane, Feb. 26, 2015, 1.
41. Administrator, interview by author, Mar. 6, 2015.
42. Faculty member, interview by author, Mar. 3, 2015.
43. "Academic Freedom Policy and Procedures," approved by the trustees on June 2016, KCR.
44. Ibid.
45. Factbook 2001–2002, 4.3.
46. Ken L. Nafziger, interview by author, Mar. 2, 2015.
47. "Sports," special issue, Crossroads, Fall/Winter 2009–2010.
48. Bonnie Price Lofton, interview by author, Mar. 2, 2015.
49. Member of president's cabinet, interview by author, Mar. 6, 2015.
50. Mark Metzler Sawin, e-mail message to author, Aug. 12, 2016.
51. Ibid.
52. Hamm, The Quakers in America, 109–19; Hamm, Earlham College, 333, 338.
53. Mark Metzler Sawin, e-mail message to author, Aug. 12, 2016.
54. Mark Thiessen Nation, interview by author, Jan. 29, 2015.
55. Andrea Wenger, interview by author, Mar. 6, 2015.
56. Andrea Wenger, e-mail message to author, Nov. 14, 2016.
57. "Why Diversity Matters at EMU," 2016 Diversity Task Force, KCR (lightly edited for style).
58. Ruayda Qadir, e-mail message to author, Oct. 20, 2016.
59. Pannell, "Mennonite Girl from Harlem," 22.

60. Statistics from EMU's Institutional Research Office, 2016.
61. Pannell, "Mennonite Girl from Harlem," 23.
62. Ken L. Nafziger, interview by author, Mar. 2, 2015.
63. *Catalog 2016–2017*, 7.
64. Fred Kniss, "Diversity and Belonging: Love and the Liberal Arts," spring convocation address, 2015, KCR (emphasis in the original).
65. Carnegie Foundation for the Advancement of Teaching, *Campus Life*; vice president for student life and dean of students, report to board of trustees, Nov. 2014, KCR.
66. *Catalog 2015–2016*, 227–28.
67. Administrator, interview by author, Mar. 6, 2015.
68. "Disciplinary Procedures," 1999–2000, B6, F14, JLL.
69. Administrator, interview by author, Mar. 6, 2015.
70. Jonathan D. Swartz, "Student Conduct and Restorative Justice Assessment," 2014–2015, KCR.
71. Lonnie Yoder, interview by author, Mar. 3, 2015.
72. Beryl Brubaker, interview by author, Nov. 5, 2014.
73. *Catalog 2016–2017*, 8 (emphasis in the original).
74. Ibid., 8, 7.
75. SACS Self-Study Response 1989, 3.1.
76. Vernon Jantzi, interview by author, June 2, 2015.
77. Vi Dutcher, interview by author, Apr. 29, 2014.
78. Bonnie Price Lofton, e-mail message to author, Mar. 3, 2015.
79. For example, see "Investing in Youth," *Bulletin*, June–July 1959, 8.
80. Lee M. Yoder, "The Diversity of Gifts and the Class of 1963," Oct. 12, 2013, KCR.
81. *Factbook 2001–2002*, 3.14.
82. "EMU Alumni by Profession and Location," University Office of Alumni and Parent Engagement, Sept. 1, 2016, KCR.
83. Mariah Martin, "I Wrestle with Empathy," *#WeAreMenno* (blog), Mennonite Church USA, June 15, 2015, http://mennoniteusa.org/menno-snapshots/wearemenno-i-wrestle-with-empathy/.
84. Blair Seitz, interview by author, July 20, 2016.
85. Orval J. Gingerich, "Internationalizing General Education: A Case Study of Eastern Mennonite College and the Global Village Curriculum" (doctoral dissertation), May 1995, MSHL; "A Twenty-Year Track Record," *Bulletin*, Spring 1994, 5.
86. Vernon Jantzi, interview by author, June 2, 2015.
87. Ibid.
88. Rachel Keshishian and Bonnie Price Lofton, "EMU Leads the Way in Requiring Cross-Cultural Study," *Crossroads*, Summer 2012, 2–6. This entire issue of *Crossroads* covers the thirtieth anniversary of the cross-cultural program.
89. Bonnie Price Lofton, interview by author, Mar. 2, 2015.
90. Bonnie Price Lofton, "From SPI to 12 Initiatives for Peacebuilding," and J. Daryl Byler, "The Amazing Ripple Effects of SPI-Type Work," in *PeaceBuilder*, 2014–2015.
91. Phil Wenger, "EMC Adds Peace and Justice Curriculum," *Weather Vane*, Sept. 15, 1978, 5.
92. For more on the influence of faith-based peacemaking at EMU, see the CJP web page introducing a new e-journal about peacebuilding: http://www.emu.edu/cjp/resources/a-genealogy-of-ideas/.
93. In addition to Lederach, Professors Howard Zehr and Ron Kraybill were hired initially through shared contracts with MCC.
94. Vernon Jantzi, interview by author, June 2, 2015.
95. James and Marian Payne played a significant visionary and sustaining role with their financial support for the development of the CTP.
96. Vernon Jantzi, interview by author, June 2, 2015.
97. The center's early women staff members included Ruth Zimmerman, Gloria Rhodes, and Cynthia Sampson, who provided administrative support and grant writing acumen, and faculty members Nancy Good Sider and Lisa Schirch.
98. "Sowing Seeds of JustPeace Worldwide" (title of map inside front cover), *PeaceBuilder*, Summer/Fall 2005.
99. Jayne Seminare Docherty, e-mail message to author, Dec. 21, 2016.
100. The CJP established the Zehr Institute for Restorative Justice in 2012. The institute promotes the key values, principles, and best practices that define the restorative justice movement through dialogue, networking, research, training, and multimedia publications.
101. Lauren Jefferson, "CJP Partners with Kellogg Foundation's New National Initiative on Truth, Racial Healing, and Transformation," Eastern Mennonite University, last updated July 19, 2016, http://emu.edu/now/news/2016/02/cjp-partners-with-kellogg-foundations-new-national-initiative-on-truth-racial-healing-and-transformation/.
102. Jayne Seminare Docherty, e-mail message to author, Dec. 21, 2016.

103. Seminary faculty member, interview by author, Mar. 3, 2015.

104. Former seminary faculty member, interview by author, Aug. 31, 2016.

105. Vernon Jantzi, interview by author, June 2, 2015.

106. Jayne Seminare Docherty, e-mail message to author, Dec. 21, 2016.

107. Vernon Jantzi, interview by author, June 2, 2015.

108. "The Mission, Vision, and Values of CJP," Eastern Mennonite University, http://www.emu.edu/cjp/about/mission-vision-values/ (emphasis in the original).

109. Initially called Abraham's Tent: A Center for Interfaith Engagement, the center focused on the world's three monotheistic religions. It emerged out of Mennonites' experiences in service and mission efforts in various religious settings worldwide.

110. For more information about CIE programs, see "Welcome to the Center for Interfaith Engagement," Eastern Mennonite University, http://www.emu.edu/interfaith/.

111. J. Daryl Byler, e-mail message to author, Feb. 3, 2017. For a listing of the Fulbright scholars, see "Join the 78 Fulbright Scholars Who Have Studied at a World-Renowned Graduate Program in Conflict Transformation," Eastern Mennonite University, https://www.emu.edu/cjp/fulbright-scholars/.

112. Corey Anderson, "A Note about This Page," Weather Vane, Apr. 8, 2004, 9.

113. "Kathleen Temple Resigns," Weather Vane, Apr. 8, 2004, 9.

114. Faculty status committee minutes, Mar. 10, 2004.

115. Loren Swartzendruber, interview by author, June 3, 2015.

116. Loren Swartzendruber, "EMU Meeting," comments at the town hall meeting, Apr. 13, 2004, KCR.

117. Ken L. Nafziger, interview by author, Mar. 2, 2015.

118. Grimsrud and Nation, Reasoning Together.

119. "Church Member Profile 2006," KCR.

120. Conrad L. Kanagy, "2014 Survey of Credentialed Leaders in Mennonite Church USA: Executive Summary," KCR.

121. For information on Pink Menno, see its website: http://www.pinkmenno.org/.

122. "Same Sex Marriage Laws," National Conference of State Legislatures, June 26, 2015, http://www.ncsl.org/research/human-services/same-sex-marriage-laws.aspx.

123. Loren Swartzendruber, interview by author, June 3, 2015.

124. Ibid.

125. Senior EMU official, interview by author, June 1, 2016.

126. Emily Sharrer, "EMU Opens Same-Sex Dialogue," Daily News-Record (Harrisonburg, VA), Nov. 16, 2013, B-1.

127. Elizabeth Eisenstadt-Evans, "Lancaster County Native Will be First Gay Pastor to Be Licensed in the Mennonite Church USA," LancasterOnline, Jan. 31, 2014, http://lancasteronline.com/features/faith_values/lancaster-county-native-will-be-first-gay-pastor-to-be/article_0281ee3e-8abc-11e3-84d4-0017a43b2370.html.

128. Paul Schrag, "MC USA Won't Recognize Colorado Pastor's Licensing," Mennonite World Review, July 1, 2015, http://mennoworld.org/2014/07/01/news/mc-usa-wont-recognize-colorado-pastors-licensing/.

129. "The Listening Process: What We Heard," June 10, 2014, KCR.

130. Dean Welty, "The Challenges in the Valley," The Forum, Spring 2014, 2, KCR; "Marriage Declaration for Eastern Mennonite University," June 11, 2014, KCR.

131. Senior EMU official, interview by author, June 1, 2016.

132. "The Listening Process: What We Heard," June 10, 2014, KCR.

133. President's report to board of trustees, June 6, 2014, KCR.

134. Chester Wenger, "An Open Letter to My Beloved Church," The Mennonite, Nov. 6, 2014, https://themennonite.org/opinion/open-letter-beloved-church/.

135. Ervin R. Stutzman, "Frequently-Asked Questions Regarding the Two Resolutions on Polity and Practice," June 18, 2015. KCR.

136. Kay Nussbaum and Loren Swartzendruber to EMU alumni and friends, "Update to Non-discrimination Policy," July 20, 2015, KCR.

137. See news releases for July 20, 2015, July 28, 2015, Aug. 29, 2015, and Sept. 21, 2015 in the CCCU archives, http://www.cccu.org/news/archives?y=2015. For an Anabaptist peace perspective on this controversy, see Jared S. Burkholder, "How Peacemaking Helps Frame the Context of Anabaptism, Sexuality, and Higher Education," The Pietist Schoolman (blog), Oct. 6, 2015, https://pietistschoolman.com/2015/10/06/how-peacemaking-helps-frame-the-context-of-anabaptism-sexuality-and-higher-education/.

138. Michael A. King, e-mail message to author, Oct. 10, 2016.

139. Michael A. King, "Response to Ervin Stutzman Statement," Jan. 22, 2014, KCR.

140. Lonnie Yoder, interview by author, Mar. 3, 2015.

141. Michael A. King, e-mail message to author, Oct. 10, 2016.

142. Mary Krahn Jensen, e-mail message to author, Dec. 21, 2016.
143. The number of graduate degrees includes theological and nontheological as well as dual degrees.
144. Kathy Evans, e-mail message to author, Dec. 21, 2016.
145. Dickeson, *Prioritizing Academic Programs*, 29.
146. Walt Wiltschek, "A Catalyst for Stewardship, Ray Martin Helps EMU and Partners to Launch the Center for Sustainable Climate Solutions," Eastern Mennonite University, Sept. 29, 2016, http://emu.edu/now/news/2016/08/catalyst-stewardship-ray-martin-helps-emu-partners-launch-center-sustainable-climate-solutions/.
147. The Southern Association of Colleges and Schools Commission on Colleges (SACSCOC) approved the application.
148. Andrea Wenger, e-mail message to author, Dec. 20, 2016.
149. Dean's Report, 1982–1983, 10.
150. Lauren Jefferson, "Celebration Bids EMU President Farewell."
151. Board of Trustees, Resolution of Appreciation for Loren E. Swartzendruber, Mar. 19, 2016, KCR; "Board of Trustees, Resolution of Appreciation for Pat Swartzendruber," May 2, 2016. KCR.
152. "Susan Schultz Huxman, PhD, Appointed as EMU's Ninth President," joint release of Eastern Mennonite University and Mennonite Education Agency, Apr. 27, 2016, KCR.

CHAPTER 12

EPIGRAPH: Faulkner, *Requiem for a Nun*, 72.
1. Hauerwas and Westerhoff, *Schooling Christians*.
2. C. H. Brunk to L. J. Heatwole, June 19, 1916, B3, F4, ADW.
3. M. T. Brackbill, "E.M.S. Different," *Bulletin*, Jan. 1947, 3–7.
4. Joe Lapp, "State of the University: Educating for Faithfulness," Aug. 24, 1989, B4, F11, JLL.
5. "Six Lessons of EMU's History," *Crossroads*, Summer 2007, 31.
6. Although the term *mission statement* belongs only to the latter part of EMU's history, it is used here for the expressions of purpose found in seven early documents: Minutes of Warwick Mennonite Institute, Jan. 22, 1913 (of which one section is titled "Constitution"), B5, F4, GRB1; Constitution and Bylaws of the Alexandria Mennonite Institute, Feb. 17, 1914, B3, F4, ADW; Charter 1917; *Announcements 1917–1918* (catalog), 2; *Catalog 1918–1919*, 15–16; *Catalog 1924–1925*, 11; Constitution 1924.
7. *Announcements 1917–1918* (catalog), 2 (emphasis added).
8. *Catalog 1918–1919*, 15 (emphasis added).
9. Ibid., 15–16 (emphasis in the original).
10. *Catalog 1922–1923*, 9 (emphasis added).
11. Ann Graber Hershberger, interview by author, Aug. 15, 2016.
12. Kraybill, *Concise Encyclopedia*, 257–58.
13. *Catalog 2016–2017*, 7.
14. Bauman, *Liquid Modernity*.
15. Joseph W. Mast, "How Computers Work," *Bulletin*, Winter 1984, 2–3.
16. Trustee minutes, Mar. 21, 2015.
17. SACS Self-Study Report 1989, 3.2.
18. Richard C. Detweiler, "Greenhouse and Laboratory," *Bulletin*, Fall 1982, 16 (emphasis added).
19. Member of president's cabinet, interview by author, June 2, 2015.
20. T. S. Eliot, *Four Quartets*, 35.
21. I am indebted to Carl F. Bowman's *Brethren Society: The Cultural Transformation of a "Peculiar People"* for the concept of symbolic transformation; however, the different types are my own construction.
22. A. D. Wenger, "Our Position on Distinctive Doctrines," *Bulletin*, Apr. 1924, 9–10.
23. EMS students would have encountered the word *discipleship* while reading Charles Sheldon's novel *In His Steps* in the 1920s and '30s. Then, in the 1940s, Harold S. Bender's *Anabaptist Vision* brought the term into currency among Mennonites.
24. *Catalog 2015–2016*, 6.
25. Member of president's cabinet, interview by author, June 2, 2015.
26. Schlabach, "Renewal and Modernization," 210; Mark Thiessen Nation, interview by author, Jan. 29, 2015.
27. Conrad G. Brunk, "A Reevaluation of Values for the Seventies," May 24, 1970, B16, F5, MSA.
28. Roth, *Engaging Anabaptism*; Charles Scriven, "The Reformation Radicals Ride Again."
29. Trustee minutes, Nov. 10, 1988.
30. *Catalog 2015–2016*.
31. Albert Keim, "EMC Functions like Medieval 'Corpus Christianum,'" *Weather Vane*, May 26, 1972, 3.
32. Albert Keim, "General Education: A Second Look," *Bulletin*, Oct. 1977, 16.
33. Albert Keim, "EMC Functions like Medieval 'Corpus Christianum,'" *Weather Vane*, May 26, 1972, 3.
34. Ibid.
35. Ben Gamber to members of the faculty council, Mar. 24, 1972, B16, F77, MSA.
36. Former faculty member to Richard Detweiler, Oct. 8, 1984, B1, F4, JLL.
37. Beryl Brubaker, interview by author, Aug. 26, 2016.
38. Administrator, interview by author, June 2, 2015.
39. Weber, *Sociology of Religion*, 269–70.

40. Ringenberg, *The Christian College and the Meaning of Academic Freedom*, 231.

41. Joe Lapp, "EMU: Stretched between the Questions," *Connections* 6, no. 12 (Oct. 1996): 8 (*Connections* was the Virginia Mennonite Conference and Virginia Board of Missions' newsletter); President's Report, Aug. 10–11, 1990.

42. Some postmodern theorists such as Jean-François Lyotard and Alasdair MacIntyre argue that the liberal arts and sciences also rest on belief but usually do not admit it.

43. C. K. Lehman, *Inadequacy of Evolution*, 8.

44. Carl S. Keener, "The Evolution of My Years: A Stream of Life in Process" (unpublished memoir), Mar. 14, 2011, KCR.

45. Statement on Creation and Natural Science, Sept. 17, 2008, KCR.

46. Faculty minutes, Dec. 18, 1962.

47. Andrea Wenger, e-mail message to author, Mar. 20, 2015.

48. C. K. Lehman, "Thy Word Is Truth," *Journal*, Sept.–Oct. 1928, 8–11.

49. Faculty minutes, Oct. 30, 1962.

50. Joe Lapp, "Thy Word Is Truth," Aug. 26, 1998, B4, F74, JLL.

51. James Bomberger, interview by author, June 3, 2015.

52. Benne, *Quality with Soul*.

53. Hughes and Adrian, *Models for Christian Higher Education*. Two other sources with templates for assessing an institution's ties with its religious denomination or heritage are Meyer, *Realizing Our Intentions*, and Ringenberg, *The Christian College: A History of Protestant Higher Education*.

54. In the fall of 2016, the university tested a program of extracurricular engagement as a graduation requirement. Chapel attendance was one activity that students could document for this program.

55. Trustee minutes, Nov. 7–8, 2003.

56. Berger, *Rumor of Angels*; Landy and Saler, *The Re-enchantment of the World*; Jacobsen and Jacobsen, *No Longer Invisible*.

57. Berger and Luckmann, *Social Construction of Reality*.

58. EMU Enrollment & Mennonite Student Data: Fall 2000 and Fall 2016, Institutional Research Office, KCR. The category "Mennonite" includes MC USA, the Brethren in Christ, Mennonite Brethren, and other Anabaptist groups in the Mennonite Central Committee constituency.

59. In those same years, the percentage of Mennonites in nontenure tracks increased from 45 percent to 53 percent. (The category "Mennonite" includes MC USA, the Brethren in Christ, Mennonite Brethren, and other Anabaptist groups in the Mennonite Central Committee constituency.) Office of the Provost, KCR.

60. *Catalog 2015–2016*.

61. Statement of Arrangements, approved by EMU trustees on Nov. 15, 2008, and by MEA on Jan. 11, 2009, KCR.

62. Related denominations include the Brethren in Christ, Mennonite Brethren, and other Anabaptist groups in the Mennonite Central Committee constituency.

63. Statement of Arrangements, approved by EMU trustees on Nov. 15, 2008, and by MEA on Jan. 11, 2009, KCR; EMU bylaws, approved by EMU trustees on June 21, 2014, and by MEA on Oct. 18, 2014, KCR.

64. EMU official, interview by author, June 2, 2015.

65. Shirley Hershey Showalter, personal communication with the author, Oct, 14, 2016.

66. Kirk L. Shisler, e-mail message to author, Sept. 7, 2016.

67. Shirley Hershey Showalter, personal communication with the author, Oct, 14, 2016.

68. "GC and MC Membership Statistics in the United States of America, 1860–2003," KCR; "Who We Are: A Quick Visual Guide," Mennonite Church USA, http://mennoniteusa.org/who-we-are/.

69. Benne, *Quality with Soul*, 179–80, 185–86.

70. Bonnie Price Lofton, "Why EMU Is Not Harvard or Duke (and Why We Feel Fine about It)," *Crossroads*, Spring 2006, 8–9.

71. Shenk to Lapp, Mar. 2, 1994, B7, F19, JLL.

72. Klaassen, *Anabaptism: Neither Catholic nor Protestant*. Walter Klaassen was a progressive, Oxford-educated scholar who taught Bible and religion at Bethel College. He later became chaplain and professor of religion at Canada's Conrad Grebel University College on the condition that chapel would be entirely voluntary.

73. Nathan E. Yoder notes that the proponents of third-way logic are wont to critique the two opposing poles of a debate and presume the third alternative is superior. Yoder, memo to author, July 8, 2016, KCR.

74. EMU strategic plan 2015–2020, approved by EMU trustees on June 21, 2014, KCR.

75. Member of president's cabinet, interview by author, June 2, 2015.

76. Loren Swartzendruber, e-mail message to EMU constituents, Dec. 7, 2015, KCR.

77. Vi Dutcher, interview by author, Apr. 29, 2014.

78. Fred Kniss, "Dare to Risk Love," matriculation address, 2016, KCR.

79. L. J. Heatwole, "The First Day at Eastern Mennonite School," *Journal*, Jan. 1928, 4.

80. Vi Dutcher, e-mail message to author, Aug. 21, 2016.

Bibliography

Ammerman, Nancy Tatom. *Bible Believers: Fundamentalists in the Modern World*. New Brunswick, NJ: Rutgers University Press, 1987.

Anderson, Benedict. *Imagined Communities: Reflections on the Origin and Spread of Nationalism*. London: Verso, 1983.

Augsburger, Esther K. "Why Nudity in Art." *Festival Quarterly*, Spring 1981, 16–17.

Barr, James. *Fundamentalism*. Philadelphia: Westminster Press, 1978.

Bauman, Zygmunt. *Liquid Modernity*. Cambridge, UK: Polity Press, 2000.

Bechler, LeRoy. *The Black Mennonite Church in North America, 1886–1986*. Scottdale, PA: Herald Press, 1986.

Bell, Sadie. *The Church, the State, and Education in Virginia*. New York: Arno Press, 1969.

Bellah, Robert N., Richard Madsen, William M. Sullivan, Ann Swidler, and Steven M. Tipton. *Habits of the Heart: Individualism and Commitment in American Life*. New York: Harper & Row, 1986.

Bender, Harold S. *The Anabaptist Vision*. Scottdale, PA: Herald Press, 1944.

———. "Bible Institute." In *The Mennonite Encyclopedia*. Vol. 1: *A–C*, 330–32. Scottdale, PA: Mennonite Publishing House, 1955.

———. "Bible School." In *The Mennonite Encyclopedia*. Vol. 1: *A–C*, 332–33. Scottdale, PA: Mennonite Publishing House, 1955.

———. Editorial. *MQR* 1, no. 1 (Jan. 1927): 1.

———. "History of Millennial Theories." In *Prophecy Conference*, 48–59.

———. *Mennonite Sunday School Centennial 1840–1940: An Appreciation of Our Sunday Schools*. Scottdale, PA: Mennonite Publishing House, 1940.

Bender, Harold S., and Ernst Correll. "C. Henry Smith's *The Story of the Mennonites*." *MQR* 16, no. 3 (Oct. 1942): 270–75.

Benne, Robert. *Quality with Soul: How Six Premier Colleges and Universities Keep Faith with Their Religious Traditions*. Grand Rapids, MI: Wm. B. Eerdmans, 2001.

Berger, Peter L. *Facing Up to Modernity: Excursions in Society, Politics, and Religion*. New York: Basic Books, 1977.

———. *A Rumor of Angels: Modern Society and the Rediscovery of the Supernatural*. Garden City, NY: Anchor Press, 1979.

Berger, Peter L., and Thomas Luckmann. *The Social Construction of Reality: A Treatise in the Sociology of Knowledge*. Garden City, NY: Anchor Press, 1967.

Bonhoeffer, Dietrich. *The Cost of Discipleship*. New York: Macmillan, 1963.

Bourdieu, Pierre, and Loic J. D. Wacquant. *An Invitation to Reflexive Sociology*. Chicago: University of Chicago Press, 1992.

Bowman, Carl F. *Brethren Society: The Cultural Transformation of a "Peculiar People."* Baltimore: Johns Hopkins University Press, 1995.

Bowman, Paul Haynes. *Brethren Education in the Southeast: An Account of the Educational Endeavors among the Brethren People in the Southeastern Region, 1857–1955*. Bridgewater, VA: Bridgewater College, 1955.

Boyer, Paul. *When Time Shall Be No More: Prophecy Belief in Modern American Culture*. Cambridge, MA: Belknap Press of Harvard University Press, 1992.

Brereton, Virginia Lieson. *Training God's Army: The American Bible School, 1880–1940*. Bloomington: Indiana University Press, 1990.

Brunk, George R. "The Drift." *ST* 1, no. 1 (Jan. 1929): 2–8.

———. Editorial. *ST* 5, no. 4 (Oct. 1933): 1, 3–4.

———. Editorial Message. *ST* 8, no. 3 (July 1936): 3–4.

———. "Faulty Fundamentalists." *ST* 3, no. 4 (Oct. 1931): 13.

———. "A Fractional Gospel." *ST* 5, no. 4 (Oct. 1931): 8.

———. Introduction. *ST* 1, no. 1 (Jan. 1929): 1.

———. "Keeping the Faith." *ST* 10, no. 4 (July 1939): 84–87.

———. "Origin of the General Conference Fundamentals." *ST* 3, no. 4 (Oct. 1931): 4–5.

———. "The Relation of Faith and Works in Present and Eternal Salvation." *ST* 2, no. 2 (Apr. 1930): 7–12.

————. *Rightly Dividing the Scriptures: Gospel Synergism*. Harrisonburg, VA: Sword and Trumpet, 1935.

————. "Scofield Errors." *ST* 8, no. 4 (Oct. 1936): 5.

————. "Virginia Conference Vigilance." *ST* 3, no. 4 (Oct. 1931): 5.

Brunk, George. R., II. *A Crisis among Mennonites: In Education, in Publication*. Harrisonburg, VA: Sword and Trumpet, 1983.

————, ed. *Encounter with the Holy Spirit*. Scottdale, PA: Herald Press, 1972.

Brunk, Harry Anthony. *History of Mennonites in Virginia*. Vol. 1: *1727–1900*. Staunton, VA: McClure Printing Company, 1959.

————. *History of Mennonites in Virginia*. Vol. 2: *1900–1960*. Verona, VA: McClure Printing Company, 1972.

"Bryan on Evolution." *GH*, July 21, 1921, 306, 316.

Burdge, Edsel, Jr., and Samuel A. Horst. *Building on the Gospel Foundation: The Mennonites of Franklin County, Pennsylvania, and Washington County, Maryland, 1730–1970*. Scottdale, PA: Herald Press, 2004.

Burkholder, John Richard. *Continuity and Change: A Search for a Mennonite Social Ethic*. Akron, PA: Mennonite Central Committee, 1977.

Burtchaell, James Tunstead. *The Dying of the Light: The Disengagement of Colleges and Universities from Their Christian Churches*. Grand Rapids, MI: Wm. B. Eerdmans, 1998.

Bush, Perry. *Dancing with the Kobzar: Bluffton College and Mennonite Higher Education, 1899–1999*. Telford, PA: Pandora Press, 2000.

————. *Peace, Progress, and the Professor: The Mennonite History of C. Henry Smith*. Harrisonburg, VA: Herald Press, 2015.

Carey, Kevin. "Academic Freedom Has Limits. Where They Are Isn't Always Clear." *Chronicle of Higher Education*, Jan. 29, 2016, A25–A26.

Carnegie Foundation for the Advancement of Teaching. *Campus Life: In Search of Community*. Princeton, NJ: Princeton University Press, 1990.

Centennial Memorial of J. S. Coffman. Scottdale, PA: Herald Press, 1949.

Charles, J. Robert. "Innocents Abroad? American Mennonite Travelers in Europe." *Mennonite Historical Bulletin* 53, no. 3 (1992): 1–8.

Church and Sunday School Hymnal: A Collection of Hymns and Sacred Songs Appropriate for Church Services, Sunday Schools, and General Devotional Exercises. Scottdale, PA: Mennonite Publishing House, 1902.

Coffman, Barbara F. *His Name Was John: The Life Story of an Early Mennonite Leader*. Scottdale, PA: Herald Press, 1964.

Coffman, John S. *Outlines and Notes Used at the Bible Conference Held at Johnstown, Pennsylvania from Dec. 27, 1897, to Jan. 7, 1898*. Elkhart, IN: Mennonite Publishing Company, 1898.

————. "The Spirit of Progress." In *John S. Coffman, Mennonite Evangelist: His Life and Labors* by M. S. Steiner, 112–30. Spring Grove, PA: Mennonite Book and Tract Society, 1903. Reprinted in *Mennonite Historical Bulletin* 47, no. 3 (July 1986): 1–6.

"Conference Report." *GH*, Nov. 16, 1916, 614.

Darwin, Charles. *The Origin of Species*. New York: Bantam Books, 1999.

Davis, Melody M. "The Woman behind *Mennonite Community Cookbook*." *The Mennonite*, Feb. 2015, 13–17.

Denlinger, Steven L. *Glimpses Past: Annotations of Selected Social and Cultural History Materials in the Mennonite* Herald of Truth, Gospel Witness, *and Early* Gospel Herald. Lancaster, PA: Lancaster Mennonite Historical Society, 1985.

Derstine, Clayton F. *The Great Apostasy, or Departing from God and the Living Word*. Scottdale, PA: Mennonite Publishing House, 1919.

Dickeson, Robert. *Prioritizing Academic Programs and Services: Reallocating Resources to Achieve Strategic Balance*. San Francisco: Jossey-Bass, 1999.

Driedger, Leo, and Donald B. Kraybill. *Mennonite Peacemaking: From Quietism to Activism*. Scottdale, PA: Herald Press, 1994.

Durnbaugh, Donald F. *The Brethren Encyclopedia*. 3 vols. Philadelphia: Brethren Encyclopedia, Inc., 1983.

————. *Fruit of the Vine: A History of the Brethren, 1708–1995*. Elgin, IL: Brethren Press, 1997.

Eastern Mennonite College & Seminary Alumni Directory, 1993. White Plains, NY: Bernard C. Harris Publishing Co., 1993.

Eliot, T. S. *Four Quartets*. New York: Harcourt, Brace, and Company, 1943.

Enns, Rebekah. "Standards of Nonconformity: Challenging Dress Regulation as a Means of Engagement—Women's Dress at Eastern Mennonite College, 1962–1972." *Pennsylvania Mennonite Heritage* 36, no. 4 (Oct. 2013): 123–36.

Evans, Christopher H. "Social Gospel." In *The Encyclopedia of Protestantism*, edited by Hans J. Hillerbrand. Vol. 4: *S–Z*, 1752–58. New York: Routledge, 2004.

Family Almanac for the Year of Our Lord 1910. Scottdale, PA: Mennonite Publishing House, 1910.

Faulkner, William. *Requiem for a Nun*. New York: Vintage, 2011. First published in 1950.

Fretz, Winfield. "Explanatory Remarks." In *Proceedings of the First Conference on Mennonite*

Cultural Problems, v–vi. N.p.: Council of Mennonite Schools and Colleges, 1942.

Fry, E. L., and J. S. Hartzler. "Change of Place to Hold General Conference." *GH*, Aug. 23, 1917, 400.

"Fundamentalism versus Modernism." *GH*, Aug. 21, 1924, 418–19.

"The Fundamental of Fundamentals." *GH*, Aug. 30, 1923, 432–33, 444.

Gbowee, Leymah. *Mighty Be Our Powers: How Sisterhood, Prayer, and Sex Changed a Nation at War*. New York: Beast Books, 2011.

Gingerich, Melvin. "Is There a Need for a Mennonite Rural Life Publication?" In *Proceedings of the First Conference on Mennonite Cultural Problems*, 60–66. N.p.: Council of Mennonite Schools and Colleges, 1942.

———. *Mennonite Attire through Four Centuries*. Breinigsville, PA: Pennsylvania German Society, 1970.

———. *Service for Peace: A History of Mennonite Civilian Public Service*. Akron, PA: Mennonite Central Committee, 1949.

Gleason, Philip. *Contending with Modernity: Catholic Higher Education in the Twentieth Century*. New York: Oxford University Press, 1995.

Gollner, Philipp. "How Mennonites Became White: Religious Activism, Cultural Power, and the City." *MQR* 90, no. 2 (Apr. 2016): 165–93.

Goossen, Rachel Walter. "'Defanging the Beast': Mennonite Responses to John Howard Yoder's Sexual Abuse." *MQR* 89, no. 1 (Jan. 2015): 7–80.

Gospel Herald. Unsigned review of *The Fundamentals*. Nov. 29, 1917, 648.

Graybill, J. Paul, Ira D. Landis, and J. Paul Sauder. *Noah H. Mack: His Life and Times, 1861–1948*. Scottdale, PA: Herald Press, 1952.

Grimsrud, Ted, and Mark Thiessen Nation. *Reasoning Together: A Conversation on Homosexuality*. Scottdale, PA: Herald Press, 2008.

Gross, Leonard. "The Doctrinal Era of the Mennonite Church." *MQR* 60, no. 1 (Jan. 1986): 83–103.

Grove, Grace S. *L. J. Heatwole: A Granddaughter's View*. Harrisonburg, VA: Campbell Copy Center, 2001.

Guzman, Jessie Parkhurst, ed. *1952 Negro Year Book: A Review of Events Affecting Negro Life*. New York: Wm. H. Wise, 1952.

Haines, Michael R. "The Population of the United States, 1790–1920." In *The Cambridge Economic History of the United States*, edited by Stanley L. Engerman and Robert E. Gallman. Vol 2: *The Long Nineteenth Century*, 143–205. New York: Cambridge University Press, 2000.

Hamm, Thomas D. *Earlham College: A History, 1847–1997*. Bloomington: Indiana University Press, 1997.

———. *The Quakers in America*. New York: Columbia University Press, 2003.

Hartman, Peter S. *Reminiscences of the Civil War*. Lancaster, PA: Eastern Mennonite Associated Libraries and Archives, 1964.

Hartzler, J. S., and Daniel Kauffman. *Mennonite Church History*. Scottdale, PA: Mennonite Book and Tract Society, 1905.

Harvey, David. *The Condition of Postmodernity: An Enquiry into the Origins of Cultural Change*. Cambridge, MA: Blackwell, 1989.

Hauerwas, Stanley, and John H. Westerhoff, eds. *Schooling Christians: "Holy Experiments" in American Education*. Grand Rapids, MI: Wm. B. Eerdmans, 1992.

Heatwole, Cornelius J. *A History of Education in Virginia*. New York: Macmillan, 1916.

Heatwole, L. J. Announcement. *GH*, July 5, 1917, 272.

———. "The Mennonite Church: Her Past and Present Conditions Compared." In *Mennonite Year-Book and Directory 1907*, 12–14. Elkhart, IN: Mennonite Board of Missions and Charities, 1907.

———. *Mennonite Handbook of Information*. Scottdale, PA: Mennonite Publishing House, 1925.

———. "Short Term Bible Course." *GH*, Dec. 30, 1915, 655–56.

———. "The Virginia Conference." In *Mennonite Church History* by J. S. Hartzler and Daniel Kauffman, 218–21. Scottdale, PA: Mennonite Book and Tract Society, 1905.

Heatwole, R. J. "Reminiscences of War Days." *GH*, Oct. 12, 1911, 444–45.

Heishman, A. G. Announcement. *GH*, Sept. 27, 1917, 488.

Hershberger, Guy Franklin. *The Mennonite Church in the Second World War*. Scottdale, PA: Mennonite Publishing House, 1951.

———. "Suggestions for Improving the Small Christian Community." In *Proceedings of the First Conference on Mennonite Cultural Problems*, 48–59. N.p.: Council of Mennonite Schools and Colleges, 1942.

Hertzler, Silas. "Attendance at Mennonite Secondary Schools and Colleges, 1949–50." *MQR* 26, no. 1 (Jan. 1952): 48–64.

Hirschman, Charles, and Elizabeth Mogford. "Immigration and the American Industrial Revolution from 1880 to 1920." *Social Science Research* 38, no. 4 (Dec. 2009): 897–920.

Holsopple, Jerry L. *7 × 7 Laments for an Age of Sexualized Power*. N.p.: printed by author, 2015.

Homan, Gerlof D. *American Mennonites and the Great War 1914–1918*. Waterloo, ON: Herald Press, 1994.

Horsch, John. *Modern Religious Liberalism: The Destructiveness and Irrationality of Modernist Theology*. Harrisonburg, VA: Sword and Trumpet, 1968. First published in 1925.

Hostetler, Beulah Stauffer. *American Mennonites and Protestant Movements: A Community Paradigm*. Scottdale, PA: Herald Press, 1987.

———. "The Formation of the Old Orders." *MQR* 66, no. 1 (Jan. 1992): 5–25.

Hounshell, David A. *From the American System to Mass Production, 1800–1932: The Development of Manufacturing Technology in the United States*. Baltimore: Johns Hopkins University Press, 1984.

Hughes, Richard T., and William B. Adrian, eds. *Models for Christian Higher Education: Strategies for Survival and Success in the Twenty-First Century*. Grand Rapids, MI: Wm. B. Eerdmans, 1997.

Itäranta, Emmi. *Memory of Water*. New York: HarperCollins, 2014.

Jacobsen, Douglas, and Rhonda Hustedt Jacobsen. *No Longer Invisible: Religion in University Education*. New York: Oxford University Press, 2012.

Jefferson, Lauren. "Celebration Bids EMU President Farewell after 13 Years." *Mennonite World Review*, July 18, 2016, 18.

Juhnke, James C. "Mennonite Benevolence and Revitalization in the Wake of World War I." *MQR* 60, no. 1 (Jan. 1986): 15–30.

———. *Vision, Doctrine, War: Mennonite Identity and Organization in America, 1890–1930*. Scottdale, PA: Herald Press, 1989.

Kalberg, Stephen. "Max Weber's Types of Rationality: Cornerstones for the Analysis of Rationalization Processes in History." *American Journal of Sociology* 85, no. 5 (Mar. 1980): 1145–79.

Kauffman, Daniel, ed. *Bible Doctrine: A Treatise on the Great Doctrines of the Bible*. Scottdale, PA: Mennonite Publishing House, 1914.

———. *Bible Doctrines Briefly Stated or 100 Points on Christian Faith*. Scottdale, PA: Mennonite Publishing House, 1922.

———. "Christianity's Greatest Foe." *GH*, Mar. 27, 1919, 921.

———. *The Conservative Viewpoint: A Message to the Members of the Mennonite Church*. Scottdale, PA: Mennonite Publishing House, 1918.

———. "A General Conference." *Herald of Truth*, Feb. 15, 1896, 50.

———. *Manual of Bible Doctrines: Setting Forth the General Principles of the Plan of Salvation*. Elkhart, IN: Mennonite Publishing Company, 1898.

———, ed. *Mennonite Cyclopedic Dictionary: A Compendium of the Doctrines, History, Activities, Literature, and Environments of the Mennonite Church, Especially in America*. Teeswater, ON: Ira J. Huber, 1980. First published in 1937 by Mennonite Publishing House.

———. "Millennium." In Daniel Kauffman, *Mennonite Cyclopedic Dictionary*, 243–44.

———. "Modernism." In Daniel Kauffman, *Mennonite Cyclopedic Dictionary*, 250.

———. *A Talk with Church Members*. Rev. ed. Scottdale, PA: Mennonite Book and Tract Society, 1907.

Kaufman, Gordon D. *Nonresistance and Responsibility, and Other Mennonite Essays*. Newton, KS: Faith and Life Press, 1979.

Kaufman, J. Howard, and Leo Driedger. *The Mennonite Mosaic: Identity and Modernization*. Scottdale, PA: Herald Press, 1991.

Kaylor, Earl C., Jr. *Truth Sets Free: Juniata Independent College in Pennsylvania, Founded by the Brethren, 1876: A Centennial History*. Cranbury, NJ: A. S. Barnes, 1977.

Kehrberg, Sarah. "Dressing Girls." *Mennonite World Review*, Nov. 23, 2015, 5.

Keim, Albert N. *The CPS Story: An Illustrated History of Civilian Public Service*. Intercourse, PA: Good Books, 1990.

———. *Harold S. Bender: 1897–1962*. Scottdale, PA: Herald Press, 1998.

Keim, Albert N., and Grant M. Stoltzfus. *The Politics of Conscience: The Historic Peace Churches and America at War, 1917–1955*. Scottdale, PA: Herald Press, 1988.

Klaassen, Walter. *Anabaptism: Neither Catholic nor Protestant*. 3rd ed. Telford, PA: Pandora Press, 2001.

Kolb, Abram B. Editorial Notes. *Herald of Truth*, Mar. 1898, 65–66.

Kraus, C. Norman. "American Mennonites and the Bible, 1750–1950." *MQR* 41, no. 4 (Oct. 1967): 309–29.

———. *Dispensationalism in America: Its Rise and Development*. Richmond, VA: John Knox Press, 1958.

———, ed. *Evangelicalism and Anabaptism*. Scottdale, PA: Herald Press, 1979.

Kraus, Jo Anne. "Holy Experiment: Mennonite Colony on the Warwick River 1897–1970." Unpublished manuscript, 2015.

Kraybill, Donald B. *Concise Encyclopedia of Amish, Brethren, Hutterites, and Mennonites*. Baltimore: Johns Hopkins University Press, 2010.

Kraybill, Donald B., and James P. Hurd. *Horse-and-Buggy Mennonites: Hoofbeats of Humility in a Postmodern World*. University Park: Pennsylvania State University Press, 2006.

Lambert, George. *Around the Globe and through Bible Lands: Notes and Observations on the Various Countries through which the Writer*

Traveled. Elkhart, IN: Mennonite Publishing Company, 1896.

Landy, Joshua, and Michael Saler, eds. *The Re-enchantment of the World: Secular Magic in a Rational Age.* Stanford, CA: Stanford University Press, 2009.

Lapp, John Allen. *The Mennonite Church in India 1897–1962.* Scottdale, PA: Herald Press, 1972.

Lapp, John E. "Amillennialism." In *Prophecy Conference,* 17–30.

Lears, Jackson. *Rebirth of a Nation: The Making of Modern America, 1877–1920.* New York: HarperCollins, 2009.

Lederach, Paul M. *A Third Way: Conversations about Anabaptist/Mennonite Faith.* Scottdale, PA: Herald Press, 1980.

Lehman, Chester K. *The Inadequacy of Evolution.* Scottdale, PA: Mennonite Publishing House, 1933.

———. "Interpretation of Prophecy." In *Prophecy Conference,* 1–9.

———. *The Last Things in the Teaching of the Bible, with Particular Reference to the Messianic Kingdom: A Defense of the Historic Position of the Christian Church on Eschatology.* Hagerstown, MD: Deutsche Buchhandlung/James Lowry, 2016.

Lehman, Harold D. *Through These Doors, a Journal of Faithfulness: Park View Mennonite Church 1953–2003.* Harrisonburg, VA: Garrison Press, 2003.

———. "To the Country Schoolhouse: Mennonite Teachers in Small Public Schools." In *Beyond the Temple of Learning: Essays Celebrating the Role of Virginia Mennonite Conference in Christian Education,* edited by Philip L. Kniss, 58–60. Harrisonburg, VA: Parkview Mennonite Church, 2010.

Lehman, J. Irvin. *Spots on My Trousers: Stories from the Life and Loves of a Mennonite Minister.* State Line, PA: Mennonite Historical Association of the Cumberland Valley, 1990.

Lehman, James O. *Lindale's Song: A Century of Harmony, Growth and Fellowship, 1898 to 1998.* Harrisonburg, VA: Lindale Mennonite Church, 1998.

———. *Mennonite Tent Revivals: Howard Hammer and Myron Augsburger, 1952–1962.* Kitchener, ON: Pandora Press, 2002.

Lehman, James O., and Steven M. Nolt. *Mennonites, Amish, and the American Civil War.* Baltimore: Johns Hopkins University Press, 2007.

Lehman, Lois M., and Rhoda E. Cressman. *A. D. & Annie: Stories, Letters, and Memories of A. D. Wenger and Annie Lehman Wenger, Their Families and Their Descendants.* Harrisonburg, VA: Campbell Print Center, 2014.

Lesher, Emerson L. *The Muppie Manual: The Mennonite Urban Professional's Handbook for Humility and Success (or, How to Be the Gentle in the City).* Intercourse, PA: Good Books, 1985.

Ley, Sandra. *Fashion for Everyone: The Story of Ready-to-Wear, 1870's–1970's.* New York: Charles Scribner's Sons, 1975.

Lindsell, Harold. *The Battle for the Bible.* Grand Rapids, MI: Zondervan, 1976.

[Loucks, Aaron]. "Report of School Meeting at Maugansville, MD, February 1914." *GH,* Feb. 26, 1914, 746.

Mack, Noah H. "The Situation in American Mennonitism." *ST* 2, no. 4 (Oct. 1930): 7–12.

Manzullo-Thomas, Devon C. "Prophet and President: Myron S. Augsburger and the Mennonite History of Evangelical Higher Education." *Pennsylvania Mennonite Heritage* 39, no. 4 (Oct. 2016): 136–42.

Marsden, George M. *Fundamentalism and American Culture: The Shaping of Twentieth-Century Evangelicalism: 1870–1925.* New York: Oxford University Press, 1980.

———. *The Soul of the American University: From Protestant Establishment to Established Nonbelief.* New York: Oxford University Press, 1994.

Marsden, George M., and Bradley J. Longfield, eds. *The Secularization of the Academy.* New York: Oxford University Press, 1992.

Mennonite Yearbook and Directory 1925. Scottdale, PA: Mennonite Publishing House, 1925.

Meyer, Albert J. *Realizing Our Intentions: A Guide for Churches and Colleges with Distinctive Missions.* Abilene, TX: Abilene Christian University Press, 2009.

Miller, D. D. "Progress of the Mennonite Church." In *Mennonite Year-Book and Directory 1908,* 10–12. Elkhart, IN: Mennonite Board of Missions and Charities, 1908.

Miller, Grant. "A Peace Witness Transformed: The Mennonite Response to the Gulf Wars in 1990–1991 and 2002–2003." *MQR* 87, no. 3 (Oct. 2013): 467–501.

Miller, James D. *A Centennial History of the Southern Association of Colleges and Schools 1895–1995.* Decatur, GA: Southern Association of Colleges and Schools, 1998.

Miller, Mary. *A Pillar of Cloud: The Story of Hesston College, 1909–1959.* North Newton, KS: Mennonite Press, 1959.

Miller, Melissa, and Phil M. Shenk. *The Path of Most Resistance: Stories of Mennonite Conscientious Objectors Who Did Not Cooperate with the Vietnam War Draft.* Scottdale, PA: Herald Press, 1982.

Miller, Susan Fisher. *Culture for Service: A History of Goshen College, 1894–1994.* Goshen, IN: Goshen College, 1994.

Minutes of the Virginia Mennonite Conference. Vol. 1. 2nd ed. Scottdale, PA: Mennonite Publishing House, 1950.

Minutes of the Virginia Mennonite Conference. Vol. 2. Scottdale, PA: Mennonite Publishing House, 1967.

"Modernism versus Orthodoxy." *GH*, July 15, 1926, 358.

"Modernism vs. Fundamentalism." *GH*, May 22, 1924, 145.

Mosemann, John H. "Fundamentalism versus Modernism." *ST* 1, no. 1 (Jan. 1929): 20–21.

Mumaw, Catherine R. "Touched by the World." In *Continuing the Journey: The Geography of Our Faith: Mennonite Stories Integrating Faith and Life and the World of Thought*, edited by Nancy Lee, 291–316. Telford, PA: Cascadia Publishing House, 2009.

Mumaw, Evelyn King. *Woman Alone*. Scottdale, PA: Herald Press, 1970.

Mumaw, John R. "Dispensationalism and the Postponement Theory." In *Prophecy Conference*, 78–86.

———. "The Mennonite Witness in the Southern High Lands." In *Proceedings of the Eighth Conference on Mennonite Educational Cultural Problems*, 71–79. Newton, KS: Herald Book Printing Company, 1951.

———. "My Faith Story." *GH*, Aug. 7, 1984, 548–51.

Nation, Mark Thiessen. *John Howard Yoder: Mennonite Patience, Evangelical Witness, Catholic Convictions*. Grand Rapids, MI: Wm. B. Eerdmans, 2006.

Newman, Mark. *Getting Right with God: Southern Baptists and Desegregation, 1945–1995*. Tuscaloosa: University of Alabama Press, 2001.

Niebuhr, Reinhold. *Moral Man and Immoral Society: A Study in Ethics and Politics*. New York: Charles Scribner's Sons, 1955.

Noll, Mark A. *American Evangelical Christianity: An Introduction*. Malden, MA: Blackwell, 2001.

———. "Introduction: The Christian Colleges and American Intellectual Traditions." In *The Christian College: A History of Protestant Higher Education in America*, edited by William Ringenberg, 17–36. 2nd ed. Grand Rapids, MI: Baker Academic, 2006.

Nolt, Steven M. "An Evangelical Encounter: Mennonites and the Biblical Seminary in New York." *MQR* 70, no. 4 (Oct. 1996): 389–417.

Nolt, Steven M., and Theron F. Schlabach. "The Facts about Nonresistance among the Mennonites of America: Challenges of Quantifying US Mennonite Responses to Military Conscription during World War II." *MQR* 90, no. 2 (July 2016): 373–84.

"No Middle Ground." *GH*, Apr. 15, 1926, 65.

"Once in a While." *GH*, Oct. 1, 1925, 529–30.

O'Neill, J. C. "Higher Criticism." In *The Encyclopedia of Protestantism*, edited by Hans J. Hillerbrand. Vol. 2: *D–K*, 866–67. New York: Routledge, 2004.

Pannell, Melody M. "A Mennonite Girl from Harlem." *The Mennonite*, Nov. 2016, 20–23.

Peachey, Paul. "A Hippocratic Mid-life Course Change." In *Making Sense of the Journey: The Geography of Our Faith: Mennonite Stories Integrating Faith and Life and the World of Thought*, edited by Robert Lee and Nancy V. Lee, 235–40. Scottdale, PA: Herald Press, 2007.

———. "Identity Crisis among American Mennonites." *MQR* 42, no. 3 (Oct. 1968): 243–59.

Pellman, Hubert R. *Eastern Mennonite College, 1917–1967: A History*. Harrisonburg, VA: Eastern Mennonite College, 1967.

———. *Mennonite Broadcasts: The First 25 Years*. Harrisonburg, VA: Mennonite Broadcasts, 1979.

Peterson, Amy T., ed. *The Greenwood Encyclopedia of Clothing through American History, 1900 to the Present*. Vol. 1: *1900–1949*. Westport, CT: Greenwood Press, 2008.

Pettigrew, Thomas F. "Our Caste-Ridden Protestant Campuses." *Christianity and Crisis* 21 (May 29, 1961): 88–91.

"Preachers of an Active Gospel." *Time*, Sept. 19, 1969, 60.

Prophecy Conference: Report of Conference Held at Elkhart, Indiana, April 3–5, 1952. Scottdale, PA: Mennonite Publishing House, 1953.

Rauschenbusch, Walter. *Christianity and the Social Crisis*. New York: Macmillan, 1907.

Riley, W. B. "Fundamentalists and Modernists Compared." *GH*, Oct. 4, 1923, 545.

Ringenberg, William C., ed. *The Christian College: A History of Protestant Higher Education in America*. 2nd ed. Grand Rapids, MI: Baker Academic, 2006.

———. *The Christian College and the Meaning of Academic Freedom: Truth-Seeking in Community*. New York: Palgrave Macmillan, 2016.

Roth, John D., ed. *Engaging Anabaptism: Conversations with a Radical Tradition*. Scottdale, PA: Herald Press, 2001.

Royce, Josiah. *The Philosophy of Loyalty*. New York: Macmillan, 1916.

Ruth, John Landis. *The Earth Is the Lord's: A Narrative History of the Lancaster Mennonite Conference*. Scottdale, PA: Herald Press, 2001.

Sack, Saul. *History of Higher Education in Pennsylvania*. 2 vols. Harrisburg, PA: Pennsylvania Historical and Museum Commission, 1963.

Sawatsky, Rodney James. *History and Ideology: American Mennonite Identity Definition through History*. Kitchener, ON: Pandora Press, 2005.

Sawatsky, Rodney James, and Scott Holland, eds. *The Limits of Perfection: A Conversation with J. Lawrence Burkholder*. Waterloo, ON: Institute of Anabaptist and Mennonite Studies, 1993.

Schlabach, Theron F. *Gospel versus Gospel: Mission and the Mennonite Church, 1863–1944*. Scottdale, PA: Herald Press, 1980.

———. *Peace, Faith, Nation: Mennonites and Amish in Nineteenth-Century America*. Scottdale, PA: Herald Press, 1988.

———. "Renewal and Modernization among American Mennonites, 1800–1980: Restorationist?" In *The Primitive Church in the Modern World*, edited by Richard T. Hughes, 197–220. Urbana: University of Illinois Press, 1995.

———. *War, Peace, and Social Conscience: Guy F. Hershberger and Mennonite Ethics*. Scottdale, PA: Herald Press, 2009.

Schlosser, Ralph W. *History of Elizabethtown College, 1899–1970*. Lebanon, PA: Sowers Printing Company, 1971.

Scofield, C. I., ed. *The Scofield Reference Bible*. New York: Oxford University Press, 1917.

Scott, Stephen. *An Introduction to Old Order and Conservative Mennonite Groups*. Intercourse, PA: Good Books, 1996.

Scriven, Charles. "The Reformation Radicals Ride Again." *Christianity Today*, Mar. 5, 1990, 13–15.

Sharp, John E. *My Calling to Fulfill: The Orie O. Miller Story*. Harrisonburg, VA: Herald Press, 2015.

———. *A School on the Prairie: A Centennial History of Hesston College, 1909–2009*. Telford, PA: Cascadia Publishing House, 2009.

Shearer, Tobin Miller. *Daily Demonstrators: The Civil Rights Movement in Mennonite Homes and Sanctuaries*. Baltimore: Johns Hopkins University Press, 2010.

Sheldon, Charles M. *In His Steps*. Grand Rapids, MI: Revell, 2012. First published in 1896.

Shenk, Henry M. "Can a Church School Promote the Simple Faith and Practice of a Plain Church?" *ST* 18, no. 3 (1950): 4–8.

Shenk, Sara Wenger. *Thank You for Asking: Conversing with Young Adults about the Future Church*. Scottdale, PA: Herald Press, 2005.

Shetler, Sanford G. *Preacher of the People: A Biography of S. G. Shetler (1871–1942)*. Scottdale, PA: Herald Press, 1982.

Shoemaker, J. S., S. G. Shetler, and J. W. Weaver. *The Christian Worker's Manual*. Vol. 1. Scottdale, PA: Mennonite Publishing House, 1915.

Showalter, Grace. "The Virginia Mennonite." *Missionary Light* 37, no. 4 (June–Aug. 1976): 2–3.

Showalter, Mary Emma. *Mennonite Community Cookbook, Favorite Family Recipes*. Scottdale, PA: Mennonite Community Association, 1950.

Sider, E. Morris. *Messiah College: A History*. Nappanee, IN: Evangel Press, 1984.

Siegrist, Joanne Hess. *Mennonite Women of Lancaster County: A Story in Photographs from 1855–1935*. Intercourse, PA: Good Books, 1996.

Smith, J. B. "The Bible." In *Bible Doctrine: A Treatise on the Great Doctrines of the Bible*, edited by Daniel Kauffman, 88–128. Scottdale, PA: Mennonite Publishing House, 1914.

———. "The Educational Problem." *GH*, Sept. 1910, 402–4.

———. "The Education of, and for, Our Young People, Part I." *Christian Monitor*, Aug. 1915, 239–41.

———. "The Education of, and for, Our Young People, Part II." *Christian Monitor*, Sept. 1915, 276–77.

———. "The God of Modernism, His Origin, History and Nature." *GH*, Apr. 1923, 66–67, 77.

———. *A Revelation of Jesus Christ: A Commentary on the Book of Revelation*. Edited by J. Otis Yoder. Scottdale, PA: Herald Press, 1961.

Sobek, Matthew. "New Statistics on the US Labor Force, 1850–1990." *Historical Methods: A Journal of Quantitative and Interdisciplinary History* 34, no. 2 (2001): 71–87.

Sprunger, Keith L. *Bethel College of Kansas, 1887–2012*. North Newton, KS: Bethel College, 2012.

Stauffer, J. L. *The Coming of the Lord and Practical Christian Living*. 3rd ed. Altoona, PA: Tract Press, [1913?].

———. *The Eternal Security Teaching*. 5th ed. N.p.: J. L. Stauffer, 1933.

———. "Fundamentals and Fundamentalists." *ST* 5, no. 2 (Apr. 1933): 16–20.

———. "Premillennialism." In *Prophecy Conference*, 31–47.

Stead, William. *If Christ Came to Chicago!* Chicago: Laird & Lee, 1894.

Steiner, M. S. *John S. Coffman, Mennonite Evangelist: His Life and Labors*. Spring Grove, PA: Mennonite Book and Tract Society, 1903.

Stoltzfus, Ruth Brunk. *A Way Was Opened: A Memoir*. Edited by Eve MacMaster. Scottdale, PA: Herald Press, 2003.

Stutzman, Ervin R. *From Nonresistance to Justice: The Transformation of Mennonite Church Peace Rhetoric, 1908–2008*. Scottdale, PA: Herald Press, 2011.

Sutton, Matthew Avery. *American Apocalypse: A History of Modern Evangelicalism*. Cambridge, MA: Harvard University Press, 2014.

Swartzentruber, Ernest. "History of the Colored Mission of Harrisonburg Virginia." *Missionary Light* 3 (Apr. 1943): 1.

Thomas, Everett J. "Church Beliefs vs. Academic Freedom." *The Mennonite*, Jan. 21, 2003, 32.

Trollinger, Susan T., and William Vance Trollinger Jr. *Righting America at the Creation Museum: Young Earth Creationism and the*

Culture Wars. Baltimore: Johns Hopkins University Press, 2016.

Turner, Victor. *Dramas, Fields, and Metaphors: Symbolic Action in Human Society*. Ithaca, NY: Cornell University Press, 1974.

"Two EMC Music Teachers Resign." *GH*, Jan. 11, 1977, 34.

Umble, John Sylvanus. *Goshen College, 1894–1954: A Venture in Christian Higher Education*. Goshen, IN: Goshen College, 1955.

Wayland, Francis Fry. *Bridgewater College: The First Hundred Years, 1880–1980*. Bridgewater, VA: Bridgewater College, 1993.

Weber, Max. *The Sociology of Religion*. 4th ed. Boston: Beacon Press, 1963.

———. *The Theory of Social and Economic Organization*. Translated by A. M. Henderson and Talcott Parsons. New York: Free Press, 1964. First published in 1947 by Oxford University Press.

Wenger, A. D. "The Mennonites a Prey of Others." *ST* 2, no. 2 (Apr. 1930): 15–23.

———. *Six Months in Bible Lands and Around the World in Fourteen Months*. Doylestown, PA: Joseph B. Steiner, 1902.

———. *Who Should Educate Our Children?* Harrisonburg, VA: Eastern Mennonite School, 1926.

Wenger, Eli D. *The Weaverland Mennonites, Including a Biography of Bishop Benjamin W. Weaver with Excerpts from His Diary*. Manheim, PA: privately printed, 1968.

Wenger, John Christian. "Chiliasm." In *The Mennonite Encyclopedia*. Vol. 1: *A–C*, 557–59. Scottdale, PA: Mennonite Publishing House, 1955.

———. *The Doctrines of the Mennonites*. Scottdale, PA: Mennonite Publishing House, 1950.

———. *Faithfully, Geo. R.: The Life and Thought of George R. Brunk I (1871–1938)*. Harrisonburg, VA: Sword and Trumpet, 1978.

———. "Millennium." In Daniel Kauffman, *Mennonite Cyclopedic Dictionary*, 243–44.

Wenger, John Christian, and Mary W. Kratz. *A. D. Wenger: Faithful Minister of Christ*. Harrisonburg, VA: Park View Press, 1961.

Wenger, Linden. "J. L. Stauffer (1888–1959)." In *Mennonite Yearbook and Directory 1960*, 8–9. Scottdale, PA: Mennonite Publishing House, 1960.

Wenger, Mark R. "Ripe Harvest: A. D. Wenger and the Birth of the Revival Movement in Lancaster Conference." *Pennsylvania Mennonite Heritage* 4, no. 2 (Apr. 1981): 2–14.

Wenger, S. B. "Observations of Goshen College." *GH*, June 13, 1908, 172–73.

Williamson, Chet. *Uniting Work and Spirit: A Centennial History of Elizabethtown College*. Elizabethtown, PA: Elizabethtown College Press, 2001.

Wuthnow, Robert. *The Restructuring of American Religion*. Princeton, NJ: Princeton University Press, 1988.

———. *The Struggle for America's Soul: Evangelicals, Liberals, and Secularism*. Grand Rapids, MI: Wm. B. Eerdmans, 1989.

Yoder, John Howard. *The Christian Witness to the State*. Newton, KS: Faith and Life Press, 1964.

———. *The Politics of Jesus: Vicit Agnus Noster*. Grand Rapids, MI: Wm. B. Eerdmans, 1972.

Yoder, Michael. "Findings from the 1982 Mennonite Census." *MQR* 59, no. 4 (Oct. 1985): 307–49.

Yoder, Nathan E. "Mennonite Fundamentalism: Shaping an Identity for an American Context." PhD diss., University of Notre Dame, 1999.

Index

Page numbers followed by *f* and *t* indicate figures and tables, respectively.

Bluffton College (University), viii, ix, 24, 91, 96, 99, 135, 258, 274, 314–15, 334–35
BMC. *See* Brethren Mennonite Council for Gay Concerns (BMC)
Board of Trustees (EMS, EMC, EMU)
  change in size and representation, 195, 230
  Eastern Mennonite seminary, 228
  General Board of EMS, 35–36, 39–41, 43, 46, 53, 353–54n22–23, 356–57n11
  and Lancaster Conference, 111–12, 230
  local Harrisonburg board, 53, 67
  and Mennonite Board of Education, 242–43
  permanent board, 68, 195, 230
  and Virginia Conference, 143–46, 230
Bomberger, Cathy, 240
Boshart, David, 241
Bowman, Lois B., 131, 260, 262
Bowman, Mary Jo, 241
Boyers, Kenny, 240
Brackbill, Maurice T. "M. T.," 58, 62, 68–69, 110, 319–20
Brackbill, Milton G., 148
Brackbill, Ruth Mininger, 259
Brethren Mennonite Council for Gay Concerns (BMC), 239, 277, 307
Bridgewater College, 6, 23, 99, 145, 177, 181, 184, 210
Brubaker, Beryl, 258, 262, 263t, 274, 285, 286, 298, 328, 342t
Brubaker, Darrell, 266
Brubaker, Mary, 55
Brunk, Christian, 55
Brunk, Christian H. "C. H.," 50, 53, 54, 60
Brunk, Conrad, 326
Brunk, George R., 7, 16, 31–34, 36–37, 39–40, 43–44, 46, 65, 92–93, 100, 101f, 105, 108, 113–14. *See also* Alexandria Mennonite Institute; Calvinism; Warwick Mennonite Institute
  criticism of Goshen College, 34, 92–93
  death, 115–16
  early career, 31–32
  J. B. Smith piano incident, 64–66
Brunk, George R., II, 145, 149, 151f, 213, 229f, 271
  dean of Eastern Mennonite Seminary, 228
  EMC investigation, 145, 147, 149–50
  Mennonite education crisis, 237–39
Brunk, George R., III, 238–39, 270, 271
Brunk, Harry A., 55, 120, 223f
Brunk, Henry, 32
Brunk, Lawrence, 151f
Brunk, Ruth. *See* Stoltzfus, Ruth Brunk
Brunk, Susan Heatwole, 32
Brunk, Truman, 65, 145
Brunk, Truman H., Jr., 215
Brunk Revivals, 150
Bulletin. See under publications
Burdge, Edsel, 223
bureaucracy, 146, 170, 242, 323
Byers, N. E., 24–25, 35, 91–92
Bylaws. *See* Constitution

Byler, Ezra, 234
Byler, Jesse, 232
Byrd, Tia, 294f

Calvinism, 114, 116, 136, 148
campus, 56f, 153f, 247, 248f, 342t
campus culture, xii, 211, 240, 290, 296, 298, 310, 332
cars. *See* motor vehicles
casting lots. *See* ordination by lot
CCCU. *See* Council for Christian Colleges and Universities (CCCU)
censorship, 171, 183–84, 291, 293, 340
  audio visuals, 161
  textbooks, x, 36, 76, 84, 93, 118, 136, 184, 237–38
Center for Interfaith Engagement (CIE), 305–6
Center for Justice and Peacebuilding (CJP), 302, 304, 306, 342t. *See also* Conflict Transformation Program (CTP)
Center for Sustainable Climate Solutions, 289t, 313
Chan, Chee Tao, 178
Chan, Wai May, 178
chapel, 63, 70, 72, 77, 109, 137, 148, 157, 162f, 164, 191, 218–20, 222, 288, 258, 332, 386n54
  compulsory, 23, 199, 219, 328, 332
character building, 42, 70, 135
charismatic movement, 226–28, 231
Charlton, Marion, 48, 58
charter, 53–54, 65, 78, 356–57n11
choice, xi, 20–22, 114, 165, 168, 180, 196, 200, 219, 222, 323–24
Church of the Brethren, 6, 23, 99, 103, 125, 170, 212, 241, 239
civil disobedience, 190, 212, 214
Civilian Public Service (CPS), 125–27, 143, 325
civil rights movement, 171–72, 192, 194–95, 198, 212
Civil War, viii, 6–7, 14, 32, 52, 172–73
CJP. *See* Center for Justice and Peacebuilding (CJP)
CLC. *See* Community Lifestyle Commitment (CLC)
Clemmer, Dean, 216f
Coffman, John S. "J. S.," 7, 9–11, 14, 24, 32. *See also* John S. Coffman Center
  "Spirit of Progress," 24
College of William and Mary, 147, 177
colleges and universities, 23, 24, 47, 135, 310, 330–32. *See also* higher education
commencement, xiv, 20, 59, 188. *See also* dress: academic regalia
communal values, 20, 164, 165
  humility, xii, 11, 21, 71–72, 105, 101, 117, 133, 164, 167, 225, 236, 281–83, 287, 291, 293
  loyalty, xii, 22, 76, 82, 107, 109, 128, 131, 137, 164–65, 184, 189, 196, 281, 300, 324, 327, 358–59n101
  obedience, 21, 42, 76, 135, 164–65, 196, 222, 242, 281, 324
  self-denial, 5, 17, 21, 71, 76, 135, 164–65, 324, 325f

RWC. *See* Religious Welfare Committee (RWC)

SACS. *See* Southern Association of Colleges and Schools (SACS)
safeguard mentality, ix, x, 25, 34, 36, 75, 101, 118, 136, 146, 180, 324, 325*f*
  constitution, 76, 136, 221, 321
  criticism of Mennonite Board of Education, 96, 101
salvation, 5, 8–9, 42, 64, 114, 138, 160, 166, 237, 275, 321
  assurance of, 166
  conversion, 20, 117
  eternal security, 114
  personal, 15, 20, 63, 238
  personal work, 9, 42
  plan of, 20
same-sex issues. *See also* Blauch, Sue; Council for Christian Colleges and Universities (CCCU); Good, Theda; Pink Menno; Purdue statement; Roth, Ken; student organizations: Safe Space; Temple, Kathleen; Wenger, Chester
  employment, 279, 308, 310
  homosexuality, 238, 240–41, 275, 277–80, 307, 309
  LGBTQ, 278, 287, 291, 306–7, 309–10, 337
  listening process, 308–9
  marriage, 277, 307, 310–11
  orientation, 178, 236, 239, 241, 277–79, 291, 307
  trustee action, 309–10
Santiago, Roland, 264
Sarco, Mike, 219
Sauder, Paul, 98*f*
Sauder, R. Clair, 246
Sawin, Mark Metzler, 294
Schlabach, Theron, 133, 135
School of Graduate and Professional Studies, 312, 342*t*
Schultz, Harold, J., 315
Schutte, Marijke, 129
science and faith, 19, 201–3, 330–31
Scofield, C. I., 7
Scofield Reference Bible, 7, 88–89
seal, 109
second coming. *See* millennial views
sectarian. *See* separatist
secular influences on EMU, 156, 242, 322, 323–24, 329–31, 333
secularization, 171, 242, 324, 329, 332–33
segregation. *See* racial segregation
Seitz, Blair, 300
Seitz, David, 207
Selective Service. *See* conscription
self, 21, 165. *See also* individualism
  self-control, 135, 165, 180
  self-denial, 5, 17, 21, 71, 76, 135, 164–65, 324, 325*f*
  self-expression, 21–22, 72, 128, 164–65, 222, 244
  self-will, 71, 184, 164
separation from the world. *See under* nonconformity; world

separatist, xi, xiii, 12, 18, 22, 47, 103–4, 200, 221, 223, 235, 322. *See also* world
Sermon on the Mount, 12, 59, 88–89
service, 70, 126–27, 194, 196, 200, 299. *See also* alumni vocations; Civilian Public Service (CPS); Mennonite Central Committee (MCC)
  alumni, 154, 201, 203, 207, 250, 303
  campus culture, 218, 248, 284, 287, 293, 296, 298–301, 321, 325–26
  YPCA, 70, 121, 121*t*, 130
sexual orientation issues, 239–42, 270, 277–81, 291, 306–11, 323. *See also* same-sex issues
SGA. *See* student organizations: Student Government Association (SGA)
Shank, Clarence, 42
Shank, Dorothy, 261, 263*t*
Shank, Duane, 214
Shank, J. Ward, 145, 147
Shank, Lester C., 214
Shank, Ralph, 174
Sharon Manufacturing Company, 111
Sheilaism, 227–28
Shenandoah. See under publications
Shenandoah Valley, 6, 16, 32, 50, 110, 235, 231
Shenk, Calvin, 301
Shenk, Daniel, 36, 37
Shenk, Emma, 133
Shenk, Henry M., 145, 147
Shenk, Jerry, 214
Shenk, J. M., 59
Shenk, Mary C., 62
Shenk, Oliver, 112
Shenk, Sara Wenger, 263*t*, 272, 276
Shenk, Steve, 336
Shetler, Samuel Grant "S. G.," 39, 48, 52
Shoemaker, Jeff, 266
Showalter, Donald, 203, 235, 247
Showalter, Edith, 132
Showalter, Grace, 112, 173, 263*t*
Showalter, Mary Emma. *See* Eby, Mary Emma Showalter
Showalter, Noah D., 57–58
Showalter, Shirley Hershey, 209, 223–24, 262, 315
Showalter, Stuart, 211
Shriner, Stephen, 206*f*
Sider, Duane, 272–73
simplicity. *See under* communal values
singing. *See under* music
Slabaugh, Laura, 70–71
Slabaugh, Moses, 119
Smeltzer, Deirdre, 262, 292
Smith, Beulah, 55, 58, 59*f*
Smith, C. Henry, 91, 168
Smith, Jacob Brubaker "J. B.," 54, 57–58, 59–61, 59*f*, 341*t*
  early career, 55
  fund-raising, 59–60, 64
  piano incident, 64–66
  president of EMS, 55–66